TRAVELLER'S GUIDE TO
AFRICA

Editor: Richard Synge

ISSN 0140 1300
ISBN 0 905268 04 0

Design: David Coetzee. Typesetting: Camden Typesetters Ltd, 31-39 Camden Road, London NW1. Printed by The Garden City Press Ltd, Pixmore Ave, Letchworth, Herts. UK.

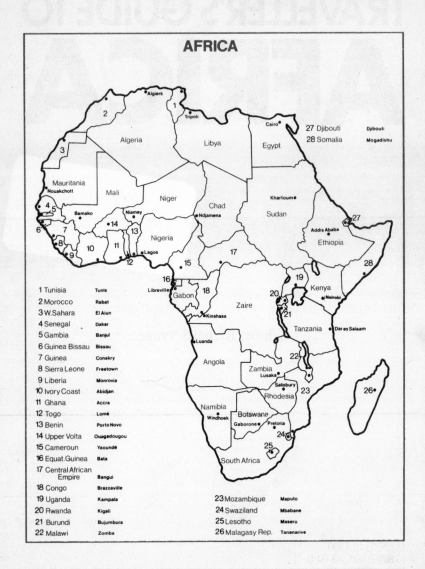

AFRICA

27 Djibouti   Djibouti
28 Somalia   Mogadishu

1 Tunisia   Tunis
2 Morocco   Rabat
3 W.Sahara   El Aiun
4 Senegal   Dakar
5 Gambia   Banjul
6 Guinea Bissau   Bissau
7 Guinea   Conakry
8 Sierra Leone   Freetown
9 Liberia   Monrovia
10 Ivory Coast   Abidjan
11 Ghana   Accra
12 Togo   Lomé
13 Benin   Porto Novo
14 Upper Volta   Ouagadougou
15 Cameroun   Yaoundé
16 Equat.Guinea   Bata
17 Central African
    Empire   Bangui
18 Congo   Brazzaville
19 Uganda   Kampala
20 Rwanda   Kigali
21 Burundi   Bujumbura
22 Malawi   Zomba

23 Mozambique   Maputo
24 Swaziland   Mbabane
25 Lesotho   Maseru
26 Malagasy Rep.   Tananarive

CONTENTS

RAINFALL·TEMPERATURE

over 16 ins. (over 400 mm) ■☐ ☐ over 100°F (over 38°C)
8—16 ins. (200—400 mm) ■ ☐ 80°—100°F (27°—38°C)
2—8 ins. (50—200 mm) ▨ ☐ 60°—80°F (16°—27°C)
0—2 ins. (0—50 mm) ☐ ☐ Below 60°F (Below 16°C)

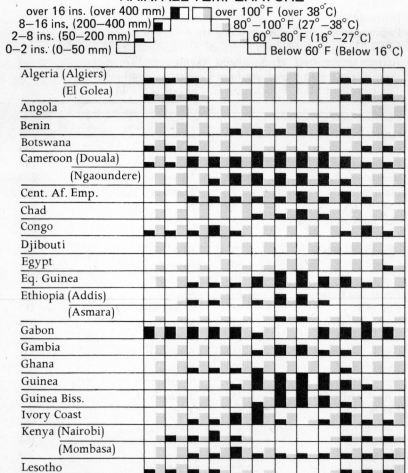

Algeria (Algiers)
(El Golea)
Angola
Benin
Botswana
Cameroon (Douala)
(Ngaoundere)
Cent. Af. Emp.
Chad
Congo
Djibouti
Egypt
Eq. Guinea
Ethiopia (Addis)
(Asmara)
Gabon
Gambia
Ghana
Guinea
Guinea Biss.
Ivory Coast
Kenya (Nairobi)
(Mombasa)
Lesotho

Liberia											
Libya											
Madagascar											
Malawi											
Mali											
Mauritania											
Morocco (Casablanca)											
(Marrakech)											
Mozambique											
Namibia											
Niger											
Nigeria (Kano)											
(Lagos)											
Rhodesia											
Rwanda/Burundi											
Senegal											
Sierra Leone											
Somalia											
S. Africa (Cape Town)											
(Durban)											
(J/burg)											
Sahara											
Sudan											
Swaziland											
Tanzania (D'Salaam)											
(Moshi)											
Togo											
Tunisia											
Uganda											
Upper Volta											
Zaire (Kinshasa)											
(Kisangani)											
(Lubumbashi)											
Zambia											

INTRODUCTION

The second *Traveller's Guide to Africa* is essentially a more practical, and much-updated, edition of the book that both delighted its readers and drove them mad.

Nearly everyone found that the binding fell off even before they had got it to Africa; they had to take out and staple together the most useful pages—there was much bartering of dismembered TGAs but it did sometimes prove to be a handy way of both travelling light and knowing your way about.

Some readers complained also that the grouping of countries into regions was too complicated and difficult to follow. But despite these and other impracticalities of the old *Traveller's Guide to Africa*, all the letters we received were encouraging and urged us to repeat our efforts. At last, after various false starts, we have now come up with what we think is the answer.

The book has been shortened without damage to its usefulness. To cut the enormous number of countries we left out North Africa, and that is now included in the brand new *Traveller's Guide to the Middle East*; we also took out much of the "heavy" introductory material. Above all we have improved the whole design, to make the *Traveller's Guide to Africa* a really useful **hand**book for travel in Africa.

Where to go?

In these days of fast political change in Africa many people who do not know the continent are put off the idea of a visit. But just as anyone who knows the Republic of Ireland will say it is still one of the most peaceful and pleasant countries and is hardly touched by the troubles in the North, so people who know Africa will tell you that the overwhelming feeling is of peaceful co-existence with the rest of mankind and a wonderful lack of animosity towards strangers, visitors and tourists. But there are places to avoid and places to which one cannot go. Writing in late 1977 it is clear that the tourist trade to Ethiopia has collapsed; that no-one in their right mind has visited Uganda for years; that the Kenya/Tanzania border is closed although both Kenya and Tanzania are still the most popular countries to visit in East Africa; that it is impossible to get permission to visit Angola; and that it would hardly be a holiday to go to the two battlefronts of the White Southern African bastion, Namibia and Rhodesia.

With these exceptions African travel is booming. Tourism is growing in Kenya,

Tanzania, Zambia, Sudan, Cameroon, Nigeria and the whole of West Africa. Package tours have blossomed as much in the Gambia as in the Seychelles, while growing numbers of young people make their own way through Africa, catching buses and staying in whatever accommodation is available. Real "African travel" is still possible though there are sometimes problems for people attempting the whole Trans-Africa run, but that adventure is dogged as much by physical difficulties as by political changes.

What has unfortunately not changed for the better is the incidence of racism among white visitors to black Africa. Many still refer to "the natives" in the derogatory way, are afraid of establishing any rapport with the people and are perhaps best off where they tend to congregate anyway, on the beaches and in the game parks.

Living close to the people breaks down all the barriers to knowing Africa and many cities provide ample opportunity for that, the most rewarding perhaps being Mombasa and Dar es Salaam in the east, Douala, Lomé, Accra, Banjul and Dakar on the West Coast with the ancient cities of Kano, Zaria, Agadez and Timbuktu in the West African interior.

Types of travel

Flying is the most practical and usually the cheapest way of getting to Africa, and there is a proliferation of air charter and cheap excursion services—from London especially—to most stepping-off points. There are immigration and exchange control delays, but that has to be anticipated. Any trip that takes you through a number of countries involves tedious rounds of embassies, getting entry permits and visas. The trouble with Africa is that there are so many countries! But it is usually easier to get your passport, visas, money and vaccination certificates organised before you ever set out on your travels.

African capital cities are increasingly short of accommodation and the top hotels are (a) always heavily booked and (b) nearly always very expensive. But if you cannot get a booking do not despair; there is rarely absolutely nowhere to stay. Taxi drivers can usually be persuaded to be very helpful in finding a hotel for you. Armed with your *Traveller's Guide to Africa* you have a full hotel list for every town at your fingertips.

Africa is a great place for collectors of attractive jewellery, carvings, ornaments, rugs, cloth and all manner of unusual things. So always leave room in your bag or suitcase for surprises for your friends, to carry the memory of Africa to cold and distant climes. A camera is useful but should never be wielded indiscriminately or aggressively, particularly in those countries with stringent laws covering where you may or may not photograph. In Zaire a camera should be well hidden at all times.

The overland trip

Anyone venturing to drive across the Sahara or through the Zaire forests on their way across Africa must be mechanically minded and able to do almost anything to a car in trouble, meticulous in carrying extra water and fuel, and should take a map showing water sources, oases and villages (eg Michelin's African series), and in the Sahara should never deviate from the marked track.

It is madness to cross the Sahara during the baking hot months (June to August), and at other times you must be prepared to cope with sandstorms and violent changes in temperature. There is only one recommended road across the Sahara, the Tamanrasset route, but even on that you should travel in a group of vehicles and not allow anyone to disappear from view. Searching for a broken-down vehicle can mean death for the rescuers too. Sandtracks are also essential for soft sand.

On the Zaire section of the Trans-Africa run you should avoid the wettest months as the narrow forest-hemmed road quickly becomes a massive quagmire for miles and miles on end. The many wooden bridges need also to be crossed with great care, or if necessary repaired first. Another problem—there is often just as much difficulty getting good drinking water in the forest as there is in the desert. And a rule for all cross-border travellers: be co-operative and polite with all immigration officials.

Overlanders whose only aim is to get to the other end by a certain date will be very bored with the 'Trans-Africa Highway'; it is a very long and very uncomfortable ride that still takes months and months. But for those who have some curiosity about the world there are some fascinating places on or near the 'Highway' that most overlanders ignore. It is their own loss.

Travelling south from the Sahara the first cultural excitement is in Agadez, where the Middle Ages live on. From then on there is no end of interest. A particularly rewarding route would take in, each for a day or two, Zinder, Daura of Katsina, Kano, Zaria, Jos, Maiduguri, Maroua, Ngaoundere, Douala, Yaoundé, Bouar, Bambari, Kisangani, Beni, Goma, Gisenyi and Mwanza. And there are all the villages in between. On such a progression through Africa you may fail to learn anything about different African cultures and countries, but you cannot fail to see that there are differences. and that's half the battle in understanding Africa.

Perhaps the most useful preparation for the Trans-Africa trip west to east would be to learn basic Hausa and Swahili—Hausa will get you friendly assistance all the way from Mali to the Central African Empire, and Swahili will guide you through Zaire, Rwanda and East Africa.

The most pleasant countryside on the Trans-Africa route is on the higher altitudes of Cameroon and the mountainous part of Eastern Zaire. It is worth planning to stay a while in both those areas and perhaps to climb Zaire's Nyiragongo volcano (if it's not erupting). There are also some sensational waterfalls and rivers in the Central African Empire and Zaire, but do not bathe in slow moving water—bilharzia is endemic. The final reward of the trip is, of course, provided by East Africa's game parks.

For those thinking of taking an Overland trip as advertised in newspapers and travel magazines be prepared for an experience that is dominated entirely by the character of the expedition leader. Beware of the man who is only interested in getting to the other end, come hell or high water and has no real interest in Africa or Africans. Some expedition leaders are more flexible. Make sure you can meet yours before you commit yourself.

At all events an Overland Expedition will be an unforgettable experience and can take you to places you would never otherwise go—but be prepared to have to spend more money than you think, to be delayed by breakdowns and to arrive a month late. Those with more confidence are recommended to take off on their own, staying wherever they want and using the whole range of African transport, from luxury buses to donkeys. But take this book with you!

Acknowledgements

Special thanks to Edwin Bourgeois, David Coetzee, Tony Hodges, Veronica Kemp, Christine Singh and Casey Synge for their help in preparing this revised edition, to Bernard Thomason for his city maps and to all the individual travellers, travel experts and government tourist officials who sent in a stream of suggestions and revisions after the first edition appeared in 1974. Many African tourist offices have also helped enormously. We will continue with our efforts for the next issue.

Richard Synge
September 1977

'The great thing about Avis is, it's the same everywhere you go. Business trip or holiday, you get the same smile of welcome, the same high standard of service. Always.'

AVIS

We try harder.

Avis rents cars in:

BOTSWANA   GABON   GHANA   IVORY COAST   KENYA
MADAGASCAR   NIGERIA   SENEGAL   SOUTH AFRICA   ZAIRE

PACKAGE TOURS

by IAN RAITT

Despite the current political problems of some parts of Africa south of the Sahara the popularity of this vast area with the holidaymaker is nevertheless being maintained. The number of tourists, for example, from Britain to Kenya in the main tourist season from January to March, 1976, (16,000) showed a 5% increase over the previous year. Other countries, notably from Western Europe, have increased their visitor figures to Black Africa. West Germany, a country which is now the largest single spender in the world on overseas tourism, sent 14,000 tourists to Kenya in the first quarter of 1976.

In the world's tourism spending league, Britain ranks fifth, with America second, France third, Canada fourth and Holland sixth.

In Africa, however, Britain occupies a more important position in terms of numbers, due mainly to the ever popular holiday traffic to Kenya and the VFR (Visiting Friends and Relatives) business to South Africa. In the first nine months of 1976, over 17,000 British nationals went to visit friends and relatives in South Africa, with another 18,000 as tourists.

Mount Kilimanjaro seen from Kenya's Amboseli Reserve

MARION KAPLAN

EAST AFRICA

Kenya

One effect of the political uncertainties in Southern and Central Africa has been to concentrate the existing tourist demand into those countries which are known to have a good record of tourism stability. In Black Africa, Kenya dominates the scene. Its visitor figures continue to increase and its tourist industry brings ever-growing foreign exchange earnings. The recent ending of meaningful tourist co-operation between Kenya and Tanzania resulting from the break-up of East African Airways and the formation of Kenya Airways is unlikely to affect Kenya's growth as much as Tanzania's.

The bulk of Kenya's tourism, both in numbers and in revenue, is now from 'stay-put' holidays on the beach as opposed to the traditional safari pattern of the sixties when an East African safari at a fairly high cost, incorporating Tanzania, Kenya and possibly Uganda, was the vogue.

A Kenya beach holiday is still as good value as it has ever been. The resorts of Nyali, just north of Mombasa, Malindi and the increasingly popular beaches south of Mombasa continue to draw visitors in their tens of thousands. Prices start from around £300. A fortnight, for example, with Sovereign Holidays at the Shelly Beach Hotel just south of Mombasa costs £325 sharing a twin-bedded room with half board. The supplement for full board is £10 per person per week.

Apart from the attractions of the palm-fringed beach and the safe swimming behind the coral reef which stretches virtually the whole length of the Kenya coast, the hotels are nearly all equipped with fresh water swimming pools and increasingly with facilities for sailing, underwater activities and tennis. A Kenya coast holiday is no longer just a 'lie on the beach' for a fortnight with the occasional intrepid trip out to the reef in a dug-out canoe. Today, the increasing sophistication of the hotels is leading to other attractions including the provision of one-day and two-day trips to nearby game parks such as Tsavo East and West.

A fortnight at a hotel such as the well-known Nyali Beach on one of the coast's most beautiful bathing beaches, cost in November, 1977, from £430 for full board in a twin room (Speedbird Holidays). This package includes what is now, in Europe, an unobtainable luxury—afternoon tea. Other companies providing beach holidays include Rankin Kuhn, Wings, and Kuoni Houlders.

Northern Kenya

Although the loss of the Northern Tanzania circuit is unfortunate for the Nairobi-based tour operators, nevertheless Kenya alone can now provide extremely interesting safari itineraries. The magnificent areas of Northern Kenya are now opening up as a result of improved roads and more lodge beds. Reserves such as **Samburu**, with its 102 sq kilometres of excellent game-watching from crocodile to Grevy's zebra, and elephant to kongoni, or **Isiolo**, formerly called Buffalo Springs, which extends over an area of 192 sq kilometres, are increasingly popular. These, together with a new reserve, **Shaba**, which adjoins the eastern boundary of Isiolo, provide incomparable game viewing in the pleasantly dry semi-desert conditions of this exceptionally beautiful part of Africa. The area is made even more romantic by the nomadic nature of the peoples such as the Turkana and the Samburu.

For the more adventurous, a new circuit has been developed by the Government—the East Turkana excursion safari. From the cool uplands of Thomsons Falls one can head northwards by Land-Rover or in a private car or minibus (except in the rainy season) to the acacia-shaded Maralal Lodge and on to Lake Turkana, formerly Lake Rudolf, a paradise for the fisherman. The return route via Marsabit Reserve and Samburu leads

*Tanzania's ancient
Kilwa Ruins*

to Nanyuki.

Other new circuits havę been opened up in Western Kenya along the shores of Lake Victoria. The 'Victoria Safari' circuit provides a blend of the Kenya uplands with the warmer equatorial climate and vegetation of the lake at Kisumu and Homa Bay.

For those who yearn for the thrill of the wild-life safari Kenya's game parks and reserves still provide an immense variety. True, there is concern about the diminution from natural and other causes of the game population in some areas, but nevertheless Kenya today still provides excellent game viewing. There is a wide choice of safaris which start from around £470 (one week on safari and one week on the coast with Speedbird).

The itineraries normally start in Nairobi and take in such ever-popular places as **Lake Naivasha**, and **Lake Nakuru**, described by ornithologist Roger Tory Petersen as the greatest ornithological sight in the world, and then over the Aberdares to one of the tree hotels in the shadow of Mount Kenya, such as Treetops, Mountain Lodge or the Ark. Returning to Nairobi the safari might head south to **Amboseli Park** under the massive, snow-covered **Mount Kilimanjaro** and then return to Nairobi via the **Tsavo Park**, the largest of its kind in Africa.

When buying your safari holiday, if possible try to pick an itinerary which does not double back on itself. Not only will this enable you to see more for your money but it will also most likely mean that the operator has taken the trouble to plan the route carefully and professionally.

Always find out before booking your safari how many passengers there are in the minibus. The ideal maximum observed by most reputable operators is five. This allows one passenger in the front with the driver and two each on the centre and back seats with plenty of room for luggage. Some operators squeeze three passengers to a bench and this is not only uncomfortable, but, if you are the unfortunate inside person for the day, your view is restricted.

One notable feature of the 1970s in tourism to Africa in general, and Kenya in particular, has been the growth of Special Interest tours. Many of these are accompanied by an expert guest lecturer whose task is to talk to his guests about the wild life, art, architecture or anthropology of the area.

Kenya is currently experiencing a wave of such tours varying from groups in search of primitive man, to farmers looking at tea and coffee plantations, botanists, and ornithologists. Recent special interest tours have included groups on tropical insects and minerology. These are in addition to the activity holidays such as mountain climbing, fishing and golf for which Kenya enjoys a reputation as an area of considerable challenge and good value for money.

Special interest holidays are naturally more expensive than the normal packaged tour. A fortnight covering a large mileage with accommodation in good quality hotels and lodges would cost from £500 upwards for two to three weeks, reaching as high as around £800 for a three-week guest-lecturer accompanied game and birdwatching safari with a firm such as W F and R K Swan (Hellenic) Ltd.

One way to holiday in Kenya is to base yourself in Nairobi at a reasonable hotel and then hire a self-drive car and plan your own mini safaris. Alternatively, you can make short safari trips with one of the many operators in Nairobi. A self-drive tour often appeals to people who have already been to Kenya for it provides flexibility and the opportunity to do something new. It is not recommended, however, for the first-timer.

Kenya today can justifiably be said to be providing a good tourist product. The climate is among the finest in the world. Food, whether sea-food at the coast or Kenya beef in Nairobi's hotels or up-country lodge, is still very good, although much more expensive relatively than it used to be.

There are, however, snags for which you should be on the alert. Don't pick a safari which rushes you around so fast that you cannot take a rest and enjoy the tranquillity and beauty of the scenery. The ideal safari should avoid too many one-night stops.

Don't imagine that you will have a 'Southern Spain' type night life at a Kenya beach hotel. The style is different. Remember, too, that there are seasons in Kenya. April and May are the time of the long rains and they are still to be avoided if you want to drive to Lake Turkana or walk up Mount Kenya. But you can still have an enjoyable holiday during the so-called rainy months if this is the only time you can get away.

Finally, when assessing the overall cost of your holiday, bear in mind that while on safari there is little to spend your money on apart from drinks and souvenirs. Thus the quoted price for a safari includes a built-in advantage; your pocket-money spending is likely to be much less than at a Mediterranean or Caribbean beach resort.

Tanzania

Tanzania possesses three of the world's most spectacular tourist attractions: the **Ngorongoro crater**, the **Serengeti Plains** and **Mount Kilimanjaro**.

Ngorongoro provides in the floor of the crater the most concentrated game viewing in Africa. The Serengeti Plains with their vast open spaces clothed by the dry savannah grass and roamed over by immense herds of game, are recognised world-wide as a priceless ecological treasure which must never be allowed to die.

Kilimanjaro, towering 19,000 feet over the great continent, pronounces its strength and majesty, particularly to the increasing numbers of visitors who seek to climb it.

Tanzania has much more to offer as well. Excellent beaches, particularly near Dar es Salaam the capital, while on the attractive, clove-producing island of Zanzibar just off the coast the gates are opening cautiously to short-term visitors. There are comfortable lodges and hotels in such cities and towns as Moshi and Arusha, the capital of the tourist Northern Circuit.

With Kilimanjaro airport available to accept the largest jets, this area is ready to receive the tourist expansion that it desires. What the outcome will be of the change in the structure of the East African safari circuits now that tours from Nairobi into Northern Tanzania are not practicable is difficult to foretell. It is clear, however, that Tanzania will need time to build up its new circuits and its operational infrastructure if it is to attract the major tour operators to introduce regular packages in significant numbers.

There is no reason why Tanzania should not create a package tour industry to rival Kenya's. The attractions of wildlife, climate, scenery and coast, are all there.

In the meantime, however, the choice of package tour, from the UK at least, is limited.

Uganda

This is one country where tourism has suffered in the past few years from the political situation. In the late 60s and early 70s Uganda was earning a substantial revenue from tourism. Its profitability per visitor was greater, for example, than Kenya's. Uganda's tourists spent more per day of stay. This was due mainly to the cost of the river and lake launch trips to see the aquatic game on the Nile at **Kabalega Falls** (formerly Murchison) and in the Kazinga channel in Western Uganda. Today there is no organised package tour operation to Uganda of any consequence. Doubtless the time will come when Uganda's incomparable wild life and scenery will once again be available for the enjoyment of substantial numbers of visitors.

Zambia

Two million gallons of water a second cascade over the **Victoria Falls**. Easily seen from the Zambia side, this mighty river is immensely impressive but Zambia is not yet a major package tour country. Indeed, it sets out, and in some ways succeeds, to encourage primarily the individual traveller. Wildlife walking safaris, for example, are a growing feature of Zambian tourism with escorted groups travelling on foot through the excellent game parks. Lasting from three to eight days in the **Kafue** or **Luangwa** national parks these wilderness trails lead from camp to camp on foot, by launch or by Land-Rover. This is the way to get the real feel of Africa. But naturally, numbers are limited.

Zambia has 18 national parks, many more than is generally supposed. They cover 59,000 sq kilometres (more than 8% of the total area of the country). The Luangwa valley parks alone have over 100,000 elephant and in Kafue Park 600 different species of birds have been recorded. Regent Holidays of Bristol had a special wildlife observation tour in con-

junction with the World Wildlife Fund in September, 1977, lasting 17 days and costing £720. It included an optional four-day walking safari in the South Luangwa National Park. Another firm offering a specialist wildlife safari is Allen and Dunn Expeditions Ltd, of Soho Square, London. The 22-day Zambezi safari, which includes Botswana in the itinerary, costs from £830. Golden Lion holidays (part of British Caledonian Airways) operate regular departure tours to Zambia for £515 for two weeks based in Lusaka and from £639 for safaris.

Small fishing village on the banks of the Zaire

Malawi

Malawi is making excellent progress in its endeavours to build up a tourist industry. Its attractions, particularly scenically, are much under-estimated. So, too, is the pleasure of a holiday at one of **Lake Malawi's** beach resorts—Salima, for example, where bathing in fresh water is safe and stimulating. It is one of the few lakes in Africa where one can enjoy oneself free from the worry of bilharzia.

In the south the slopes of picturesque

Mount Mulanje provide good walking, bird watching and fishing. Wildlife is not the country's strongest point, but there is enough to give the visitor 'the feel' of Africa and the scenery and intimate atmosphere of this small and interesting nation will do the rest. Package tours are operated by Martlet Holidays.

WEST AFRICA
Ghana

It is surprising that Ghana has not gone out to win a greater share of the tourist market to Africa. An attractive and orderly country, its beaches, colourful towns, lakes and rivers all provide a feeling of spirit and life which is captivating to the visitor. Rich in history from the early trading days of the European maritime nations, the ancient castles founded by Danes, English and Portuguese, are of real tourist value. Accra itself, the capital, is picturesque and the breeze sweeps in from the sea to lessen the heat and make it one of West Africa's most pleasant cities.

The introduction recently of low cost ABC air fares (starting at £190 return with British Caledonian or Ghana Airways) has meant that it is easier to reach Ghana as an individual traveller. Consequently, the package tour industry has not developed as might be expected. A further reason is the shortage of hotel beds. Ghana nevertheless is a land of beauty and will doubtless one day build up its tourist industry to an important level eonomically.

Sierra Leone, The Gambia

Sierra Leone likes to describe itself as the Heartbeat of Africa. The country is full of rhythm and its palm-fringed villages and gloriously empty beaches are vibrant with colour and life. The beaches, with the Hotel Cape Sierra and the new Bintumani Hotel, remain the main tourist centres but there is much of interest in Freetown, the capital, where you can shop in the market for exotic fruits, or attractive leather goods and giftware.

The great advantage of the country is the low price combined with the warm tropical climate. Two weeks accommodation at the Hotel Bintumani with Golden Lion Holidays of British Caledonian, flying on scheduled air services, cost from £274 half board.

Kuoni Holders also operate to Sierra Leone. Their tours are based either on the Cape Sierra Hotel, or the Bintumani. A most important point about Sierra Leone is that you can fly there for only seven nights if you wish, a plus factor for the busy person who cannot get away for a fortnight but wants to reach a warm climate in the shorter time available.

The Gambia spreads along a 300-mile length of the Gambia river and if you want peace and quiet and a marvellous 30-mile long Atlantic beach swept by immense rollers, then this is an ideal country wthin easy time/distance reach of Europe. You can also go on launch trips on the river. But remember that from May to October this part of West Africa experiences its rainy season. The best time for a holiday here is during the European winter. Two hotels used by package operators, both near Banjul, the capital, are the Atlantic Hotel and the Hotel Fajara. Golden Lion package holidays are for 10 nights and start from £232. Kuoni Holders also run tours.

Senegal and Ivory Coast

The two francophone West African countries with meaningful tourist industries are Senegal and the Ivory Coast. The latter, however, is a very prosperous country and consequently expensive for the British holidaymaker. There are unfortunately no package tours to enable the British visitor to reach its pleasant capital, Abidjan, or to enjoy the facilities of the nearby Club Méditerranée, increasingly popular with the French visitor.

Senegal, however, is different. It has been receiving a limited number of British package tours for some time. Golden Lion operate 12-night holidays, including four nights at the Pointe St. Georges Holiday Village, which is reached by an interesting launch trip. The last three nights are spent at the beach hotel of Cap Skirring.

Senegal is a fascinating holiday area and to the traveller accustomed to anglophone Africa, a stimulating experience. But it is expensive. Golden Lion holidays start from the mid £400s for 12 nights.

You can also reach some West African countries, such as Senegal, the Gambia and Sierra Leone by fly/cruising. British Caledonian, for example, operate fly/cruises in conjunction with Finnlines.

SOUTHERN AFRICA
South Africa

Tourism to South Africa saw the ending of an epoch in 1977 when the last Union Castle liner sailed with its last passengers to Table Bay. From now on tourism to South Africa will be almost completely in the hands of the package tour operators. Of these, there are several reliable and notable names, including Sovereign, Speedbird, Rankin Kuhn, Ellerman, Far Horizons, Kuoni Houlders, Peltours, Swans Status Holidays and Martlet, and for the specialist who wishes to be escorted by a guest lecturer, W F & R K Swan (Hellenic) Ltd.

South Africa has always provided one constant in its long history as a tourist country—value for money. Even after the effects of today's worldwide inflation one can buy a meal, a bottle of wine, hire a car, or find a room in a small hotel at prices which pleasantly surprise the first-time traveller from Europe.

The air fare element, of course, being a 6,000-mile journey each way, lifts the price of the overall package but nevertheless South Africa today remains a highly popular tourist destination, whether for the stay-put beach holiday at the Cape or in Natal, or for a touring holiday along the glorious garden route or a stay-put holiday in a modern city such as Johannesburg.

A fortnight at the Elengani Hotel in Durban with Martlet Holidays starts at £454 or at the prestigious President in Cape Town from £537. A two-centre holiday with Kuoni, comprising a week in Johannesburg at the Landrost Hotel, followed by a week on Durban's sunny beaches starts at £459. Rankin Kuhn's

Zebras in one of Tanzania's great game parks

TANZANIA INFORMATION

two-week Garden tour holiday begins at £537. You can stay in private accommodation too. The lead-in price for these holidays, which normally provide bed and breakfast for two weeks in Johannesburg or a week in Johannesburg followed by a week in either Cape Town or Durban, is now around £325. This is still a reasonable price for flying half way across the world and having a bed for two weeks as well.

South Africa's tourist industry has not, as yet, suffered appreciably from the political problems of Southern Africa but there are indications that this may be changing.

"Leopardman", Ivory Coast

Swaziland, Lesotho, Botswana

These three African countries, small either in area or population or both, are all aiming to build up useful tourist industries. Particularly in the case of Swaziland, they are now catering for increasing numbers of visitors, mainly from the Republic of South Africa.

Swaziland is an extremely picturesque country with high rolling hills and mountain ranges and a welcome cool air to contrast with the heat of the Transvaal plains. Mbabane the capital offers good

accommodation and a casino which is highly popular with South Africans. The city provides lively night clubs and a stimulating multi-racial life. Motels are springing up to cater for the influx of short and long stay holidaymakers anxious to enjoy a holiday or a weekend with a difference from the more formal entertainment of the wealthy cities of Johannesburg and Pretoria.

Lesotho too can provide a pleasant change for the tourist. The open rolling hills around the capital Maserb are ideal for walking and fishing, or for riding the sturdy Basuto ponies. There is climbing too on the Lesotho side of the Drakensberg. For those with the gambling spirit this delightful little country also offers the sophistication of a casino.

Botswana is well endowed with opportunities for game watching but mainly on the basis of individual safaris of the four wheel drive type. The areas around the Okavambo swamp in the North provide good game viewing. The country is contiguous to Rhodesia and the intending traveller will therefore have to keep abreast of the political situation.

There are no package tours from Europe to these three countries but they can be reached easily from South Africa. Several weekend safaris to Losotho and Swaziland are available all the year round from Johannesburg. A three-day Swaziland weekend tour costs from £58 with Martlet Holidays.

SEYCHELLES

The Seychelles are a major success story in international tourism. Much of the credit for this must go to the planners of the islands' tourism industry in the late 60s and early 70s who drew up a policy prior to the opening of the airport in 1972 to ensure that the natural beauty of the islands was not exploited. The height of hotels was carefully controlled and there are still no high-rise buildings. Certain islands were designated as reserves or non-vehicle islands and the growth of the industry was controlled over a period so that expansion proceeded alongside the ability of the islands to cope with the numbers.

There are now 2,000 tourist beds in the island archipelago and this number is planned to increase in the coming years. New internationally managed hotels will form the bulk of the increase but there are plans for chalet type units on some of the islands.

The sudden change of government in the middle of 1977 is not expected to alter the attitude to tourism, one of the largest operators from Britain, Kuoni, report that out of 1,000 bookings at the time of the coup they only received one cancellation.

The Kuoni 1977 programme starts from as low as £237 for 14 nights in private accommodation on Mahe, the main island. Hotel holidays start at £384 for two weeks at the Coral Strand, £428 at the Mahe Beach and £474 at Fishermen's Cove. Other tour operators prominent in arranging groups to the Seychelles include Speedbird, Martlett and Sovereign Holidays. Accommodation with half board at the Mahe Beach Hotel with Sovereign in September and October 77 costs, for example, from £440.

The Seychelles are beginning to attract special interest groups. The islands are a paradise for the ornithologist and botanist. It is perhaps therefore not surprising that Swan Hellenic have now launched a guest-lecturer accompanied ornithological and botanical tour, the first being in October 1977, with several more scheduled. The price is £669 for 17 days and includes flights to Praslin Island, thought by General Gordon of Khartoum to be the original garden of Eden, and to Frigate and Bird Islands.

MAURITIUS

Mauritius deserves to do better touristically. Sunsets over the mountains, the glorious gardens of the Old French Chateau of Pamplemousse, the excellent beaches, the charm of the different races in Port Louis, all combine to make the island an exceptionally interesting and enjoyable holiday destination.

The size of the island is an important factor. It is large enough (about 40 miles from north to south and 30 from east to west) to enable you to hire a car and drive to a different beach each day, yet it is small enough to give you the feeling of being on a romantic island, with relics of ancient sea fights between French and English in Mahébourg, and with the "elegance" of 18th and 19th century colonial life reflected in the architecture of Port Louis. Yet Mauritius has undoubtedly lost some of its tourism to the Seychelles and its dependence on the South African market has been a weakness.

Several British operators run tours to Mauritius including Flairworld (a member of the THF Travel Group) who offer two and three week holidays at the Auberge Isle de France starting from £468 and High Society Tours who can provide you with a holiday at the Dinarobin for two weeks from £557, or at four other hotels.

Kuonis, one of the biggest operators from the UK to Mauritius, offer for example two weeks at Le Morne Brabant, a delightful hotel on the South East coast of the island, for £496. Sovereign Holidays start at £475 at the Merville Hotel. Martlett also operate to Mauritius. Several operators provide joint tours to the Seychelles and Mauritius, a good way to combine on one holiday these two attractive destinations. Kuonis tour of Mauritius and Seychelles, with a week in each, starts at £498.

10 hints for package tourists to Africa

1. Plan your holiday well ahead. Don't wait until the last moment. You will end up by paying more and possibly

Mogadishu's waterfront, Somalia

make a wrong decision.

2. Study the country and the political situation there before you make up your mind.

3. Watch for seasonal price changes. You can save a great deal by delaying your holiday for a week or two. Also watch out for special offers such as three weeks stay for the price of two. These are often' genuinely good value.

4. Talk to those who have been on holiday to Africa in the recent past and ask their advice.

5. Choose your airline carrier carefully. An IATA carrier is the most reliable for long-haul travel to Africa. The special charters may sound attractive in price but they can let you down.

6. Don't cross more international boundaries than you need in your holiday or safari itinerary. Apart from wasting time at the border posts there are increasingly annoying currency restrictions.

7. Don't leave your inoculations until the last minute. Get them done at least two or three months in advance.

8. Preferably book your tour with an established and respected tour operator who is a member of ABTA. If you use a travel agent, use an ABTA one.

9. Don't carry too much cash around with you. Traveller's cheques are safest. The UK banks can telex or telegraph the money to you within hours if you lose them.

10. Above all, make allowances for Africa. The pace is not the same as many capitals or resorts in Europe. That is part of the charm of the continent. The people will be invariably courteous and friendly to you if you are to them. Most African countries welcome tourists but they are naturally sensitive to criticism. Remember that in some countries you are not allowed to criticise the Government or the Head of State. Don't get mixed up in local politics; just enjoy yourself as a genuine holiday-maker. After all, that is what you're there for!

FESTAC

The Second World Black and African Festival of Arts and Culture

by JULIET HIGHET

Lagos, Nigeria, was the magnet for the greatest pilgrimage this century of black people, meeting from January 15th to February 12th, 1977, for the Second World Black and African Festival of Arts and Culture.

Ambroise Mbia, the Secretary General of the International Festival Committee, gave a Welcome Message which summarises most of the aims of this unforgettable experience:

'For the first time, African countries and black communities from all over the world will be brought together. Thus, for one month, artists, writers, thinkers and political leaders representing over 60 African nations and black communities with a population almost 800,000,000 people will assert before the whole world the existence of their cultural identity, their solidarity, the vitality of their creative genius, and their profound aspira-

tions. This is what will make this festival a cultural and artistic event of an inestimable scope. Events, exhibitions and above all, a Colloquium, whose theme is "Black Civilisation and Education", make up the cultural programme of the festival.

'Seen as a cultural event, the Lagos Festival will be the greatest gathering of all black and African people in the history of the 20th century.

'The Festival is not meant to be an arena for an ideological or political competition. Its aim is to bring about a reconciliation between men for the salvation of the spiritual values of mankind and the promotion of peace. To attain this objective, the Lagos Festival has been the handiwork of all our peoples, artists, writers, thinkers; of all our youth who are already anxious to make history. In this festival, it is not a question of proving that we have a civilisation, for it has already imposed itself on the world, and no serious-minded person today can deny the existence, the originality and the priceless values of black and African civilisations. What we propose to do, is to make a survey of the richness of our heritage and to draw therefrom the necessary resources for the revival of our peoples, and—why not—for the revival of mankind in general.

'We want to turn over a new leaf in the history of black and African civilisation, to a page as beautiful as those bequeathed to us by our ancestors. This is what the world expects from this festival.'

And did Festac '77 fulfil its promise? What did it really mean to the world, to the participants, to black people in their home countries and to Nigerians in whose country it was held?

The most important thing about Festac is that it happened at all. Its two main achievements were first to pinpoint to themselves and to the world just where black people are at ideologically. Secondly, that it helped in the creation of what might be termed a black aesthetic. By holding Festac, black and African peoples made the celebration of their cultural heritage the focal point of their oneness and strength.

'Talking Together'

Time and again in pre-Festac publicity, it was reiterated that the 'Colloquium' (meaning 'talking-together') was to be the kernel of the festival. No matter what reservations there may be over Festac, no matter how the Colloquium did not, indeed could not, 'solve' anything, both served a historical purpose as a barometer of what is going on in the black world, particularly in its ideological tendencies.

The Colloquium proved to be a battle-ground between the supporters of Negritude and the socialists. The socialist position was that freedom from domination by racist, neo-colonial or capitalist forces was of pre-eminent importance. They refuse to accept any aspect of the black heritage that could possibly be tainted, in the formation of future socio-political models. Based on a transcendental concept of black unity, the Negritude movement affirmed the historical worth of African culture in response to accusations that black people have no civilisation. At Festac, its exponents proposed that traditional structures should be the basis for African society of the future.

In essence, Festac and the Colloquium showed that black peoples are historically aware that at this moment in time, freedom is what counts; not just that the continent must be black from cape to coast, but that the enemies within independent nations must be sought out.

To understand the significance of the ideological split in the Colloquium and Festac, one has to trace the history of Arts Festivals in Africa, and indeed, the themes of their Colloquia.

The First World Festival of Negro Arts in Dakar in 1966 was organised by the poet President Leopold Senghor of Senegal, arch-exponent of the philosophy of Negritude. During this Festival, there was a Colloquium on the theme 'Function and Significance of Negro African Art in the Life of the Masses and for the Masses'. At the time such concerns, which smack of a rather non-African separation of life from art, had particular relevance for the recently-independent African states, in affirming the sovereignty of black peoples over their cultural heritage.

Right from 1956 when the first Congress of Negro Writers and Artists had met in Paris, battles had raged between countries and intellectuals who insisted on Negritude and those who opposed it.

Then, in 1969, the socialist side presented their case through the First Pan-African Cultural Festival in Algiers, quite a different kettle of fish, where the theme of that Colloquium was: 'The Realities of

Osibisa, from Britain, on stage at Festac

African Culture' and 'The Role of African Culture in the National Liberation Struggles and in the Consolidation of African Unity.'

Where Dakar was supposed to have placed culture above politics, Algiers was overtly and militantly political. Where Dakar was Negro (a word which even at that time was dangerously unfashionable), Algiers was African, set up by the Organisation of African Unity (OAU), which meant Arab and African together.

This unity led to pre-Festac differences between Senegal and Nigeria, the former proposing that the Arabs had nothing to do with "Negro" arts. As *The Times* of London pointed out in a Black Arts and Culture supplement issued at the time of Festac, the difference between the two festivals was perhaps most clearly seen in the kinds of Black Americans represented at each.

"Whereas at Dakar there was Duke Ellington (of whom President Senghor once wrote: 'Just play me "Solitude", Duke, and let me cry myself to sleep'), in Algiers there was the progressive jazz trumpeter Archie Shepp, communicating with traditional African musicians in the Casbah. There was also Miriam Makeba (who re-appeared at Festac), and who, with the Guineans, had boycotted Dakar; the Cubans, who had not been invited to President Senghor's festival; and, for good measure, Stokely Carmichael, Eldridge Cleaver and Al Fatah."

Perhaps Festac, with its huge financial investment, and the consequent public relations dreams of its sponsors, the Nigerian Federal Military Government, tried to be all things to all people, and therefore, just a bit too safe. No wonder everyone felt so ambivalent towards it; small surprise that the resolutions, patterns of discussion and division of the Colloquium reflected the deep ideological divide permitted by Festac, which had been predetermined by previous conferences and debates on African culture.

What was unfortunate in the context of the historical importance of Festac, was that so many radical Nigerians pulled out. Talking to Fela Anikulapo-Kuti, Afrobeat king of Africa, whose 'preaching' and way of life are daily more militant politically, and to the Ghanaian filmmaker Alex Oturo, who has just completed a film biography of Fela's life, I was told that they would have nothing to do with Festac because it cost too much and lacked ideology.

Fela refused to be included after he was told he could not perform with his own Africa '70 band. He told the Nigerian government that he would play if they gave out free books to all local schools, but the Government refused. (Schoolchildren had been given a month's holiday, which annoyed many parents.)

Guinea came on at the Opening Ceremony of Festac with its colours flying, serving warning of the impending conflict, by displaying placards saying: 'To every country their culture. No Whititude; No Negritude.'

Although 50 countries and over 700 participants took part in the Colloquium, only about ten delegates featured prominently. In essence, it became a gladiator event between the 'moderates'—the supporters of Negritude—Senegal, Zaire and Gambia—and the socialist delegations from Guinea, Somalia, the United States, Cuba and Kenya.

Negritude came under fire from the socialists as an emotional escape. They refused to accept that contemporary African culture should be based on it. They described it as idealist, abstract and outdated. As Professor Ron Karenga, a university teacher from the US put it: 'Programmes and proposals for a "return to source" are often no more than substitutes for real struggle against oppression and exploitation. Often it means bogging down in air-conditioned conference halls, discussing, peddling and pimping a traditional culture which long ago has been abandoned for Brook Brothers in New York; Christian Dior and Jacques Fath in Paris; Cecil Gee in London and Gucci in Rome.'

Professor Karenga went as far as to deny that there was any greater reason for Black and African unity than the need to struggle for genuine freedom. 'The African world, if it is anything, is a community which shares a common experience at the hands of capitalism and racism, and thus, a common need to free ourselves of their various forms of rule and ruin.'

But the other side was not inactive. As Bassey E. Bassey pointed out in *New Breed*: 'Word got round that the Negritude group had influenced the composition of the executive committee of Festac. This connection made it possible for the committee to reject radical papers (allegedly) under some understanding with the writers' home governments. The explanation offered was that the committee was determined to keep the discussions at the Colloquium strictly academic'.

The Brazilian Professor Do Nascimento, whose paper was rejected by the Colloquium, denounced his country as fascist, spoke of the economic basis of racism in Brazil, and alleged that his country had had a hand in his paper's rejection.

What happened at the end of the Colloquium was in the nature of a silent coup by the 'moderates', from which the socialists immediately dissented.

Professor Mveng, the Rapporteur-General from Cameroon, had throughout the Colloquium showed definite sympathy towards the conservatives. His report excluded resolutions on political parties, on ideology, control of the economy, and other important polemical issues that had come up. It was dutifully greeted by applause.

In a dramatic moment, Colonel Ali announced that there would be no debate, no proposals of amendment. It was passed as it stood—by applause!

But during the recess that followed, there was feverish activity as the working groups consolidated their opposition, discovering how the general report was totally at variance with the resolutions passed earlier in the Colloquium. Two of the five heads of delegation who were allowed to speak, voiced vigorous protest. Professor Kerenga pleaded that the general report was a negation of what they had had sleepless nights working for: 'I look at it and cannot find myself in there'.

Professor Adam, a Marxist Somali university teacher, said that if the report stood as it was, there was no justification for the distance they had travelled to take part in the Colloquium. He demanded that the report be accompanied by the resolutions and reports submitted by the various working groups. All accepted. Professor Adam emphasised the importance of the dissent from the influential supporters of Negritude, in an interview for *New Breed*: 'The general report that was read by the rapporteur-general (Professor Mveng) of Cameroon was his own selected summation of the whole. It was his personal opinion, not that of the Colloquium. The report was not discussed, it was not amended, it was not

23

National Dance Troupe
of Cuba

submitted to usual democratic procedures.

'On the other hand, the reports of the five working groups which should have constituted the material for the general report, had passed through the democratic grind. They include concrete resolutions which came as a result of discussions and debates which went on late into the night. Each resolution was adopted after thorough discussion.

'We want to emphasise that these resolutions form the heart of Festac '77 Colloquium. They are the valid materials to be submitted to heads of government and the OAU. There is the resolution calling for socialism. There are others concerning a new world economic order, the question of having militant and relevant political parties, supporting liberation movements, popular control of the economy. We emphasised our Africanness in the context of our anti-imperialist identity. This was a deadly blow to Negritude.'

It was always dreamed that Festac's Colloquium would not be just another ivory-tower conference and that the impact of the festival would not end with the closing ceremony. Having arrived at conclusions, it was recommended that the resolutions should be presented to governments for action. So how could the

Colloquium change the lives of black and African peoples?

It did come to the conclusion that all black countries should have education syllabuses more pertinent to black culture and civilisation. Training programmes for teachers and all those involved in African education are to take this view into consideration. Another proposal was the adoption of Swahili as a *lingua franca*. Through the haze of proposal and dissent, the Colloquium does seem to have suggested that Swahili should be taught, at least in universities (it already is in some.) It was Wole Soyinka, the renowned Nigerian writer, who proposed the adoption of Swahili in his paper "The Scholar in African Society", after he had done his bit to demolish Negritude by reiterating his now-famous remark: 'The tiger does not proclaim his tigritude. He just pounces.'

But like a lamb at the slaughter, Professor Soyinka was leapt upon by others more militant than he, who felt there were other far more pressing problems to address in Africa and the Third World, and that to propose the teaching of Swahili was nothing short of diversionary.

The priority in the struggle was felt to be the neo-colonial status of most African countries, and as Professor Adam pointed out, the primary contradiction to be resolved is the communication gap in each African country. 'When it comes to communications between the elite in the various countries, you can start discussing a continental language. . . . By itself it cannot solve our problems. That was my reason for disagreeing with Wole Soyinka. He made it appear as if adopting Swahili would change our dependance status. In fact he said so.

'My first language is Swahili, I am more fluent in it than either Somali or English, but that does not blind me to the real composition of our continental problem of poverty and dependence. It doesn't lead me to the stupid illusion that if every African spoke Swahili, our problems will melt away. This does not mean that we should not encourage Swahili.'

The writer Andy Akporugo brought up the subject to which many Africans outside Festac felt that the Colloquium should have been addressing itself—the development of African technology: 'It is difficult to see what useful purpose the adoption of one indigenous language (say Wole Soyinka's Swahili) is meant to serve for Africa. Is it because Africa speaks so much English, Arabic, Portuguese and French that she has been unable to register any noteworthy invention yet? It is not known that Britain, France and Germany had to use a common language to be almost simultaneously encapsulated into the Industrial Revolution. . . . And surely, the Americans, also former colonial people, have, without bothering about an alternative to the language of the English, demonstrated to the English and to the rest of the world that technolgical advancement requires much more objective inputs.'

The Festival

The greatest show on earth was on! For 29 days, including Saturdays and Sundays, Festac covered 50 drama plays, over 150 orchestral, jazz, song and dance

Festac Regatta boat

JULIET HIGHET

shows, 80 films and documentaries, 200 poetry and literature sessions, 40 exhibitions of sculpture, paintings and popular crafts. The Colloquium on Black Civilisation and Education was attended by 700 academics from over 50 countries. The diversity and level of cultural achievement was staggering as each country presented the cream of its artists. Or did it? Does the very fact that it was government-sponsored and the invitations extended and answered at governmental level automatically necessitate non-controversiality? Did the selection process produce 'safe' delegations, who lacked ideology, and whose more militant brothers and sisters were excluded?

Why for instance was there no Reggae music? Couldn't Festac take the 'dreadlocks'? Seems like Rasta music was not music to the ears of the Jamaican Government. Instead the Mighty Sparrow, the Trinidadian king of Calypso in the 1950s (and still going strong) entertained us. And why was the modern Nigerian music at Festac such a travesty of what that country has to offer, just a group of tired old hustlers on the bandwagon?

It is important to consider why there were so many persistent criticisms both during Festac and after. The ambivalence of most people's reactions (including my own) may in part reflect the ambivalence of the Nigerian Government in staging the affair. What did it really achieve for them—the government? Is it enough to mount the grandest public relations gesture of all time? What is the point of such a festival of the arts at all, of raising black consciousness, if there is to be no follow-on? Five years is an awfully long time to wait before the next scheduled festival in Ethiopia. The concept could have been engendered and projects set up for smaller more specialised festivals each year, to keep alive the Festac spirit. Was Festac really just a 'song and dance affair'?

And then there is the question of finance. Can such an expensive festival be justified when the Third World has so many pressing needs? The staggering bill is enough to trigger the controversy—at between £700 million and £1,000 million; at the lower estimate, this exceeds the total gross national product of many of the black African and Caribbean countries represented.

The Students' Union of the Ahmadu Bello University at Zaria, Nigeria, as early as June, 1975, described Festac as 'an exercise in financial recklessness'. And as everyone knows, the more urgent it became to complete the projects, the faster the money flowed into private pockets. Opportunities abounded for personal enrichment. Nigerians were not slow to take them up.

The main venues for Festac were Lagos and Kaduna, though many of the States held mini-festivals. The National Theatre in Lagos, a permanent structure costing approximately £35 million, was the main centre, and offered a theatre hall with 5,000 seats, a Conference hall of 1,000 seats, two cinema halls, each with 800 seats, four snack and cocktail bars, two large exhibition halls (as well as a sometimes over-zealous security check).

At Kaduna, the recently-completed Durbar Hotel and the Hamdala Hotel accommodated visitors to the Durbar. The Festival Village provided about 18,000 people with food and accommodation for four weeks and has since become a low-cost housing project.

Festac's staggering cost also means that never again will there be a festival of the same magnitude. Indeed, Ethiopia, destined to be host country of the next festival in 1981, has not yet given a firm commitment. Certainly its economy is in a very different condition than that of the oil-rich Nigeria. Festac was planned in the days of General Gowon; were it not for the fact that they would have lost so much face, and that there had already been so much money spent, the present more realistic regime of General Obesanjo, would never have mounted such an affair. Indeed its scope was cut down.

With entrance tickets to almost all Festac events at first costing three naira—in effect £3—an unacceptably elitist debarment which was later altered, most Lagosians felt excluded from their own festival, and became increasingly resentful as the millions of their tax money seemed to be frittered away on bare breasts and war dances, because this was about all the local press reported to their people (the international press largely ignored Festac).

True, Nigerians are still watching it on television; it was pretty comprehensively covered; in spite of unannounced switches from event to event and totally uninspiring camera-work.

Curiously it was the middle-class Nigerian who felt alienated from Festac and its meaning, whereas the working-class man and woman were incredibly proud that it had happened at all and on the scale that it did. They were intrigued to see all the foreigners in their city and felt that they were learning a lot from other blacks from far-flung places. The market women of Lagos held a spontaneous rally in honour of Festac. Perhaps if Nigerians had been more included in the event, if it had been less superficially reported, it would have meant more to them.

Since there are as yet no conditions for a Pan-African economic or military community, the most concrete exchange is through culture. Subtly underlying the somewhat questionable value of culture was the wider political implication. Nigeria, already the headquarters of ECOWAS, the economic community of West African states, consolidated its position as the wealthy colossus of Africa. It also showed itself to be dominant in the trend towards African integration.

The search for a common black identity was inevitably intertwined with the struggle for political emancipation in Africa and civil rights in the United States and elsewhere in the black diaspora. One of the most significant changes of Festac

'77, was that despite the objections of the Senegalese, it came to include Ethiopians and the Arabs, though 'Arab' was defined purely geographically. No Arab state east of Suez was included.

The original Secretary-General of the International Secretariat, the Senegalese Dr Alioune Diop, was relieved of his duties after his government had temporarily pulled out of Festac. Senegal was both affronted at the inclusion of all OAU members and liberation movement participants and at the level of personal and public corruption they alleged over Nigeria's financial involvement.

How important is the self-confidence and solidarity engendered by Festac? The colonialism brought Africans in close contact with Western civilisation and values, inferring all the time that these were superior to the native ones, and certainly conferring on black people the sense that to get ahead materially in the white man's world, one needed white education and Christian religion.

Urban development exacerbated a process which the slave trade had set in train. Both forces had the effect of imposing Western concepts on black people, giving them a sense of inferiority, as people with no cultural roots.

It is in this context that we can see Festac performing a vital function, not as an orgy of self-love, but as a pinnacle of world-wide black aesthetic achievement. Even if it only happened for one month out of a lifetime, it was important that it happened, on that scale, a vindication of what African and black people have always had in their backgrounds of which to be proud. A culture that was never crushed by outsiders, and what black people have to offer themselves and to the world—the creation of a black aesthetic, unique because it was born out of just those painful experiences that were supposed to have decimated it. Soul music is just that.

For many black peoples of the New World, their Festac experience was a pilgrimage, a soul-to-soul reunion with the land of their ancestors. There is a great interest in the US at the moment in tracing genealogical roots. As Dr Jeff Donaldson, deputy president of the American entry to Festac and head of the art department at Howard University in Washington, put it: 'Black people are the only group that did not come to this country voluntarily, and so had our roots obscured. That's not healthy when everyone else here looks back to some other country to find their heritage.' He felt that the African heritage had been shrouded in romanticism. Although there was a danger of disappointment in the culture gap between Americans and Africans, it is important for Americans to separate myth from reality, and exposure

JULIET HIGHET

Participants in the Regatta,
Ikoyi Island

to contemporary African realities could help clarify their identities and add renewed vigour to their work.

Recent movements in the arts had drawn more and more on the conscious following of traditional African art forms—the mask, percussive polyrhythms, and on subconscious survivals of the original heritage.

Festac's opening ceremony at the Stadium took off like a cultural Olympics, but so much more exciting an opening, with its diverse music, extravagant costumes, dancers hugging each other with

sheer joy to be there. It was tangibly moving; everyone felt thrilled and proud to be finally present at this most important of all black festivals—that so many nations representing such different ideologies were there was significant enough in itself—but even more meaningful was the realisation that here was an amazing diversity, an unparalleled level of cultural achievement, unified by the celebration of black culture.

Lagos, never a beautiful city, looked resplendent in its Festac decorations, all along the highways and over every public building. Erhabor Emokpae, one of Nigeria's foremost artists, had won a 4 million naira contract for these decorations, which included thousands of gilt-coloured plastic moulds of the Festac mask and of the famous medieval bronze panels from Benin.

The tone of the Opening Ceremony was somewhat marred by violence of the soldiers, who beat up unoffending queues of Nigerians, and threw people over the heads of the audience, like human cannon-balls. An aggressive atmosphere was never very far away.

A Festac held in Lagos naturally enough couldn't help but be a reflection of the urban stress of Lagos, but Festac also reminded the whole world who was in charge of Nigeria.

The military high command arrived at the Opening Ceremony escorted by their tanks. Festac '77 was happening, the African contingents giving a foretaste of their song-and-dance shows, with colourful masquerades, acrobatics and stilt-dancing. The despotic President Marcias Nguema of Equatorial Guinea was so determined to present his personal publicity via Festac, that his contingent carried giant-sized portraits of him.

The troupe calling themselves the Black People of Great Britain received tremendous applause, partly because it contained the immensely popular Afrobeat band Osibisa. They gave several superb concerts at Festac, playing to capacity audiences who must have given them the critical feedback they needed, for I have never heard them play better than on their own home-soil.

The Presidential box was loaded with an assembly of African heads of state, including Kenneth Kaunda of Zambia and the Ivory Coast's Houphouet-Boigny. After the ceremony, they travelled in one of the hundreds of smart new Festac buses to the National Theatre to see Nigeria's dramatic presentation 'Langbodo' by Wale Ogunyemi, one of the stream of dramas on the subject of the colonial expulsion, a safe Festac theme, which became dreary through

was a modern dance drama from Brazil presented by the Clyde Morgan Contemporary Dance Company. Based on a traditional African folk-tale, the show spanned witchdoctors and their magic, a meeting between man and woman, black and white, aggressive and lyrical qualities. Their costumes were most unexpected and creative, their music a fusion of tape and a surrealistic, evocative group on stage. The exuberant dancing turned us all on so much that the audience joined the drama.

It had been preceded by an informal jam session of musicians who just happened to have their instruments around,

Mozambique folklore troupe

endless repetition.

Dramatic experiences

My experience of Festac events began with traditional music from Ghana and Algiers. I was happy to have been present at some of these song-and-dance affairs, but pretty soon grew a bit bored with the apparent similarity. I gravitated more and more to the contemporary dance dramas and to hear modern black fusion music and to see African and Black movies.

The first event that really moved me

a spontaneous get-together that burst out again and again at Festac.

Apparently the present regime in Brazil does not care to acknowledge the huge black cultural presence in their country and so sent a small 'censored' contingent. What they lacked in numbers, they made up for in power.

Omo Alakatu, priestess of the Yoruba cults still influential in Brazil, brought over a troupe of fellow priestesses, quite elderly ladies, who represented different gods or life-forces in the Yoruba pantheon, in ritual dance patterns and music, full of spiritual force.

Gilberto Gil also finds inspiration in the Afro-Brazilian cults, and played fabulous Afro-Latin music ranging from the religious, to a ballad dedicated to his mother, to up-tempo dance music. He called his band 'Very Very Happy' because that was how they felt to be in Nigeria at Festac. He said that he would have come anyway, even if he had not been a part of the official contingent, 'because I have a great desire to intensify my cultural links with Africa and to make them physical'. Paulo Moura and Refazenda, both of Brazil, also gave distinguished performances.

It became evident that certain contingents were getting the audience on their feet for every one of their events, and these really seemed to be a reflection of the revolutionary nature of their societies, and of their recognition of the value of culture (or—as in the case of Brazil—in spite of the policies of their government).

Cuba has long recognised the importance of culture, both as a release for its people and as part of the revolutionary armoury. Cubans see their National Dance Troupe as including the best of Cuban traditions, as well as the search for new forms of expressing the new reality, and with the definite aim of becoming an instrument against cultural colonisation, in order to contribute to the rescue of the Cuban identity.

One of their dances called 'A panorama of Cuban Dance and Music' traced these forms from colonial times up to date, celebrating the coming-together of African and Spanish culture in a transformation into Creole. Another called "Okantonri" was inspired by Ife and Benin Nigerian sculptures. Another called "Sulkary" combined in its dance movements African sculpture, Afro-Cuban dance, Yoruba and Arara influences, as well as specifically contemporary Cuban techniques, which are innovative, sensual and lyrical.

At the exhibition of contemporary art, Cubans used photographic images culled from international magazines in startling juxtaposition, to comment on pressing Third World problems. The bony face and strained expression of a Vogue model looked sickeningly familiar to that of the starved child. These graphics were the only images I saw that made any attempt to shock the viewer out of complacency, to express any degree of urgency—indeed the one realistic and serious note in a Festac that was otherwise really rather escapist.

Guinea's paintings at the Contemporary Arts Exhibition had more substance and aesthetic merit than most of the other countries.

The sizeable delegation included the exiled South African singer Miriam Makeba, who enthralled capacity crowds with her powerful magic. Nothing less than the Queen of African song, she moved her audience to tears, recalling dead heroes like Murtala Mohammed. She was larger than life, super-professional, her act a mixture of wit and experience. It ranged in scope from the most universal of themes, of revolution, hope and despair, to the most personal, of love. For, as she said, there should always be time for love within the revolution.

Guinea scored again musically with its Bembeya Jazz. The jazz group was followed by a terrific all-female band of Highlife musicians called Les Amazones, from the Guinean Army.

For me the ultimate Festac 'song and dance' was Les Ballets Africains, also from Guinea. A masterpiece of dramatic choreography and tight production, they really raised a storm.

In spite of the extraordinary anomaly of the reappearance in Lagos of the apartheid-backed Ipi Tombi, the liberation movements did remind Festac that Africa was not yet free. The ANC (the African National Congress) promoted music and dance shows.

Mozambique and Angola laid emphasis in their shows on ideological militancy. The liberation of Angola generated new dance steps and poetry, celebrating the departure of the Portuguese, while the dance-drama of Mozambique was near to militaristic in its parade-ground quality of opening dances: the clenched fists, taut direction, aggressive build-up into set-pieces for the women encouraging their men to go to war, the martial stamping, and fierce expressions actualised into series of set-piece war dances.

The USA was expected to dominate Festac, but kept a low profile, disappointing many by the reduction in its contingent. Two thousand were expected but only about 350 showed up. However, in sheer range and diversity, the Black American representation was unsurpassed, except by Nigeria's own. All forms of art were represented: in drama, several three-act productions, puppet drama and mime. Twenty dance groups came, ranging from flying trapeze artists and modern black movement to ballet and simple street rope-dancing. There were 21 films, made by blacks, starring blacks or about the black experience. Contemporary black writing was represented by about 40 prominent writers and poets. In the visual arts, 26 printers, sculptors, painters, photographers and fashion designers exhibited.

The most popular entry on the mainstream of black and African culture was the US musical contingent. Stevie Wonder came under his own steam, giving a momentous concert with Miriam Makeba and Osibisa, and others for blind people. He was tumultuously acclaimed by the young anti-Festac brigade in the Lagos nightclubs. In turn, so moved was he by his reception and at the spirit of Nigeria, that he asked permission to build a home there. Other musicians who created a deep impression included Richard Abrams, influential leader of the Chicago movement in new black music; Sun ra, one of the original exponents of experimental black music; Donald Byrd and the Blackbyrds—a heady jazz-rock band; Nation with jazz poetry; Gil Scott Heron, a poet-musician; and the Art Porter Trio, among many others.

So in a most positive way, Festac furthered the international musical cross-fertilisation. Those African origins embedded deep in virtually all kinds of contemporary Western music had come flocking home in their new clothes, in turn bringing new directions to young African musicians, who have already been annexing them in their Afro-beat fusions.

Black American artists, though feeling themselves to be essentially outcasts of American society, have become increasingly aware that they have a unique and valuable aesthetic contribution to make. The American art-market may be white-dominated and the realisation may have dawned that there is a considerable discontinuity from their African heritage, but Afro-Asians none the less found that Festac increased their perception of themselves as African American artists and strengthened their roots-confidence through the ancestral tie with Africa.

One aspect of the contemporary black aesthetic is its commitment to a subject matter that is profoundly political, without being didactic. The Black American contingent may have come almost humbly to Festac, but it was noticeable that few of their offerings were art for art's sake, from painting to the music of 'Tribe' to the drama 'The Long Black Block', it had a message.

What did Festac do for the black aesthetic? Such a multilateral festival inevitably speeds up the process of transition in the performing arts from traditional through neo-traditional to contemporary. When dancers, masqueraders and musicians perform in front of their home audiences, they are subject to articulate criticism from discerning authorities, who share the ethics and customs that give rise to the performance.

In the participatory experience time is elastic, the audience and the performers go on until every phase and transition of feeling is lived through. It can sometimes be up to eight days of continuous drumming. Each aspect of the performance has a specific function, whether of dress, dance step or musical pattern.

Although styles were in a constant process of evolution and traditional culture was never stagnant, the performance represented a repository of societal and religious values.

As soon as a performance is lifted into an alien setting such as a civic, national or international festival, a process which has been going on in Africa for at least 20 years, it mutates. The costumes and dance patterns are subtly altered to become more dramatic, movements are changed to accommodate a proscenium arch theatre, repetition is avoided and strictly local features disappear to make way for a more spectacular entertainment, which in many cases performs the role of cultural ambassador to unfamiliar audiences.

So what one began to recognise at Festac was a polarisation between the traditional forms and the contemporary dance-drama, which such festivals have helped to create. And the traditional was so very similar throughout the world, that it really became boring so see yet more 'natives' jumping up and down with what seemed to be the same bells, feathers and beads, to what surely must have been the same dance steps, to the same endless drum-beats.

Once Black people had got over the heartening solidarity of their traditional culture from New Guinea through Rwanda to Surinam, it became evident that such locally-based success stories are better seen where they come from, where they have a function. Their static, uniform quality at Festac was in direct comparison with the innovative contemporary dance-dramas. Offerings from Brazil, Cuba, the US, Nigeria, indeed from all over the place, took on a dramatic life of their own, truly a reflection of the syntheses at work in the polyglot cultures that produced them.

Choreographers in Africa, too, have, during the past ten years, felt free to borrow elements from all over the place, brewing a new African aesthetic vitality and originality that becomes a springboard for ongoing experimentation. They use songs and words too, specialisation in theatre arts being foreign to African audiences. Traditional myths and legends still frequently provide rich themes for such dance-dramas and musical offerings, and so universal can they become that

National Dance Troupe,
Ivory Coast

they assume heroic porportions, automatically appealing to the spiritual journey going on within the heart of every man and woman.

Theatre

The core of the festival proved to be drama. By looking at just what drama there was, and at what was excluded, we get an idea of the selection processes at work, of the forces of nationalism, rather than community. there is also another significant process at work in such festivals, symbolised by the plays we saw, and that is the transition of Black and African arts from communal to individual.

There were two basic types of drama at Festac, which more or less mirrored the state of theatre in Africa—the locally-based traditional masquerade with its vigorous contemporary counterpart, and the intellectual, often elaborately-staged theatre of ideas, in which individual playwrights present the problems facing black people today, their aspirations in the new Africa, using the play as a vehicle for personal introspection and social abstraction. Obviously plays from the black diaspora tended to be individually- rather than community-based, since these 'expatriates' live in non-communal conditions, for the most part.

But theatre in Africa is not a commercial middle-class enterprise; it is not a metropolitan theatre like the National Theatre in Lagos. In fact the theatre of ideas is often subsidised by universities. African theatre is of the people and has to go to the people and not expect them to come to it.

Locally-based travelling theatre companies, often members of an extended family in West Africa, travel arduously, squashed into Mammy Wagons with their props and costumes. They are rapturously received by huge audiences who respond to a familiar dramatic millieu and to a language they can understand.

It is a classless drama whose audience and participants come from all social levels.

The plays performed are concerned with all sections of society. It is essentially community-based and springs from an ancient tradition of masquerade that was permitted to be highly critical of its rulers and even to demand their removal.

Tanzanian popular drama is actively developed through amateur groups in factories and co-operatives, often helped by theatre arts graduates who carry the work into the *Ujamaa* villages and give

Omo Aleketu, from Brazil

expression to practical problems, suggesting potential solutions through the drama.

Village theatre is used by Frelimo forces in Mozambique to awaken people to the difficulties and responsibilities of independence.

None of this popular drama was seen at Festac. What we saw were the intellectual play-texts, the safe ones, chosen for technical proficiency rather than content. On the whole the new dramatists in Africa are committed to the nationalist ideas of their countries, with the notable exception of two Nigerians—Hubert Ugunde, who has had a travelling theatre company for over 30 years, and who has been in and out of jail for his outspokenness, and has had plays and records banned. The other is Wole Soyinka, celebrated novelist, poet and playwright who has suffered in prison for his criticisms. His contribution at Festac was limited to his paper at the Colloquium. But most of the African plays were both nationalistic and individualistic.

Film-makers as pioneers

Festac showed us that at last film has come of age as a significant mass medium in Africa. Africans adore cinema and will flock to see anything, particularly if it has a local context. But their diet has for long been one of third-rate American, Indian and karate films. This has largely been due to the lack of finance available for African film-makers and the controlled distribution networks, often in the hands of foreign distributors. But at Festac we saw many excellent African (and Black) features and documentaries, many using the medium as a political and social voice. As Sembene Ousmane, the renowned Senegalese film-maker and novelist said, cinema should be the evening classes of Africans. Films should be a weapon in the fight for awareness and progress. Cinema could replace the folktale told at night.

Many of the films made in Francophone Africa, like those of Sembene Ousmane and the Camerounian Jean-Pierre Dikiongue Pipa, concern aspects of social oppression, the African bourgeoisie, Islamic exploitation of child-labour under the guise of Koranic education. The number and variety of films at Festac from all over the black world indicate the vitality of the industry. But as Francoise Balogun, co-producer and wife of the Nigerian film-maker Ola Balogun, points out: 'The African film-maker is a pioneer, working with inadequate budgets and facilities. The lack of finance, equipment and qualified technicians are responsible for the weaknesses to be observed in most African films. The director is in most cases the producer and even the cameraman and sometimes the scenarist and scriptwriter too. Sometimes he has to spend years on a film, working on a day-to-day basis as finance becomes available.'

One of the films at Festac provokes consideration of another aspect in the discussion of a black aesthetic. 'Shehu Umar', a Nigerian movie was written by the late premier Sir Tafawa Balewa. The story of an Islamic teacher and holy man, it had a fine contemplative feel, it let the panoramic landscape speak to the camera. Its timing was lengthy, it was spacious and very African, differing radically from a typical Hollywood movie, which alternates different kinds of shots—panning, zooming, close-up, its hurried build-up to one climax after another.

In this film and several others in the Festac presentation, the camera often stayed in one place and allowed the action to happen to it. Of course this technique can easily become an excuse for lazy and unimaginative film-making, as is the case with Nigerian television cameramen, for all their expensive new equipment.

Television and radio couldn't really be exhibited at Festac but are immensely important media in Third World countries. Nigeria's television coverage of Festac was non-controversial to the point of becoming non-comment. However, the best thing about it was Alfred Opubor's nightly summing-up of the Colloquium. The Head of the Institute of Mass Communications at Lagos University, he made a neat job of introducing the most important topics of the day and conducting a dialogue with that day's most important speakers.

Big spectacles

Nigeria's big contributions to the events of Festac were in the field of spectacular popular art—the Durbar and the Regatta. At the Durbar, more than 2,400 horses, camels and riders paraded around the Northern town of Kaduna. Themes stemming from the predominantly Hausa and Muslim culture of the ten Northern states were expressed through traditional shows of horsemanship.

The horse was vital in these ancient Sudanese states of the Savannah, both for communications and for military purposes. As a display of traditional pageantry, the Durbars have no equal in Africa. Every traditional ruler was accompanied by his household retinue, by mounted musical bands playing huge ancient trumpets, by dancers, acrobats and court jesters, all in a dazzling variety of costume. Their horses too were sumptuously robed and decked in the ornate leather work for which the Hausas are famous.

The regatta of 2,000 boats, drawn from eight of the 19 states, passed along the picturesquely-named Five Cowries Creek on Ikoyi Island, Lagos, in a variety of traditional boats. All were gaily decorated with cloth and flags, and manned by masqueraders. Men and women danced in the boats, accompanied by musicians. Women from the Creeks region leant right back in the water while continuing to row past; men swam by upheld by giant gourds. It was all extremely colourful and exciting.

Although the exhibition at the National Museum, Two Thousand Years of Nigerian Art, was small, due to lack of space, and limited itself to the media of bronze, terracotta and stone, the antiquities exhibited were the absolute cream of the Nigerian heritage. Deprived of the controversial Festac mask, a sensitive ivory pectoral from the court of the kingdom of Benin, now in the British Museum, and notwithstanding the fact that most of Africa's antiquities lie in foreign museums and collections, this was a momentous show indeed, beautifully lit and presented.

There was an awesome, inevitable quality about these sculptures; I detected the feeling of hushed solemnity amongst the viewers that I've noticed previously when art is of such calibre, so spiritually elevating, that it crosses all boundaries of culture, stunning us 2,000 years later. Festac's exhibitions of traditional art reiterated to all doubters the international standards of excellence Black culture has attained.

The National Museum also presented craftsmen at work, charging special Festac prices. Each country had an opportunity to exhibit crafts and national dress at Tafawa Balewa Square. Other traditional art exhibitions included the French contribution—the effect of African art on European—and the enormous and lively Ethiopian one. Successfully staged to simulate Ethiopian environments such as a church carved out of the rock, the Ethiopians even had a group of live musicians playing among the artifacts.

Apart from a most instructive and beautiful exhibition of African architectural photographs, I was disappointed by the other exhibitions of contemporary visual art. Nothing except the Cuban graphics really moved me. Was it the fault of the selection committees? Did they pick "safe" artists? Few of these were well-known. Or is the Black aesthetic just too amorphous a concept for the visual arts?

Finally one has to judge paintings and sculpture by world standards, and there were just no excuses to be made for rather amateurishly-daubed idealised or artificially-extracted canvasses with repetitive themes of the return to the mother land.

Of course some individuals stood out, notably Taiwo Jegede's impressive wood and bronze sculptures. He is a Nigerian living in London. The Sudanese Ibrahim-el-Salahi's paintings based on developments of Koranic calligraphy, and the marvellously mature bronze reliefs of the Nigerian Bruce Onobrakpeya, were works which seemed to represent high points of their creators' careers. But otherwise this was art school stuff, near to tourist art, a travesty of the artistic heritage of the African countries represented.

The Republic of Benin even had a monstrous figure that moved after the insertion of money. And I fear that it was not a send-up. Of course the Third World and the US participants do have a problem—what and how to paint? Shall they be black, international, or uniquely themselves?

It is a significant aspect of the African end of the Black aesthetic that contemporary artists return again and again to traditional themes for their subject matter. Constantly at Festac, the inspiration for the new aesthetic rested on the sure foundation of the gods, the ancestors, local mythology, the influence of the family and of natural elements—the earth, rivers and forests, and to the artists' inner dream worlds. But with urban folk art, which was missing at Festac, there is another important factor, whose combination with the traditional,

National Theatre, Lagos,
main venue for the Festival

makes it unique. These are the allusions to the "sweet life", of cities, the cars, motorbikes—the objects on which admiration for the West has chiefly rested. But for the concepts and the spiritual platform of the new art—it is Africa that gives rise to its own cultural renaissance.

Never have I heard so much good music as at Festac; it seemed like a lifetime's exposure in one month. A typical day would be to start with the radio in the morning and hear Nigerian juju music; turn on the television to catch up with the previous day's Festac presentation of the

Golden Sounds of Cameroon; take a taxi down to Tafawa Balewa Square to hear Rocking Dupsie and the Twisters from the USA.

In the evening we caught Oscar Peterson at the National Theatre and lastly ended the night at the Surulere Nightclub, where exiled South African musicians like Louis Maholo and Dudu Pukwana were creating their own musical fusions with locally-based Nigerian talent. A feast indeed.

Another memorable night, after hearing Nigerian musicians play soul in a Lebanese nightclub, we went to the Africa Shrine, where Fela Anikulapo-Kuti had invited some far-out American musicians to share the stage in an African-American Solidarity night.

It became an alternative Festac, with Fela 'preaching' against corruption, openly smoking 'weed' on stage, his go-go girls writhing away in their wooden cages, the place totally packed with hip Lagos youth, the big-time prostitutes, Fela's respectable family and of course hundreds of Festac visitors eager to see where Nigerian music was really at.

Professor Adam of Somalia summed up the Colloquium and the festival thus: 'Memories of healthy ideological debates on issues that are crucial to the survival of African and other peoples, especially in the Third World. Memories of once in a life-time contacts I have made with excellent intellectuals and artists. The art part of it has also been of tremendous significance, not only for the enjoyment, but also for learning. Our artists have been able to teach each other and learn from each other. It shows we have a lot to be proud of, but it also shows the need to take our arts higher, to further modernise them. Memories of marvellous performances by our artists, poets, musicians. Memories of Nigeria, of its generous and lively people, the friendly African people of Nigeria, and of the great potential Nigeria has if its immense resources are freed from external exploitation.'

AFRICAN MUSIC

by Prof. J. H. KWABENA NKETIA*

The duality of old and new, indigenous and foreign that characterises social and cultural life in Africa today is reflected in the music of the continent. Various forms of traditional music which have survived the impact of social change are practised by different ethnic groups in urban and rural areas. Some of these are purely indigenous in style, while others practised in some parts of the Savannah belt of West Africa, the east Horn and the East African littoral show traces of Africa's contact with Islam and Arabic culture.

Alongside traditional music are contemporary forms of African music practised largely in urban areas and which reflect Africa's response to western popular and art music as well as the impact of certain institutions transplanted in Africa. These new forms vary in style and are identified by different names such as Highlife in West Africa, Sabasaba and Kwela in Southern Africa.

The features which set traditional and contemporary musical expressions apart lie mainly in the kind of instruments and types of multi-part structures that are used.

Traditional music limits itself to instruments made by local craftsmen out of indigenous resources, even where the models come from elsewhere. These instruments include a wide variety of idiophones—that is, instruments such as rattles, bells, stick clappers, scrapers, friction sticks, stamping tubes, slit drums or gongs, and tuned idiophones—the *mbira* or hand piano (also called *sansa* in the literature), and the xylophone.

Africa is also very rich in membranophones (drums with parchment heads). They appear in a variety of shapes and sizes. There are single-headed and double-headed drums, cylindrical, semi-cylindrical, goblet and hourglass shaped drums as well as kettle drums and frame drums. These instruments are used not only for playing music, but also for giving special signals or for talking, that is, for

---

*Director, Institute of African Studies, University of Ghana, Legon

reproducing speech texts.

Aerophones (wind instruments) are also found. They include flutes, pan pipes (found in only a few places), horns made out of the tusks of elephants or animal horns, and trumpets carved out of wood or made out of conch shell, cones of calabash or out of metal.

Single reed pipes made out of the husks of millet and double reed pipes borrowed from Arabic culture are played in the Savannah belt of West Africa and the East African littoral.

A variety of chordophones (stringed instruments) are also found. Of these the musical bow is the most widespread, but there are also bowed and plucked lutes as

KENYA INFORMATION

Traditional horn, Kenya

well as varieties of zithers, harps and lyres.

It must be pointed out, however, that African societies tend to limit their choice of instruments to a selection of the above. As far as it is known, all societies make use of idiophones of some sort, while drums, musical bows and horns appear to

be widely used. However, there are a few societies that either possess no drums at all or appear to have adopted them in more recent times. Moreover not all societies have flutes, trumpets, lutes, zithers, harps or lyres.

Another characteristic of traditional music is the variety of scales it employs. There are four, five, six and seven tone scales, though every society limits itself to one or two of them. The musical intonation of these scales and the way the scales are used differ considerably from contemporary usage. Singing may be in unison or in fairly simple polyphony.

In addition to the foregoing, one must take note also of the complexity of rhythmic organisation in traditional music. The use of cross rhythms and polyrhythms which find their highest expression in drumming is the hall mark of traditional music.

In contrast to the foregoing, contemporary musical expressions tend to lean very heavily on Western instruments, especially guitars, wind and percussion sets, and more recently on electronic instruments. They employ western harmonic techniques or their approximations. Their creative models and style of performance are drawn from jazz and popular music of the New World and the Caribbean.

It is in melody, rhythm and the use of song texts that contemporary expressions maintain in African character. The use of a rhythm section—an African practice which has survived in the music of peoples of African descent—is emphasised in contemporary forms of African music.

It is not only in style and resources that traditional and contemporary musical expressions are differentiated but also the contexts of performance. The two traditions complement each other. Contemporary musical expressions are associated with modern institutions of leisure—the night club, the cafe, the ballroom, the theatre—as well as educational institutions, and the Christian church.

Traditional music, on the other hand,

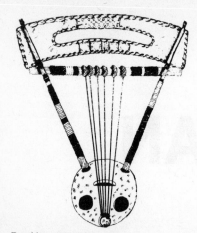

Bowl lyre, 4ft 6ins high

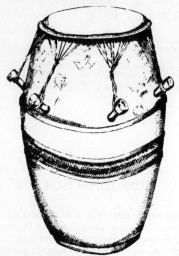

Ashanti drum, 3ft high

Xylophone, 4ft long

is used in connection with traditional institutions, rituals and ceremonies, for in traditional society, music and social life are very closely integrated. There is not only music for different social occasions but also music for different social groups. There is music for young and adults, men and women, warriors, hunters and other occupational groups, the leaders of the community and their gods.

Because of this arrangement, in traditional society music making is community oriented. A lot of scope is given to social interaction, for in addition to its aesthetic function, music provides an avenue for the expression of group consciousness. In contemporary society, on the other hand, economic considerations often provide the motivation for performances, particularly in the field of popular music. Much of the music is, therefore, commercialised. Hence it is more readily available in the form of commercial recordings.

Arising out of all these is the question of continuity and patronage. Because of the close identification of traditional music with social life, changes in social organisation, attitudes, outlook and way of life inevitably affect the practice of traditional music. Although a great deal has survived, traditional music faces difficult problems of continuity, for it is not the music that is patronised by the literate youth and urban communities in their leisure hours. Because of this and the fact that traditional music provides a clearer basis for the assertion of political and cultural identity, many African governments now pay particular attention to its promotion, preservation and dissemination. National dance troupes specialising in traditional music and dance have been formed in many African countries.

The celebration of the anniversary of political independence and other national occasions invariably features traditional music and dance in the programmes. The organisation of festivals of arts on local, regional and national levels has become a feature of cultural life in Africa.

WEST AFRICAN POP MUSIC

by JOHN COLLINS

In the past few years a number of West African bands have either recorded in or toured around Europe and America and some, like Osibisa, the Funkees, Boombaya and Twin Seven Seven have been based there. From Ghana there have been visits from E. T. Mensah's Tempos with its big band Highlife, and the African Brothers with their guitar-band variety. Four years ago the master drummer Mustapha Tetty Addy and his Obuade group released an excellent LP of traditional Accra dance-music such as Gome music and Kpanlogo.

Nigeria boasts Fela Anakulapo-Kuti whose Afrobeat is taking over from High-life throughout West Africa and is just beginning to be known to western pop-fans. Two other big names in the Nigeri-an pop scene are Sonny Ade, who spread Juju music around England on a three-month tour and Victor Uwaifo who is releasing an LP for the international market. Finally there is the Cameroonian sax player Manu Dibango who recorded the smash hit "Soul Makossa".

This is a pretty confusing array of styles, for it ranges from traditional West

African music through to the multitude of westernised types like Highlife, Juju and Afrobeat. This article will therefore give a brief survey of westernised African dance-music, starting with the first to emerge, Highlife.

The beginning of Highlife

Highlife grew out of the music styles present in the coastal towns of West Africa during the last century which led to a fusion of indigenous dance rhythms and melodies with influences from the West. One source of this outside influence was the regimental bands associated with the forts and composed of European-trained African musicians—these played military marches, polkas and popular ballads of the time.

Another source was the sea-shanties and folk-songs introduced by sailors of every nationality, including black seamen from the West Indies and Americas. In fact some of the earliest Highlife was played on a combination of African percussion instruments and sailor's instruments like the guitar, concertina and harmonica.

Finally there was the affect of the piano music and church hymns of the educated elite.

By the beginning of the century these foreign influences at work on the local music scene led to a number of "proto-Highlife" styles such as the Osibisaba of the Fantis of south-western Ghana, the Ashiko and Gome (Gombe) music of the Accra people, the "Dagomba" guitar songs of Liberian sailors and Creole melodies from Sierra Leone. By the First World War period these became known collectively as Highlife.

By the 1920s Highlife became firmly established, especially in Ghana where it was played by three distinct types of band. One was the brass and fife band playing regimental marches and Highlifes at Empire-day parades, picnics and other town functions. The large towns like Accra, Cape Coast and Kumasi also had

Les Amazones, an all-female band from Guinea

prestigious ballroom orchestras which played Waltzes, Foxtrots, Quicksteps, Ragtimes, Rumbas and Highlifes to a black elite audience complete with top-hats and evening-dress. It was in this context of local melodies, being orchestrated for a high-class audience that the term "Highlife" was coined.

A third type of Highlife band was the guitar-band which combined acoustic guitars with local hand-drums, rattles and hand-pianos. In the rural hinterland of southern Ghana and Sierra Leone literally scores of these groups appeared which played a less westernised Highlife than the posh urban bands. In Nigeria, during the thirties, a similar process occurred with guitar bands there playing a Yoruba music related to Highlife, called Juju music.

The Second World War had a big impact on the dance-band scene as Commonwealth and American troops stationed in West Africa brought in new musical ideas, particularly Swing. The Swing bands played mostly at the army clubs and European clubs, but by the end of the war when the foreign troops had left they became Africanised.

The most important was the Tempos which by 1947 was fully African and

41

besides Swing and ballroom music started playing Highlife. The leader was E. T. Mensah and the drummer Guy Warren, and between them they introduced a Latin percussion section of bongos, congas and maraccas and enlarged the band's repertoire to include Calypso. Subsequently this band became the prototype for the numerous post-war Highlife bands that sprang up throughout West Africa. For example it was only after the Tempos had toured Nigeria in the early fifties that bands like Bobby Benson's, Victor Olaiya's and Rex Lawson's started playing Highlifes. Consequently E. T. Mensah became known as the "King of Highlife".

Meanwhile the acoustic guitar-bands continued to grow in popularity. In Sierra Leone there was Kalenda's group which played local Meringues and Highlifes. In Nigeria Juju music kept gaining converts, especially after I. K. Dairo formed his Blue Spots band in 1957 although it was never allowed at the expensive hotels.

One feature of both the dance-bands and guitar-bands has been their continual assimilation of foreign musical ideas and styles, in particular the influence of black American music. Black music from both sides of the Atlantic is almost exclusively dance-music and places great emphasis on rhythm, in other words they have a lot in common. Another interesting synthesis is that of Africa and Latin to create Congo. It first appeared in Zaire about 25 years ago and then spread throughout French-speaking Africa. A present-day example is the Afrobeat explosion sparked off by Soul.

For many years Jazz experts have traced the African heritage of black American music and more lately have noted the increasing "Africanisation" of western Pop music (ie Jazz, R & B, Soul, Reggae, etc), music that is indirectly African in origin.

Feed-back is a third aspect of the cross-cultural musical exchange between Africa and the West and is a factor likely to lead to the direct impact of African music on western Pop.

Pop group on stage at Festac in Nigeria

JULIET HIGHET

West African Pop bands

By 1960 Rock and Roll was being widely played and after 1962 dozens of distinct pop groups appeared, formed by school students and encouraged by promoters who organised competitions. The next stage was the introduction of Soul. By the later sixties numerous pop bands were around playing Rock, Soul and Underground music—the Echoes and Akpata Jazz of Sierra Leone, the Saints, Psychedelic Aliens and El Pollos of Ghana, the Super Eagles from Gambia and the Strangers, Hykkers International and Segun Bucknor's Soul Assembly from Nigeria.

The only problem with them was that, except for the occasional Highlife and Congo number, they only played "copyright" music, that is exact copies of western pop records.

Since the sixties pop bands have moved towards a more creative and experimental attitude, with two main factors being catalytic.

First and foremost is Afrobeat, a fusion of African music and soul pioneered by Fela Anakulapo-Kuti.

He was first the leader of the Koola Lobitos which tried to fuse Jazz and Highlife, but then after a trip to the States in 1969, during which he "found his faults", he returned, changed the band's name to the Africa Seventy and concentrated exclusively on his Afrobeat.

Many LPs have followed his first release of 1970 called "Chop and Quench". All the lyrics are controversial whether in Yoruba or pidgin English. "Shakara" is about the sex war in modern Nigeria and "Confusion" is about the hectic life in overcrowded Lagos. A recent release refers to a brush he had with the police involving Indian Hemp. His large band, based at his Africa Shrine club in Lagos, consists of guitarists, drummers and a front-line of trumpet and saxes.

Fela sings and plays electric piano or tenor sax and is accompanied by six girl singers and a variable number of "Afrosexy" dancers. He is the most popular musician in West Africa at the present time.

Another factor encouraging pop musicians to turn towards their own African music for inspiration is the Latin Rock of Santana. In 1971 this group played at the Soul to Soul concert in Accra and their "Afro" sound started off a number of Ghanaian pop bands using Latin and African drums.

The net result of the various influences has been the growth of bands that combine African instruments like the drums, rattles, flutes and xylophone with electric guitars and play a multitude of styles that go under the name Afrobeat, Afro Rock, Afrodelic Funk and so on. From Ghana come the Big Beats, Boombaya and Hedzoleh, from Dahomey the Polyrhythmic Orchestra, from Nigeria Mono-Mono, Ofege, Ofo and the Funkees, and from Cameroon Manu Dibango.

The simultaneous revival of folk-music and appearance of Afrobeat has also started to bring together the very separate traditions of the folk guitar-bands and the western Pop-influenced ones. For instance in Ghana Ampadu, leader of the African Brothers, has brought out a synthesis of Highlife and Afrobeat which he calls Afro-hili. Similarly, Manu Dibango has fused Soul with Cameroonian Highlife music called Makossa. In Nigeria Sonny Ade has developed a style of Juju music influenced by Afrobeat and Sonny Okosun has created Ozzidi music or "Jungle Rock" developed from Victor Uwaifo's version of Highlife.

While Highlife evolved in a colonial situation with the urban African musicians copying Western music, today West Africa is independent and local music is being given its rightful place. The western music being assimilated now is black American music looking towards Africa for inspiration. Things have come full circle.

THE CRADLE OF MAN

by RICHARD E. LEAKEY*

What was Africa's contribution to the world we know? Not the wheel, nor the aeroplane but the creature that contrived both, together with every other technological device! Mankind originated in Africa, and the complex behaviour that embodies technology was a product of man's adaptation to prevailing circumstances in Africa millions of years ago.

To discern why man's origin should have begun on the African continent one must go back well before the first appearance of man-like creatures to a time when the early mammals were establishing themselves. At this time the Americas were splitting away to become distinct and separated land masses. The continent of Africa thus formed, retained populations of mammals from which the Old World primates developed. As time went on, there evolved more specialised groups, one of which includes apes and man himself. These early Old World primates spread into Europe and Asia and, at different points in time, there was a remarkable diversity of primate types in Africa and Asia.

The fossil record for early primates and early man in Africa is spectacular, and from the available evidence, it seems certain that Africa was the crucible for man's development at a number of stages—the first differentiation from the apes, the subsequent appearance of man-

like forms, the emergence of tool making and tool using, and ultimately the development of the 'wise man' *Homo sapiens.*

Man's forebears appear to have travelled between continents as there are records of early man in southern Europe, Asia and the Far East. Nevertheless, it was from Africa that these populations appear to have originated. The study of man's origin in Africa got underway in 1924 with the discovery of a child's skull in a limestone quarry at Taung in South Africa. Robert Broom and Raymond Dart worked various sites in South Africa in succeeding years and a very large collection of fossil remains of early man resulted. The fossils were variously classified but essentially, two 'types' were identified—*Australopithecus robustus* and *Australopithecus africanus*. These discoveries were all made at a time when research in eastern Africa was severely hampered by lack of finance and it was not until 1959 that the position changed significantly.

The South African fossils are very important but they unfortunately lack certain details which restrict their value in the documentation of man's evolution. The fossils were all recovered from limestone cave deposits which were quarried

Administrative Director,
National Museums of Kenya

by means of dynamite. Thus in general their temporal relationships cannot be accurately determined. Furthermore there are no minerals suitable for dating studies so that the age of the fossil material is unkown.

The situation in East Africa is very different. Since 1959 when the first major find was made in Tanzania at Olduvai Gorge, a wealth of specimens has been recovered from a number of sites. The fossil material is not as plentiful as in South Africa but the specimens are generally better preserved and more complete, providing vital clues to many aspects of human origins that had previously eluded scientists.

The East African sites are numerous and all have one important feature in common—the fossils are recovered from soft rock or sediments that are well stratified and which are associated with volcanic rocks that provide a basis for dating. Many of the sites lie in the Rift Valley, a geographical feature stretching from the Zambezi River northwards through Tanzania, Kenya and Ethiopia to the Red Sea. In addition to sites that have yielded remains of early man, there are many sites where stone implements occur, providing valuable data on man's early technological skills.

The most famous East African sites for early man are the Olduvai Gorge in Tanzania, East Rudolf in northern Kenya and the Omo Valley in southern Ethiopia. All of these deserve additional comments but it seems appropriate to mention briefly some of the other sites first.

In Tanzania, one important locality is Laetolil, lying to the north east of Lake Eyasi, not too distant from Olduvai Gorge. Other sites in this region are Lek Lagarga and Lake Ndutu, situated at the westerly end of the Olduvai river. These three sites have produced some evidence of man and his stone implements and future studies may well provide additional material. To the north east of Olduvai, the Peninj site on the western shore of

Lake Natron has provided a superb jaw of *Australopithecus* as well as many stone implements dated at just over 1.2 million years.

North from Lake Natron, across the border into Kenya there are a series of sites associated with Lake Magadi. The most important of these is Olorgesaillie, a distance of 60 kilometres from Nairobi where thousands of hand axes and other tools can be viewed as they were when discovered. This site is a popular attraction and provides an excellent example of man's technology as developed about 500,000 years ago. A similar but smaller site can be seen at Kariandusi near Lake Elementaita on the main road north from Nairobi towards Lake Nakuru.

Lake Baringo, also situated in the Rift Valley is an area where a number of important sites are now known. To the west of the lake, Chemeron and Kapthurin have both yielded fossil remains of man and Chesowanja to the east of the basin has also provided an important fragment of a cranium and a large number of archaeological sites. The Baringo sites are all quite small and situated in thick thorn bush which makes access very difficult.

Two sites are known to the west of Lake Rudolf and these are relatively early in time—Kanapoi being dated at just over three million years and Lothagam approximately five million. The evidence for man at this time range is so far very scanty but it is quite probable that the key to the later developments in man's evolution will eventually be traced back to somewhere near five million years. It is unfortunate that very few localities are known where fossils of this time range can be found. The most recently discovered site is situated in northeast Ethiopia in the Afar region of the Awash Valley. Preliminary reports point to the potential of this site as being likely to yield evidence of man at a time range older than three million years. Many questions have resulted from the studies of younger material and the scientific community is anxiously awaiting new discoveries from the Afar.

Let us now turn to the three most well known East African sites—Olduvai, East Rudolf and the Omo Valley. These three localities provide a very comprehensive picture of early man, his technology, his environment and the animals that lived with him in East Africa between three million years ago and the present time. The story that unfolds is complex and new questions are posed as the research progresses.

The programme at Olduvai was started by the late Dr. L. S. B. Leakey in 1931 and is begin continued by his wife Dr. Mary Leakey. More than 40 years of work have produced a very complete story and the study is probably the most comprehensive that has ever been undertaken in the broad discipline of prehistory. The Olduvai evidence begins at 1.8 million years and the youngest strata are less than 100,000 years, well into the period when modern man or *Homo sapiens* was well established in Africa.

From the earliest levels at Olduvai, a wealth of data has been collected on man's stone tools and living sites. From these, it is possible to reconstruct some aspects of man's life style for the period—for example what he ate, the probable density of the population, the techniques he used when making implements and many others. It seems that at Olduvai, there were at least two distinct kinds of early man living in the same habitat at the same time. One of these, the ape-like *Australopithecus (Zinjanthropus) boisei* was not common and almost certainly did not make stone tools. Present thinking suggests that this type of man became extinct about one million years ago and the *Australopithecus boisei* was primarily vegetarian, rather than a meat-eating omnivore. The other form of man *Homo habilis* was more advanced, surely the maker of the tools and it seems likely the *Homo habilis* was a precursor of later

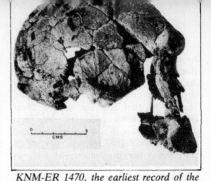

KNM-ER 1470, the earliest record of the genus homo

forms of man such as *Homo erectus* and *Homo sapiens.*

The Olduvai Gorge has also yielded evidence for *Homo erectus* living just over one million years ago. The presence of this form in East Africa at this time is of the greatest interest because previously, the only material known was from Peking and Java in the Far East. The ancestry of *Homo erectus* is not fully understood but it seems quite likely the the Asiatic material originated in Africa. The 'hand axe' technology or Acheulean industry is normally attributed to *Homo erectus* and this can be established as an African development that moved into Europe and Asia.

To go back further in time, one must move from Olduvai to East Rudolf and the Omo Valley where stratified deposits cover a longer time span, beginning at just over three million years. At the Omo, an international team of scientists have carried out research since 1967 and results have been reported by the team leaders Dr. Y. Coppens (France) and Dr. F. C. Howell (USA) and their associates. At East Rudolf, an international group has undertaken research since 1968 through the offices of Kenya's National Museum with support from the National Geographic Society, the National Science Foundation and other grant-giving bodies. The final results of this research in the Rudolf basin are yet to be fully assimilated and studies are continuing. Several important milestones in our knowledge can be noted, however, from evidence from these two sites, and there is little doubt that mankind is today closer to understanding his origin that at any time before in the history of the species!

The ungainly looking *Australopithecus boisei* was fairly well spread through Africa from between three million years ago. The East African variety is very similar to the form in Southern Africa *Australopithecus robustus*. These creatures had small brains, large molar teeth and while they moved about on two legs, they were probably less inclined to stride out on long distance moves. A large number of scientists consider it likely that these creatures occupied a very specialised niche in the ecology and that the dental characteristics imply a rough, vegetarian diet. There is evidence that the individuals varied in size, especially between sexes; similar dimorphism is evident in other living primates such as the gorillas. There is no sign of any significant evolution occurring during the period and it is probable that the specialisation occurred earlier than three million years ago with the inability to further specialise resulting in extinction at about one million years ago.

The evidence for a second species of *Australopithecus* in East Africa is more tenuous but recent work suggests that there may well have been a small brained, gracile hominid comtemporary with *Australopithecus boisei*. In South Africa, there is clear evidence for this smaller species and it would be surprising if the same situation did not exist further north. The big question is whether *Australopithecus africanus*, the gracile form, was really ancestral to *Homo habilis* and *Homo erectus* as has been proposed. There is sufficient evidence to seriously question this hypothesis and possibly we will have to accept that a common ancestor for *Homo habilis*, *Australopithecus africanus* and *Australopithecus boisei* has yet to be discovered and will be found at an earlier time level than three million years.

At East Rudolf, there is excellent evidence for an early form of *Homo* at three million years. The now famous skull KNM-ER 1470 is the most dramatic example but other specimens are known and establish beyond doubt that *Homo* was a contemporary of *Australopithecus* from at least three million years ago. The relationship between the '1470' type of *Homo* and *Homo habilis* has not been established but they were clearly very similar. As the story before three million years, there are too few specimens at present to enable detailed interpretation. It does appear that there is presently no definitive evidence for *Australopithecus* earlier than three million. The few fragments that are known are too incomplete to allow conclusive identification and all that is possible is to confirm the presence of man in broad terms. The earliest evidence for 'man' as opposed to 'ape' is from Ft. Ternan in western Kenya where the late Dr. L. S. B. Leakey recovered specimens of a creature called *Kenyapithecus wickeri*. There is little doubt that this form was already differentiated as an hominid and the dating places the material at 14 million years. Further material is required to fully document this stage of man's past.

In summary, it can be shown that a great wealth of evidence has been uncovered in Africa and all of this confirms the contention that man is a product of evolution in Africa. There is more to be studied and questions outnumber answers. Man's future as species on this planet is complex and it is certain that we are all committed to the same destiny. Too often, men forget their bonds in common and dwell instead upon superficial differences which are unimportant in the context of time.

Man today is a single species and we have both a common evolutionary heritage and origin. The ultimate success of our species must rest upon our ability to recognise our dependence upon unity and co-operation between all people.

ANGOLA

After many years of struggle against Portuguese colonisation the people of Angola won their independence in November 1975, but there was immediately civil war between the different nationalist movements. The Popular Movement for the Liberation of Angola (MPLA) won this war in March 1976 after contending with an armed invasion from South Africa and mercenary forces who backed its enemies, the National Front (FNLA) and the National Union (UNITA). The MPLA called upon Cuban forces to help it repel the invaders and it refused to negotiate with the rival movements.

Since the civil war ended the MPLA has concentrated on consolidating its power, restoring order and rebuilding the damaged economy, and it has no intention of allowing tourism for several years to come. It is at present impossible for anyone to visit Angola except on Government-approved business, and there is no reliable information available on travel facilities.

GENERAL INFORMATION
Area: 1,246,700 sq. km.
Population: 6 million.
Altitude: From the narrow coastal belt mountains rise to about 2,000m, levelling to a plateau of about 1,300m.
Capital: Luanda.

Head of State: President Agostinho Neto.
Government: Controlled by the MPLA.
Languages: Portuguese is the official language. The main African language groups are U-Mbundu, spoken by the Ovimbundu of the central plateau around Nova Lisboa; Ki-Mbundu, spoken by the Mbundu in Luanda and its hinterland; Kongo in the north; Chokwe (Kioko) in the east. In the south are smaller linguistic groups such as the Olambo, Ngangela, Nyaneka-Humbe, Cuanhama Herero.
Religions: Christianity and traditional beliefs.
Currency: Kwanza (=100 lwei).
Time: GMT + 1.

HISTORY

The famous Kongo kingdom was extended over northern Angola by Wene in the 14th century. The empire was still flourishing when Diogo Cao, a Portuguese explorer, reached the mouth of the river first known as Zaire (later Congo) in 1482. The Kongo kings, notably Afonso I (1506-43), were very interested in the foreigners and asked for missionaries and craftsmen to be sent from Europe. They in turn sent their sons to Lisbon for education, and one returned as the first African bishop. By the 17th century, however, the slave trade and unscrupulous traders had undermined the central authority in the kingdom and destroyed any trust between the two countries.

The invasion of the Jaga in 1568 also weakened Kongo. Soon the Ndongo State, ruled by a king known as the Ngola, rose to prominence around the Lucala River. The Ngola became the major target of Portuguese attacks from the coast—400 settlers had arrived in Luanda in 1575. Throughout the 17th century they drove inland, building first Massangano and then Cambambe forts. They followed the navigable Cuanza River looking for elusive mines.

When defeat at the hands of these settlers was inevitable, Nzinga, queen of Ndonga, moved towards the Cuango River to remain an independent "middleman" in the lucrative trade between the coast and the interior.

Angola was useful to the Portuguese solely as a source of slaves for Brazil—about one million were shipped between 1580 and 1680. The strongest tribes joined the slave raiders, and some areas were devastated. The country saw no economic advance. Other Europeans took part in the drive for slaves: the Dutch where they could, the English at Ambriz and the French at Cabinda.

Meanwhile the Portuguese expanded from Benguela to build Caconda fort in 1682. Their Eurafrican agents *(pom-beiros)* travelled far and wide to discover new markets.

The independence of Brazil in 1822 brought the formal abolition of the slave trade (1836) but in fact it made no difference to its continuance. The Ovimbundu became adventurous traders from the Zaire River to the Great Lakes and from Zambia to the Kalahari. They switched, equally profitably, to collecting wild rubber for sale.

The loss of Brazil inspired some Portuguese to intensify Angola's process of colonisation.

When other countries joined the scramble for Africa in the 1870s, Portugal expanded into the Lunda area, but lost its claim to the rest of the Zaire basin to Leopold II of Belgium, and western Zambia to Britain. Within the sphere recognised by Europeans to be Portuguese, various African peoples (Ovimbundu, Dembo, Cuanhama) put up long drawn-out resistance until 1918.

In 1961 a rebellion on the coffee plantations near Carmona, encouraged partly by the new independence of other African countries, was savagely suppressed and 50,000 Africans were slaughtered. The rebellion did, however, awaken the authorities into abolishing forced labour and providing better educational, health and agricultural opportunities for Africans.

The guerrilla war moved during the 1960s from the north to the east and the most active nationalist movement throughout this period was the MPLA. When the Portuguese government of Dr. Marcello Caetano was overthrown in April 1974 Angola was thrown into confusion, with the smaller nationalist parties manoeuvring for power and influence.

The MPLA finally emerged the victor after a period of great uncertainty in 1975 and civil war in early 1976. Its policies are uncompromisingly Marxist-Leninist and it still faces internal and external opposition.

BENIN

For travellers without the time and patience to discover Africa slowly the People's Republic of Benin has perhaps more sights per square kilometre than any other African country. Geographically, it is conveniently established at the crossroads between English and French-speaking West Africa, and it is traversed by the beautiful palm-tree lined coastal highway from Lagos (Nigeria) to Accra (Ghana).

There are important centres of culture dating from the pre-colonial period and the artistic and musical traditions remain very strong. Known for centuries as the 'Slave Coast' with its great slave market and European forts at Ouidah, this was also the home of the powerful Voodoo cult which spread to the New World.

After gaining its independence from France in 1960 as Dahomey this small, overcrowded, politically volatile country experienced six coups, six constitutions and eleven governments leading to the military regime under Lt-Col. Kerekou. The name was changed from Dahomey to Benin in 1975 as part of a campaign to break with colonial ties. The name is, however, purely symbolic and not historically consistent since the ancient Kingdom of Benin covered an area that is now part and parcel of modern Nigeria.

Potential visitors should take into account the possibility of being cut off from the rest of the world for a number of days as there have been alleged or attempted coups in recent months, followed by security clamp-downs. On the other hand, there is no reason to feel that there is any extraordinary risk in visiting what is a fundamentally friendly and peaceable country.

THE LAND AND THE PEOPLE

The People's Republic of Benin is a long narrow strip of country, stretching 700 km from the Bight of Benin to the Niger River. The sandy, coastal strip, planted with waving coconut palms, soon gives way beyond the lagoons of Porto Novo, Nokoue, Ouidah and Grand Popo to a plateau rising gradually to the heights of the Atakora Mountains, with altitudes from 500-800 m.

Much of the country across the plateau is rich agricultural land covered in plantations of oil palm, cotton, coffee and tobacco. Farther north, as the land dries out into savannah, karite nuts are cultivated for oil, and stock rearing is possible, being free from the tsetse fly.

From the Atakora highlands in the north-western part of the country run two tributaries of the Niger, the Mekrou and Alibori; while southwards the Oueme flows down into the Nokoue lagoon.

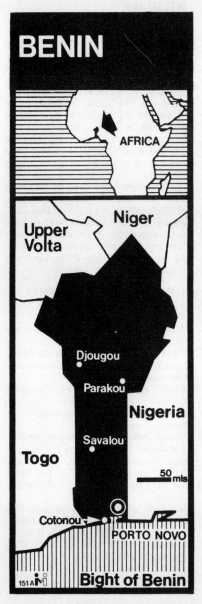

Another river, the Mono, flows into the sea at Grand Popo and is the frontier with Togo along much of its course.

Three major ethnic groups dominate the population of three million: the Fon (and the related Adja), the Yoruba and the northern group composed of Bariba and Somba.

The Fon, the most numerous group, constituted the former kingdom of Abomey; now they are spread throughout the country and are mainly farmers. The Yoruba are settled along the eastern border with Nigeria; a great Yoruba kingdom was centred on Porto Novo; its people have always been merchants and traders. Bariba dwell in the north-east, a farming people whose kingdom was Borgou, while in the Atakora region live their brothers, the Somba—naked warriors who build their houses like two-storey fortresses and cluster together in large villages.

CULTURE

The cult of Voodoo, the best-known of the traditional religions, was born in Benin. It is a highly organised religion with a hierarchic structure. At the head stands God the Creator, Mahou, from whom emanates the secondary divinities, or Voodoo, who act on human destinies. Formidable supernatural powers are attributed to them. Among the Voodoo are Hebioso, the God of Thunder, and Sakpata, the God of Smallpox.

A step below the Voodoo come the spirits of the dead who dwell on earth. Only the priests can communicate with the Voodoo and the spirits of the dead; their social and political power is consequently enormous. The priests are trained in monasteries and convents, often recognisable by the white cloth hanging over the doorway. The Voodoo priest will select novices from among the young village girls. They undergo rigorous training away from their families and spend their lives in the service of the cult.

Benin's most famous art forms are silver, bronze or tin figures and objects, and the royal Abomey tapestries. Until the 19th century, the Fon kings did not allow metal objects, or their famous embroidered tapestries, to be made outside the Abomey Palace walls. The palaces are full of royal statues and animal effigies, beautifully fashioned; the common people were traditionally only allowed to carve wood and calabashes. After 1900, tin was used by craftsmen to make the long, elongated figures of men and animals that characterise Beninese metalwork. They are curiously naturalistic, with animal fur and men's clothes often point-engraved upon them.

Statuettes of a horseman armed with a lance represent Shango, a dreaded king who became transformed in his people's memory as a God of Thunder. Eshu, a demon, is portrayed as a man with a pointed bonnet and flute. Perhaps the most famous figure is the God of Medicine, the bird Osanhim, perched on a stick and gracefully swaying on a mobile.

The remarkable tapestries that hang in the Abomey Palace tell the history of its kings and their exploits. A flourishing industry produces gaily coloured patchwork and embroidered tapestries. A figure often depicted is the male panther-god Agassou, from whom Abomey kings claim descent. Other emblems adopted by the kings were 'Buffalo wearing a tunic' and 'Bird with tam-tam'. Behanzin (1889-1894) had as his personal emblem a shark and an egg: 'Here is the king we have awaited so long for great achievements. . .the world holds the egg for which the earth craves.'

Abomey is the place to witness traditional dances, but there are many cultural events throughout the country during the year. The Bariba people have horse-riding displays, for example, while in Porto Novo there is a spectacular carnival in December.

WILDLIFE

The southern half of the country is in general too cultivated and populous for many wild animals but the open savannah of the north is some of the best game country in West Africa. Here reserves extend along the Niger River and its tributary, the Mekrou, as well as the Oti in the east. The famous 'W' Park, named because of its shape, has been jointly developed by Niger, Upper Volta and Benin. The Pendjari Park (adjoining the Arly in Upper Volta) has a modern hotel and can also be visited from nearby Porga.

In the light forest land of the parks there are herds of elephant, buffalo, giraffe, antelope and Buffon's kob. Lion, leopard and cheetah come down to drink at the waterholes. There are many monkeys and numerous species of birds. In the slow-running Niger River, hippo and crocodiles bask in the sun.

GENERAL INFORMATION

Area: 116,000 sq. km.
Population: 3 million.
Altitude: Most of the country lies below 500 m.
Capital: Porto Novo remains the official capital although the effective capital is Cotonou.
Head of State: Lt-Col. Matthieu Kerekou.
Government: Military, claiming to be Marxist-Leninist.
Date of Independence: 1 August, 1960.
Languages: French (official). The three main languages are Fon, Yoruba and Bariba but the language of the Dendi who live near the Niger is also widely spoken.
Religions: About 68% traditional; 17% Christians, predominantly Roman Catholic; 15% Muslims (mostly in the north).
Currency: CFA franc. £1=428 CFA francs. $1=249 CFA francs.
Time: GMT+1
Electricity: 220V.

HOW TO GET THERE

By air: There are regular services by UTA and Air Afrique from Paris and by Pan Am from New York. There are also regular services from Abidjan, Accra, Bamako, Douala, Lagos, Lomé, Monrovia and Ouagadougou. The airport is 6 km from Cotonou. Taxis and car hire firms meet international flights. Taxi fares should be agreed before starting any journey. There are supposedly fixed and cheap rates for rides within Cotonou.

By road: There are good tarred coast roads from Lagos (Nigeria) and Accra (Ghana) and the traveller can easily take a taxi from Lagos or Lomé (Togo). The border normally closes at 1900 hours. Visitors travelling by private car can easily obtain a *laisser passer*, which is also valid in Togo. There is a thrice-weekly bus service on the other main entry route from Niamey (Niger) to the railhead at Parakou run by the Société Nationale des Transports Nigeriens.

By sea: Several shipping lines run regular cargo services with limited passenger accommodation from Marseilles to Cotonou and local shipping from Lagos arrives in Porto Novo.

Visa and health regulations

Nationals of France, French-speaking Africa and Nigeria require only a national identity card or passport; nationals of all other countries must possess a valid passport and entry visa obtainable from Beninese or French Embassies abroad. Visitors should have a return or onward ticket or repatriation guarantee.

All visitors must have international certificates of vaccination against smallpox, yellow fever and cholera.

Dutiable goods

In addition to personal effects, the following may be brought in duty-free: 50 cigarettes; two cameras with 10 rolls of film per camera, one movie camera, one record-player, one radio, one tape-recorder, sports equipment.

Currency regulations

There is no limit on the amount of foreign or local currency which may be imported. A declaration should be made on arrival. On leaving the country, not more than 25,000 CFA francs in local currency per person may be taken outside the franc zone. Any unused foreign currency may be taken out. French franc notes are normally accepted at par value.

CLIMATE

The south of the country has an equatorial climate and the north a tropical one. The south is very humid, especially on the coast, and the mean temperature is 25°-28°C. There are four seasons: dry January to April; rains May to July; dry in August; rains September to December.

In the north, temperature variation is more extreme, rising sometimes to 46°C in the day in March and April and falling to 10°-15°C in December and January, when there is often a dusty and cool harmattan wind from the north east. There are two seasons in the north: dry November to June and rain July to October.

What to wear: Plenty of lightweight cotton or linen clothes are needed. Avoid synthetic fibres. Take a light raincoat or umbrella in season and a warm wrap for cooler evenings.

Health precautions: Take anti-malaria prophylaxis a fortnight before, during, and a fortnight after the visit. Vaccination against typhoid (TAB) is advisable and tap water should be boiled before drinking.

ACCOMMODATION AND FOOD

The main hotels in Cotonou are pleasant but elsewhere there is very little accommodation for visitors, even in coastal towns. Abomey has only a small hotel and motel and Parakou two small hotels; there are two good establishments for game viewing near the Pendjari National Park. Food at hotels and restaurants is generally in the French style although some also serve local African specialities.
Tipping: The normal tip at hotels and restaurants is 10%.

TRANSPORT

Air: Escadrille Beninoise provides regular services from Cotonou to Parakou, Natitingou, Kandi and Abomey and in the dry season to Porga (from which Pendjari Game Park may be reached). They and the Aeroclub, Cotonou, will also charter out two-seater Piper PA 18s.

Road: The principal roads in the south are tarred. Other roads are gravel and impassable in heavy rains. When travelling, especially in the north, take good supplies of drinking water and spare petrol; filling stations are rare.

There are plenty of taxis in Cotonou, Porto Novo, Abomey and Parakou. Coast services run on the main road north of Parakou to Niger and also to Natitingou as well as along the coast from Cotonou to Lomé (Togo).

Rail: Daily services run along the coastal railway. On the line from Cotonou to Parakou railcars with second and third class coaches run every day and first class coaches with reclining seats three times a week.

Car hire: Vehicles may be hired in Cotonou from: **Locar Benin,** B.P. 544, tel: 31.38.37; **Onatho,** B.P. 89, tel: 31.26.87; **Sonatrac,** B.P. 870, tel: 31.23.57, **Locauto** (M. Pion) B.P. 117, tel: 31.34.42;

Soda Locar, B.P. 8119, tel: 31.31.57.

An international driving licence is required for self-drive cars. A French make of car is advised for a journey into the bush, for the magician-mechanics are best at 'doctoring' these.

BANKS AND COMMERCE

The Société Beninoise de Banque has branches in main towns.

Business hours: Banks: 07.30-11.30; 14.30-15.30 Monday to Friday. **Government and commerce:** 08.00-12.30; 15.00-18.30 Monday to Friday. **Shops:** 08.00-12.00; 15.30-19.30 Tuesday to Saturday; 09.00-11.00 Sunday.

PUBLIC HOLIDAYS

New Year's Day, Easter, Labour Day 1 May, Independence Day 1 August, Benin Day 30 November, Christmas Day, Harvest Day 31 December. Variable dates: Tabaski—Commemoration of the Sacrifice of Abraham (the Fete du Mouton); Id-al-Fitr.

FOREIGN EMBASSIES

France; B.P. 966, Ave. General Leclerc, Cotonou.
W. Germany; B.P. 504, Route Inter-Etats, Cotonou.
USA; B.P. 119, Rue Caporal Anani, Cotonou.

COTONOU

In this pleasant and relaxing capital you are rarely out of sight or sound of the Atlantic Ocean and the long palm-fringed beach. The beauty is so far unimpaired by large-scale hotel development. There is great activity in the port where you can watch fishermen launch their dugout canoes into the Atlantic breakers. The town itself is a trading centre and the markets are full of life and interest. Cotonou is a good base for day trips to Porto Novo, Ganvie, Ouidah, Abomey or even Lomé (in neighbouring Togo).

Hotels

Hotel du Lac, B.P. 184, tel: 31.49.70; 40 rooms, night-club, swimming pool, restaurant, bar.

Hotel de la Plage, B.P. 36, tel: 31.25.60; the oldest and most prestigious of Cotonou's hotels and a favourite with businessmen. On the beach yet only a few yards from the town centre; 55 rooms, swimming pool, restaurant, snack-bar.

Motel du Port, B.P.884, tel: 31.42.43; 52 rooms, 6 bungalows, night-club, swimming pool, restaurant.

Croix du Sud, B.P. 280, tel: 31.29.54; a modern hotel near the Ministerial block and the Presidency; 55 rooms, night-club, swimming pool, restaurant.

Hotel le Concorde, B.P. 1557, tel: 31.33.13; 20 rooms, restaurant, bar.

Le Nokoue, 130 rooms, restaurant, bar.

Le Trianon, 14 rooms restaurant, bar.

Babo, 30 rooms, restaurant.

Benin Palace Hotel, 12 rooms, restaurant, night club.

Cave-Club Hotel, 9 rooms.

Restaurants

The best restaurants are at the **Hotel de la Plage** and the **Hotel du Port.** A good café in the commercial centre sells croissants and cakes. Other eating places are the **Pam-Pam** and the **Capri, Pepita, Paris-Snack, le Calao,** and **Edelweiss.** For good African food, try **Les Trois Paillottes** on the road to Porto Novo.

Entertainments

Night-clubs: Cave-Club, Cosmos, Rive-Gauche, Play-Boy, Safaris (Hotel Croix du Sud).

Sports: Water sports. Only the best swimmers are advised to bathe in the ocean, which is extremely dangerous. Swimming pools at several hotels. Tennis at the Club du Benin. Sailing at the Yacht Club.

Shopping and markets

Between the Hotel de la Plage and the Hotel du Port, along the Marina, there are many stalls selling crafts and souvenirs, but no real antiques. The Dan Tokpa market borders Cotonou Lagoon and is stocked with many goods from Nigeria and the outside world as well as traditional medicines and artifacts.

Tourist information

Onatho (Official Tourist Office) B.P. 89, tel: 31.26.87 and 31.32.17.

Travel agents: Delmas Vieiljeux, B.P. 213, tel: 31.33.27; Transcap, B.P. 483, tel: 31.28.38.

PORTO NOVO

Only half an hour's drive from Cotonou, Porto Novo is the administrative capital. It has a rich history as the city of the kings of Porto Novo. Claude Tardits described it thus: 'The city forms a crescent moon, on a plateau whose southern face falls 30 feet into the lagoon, where houses and boats share a landscape of grass and water' It retains its appearance of a small fishing village until one reaches Jean Bayol square with its two-lane road lined with shady mahogany trees. The new city centre is Independence Square.

The narrow streets, lined with the red earth walls of the old houses, call for exploration and reveal the spacious old houses of the Yoruba merchants, hidden behind high walls and surrounded by leafy gardens. Many of them were built by the Portuguese who made Porto Novo their headquarters for slave and tobacco trading with Brazil.

There is an ethnographic museum. When you visit the Palace of King Toffa you must ask for permission to use your camera inside, and you will be asked to make a donation.

Hotel Beau-Rivage, 19 rooms, restaurant, bar.

GANVIE AND SO-AWA

These lake villages, built high on bamboo stilts, are unique on the African coast. The best approach is by a hired dugout canoe (without a motor to be even more romantic) from Cotonou or Abomey-Calavi, 18 km to the north. If you leave as dawn is breaking, you will see the morning dew rise and a white mist swirl among the stilts of the houses. When you climb the ladders leading up to the villagers' homes there is a surprising amount of space high above the water. The homes are well laid out and airy. Huge earthenware ovens on the bamboo floors dry and smoke the fish which constitute the main livelihood of the villagers. They also produce attractive wood carvings.

Ganvie was created by a group of local people to escape the French tax collector. Today villages like these thrive and even have their own schools. The tradition of tax evasion remains strong.

GRAND POPO

Some 30 km west of Ouidah on the road to Togo, Grand Popo is famous for its wonderful, almost Polynesian, beaches. From here one can take a canoe to the Bouches du Roy (King's Mouth) where the River Mono flows into the lagoon, past golden shores dotted with silky palm trees and little fishing villages, behind which pounds the Atlantic surf.

OUIDAH

Some 40 km west of Cotonou Ouidah remained, in Lisbon's eyes, Portuguese until 1963. Throughout French rule, the Portuguese 'Governor' remained ensconced in his white fortress overlooking the sea, and solemnly hoisted the Portuguese flag at sunrise. Finally a Portuguese frigate was sent to evacuate him and his family. But before he abandoned the old fort, the 'Governor' set fire to all the possessions he could not carry with him, including his car, the blackened frame of

which is still on display inside the walls.

One of the oldest of the Portuguese forts along the coast, Ouidah is also known as 'Glenhoue—the house of many gardens'. It was thus baptised by a former king who wondered at the rich vegetable and fruit gardens planted within and without the walls by the Portuguese and later by the Dutch. They are still there, unforgettably beautiful. Within the fort itself is a small museum and a shop which sells souvenirs.

The town's narrow streets are flanked

Ganvie lake village

by old brick houses and wooden galleries running along outer walls and inner patios. There are two forts nearby—the Danish fort and the British Fort Williams, both now occupied by trading companies. Not far off is the cathedral and the famous Temple of Sacred Pythons; a humble earth structure housing the most popular fetish of the coastal regions.

Ouidah is a centre of many local festivals, which pulsate with rhythm and colour.

ABOMEY

Abomey was for centuries the centre of a powerful kingdom and sheltered the palaces of kings such as Agadja, called the 'Black Alexander' because of the size of his kingdom. His great palace walls, 10 m high and 2 m thick, enclosed a court of 10,000 people on 40 hectares, the king's wives and children, the Amazon bodyguard (women were thought to be less treacherous than men), Ministers, fortune-tellers, and palace eunuchs.

The palaces of King Ghezo and King Glele have been restored as a setting for collections of objects belonging to the old dynasty. The museum is inside the palace precincts. Behind the great thrones hang the famous Abomey royal tapestries, depicting the country's history. The visit concludes with a tour of the Royal Sepulchres. *Written permission is needed to take photographs inside the buildings.*

Around Abomey are many small villages. Eastwards, you can visit the bronze craftsmen of Cove, or the woodcarvers of Baname who sculpt the wooden tables, supported by caryatids, so typical of Benin.

Hotel Villa Gardela, 46 rooms, swimming pool, tennis.
Motel D'Abomey, 6 rooms, restaurant, bar.

THE NORTH

The Atakora Mountains are a wonderful sight, full of fast-flowing mountain rivers plunging into deep gorges, huge waterfalls and sparkling lakes fringed with flowers. The mountains stretch from Natitingou towards the Pendjari National Park, and are inhabited by the Somba people—warriors and hunters who walk naked and live in square two-storey houses flanked by round corner towers, giving them the appearance of miniature fortresses. A strong vehicle and plenty of time are needed to visit this area.

Parakou is the main centre for the north and the limit of the railway from the coast. It is a bustling town, whose main commerce is in groundnuts. It is not uncommon to see the proud Bariba horsemen, resplendent in colourful robes, riding through the wide shady avenues.

Parakou has two small hotels, the **Hotel Les Routiers** and **Buffet-Hotel.**

NATIONAL PARKS

The two National Parks in the north are among the best in West Africa. The roads through them are not good but quite usable during the dry season. Do not forget to carry a stock of petrol.

The Pendjari Park lies at the source of the Oto River, which flows into the Volta, separated from the rest of Benin by the Atakora Mountains. There are elephant, buffalo, lion, cheetah, many kinds of antelope, warthog, monkeys, hippo and crocodile. The park is negotiable only in the dry season and tracks are closed from 1 June to 1 December. Escadrille Beninoise operates twice-weekly flights to Porga where Land-Rovers may be hired if booked in advance.

At Porga there is a *campement* with 21 rooms. In the park, on the frontier (24 km from the Arly encampment in Upper Volta), is the **Hotel de la Pendjari**, 25 rooms, restaurant, swimming pool.

The Beninese part of the 'W' Park is less developed (no nearby accommodation).

Hunting
Special tourist hunting licences may be obtained from the Administration des Eaux et Forêts at Cotonou or Porga.

HISTORY

The peopling of the present-day Republic of Benin has taken place over the past two thousand years through a series of migrations, mainly from the east. The growth of the Yoruba civilisation in the past thousand years has had a particularly strong influence, particularly in the establishment of the Dan-Homé (Fon) Kingdom of Abomey, which survived from the 15th century to the 19th century under pressure from both coastal slave-raiders and the Yoruba Kingdom of Oyo.

Dahomey's independence was granted by France in 1960. Ethnic and socioeconomic tensions caused a succession of governments to fall until on 26 October, 1972, a revolutionary military government took control, changing the country's name to the People's Republic of Benin on 30 November, 1975.

BOTSWANA

The lonely Kalahari Desert covers most of this vast, sparsely-populated country, bounded by South Africa, Namibia and Rhodesia and touching Zambia. In the north lies the Okavango Delta, alive with birds and game, and potentially a huge source of water in a thirsty land. In the Okavango is the Moremi Wildlife Reserve and nearby the excellent and more accessible Chobe National Park, only one-and-a-half hours' drive from the Victoria Falls. For the truly adventurous visitor the tough journey to the Tsodilo Hills brings a rich reward in a treasure-house of Sarwa (Bushman) cave paintings.

Botswana, formerly known as the Bechuanaland Protectorate, became independent from Britain in 1966 under the leadership of Sir Seretse Khama. After years of neglect and poverty, the people are now experiencing an increase in national wealth from the newly-discovered copper-nickel and diamond mines.

In 1977 there was growing insecurity in areas adjoining Rhodesia and as a result the Chobe Safari Lodge was closed in April. However, tourism in general has not been affected and is unlikely to be spoiled by this temporary phase.

THE LAND AND THE PEOPLE

A land-locked, semi-arid tableland, about the size of France or Texas but with a population of only 700,000, Botswana is a country of great contrasts.

Most of the population live on the eastern rim of the arid Kalahari sandveld which occupies a vast tract of land in central, southern and western Botswana—the 'Thirstland' of the early pio-

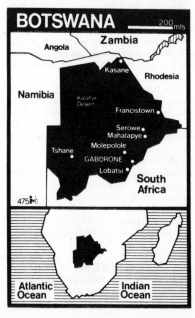

neers. Rainfall averages are very low in this area, about 220mm per annum in the far south-west, increasing towards the east and the north, and reaching 680mm per annum in the Chobe district of the north.

As the rainfall varies, so does the aspect of the country. The major part is covered with bush savannah: thorn acacias and mopane trees, low scrub growths beaten down by the sun into the red and brown sandy soils. There are a few low rocky hills scattered in the east. The average altitude is 1,000m rising to 1,225m in places. In Ngamiland in the north there is an area of indigenous forest and dense bush, giving way in the north-west to the lush expanses occupied by the Okavango Delta. Here the Okavango River fans out into innumerable waterways and lagoons, swollen each year by the winter floods from the Angolan highlands, and extending over 10,400sq km to create one of the wildest and most beautiful nature reserves in Africa.

In the east, 80% of Botswana's population is concentrated into traditional towns: Serowe, capital of the Ngwato tribe; Kanye of the Ngwaketse; Molepolole of the Kwena. To the west is the Kalahari, whose vast tracts are virtually unpopulated, apart from nomadic groups of Bushmen and some scattered villages clustered around boreholes or seasonally filled pans. In the far south there are a few settlements of Coloured people.

The Bushmen, of which there are estimated to be some 4,000 still living in the Kalahari, are the earliest known inhabitants of Africa. Place names and rock paintings record their presence all over the southern part of the continent. The Kalahari is their last refuge. They live by tracking game and by following seasonal pans of water, moving on as they dry up.

The majority of the people belong to the eight branches of the Tswana people and still follow a traditional pattern of life. Cattle-rearing is the mainstay of their economy.

CULTURE

Perhaps because of the harshness of the climate and the aridity of the land which combine to make subsistence a lifelong pre-occupation, the Batswana have never had any particularly distinctive artistic traditions. Handicraft production has practically died out in the face of competition over the years from cheap imported manufactures in the local stores. However, fine basketwork is still produced in Ngamiland, and beautiful furs, or karosses, and skin mats are made in the Kalahari. There are still a few people who make magnificent large earthenware pots for cooking and beer-brewing.

Traditional dancing and singing still take place on important occasions, and fine *leboko*, or praise poems, are sung.

The Bushmen are well known for their lifelike rock paintings which can be seen at places they used to inhabit, such as Tsodilo Hills.

WILDLIFE

Because of its vast area and tiny population, Botswana is peculiarly suited to the conservation of wildlife in an environment as undisturbed by man as is possible anywhere in the world. The Department of Wildlife and National Parks in Gaborone administers a network of national parks and game reserves protecting wildlife across one-fifth of the total area. The protected areas in the north and in the Kalahari remain as they were over a hundred years ago, with large herds of buffalo, elephant, rhinoceros and wildebeeste as well as the larger varieties of antelope.

Outside the protected areas, the country is divided into 40 hunting blocks, each with a small quota of animals which may be shot annually. Hunting licences are strictly limited.

The waterways of the Okavango Delta teem with a variety of fish, including tiger fish, bream, pike, barbel and squeakers.

No licences are presently required, nor is there any closed season for angling. The Delta is also rich in birdlife.

GENERAL INFORMATION

Area: 570,000sq km
Population: 661,000
Altitude: 1,000m
Capital: Gaborone
Head of State: Sir Seretse Khama
Government: Republic and multi-party democracy
Date of Independence: 30 September 1966
Languages: English and Setswana
Religion: Traditional beliefs and Christianity
Currency: Pula, at par with SA Rand. £1 = 1.49 pula. $1 = 0.87 pula
Time: GMT+2
Electricity: 240V

HOW TO GET THERE

By air: There are regular services to and from Johannesburg on Mondays to Saturdays, operated by South African Airways who also fly direct from London to Gaborone on Sundays. Zambia Airways and Air Botswana fly to and from Lusaka. Air Botswana operate a regular service from Johannesburg to Selebi-Pikwe, Francistown and Maun. Most of the main towns and game reserves have airstrips served by light aircraft operated by charter companies.

By road: A tryptique or carnet de passage is required for vehicles entering the country. Normal car insurance from the country of origin, provided it includes third-party risks, is valid in Botswana. Visitors holding valid driving licences issued in their own countries may drive in Botswana for up to six months. The roads from South Africa and Bulawayo leading to the more developed south-east are gravel and fairly good. A new road from Francistown has been built to the Kazungula ferry on the Zambian border.

By rail: The railway from South Africa to Rhodesia passes through Botswana, offering regular passenger services, and arrives in Gaborone at midnight.

Visas and health regulations

No visa is required for nationals of Commonwealth countries, Austria, Belgium, Denmark, Finland, France, Federal Republic of Germany, Greece, Iceland, Eire, Israel, Italy, Liechtenstein, Luxembourg, Netherlands, Norway and colonies, San Marino, South Africa, Sweden, Switzerland, USA and Uruguay. Others must have visas, obtainable from the Immigration Control Officer, Box 534, Gaborone, or a Botswana Diplomatic Mission. Visitors to Botswana are permitted to stay in the country for seven days without requiring any permits. If they wish to remain longer application should be made in the country from an Immigration Control Officer or police station.

A valid International Certificate of Vaccination against smallpox is required, and a certificate of vaccination against

Horn bangles and rings from Botswana

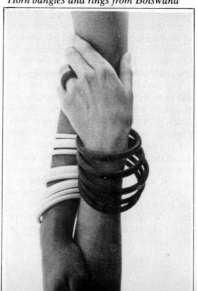

cholera for those travelling from infected areas.

Dutiable goods

Between Botswana, South Africa, Lesotho and Swaziland there are no restrictions on the movement of goods, except for liquor, firearms and ammunition, for which permits must be obtained from the relevant Botswana District Commissioner, as well as a general import permit for firearms, obtainable from the Central Arms Registry, Box 516, Gaborone.

Export permits are required for game trophies and skins, and these are obtainable from the offices of the Department of Wildlife and National Parks. In certain cases an export fee is payable. For those entering from Zambia there are customs formalities but personal effects are duty-free, as are new goods for personal use up to R50 in value.

CLIMATE

Most of the country lies in the temperate zone but becomes tropical in the north. Most wildlife parks are open all the year round, but from December to April parts may become impassable and water-logged. From May to September (the winter) the days are sunny, dry and dusty, with temperatures around 25°C; early mornings and evenings may be cold and even frosty. The summer (October to April) is hot, often reaching 38°C in December and January. This is the rainy season, but Botswana has a very low rainfall.

What to wear: Light-weight summer clothing can be worn during the day throughout most of the year but visitors between May and September should bring sweaters for the sudden drop in temperature, and coats and warmer clothing for the evenings.

Health precautions: As a general rule water outside the main towns should be boiled. Swimming or paddling in stagnant water should be avoided because of bilharzia. In the northern wildlife parks malaria is prevalent and prophylactics must be taken before and during one's stay. In the Moremi Wildlife Reserve, other parts of Ngamiland and western parts of Chobe National Park, tsetse fly, which can cause sleeping sickness, is a danger. The visitor should wear protective clothing, have a fly-spray handy and keep the vehicle's windows shut.

TRANSPORT

Air: Air Botswana at present operates a regular flight from Johannesburg via Selebi and Francistown to Maun. All other internal flights are operated by charter. There are airports at Gaborone, Lobatse, Francistown, Orapa, Selebi and Maun, airstrips at Molepolole, Kanye, Serowe, Palapye, Mahalapye, Ghanzi, Rakops, Shakawe and Kasane, and emergency landing strips at Tshane, Tshabong, Mamuno and Okwa in the Kalahari, Mosomane, Machaneng and Mmadinare in the east and at Mosetse, Mata, Gweta, Bushman Pits, Tsau, Nokaneng and Gomare in the north and north west.

Road: A tarred road runs from Gaborone to Lobatse in the south. There are good all-weather roads between Gaborone—Lobatse—Kanye, Gaborone—Palapye—Mahalapye—Francistown, Francistown—Gweta—Maun, and Francistown—Kazungula.

All roads from South Africa via the main border posts into eastern Botswana are all-weather roads. Petrol is available at all the towns mentioned. Four-wheel-drive is necessary for minor roads, particularly those through the Kalahari, and for the wildlife reserves. Petrol is available in the Kalahari at Ghanzi, Kalkfontein, Kang and Mamuno, and in the north and north-east wildlife area at Sehitwa, Toteng, Kasane, Nata, Orapa, Ramokgwebana, Tsheshebe, Sebina and Serule.

Car hire: Trucks and Land-Rovers can be hired from Safari companies. **Botswana Game Industries**, P.O. Box 118, Francistown, will sometimes hire out vehicles, as can the **Botswana Development Corporation**, P.O. Box 438, Gaborone; and **Cliff Engineering**, P.O. Box 282, Gaborone; **Leonard Motors**, P.O. Box 252, Gaborone.

Safari Companies: There are many safari companies for photography and sightseeing. These can be found in Maun, Gaborone, Francistown and Kasane. Others operate from Johannesburg.

BUSINESS HOURS
October—April: 07.30-12.45 and 14.00-16.30.
April—October: 08.00-13.00 and 14.15-17.00.

PUBLIC HOLIDAYS
New Year's Day; Good Friday; Holy Saturday and Easter Monday; Ascension Day; President's Day, end of May; Whit Monday; Commonwealth Day, in June; last Monday in August; Botswana Day 30 September; United Nations Day 25 October; Christmas Day; Boxing Day.

FOREIGN EMBASSIES
UK: B.P. 23, Gaborone.
USA: P.O. Box 90, Gaborone
Zambia: P.O. Box 362, Gaborone
Nigeria: P.O. Box 274, Gaborone
Sweden: P.B. 17, Gaborone.

Others are represented in Pretoria (South Africa), Lusaka (Zambia) or Dar es Salaam (Tanzania).

GABORONE
Gaborone was built in 1964 to be the capital of Botswana on independence in 1965. It is divided in half by the main axis, the Mall, a pedestrian shopping area flanked by parking lots and two streets running down from the National Assembly building and Government offices at the top, to the Town Hall at the bottom.

Near Gaborone is an artificial lake ('the dam') lying in a pretty valley flanked by hills; it is a favourite spot for bird watchers. There are facilities for sailing, water-skiing and fishing. Many stone-age implements were discovered during the construction of the dam and these are exhibited in the National Museum. There are some worthwhile day trips to be taken from Gaborone: to Manyana where there are Bushmen paintings on a rocky outcrop outside the village, and to the Kolobeng, where there are remains of a mission which was established by Livingstone.

Gaborone airport

Khutse Wildlife Reserve, 232 km from Gaborone via Molepolole and Lothlekane, is in the Kalahari sandveld and holds large herds of drought-resistant wildlife, such as kudu, hartebeeste, springbok, lion, leopard, hyena and the bat-eared fox. They move around a good deal, and numbers depend on conditions in the reserve. Four-wheel-drive vehicles are necessary. Fill up with petrol and water before you leave Gaborone or Molepolole and carry extra supplies of both with you, as well as camping equipment and food, as there is neither accommodation, shopping nor petrol in the Reserve.

Hotels

President Hotel, on the Mall, P.O. Box 200, tel: 2215, 24 rooms and suites.

Holiday Inn, on the outskirts of town next to the golf course and near the airport, P.B. 16, tel: 2221, or Johannesburg 212011, 119 rooms. Swimming pool, night club and casino.

Gaberones Hotel, at the station, one mile from centre of town, with 22 beds.

Tourist information

Holiday Inn Safaris run services between the hotel and the airport and the centre of Gaborone, and arrange sightseeing in and around the city. They also arrange for the hire of cars and air charter flights.

MAUN

The main town of Ngamiland and the centre for most of the wildlife viewing and hunting areas of the north-west, Maun is on an all-weather road from Francistown. It is linked to the rail and road network running into the rest of Botswana, Zambia, Rhodesia and South Africa. Moremi and the Okavango Delta are accessible from the town (see NATIONAL PARKS), and other trips from Maun include Nxai and Makarikari Pans.

Nxai Pan is a fossil lake, lying 32 km north of the Francistown—Maun road, and is accessible by Land-Rover. There is wildlife during the rainy season (November-April) when large herds of oryx, zebra, springbok and wildebeeste congregate there in enormous numbers—it is possible to see up to 5,000 head of game at one time.

Makarikari Pans lie due south of Mxai on the southern side of the Francistown—Maun road. The huge salt pans are seasonally filled with water between May and October to a depth of a few inches; then huge flocks of flamingos visit the pans.

Tsodilo Hills, 400km from Maun along roads passable by four-wheel-drive vehicles are the most interesting and spectacular prehistoric site in Botswana. They comprise a micaceous quartzite schist ridge, rising at one end sheer by 400m and extending for about 18 km, varying in colour from grey to soft yellow, streaked with purple and red. Implements from the middle and late stone ages and iron age, glass and clay beads and pottery can be found there, but the Hills are most famous for their rock paintings, of which there are about 2,000, the majority concentrated on the second, or female, hill. The paintings are attributed to the Bushmen and Tsodilo is one of the last places where both paintings and Bushmen are still found in the same area.

Most of the paintings are of animals in silhouette, with a few scenes such as an elephant hunt and a rhinoceros hunt. Only in one place do pictures overlap, giving some idea of the order of succession of the many different styles found in the paintings. Although their age is uncertain, the style is similar to Transvaal paintings which have been dated back 4,000 years.

Lake Ngami is south-west of Maun on the road to Sehitwa; a four-wheel-drive vehicle is necessary. The amount of water varies in the lake and in some years it is completely dry. When Livingstone saw it, it was 240 km wide. It is a paradise for anglers, and for bird-watchers.

Riley's Hotel, P.O. Box 1, tel: Maun 2.

SEROWE

The town lies on a good, all-weather gravel road between Gaborone and Francistown. It is the chief town of the Ngwato and a fine example of a traditional Tswana village. Huts fan out in ordered patterns from the *kgotla*, or central meeting place, and the hill is where the Chiefly family, the Khamas, are buried. **Serowe Hotel**, P.O. Box 150. Accommodation should be booked in advance.

LOBATSE

On a good all-weather gravel road to Mafeking (South Africa), 64 km from Gaborone, Lobatse was once planned to be Botswana's capital. It is on the railway line from South Africa.

The High Court is situated here, as well as Botswana's large export abattoir. **Cumberland Hotel**, P.O. Box 135, tel: 281, cinema, sauna baths, badminton, rooms with bath, bed and breakfast. **Lobatse Hotel**, P.O. Box 13.

FRANCISTOWN

The industrial and commercial centre of Botswana, Francistown grew from the gold rush to the first mine discovered in southern Africa in the 1880s, and it still carries many of the trademarks of that period—whites living one side of the river, Africans on the other; a main street flanked by dilapidated buildings running parallel to the railway; scruffy hotels with thriving bars.

Places of interest in the town are the Botswana Game Industries' factory and shop, and Lekgaba Centre, the only art centre in Botswana, about a mile from the main street, where craftwork in wood and ivory is sold. There are ruins north of the town, thought to be contemporary with Zimbabwe.

Francistown, on the main road and rail routes across Botswana, is the taking-off point for the great wildlife areas of Ngamiland.

Tati Hotel.
Grand Hotel.

NATIONAL PARKS

Chobe National Park. This is open all the year round, but some areas are closed during November-April; the best time is between April and November when lack of rain concentrates the wildlife on the river. Habitats vary from the flood grasslands and thickets by the river to a series of pans. All species of animals and birdlife abound here, from giraffe and elephant, white rhinoceros, lion, leopard and cheetah to the rare Chobe bushbuck, unique to this area. The fishing is superb. There is a good network of roads through the Park which make wildlife viewing easy.

Accommodation
Chobe Safari Lodge (temporarily closed in 1977) at entrance to Park at Kasane, P.O. Box 10, Kasane, tel: Kasane 6; 66 beds in cottages and rondavels, swimming pool, tennis, restaurant, bar and water-skiing facilities. Guided tours are arranged into the park for hunting, photography and wildlife viewing and there are launch trips up the river. The fishing is excellent.

Southern Sun Hotel: 8 km inside the park. First-class hotel, 100 beds; all amenities plus full air-conditioning. P.O. Box 32, Kasane.

Access: There is an airstrip for light aircraft at Kasane, at the entrance to the park. By car from Livingstone (Zambia) take the Mombova road and turn off at the sign to Chobe, crossing the ferry to Kasane at Kazungula.

Moremi Wildlife Reserve. Situated at the edge of the Okavango Delta where riverine grassland begins, it is bounded by the Khwai, Santantadibe, Gomoti and Mogogelo Rivers, and belongs to the Tswana people who created it to preserve their animals. It is perhaps the most spectacular reserve in southern Africa.

There are only tracks and a guide is essential; one can be picked up at the entrance on the Maun road. Visitors may go where they like and camp where they like, but a vehicle with four-wheel-drive is advisable. The Reserve is closed during the rainy season, approximately December to April. The wide variety of wildlife ranges from lion, cheetah and leopard to vast herds of zebra, wildebeeste, lechwe, kudu and eland, and at least 80 species of birdlife.

Accommodation

Khwai River Lodge, situated on the banks of the Khwai River just outside the Reserve, P.O. Box 100, Maun, tel: Maun 46; 32 beds, in 16 double units. Swimming, water-skiing, fishing trips, launch trips into the Delta, Land-Rover trips into the Reserve for hunting, photography and game viewing. The Lodge is closed 15 January to 30 March.

Crocodile River Camp on the Thamalakane River just outside Maun, P.O. Box 46, tel: Maun 53, 24 beds, full board. Water skiing and fishing trips can be arranged into the Delta as far north as Shakawe, which takes 10 days, and into the Reserve.

Access: Airstrip for light aircraft just outside the Reserve. It is possible to drive as far as Maun in an ordinary vehicle from Francistown, but the road from Maun to Moremi requires four-wheel-drive.

The Okavango Delta. The Delta consists of 16,000 sq. km of waterways caused by the flooding of the Okavango River which flows into Ngamiland from the Angolan highlands. The flood reaches its peak in May, raising the level of the Delta by several feet, and overflows into Lake Mgami and down the Botetli towards the great salt pans of the Makarikari in the south.

Papyrus blocks many of the Delta's waterways in the north, making it impenetrable except by *mekoro*, the dug-out canoes used by the Yei and Mbukushu people who have settled on the periphery of the Delta. Hippo, by breaking their way through the papyrus, keep the channels open.

Accommodation

Crocodile River Camp, mentioned above under Moremi Wildlife reserve, is a good place from which to approach the Delta. There is also **Riley's Hotel** in Maun itself. Most of the safari companies operating in Botswana are centred on Maun, and sightseeing or hunting trips up the Delta can be arranged through them.

HISTORY

The ancestors of the nomadic Sarwa (Bushman) who roamed the bush following game and gathering fruit were probably the first inhabitants of Botswana. They engraved and painted pictures of themselves and animals in caves like those in the Tsodilo hills.

Sotho ancestors of the Tswana came to the Transvaal between the 11th and 14th centuries. Of the Tswana, the Rolong (mostly in the northern Cape) and Hurutshe (mostly in the Transvaal) are regarded as senior branches. The Kwena quarrelled with the Hurutshe and later, perhaps in the 18th century, some of them came to Botswana.

Early 19th-century travellers were struck by the number of ruins and by places like Dithakong (Old Lattakoo) north of Kuruman with perhaps 3,000 huts partly built of stone. In Botswana there are still some ruins in the south-east but elsewhere no convenient stone is to be found.

Between 1810 and 1830 travellers and

The towers of a copper and nickel mine stand above traditional huts

missionaries began to penetrate the northern Cape and Botswana from the south. The inhabitants suffered a succession of invasions by Mma Ntatisi, the Ndebele and the Afrikaner Voortrekkers.

Mma Ntatisi was a warrior chieftainess who led her people from the Lesotho area when invaders began pouring over the Drakensberg to escape from the bloodshed of Shaka's Zulu wars. She, in turn, spread chaos among the Tswana but was finally defeated in 1823 by the Thlaping in the northern Cape.

When the Afrikaners ended their Great Trek in the Transvaal they drove the Ndebele to Rhodesia and caused the flight of many groups of Malete, Tlokwa and Kgatla to Botswana throughout the 19th century. By the 1840s Livingstone and others had set up a mission among the Kwena at Kilobeng (west of Gaborone). Further north, the son of the Ngwato Chief went to school and became an ardent Christian. He was Khama the Great, who succeeded to the chieftaincy in 1872. He built up a strong army and united many of the Tswana under him.

Meanwhile the Afrikaners' interest in Botswana was increasing because of gold-finds at Tati. The British missionaries, however, were anxious to keep a right of way through to central Africa and encouraged the Chiefs to seek British protection against the Afrikaners. Thus, in 1885, the British Government reluctantly agreed to declare the Bechuanaland Protectorate over Khama's peoples and to annex the other Tswana territory of the northern Cape (British Bechuanaland) as part of the Cape Colony.

Khama's aim in seeking British protection was military. He intended to remain in full control of administration, law and justice in his area. He firmly opposed granting any mining concessions, and successfully resisted proposals that Cecil Rhodes's British South Africa Company, which was ruling in Rhodesia and later in Northern Rhodesia (Zambia) should take over his territory. Later the Chiefs successfully opposed union with South Africa.

Until the 1950s the Protectorate was expected to pay its own way from its meagre resources. The development of education and health services was by missionaries and was totally inadequate. Years of neglect left Botswana at its independence in 1966 with an almost completely white civil service, even down to typists and post office clerks, and with only 35 locally-born graduates.

Its geographical position makes Botswana inevitably dependent on South Africa, but the historical links with Britain remain strong. President Seretse Khama (descended from Khama the Great) has striven to encourage other western countries, especially the United States and Scandinavia, to invest. Although powerless against South Africa, he has constantly condemned apartheid and has refused to send a representative to Pretoria or to recruit expatriate personnel from there. He has worked to extend his links with Zambia and the rest of black-ruled Africa.

BURUNDI

Burundi is a beautiful hilly country nestling at the heart of Africa overlooking the great waterway of Lake Tanganyika. Its recent history has been marked by bloody conflict between the ruling Tutsi and the majority Hutu people and for this reason it is still not considered the tourist paradise it could conceivably become.

THE LAND AND THE PEOPLE

The majestic hills and valleys of Burundi are covered with eucalyptus trees and banana groves, with homesteads scattered among cultivated fields, and with patches of luxuriant pasture. The climate of most of this high, though tropical, country is warm and pleasant. In the east the fertile area gives way to savannah grassland and to the valley of the Ruvubu which receives most of the water from the rivers flowing into the Kagera and Lake Victoria. On the southern frontier the land slopes towards the Malagarasi River which flows into Lake Tanganyika.

Running from north to south is the 2,000-2,500m high mountain range marking the Nile-Zaire watershed. Little primary forest is left on the ridge, which is now used for cash crops of coffee and tea. Descending steeply on the west it affords extensive views over Lake Tanganyika. A strip along the lake shore dips as low as 774m and is hot and arid while the

mountains behind receive most of the rain (1,500mm compared with 900mm by the lake). At the north end of the lake the Ruzizi River enters through a fertile plain where the capital and only large town, Bujumbura, has developed.

The people speak Kirundi but are divided socially by their ancestors' origins: the Hutu (85% of the population) descended from agriculturalists who long ago came from Zaire; and the Tutsi

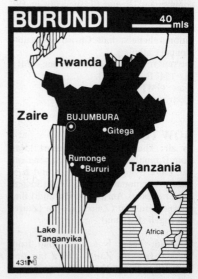

(14%) are tall slender pastoralists who came perhaps from southern Ethiopia. The Tutsi are themselves hierarchically divided and, in fact, the most significant gulf in the past was between the *ganwa* ('princes of the blood') and the rest. The main group are concentrated in the Bu-Tutsi district where they form over 80% of the population, occupying all levels of society.

Less than 1% of the population are Twa, a neglected pygmy people.

GENERAL INFORMATION
Area: 27,834 sq. km.
Population: 3.8 million
Altitude: Most of the country averages 1,500m but the lakeshore and Ruzizi valley drop to about 800m.
Capital: Bujumbura.
Head of State: Col. Jean-Baptiste Bagaza.
Government: Military.
Date of Independence: 1 July 1962.
Languages: Official languages are Kirundi and French. Swahili is spoken as a commercial language, especially in Bujumbura.
Religions: Half the population follow traditional beliefs, half Christian (mainly Roman Catholic).
Currency: The Burundi Franc (FB). £1 = 154FB. $1 = 90FB.
Time: GMT + 2.
Electricity: 220V.

HOW TO GET THERE
By air: The international airport 15km from Bujumbura is served by Sabena and Air Zaire flying from Brussels and Kinshasa. A national airline STAB (Société des Transports Aeriens du Burundi) flies between Bukavu (Zaire), Goma (Zaire) and Kigali (Rwanda).

By road: There is a good road from Bukavu (eastern Zaire) and a fair one from Rwanda and thence to East Africa.

Land communications with Tanzania are poor. Motoring is difficult in the rainy season.

By lake: Cargo steamers, which also carry some passengers, ply between Kigoma (Tanzania) and Bujumbura, taking one night or one day. There are less frequent services from Kalemi in Zaire (three days via Kigoma).

Visa and health regulations
Visitors must have a valid passport and visa and a return or onward ticket. Visas should be obtained well in advance from Burundi Embassies, e.g. in Brussels, Paris, Bonn, Kampala (Uganda) or Washington. Passengers arriving without a visa may be put on the next international flight leaving Bujumbura regardless of destination. Travellers intending to visit other countries and to return to Burundi need to hold a visa valid for several journeys, or to obtain a further entry visa in Bujumbura from the Immigration Service.

Visitors must possess valid international certificates of vaccination against smallpox and yellow fever; inoculation against cholera and typhoid is not compulsory but recommended.

Dutiable goods
All baggage must be declared. Cameras, radios, tape-recorders, etc., are liable to duty, but visitors staying only a few days are usually allowed to take them into the country duty-free. The import of arms without prior customs permission is forbidden.

Currency regulations
Visitors must declare all Burundi or foreign currency. There are no restrictions on the amount that may be imported. All exchange transactions must be conducted through one of the main banks or at Bujumbura airport.

CLIMATE

The climate near Lake Tanganyika and in the Ruzizi River plain is equatorial—hot (around 23°C) and humid though often windy on the lake—but in the rest of the country mild and pleasant (average 20°C). The long dry season lasts from June to September while the rains of October to May are interrupted by the short dry season from December to January. The best time for a visit is June-September or January-February.

What to wear

Lightweight clothing is essential with a cardigan for evenings and a light raincoat in the appropriate season.

Health precautions

Anti-malarial prophylactics should be taken. Tap water is unsafe for drinking.

ACCOMMODATION & FOOD

Good hotel facilities exist in Bujumbura where meals, although reasonably good, are expensive. Elsewhere in the country there is virtually no accommodation for the visitor.
Tipping; As a rule no service charges are levied, and 10% of the bill is a normal tip at a restaurant.

TRANSPORT

There is no commercial internal air service although air charter facilities are available. Roads are poor, dusty or muddy according to season since only 100km are tarred. The road to the north from Bujumbura is being improved, as is that to Gitega. Repair facilities for vehicles outside Bujumbura are meagre and there is no system of public transport.

BANKS AND COMMERCE

Commercial banks, which operate only in Bujumbura, are Banque Belgo-Africaine du Burundi, Banque Commerciale du Burundi, and Banque Credit de Bujumbura.
Business hours: Banks open in the mornings but are normally closed for cash transactions in the afternoon. They close on Saturdays. Government offices close at noon and all Saturday. Most commercial offices work 08.00-12.00 and 14.00-16.30 Monday to Friday, and 08.00-12.00 on Saturday.

PUBLIC HOLIDAYS

New Year's Day; Easter Monday; Labour Day; Ascension Day; Whit Monday; Independence Day, 1 July; Assumption; UPRONA Day, 18 September; Rwagasore Day, 13 October; All Saints' Day; Christmas Day.

FOREIGN EMBASSIES

All in Bujumbura:
Belgium: Ave de l'Industrie, B.P. 1920, tel: 36.76.
France: B.P. 1790, tel: 31.76.
Federal Republic of Germany: Tel: 32.11.
Netherlands: Tel: 23.58.
Sweden: Tel: 26.41.
UK: B.P. 1750.
USA: B.P.1720, tel: 34.54.

BUJUMBURA

The capital, a trading and industrial centre as well as a port, was founded in 1899 by the Germans as Costermansville. It is now a bustling, cosmopolitan town of over 100,000 inhabitants, attractively located on the shores of Lake Tanganyika with high hills rising behind it. It is well placed for water sports—sailing, skiing and fishing. The public beach lies about 5 km from the town towards the west. Sights in the town include the Postmaster's House, recalling the German period, and the striking modern Parliament Buildings.

The French and Greek restaurants are exceptionally good.

Hotels
Hotel Burundi-Palace, Ave de l'Uprona, B.P. 225, tel: 29.20.
Hotel Paguidas-Haidemenos, Ave du Peuple Burundi, B.P. 2, tel: 22.51.
Hotel Central, Place de l'Independance, tel: 26.58.
Hotel Grillon, Ave du Zaire, B.P. 34, tel: 25.19.
Hotel Residence, Ave de Stanley, B.P. 405, tel: 27.73.
Hotel Tanganyika, Tel: 44.33.

Entertainments
There are several nightclubs.
Sport: *The Entente Sportive* club offers tourist membership for swimming, tennis, volleyball, basket-ball, golf. It also has a restaurant and bar. For information on water sports contact the **Cercle Nautique.**

Tourist Office
Office National de Tourisme, B.P. 902, tel: 20.23/30.84.

INLAND
The main road east from Bujumbura climbs over the great Nile-Zaire watershed to Muramvya, which was once the royal city of Burundi. To the south (111km from Bujumbura) is Gitega, also a former residence of the king and, for a few months after independence, the capital.

About 100km south of Gitega, near Rutana, is a pyramid marking the source of the Nile. It was set up in 1937 by Burkhart Waldecker. Although the definitive source of the White Nile is much disputed (see RWANDA), this Kigira River is the most southerly of the many rivers running into the Ruvubu, then Kagera and Lake Victoria.

HISTORY
Burundi was one of the Interlacustrine Kingdoms, akin in origin and customs to those set up by Tutsi and Hima pastoral invaders in Uganda and Rwanda. Burundi society, maintained by clientship ties, was not as strictly segregated by caste, nor was the kingdom (dating back to about 1675) as militarised or centralised as Rwanda. Rather, it was a loose unit frequently rent by factions among royal princes.

Although the main Zanzibari traders' route to Ujiji (Tanzania) lay just south of Burundi, they rarely entered the area. Burton and Speke came in 1858. Henry Stanley, after finding David Livingstone near Ujiji, travelled with him round the north of the lake, finding to their disappointment that it did not flow north to the Nile.

The Germans arrived amid continuing internecine strife. They were followed in 1916 by the Belgians who ruled Ruanda-Urundi under a League of Nations mandate in close association with the Belgian Congo (Zaire). Burundi attained its independence in 1962 without the violence suffered in Rwanda, but in the next four years seven governments attempted to rule and two Hutu Prime Ministers were assassinated. King Mwambutsa tried to maintain a balance between Hutu and Tutsi but he was overthrown in an army coup led by Colonel Michel Micombero with the support of the King's son who was installed as Ntare V. But he, too, was soon deposed, a Republic declared, and full military rule instituted under Colonel Micombero in 1966.

Micombero's rule, which was by no means popular with all the Tutsi clans, failed even more conspicuously than the royal rulers to win over the Hutu majority and to unify the country. The Hutu rebellion in 1972 was repressed with extreme violence—between 80,000 to 100,000 Hutu and Tutsi died in the upheaval.

On 1 November 1976 Micombero was overthrown by Col. Bagaza, who promised to work towards inter-communal harmony.

CAMEROON

A unique corner of Africa, with many of the qualities of other parts of the continent and spectacular scenery, Cameroon is an increasingly popular country with tourists. Its triangular shape embraces equatorial forest, a beautiful coastline, mountain ranges and semi-desert. The diverse cultures of the people, their great friendliness and the wealth of wildlife in the Game Parks make a visit to Cameroon a memorable experience.

THE LAND AND THE PEOPLE

With an area of 476,000 sq. km. Cameroon is larger than it looks on the map. The north is more or less semi-desert, with the rainfall sometimes below 500mm annually. It broadens into the vast Maroua plain—with its game reserves and mineral deposits—which is bordered by the majestic Mandara Mountains to the west, and the vegetation is nourished by the broad Benue River, which flows west to join the Niger.

Further south and to the west are the savannah uplands of the Ndop plain and the Bamenda grasslands—high and cool, hills with glorious views across plains that are fertile enough to grow tea and sufficiently free of disease to support cattle.

To the east and south is the forest—dense, almost uncontrollably fertile. Yet in the coastal area the tropical richness and heavy rainfall have made possible the cultivation of cocoa, rubber, timber, coffee and bananas in profusion. Debundscha, on the western slopes of Mount Cameroon (4,070m), has the second highest rainfall in the world. The riverine confluences and estuaries have made possible the ports and hydro-electric power schemes that provide the base for industrial growth.

Around Kribi, to the south of the ports of Douala and Victoria, are many exquisitely beautiful palm-fringed beaches.

71

The big cities, Douala and Yaounde, and the towns, whether industrial or commercial, like Edea, Nkongsamba, Ebolowa or Sangmelima in the French-speaking areas, or Victoria in the English-speaking part; or administrative like Garoua, Ngaoundere and Bafoussam (francophone) or Buea, Bamenda, Kumba and Mamfe (anglophone) contain the urbane and sophisticated people one would expect to encounter in the centres of any developing country. The difference is that there is often a local ethnic predominance in the smaller towns—the Bassa around Edea; Bakweri around Victoria and Buea; Fulani in Garoua; Bamoun in Bafoussam; Bafut and Bali near Bamenda and so on.

The capital city, Yaounde, is too complex to type-cast in this way. The administrators, politicians and traders who have flocked to it from all over the country have brought with them relatives and friends in profusion, and they make up a sizeable proportion of this multi-ethnic city.

This is even more true of Douala, where the indigenous Duala have a minority in the country's biggest city. One people alone bid fair to outnumber the original inhabitants of both major cities—the Bamileke, who come from the grassland areas and the plains of the centre south; they are ubiquitous in commerce and professions, and thrive as traders.

For sheer ethnic diversity Cameroon is unrivalled. Its population of six million (about a quarter in the anglophone areas, the rest in the francophone areas) includes over 130 different peoples.

The Semitic groups in the north (Arab, Chadic and Fulani) are for the most part Muslim, though the bulk of the people of the north are non-Muslim and collectively known as Kirdi. There are two groups of Bantu—the equatorial Bantu in the areas between the Congo basin and the plateaux of the interior, and the semi-Bantu peoples in the west and centre of the country (including the Bamileke).

There are also small hunting bands of pygmies (the original inhabitants of Central Africa) in the remote southern forests.

CULTURE

Cameroon's rich ethnic diversity is matched by its wealth of culture in the form of dances, festivals, carnivals, folklore and just plain expressions of the enjoyment of life. Musical instruments abound—horns, harps, drums, thumb-pianos, balafons and xylophones—and are played whenever there is a suitable occasion; even a funeral can be a musical event.

But it is sculpture that makes Cameroon exceptional. Masks, fetish-figures, ancestor memorials are everywhere and their materials include wood, ivory, bronze, stone and clay. The range of local handicrafts is also remarkable: highly decorated pots, drinking horns, jugs, bottles and cups, great earthenware bowls and delicate pottery, dishes and trays; mats and rugs woven from raffia, grass, camel-hair or cotton, and beadwork garments. Each differs according to the local significance. Even paintings can be outstanding—some old and functional-decorative and some new like that incorporating the unique and original Bamoun calligraphic script.

WILDLIFE

Wildlife conservation has been part of Government policy. Huge areas—like the famous game park at Waza—have been set aside for tourists and strict control is maintained over hunting. Cameroon still abounds in wildlife, and the area north of Ngaoundere offers the richest game country.

The network of rivers is extensive. Some, like the Sanaga and the Nyong, are broken by spectacular falls and teem with fish. The Longone is one of the richest fishing rivers in the world. Along the coast—in the creeks behind Mount Cameroon, along the Wourri estuary, or from the beaches near Kribi or Grand Batanga—there are rich sea fishing areas, either from the shoreline of from boats which can be hired from local fishermen. Among the great variety of fish there are the tarpon and barracuda.

GENERAL INFORMATION

Area: 476,000 sq. km.

Population: 6.5 million.

Altitude: Sea level to 4,070 m (Mount Cameroon).

Capital: Yaounde; biggest city is Douala (population 500,000).

Head of State: El Hadj President Ahmadou Ahidjo.

Government: Single ruling party (Union Nationale Camerounaise/Cameroon National Union—CNU/UNC).

Date of Independence: 1 October 1961 as a federal state. The francophone area became independent first as the Republic of Cameroon on 1 January 1960.

Official Languages: French and English. Few people are bilingual.

Religions: Islam, Christianity (Catholic and Protestant) and animist.

Currency: CFA franc. £1=428 CFA francs. $1=249 CFA francs.

Time: GMT + 1.

Electricity: 110V and (mainly) 220V.

HOW TO GET THERE

By air: There are scheduled flights daily to Douala from Paris or other European capitals or weekly from New York. Airlines: UTA, Air Afrique, Cameroon Airlines, Alitalia, Lufthansa, Swissair, Sabena, and Iberia. There are interesting stop-overs almost anywhere along the west coast of Africa when starting from New York; or in Paris, Marseilles, Nice, Rome, Ndjamena, Lagos or Malabo.

Douala's airport is about 4 km from the town, Yaounde's 7 km. Airport tax: 560 CFA francs for inter-African, 3,500 CFA francs for inter-continental flights.

Hotels will collect passengers with bookings, but taxis are plentiful. Settle the price in advance.

By sea: Irregular sailing from European ports to Douala take between two and three weeks, with stops in the Canary Islands and West African ports. There are also connections on cargo boats, some of which have places for between six and 12 passengers.

By road: It is possible to enter from Nigeria, Chad, the Central African Empire and Gabon—but a great deal depends on the weather. Things will improve when the Trans-Africa Highway from Kenya to Nigeria is developed. At present a four-wheel-drive vehicle is recommended for any overland journey into Cameroon.

Visas and health regulations

A tourist visa valid for 10 days can be obtained free on arrival, provided visitors are in possession of a valid passport and a ticket for continuation of their journey (failing an onward ticket, a deposit is required). This visa can be extended for up to a month at the local Service d'Emi/Immigration, police station or frontier post.

Transit visas, valid for up to 48 hours, may be obtained at Douala airport on arrival; but visitors intending to stay longer than 10 days should obtain a visa (valid for a maximum of three months) from a Cameroon diplomatic mission abroad. There is a nominal charge.

Holders of passports issued by, or containing visas valid for entry to, Rhodesia or South Africa are forbidden to enter Cameroon.

Valid international certificates of vaccination/inoculation against smallpox, yellow fever and cholera are essential. Smallpox certificates must be dated not less than 14 days and not more than three years prior to entry.

Dutiable goods

Vehicles are admitted as long as they are accompanied by a tryptique or carnet de passage. In addition to personal effects, the following items may be taken into the country duty-free: 50 cigarettes, 1 litre of spirits per person; 1 camera (plus accessories); 1 radio; 1 tape-recorder; 1 pair binoculars.

Export of goods other than personal effects and curios is subject to investigation. Objects of artistic interest may be scrutinised, as will be gold and ivory.

Importation of firearms is subject to prior authorisation by a Cameroon diplomatic mission.

Currency regulations

There are no restrictions on bringing in foreign currency though the total amount imported should be declared. Up to 25,000 CFA francs may be taken out if visitors are going to a non-franc country, but they are difficult to convert outside the CFA area. It is better to change money back into French francs (or some other foreign currency) before leaving.

CLIMATE

Hot, though not difficult to get used to, especially when away from the humidity at the coast. Yaounde is pleasant, particularly towards evening. Douala/Victoria can be sticky and uncomfortable although there is always the opportunity of escaping to the cooler temperatures of Buea on the slopes of Mount Cameroon.

In the south there are three seasons: a long dry one from November to February—a season of not-so-heavy rain from March to June: and a long, heavy rainy season from July to October. The mean temperature in the south is 26°C, but it feels hotter because of the humidity.

The north can be both hotter and a bit cooler—around Garoua, it averages 29°C; on the Adamaoua plateau it drops to about 22°C, and can be cold at night. The north is always drier, but there is a long rainy season from May to October. The grassland areas—Bamenda, Bafoussam and the Ndop plain—are always much cooler than the coast. Overall, the best time to visit Cameroon is between November and April.

What to wear

Lightweight cotton clothes (avoid nylon and synthetic fabrics), canvas or light leather shoes or sandals; plus (if you're going away from the coast) a light woollen sweater and, always, a raincoat.

Health precautions

Cameroon is in the endemic malaria zone, and it is essential to have an adequate supply of Paludrin or Nivaquin. Start taking it before your arrival and continue for two weeks afterwards. A good supply of an anti-spasmodic or stomach-settling substance is helpful, just in case.

There are 24 hospitals in Cameroon, mostly in the big centres, private nursing homes in Yaounde and Douala, and plenty of private doctors. Treatment is competent, but not cheap; medicines are in plentiful supply in big towns, but come in French dosages and are expensive.

Water should be boiled or filtered before drinking. Or stick to the bottled varieties—Perrier, Evian, etc—which are on sale everywhere.

ACCOMMODATION AND FOOD

Excellent in most towns. There are hotels of international standard in Douala, Yaounde, Bamenda and Kribi, with Buea a bit on the English provincial side. There are many restaurants of high quality in the big cities; but expect to pay high prices for anything of a luxury nature. The cooking is often French or Lebanese but local foods can be very tasty. The country abounds in avocado pears, citrus fruits, pineapples and mangoes, and there are delicious prawns in the south. The cuisine, however, varies. A 10% tip is the rule.

TRANSPORT
Air: Daily return flights from Douala to Yaounde. Flights are less frequent to other places in the interior, Ngaoundere, Maroua and Garoua being the best served. There are also flights to Malabo from Douala and local air charter.

Rail: Rail travel is slow but cheap. The best served route is Douala-Nkongsamba, a distance of 172 km which takes five hours. Douala-Yaounde takes longer. The Trans-Cameroon railway up to Ngaoundere has now been opened and provides a scenic route for those with days at their disposal.

Roads: Cars drive on the right. There are still only limited stretches of paved roads but the main centres are well served by all-weather roads. Main tarred roads link Douala to Bafoussam, Douala to Buea, Douala to Edea, and Yaounde to Sangmelina.

The main trunk routes, tarred or partially tarred are: the western route from Douala through Nkongsamba, Foumban, Banyo and Tibati to Ngaoundere, Garoua and Maroua; the central route from Douala through Edea, Yaounde, Bangangte and Tibati to Ngaoundere and beyond; the eastern route from Yaounde through Bertoua, and Garoua Boulai (for Central African Empire) to Meiganga and Ngaoundere.

In the south there are scenic routes, preferably tackled in the dry season, from Douala and Yaounde to Kribi, from Yaounde to Bafoussam, from Kumba to Mamfe and on to Calabar or Enugu in Nigeria. The Bamenda-Mamfe road goes only one way on alternate days.

In the north there have been considerable improvements between Ngaoundere and Maroua, but north of Maroua there are likely to be delays in the wet season, especially on the road to Maiduguri in Nigeria, via the town of Bama.

As a general rule the improved laterite roads are controlled by frequent rain barriers, which hold back lorries for up to four hours after a heavy storm. Overlanders planning to cross Cameroon between June and October should allow extra days for such hold-ups.

Taxis are plentiful in the big towns, with ranks and cruising cars both in Douala and Yaounde. Prices are fixed in terms of Government-ordained zones within each city.

Car hire: Difficult outside Douala, Yaounde and Victoria, and expensive there. Try **Locamat, Autolocation** and **Lovoto** in Douala; **Autolocation** in Yaounde; **King** or **John Holt** in Victoria; **CEAC** or **CIACAM** in Garoua.

BANKS AND COMMERCE
In Douala and Yaounde are branches of the main banks, the Banque Internationale de l'Afrique Occidentale (BIAO) and the Banque International pour l'Industrie et le Commerce (BICIC), Banque Camerounaise de Développement. Other banks in most main towns are the Société Camerounaise de Banque and Société Général de Banque.

Business hours: In the francophone areas: 0800-1200, 1430-1730, closed Saturday afternoons. Banks: 0800-1130, 1430-1530 Mondays to Fridays only. In the anglophone areas: Government, 1730-1430 Mondays to Fridays, 0730-1200 Saturdays. Business: 0800-1200, 1400-1630, Mondays to Fridays, closed Saturday afternoons. Banks: 0800-1330, Mondays to Fridays only.

PUBLIC HOLIDAYS
A large number, only some of which are predictable, partly because the Muslim calendar varies from the Christian (and both sets of festivals are observed) and partly because of the existence of 'ponts' (bridges)—an extra day inserted between

a rest day (Sunday or Saturday) and a holiday to make a continuous period like a long weekend. The following are also observed compulsorily: Independence Day, 1 January; Youth Day, 11 February; Labour Day, 1 May; National Day, 20 May; Reunification Day, 1 October; Human Rights Day, 10 December.

FOREIGN EMBASSIES

Embassies in Yaounde: (tel. numbers in brackets).

Belgium (222788), Benin (224898), Canada (222922), Central African Empire (225155), Chad (220624), China PR (224198), Egypt (223922), France (221822), Gabon (222966), West Germany (220566), Ghana, Italy (223376), Liberia (222001), Nigeria (223455), Netherlands (224704), Spain (223543), Switzerland (222896), UK (220545), USA (221633), USSR (221714), Zaire (225103).

DOUALA

This is the biggest, most populous (485,000) and most thriving commercial centre and port. Situated about 25 km from the sea, it spreads from the Wourri estuary into the interior. The town has many big, modern buildings, beautiful shops and interesting markets, museums and monuments. The weather is hot and sticky but it is easy to get away from, to the beautiful cool and (nearly always visible) slopes of Mount Cameroon, or to the beaches of Victoria.

Hotels

Hôtel des Cocotiers, Ave. des Cocotiers, B.P. 310, tel: 42.58.00, luxury food and accommodation, views over the estuary to the mountain, 56 rooms, swimming pool, nightclub.
Akwa Palace, Ave. Poincare, B.P. 4007, tel: 42.26.01, more than just a comfortable commercial hotel, in the centre of town, 90 rooms.

La Falaise, B.P. 5300, tel: 42.46.46.
Residence Joss, B.P. 1218, tel: 42.17.50.
Hotel Beausejour, Rues Joffre and Alfred Saker, B.P. 5368, tel: 42.27.02.
Deido Plage, B.P. 69, Deido, tel: 42.51.45.
Hotel de Douala, B.P. 780, tel: 42.54.78.
Cameroun Hotel, Carrefour des Flèches, B.P. 5412, tel: 42.17.67.
Hotel des Palmiers, B.P. 56, New Bell, tel: 42.40.58.
Hotel de Lido, Rue Joffre, B.P. 210, tel: 42.62.45.
Hotel le Coin de Plaisir, B.P. 5300.
Hotel Arystha, B.P. 140.

Entertainment

Two air-conditioned cinemas, the **Wourri** and the **Paris**, as well as numerous nightclubs, among which the best are: **La Jungle, Le Castel, Le Scotch Club** (Hotel des Cocotiers), **La Bodega** and the **Deido Plage**. Most double as restaurants, but there are literally dozens of these—ask anyone who knows (travel agent, concierge, or taxi driver), mentioning, if you like, the special cuisine you prefer.

Shopping and markets

You are likely to be able to find something to suit all tastes—from the *folklorique* and *haute couture* to a bunch of bananas—in any of the countless shops and markets.
Travel agents: Camvoyages, Rue Joffre, B.P. 4079; **Delmas-Vieljeux**, Rue Kitchener, B.P. 263; **SOCOPAO**, Rue de Brazza, B.P. 215; **Mory**, Rue Joffre, B.P. 572.

YAOUNDE

This is the capital city with more bureaucrats and politicians and fewer businessmen. It is a big city (population 270,000), set among beautiful hills, with the really spectacular Mont Febe overlooking it, and the dense jungle only a few miles beyond. Mont Febe has all the trimmings—a luxury hotel (plus night-club and casino), a superb restaurant-cum-nightclub, botanical gardens and a golf course.

Hotels
Sheraton Mont Febe Palace, B.P. 4178, tel: 22.42.24, six km from centre, luxury, 219 rooms, swimming pool, nightclub.
Hotel Central, B.P. 6, tel: 22.36.11, luxury, particularly good food, 26 rooms.
Indépendance, B.P. 474, tel: 22.29.24.
Terminus, B.P. 21, tel: 22.00.11.
Grand, B.P. 714, tel: 22.49.33.
Safari Mont Febe, B.P. 84, tel: 22.08.02.
Hotel des Deputies, B.P. 1034, tel: 22.49.65.
Hotel de l'Unité, B.P. 1034, tel: 22.48.65.
Imperial, B.P. 977, tel: 22.35.66.
Bellevue, B.P. 124, tel: 22.29.42.
Idéal, B.P. 868, tel: 22.03.04.
Aurore, B.P. 152, tel: 22.08.66.
Hotel de la Paix, B.P. 106.
Flamenco, B.P. 4005, tel: 22.01.80.
Repos du Mahomy, B.P. 2434, tel: 22.29.20.

Tourist information
Commissariat General au Tourisme, Ave. du 27 Aout 1940, B.P. 266; Office National du Tourisme Camerounaise.
Travel agencies: Camvoyages, Ave. Mgr. Vogt, B.P. 606, **Mory**, B.P. 280.

VICTORIA

A pleasant, seaside town whose rather sleepy, lazy appearance masks a fair amount of commercial activity, mainly the result of the local rubber, palm oil and banana plantations, and the fact that it is an important port. It has one unique feature—beaches with black (pitch black) sand, the result of volcanic fall-out from the nearby Mount Cameroon. The town has a hot and sticky climate like Douala, but the sea breezes and the swimming are more than fair compensation.

Hotels
Park Hotel Miramare, P.O. Box 63, tel: 33232, the only luxury hotel, 37 rooms, swimming pool, nightclub.
Oceanic Hotel, P.O. Box 90, tel: 32249, 17 rooms, 6 chalets.
Victoria Hotel, in the town.
Airport Hotel, P.O. Box 3, tel: 51219.

BUEA

Lovely, tiny, old world former capital of the German colony and later capital of the anglophone West Cameroon, the town has a *schloss* (now the Governor's residence) and other memories of bygone ages—like a Bismark memorial and a postbox with E II R on it. It is set right up against Mount Cameroon with views across the Wourri over the creeks of Tiko to Douala. The weather is cool, pleasant and the atmosphere is relaxing.
Buea Mountain Hotel, P.O. Box 71, tel: 322251, 56 rooms and chalets.
Parliamentarian Flats, from the days when there was a separate parliament in anglophone West Cameroon, 30 rooms, snacks only.

BAMENDA

Up to the grasslands, set in the hollow created by the surrounding hills and providing glorious views, the town is a relaxing, cool, upland administrative (rather than commercial) centre.
Skyline Hotel, the only luxury hotel, tel: 361158, superb views, 22 rooms.
Ring Way Hotel, in the middle of the town, 18 rooms.
Fort Hotel, situated on top of a hill near the Government offices, 6 rooms and chalets.

DSCHANG

This is the francophone equivalent of the Bamenda grassland resort, with the added advantage of the cuisine. Visit the Baleng lake, Bamileke Museum and the Sunday market.
Centre Climatique, 44 rooms.

KRIBI

A palm-fringed beach resort, for fishing and bathing. The main beaches north of the town are Mpouloungou beach and Londji beach. South of Kribi are Ebome, Bouambe and Lobe Falls beaches.
Palm Beach, luxury, 112 rooms.
Kribi Plage, 17 rooms.
Azur Plage, 10 rooms.
Londji Plage, 9 rooms.
Hotel de la Paix, 5 rooms.
Maison du Tourisme, 4 rooms.
Chez Annette, 8 rooms.

THE SOUTHERN TOWNS

Edea. This small industrial town is 90 km. from Douala by a good road or by rail. It is in the heart of the equatorial forest. **Case de Passage**, 6 rooms.
Mbalmayo. A centre of cultural interest and for wildlife viewing. **Hotel de la Poste**, 9 rooms.
Ebolowa. A thriving commercial town on a good road from Yaounde. Situated in the equatorial forest it is the centre of the timber industry. **Splendid Hotel**, 15 rooms. **Hotel la Jungle**, 20 rooms.

Sangmelina. On the way from Yaounde and Ebolowa to Kribi by a not very good road. It is scenically beautiful (Mezesse rocks and Mekok caves) and there is a monastery where the nuns sing a beautiful Gregorian Mass accompanied by drums and in local rhythms. **Maison du Tourisme**, 4 rooms.

Foumban. There is lots of local interest in this, the major city of the important Bamoun culture. The Sultan's Palace and the museum are well worth seeing. It lies in the grasslands at an altitude of 1,200 m. and is free from humidity. **Beauregard Hotel**, 24 rooms, expensive but recommended. **Auberge**, 10 rooms.

Nkongsamba. Main town of the Bamileke area and railhead for much of Cameroon's cocoa and coffee production. **Hotel du Moungo**, 24 rooms. **Le Relais**, 12 rooms. **Hotel du Centre, 18 rooms**.

BAMILEKE COUNTRY TOWNS

Bafang is near enough to Dschang and Nkongsamba for one to be able to stay in either of the towns but there is **Le Paradis** restaurant, bar, 14 rooms; **Auberge du Haut-Nkam**, 8 rooms; **Hotel Pouleau Victor**, 6 rooms.

The same applies to **Bafoussam**, though there are the rather more impressive **Carrefour de l'Ouest**, restaurant, bar, 40 rooms; **Hotel du Cheval Blanc**, 8 rooms; and the **Mifi**, bar, 8 rooms.

Bafis has the **Campement Auberge**, 7 rooms, **Mbouda** has the **Relais Touristique**, 8 rooms, and **Bangante** has the **Auberge de Noe**.

THE NORTH

The exciting mountain scenery of this region is matched by its cultural diversity, from the ancient Islamic emirates and Foulbe (Fulani) villages and towns, to the remote non-Islamic communities, who can boast some of the finest indigenous African art in the Continent. The Kirdi peoples live in the mountains north of Garoua. The Kapsiki mountain range makes an unforgettable tourist circuit with its little cliff-hanging villages, where the Kirdi stage unique dances, amid the pinnacles and craters of extinct volcanoes.

The Mandara people live around Mora on the flat plains below the mountains that bear their name. Their culture bears a superficial similarity to the Kanuri lifestyle of north-eastern Nigeria, but it has its own traditions. This is the region where tantalising finds have been made of artifacts from the 10th century, presumed to belong to the mythical Sao people who first peopled the Lake Chad

Oudjila dancers, N. Cameroon

area. Some of their clay objects can be seen in the Maroua museum.

The Foulbe have penetrated from the far north of the country to the Adamaoua Plateau bordering the Central African Empire. The Foulbe villages with their ordered and expansive compounds have an air of prosperity, with neat gardens, decorated and furnished huts, in contrast to the more rudimentary villages of the Kirdi.

The dramatic peaks of the far north give way to the rolling mountain scenery of the Adamaoua Plateau. The area is interspersed with some fine game parks and open game country. Even from the main roads it is not unusual to see huge troops of baboons and monkeys. Here one finds the astonishing horizons and skies normally associated with East and Southern Africa. The Adamaoua Plateau proper has scattered volcanic craters forming round green hills.

NGAOUNDERE

The rail-head of the new Trans-Cameroon railway and a growing commercial centre, Ngaoundere lies in hilly surroundings, with several attractive lakes in the immediate neighbourhood, such as Lac Tison lying in a volcanic crater. Other sights are the Tello Falls, Vina Falls, and Rey-Bouba, the capital of the local Islamic sultanate. A typical town is Meiganga, accessible by a good road in the direction of Garoua-Boulai; as elsewhere the Foulbe dominate economic and religious life, while the local Baya sultan presides over civil affairs from his imposing palace compound; the Bororo (descendants of an earlier Foulbe invasion) live a separate and nomadic existence in the bush, while the Baya act as a workforce for the aristocratic Foulbe.

Hotel de l'Adamaoua, 16 rooms.

Hotel des Hauts Plateaux, 12 rooms.

Ngaoundere Ranch, near a crater and out of town 36 beds in chalets.

GAROUA

Regarded by people further north as a 'veritable Paris' Garoua is merely a traditional trading city with some modern facilities. Less attractive than Maroua, it is still a good centre for reaching points west and north. Being situated on the Benue River, Garoua has a considerable river trade and it is not uncommon to see dug-out canoes being carved by the roadside.

Hotel de la Benoue, luxury, 42 rooms.

Relais St. Hubert, 23 rooms.

MAROUA

This quiet and relaxed capital of the Diamare region presents a contrast with the more modern cities further south. The overriding culture is Foulbe and the religion Islam. Away from the neat central market the shady streets and traditional mud houses spread in every direction. During the rainy season the rivershore makes a very pleasant walk.

The fascinating little museum (in a prominent red building at the market entrance) presents a disorganised jumble of treasures from the 10th century Sao beside 19th century Foulbe and present-day Kirdi, Mandara and Yagoua artifacts, including weapons, ritual regalia and agricultural implements. If not open, go to the Centre Artisanal next door and ask for M. Hamadou Mallé, the helpful

curator. The Centre itself is a must for a complete picture of local crafts, which are sold at fixed but reasonable prices. Outside town is a clothweavers' collective, whose produce is of excellent quality.

Maroua is the best centre for the beautiful Mandara and Kapsiki mountains.

Relais du Kaliao, dry season only, 16 rooms.

Relais de la Porte Mayo, good restaurant.

Hotel Le Sare, luxurious and expensive.

The best of a number of small restaurants is **Chez Pierrot**. A bar/nightclub called **Chez Bossou** is one of the best in the north and presents some excellent coastal music.

There are small but inexpensive hotels in Mora, Mokolo and Rhumsiki, the best towns to visit for a taste of the north's cultural and scenic variety.

NATIONAL PARKS

Waza National Park

North of Maroua, this is Cameroon's most impressive nature reserve and game park. It was established in 1934, covers 170,000 hectares and is accessible not only by air from Douala and Yaounde, but from Ndjamena in Chad or Maiduguri in Nigeria. Great care has been taken over nature conservation and it is considered one of the best game parks in West Africa.

The park is organised to encompass two distinct regions, a forest area and a vast expanse of grassy plains. With the natural lushness of the former, and the flooding between February and August of the plains by the rivers flowing into Lake Chad, it has been possible to include the entire range of West African fauna—elephant, giraffe, antelope, hartebeeste, kob, lion, cheetah, leopard, wart-hog, all manner of large and small snakes, ostrich and a rich variety of exquisite birdlife (ibis, guinea fowl, geese, cranes, osprey, pelicans).

The park is open from November to June. Camping is forbidden, but there is the **Hotel de Waza** (100 beds in chalets, restaurant, bar) just outside the park, which offers excellent facilities for viewing game *au naturel*. Within the park there are special lookout posts near all the main pools where animals come to feed and drink. Hunting is strictly forbidden. The park has 400km of passable tracks.

Boubandjidah National Park

A relatively new and smaller park near Rey-Bouba, where you can see rhino and the Derby eland (one of the largest and most beautiful antelopes) in profusion; also buffalo, giraffe, lion, leopard, cheetah and other varieties of antelope.

Guides are available, and the Park's camp, on the banks of the Mayo Lidi River, offers eight four-bed chalets and a dining room.

Benoue National Park

Also well-endowed with wildlife, like the Waza and Boubandjidah Parks, it is less far north—on the Ngaoundere to Garoua road.

Kala Maloue Reserve

This small reserve is situated only 11km from the Ndjamena airport (in Chad), and is well worth an excursion to see the elephant, hippo, giraffe and the varieties of antelope whose natural habitat is the savannah.

HISTORY

Cameroon is the home of some of the earliest archaeological artifacts of pre-history, and of the Sao sculpture of a later period. The land was mentioned by Hanno the Carthaginian who described Mount Cameroon in the 6th century BC (when it was still an active volcano) as the Chariot of the Gods.

The history of the north was determined by the contest for power between the great empires of the 11th to 18th centuries, which saw the spread of Islamic culture under the aegis of both Kanem-Bornu and the Fulani, who established their authority through emirates in Dikwa and the Benoue and Adamaoua plateaux. The south was for many years ravaged by the slave and ivory trades, stimulated first by Portuguese and later by Dutch, Scandinavian and British traders. In this way were created the great kingdoms of middlemen, the Kings of Akwa and Bell at the coast, and the Bamileke and Bassa confederations in the centre.

In the 19th century, Cameroon was a prize to be won in the scramble for Africa—with France, Germany and Britain all competing. Germany won, and ruled over the country until defeated in World War I. The country was then divided and ruled separately by Britain and France under the mandate system created by the League of Nations. In 1945, each part became a Trust Territory under the supervision of the United Nations; they were in fact ruled just like any other colonial possession.

An anti-colonial unification movement grew up in the French Cameroon in the 1950s and was still in progress when the French finally agreed to hand over power to the present Head of State, El Hadj Ahmadou Ahidjo, and his *Union Camerounaise*. He put down the radical rebellion with considerable ruthlessness and then went on to pursue the goal of unification with British-ruled Cameroon, which was being administered as a part of Nigeria.

In a referendum conducted in 1960, the northern part of the British Cameroon voted to remain in Nigeria, while the southern part agreed to federate with the francophone Republic of Cameroon. The country continued as a federation with domination by the larger, richer and more populous francophone section from October 1961 until May 1972. Then, in another referendum, the population voted to create a single, unitary state. There is no freedom of the press, of speech or of political association.

CAPE VERDE ISLANDS

Being an Atlantic Ocean extension of the drought-ridden Sahel, the Cape Verde Islands are dry, barren and rather inhospitable to the visitor. Since 1968 little rain has fallen, the country's agriculture has been decimated and the 300,000 islanders have depended entirely on international aid to avoid starvation.

The archipelago consists of ten major islands and four uninhabited islets strung in a curved volcanic chain 500km off the West African coast. Bon Vista and Sal Islands (the latter with the international airport) stand nearest the mainland. The northern side of the chain, called the Windward Group, includes Santa Antao, Sao Vicente, Santa Lucia and Sao Nicolau. The southern or Leeward Group consists of Brava, Fogo, Sao Tiago (Santiago) and Maio.

With variations among them, the islands are generally rocky, arid, eroded and agriculturally unproductive. The largest island, Sao Tiago, has the capital, Praia, and occupies about a quarter of the total area. Most of the islands have mountain peaks, dominated by Pico do Cano, an active volcano on Fogo.

Uninhabited when the Portuguese reached them in 1456, the islands now have a population of mixed European and African descent. Portuguese planters imported a workforce of West African slaves and European convicts. The first recorded slave expedition raided the Guinea coast in 1461; the last slaves were freed in 1876.

Until July 1975 the territory was administered as an 'Overseas Province' of Portugal. Nationalist dissent was fiercely repressed. The African Party for the Independence of Guinea-Bissau and the Cape Verde Islands (PAIGC) was prevented from sinking roots in the islands—although its founder, Amilcar Cabral, was an islander (he was assassinated by Portuguese agents in Conakry in 1973).

The turning point in the islands' history came after the April 1974 coup in Portugal, which sparked a wave of nationalist agitation in the islands. Portugal and the PAIGC came to terms in December 1974 and independence followed in 1975. Since then the PAIGC has built up a

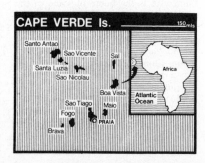

CAPE VERDE Is.

strong party apparatus and an associated array of mass organisations. The Government plans eventually to unify the Cape Verde Islands with Guinea-Bissau.

The new government has refused to allow the establishment of foreign military bases, although the islands have an obvious strategic potential. It has, however, courted both Western countries and the Soviet bloc for aid and trade.

The islands have always suffered from drought. In one famine, between 1860 and 1866, nearly half the population starved to death. Thousands of islanders have been forced to emigrate so that today there are as many Cape Verdeans abroad as at home. These emigrés remit money to their relatives at home.

The present drought is the longest ever. Production of the staple food, corn, is now less than a tenth of its normal level, and thousands of goats, cows, horses, pigs and sheep have perished. Food that the country cannot afford has to be imported to keep the population alive. The Cape Verdian people have an individualistic creole culture which finds expression in music, dancing and lyrical *crioula* poetry.

GENERAL INFORMATION

Area: 4,000sq km.
Population: 300,000.
Altitude: Sea level to high volcanic peaks. Pico do Cano 3,000m.
Capital: Praia (Sao Tiago).
Government: African Party for the Independence of Guinea-Bissau and the Cape Verde Islands (PAIGC).
Head of State: President Aristides Pereira.
Languages: Portuguese is the official language but the majority speak *crioula*, derived from Portuguese and African languages.
Religion: Roman Catholic.
Currency: Cape Verde Escudo. £1=66.50 escudos. $1=32.95 escudos.
Time: GMT −2.

HOW TO GET THERE

By air: Regular flights to Sal International Airport by TAP from Lisbon, the Cape Verdes' airline TACV from Bissau, and from London and Johannesburg by South African Airways.
By sea: Regular passenger service to Mindelo (Sao Vicente) from Lisbon and Bissau by SGT.

TRANSPORT

Boats ply regularly between the islands and there are airstrips on Sao Tiago and Sao Vicente served by the local airline. Taxis and buses operate on the main islands.

ACCOMMODATION

There are small hotels at Praia (Sao Tiago) and on Sal island. The country's principal port and commercial centre is Mindelo, which has some accommodation for visitors.

Antao's rugged volcanic peaks

CENTRAL AFRICAN EMPIRE

A fascinating expanse of Africa almost untouched by the 20th century, Central Africa is being visited more and more by trans-African travellers.

While the sophisticated enclave, of Bangui, the capital, has most modern facilities, you only have to travel a few kilometres out of the city to discover an Africa that has practically no administration, modern education or health facilities. The people live at a subsistence level, growing or hunting their food, with little or no incentive to trade or to enter into a modern way of life. Perhaps because of this, the Central African villagers are among the most welcoming and charming people to meet on travels anywhere in the world.

THE LAND AND THE PEOPLE

The Central African Empire (of Emperor Bokassa) is a huge territory of largely uninhabited forest and bush, lying between latitudes 4° and 11°N. The southern border is the Oubangui River and the M'boumou. The watershed with the Chari River running into Lake Chad cuts through the centre from east to west. More than half the country lying east of a line joining Bangassou—Fort Crampel—Batangafo is almost uninhabited and this is where the big game reserves and parks are situated.

Groups of nomadic Fulani, Chad Arab and Sudanese cattle-peoples move through the country and in and out of neighbouring Cameroon, Chad and Sudan with no regard for political frontiers.

The country rises in mountainous forest towards Cameroon, with altitudes up to 2,000m west of Bocaranga in the north-west corner. There is fairly dense tropical rainforest in the south-west, in the inaccessible districts of Haute Sangha and Lobaye towards the Congo border, but most of the country is rolling or flat pleateau, at altitudes of about 500m, covered with dry deciduous forest where this has not been reduced to grass savannah, or completely destroyed by annual bush-fires. To the north-east the country becomes sub-desert, with a Sahelian flo-

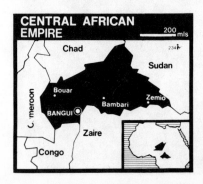

ra, and mountainous in places. The frontier with Sudan runs mainly above a watershed.

The population is probably about two million, but since many people live in the forest out of reach of the administration and others move in and out of neighbouring countries, this figure is approximate. The Baya and Banda peoples make up about half the population. Other prominent groups are the Baka and the Zande.

Probably the main food crop is cassava, but coffee, cotton, tobacco, bananas and oil-palm are also grown. Cattle are reared in many parts of the savannah belt.

The Central African Empire is one of the few African countries with an almost nationally understood language, Sango. It originated as a trading language along the Oubangui River, and is related to Lingala, one of the four main languages of Zaire. Although French is the official language, Sango is widely used in administration, and almost entirely on the radio.

A striking feature of Central Africa is the widespread continued use of the 'talking drum' to convey messages from village to village—a system far more relevant than any multi-million dollar telecommunications scheme.

CULTURE

Each ethnic group has its own lively dancing and characteristic musical instruments. To see these, you have to travel in the bush and hope to happen on one of the frequent village ceremonies. The villagers make for their own use some beautifully simple but practical basketwork and furniture (stools, chairs and beds).

There are quite a number of woodcarvings; those from the forest near the Congo border are among the best, but they are not of the high standard found in Zaire. Traders offer a wide variety of animal and snake skins, and also ivory objects. On the pavements in Bangui, Hausa traders offer sandals, belts and other fine leatherwork, much of it from Cameroon.

The Boganda Museum in Bangui is stuffed full with a vast range of traditional implements, drums, religious objects and weapons from all over the country. A morning spent in this museum is more worthwhile than any academic course in African anthropology.

WILDLIFE

The Central African Empire is still probably one of the finest game countries in Africa.

The wildlife is at present preserved because almost two-thirds of the country is uninhabited rather than because of Government policy. Hunting for food by small groups of villagers with spears, nets and bows and arrows is vigorously carried on, especially in the centre and centre-west regions.

Thousands of hectares of forest are burned each year during hunting, which accelerates the destruction of natural vegetation, and hastens the extermination of many animal species.It was not until the 1950s that seven wildlife reserves, three national parks and one *reserve integrale* was established.

The number of animals can still compare with that of the East African reserves.

All kinds of antelope are represented by big herds: waterbuck, hartebeeste, roan antelope, Buffon's kob, Derby eland and great kudu. There are large numbers of lion, leopard and cheetah as well as elephant, giraffe, hippo and rhino.

The Central African Empire is fine fishing country because of its many rivers.

It is also remarkable for its thousands of brightly-coloured butterflies, many of them unique to the region. They are found all over the country, and especially in the south-west.

GENERAL INFORMATION

Area: 617,000 sq. km.

Population: 2 million.

Altitude: Mainly about 600 m but rising in places about 1,500 m. Bangui 500 m.

Capital: Bangui.

Head of State: Emperor, Field Marshal, Jean-Bedel Salah Addin Ahmed Bokassa 'the First'.

Government: Military.

Date of Independence: 13 August 1960.

Languages: French (official), Sango and other local languages. Swahili is used in the east, Arabic in the north and Hausa among traders.

Religions: Traditional, Roman Catholic and Muslim.

Currency: CFA franc. £1 = 428 CFA francs. $1 = 249 CFA francs.

Time: GMT + 1.

Electricity: In Bangui 220V, but erratic.

HOW TO GET THERE

By air: From Paris: UTA, Air Afrique and ACAV. From Moscow: Aeroflot (via Cairo and Khartoum). From Douala: Air Centrafrique (irregular). From Brazzaville: Air Centrafrique. From Kinshasa: Air Zaire (irregular and unreliable).

By road: The only way across Africa from west to east lies through Bangui. From Ndjamena you can drive south to Bangui through Bossangoa. From Douala you can drive via Yaounde to Bouar and Bangui. The roads are in reasonable state of repair, although there are stretches that become difficult during the rains. One almost impassable section is, ironically, at the entry point to the country from Garoua-Boulai in Cameroon.

From Zaire there are no bridges across the Oubangui River and vehicles must be transported by ferry, either at Bangui, Bangassou or Zemio.

By river: There is transport upriver from Brazzaville to Bangui, and a passenger ferry across the river from Zongo in Zaire.

Visas and health regulations

Visas are required by all nationals other than French and Africans from francophone States. Where there is no Central African Empire Embassy, the French Embassy should be able to deliver a tourist visa, but usually for only 48 hours. This has to be renewed after arrival in Bangui.

While immigration controls are normally conducted at Bangui airport, visitors arriving by road should be prepared for the unpredictable at entry points such as Bangassou, or coming from Chad. The Cameroon border controls appear to be normal. The numerous barriers set up on the main roads to control the movement of traffic may be the source of some delay. The worst is kilometre 12 on the road north out of Bangui. Here everyone moving in or out of Bangui is stopped and 'controlled', though the object of this is uncertain. Foreigners arriving by road have to present passports and car tryptiques all over again as when arriving at the frontier.

Yellow fever, cholera and smallpox certificates are required.

Dutiable goods

While you can in theory bring in the usual personal goods and belongings, unpredictable behaviour of military personnel at entry points should be expected. Firearms on no account should be brought.

Currency regulations

There is no limit on the amount of foreign currency or travellers' cheques which can be taken into the country, although a declaration must be made. Unused foreign currency may be taken out again. Similarly there is no limit on the import or export of French francs or CFA banknotes.

CLIMATE

The climate is generally hot with a marked dry season. Mean annual temperatures are about 25°C in Bangui, but rise to nearly 30°C in the north-east. The rains in the south are from May to October, the season shortening as one approaches Chad and the Sudan. Mean annual rainfall varies from 1,636 mm in Bangui to 2,070 mm in Bangassou. In the north the dusty but cooling harmattan is felt in January and February, but it does not affect Bangui.

Health precautions
Anti-malarial precautions are essential. Bilharzia is found almost everywhere, so water should be filtered or boiled, even in Bangui. Various kinds of intestinal disorders can be picked up in the bush.

ACCOMMODATION AND FOOD
The only regularly-functioning hotels are in Bangui, where they are very expensive.

The only European-style restaurants are in Bangui but local food is available. There are numerous local bars.

TRANSPORT
There are 19,207 km of roads and tracks, including 5,018 km of well-surfaced main roads passable throughout the year. Traffic drives on the right. If driving through the country it is essential to carry the maximum of petrol. There are pumps in many centres but these are very often out of petrol for long periods. Portuguese-owned stores (such as the chain of Moura and Gouveia) can supply quite a good range of supplies, but may be out of items like sugar or oil.

There are very few garages outside Bangui and spare parts for cars are practically unobtainable. When a car has an accident, its owner usually breaks it up and sells the parts at a good profit.

Taxis are available in Bangui. They do not have meters and it is advisable to settle the fare before starting your journey.

Car hire: Self-drive cars are available from **Tsiros Location**, B.P. 68, Bangui, tel: 29.86 and **Auto Service**, B.P. 13, tel: 22.57.

BANKS AND COMMERCE
UBAC, BIAO and BNCD.

Business hours: Markets and shops are generally open 0800 to 1200 and 1430 to 1700 except on Sundays.

PUBLIC HOLIDAYS
As well as Christian feastdays the following holidays are observed: Anniversary of President Boganda's death 29 March; Anniversary of first Government 14 May; Independence Day 13 August.

The cotton festival of July/August is celebrated throughout the country. Muslim festivals are observed in the north.

FOREIGN EMBASSIES
Belgium: Pl. de la Republique, B.P. 938, Bangui.
France: Blvd. du General de Gaulle, B.P. 784, Bangui.
USA: Pl. de la Republique, B.P. 924, Bangui.
West Germany: Ave. du President Nasser, B.P. 784, Bangui.

BANGUI
The capital takes its name from the rapids on the Oubangui River where it squeezes through a range of low hills. The town is rapidly spreading, with modern blocks and broad avenues, shaded by mango trees and flamboyants. The central market is a bustling and colourful focus of activity. The Grande Corniche leads to the banks of the Oubangui, where fishermen have their canoes.

Two elegant shops stock fine ivory and ebony art objects, as well as traditional artefacts. Anyone interested in African culture should not miss the Boganda Museum.

The main activity and vitality of Bangui is concentrated in the quarter known as 'Kilometre Cinq'.

The dramatic Boali Falls are 90 km north of Bangui by good road.

Hotels

Safari Hotel, B.P. 1317, tel: 30.20. On the Oubangui River, about 1 km to the east of town. Designed as a luxury hotel, it has a reasonable accommodation and bar service. The food is moderate, but prices exorbitant for what is offered. There is a pleasant bar, serving also *mechoui*, on an island in the river reached by a causeway from the hotel. 51 rooms.

Rock Hotel, B.P. 569, tel: 20.88, between the 'Safari' and town, has a pleasant shaded garden on the edge of the Oubangui River where drinks and meals are served. All food is imported, strictly French and quite unsuited to the climate. Well-run but very expensive. 38 rooms.

Minerva Hotel, B.P. 308, tel: 26.62, an old colonial style hotel in the centre of town. Has large cool rooms, a good bar and atmosphere, but no meals. 23 rooms.

New Palace Hotel, B.P. 108, tel: 23.77 in the centre of town, has a much-frequented terrace in the evenings, not smart but has a distinct atmosphere. The restaurant serves quite good, simple and inexpensive meals. A few rooms in the colonial style, but the hotel is next to its own cinema and is noisy.

Hotel St. Sylvestre, B.P. 1015, tel: 38.00, a recent and pretentious hotel in the middle of town. Rooms are small, expensive, air-conditioned boxes. No restaurant. Bad service, poor bar, no atmosphere. More expensive than the

Minerva, but cheaper than the Rock. 75 rooms.

National Hotel:, B.P. 823, tel: 33.76.

Restaurants
Apart from the hotel restaurants there are: **L'Orient, La Banquise, Le Dragon d'Or** or the airport restaurant.

Entertainment
In the smart clubs (in the main hotels) drinks are very expensive. Local night-life is found in the quarter at 'Kilometre 5'.

There are sports at the Rock Club, including swimming, tennis, golf and riding.

Tourist information
Office National du Tourisme, B.P. 655. Bangui-Tourisme, B.P. 875, tel: 34.24.

BOUAR
In a fine position on the edge of the plateau that extends into Cameroon and on the main road between Cameroon and Bangui, this delapidated town has an ancient and mysterious history. The whole area around Bouar is dotted with evidence of a megalithic culture that flourished thousands of years ago before any of the present peoples started to arrive. This ancient civilization has hardly been investigated, but the stone monuments that now stand neglected or overgrown in the rocky landscape seem to point to a link with megalithic cultures elsewhere in the world, perhaps with those of Egypt or western Europe.

No less than 70 individual groups of standing stones in varying arrangements have been found in the Bouar area, which straddles the watershed between the Zaire River and Lake Chad basins. Generally placed at the head of streams, 60% of these granite monuments are on tributaries of the Zaire and 40% are on tributaries of Chad rivers. Several individual stones weigh three or four tonnes and would have had to be transported at least three kilometres to each site. Archaeologists have calculated that the moving of the stones would have required a greater population in the area than is now present. Some of the finest examples of the Bouar megaliths are on the outskirts of the town itself.

Bouar has also featured more recently in world events. It was the Central African headquarters of the free French forces in World War II under General Leclerc, but now it is completely run down, both as a commercial centre and as a tourist resort. The people in this area are mainly Baya, but there are Hausa and Fulani communities.

BAMBARI

A typical Central African town, once with a semblance of prosperity, now completely run-down, but still pleasant by virtue of its position on the Ouaka River. The people in the area are Banda. The countryside consists of rolling green

grassy hills. To the south is some beautiful scenery with neat Banda villages nestling among fields of coffee and food crops. By the rivers the fishing communities have a life-style and vitality of their own.

Hotel des Chasses, restaurant, bar. 8 rooms.

BANGASSOU

Another sleepy run-down town but the usual point for overlanders to cross the Oubangui River to or from Zaire. On the road from Bangui are the spectacular Kembe Falls on the Kotto River; a good spot for washing but fatal for anyone attempting to swim.

La Palmeraie, Bangassou, 4 rooms, restaurant and bar.

GAME RESERVES

Zemongo is on the Sudan border in the east of Central Africa. Almost inaccessi-

River boats on the Oubangui

R. SYNGE

ble except in certain seasons by four-wheel-drive vehicles from Bangassou via Zemio on the road to Obo. Open grass savannah with 'plains game', similar to the Garamba Park near Faradje in Zaire.

Yata Ngaya is farther north, also on the Sudan border. Contains the **Andre Felix National Park**. Mountainous.

Ouandjia Vakaga—100 km to the west of the above—and **Aouk Aoukale**, 50 km to the north-west. Between these two reserves is the small **St. Floris National Park**

The above three reserves and the national parks are accessible from Birao by four-wheel-drive vehicles in certain seasons. Birao can be reached, also by four-wheel-drive vehicles, from Bangui via Bambari and Bria (about three days' drive).

Another group of game reserves is situated near the Chad border and can be reached by road (four-wheel-drive) from Bangui, via Fort Crampel and Ndele. **Miamere Miadiki** and **Gribingui Bamingui** consist of wooded savannah and contain varied game and elephant. Between these two reserves is the large **Bamingui Bagoran National Park**, in which is the *reserve integrale* of Vassako Bolo.

Nanya Barya, a small game reserve on the Chad border, about 120 km north of Bossangoa, is the most accessible.

The game population of these reserves is impressive, and includes large numbers of elephant, buffalo, lion and antelope. The birdlife is very prolific.

There is no possibility of accommodation. All food, water, bedding and petrol should be taken in a very reliable four-wheel-drive vehicle. While it is sometimes said that there are 'resthouses' in Central Africa, and these even appear on maps, you will be lucky if you find a ruined bat-infested building. You may have to be content with a bank-breaking safari organized by the UTA, or possibly you may be able to obtain a permit to visit the reserves from *Le Directeur, Service des Eaux et Forêts*, Bangui.

HISTORY

Little is known about the peopling of Central Africa until the 18th century. The Bandia were one of the more powerful groups, giving rise to the Zande nation of the east in the 19th century, but the whole area was subjected to slave-raids from Sudan and Chad. The French called the territory 'Oubangui-Chari' when Equatorial Africa was established in 1910 out of a confusion of territorial claims arising from military penetration since 1886.

The colony was under-administered, except in the plantations where forced labour provoked a series of rebellions that were savagely repressed by the French. With vast expanses of wild uninhabited country, Oubangui-Chari was a favourite big-game hunting ground for French administrators and army officers. A large military base established at Bouar near the Cameroon border played an important part as a depot during the Free French operations under General Leclerc in the 1939-45 war.

The territory was educationally, economically and administratively unprepared for its political independence in 1960. It was further handicapped by the death in an air-crash in 1959 of Barthelemy Boganda, its outstanding political leader. He was succeeded by David Dacko, whose administration depended almost entirely on French technical assistants, and on a substantial French subsidy. Dacko was overthrown on 31 December 1965 by General Jean-Bedel Bokassa in a military coup. Parliament was dissolved and Bokassa has since ruled as a dictator with a strongly personal and quite unpredictable style.

France still gives technical and military and financial support, mainly to prevent the total collapse of the administration.

CHAD

Chad is a huge basin, once covered by water. Lake Chad and the small rivers are still fished in traditional canoes and papyrus boats. All over the southern savannah there is varied and abundant game, while for the more adventurous traveller the torrid red mountains of the central Sahara are a treasury of ancient rock art.

The country's vast size, poor communications, sparse population and lack of natural resources make Chad among the world's poorest countries. These conditions have been exacerbated by a tenacious rebellion among some of the people in the Muslim north.

THE LAND AND THE PEOPLE
Over twice the size of France, Chad stretches from the borders of the equatorial forest to the mid-Sahara. Lake Chad is the 11th largest in the world—at its maximum, 25,000 sq km. Evaporation sometimes reduces it to 10,000 sq km. It is choked with papyrus and covered with floating islands of vegetation which occasionally take root on the shallow bed (maximum depth 4 m). The water is sweet for cattle but the salts build up into valuable natron deposits in the north.

The south is watered by the Chari, Logone, Salamat and Aouk rivers and their tributaries. They are mostly dry beds except in the few months when they flood the surrounding land; only the Chari below Ndjamena remains navigable all year.

The Chad basin is bounded to west and south by the Adamaoua and Mandara

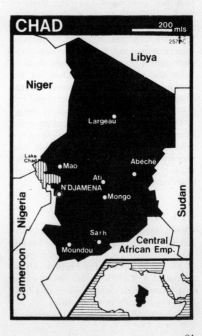

Mountains (Cameroon) and the Central African Empire plateau, and for the rest by mountains within Chad's borders. In the east the crystalline range of Ouaddai reaches 1,500 m; in the north-east lie the pink sandstone heights of Ennedi; and in the north the volcanic chain of Tibesti where sheer cliffs, ravines and canyons of twisted curiously-formed rocks rise out of the sand dunes of the Sahara to the peak of Emi Koussi (3,415 m). The north is rich in fossil remains, such as the skull of *Chadanthropus* , as well as rock art—a reminder that the desert once bloomed. Other hill ranges such as Guera rise in the centre of Chad.

The most populous region is the largely Negroid agricultural south, the Sarh region, where the Sara people predominate as farmers self-sufficient in millet, sorghum, rice and groundnuts. Since the 18th century they have resisted the northern empires' attempts to subjugate them.

In the south-west—once the home of the Sao civilization—live the Kotoko fishermen who occupy fortified villages and fish with huge nets attached by poles to their canoes, and the Massa who build curious huts shaped like artillery shells.

On the islands of Lake Chad live the Boudouma and Kouri who use papyrus both for huts and raft-like boats, and live off fish and their strong-swimming cattle.

The Sahel region of the centre is the home of the pastoral peoples—semi-nomadic horsemen who herd cattle and sheep and who still hunt with spears, but the recent droughts have threatened their traditional way of life.

CULTURE

Chad's fascinating history at the crossroads of African and Arab culture has left many material traces. The great empires of the centre spread the Muslim culture to almost half of the entire country; the rest follow traditional religions or Christianity (especially in the south).

The rock engravings and paintings of the Tibesti and Ennedi Mountains, dating from 9000 BC, show that elephant, rhino and hippo once inhabited the Sahara, which must then have had a humid climate and dense vegetation. There are two epochs of artists: the first a time of hunters, who gradually evolved with the use of more sophisticated hunting techniques and the aid of dogs; the second, a time when the hunters also became pastoralists with domesticated cattle, goats and sheep. The best art is found at Gonoa, Oudingueur, Bardai and near Zouar and Aouzou.

In the fertile riverine area south of Lake Chad archaeologists have found distinctive pottery funeral urns topped by grotesque busts and other artefacts dating between the 9th to 16th centuries AD which have been called Sao after a people known in oral tradition as giants who once lived here.

Muslim influence has encouraged craftsmen to make very fine carpets, embroider hand-woven cotton, and to make articles of camel-hair and leather.

Highly developed styles of music and dancing are to be found among the Toubou of Tibesti, the Kanembou of the centre and the Sara of the south.

WILDLIFE

The variety and abundance of Chad's fauna and the diversity of its terrain make it a fascinating country for the naturalist. The savannah—merging into the southern Sahel, which incorporates one of the richest game parks in Africa, the Zakouma National Park—is a paradise for elephant, buffalo, giraffe, all kinds of antelope, ostrich, lion and hyena. In the rivers and Lake Chad there are hippo, crocodile, python and myriad birds such as pelicans, marabou storks and huge numbers of fish such as the capitaine, binga and catfish. Hunting is forbidden.

The country dries out through the thorny Sahel pastureland to the desert and mountains of the north which are inhabited by rare animals such as the addax, oryx, various gazelles and leopard.

GENERAL INFORMATION
Area: 1,284,000 sq. km.
Population: 4 million.
Altitude: Lake Chad lies at 250m above sea level and the land rises to c.1,800m in the mountains, topped by Emi Koussi at 3,415m.
Capital: Ndjamena.
Head of State: General Felix Malloum.
Government: The Supreme Military Council.
Date of Independence: 1 August 1960.
Languages: The official language is French. The people speak a variety of African languages, notably Sara. Arabic is used in the north.
Religions: 45% Muslim; 10% Christian and the remainder Traditional.
Currency: CFA franc. £1=428 CFA francs. $1=249 CFA francs.
Time: GMT +1.
Electricity: 220V.

HOW TO GET THERE
By air: An international airport, used as a stopping place for traffic from Europe to francophone Africa, lies 2 km from Ndjamena. Taxis and hotel transport meet flights. UTA and Air Afrique run four flights a week to Ndjamena from Paris. There are flights from Douala, Kinshasa and Bangui.
By road: There are passable roads from the Central African Empire, Cameroon and Nigeria. The motorist needs a carnet de passage issued by the Tourist Association in the country of origin, an international driving licence and either a green card for insurance or all-risks insurance obtained in Chad. Petrol is expensive.

Visas and health regulations
Citizens of France, Andorra, Monaco, West Germany, former French colonies and Zaire only require a passport. All others must also obtain a visa from a Chadian Embassy or, where none exists, from a French Embassy. The visitor should possess an onward or return ticket or repatriation guarantee. A Government permit is necessary to go to the northern frontier zone beyond Fada and Zouar where the rebellion has not finally been broken.

International certificates of vaccination against smallpox, yellow fever and cholera are required.

Dutiable goods
Personal effects may be brought in, including 400 cigarettes, two cameras with 10 rolls of film each, a cine camera and a record player.

Currency regulations
All currency must be declared at the frontier. There is no limit to the amount imported.

Unused amounts of foreign currency may be taken out together with 10,000 CFA francs. (CFA francs are not easily exchanged in non-franc zones).

CLIMATE
The country has one rainy season: in the south c. 1,000mm fall in May to October; in the centre the season lasts from June to September with less precipitation, while the north has very little rain at any time of the year. Temperatures average 20-25°C.

The dry season brings cloudless skies, often with a wind from the east when nights can be cold, but day-time temperatures can rise to 40°C. It is especially hot just before the rains.

The best time to visit Chad is November to May.
What to wear: The heat demands linen and cotton light clothing, although woollens may be needed in the cool evenings. A light raincoat is advisable in the rainy season.

Health precautions:
Visitors should take malaria prophylactic tablets a fortnight before the visit, during their stay and for a fortnight afterwards. Water is drinkable in Ndjamena but elsewhere it should be boiled first.

ACCOMMODATION
There are three good hotels in Ndjamena, but accommodation elsewhere is very limited.

There are two small hotels at Sarh, a modern hotel complex in the Zakouma National Park and various small hunting hotels in the south-west.

TRANSPORT
Air: Air Tchad operates regular flights to Ati, Am Timan, Abeche, Bol, Bongor, Faya-Largeau, Mongo, Moundou, Mao, Pala, Sarh and Zakouma. Bol (on Lake Chad) is also served by air taxi.

Road: The road network over the vast distances of Chad is at present inadequate and plans to improve at least the main arteries connecting Ndjamena, Sarh and Abeche have not yet reached fruition.

All roads are earth (except in Ndjamena). The south is cut off from the north during the summer rains for four months.

Car hire: For travel in the city and its vicinity cars may be hired in Ndjamena from **Tchad Tourisme,** Rue du Sultan Mohammed Ouradah, B.P. 894, tel: 34.10; **Sympatic Taxis,** B.P. 707; and **Texaco Taxis,** Pl Sultan Kasser, B.P. 873, tel: 30-08.

BUSINESS HOURS
Banks: 0700-1130 Monday to Saturday. **Post Offices:** 0730-1130 or noon; 1430-1630 or 1700. **Shops:** 0800 to 1200 and 1600 to 1900 (including Saturdays). Most shops are closed on Mondays. Food shops open on Sunday mornings.

PUBLIC HOLIDAYS
New Year's Day; National Holiday 11 January; Easter Monday; Labour Day 1 May; Ascension Day; Africa Liberation Day 25 May; Whit Monday; Independence Day 11 August; Feast of the Virgin Mary 15 August; All Saints' Day 1 November; Day of the Proclamation of the Republic 20 November; Christmas Day.

Variable holidays are: The Muslim New Year; the end of Ramadan; and the Fête du Mouton (71 days after the end of Ramadan).

FOREIGN EMBASSIES
(All in Ndjamena)
France: B.P. 431, tel: 25-76/8.
Federal Republic of Germany: B.P. 893, tel: 23-77/8.
U.S.A.: B.P. 413, tel: 30-91/4.
Others: Sudan, Nigeria, Libya, Zaire, Egypt, Central African Empire.

TOURIST INFORMATION
Direction du Tourisme, B.P. 86, Ndjamena, tel: 28-17.
Tchad Tourisme, B.P. 894, Ndjamena, tel: 34-10.

NDJAMENA
The modern capital preserves an historic quarter of traditional mud-brick houses where the colourful daily market is a picturesque sight. The Museum has rich ethnographic and archaeological collections of the Sao culture dating back to the 9th century, as well as samples of rock engravings from the north.

Lake Chad (120 km) can be reached by air (to Bol) or by rough road; there are hippo and elephant, colourful birdlife, and, in the sand dunes, large flocks of ostriches.

Nomads of the Sahel region

Hotels
La Tchadienne, B.P. 109, tel; 33-11, on river 1 km. from city, 104 rooms.
Le Chari, B.P. 118, tel; 28-20, on river 1 km. from city, 32 rooms.
Le Grand Hotel, B.P. 108, tel: 38-88, in city centre, 30 rooms.
Air Hotel, B.P. 22, tel: 20-58, 9 rooms.

Restaurants
For French cuisine: **Air Hotel, Bar de la Poste, le Saloon,** as well as all hotels above. There are, too, the **Cabrini Restaurant** (Italian), **Naufal Snack** (Lebanese) and **Le Lotus** (Vietnamese) and **Kim Son.** In most you will find the famous local capitaine fish.

Entertainments
Nightclubs are **Baby-Scotch, Hi Fi Music, Le Mecreant.** There are facilities for swimming, bowling and volley-ball and excellent fishing.

No permits are required and the rivers are packed with fish, the commonest being capitaine, binga and catfish.

Shopping
In the market and elsewhere you will find souvenirs produced by Chad's flourishing craft industry: camel-hair carpets, all kinds of leatherware, embroidered cotton cloths, finely decorated calabashes, brass animals, knives, weapons and pottery.

SARH
A large town in the south (formerly called Fort Archambault), Sarh lies at the intersection of trade routes, especially that linking Chad with the Central African Empire and Zaire. It is a popular base for hunting trips.
Hotel des Chasses, B.P. 25, tel: 354, 8 rooms, swimming pool.
Hotel Safari, tel: 273, 12 rooms.

ABECHE
This large semi-desert town, full of mosques and old markets (souks), is frequented by nomad caravans with their multi-coloured tents. It was once capital

of the Ouaddai empire. Its craftsmen are famed for their camel-hair blankets.

Some kilometres away is Ouara, an early capital, approached by narrow passages through a maze of rocks. A huge town wall, 6m thick, surrounds the remains of a palace and mosque and the sultan's tombs.

GAME PARKS

One large game park—Zakouma—is well laid out for visitors. Other smaller ones near the towns make pleasant short expeditions.

Zakouma National Park: Huge grassy plains, dotted with forest, drain down to the Bahr Salamat through watercourses that dry up for most of the year, leaving only drinking pools for the myriad animals which inhabit the 297,200 ha park. the park is open from 15 December to 31 May.

There are great numbers of elephant, buffalo, giraffe, lion, many kinds of antelope, including greater kudu in the extreme south-west. There are, too, a few rare rhinoceros and leopards, as well as numerous birds—ostrich, pelicans, marabou storks. Water fowl inhabit the ponds where crocodiles and pythons reign.

Accommodation is in large, air-conditioned rondavels, providing 56 beds as well as a few beds in a former hotel. There is a restaurant nearby.

Other reserves: Near Ndjamena, **Douguia** (80 km) is an interesting reserve near Lake Chad equipped with bungalows, providing 20 rooms. A tour of the lake may be made from this base.

Other parks at **Mandelia,** 35 km. from Ndjamena, with large herds of elephant, and **Kala-Malou.** In addition, **Waza** National Park in Cameroon is within easy reach of Ndjamena.

Manda, 27 km from Sarh is being developed with some game-viewing tracks already laid out and more under construction. The public may enter free and drive around in their own cars. The nearest hotels are at Sarh.

HISTORY

Throughout history the area of modern Chad has provided a link between northeast Africa (Egypt, Libya and Sudan) and West Africa. It is also a salt-producing area and various empires have been built on trans-African commerce. A thousand years ago the Saharan ancestors of today's Kanuri people (of northern Nigeria) formed one such empire east and north of Lake Chad. This came under pressure from Bulala warriors and entrenched itself to the west in Borno in the 16th century. This was also the time that the powerful Muslim state of Ouaddai came into existence, with its capital first at Ouara and then at Abeche.

Ouaddai was founded by traders from Darfur in Sudan and became wealthy from the extensive commerce in the area. It remained invincible even into the 20th century, but was finally conquered by the French in 1911. The colonial period saw a reversal of the former Muslim dominance in the area when southerners took more readily to Christianity and hence to Western education. At independence in 1960 the southerners were dominant in the Government.

Opposition parties were abolished in 1963 but by 1965 the Government's opponents had turned to guerrilla tactics in the north and east. They united loosely in the Front for the National Liberation of Chad (Frolinat). Some elements in Frolinat tried to turn their struggle into one of Muslims versus Christians to appeal for Arab support. French troops, called in by President Tombalbaye in 1968 were mostly withdrawn by 1972, but the north is still in a state of rebellion. The new Government of General Felix Malloum, who overthrew Tombalbaye in April 1975, has attempted to pursue a policy of reconciliation.

COMORO ISLANDS

A string of beautiful islands of volcanic origin, surrounded by coral reefs, the as yet unspoilt Comoro Islands stretch across the north of the Mozambique channel, between Madagascar and East Africa. The archipelago comprises the four islands of Grande Comore, Anjouan, Moheli and Mayotte. Despite Comorian protests, the French continue to hold on to Mayotte as a naval base.

The special atmosphere of the Comoros is attributable both to the beautiful scenery and to the unique racial mixture, which reflects the successive invasions of sea-faring people in this part of the world: Arabs, Persians, Malays, Malagasy and Africans. The strongest influences are Arab and African and for this reason the main religion is Islam and the predominant language is Swahili.

Each island was dominated for centuries by its own Arab aristocracy, but between 1841 and 1908 the French gradually installed their rule over the islands and incorporated them into the colony of Madagascar until 1947—when they became an 'Overseas Territory' of France. In 1975 they gained their independence.

The mainstay of the islands' economy is plantation agriculture, producing perfume oils, copra, spices and vanilla, but many Comorians have to go to East Africa or France to find employment.

A big attraction of the Comoros to visitors is the scope for fishing: tuna, barracuda, shark, grouper, scad and, occasionally, the coelacanth.

GENERAL INFORMATION
Area: 2,236 sq. km.
Population: 300,000.
Altitude: Sea level to 2,400 m. on Grande Comore (Karthala volcano).
Capital: Moroni (Grande Comore).
Head of State: Ali Soilih.
Government: The National Executive Council, a civilian regime.
Date of Independence: 6 July 1975.
Languages: Swahili, French and Arabic.
Religion: Islam.
Currency: CFA Franc. £1=428 CFA francs. $1=249 CFA francs.
Time: GMT+3.

HOW TO GET THERE
By air to Moroni: From Madagascar, connecting with Paris, Djibouti, East and Southern Africa, Western Europe and other Indian Ocean islands: Air-Comores, Air France and Air Madagascar (twice weekly). From Tanzania and Kenya: Air Comores (twice weekly), connecting with most European flights.
By sea to Moroni and Mutsamudu: From France: freighters of Nouvelle Compagnie Havraise Peninsulaire and other

97

French and Scandinavian lines, mostly via Madagascar. From East Africa and the Indian Ocean: the lines mentioned as well as some British freighters at Mombasa, Dar es Salaam, or Mauritius; Arab dhows hired at Majunga or Zanzibar.

Visas and health precautions

Entry visa for Comoro Islands costs 1,250 CFA (equivalent to 25 French francs). This can be bought on arrival at the airport. The entry visa is valid for three months' stay.

An international certificate of vaccination is required, showing immunization against smallpox, as well as against yellow fever and cholera if the traveller is arriving from an infected area. Precautions against malaria are essential. Medical facilities are scarce on the Islands.

Dutiable goods

Personal effects and restricted amounts of tobacco and alcohol are admitted free of duty.

Currency regulations

There is no restriction on the amount of foreign currency taken into the Comoros, but a declaration must be made and the amount not used may be taken out again. The same applies to travellers' cheques.

Any amount of local currency may be taken into the Comoros but only 50,000 CFA francs may be taken out again, unless one is travelling direct to another franc zone country.

CLIMATE

The most pleasant period for the Comoros extends from May to October. November and December are best for deep-sea fishing, and August and September are best for diving. The coasts swelter in the austral summer (December to March) although the rains at this time of year bring some relief—as well as the occasional cyclone. Higher points on the islands are cooler, especially at night, but

the hills also attract greater rainfall.

What to wear: If you are climbing the Karthala or M'Tingui Mountains, you will need sweaters, thick trousers for protection against thorns, and a rainproof hat. Sturdy shoes are invaluable for walking anywhere on Grande Comore's hard-lava surface. Otherwise, bring light clothing with little concern for formality. Women should remember general Muslim objections to the over-exposure of the female body—although French residents and tourists usually dress as they please.

ACCOMMODATION, FOOD

A few hotels on Grande Comore, Anjouan and Mayotte handle the needs of travelling businessmen, Government officials and other visitors. There are simple shelters *(gites)* on Mayotte and on the slopes of the Karthala.

The restaurants serve good food with local spiced sauces, rice-based dishes, cassava, plantain and couscous, barbecued goat meat, plentiful seafood and tropical fruits.

TRANSPORT

Road: Travellers depend on the all-purpose *taxi-brousse* (bush taxi) hired vehicles or private cars to circulate on the islands. Only Grande Comore and Anjouan have any tarred roads worth noting, so four-wheel-drive vehicles are advisable for the outlying islands and the interiors, especially in the rainy season.

Air: Each island has an airfield served by Air Comores' scheduled and charter flights; there are daily connections between Moroni and Anjouan, six weekly flights between Moroni and Dzaoudzi, and five to Moheli.

Sea: Travellers can hire motorboats, sailing craft or canoes *(pirogues)* in port villages and towns; a boat can be especially useful for Moheli, where the road system is rudimentary. Mayotte, Pamanzi and Dzaoudzi are linked by a regular

ferry service.
Car hire: Moroni—Omar Cassim and Sons, B.P. 700, tel: 23-82.

BUSINESS HOURS
Banks: 0700-1200 Monday to Friday. Offices and shops close between 1200 and 1500 and close Saturday afternoons.

PUBLIC HOLIDAYS
Independence Day 6 July; 'Coup d'Etat' 3 August; 12 November, plus Holy Days of the Muslim Calendar.

FOREIGN EMBASSIES
There are no embassies or consulates in the territory. The nearest UK, European and USA representatives are in Dar es Salaam, or Antananarivo.

TOURIST OFFICES
Direction du Tourisme, B.P. 428, Moroni, tel: 2445. Société hoteliere et touristique des Comores, and Air Comores, Moroni. In Paris: Senegalese Embassy, tel: 525-7032.

GRANDE COMORE
Moroni, the territorial capital, has a quiet, whitewashed charm not unlike that of Zanzibar. A few broad squares and a modern Government complex are surrounded by narrow winding alleys with a picturesque market place, several handsome mosques, a sleepy port of dhows and *boutres*, and villas and gardens on the Karthala's slopes.

There is a fine view from the top of the Vendredi Mosque. Important marriages and neighbourhood festivals often bring out a steady, stately sense of ceremony in

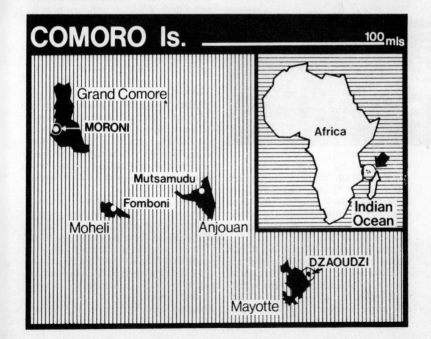

the Comorians; drumming is sometimes 'in the air', and the dances of the men are dignified, contemplative and rhythmic.

A climb up the Karthala and a descent into its crater can be made with one overnight stop—usually at the shelter maintained by the *Société Anonyme de la Grande Comore*; the SAGC also arranges for guides, provisions and transport to and from the point of ascent.

The Tourist Office often commissions dance performances by the men of Itsandra, a rugged fishing village with rough lava walls and a fine beach 6 km from Moroni. Comorian products can be seen and purchased at the Government Crafts Centre on the Moroni-Itsandra road; these include jewellery in gold, pearls and shells, woven cloth, embroi-

View over Moroni

dered skull-caps *(coffias)* and slippers, carved chests, panels and *portes-Cran* (lecterns), pottery and basketry. Most items can be purchased in the villages where they are made—particularly the boat models carved at Iconi.

Travellers should stop at the Bongoi Kouni Mosque, a pilgrimage site; the attractive northern town of Mitsamiouli where Comorian dancing reaches its peak of elegance; the fishing villages of Chindini and Foumbouni; and the Trou au Prophete for diving.

Hotels

Hotel Itsandra, 7 km north of Moroni, extensive sporting facilities, palm grove and good food. B.P. 3, tel: 23.65.

Maloudja, Mitsamiouli, 40 km north of Moroni, bungalows, water sports, 12 rooms, B.P. 422, tel: 23.59.

Le Coelacanthe, Moroni, B.P. 404, tel: 22.75.

Le Karthala, B.P. 53, tel: 20.00.

Restaurants: Apart from the hotels, there are the *Bamboo*, *Allaoui*, *Mimosa* and the *Islam* in Moroni and the *Safari* in Itsandra.

ANJOUAN

With its waterfalls and luxuriant vegetation, Anjouan lures visitors from Moroni for a day or two at least. Its town, Mutsamudu, is an epitome of Swahili-Shirazi style, with 17th century houses on serpentine alleyways, carved doors, mosques, conical-shaped tombs, a citadel and a dash of colour in the gowns of its veiled women.

Hotel Al Amal, Mutsamudu, similar to the Itsandra on Grande Comore, with a fine view from a bluff overlooking the sea, 24 rooms. B.P. 59, tel: 65.

MAYOTTE

Mayotte is a place of the sea, with its neighbour Pamanzi and the rock-town of Dzaoudzi between them. Here are beaches, streams, coral reefs, excellent skin-diving and an occasional *pirogue* race. The island is surrounded by a coral reef, forming one of the most beautiful lagoons in the world.

Pamanzi is a lush, scented forest islet, 5 km across the straits from Mayotte with the lovely Dziani lake at its centre. Dzaoudzi has some fine old fortifications. There is a beach sports centre with bungalows on Mayotte, and the Restaurant Foucault in Mamutzu, Mayotte's principal town. Sada in Mamutzu is a good shop for jewellery.

Hotel Le Rocher, Dzaoudzi, B.P. 42, tel: 10.

CONGO

Congo, formerly a French colony, is a poor, though relatively urbanised, country dependent on forestry and agriculture. Most of it is uninhabited swamp and jungle. Noted for its art and music, both traditional and modern, it offers attractions like the rapids of the Congo River and game fishing off the coast; but it is not developed for tourism and road communications are difficult.

THE LAND AND THE PEOPLE

Congo, a little bigger than Britain, has a seaboard on the Atlantic, flanked by the Angolan enclave of Cabinda and by Gabon; the rest of the southern frontier is marked by the Congo River and by the Oubangui, which divide Congo from Zaire (the former Belgian Congo). These rivers are vital means of transport, both by steamer and the traditional dugout canoe. The Congo River (known across the river as the Zaire) forms a lake-like expanse, 33 km by 25 km, at Stanley Pool before rushing into rapids for most of the remainder of its journey seaward. The two capitals of Brazzaville and Kinshasa (Zaire) were built on opposite banks of the Pool to become the terminal for two railways from the coast. Above the Pool steamers ply upriver as far as Bangui and Kisangani (Zaire).

The narrow, sandy coastal plain,

broken by lagoons, has low rainfall and grassland vegetation, due to cool sea currents. Behind, the deep forest-clad gorges of the Mayombe Mountains rise abruptly 500 to 800 m until, beyond Loubomo, the landscape dips to the fertile alluvial depression of the Niari valley where the main agricultural crops, especially sugar, are grown.

Brazzaville itself lies to the south of the dry, grassy unproductive BaTeke plateau through which rivers cut deep valleys to the Congo. The whole northern half of the country is by contrast swamp and

101

forest of the Congo basin, almost constantly flooded. Predictably, three-quarters of the one million Congolese live in the south, while one-third of the total population is concentrated in the four large towns: Brazzaville, Pointe-Noire, Loubomo and Kayes. The forests are uninhabited.

The Kongo people, who are also found in Zaire, Angola and the Cabinda enclave, form 45% of the population and live predominantly around Brazzaville. They were part of the 15th-century Kongo kingdom, with its capital of Sao Salvador (Angola). The Vili on the coast were once united in the Loango kingdom which fell under Kongo and Portuguese domination at that time. The Teke (20% of the population) on the plateau north of Stanley Pool were once loosely knit under the Anzico kingdom, but by the 19th century this had fallen apart, long before Count Savorgnan de Brazza, the explorer, was claiming that his treaty with their chief Makoko conferred rights to the whole plateau. Other ethnic groups are the Boutangui, the Sanga, the Lari (who straddle both banks of Stanley Pool), and the M'Bochi of the far northern Likuala basin. There are also a large number of Gabonese and some 10,000 non-Africans, mainly French.

CULTURE

Carved wooden masks and figures are the Congo's best-known art form. Similar figures were cut into the soft stone lids of tombs. Kongo art was Christianised early so that, for example, figures of the mythical ancestress of mankind were translated into the Madonna and Child. The M'Bochi made long dancers' staves with a human head for festivals honouring Djo, the Creator, who was envisaged as a snake. Much of the carving was deliberately horrific, such as the monstrous caricature masks of the Vili or the Kongo and the Teke animal figures which bristle with nails and knives, or are hung about with rags and beads for use as charms.

Modern artists, combining western art with African art, have also made a name for Congo—notable the sculptor, Benoit Konongo.

Painting has developed as a new art form. Some of the best modern work can be seen and bought at the Poto Poto arts and crafts centre in Brazzaville. In addition to traditional dance forms, modern song and folklore groups play the Congolese style of music which is popular throughout Africa.

WILDLIFE

Elephant, buffalo, hippo and sitatunga abound in the savannah land of the coast, while the forests support the rare bongo, chimpanzees and gorillas as well as multicoloured parrots and butterflies. Animals such as buffalo and antelope can be seen near Stanley Pool, but the two main reserves, Lefini and Divenie, are hardly organized to cater for tourists.

Fishing on the other hand is good. The sea and lagoons are full of large species such as tarpon, barracuda, red tuna fish, sword-fish, grouper, horse mackerel, shark and skate. Pointe-Noire is proud of its world record tarpon, 2.38 m long, weighing 101 kg. The rivers offer Nile perch and binga, some exceeding 50 kg.

GENERAL INFORMATION

Area: 342,000 sq.km.
Population: 1.3 million.
Altitude: The coastal zone lies below 100 m and the mountains behind rise to 800 m. Brazzaville lies at about 300 m.
Capital: Brazzaville.
Head of State: Col. Joachim Yhombi-Opango.
Government: People's Republic.
Date of independence: 15 August 1960.
Languages: French (official) and African languages of the Bantu group, the main ones being Kongo, Teke and Boutangui.

Religion: Nearly half the population is animist, one-third Catholic, the remainder Protestant or Muslim.
Currency: CFA franc. £1=428 CFA francs. $1=249 CFA francs.
Electricity: 220-230V.

HOW TO GET THERE

By air: Maya Maya airport is 4 km from Brazzaville, The only transport to town is by taxi. Regular flights are operated from Europe by Air Afrique, UTA and KLM; from north-east Africa by Aeroflot and Air Algerie, and from West Africa by Air Mali and Air Cameroon. Transgabon flights arrive at Pointe-Noire.
By sea/river: Cargo ships dock at Pointe-Noire. A half-hourly car ferry operates between Kinshasa and Brazzaville across the Congo River; it takes 20 minutes.
By road: There is a road connection from Lambarene in Gabon to Loubomo and Brazzaville. The surface is not completely tarred. The road from Cameroon is only passable in the long dry season.

Visas and health regulations

French and francophone African nationals may enter with a national identity card. Others must produce a valid passport and visa. Visas may be applied for from Congolese or French Consulates abroad; allow several weeks for issue. (In no case may a visa be issued on arrival; neither can it be obtained through an airline company.) An onward or return ticket or repatriation guarantee is necessary.

Smallpox, yellow fever and cholera vaccination certificates are required.

Dutiable goods

In addition to personal effects, the following may be taken in free of duty, if they are declared: 1,000 cigarettes, two cameras, 10 films, a tape-recorder, one movie camera, a pair of binoculars.

Currency regulations

There in no restriction on the amount of foreign currency brought in or taken out, but on arrival visitors must declare all moneys being brought into the country.

CLIMATE

Most of the country has a hot, humid, equatorial climate. The Teke plateau has a longer, cooler dry season and temperatures vary from $21°$-$27°C$, whereas the Congo basin is more humid with c. 1,600 mm of rain per year and temperatures of $24°$-$30°C$. The average rainfall is 1,000-1,200 mm per year.

There are four seasons: the long dry season from May to September; short rains October to mid-December; short dry season mid-December to mid-January; long rains mid-January to mid-May. The best time is June to September.
What to wear: Practical lightweight cottons and linens are essential, leather or canvas shoes, and a light raincoat or umbrella in the rainy seasons.
Health precautions: Malaria prophylactics must be taken daily a fortnight before, during and a fortnight after the visit. Water is drinkable in towns.

ACCOMMODATION AND FOOD

There are adequate hotels in Brazzaville, Pointe Noire and Loubomo; elsewhere there is little accommodation for visitors. Restaurants in these towns provide mostly French cuisine and the coast has excellent fish, giant oysters and shrimps. Some restaurants—those at Nanga Lake and the Grand Hotel in Loubomo—specialize in African dishes such as piri piri chicken (with pepper), Mohambe chicken in palm-oil, palm cabbage salad, cassava leaves or Paka Paka in palm oil. A 10% tip is customary.

TRANSPORT

By air: The local airline Lina-Congo flies

from Brazzaville to Loubomo, Owando, Impfondo, Kayes, Loukolela, Makabana, Moanda, Ouesso, and Pointe-Noire.

By road: Roads are mostly earth tracks, sandy in the dry season and impassable in the wet, suitable for Land-Rovers only. There are 243 km of tarred road. The main road from Brazzaville to Loubomo is uneven in quality although it is being tarred. It continues to the Gabon border, but the branch to Pointe-Noire is passable only when dry.

By river: Inland steamers ply from Brazzaville up the Congo and the Oubangui.

By rail: The Congo-Ocean railway company runs a daily railcar, with dining and sleeping carriages, between Brazzaville and Pointe-Noire and a weekly railcar from Pointe-Noire to Mbinda.

BUSINESS HOURS
Banks: 7.00-11.30 weekdays only. Post Offices: 7.30-11.30 and 14.30-16.30. Shops:7.00-12.00 and 15.00-17.30, closed on Sunday afternoon and Monday.

PUBLIC HOLIDAYS
In addition to Christian holidays there are: Labour Day; Anniversary of the People's Army 22 June; Anniversary of the Three Glorious Days 13-15 August; Birth of the PCT (Party) 31 December.

FOREIGN EMBASSIES
Algeria, Belgium, Central African Empire, Chad, China (P.R), Cuba, Denmark, Egypt, Equatorial Guinea, Ethiopia, France, Gabon, W. Germany.

BRAZZAVILLE
There are splendid views over the town, the brightly lit city of Kinshasa and upriver to Stanley Pool from the cathedral of St. Firmin, built in 1892, and the house occupied by General de Gaulle

during World War Two. Other places of interest are: the Basilica of St. Anne du Congo (1943-9), built in a combination of European and African styles; the National Museum of History and Ethnography; the colourful markets; the fascinating arts and crafts centre at Poto Poto (the former African township laid out in 1900) which displays and sells local paintings, masks, carvings, etc. There are also performances of African dancing.

Hotels
Hotel Cosmos, Ave du Beach. B.P. 2459; tel:39.61, in centre of town; 109 rooms.
Relais Aeriens de Maya Maya, Blvd. Lyautey, B.P. 588; tel: 34.53; 1 km from centre, magnificent view; 64 rooms.
Hotel M'Foa, Ave du 28 Aout 1940, B.P. 297, tel: 20.54; town centre; 21 rooms.
Hotel Olympic Palace, Ravin de la Mission, B.P. 728, tel: 36.71; 27 rooms.
Le Petit Logis, B.P. 318, tel: 28.74; central, 21 rooms.

Restaurants
French cuisine at **Alex 'Ma Campagne', Les Ambassadeurs, Relais Aeriens de Maya Maya, Petit Logis 'Chez Simone', Pam Pam** (snack bar) and **Le Mistral**. Italian cooking at **La Pizzeria, O'Sympathic Bar** and **M'Pila.** Vietnamese restaurant: **L'Exotic.**

Entertainments
Local groups singing Congolese music are popular and heard everywhere. There are night-clubs at the **Scotch Club, Hotel des Ralais, Hotel Cosmos** and **La Saturne.**
  There are also opportunities for sailing, horse riding and golf.

Markets
The two main markets are Moungali (go in the morning) and Ouendze. The Avenue Foch is crowded with street vendors. For those interested in curios, there is the Poto Poto centre and the artisan school on the banks of the Congo.

Tourist information
Office National Congolais du Tourisme, Plateau, B.P. 456, tel: 27.13. **Syndicat d'Initiative,** Ave. du 28 Aout 1940, B.P. 173; tel: 31.78.
Travel agencies: Congo Voyages, Ave Foch, B.P. 91, tel: 29.99/24.90. SOAEM, Pl du Central Bar, B.P. 284, tel: 48.48.

EXCURSIONS FROM BRAZZAVILLE

M'Pila (3 km) is a fishing village, with potteries and an open air market among baobabs overlooking Stanley Pool. Boat trips on Stanley Pool from M'Pila pass the M'Bamou island where huts are built on poles. The Rapids are 10 km away by tarred road. Foulakari Falls (85 km by earth road) is a good picnic spot. There is a motel (10 rooms). Makana is a village of basketworkers on the main Kinkala road. From there one can drive to the panoramic Trou de Dieu, probably formed by a meteorite (60 km).

POINTE-NOIRE

The main port, commercial and industrial centre, whose name derives from the black rock of the headland, is of particular interest to anglers; the lagoons along the coast abound in tarpon, barracuda, tuna, swordfish and skate, while the rivers hold Nile perch and binga.

The Plage Mondaine is a protected beach resort, with water-ski-ing and yachting. The lagoons of Gounkouati are a paradise for fishing and shooting. Lake Nanga (9 km) provides good angling and has an excellent restaurant. To the north, Loango was the capital of the old Vili kingdom and site of the first Catholic mission (1883). The red gorges of Diosso (31 km) form a semi-circle of cliffs facing the sea. Lake Cayo is 25 km from the town. At Djeno, 21 km to the south, one can fish from the beach. Farther away (150 km)—accessible only in the dry season though also visible from the

train—are the abysses, canyons and sombre forests and characteristic flora of the Mayombe Mountains.

Hotels
Hotel Atlantic Palace, B.P. 939, tel: 24.35, near beach, 41 air-conditioned rooms.
Hotel Victory Palace, B.P. 124, tel: 24.49; centre of town, near beach, 35 air-conditioned rooms.
Hotel du Plateau, B.P. 1060, tel: 28.30, 24 air-conditioned rooms.
Hotel Sole & Mare, B.P. 907, tel: 22.49, centre of town, 16 air-conditioned rooms.

Restaurants
French cuisine at **Duchesse de Bourgogne, Restaurant de l'Aerogare, Victory, Chez Paulette, Atlantic, Station Balneaire La Rotonde** (snack bar); tourist restaurant at the **Nanga Lake.** Night-clubs: **The Sea Club, La Licorne** and **Le Mikado.**

Tourist information
Syndicat d'Initiative, opposite the Post Office.

LOUBOMO

Grand Hotel, B.P. 26, tel: 21.02, town centre, 25 rooms.
Hotel de France, BP. 76, tel: 20.12, town centre, 12 air-conditioned rooms.

HISTORY

The period after independence was marked by considerable tension and some fighting between parties representing different ethnic and other interests. The first President, Abbe Fulbert Youlou, was forced to resign by demonstrations and a general strike on the 'Three Glorious Days' of 13-15 August 1963. The Government led by Alphonse Massamba-Debat was more radical although its professedly Marxist-Leninist party was deeply divided. In 1968 the army seized power and Major Marien Ngouabi took over. He was assassinated in 1977.

DJIBOUTI

Having remained closely controlled by France until 1977, this country's birth into the family of independent nations at such a late stage is proving difficult, particularly with the increasing insecurity in neighbouring Ethiopia. Until the political situation calms it would be unwise to consider visiting Djibouti for a holiday. However, as an important port at the mouth of the Red Sea, the city of Djibouti will clearly continue to be cosmopolitan in its contacts after the present uncertainty has evaporated.

THE LAND AND THE PEOPLE

The hinterland of Djibouti is a barren strip of land around the Gulf of Tadjoura, varying in width from 20km to 90km, with a coast line of 800km, much of it fine white sand beaches. The land is semi-desert, with thorn-bush steppes and volcanic mountain ranges

Millions of years ago this part of the world was ocean-floor. Submarine volcanic activity caused the contorted rock and lava formations that stand there today. Even now part of the territory is below sea level. Evaporation has left vast deposits of salt; this is collected by the Afar people who still distribute it as currency throughout the region.

The total population is small, divided almost equally into Afars and Issas. The Afars are known across the Ethiopian border as Danakil, where they form an independent-minded minority. The Issas are a Somali group, and they predominate in the capital, Djibouti, which is a busy and modern port.

In the surrounding countryside the people lead a nomadic existence, taking their flocks and herds from pasture to arid pasture. The soil and the climate prevent cultivation of all except dates and small amounts of fruit and vegetables.

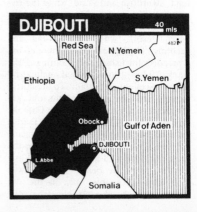

GENERAL INFORMATION

Area: 21,782sq. km.
Population: 220,000
Altitude: Sea level to 2,063m.
Capital: Djibouti.
Head of State: Hassan Gouled.
Languages: French (official), Somali, Afar and Arabic.
Religion: Islam.
Currency: Djibouti franc (Fr Dj.) £1= 280 Fr. Dj. $1=163 Fr. Dj.
Time: GMT + 3.
Electricity: 220V.

HOW TO GET THERE

By air: Djibouti airport, 5km south of the town, is served by Air Djibouti from Ethiopia, Somalia and both Yemen republics. There are flights from Europe, Africa and the Middle East by Air France, Air Madagascar, Yemen Airways, Al Yemda, Ethiopian Airlines and Somali Airways.

By rail: The Franco-Ethiopian railway provides regular services from Addis Ababa and Dire Dawa three times a week. It is a long slow journey, but comfortable sleeping accommodation is available in first-class carriages.

By road: There are good roads from Assab and Dire Dawa in Ethiopia, but it may be impossible to enter from Ethiopia and Somalia in view of political conditions in both countries.

Visas and Health regulations

Potential visitors should enquire at a French Embassy about the latest visa regulations.

International certificates of vaccination against smallpox, yellow fever and cholera are required.

Dutiable goods

Personal effects are admitted free of duty.

Currency regulations

An amount of local or foreign currency may be taken into or out of the territory. US dollars and French francs are welcomed. Djibouti francs are of little value outside the territory.

CLIMATE

One of the hottest places on earth, Djibouti is particularly parched between June and August when the temperature can reach 45°C and the dusty Khamsin blows from the desert. Between October and March it is slightly cooler, with occasional light rain.

Clothing should be very light. Avoid synthetic fabrics.

Health precautions: An anti-malaria prophylactic should be taken before, during and after one's visit. Water should be boiled or filtered before drinking. Precautions should be taken against prickly heat.

ACCOMMODATION AND FOOD

The air-conditioned hotels in Djibouti are expensive, but the service is generally good. There are restaurants to suit all tastes, serving French, Vietnamese, Chinese, Arab and local specialities. Hotel and restaurant staff are normally tipped 10% of the bill.

TRANSPORT

Road: The best roads are from Djibouti to Arta and the coast road from Djibouti towards Assab in Ethiopia. Most other roads are rough but passable throughout the year. There are taxis in Djibouti.

BANKS

The main banks in Djibouti are the **Banque de l'Indochine**, the **Banque Nationale pour le Commerce et l'Industrie,** and the **British Bank of the Middle East.** They are open 0700-1200 Monday to Saturday.

PUBLIC HOLIDAYS
Christian holidays and Muslim feast days are observed.

CONSULATES
Ethiopia: Rue Clochette, B.P. 230, tel: 23.18.
Somalia: Rue Bourhan-Bey, B.P. 549, tel: 34.21.
Yemen: Plateau du Serpent, B.P. 194, tel: 31.75.
Belgium, B.P. 76, tel. 23.60;
Italy, B.P. 462, tel. 24.62;
West Germany, B.P. 519, tel. 22.07;
Netherlands and **Sweden,** B.P. 89, tel. 28.22

DJIBOUTI
The capital of the territory lies on a peninsula separating the Gulf of Tadjoura from the Gulf of Aden. The town centre contains a lively and colourful market near the Mosque. Out of the town there are pleasant walks to the Ambouli palm grove and gardens.

Hotels
La Siesta: B.P. 508, tel: 28.88, on the seashore at Plateau du Serpent, 34 rooms.
Le Palace, Blvd de Gaulle, B.P. 166, tel: 23.82, 31 rooms.
Continental, Pl Menelik, B.P. 675, tel: 20.46, 25 rooms.
Europe, Pl Menelik, B.P. 83, tel: 21.76, 16 rooms.
There are other hotels.

Tourist information
Office de Developpement du Tourisme, Pl Menelik, B.P. 1938, tel: 34.90.
Travel agencies: Air Djibouti, B.P. 505. Djibouti Tours, Blvd. de Gaulle.

OUTSIDE DJIBOUTI
About 30km from Djibouti port by tarred road is **Arta,** a summer resort in the mountains overlooking the Gulf of Tadjoura.

100km from Djibouti is the eerie **Lake Assal,** below sea level and encircled by mountains. The cold, dead waters are surrounded by a crystal bank of salt and gypsum. Jagged needles of rock give the landscape a moon-like appearance. On the Ethiopian frontier is **Lake Abbe,** another almost unearthly sight, the home of flocks of flamingos.

One can reach the opposite side of the Tadjoura Gulf by the coast road or by ferry from Djibouti to the settlements at Obock and Tadjoura itself. In the Goda Mountains behind there is a fossilized forest and a wealth of rare plants.

HISTORY
In ancient times the territory formed part of the Abyssinian empire, with which it was only tenuously linked; but because it provided the easiest access to the sea it was of obvious strategic value to the largely landlocked empire.

It was first explored in more modern times by a Frenchman, d'Hericourt, in the 1840s. France immediately laid claims to the coastal strip and conducted military campaigns against the inhabitants between the 1860s and the 1890s. Obock became their first base. In 1897 the Franco-Ethiopian railway was commenced from Djibouti, finally reaching Addis Ababa in 1917.

France held controversial referenda on the issue of independence in 1958 and 1967. The published results were 75% and 60% respectively in favour of a continuing French presence. Several waves of riots were put down by French troops.

In 1976 France agreed to the principle of independence, and a new government headed by Hassan Gouled took power in 1977.

EQUATORIAL GUINEA

Few visitors are likely to want to stay long in Equatorial Guinea. Macias Nguema island (Fernando Poo) is, however, an attractive place with dramatic mountain scenery and many beautiful beaches. A brief flight from Douala (Cameroon) to Malabo (Santa Isabel) might provide an adequate sample. The intensely humid climate, the poverty and the atmosphere of political repression are not altogether conducive to a pleasant stay.

THE LAND AND THE PEOPLE

The mainland province of Rio Muni is mainly forest, with plantations on the coastal plain and one or two mountain peaks. There are three small offshore islands, Corisco, Elobey Grande and Elobey Chico. The majority of the inhabitants belong to the Fang group—also Gabon's dominant ethnic community. The coastal peoples are mainly the Kombe, Belengue and Bujeba.

Macias Nguema is an island 34 km off the coast of Cameroon, rising steeply to two main peaks in the north and south. The southern part is very rugged, inaccessible and little inhabited, leaving cultivation and settlement to the slopes of the north, west and east. Forest remains thick above the cultivated slopes.

The original islanders were Bubi, but the island's chequered history of slavery and plantations, and of British and Spanish influence has left a mixed population: Bubi, Fang, Fernandino (descendants of freed slaves, many with names of English origin) and immigrants from West Africa.

The remote island of Pigalu (Annobon) resembles Macias Nguema in terrain and population, but is becoming overpopulated.

CULTURE

Traditional magic still has a strong hold on the Fang of the mainland. There are unique ceremonies of spiritual cleansing and frenzied dancing. The costumes have changed little—grass skirts, belts made from hide, bracelets of many different

EQUATORIAL GUINEA   50 miles

Nigeria

Malabo

Cameroon

Macias Nguema

Bata

RIO MUNI

Atlantic Ocean

Gabon

730

materials on both arms and legs and feather head-dresses.

The Bubi on Macias Nguema island have maintained their customs, including yam and other harvest festivals and dances. The Belele dance is one of the most exciting to be seen anywhere in Africa. The Bubis are skilled at making miniature charms, arrows, shields and in basketwork.

WILDLIFE
The mainland province of Rio Muni has a wide variety of animals from otters to elephants, as well as a host of beautiful forest birds. There are a few protected gorillas left. Hundreds of varieties of fish are found in the rivers.

Macias Nguema has a few antelopes in the foothills of its mountains, as well as monkeys. There is a game reserve on the slopes of Mount Santa Isabel.

GENERAL INFORMATION
Area: 28,051 sq. km.
Population: 300,000.
Altitude: Rio Muni—sea level to 1,200 m. Macias Nguema—sea level to 3,007 m.
Capital: Bata (Rio Muni) and Malabo (Macias Nguema).
Head of State: Life President Francisco Macias Nguema.
Government: Presidential rule, supported by Council of Ministers, and single party.
Date of independence: 12 October 1968.
Languages: Spanish, Fang, Bubi, pidgin English.
Religion: Predominantly Roman Catholic.
Currency: Ekpwele equivalent to Spanish Peseta. £1=118 pesetas. $1=69 pesetas.
Time: GMT+1.

HOW TO GET THERE
By air: There are weekly flights from Madrid to Malabo by Iberia. The local LAGE airline flies several times a week between Douala (Cameroon), Malabo and Bata. Air Cameroon also flies from Douala to both main towns. Transgabon flies from Libreville to Bata.

By sea: Malabo and Bata are served by ship from Spain. There are also irregular sailings from Douala and Calabar.

By road: The only passable road into Rio Muni enters at Ebebiyin (accessible from Cameroon or northern Gabon). Information on entry formalities should be obtained in Douala or Libreville before setting out.

Visas and health regulations:
A valid passport and visa are essential for entry. A visa may be obtained from Equatorial Guinea's representative in Madrid, Douala, or Libreville.

International certificates of vaccination against smallpox, yellow fever and cholera are required.

CLIMATE
There is persistent heavy rainfall and humidity throughout most of the year, with the exception of December, January and February. This short dry season is very hot on Macias Nguema island but cooler in Rio Muni. Total annual rainfall on Macias Nguema is 1,500 mm rising to 2,000 mm on mountain slopes. The average temperature is 26°C.
What to wear: Lightweight cotton clothes are essential. Synthetic fabrics should be avoided.
Health precautions: Only boiled or filtered water should be drunk. An anti-malaria prophylactic is essential before, during and after a visit.

ACCOMMODATION AND FOOD
There is a handful of hotels in Malabo and Bata, all of them cheap for the standard which they offer.

The Spanish influence has pleasantly influenced local cooking. Olive oil is used rather than palm oil and fish rather than meat but otherwise the peppers and spices are unmistakably tropical. There are one or two European-style restaurants in Malabo.

The traditional drink is *tope*, resembling palm wine.

TRANSPORT

The only tarred roads run a short way east and west from Malabo, and from Bata to Mbini. Other roads in the country tend to be washed out during heavy rain.

There is very little traffic. Taxis and minibuses provide irregular public transport.

Flying is the usual mode of travel between Bata and Malabo, but small ships and fishing boats occasionally make the crossing taking passengers.

PUBLIC HOLIDAYS

Catholic holidays, plus Independence Day, 12 October.

MACIAS NGUEMA ISLAND

The island is dominated by Mount Santa Isabel, rising 3,000m behind the main town, Malabo. This extinct volcano is not difficult to climb and commands views of the Cameroon coast and, on a clear day, even Nigeria. On its slopes the thick forest has been cleared for plantations, mainly of cocoa.

Malabo is a small but clean town with shops and lively markets. The curved shoreline is formed by a half-submerged volcano, making pleasant beaches and a perfect natural harbour.

Macias Nguema has hundreds of quiet, idyllic beaches around its shores. A circuit of the island by road takes one south west to Luba (San Carlos), where a road leads over cultivated plateau-land to the east coast at Ri-Aba (Concepcion), past the Moka Mountain (1,980m) and the Moka valley (containing a crater lake).

Hotel: Ureca, Malabo.
Restaurants in Malabo: Flamenco, Rosaleda, Riakauba.

RIO MUNI

A thickly-forested chunk of equatorial Africa, Rio Muni has few conventional attractions for the visitor, except peaceful palm-fringed beaches, stretching south from Bata and surrounding the island of Corisco and Elobey Grande. The cultural heritage has been sustained in Rio Muni and there are plenty of original artifacts to be found, including magic symbols and ornaments, musical instruments, wrought-iron sculptures and wooden carvings.

Bata has the **Panafrica Hotel**.

HISTORY

Spain took possession of Fernando Poo (now Macias Nguema island) in the 18th century. Its port was used by ships of all nations, including British squadrons suppressing the slave trade. Slavery however existed on the island's own plantations long after abolition.

Spain was finally pressed into granting independence in 1968 both by Equatorial Guinea's internal political forces and the need for respectability abroad. Power went to the election victor, Francisco Macias Nguema, a Fang from Rio Muni. After only four months in office he accused Spain of trying to overthrow him by exerting pressure on Bubis of Fernando Poo to secede. At that time expatriate influence on the island remained very strong and a force of Spanish *Guardia Civil* was maintained for their security.

Relations with Spain are now back to normal and aid has been resumed. The President keeps tight control over his subjects with the help of a militant 'Guinea Youth' movement.

ETHIOPIA

Through the centuries Ethiopia has exercised a strong fascination over the world, and the magic still persists. For long periods of time, partly because of its difficult terrain and partly because of the wish to avoid foreign intrusion, the country was largely inaccessible and thus acquired the allure of mystery and became a land of legends and myths. Its ancient history and cultures make it unique. Ethiopians today retain a pride and a love of life reflected in their distinctive and colourful art and culture. The country is poised between the old and traditional society and its modern age: both have much to offer. Since the overthrow of Emperor Haile Selassie in 1974 and the subsequent military *coups d'état* a lot of changes have taken place, affecting life throughout the country as well as exacerbating old conflicts. In 1977 there was widespread insecurity in the Ogaden and in the northern province of Eritrea (spilling over into Tigray and Begemdir) which has limited the possibility of travel to some of the renowned historic sites and to the Red Sea coast.

The potential visitor is recommended to contact an Ethiopian Embassy or Ethiopian Airlines office to check on current conditions affecting tourists.

THE LAND AND THE PEOPLE

The central core of Ethiopia is a vast highland region of faulted volcanic rocks thrown up in the Tertiary Period when the Great Rift started to open and extend from Palestine down the Red Sea, through the Rift Valleys of Ethiopia and Kenya and on to Malawi. The highland

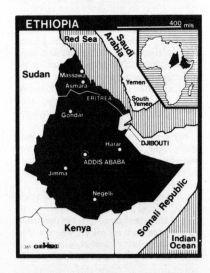

areas alone cover an area roughly the size of France and form a watered, temperate world of their own, surrounded by hot, inhospitable deserts which only the most determined have crossed with success.

The escarpments on either side of Ethiopia are steepest in the north, and the highland terrain there is exceedingly rugged. To the south the contours are generally softer and agricultural potential is much richer.

Along the Eritrean coast and in the northernmost highlands are people who speak Tigre, a Semitic language closest to the ancient Ge'ez which otherwise only survives in church literature. In Tigray Province, in which Axum lies, another Semitic language, Tigrigna is spoken; the centre of the country is the home of the national language Amharic; and further south Guragigna, a Semitic language, is spoken by a people of Hamitic origin.

To the east and south are people who speak Cushitic languages: Oromigna, Denakil and Somali and what is called the Sidama group of languages. These languages form the so-called Eastern Cushitic group of the central Southern Highlands—between the Rift Valley lakes and Lake Turkana on the Kenya border.

Prior to the mid-16th century there was no recorded mention of the Oromo peoples, who make up nearly half the population of the country, nor do the chronicles record conflicts with people fitting their description. And, although the various Oromo groups and peoples have remained socially distinct, their culture is a fascinating one, adding much to the richness of the Ethiopian cultural scene.

To the far west and south west are the Nilotic peoples: the Nuer and Anuak near Gambele, and the Geleb and other tribes in the south, each with their own languages.

Within this broad outline there are to be found numerous variations and nonconforming communities whose language and culture reflects some individual quirk of history. One such group is the Fala-shas, the 'Black Jews' now living near Gondar, whose culture reflects Ethiopia's early links with Judaic Palestine.

The Christian Amharas and the Tigreans have traditionally dominated the country. Although their culture is remarkably similar, each still clings strongly to their own heritage. At one period in Ethiopian history the Tigreans provided the country's king of kings, and their ancient capital of Gondar was the centre of the empire. But the pendulum swung in the 19th century towards the Amhara who centred the new kingdom on Addis Ababa. Considerable intermarriage and continuous acculturation occurs between these two peoples. The Amharas comprise about a fifth of the total population and the Tigreans a tenth.

Although at least one-third of the country is Muslim and another substantial proportion pagan, the Christian Church remains a dominant factor.

The country still retains the Julian calendar (named after the Roman Emperor who acquired it from the mathematicians of Alexandria, whence Ethiopia got it direct) which is divided into 12 months of 30 days each and a 13th month of five or six days at the end of the year. Taking for its starting point the birth of Christ, the Ethiopian calendar is seven years and eight months behind that of the west. Several Church festivals are of considerable interest.

CULTURE

Ethiopia shares with Egypt the visible remnants of a rich ancient culture; but whereas Egypt's golden age was most closely associated with the Pharaohs, Ethiopia's earliest art sprang from its early Christian heritage with which much of it remained closely involved until recent times. In a land of 15,000 churches religious art permeated much of the culture, especially of the highlands, and priests share with warriors a love of richly embroidered costumes. Places of worship are often living museums of lovely vestments.

The modern dress is often quite different from any other costumes to be found in the world. The *qemis* and the *shamma* are the traditional garments. Handwoven of a tough local cotton fibre bleached snow-white, with a coloured woven border called a *t'ibeb* the *qemis* (dress) is sometimes embroidered at the neck, the sleeves and the hem, usually in a geometric design, but can include crosses, wheat-sheaves or the national Mesqel flower.

The Ethiopian love of design and beauty is reflected not only in dress but in ornaments and in everyday objects. The country is a treasure-house of jewellery, especially in the monasteries and churches. Formal jewel-studded crowns and diadems, daggers and shields set with rubies and emeralds find their more mundane equivalent in the rich artistry of the silver biriles for drinking *t'ej* and in beautifully designed goblets and tableware. Jewellery and ornaments are an important part of Ethiopian dress, so keeping alive the old traditional crafts of the goldsmiths and silversmiths, as well as the humbler but no less impressive skills of the rural weavers of grass, leather, hair, glass and shells.

The monasteries of Ethiopia produced the earliest illuminated parchments, which have reached high standards in book illustrations and contributed to establishing a traditional style of painting on parchment.

Ethiopia's music and dances have their own distinctive characteristics and are tremendously varied according to the region and the event.

WILDLIFE

Ethiopia's geographical location and remarkable physical features have endowed it with a rich and varied natural heritage of vegetation and wildlife. There are a number of animals found nowhere else in the world—the Walia ibex, the Simyen

fox, the mountain Nyala and the gelada (bleeding-heart baboon)—and 23 species of birds unique to Ethiopia.

The Walia ibex and gelada baboon are found only in the mountain massif. It is here that the Simyen National Park has recently been established. The Nubian ibex is found in the Red Sea hills of northern Eritrea and further north along the Sudan coast. The rare and shy Somali wild ass ranges the Denakil country to the north east.

The Awash National Park and the surrounding reserves abound in game. The Beisa oryx is the most common species, while Soemmering's gazelle, Grevy's zebra, greater and lesser kudu, gerenuk, waterbuck, klipspringer, Chan-

PETER FRAENKEL

Africa Hall, home of the Organisation of African Unity in Addis Ababa

dler's reedbuck and the elegant dikdik occur in considerable number.

The remote Omo National Park, on the Omo River which flows into Lake Rudolf, is one of the richest (and least visited) wildlife areas in eastern Africa. Eland may be seen in herds of several hundred, and oryx, Burchell's zebra, Lelwel hartebeest, as well as buffalo, giraffe and elephant, and common species such as waterbuck, kudu, lion, leopard and cheetah.

The Rift Valley, which cuts diagonally through the highlands of Ethiopia and connects the Denakil Desert in the north east to Lake Turkana in the south west, has its own distinctive features. Lakes Abyata and Shala are being formed into the Rift Valley National Park in which the emphasis is upon the abundant bird-life around the alkaline lakes, an important migration route for birds of the northern hemisphere providing a temporary home for many varieties of geese, duck and waterfowl, which are to be seen by the thousand in the winter months of January and February.

GENERAL INFORMATION

Area: 1,221,900 sq km.
Population: 27,800,800.
Capital: Addis Ababa.
Head of State: Col. Mengistu Haile Mariam.
Government: Provisional Military Administrative Council.
Languages: The national language, Amharic, is spoken throughout Ethiopia and has its own script. English is the second official language and is understood in the main towns. French, Italian and Arabic are also widely understood.
Religions: Ethiopian Orthodox Church, Islam, freedom of worship for all creeds.
Currency: Ethiopian *birr.* £1=3.56 Birr. $1=2.09 Birr.
Time: GMT +3.
Electricity: 220V/380V in most places, but 127/220V in Eritrea and 125V in Gondar.

HOW TO GET THERE

By air: Ethiopian Airlines: flights to and from Accra, Athens, Abu Dhabi, Bahrein, Bombay, Cairo, Dar es Salaam, Djibouti, Douala, Entebbe, Frankfurt, Jeddah, Kigali, Kinshasa, Khartoum, Lagos, London, Nairobi, Paris, Rome, Shanghai, Sanaa and Seychelles.

Ethiopia is also served by Air Djibouti, Air France, Air India, Alitalia, British Airways, Egypt Air, Lufthansa, Saudi Arabian Airlines, and Yemen Airlines.

Sudan Airways suspended flights in early 1977.

Bole airport is about 8 km from Addis Ababa. Airline transport and taxis are available to the city centre. Passengers leaving Ethiopia must pay airport tax of 3 Birr.

By road: The all-weather road from Kenya, via Moyale, Yabello and Dilla is open. Roads from Sudan and Somalia are likely to be closed for political reasons.

A temporary Ethiopian driving licence will be granted on production of a valid licence from your home country—although this is only necessary for visitors staying more than one month: for visits of less than this, the home licence is accepted. Vehicles may be imported duty free for a period of six months. Ownership certificate of vehicle and valid driving licence are all that are required.

By rail: There is a railway to Addis Ababa from Djibouti (accessible by sea) which used to be almost the only means of access for travellers in the early part of this century. It is painfully slow but a unique introduction to the country—comfortable seating is available.

By sea: Ethiopian Shipping Lines and other companies operate regular sailings between several European ports and Massawa and Assab. Djibouti is also an international port of call, but its only connection with Ethiopia is by the railway (see above).

Visas and health regulations: Visitors holding valid passports can obtain a 30-day tourist visa on arrival at either of the international airports, Addis Ababa or Asmara. The visa fee is 10 Birr. Alternatively tourist and business visas, valid for three months, can be had from any Ethiopian mission abroad.

Visitors who stay more than 30 days must register with the Immigration Office and secure an identity card (10 Birr and 2 photos), also extending their visas if necessary. Exit visas are issued automatically and free of charge for visitors who stay in Ethiopia less than 30 days. For visitors who stay more than 30 days the exit visa is issued free of charge upon surrender of the ID card to the Immigration Office.

Visitors entering and leaving Ethiopia must have valid certificates of vaccination against smallpox and yellow fever. Vaccination against typhus, typhoid and tetanus is also advisable.

Visitors should also have tickets to a point beyond Ethiopia and the requisite health certificates and visas for that country.

Dutiable goods: Travellers' personal effects are not subject to duty, but a declaration form must be filled for cameras and other valuables which may not be sold in Ethiopia unless duty has been paid. One litre of acoholic liquor and 100 cigarettes are also allowed in free of duty.

There is a duty-free shop at Bole International Airport for departing passengers, where items may be paid for with up to 100 Birr in Ethiopian currency, the rest being payable in foreign currency.

Currency regulations: Foreign currency must be declared on arrival. The amount taken out must not exceed that taken in. Foreign currency in notes or coins can only be changed at the National Bank of Ethiopia, but travellers' cheques can be changed at any bank, main hotel or large shop.

The maximum amount of local currency which may be taken into or out of Ethiopia is 100 Birr.

CLIMATE

In Ethiopia the climate depends entirely upon where you are, the main determining factor being, of course, the altitude. The coastal regions and the Denakil plains are among the hottest places in the world. But on the plateau, including Addis Ababa, and the highland historic sites, the climate is a pleasant 10°C. to 23°C. throughout the year. Some time between February and April the 'small rains' are due—a scattering of showers, in no way off-putting. The 'big rains', which account for about 80% of the country's rainfall, occur from mid-June to September. During these months moderate to heavy showers should be expected for part of most days.

What to wear: In the lowland areas the lightest possible clothing, with a hat and sunglasses is all that is required. In Addis Ababa and throughout the highlands, where the climate is more like that of the Mediterranean in the spring or London, say, in early summer, light to medium weight clothing is appropriate. Ethiopians tend to be fairly formal and conservative in their dress—suits and ties being standard in Government and business offices. During the 'big rains' an umbrella or raincoat is more or less essential, and a sweater, as the evenings may be quite chilly.

Health precautions: Prophylactics against malaria should be taken (not in fact necessary in Addis Ababa as the town itself is above the malaria line, but advisable if any trips into the country are envisaged); it is wiser to drink only boiled water or the bottled mineral waters that are available everywhere; sudden dips in country lakes or rivers should be resisted as there is always a danger of contracting bilharzia, a tedious and unpleasant disease whose effects can last a long time. The various hot-water springs and the alkaline lakes Debre Zeyt (Bishoftu) and Langano are quite safe to swim in.

The high altitude of most of Ethiopia puts strain on the heart and nervous system until one is acclimatised. So avoid any physical exertion for the first few days. Sufferers from heart ailments or high blood pressure should consult a doctor before going to Ethiopia.

Avoid contact with stray dogs or cats as a precaution against rabies.

USEFUL PHRASES

There is a useful English-Amharic Conversation Manual, prepared by the Ethiopian Tourist Organisation, widely available for 0.50 Birr and recommended. A few phrases in Amharic will help the visitor feel at home. Perhaps the most useful are:

Hello	*Tenastellign*
How do you do?	*Endemenalu*
How much is this?	*Sint no?*
All right or yes	*Ishi*
It is expensive	*Wood no*
No!	*Yellem*
Please	*Ebakwon*
Wait a moment	*Tinnish Koya*
Please hurry	*Tolo bel*
Thank you	*Igzer yist'illig*

ACCOMMODATION AND FOOD

There are international standard hotels in Addis Ababa and good hotels in tourist and business centres.

The low-budget traveller will find plenty of cheap hotels. Addis Ababa has a YMCA but no provision for campers. It is, however, possible to camp elsewhere in Ethiopia, but bring a tent and be prepared to employ a local guard to keep an eye on it if you are away. In this you are participating in local custom; an Ethiopian camper would do the same.

In the best hotels the menus follow normal international practice. Addis Ababa also has a number of good restaurants serving Chinese, Italian and Indian food.

Ethiopian food centres on dishes, called *we't*, which may be of meat, chicken or vegetables, cooked in a hot Ethiopian pepper sauce to be eaten with, and traditionally upon, a flat, spongy bread called *injera*. While chicken *we't* is probably the single most typical Ethiopian dish, a meal will consist of a number of dishes. There are restaurants in the larger cities, such as the **Addis Ababa** or **Maru Dembia** restaurants in the capital, where Ethiopian food may be had in the grand manner (and it is a recommended experience). More simple Ethiopian food may, of course, be had very cheaply in all parts of the country.

Tipping: In most hotels and restaurants a service charge is added to the bill. Tipping is a fairly frequent custom, but the amounts are small—say 5-10% on restaurant bills and 10-15% for small services.

TRANSPORT

Air: Probably the most convenient, and sometimes the only, way of travelling is by air. Ethiopian Airlines operates regular flights to and from over 40 towns throughout the country.

Road: There are now all-weather roads to all the provincial capitals and to most of the business and tourist centres. Motorists will find the usual roadside facilities. Drive on the right in Ethiopia, and abide by normal 'Continental' rules of the road (except that traffic on a roundabout has the right of way). But drive slowly and make allowances for unexpected animals and people at all times.

A good and cheap network of buses operates throughout the country. Bus schedules and prices are now standardised whether the company is government or privately owned. Schedules and tickets may be obtained at the Bus Terminus in the market (preferably a day beforehand). In addition there are, of course, a number of straightforward package tours by which the principal tourist centres may be visited in luxury coaches and, usually, with the services of a guide.

With the help and promotion of the Ethiopian Tourist Organisation (ETO), there are several travel agencies and tour operators offering a wide variety of tours. The central feature is Ethiopian Airlines' Historic Route by which, for a relatively small supplement, the visitor can make overnight stops at Axum, Lalibela, Gondar, and Bahir Dar en route between Addis Ababa and Asmara. To get a broader look at the whole country many tours also arrange for visits by air and coach to Dire Dawa and Harar, the Awash National Park and then if time permits, down the Rift Valley to the Rift Lakes National Park and to the Lakes Langano or Awasa.

A number of more specialised tours focus on one particular interest—the birdlife of the Rift Valley; the game and people of the Denakil Plains; around Gambella; the Omo River region; a mule trip up into the fantastic Simyen Mountains; or to examine in depth some of the rock churches and their treasures in Tigray Province. Such tours are usually organised in the country of the visitor's origin—but ETO will provide liaison facilities to put any possible visitor in touch with knowledgeable agents in Ethiopia or their own country.

Another way of seeing Ethiopia is to hire a Land-Rover or VW car or Microbus and camping equipment, and take off on your own. Such arrangements can be made through United Touring Company (Box 3092, Addis Ababa). More adventurous hunting or photographic safaris to the more remote areas can be arranged through the Eastern Travel and Tourist Agency (Box 1294, Addis Ababa) or UTC. It would also be wise to consult the Ethiopian Tourist Organization.

Car hire: There are a number of car hire firms in Addis Ababa. Amongst those catering regularly for international visitors are: **United Touring Company (Hertz):** P.O. Box 3092, tel: 151122. **Ras Rental:** P.O. Box 2180, tel: 155150. **Forship Travel Agency:** P.O. Box 957, tel: 112159.

BANKS
The Commercial Bank of Ethiopia and the Addis Ababa Bank have branches throughout the country.

Business hours: Banks: 0830-1230 and 1430-1630 and Saturday mornings. Offices: 0900-1300 and 1500-1800, and Saturday mornings. Shops: 0900-1300 and 1500-2000, and all day Saturdays.

NATIONAL HOLIDAYS
7 January—Christmas Day; 19 January—Feast of the Epiphany (Timqet); 2 March—Commemoration of the Battle of Adwa; variable—Good Friday, Easter Sunday, Id Al Fitre (end of Ramadan), Id Al Adha (Abraham's sacrifice of his son), Mawlid (Birthday of the Prophet Mohamed); 6 April—Liberation Day; 1 May—May Day; 11 September—New Year's Day; Return of Eritrea; Feast of St. John the Baptist; 12 September—Popular Revolution Commemoration Day; 27 September—Mesqel (Feast of the Finding of the True Cross).

FOREIGN EMBASSIES
All African countries are represented in Addis Ababa.

Belgium: Fikre Mariam Street, P.O. Box 1239.
Canada: Churchill Road, P.O. Box 1130.
Finland: Old Airport, P.O. Box 1017.
France: Omedla Road, P.O. Box 1464.
Federal Republic of Germany: Qebena Street, P.O. Box 660.
Italy: Qebena District, P.O. Box 1105.
Kenya: Fikre Mariam Street, P.O. Box 3301.
Netherlands: Near Old Airport, P.O. Box 1241.
Sudan: Mexico Square, P.O. Box 1110.
Sweden: Ras Tesemma Sefer, P.O. Box 1029.

Switzerland: Near Old Airport, P.O. Box 1106.
UK: Fikre Mariam Street, P.O. Box 858.
US: Int'ot'o, P.O. Box 1014.
Yemen: Jimma Road (Near Old Airport) P.O. Box 889.

ADDIS ABABA

Located almost in the centre of the country, Addis Ababa (population 1.32 million) is not only the political capital but also the economic and social nerve centre of Ethiopia.

Founded in the 1880s by Emperor Minilik the city still bears the imprint of his personality: he was a big, sprawling, generous man, and Addis Ababa is such a city. Built on the side of the Int'ot'o mountain range, which rises just behind the city to over 3,000m above sea level, the city rambles across a number of gullies and mountain streams, and covers an area of 10km by 8km. Most parts of the city lie between 2,200m and 2,500m above sea level (7,500-8,500ft).

While there was clearly little preparatory planning for so large a city, it has grown in a very natural way, with no social or economic segregation. Thus the most modern buildings, gleaming in their marble and anodised aluminium, lie adjacent to simple country-style houses with chickens and perhaps a sheep or two. Everywhere there are the eucalyptus trees which give the city much of its character and charm.

Places of Interest:
Africa Hall: birthplace of the Organisation of African Unity, whose charter was signed here on 25 May 1963. The building behind Africa Hall houses the UN Economic Commission for Africa. The OAU's offices are in a new block beyond Mexico Square.

Addis Ababa University: Up beyond Siddist Kilo, the main campus occupies the house and grounds of a palace. The Institute of Ethiopian Studies museum is well worth a visit. The Kennedy Library was donated by the U.S. Government.

St. George Cathedral: Built in 1896 in the traditional octagonal shape in commemoration of St. George, the dragon killer and patron saint of the soldier (because of Ethiopia's success at the battle of Adwa). In 1937 the Italian Fascists tried to burn it down (not very successfully—it is built of stone!) and it was restored after the war. It houses some interesting paintings by Ethiopia's internationally-known artist Afework Teklje and others.

Trinity Church and the Minilik Mausoleum: just behind the Old Gyibbi Palace lies the mausoleum built in 1911 in which Emperor Minilik II lies buried with his wife Empress T'aytu. Not far away, on the other side of the parliament building, is Trinity Church built in 1941 to commemorate Ethiopia's liberation from Fascist rule. Its interior resembles that of many European churches, but is divided into the three traditional areas—the outer ring, occupied by pews, the inner ring beneath a magnificent chandelier, and the sanctuary beyond.

The Market (Mercato): Covering a vast area to the west side of the town, it is one of the largest markets in Africa and presents the visitor with a confusing, fascinating kaleidoscope of impressions and experiences. It is divided into areas specialising in types of goods and produce.

While that of most interest to visitors is probably the section dealing with Ethiopian arts, crafts and antiques (for beautiful crosses, manuscript books, old swords), other parts of the Mercato should also be seen.

Int'ot'o: A visit to the site of Minilik's earlier capital on the top of the mountain range behind the town is well worthwhile. Little remains of the town here except the two churches, Int'ot'o Mariam, where Minilik was crowned in 1882, and Int'ot'o Raguel which may be difficult to enter but which has some fine paintings. The views from here are marvellous.

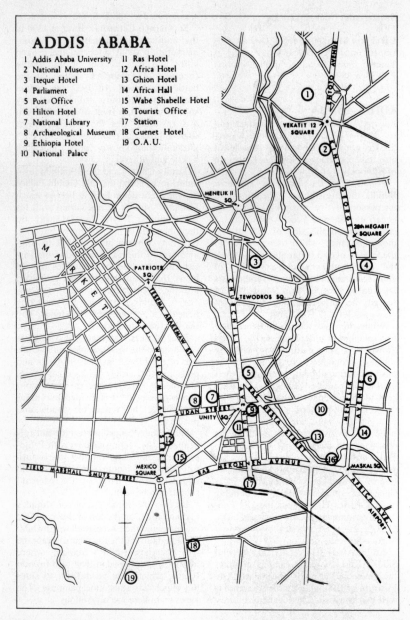

ADDIS ABABA

1 Addis Ababa University
2 National Museum
3 Iteque Hotel
4 Parliament
5 Post Office
6 Hilton Hotel
7 National Library
8 Archaeological Museum
9 Ethiopia Hotel
10 National Palace
11 Ras Hotel
12 Africa Hotel
13 Ghion Hotel
14 Africa Hall
15 Wabé Shabelle Hotel
16 Tourist Office
17 Station
18 Guenet Hotel
19 O.A.U.

ETHIOPIAN AIRLINES

18th Century castle at Gondar

Excursions:
Debre Zeyt (Bishoftu): An hour or so away, centring on some interesting volcanic crater lakes with swimming and sailing facilities.

Menagesha National Park: About 35km from Addis Ababa, a forest sanctuary for birds and wildlife. To go far into the park a four-wheel-drive vehicle is recommended.

Hagere Hiwot (Ambo): About 125km from Addis Ababa on the same road as the Menagesha National Park, it has a hot-water spring and swimming pool which attracts many people at weekends. Some 30km beyond is the breathtakingly beautiful crater lake of Wenchi.

Debre Libanos: About 100km north of Addis Ababa, the revered monastery of Debre Libanos is set on the edge of an immense gorge of one of the Blue Nile tributaries, and well worth visiting.

Hotels
De luxe
Addis Ababa Hilton, P.O. Box 1164, tel: 448400, 247 rooms.

First class
Ghion Imperial, P.O. Box 1640, tel: 447130, 180 rooms.
Ethiopia, P.O. Box 1131, tel: 447400, 100 rooms.

Wabe Shebelle, P.O. Box 3154, tel: 447187, 120 rooms.
Africa, P.O. Box 1120, tel: 447385, 74 rooms
Harambee, P.O. Box 3340, tel: 154000, 50 rooms.

Tourist class
Ras, P.O. Box 1622, tel: 447060, the oldest 'modern' hotel, a friendly atmosphere, 110 rooms.
Itegue, the only central hotel in Addis Ababa, P.O. Box 7, tel: 113240.

Student class
International, P.O. Box 409, tel: 110122, 72 rooms.
Y.M.C.A., P.O. Box 2117, tel: 112300, open to single men and women.

Restaurants
There are a considerable number, of which the **Addis Ababa** restaurant and **Maru Dembia** (Ethiopian food), the **Hong Kong**, **Chung Hwa** and **China Bar and Restaurant** (Chinese), the **Cottage** (Austrian), **Omar Khayam** (Middle Eastern), **Castelli's** and, a little out of town, **Vila Verde** (Italian) are probably the best.

Entertainments
There are several cinemas showing a wide range of international films, either in English, or with sub-titles in English. There are several night-clubs, the most interesting of which are the **Ghion**, **Ras Night** and **Wabe Shebelle** and **Sheba Night Club**.

Shopping and markets
The shops are well stocked with almost everything that can be required. Especially desirable is the local jewellery (sold by the actual weight of the gold or silver). The Mercato has a wonderful range of goods and produce, as well as Ethiopian art and curios. In the market places a certain amount of bargaining is expect-

ed—so allow time for it. At shops in town, however, prices are fixed, although a small discount is often allowed on large purchases. The Ethiopian Ceramic Workshop, three kilometres from the centre on the Bole International Airport Road, welcomes tourists at its factory.

Tourist information

Ethiopian Tourist Organization, P.O. Box 2183.

Travel agents and tour operators:

Adulis Travels, P.O. Box 2719, Addis Travel Agency, P.O. Box 2282, Eastern Travel and Tourist Agency, P.O. Box 1136. ITCO Tourist and Travel Agency, P.O. Box 1048. Seco Travel Agency, P.O. Box 264. United Touring Co., Churchill Road, P.O. Box 2465.

ASMARA

The capital of the province of Eritrea, Asmara (population 290,000) is the second largest city. At an altitude of 2,300m above sea level, its climate is typical of the Ethiopian highlands. Prior to the Italian occupation in 1889, it had been a small Coptic village and the camp of Ras Alula, the Governor of Hamasien. Under the Italians it developed into a substantial town with a 'native quarter', now the Market, and a European section, the main part of the present town.

Liberated by British forces in April 1941, Eritrea was administered by a British Military Administration until 11 September 1952 when, under a United Nations resolution, Eritrea was federated with Ethiopia. Eritrea was incorporated into Ethiopia on 14 November 1962. Thereafter a rebellion broke out which has caused increasing problems both for the Haile Selassie regime and its successor, the Provisional Military Administrative Council.

The Asmara Archeological Museum houses an excellent collection of historical objects from the pre-Axumite and

Axumite periods (1000BC—AD1000) found at sites in Eritrea and Tigray.

Hotels
First class
Nyala, P.O. Box 867, Ave Queen Elizabeth II, 110 rooms.
Amba Soyra, P.O. Box 181, 50 rooms.
Tourist class
Adulis, 63 rooms.
Keren, old family hotel with a nice atmosphere and excellent restaurant.

Restaurants

There are several good Italian restaurants in Asmara, the most notable being the **Esposito**, **San Giorgio**, **Rino's**, the **Capri**, and the restaurant in **Keren Hotel**. Local food may be had at the **Shoa** restaurant and at the **Sport** restaurant.

Travel agent

Ufficio Viaggi, P.O. Box 877.

MASSAWA

The island of Massawa was occupied by the Turks in the 16th century. Around 1850 control passed from them to Egypt, from whom the Italians took it over by arrangement in 1885. A causeway now connects Massawa to Taulud Island and another causeway runs from Taulud to the mainland. Arkiko, now just a village on the mainland and a mile or so south, was the main port of entry for Ethiopia until the 1850s. While some of the smaller buildings on Massawa Island are several hundred years old, most of the larger ones date from 1870-1890: the Imperial Palace was built around 1871-3 by Werner Munzinger, a Swiss scholar and businessman employed by the Egyptian Khedive as Governor of Massawa.

In the bay, a short boat-trip from Massawa is Green Island which has a pleasant beach. Gurgusum Beach, complete with two small hotels, bars and food, lies about 15 minutes' drive northwards along the coast.

Hotels:
Red Sea, first class, 54 rooms.
Luna, tourist class, clean and modern.

HISTORICAL SITES

South from Asmara to Senafe and Adigrat lies, first, at 116km, a small site of ancient Axumite buildings. Pillars of an Axumite buildings can be seen on the right side of the road. Between the 121 and 122km posts, a track leads off to the left to one of the most famous ancient cities in Ethiopia: Qohayto (or Coloe as the Greeks called it). Extensive remains of buildings, tombs and a beautifully cut reservoir remain, and in the cliffs nearby are some interesting cave-paintings.

Matara, near Senafe and 135km from Asmara, is the only undisturbed site of an Axumite city. The ruins include walls and staircases in near-perfect condition, and an obelisk carried one of the earliest examples of Ge'ez writing. Excavations are continuing. On the road from Adigrat to Axum is the monastery of Debre Damo (from which Judith seized the sons of the last Axumite king late in the 10th century) and the oldest surviving Axumite building at Yeha (5th or 4th century BC).

The Department of Antiquities imposes fees on visitors to the sites at Axum, Lalibela, Gondar and Bahir Dar.

AXUM

Capital of the ancient kingdom of the Queen of Sheba, Axum is a town of dramatic contrasts. Over the ancient city sprawls a small country town, apparently unaware and uncaring of the relics all around. The old (probably 15th century, but on a very ancient site) Cathedral of St. Mary of Zion is interesting. The new Cathedral is impressive. Here are kept the crowns of many of Ethiopia's former Emperors. Here, too, according to legend is the original Ark of the Covenant.

But the most astonishing relics of all are the obelisks or stelae, some still standing made of single blocks of granite and carved to represent multi-storey buildings. The tallest, now fallen, was over 33m in height and represented 13 storeys. The largest still standing is 20m in height and shows 10 floors. The carving is deep and totally clear, showing the floor-beams for each floor and the windows. The style of construction is similar to that in use in the Hadramoyt (South Yemen Republic) today .

While the origins and purposes of these stelae is still debated, it is probable that the statues were erected by the early Axumite kings in remembrance of the sort of houses they had before crossing the Red Sea. Along the Sabean coast, where land was scarce, it made sense to build skyscrapers, and it may be supposed that each king built a new one in the same way as, in the 17th and 18th centuries, each of the Ethiopian Emperors built his own castle at Gondar.

Other sites of interest include the grave of King Kaleb and Gebre Mesqel, the so-called Queen of Sheba's Bath, and the ruins of the vast Royal Palace over which, sadly, the road to Gondar now passes. The market has interesting curios and, often, recently-found coins for those willing to ask around. The Axum Hotel is of tourist class; as it is often full, it is advisable to make reservations in advance.

MEQELE

Capital of Tigray Administrative Region, Meqele has the old castle of Emperor Yohannes IV. Another castle of the same period at the other end of the town has been turned into an excellent hotel. As the **Abraha W'atsbaha Hotel** is often full, booking (tel: Meqele 62) is advisable. There are several simple hotels in the town. The new **Gere'alta Lodge**, in Dugam, is an excellent base.

Expeditions to the 130 rock churches in ·

Tigray can best be arranged from Meqele.

LALIBELA

The best way to get to Lalibela is by plane, followed by a 45 minute trip in a Land-Rover to cover the 8km from the airstrip to the town, or a three-hour journey by mule along a beautiful mountain trail. But either way, it is worth it: the country here is among the most rugged and mountainous anywhere. It is an astonishing terrain in which to find the ancient town of King Lalibela, who initiated the spate of rock-church buildings, which has left 11 such churches of the 12th and 13th centuries in the town itself. Their incredible execution (one cannot say 'construction' since they were simply carved, inside and out, from the solid rock to look as though they had been constructed), their rich ecclesiastical treasures, and the priests who serve in them, somehow expresses all that is most fascinating about Ethiopia's Middle Ages. During the 'big rains' (June-September) the town is inaccessible but a visit at Easter, Timqet or some other church festival is particularly exciting. As the only tourist hotel is the **Seven Olives**, booking (via Ethiopian Airlines) is essential. The new **Roha Hotel** is under construction.

For the vigorous there are a number of other rock churches in the vicinity for which mule trips can be arranged.

GONDAR

Capital of Ethiopia from the time of Fasile (1632-1665) until the rise of Tewodros (1855-1868), Gondar's unique Imperial Precinct contains a number of castles, built by various Emperors throughout this period, which seem, in their typical plateau setting, quite astonishing. Although the earliest of these was built by Fasile just after he expelled the Portuguese, it appears at first to reflect Moorish/European influence, but closer study reveals both interesting architectural traits of the Axumite traditions and also strong connections with the great castles of South Arabia of about the same period. An element of real mystery remains as to the intellectual parentage of the ideas and skills with which these fine castles were erected.

Elsewhere in the town is the palace known as Ras-Beit which was built in the 18th century as the private residence of a famous Lord of Tigray, Ras Mikael Sehul, and which has been in continuous occupation ever since. A short distance away is the Bath of Fasile, and the so-called House of Chickens.

Within easy range of the town lies the monastery and ruined palace at Qusqwam and the church of Debre Birham Silasie with its glorious painted roof and walls. The town itself seems dominated by a decaying Italian square, but it has a lively and interesting market.

The only tourist class hotel is the **Tarara**, although there are some simple hotels in the town.

DIRE DAWA

To the east of Addis Ababa, approximately half-way by train to Djibouti, Dire Dawa has a warm, dry climate, which gives it a most relaxing atmosphere. The market is frequented by Oromo, Somali and Afar peoples with their camel caravans.

Dire Dawa has three good hotels—the new' and excellent air-conditioned **Ras Hotel**, the old but intriguing and comfortable **Continental** and the **Omedla.**

HARAR

The 54km drive up the edge of the Rift Escarpment to Abse Tafari and Harar is a memorable experience. The warm, desertlike atmosphere of Dire Dawa soon gives way to rolling, rich green farmlands. The road passes Lakes Adele and

Alemaya. In these mountainous areas some of Ethiopia's best coffee is grown—as well as *ch'at*, a mild stimulant if chewed to extract the juices.

The whole setting of Harar, with its medieval walls tightly holding the ancient city together, its rich and exciting market (for the variety of tourist goods probably the single most exciting market in Ethiopia), the broad sweeping views to the mountains around, and the glorious, cool climate, make it an ideal place to spend a day or two.

The **Ras Hotel** is large and comfortable.

From Harar the road to Hargeisa (Somalia) leads to Jijiga, an important market centre for much of the Ogaden, and on to the border at Tug Wujale.

RIFT VALLEY LAKES

The lakes of the Rift Valley, and especially the alkaline Lakes Abyata, Shala and Langano, provide one of the most exciting bird sanctuaries in the world. This region is well provided with hotels. The chain of Bekele Molla Hotels has one in almost every town, large or small, from Mojo to Arba Minch. These are good, if simple, tourist hotels. The one at Lake Langano occupies an especially delightful site on a beach with safe swimming.

RECENT HISTORY

Under Emperor Haile Selassie—who became regent in 1917 and Emperor in 1930—Ethiopia was gradually introduced into the twentieth century. A parliamentary constitution was published in 1931, but in fact the Emperor had a close personal hold on power with the help of traditional aristocratic families.

Anti-slavery legislation was enacted, a few schools were built and the children of wealthier families went to Europe and America for further education. This be-

came the main impetus for reform, not only of the archaic feudal structures, but also of the economy.

After liberation from the Italians in 1941 Ethiopia had to contend with the economic disruptions of war and also found itself at odds with Britain, which claimed a role in administering the country. In fact British occupation of some parts of Ethiopia did not end until 1954. However, the British influence was replaced in the 1950s and 1960s by considerable US involvement in military and civil spheres.

By 1973 the Emperor's personal control of the country was slipping and the vested interests of the land-owning elite prevented meaningful change. When the Government failed to react to the Wollo drought of 1973, and 400,000 people starved to death, there was a rapid build-up of discontent that spread to the inflation-hit urban community and, most significantly, the armed forces.

In June 1974 armed forces officers began to arrest leading political figures and the Emperor's associates. In September 1974 the Emperor was deposed, the constitution abrogated and Parliament dissolved. A Provisional Military Government was established under the chairmanship of General Aman Andom, but he was executed along with dozens of former political leaders in November 1974.

Thereafter Ethiopia was proclaimed a socialist state and many companies were nationalised. Land was nationalised and students were sent into the countryside for mass education of the peasantry. The Government moved to control the unions and to operate without the advice of the political forces that had contributed to the downfall of feudalism.

General Teferi Benti was chairman of the ruling Military Council (the 'Dergue') in 1975 and 1976 but he too was executed in fighting on 3 February 1977 as power was consolidated into the hands of one man, Colonel Mengistu Haile Mariam.

GABON

A land of dense forests and rivers, Gabon would be of little significance in the world today had it not been found to contain valuable minerals, including petroleum. Now it is one of the wealthiest countries in black Africa and its small population means that modernisation will come fast. Already the infrastructure is being expanded with the construction of a Trans-Gabon railway to open up the inland forest and mining zones, rich in iron-ore, manganese and uranium.

Rapid development in Gabon has almost ruled out the possibility of casual tourism. The capital, Libreville, is one of the most expensive cities in the world and the accommodation available is only in the 'international' bracket. Moreover the remoteness of the interesting inland towns makes travel by air the only feasible means of getting there. Thus at the moment the only tourists are local residents or a handful of jet-setting big-game hunters.

THE LAND AND THE PEOPLE

The dense equatorial forest has a variety of exotic trees. The *okoume* tree, unique to this area of equatorial Africa, was for years the mainstay of the economy; but there are also the valuable *akajou*, *izogo*, *iroko* and *tchikola*. The forest covers ancient pre-Cambrian rocks which form a

plateau 600m. in altitude, rising here and there to mountains like Monts de Cristal in the north west and the Monts du Chaillu in the south, topped by Mont Iboudji. Minerals like manganese, uranium and iron have been discovered, but poor communications have enabled only the south east to profit from them so far.

The sandy coastal strip, sometimes 200km. in width, is a series of palm-fringed bays, lagoons and estuaries—the shape of one of which gave Gabon its name, from the Portuguese for 'cloak'. The lush tropical vegetation gives way in parts to savannah plains. Settlements grew up along the banks of the many rivers and now, as in the past, they are

GABON

Cameroon

Equatorial Guinea

• LIBREVILLE

Lambarene
Port Gentil •

Mouila •

Congo

Atlantic Ocean

Zaire

100 mls

the main communication routes. The canoe is still the major means of transport, but the Ogooue itself, 1,200km. long, is navigable by larger craft for 350km. up to the first rapids at Ndjole.

Much of the small population lives in the towns. Libreville's long connection with France, and its prosperity, have created a sophisticated society, whose elite has adopted western customs. There is also a large French community.

The original inhabitants of the northern coast were the Mpongwe, whose territory was invaded in the late 18th century by the Fang, coming from north of the Sanaga River, and who form a third of Gabon's population as well as living in neighbouring northern countries.

CULTURE

Gabon is the home of the Fang style of carving which influenced Pablo Picasso. Its characteristic is the distinctive heart-shaped face where a straight nose divides into half-moon eyebrows and is prolonged into the curves of the cheeks. Often the face is topped by the elaborate hair styles, discs and spikes, still to be seen in Kota and Fang areas and along the Ogooue River.

Other masks show spirits disguised as fantastic animals and were used by dancers for ceremonies of secret societies or cults such as the *mangala* on the upper Ogooue or the Fang *ngil*. Visitors may not attend these ceremonies unless specially invited.

The culture which produced this style has, however, changed and the art has died. Everything of real value has been bought up by collectors, and the only truly original modern work is the stone sculpture—figures and busts—made at Mbigou in the south.

The people also continue to make iron tools and weapons for their own use as well as clay pots and a variety of drums, xylophones and stringed instruments.

Dance and song, and the relating of poems and myths remain as important as ever.

WILDLIFE

The largely inaccessible forest abounds with elephant, buffalo, hippo, crocodile, gorilla, chimpanzee, monkeys and innumerable snakes and birds. On the savannah of the national parks one also finds many antelope including the rare *sitatonga* on the coast (Petit Loango and Wonga Wongue) and the *bongo* inland (Okanda National Park). Near the parks are hunting areas where the main game animals are elephant and buffalo. The sea, too, teems with large fish such as tarpon, barracuda and shark.

GENERAL INFORMATION

Area: 267,667 sq. km.

Population: One million.

Altitude: Apart from the low coastal plain, most of the country is about 500m. above sea level with mountains rising to 1,200m.

Capital: Libreville.

Head of State: President Omar Bongo.

Government: The President and Vice-President are both elected by universal suffrage for a seven year term and together with the Council of Ministers form the executive. The legislature is a National Assembly of 47 members, all of whom belong to the *Parti Démocratique Gabonais*.

Date of independence: 17 August, 1960.

Languages: The official language is French. Fang is spoken by about a third of the population, mostly in the north; Mpongwe on the coast; also Adouma, Okande, and Kota.

Currency: The CFA franc. £1=428 CFA francs. $1=249 CFA francs.

Time: GMT +1.

Electricity: 110V and 220V.

HOW TO GET THERE

By air: Gabon's international airport, 12km. from Libreville, is linked by almost daily flights to Paris, Rome and Geneva by Air Afrique, UTA, and Swissair. These companies and Air Zaire also operate flights from Brazzaville, Douala, Kinshasa and Johannesburg. Hotels in Libreville do not organise transport from the airport, but there are taxis (not fitted with meters) and buses.

By sea: Freighters with passenger cabins call at Libreville and Port-Gentil en route from Genoa, Marseille and other European ports. Motor boats bring the passengers from the ship to the quay.

By road: The main road through Gabon arrives from Yaounde (Cameroon) in one direction and Brazzaville (Congo) in the other. A traveller by car requires an international insurance certificate against all risks, obtainable in Gabon, and an international driving licence. Driving is on the right.

Visas and health regulations

French and West German nationals require an identity card or a valid passport; all other visitors need a visa as well as a passport. Visas are obtainable at Gabon missions abroad on production of a return or onward ticket or repatriation guarantee. Applications should be made at least one month in advance. Vaccination certificates are needed against smallpox, yellow fever and cholera.

Dutiable goods

Visitors may import a reasonable quantity of personal effects. Works of art, etc, may be exported.

Currency regulations

Visitors may import any amount of Gabonese or foreign currency but must declare it on entry; up to 25,000 CFA francs in local currency may be exported from the franc zone or any amount of foreign currency that has not been used during their stay.

CLIMATE

The climate is tropical and varies little through the country. The average temperature is 25°C. The most pleasant time for a visit, especially for a beach holiday, is the cooler dry season from mid-May to September. This is followed by the short rains from October to mid-December, a short dry season mid-December to mid-January, and long rains from mid-January to mid-May.

What to wear: Lightweight non-synthetic materials like cotton and linen are essential. A light raincoat or umbrella is required in season.

Health precautions: Malaria prophylactics must be taken. Visitors on hunting safaris are advised to take a first-aid kit containing anti-tetanus and anti-venom serum.

ACCOMMODATION AND FOOD

The few hotels in Libreville are not only fiendishly expensive but also completely booked up the whole year round. Businessmen have to book months in advance, and even then cannot be sure of a bed when they arrive. There is as yet no solution to this problem, apart from the expansion of the existing hotels. Like the hotels, most restaurants are French-run and expensive.

TRANSPORT

Air: Air transport is much used in this land of thick jungle, and there are 115 airstrips in all. Air Gabon, the domestic air service, operates regular flights between Libreville and Lambarene, Makoukou, Mekanbo, Moanda, Franceville, Ndjole, Port-Gentil and Tchibanga.

Road: There are nearly 5,000km. of roads, but three-quarters of the country is still impenetrable rain forest and the roads are not of a high standard. There is no road to Port-Gentil. Travellers should not attempt road travel in the rainy season except on the following routes: Libreville—Lambarene—Ndende; Libreville—Booue and Libreville—Bitam.

Rail: Work was begun in 1973 on the Trans-Gabon Railway—it is not yet complete.

Car hire: Cars may be hired in Libreville from the leading hotels or **Autos-Gabon**, B.P. 747, tel: 22456; **Europe-Cars**, B.P. 161, tel: 21326; **Hertz**, B.P. 391, tel: 32011. A national or international driving licence is required for self-drive hire and a deposit must be paid.

BANKS AND COMMERCE

The main banks are Union Gabonaise de Banque; Banque International pour le Commerce et l'Industry du Gabon; Banque International pour le Gabon and Banque de Paris et des Pays-Bas.

Business hours: Banks: 0730-1130, 1430-1630 Mondays to Fridays; Government: 0800-1200, 1500-1800 Monday to Friday, and 0800-1300 Saturday; Private sector: 0730-1230, 1430-1730 Monday to Friday, and 0730-1230 Saturday.

PUBLIC HOLIDAYS

1 January; Renovation Day, 12 March; Easter Monday; 1 May; Ascension; Whit Monday; 15 August; Independence Day, 17 August; All Saints Day, 1 November; Christmas.

FOREIGN EMBASSIES

Central African Empire; Congo; Equatorial Guinea; France B.P. 25 Libreville; Federal Republic of Germany B.P. 299, Libreville; Italy; Malta; Spain, U.S., B.P. 185, Libreville; Zaire.

LIBREVILLE

The town was bought from the local Kings Louis and Denis in 1839 and, as its name suggests, soon became a haven for slaves freed by the French. After many years of obscurity the past decade of prosperity has seen very rapid development, and modern villas and hotels have sprung up beside the older French-style houses. The town of 165,000 people extends amid lush tropical vegetation along the hills and valleys of the Atlantic coast. The visitor can enjoy the colourful markets, the, sculptors' village, nightclubs, and the beach, surrounded by coconut palms and strewn with *okoume* logs. There is also an interesting museum of art, ethnography and history.

Hotels
Hotel du Dialogue, B.P. 3947, tel: 32111.
Okoume-Palace-Intercontinental, B.P. 2254, tel: 32023, on the sea 5km. from the centre, 133 rooms.
Hotel Gamba, Blvd de Nice, B.P. 32267, tel: 10074, near the airport and the sea, 12km. from town, 104 rooms.
Hotel Tropicana, B.P. 300, tel: 32511, 11km. from town centre and 1.5km. from airport.

Restaurants
Apart from the hotels there are a number of expensive restaurants: **Brasserie de l'Ocean, Le Corsaire, Le Surcouf** and **Le Komo**.

Markets
Nombakele and Mont Bouet are bustling markets. On the outskirts of the town a group of stone carvers has adapted traditional techniques for the tourist market. Outside the large stores street vendors sell carvings from the villages.

AROUND LIBREVILLE

Cap Esterias, 35km. along a lovely road through forest reserve past fishing villages, is a rocky headland. There is an inn.

Owendo Port (12km.) is a newly established harbour which will become the railhead for iron ore from Belinga. It is now used for fishing and timber loading. Boat trips may be taken to the island of Coniquet, with caves which once served as refuge for slaves, and Perroquet, as well as Pointe Denis with its old royal graves and fine sandy beach where one can go skin-diving.

Kinguele Waterfalls are on the Mbe river, 115km. from Libreville along a tarred road.

Cocobeach, the northernmost point of Gabon, has an hotel. It offers fishing and hunting.

PORT-GENTIL

The oil city and industrial and commercial centre of Gabon lies at the mouth of the Ogooue and has beaches with water-skiing facilities and game fishing to tempt the tourist. The island is not connected by road with the hinterland and can be reached only by air or sea.

Hotels

Relais du Grand Tarpon, Blvd de Chavannes, B.P. 336, tel: 52103, amid coconut palms by the sea, 35 rooms.

Le Provencal, B.P. 393, tel: 52121, in the town centre, 10 rooms.

LAMBARENE

The town has become world-famous because of the mission hospital, built there in 1926 by Albert Schweitzer. This is still in use, although a new one with modern equipment has virtually replaced it. The town is situated on an island in the middle of the Ogooue river and is served by a car ferry, while the hospital, on the north bank of the river, can be reached by boat from the town or, in the dry season, on foot from the main road (20 mins.). An application must be made before a visit.

Hotel de l'Ogooue, B.P. 43, tel: 46, in the town centre with a view over the river, equipped with launch for lake-cruising. 15 rooms.

GAME PARKS

Wonga Wongue: This relatively new reserve stretches from the Atlantic coast to Lakes Azingo and Alombie between Port-Gentil and Lambarene, and can be reached from either of these or from Libreville by air or by boat, but not by road. Its plains are stocked mostly with buffalo and elephants, which can also be hunted from the lodge, near Lake Alombie. Guides and Land-Rovers are available.

Petit Loango: This is a small game park on the Atlantic coast specialising in photo-safaris. Hunting is organised in nearby areas. There are small hunting lodges. Reservations must be made several months in advance. The big game is elephant and buffalo.

The hunting season lasts all year but the best season is May and September. The lodges can only be approached by Air Gabon charter services from Port-Gentil. (B.P. 240, Port-Gentil).

HISTORY

Like much of this part of equatorial Africa, the area now known as Gabon suffered from the European slave-trade until the 19th century. In 1839 the French established Libreville as a settlement for freed slaves. The French then began to explore the Ogooue river and to make treaties with local chiefs, paving the way for colonisation in the 1890s.

Gabon's 'father of independence' was Leon Mba, who died in 1967 handing over to his Vice-President, the present Head of State, Omar Bongo. Relations with France remain close.

GAMBIA

The Gambia is developing as an easy-going holiday spot for Northern Europeans wanting a brief respite from their cold winter. The climate between October and March is warm and dry, the beaches are clean and generally safe for swimming in the warm Atlantic, and the Gambian people are welcoming and friendly. If there is nothing spectacular about The Gambia it has the great advantage of small countries—there is time enough for everything. There is no need to feel harassed or rushed as you enjoy the pleasures of the coast or wander through the markets of the small towns or take a trip to the sites upriver.

An attractive aspect of The Gambia's modesty is in its prices. Tourism has been developed for the low budget visitor (mainly by Scandinavian companies) and there are apparently no plans to construct extravagant tourist complexes like those in neighbouring Senegal.

THE LAND AND THE PEOPLE

Forming an enclave cutting into Senegal, The Gambia is a strip of land 200 miles

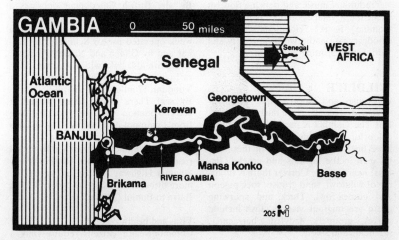

long straddling the Gambia River (with a short seaboard on the Atlantic) about 30 miles wide near the river mouth and only 15 miles wide further inland. Mangrove swamps line the river banks for the first 100 miles from the sea. In places mangrove has been cleared for rice cultivation. Further upstream, the country becomes more open, and there are cliffs of red ironstone. Away from the river are bamboo forests, thick scrub and cotton trees; further inland, groundnuts and millet are grown on the light sandy soil. The country is mainly flat, particularly at the western end.

The river, tidal for 100 miles in the rainy season and for a further 37 miles in the dry season, is navigable through the whole country for craft drawing less than 6 ft, while vessels drawing up to 19 ft can reach Kuntaur, 150 miles upstream, all the year round.

The main ethnic group is the Mandingo, followed by the Fula, Wolof, Jola, Serahuli and Aku. Most of the population of Banjul (formerly Bathurst), the capital, are Wolof. About 90% of the people are Muslim; there are some Christians, and a small number still follow traditional religion.

Traditional music and dancing flourish in the many villages on both banks of the Gambia River. Handicrafts include woodcarving, leatherwork, jewellery and 'batik' cloth printing and dyeing.

WILDLIFE

Crocodiles and hippo can be seen upstream, and monkeys are fairly abundant. But The Gambia is particularly rich and colourful in birdlife: over 400 species have been recorded. Many of these can be seen in the lagoons and creeks (*Bolons*) near Banjul. Upriver there is shooting of wildfowl, sand grouse, rock pigeon and guinea-fowl. Duck and spurwing geese are migrant visitors. Fish include mullet, groupers, ladyfish, barracuda, seabream and sole.

GENERAL INFORMATION

Area: 4,262sq miles.
Population: 500,000
Capital: Banjul (formerly Bathurst).
Head of State: The President, Sir Dawda Jawara.
Government: Independent Republic within the Commonwealth. Parliament consists of 32 members, four Chiefs, three nominated members and the Attorney-General. A small opposition party is represented.
Date of Independence: 18 February 1965.
Languages: English is the official language; the local languages are Mandingo and Wolof.
Religions: Almost 90% are Muslims; Christians include Anglicans, Methodists and Roman Catholics; there are a few animists.
Currency: The dalasi (D), divided into 100 bututs. £1=4 dalasi. $1=2.34 dalasi.
Weights and Measures: Imperial.
Time: GMT.
Electricity: 230/40V.

HOW TO GET THERE

By air: British Caledonian operates a twice-weekly flight to Banjul from London (Gatwick). There are several flights a week operated by Air Senegal from Dakar and by Ghana and Nigeria Airways. There are also links with Freetown, Sierra Leone. The international airport is at Yundum, 17 miles from Banjul.
By sea: There is occasional passenger accommodation on cargo boats sailing from Liverpool or London. Cruise ships occasionally call.
By road: Banjul can be reached by tarred road from Dakar, either by the Trans-Gambia Highway (300 miles) or by the more direct route using the car ferry from Barra to Banjul (200 miles).

Visas and health regulations
Commonwealth citizens require only a

valid passport; others require a visa. Collective visas are obtainable for organised groups. A Visitor's Pass is issued on entry, valid for one month, but can be extended on payment of D5. A return ticket or a document guaranteeing the return journey is required.

Valid international certificates of vaccination against smallpox and, for those coming from an infected area, yellow fever, are required. Inoculation against cholera is also advisable.

Dutiable goods

Personal belongings are admitted free of duty, as well as one quart of perfume and spirits, two quarts of wine or beer and 8 ozs of cigars, cigarettes or tobacco.

Currency regulations

Not more than £50 in value of Gambian currency and/or sterling can be taken out of the country, and not more than £250 in value of any other currency.

CLIMATE

The dry season from early December to the end of April is best, with uninterrupted sunshine, cooling breezes and an average temperature in Banjul of 24°C. This cool season is shorter upriver, lasting only until February. Between March and October the average temperature is 29°C in Banjul, and can rise as high as 43.3°C upriver. The rainy season lasts from July to October, when there is high humidity. Annual rainfall averages 40 ins on the coast and decreases inland.

What to wear: Lightweight clothing of cotton. Shirts and underwear of synthetic fabrics are not suitable. Light woollens are needed for evenings and for the cool season, and a lightweight raincoat or umbrella for the rainy season. Dress is very informal, but women should avoid wearing scanty beach clothes in the street. Hats and sunglasses are necessary.

Health precautions: Visitors should start taking a prophylactic against malaria 14

days before arrival and continue taking it during the stay and for 14 days afterwards. It is advisable to sleep under a mosquito net. Drinking water must be filtered or boiled, and fruit well washed before eating.

Outdoor market

TRANSPORT

Road: Roads around Banjul are tarred. Between other main towns there are good all-weather roads. The Trans-Gambia Highway connects the north and south regions of Senegal, crossing the river by ferry. It is linked with Banjul by the south bank trunk road which extends to Basse in the east. There is also a trunk road along the north bank of the river, from Barra to Georgetown, through Kerewan and Farafenni, where it crosses the Trans-Gambia Highway.

A bus service is operated by G.L.A.T.C. Taxis do not have meters, and the price of a journey should be agreed before setting out. Car hire can be arranged through the VW company.

River: The Government-owned steamer, *Lady Wright*, makes the 250-mile trip from Banjul to Basse every ten days, carrying passengers, cargo and mail. It has cabin accommodation and simple but adequate catering arrangements. Reservations must be made in advance through the Director of Marine, Banjul.

An hourly ferry service runs between Banjul and Barra. The crossing takes about 20 minutes.

BUSINESS HOURS

Banks: Monday to Friday 0800-1300 and Saturday 0800-1100. Shops: Monday to Friday 0800-1200 and 1400-1700; Saturday 0800-1200. Government offices: Monday to Thursday 0800-1445; Friday and Saturday 0800-1245.

PUBLIC HOLIDAYS

In addition to the main Muslim and Christian feastdays, the following are observed: Independence Day 18 February; Workers Day 1 May.

FOREIGN EMBASSIES

Senegal: Cameron, corner Buckle Street, Banjul.
UK: 78 Wellington Street, Banjul.
US: Cameron, corner Buckle Street, Banjul.
Other embassies: Sierra Leone, Nigeria, Guinea, Libya and Mauritania.

ACCOMMODATION, FOOD

The Gambia has many hotels, most of which are situated along the Atlantic coast near Banjul. Only a limited number of air-conditioned rooms are available.

Most hotels have bars and restaurants which serve both African and European dishes. There are few restaurants in Banjul. Food is relatively cheap; meat, fish and shellfish are plentiful. A Gambian speciality is *benachin*, also called jollof rice—a spiced rice dish with either meat, chicken or fish, cooked with tomatoes and other vegetables.

In some cases a service charge of 10% is included in hotel bills; in other cases tipping is necessary. It is not normal to tip taxi drivers.

BANJUL

The capital is the only sizeable town. Originally named Bathurst (until May 1973) after a former British colonial secretary, it was founded on a sandbank at the mouth of the Gambia River in 1816 as a settlement for freed slaves. The island's local name was Banjul (Bamboo Island) but the British renamed it St Mary's. On the north bank of the Gambia, near the ferry landing at Barra, is Fort Bullen, built in 1826 to protect the settlement.

Travelling by steamer, 20 miles upstream is Fort James Island. The fort, now ruined, was built in 1651 by the German Duke of Kurland. In 1659 it was captured by a French privateer and the following year recaptured by Kurland. In 1661 an English naval force took the island and named it after the then heir to the throne.

On the north bank of the river, opposite the island, is Albadarr, a French trading post between 1763 and 1857; and above Kau-Ur, 120 miles upstream, the Senegambian Stone Circles, consisting of stone pillars 3-10ft high, and of so far unexplained origin. Georgetown on MacCarthy Island was founded in 1857. The steamer trip ends at Basse.

Hotels:
BANJUL
Atlantic, Marina Road, tel: 8241; 77 rooms.
Banjul, 10 Cameroon Street, tel: 8384; 14 rooms.
Adonis, 23 Wellington Street, tel: 262; 32 rooms.
Apollo, 33 Buckle Street, tel: 8184, 44 rooms.
Carlton, Independence Drive, tel: 231, 88 rooms.

OUTSIDE BANJUL

Sunwing, Cape Point, Cape St Mary, tel: (93) 2428; 200 rooms.

Fajara, Atlantic Road, tel: (93) 2551; 275 rooms.

Palm Grove, Mile 2, Banjul, tel: 8119; 22 rooms.

Wadner Beach, Mile 3 Banjul, tel: 8199; 120 rooms.

Bungalow Beach, Kotu Strand, Fajara, tel: (93) 2288; 144 rooms.

African Village, (Club 98), Bakan, tel: (93) 2384; 43 rooms.

Tropic Bungalows, Atlantic Rd, Fajara, tel: (93) 2311; 70 rooms.

Riviera Hotel, 78 Atlantic Rd, Fajara, tel: (93) 2284; 16 rooms.

On the north bank, not far from Barra, there is a camping site at Tendaba, with full amenities including a restaurant. There are rest-houses at Mansa Konko, Georgetown and Basse.

Entertainments

There are miles of sandy beaches around Banjul, inluding the Mile 3 Beach (with beach huts and refreshments), Mile 5 Beach, Brufut (16 miles from Banjul), Tanji (17 miles) and Gunjur (33 miles). In some places, such as Cape St Mary (10 miles from Banjul) there are dangerous currents and swimmers should always be careful. Taxis can be taken to any of these beaches; standard fares have been laid down. Bathing is also possible at Barra Point near the ferry landing on the north bank.

There is sailing (Bathurst Sailing Club); riding at Yundum; golf at the Golf Club at Fajara. Tennis is played all the year round, and cricket and football are popular. There are plenty of opportunities for offshore fishing and for shooting in the upriver areas.

Temporary membership can be obtained at the Casuarina Club at Fajara, eight miles from Banjul on the coast (closed May to November). There are several night-clubs in Banjul, Fajara, Bakau and Serrekunda.

Shopping and markets

Banjul has a colourful market where sandals, dyed cloth, and hand-printed shirts can be bought, as well as handcrafts, including woodcarvings, gold jewellery, beaded belts, handwoven fabrics and snakeskin handbags.

Tourist information

The Government Tourist Board is in Bedford Place, Banjul, and there is an information office at Marina Parade.

NATIONAL PARKS

The Abouko Nature Reserve, run by the Ministry of Agriculture, is situated about 15 miles from Banjul. It has monkeys, crocodiles and pythons, as well as a wide variety of birds. A National Park has been proposed at a site about 100 miles from Banjul in the Kiang West district.

HISTORY

The Senegambian Stone Circles and other archaeological remains prove that both banks of the Gambia River have been inhabited for many centuries. By AD 1000 the small groups of people in the area had established their own methods of farming, fishing and metal-working and individualistic styles of dancing, music and sculpture. They were, however, on the outer rim of West African civilization at the time, with the ocean a barrier to the outside world. One of the main groups in the area was the Barra. Upriver were Mandinka traders.

The first Europeans to arrive were the Portuguese in 1455. In the 16th century the English began to trade on the coast and in 1661 the first English settlement on the West African coast was established at Fort James by the Royal Adventurers Trading to Africa.

The Gambia formed part of the Crown Colony of Senegambia between 1765 and 1783 and was governed from Saint-Louis at the mouth of the Senegal River. After

On the Gambia River

the Peace of Versailles in 1783 when Saint-Louis was handed back to France, Senegambia ceased to exist and The Gambia was declared a British possession.

It was not until 1889 that a boundary settlement was reached with France, determining the country's character as an enclave almost bisecting Senegal.

Since the administration was inevitably on such a small scale, British colonial rule had little impact on the economy and social structure of the territory. However, during the 1950s, improvements were made to the road network, Bathurst (Banjul) harbour and to the social services.

Pressure from Gambian political organisations led to increased autonomy, and a House of Representatives was established in 1960. The political parties formed during the 1950s—the Democrat-ic Party, the Muslim Congress Party and the United Party—all drew their support from the Wolof of Banjul. The first party to base its strength on the people of the hinterland, the numerically dominant Mandingo, was the People's Progressive Party (PPP), founded in 1960 and led by Dawda Jawara.

Full internal self-government was granted in 1963 and independence was achieved in 1965, under a coalition led by Jawara and Pierre N'Jie, founder of the United Party (UP).

The Gambia has enjoyed remarkable stability since independence and is the only former British West African territory not to have experienced a military coup.

The PPP has stayed in power since 1966, with the UP in opposition. In 1970 the Gambia became a Republic, with Sir Dawda Jawara as President.

GHANA

An up-and-coming tourist centre, Ghana is one of the most pleasant countries in Africa for every sort of visit, whether two days, two weeks or two months, whether business or pleasure.

It is a country of interest wherever you go: the great cities of Accra, Kumasi, Takoradi, the many lively towns and villages, the coastal beaches and historic forts or the forests, plains, rivers and lakes of the inland areas. Everywhere there are markets, bars and clubs with something different to offer.

Although a sophisticated society, Ghana retains many African traditions and none so strongly as that of friendliness towards visitors. The traveller with a genuine interest in Ghana will be rewarded with memorable experiences.

THE LAND AND THE PEOPLE

A rectangular country in the middle of the Guinea Coast, Ghana extends over 600 km. south to north and 480 km. east to west at its widest point. A narrow grassy plain stretches inland behind the curving beaches and lagoons, widening to about 30 km. on the east.

Rain forest stretches inland, covering a total of 64,000 sq. km. mainly in the south and west. Behind Accra the road climbs steeply up an escarpment from where one can appreciate the stunning differences in African scenery. Northwards the forest and hills roll on as far as the eye can see. Only when you are past the forest does the climate become really hot and dry and the land breaks into savannah and open woodland. The northern area of Ghana is plateau, averaging 500 m. in height.

In the east the Akwapim-Togo hills

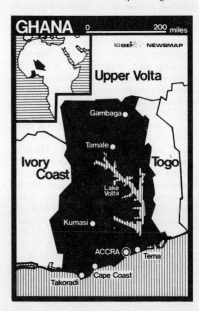

GHANA   0   200 miles
163 GEM   NEWSMAP
Upper Volta
Gambaga
Tamale
Ivory Coast   Togo
Lake Volta
Kumasi
ACCRA   Tema
Cape Coast
Takoradi

137

stretch from a few miles inland from Accra to the Togo border. This range has deep valleys.

The Black and White Volta rivers enter Ghana from Upper Volta, merging in the largest man-made lake in the world, the Volta lake, covering 8,000 sq. km. behind the Akosombo hydro-electric project.

The people of Ghana are generally of negroid stock; only in the north are there Hamitic strains introduced by the nomadic Fulani. The peopling of the land was generally from the north, though the Ga of Accra and the Ewe of the Volta Region originate from the east.

The Akan group is predominant in the south and west, with Fanti on the coast, and the Ashanti and their sub-groups in the forest area. The latter are responsible for much of Ghana's 'traditional' character. At the height of their power the Ashanti controlled a large tract of land from the coast to northern Ghana; but their heartland has always been around Kumasi, a region of rich soil, forest produce and minerals. These are not only exploited for the practical purposes of survival but also used creatively. Most Ghanaian farmers are also excellent craftsmen, able to turn their hands to working gold, weaving the rich *Kente* cloth, or carving wood and making drums and other instruments. The symbol of the Ashanti people is the golden stool of their king, the Asantehene.

The northern peoples differ markedly from those of the forest in their traditions, appearance and dress. They include the Mamprusi, Dagomba and Gonja in the centre and north east, the Kassena, Nankani and Builsa in the northern frontier zone, and the Wala, Dagarti and Sissala in the north west.

Ghana's towns are often the headquarters of a people or clan, with a chief in residence. A 'town' may have a smaller population than places designated as villages, but each of these capitals has a distinctive character. For example, Nkawkaw, the centre of the Kwahu people, is known as a flourishing business centre, while Kibi (not far away) rests on its age-old traditions as capital of the Akim Abuakwa state.

The markets express the country's real character. Noise, colour and movement are everywhere. The locally produced cloth is of high quality. There are many traditional handicrafts on sale, carvings, leather work, baskets, furniture. Moreover as proof that Ghana is basically an agricultural country, there is a wealth of local foods.

CULTURE

Ghanaian festivals sometimes have their origins in historical events. They may commemorate outstanding battles, but more often they mark the harvest, or the purification of ancestral stools or the pacification of a god. A festival involves drumming, dancing, feasting and the pouring of libations (or spirit) with incantations and perhaps the sacrifice of an animal.

Different cloths are worn for different occasions and the more intricate patterns are rich in symbolism. Similarly each movement in a dance conveys a recognisable message and meaning. For Ghanaians dancing is a dramatic expression of life itself; it is as important as language and can convey the whole gamut of experience. Drumming and singing are essential accompaniment to a dance, setting the scene and creating the mood. The dancing sometimes follows the music but it can be in opposition to it—for dramatic effect.

Religion enters significantly into Ghanaian life. There are many sects of Christianity—some new, some old—but they all make full use of local musical talent, and there is a great gusto and depth of feeling in church services. Islam also has a strong hold in the north.

Ghana has a high rate of literacy for Africa, and a considerable number of newspapers and magazines. Freedom of

*Independence Arch in
Black Star Square, Accra*

the written word is not as restricted as in other African states, and eloquent freedom of speech is unlimited.

Every tiny village in Ghana has its bar, which is central to village life, particularly after dark. There is always music from a wireless or records, and it is the best place to get to know people. In the large towns there are casinos, restaurants and nightclubs, some with live bands playing a stimulating West African blend of music from other parts of Africa, from America and Europe.

WILDLIFE

The Mole National Park in the north west is rich with game in the dry season from December to May, with animals concentrated around the water holes and saltlicks. The more common species are oribi, bushbuck, hartebeeste, duiker, waterbuck, kob, roan antelope, baboon, buffalo and warthog. Elephant, lion and leopard are occasionally seen.

There are a number of small parks and reserves scattered throughout Ghana, but in all rural areas one can find a fascinating variety of wild animals and exotic birds.

There is a great variety of fish in the sea, the Volta lake and the many rivers. Fishing enthusiasts will find their counterparts in Ghana.

GENERAL INFORMATION
Area: 235,500 sq. km.
Population: 10 million.
Altitude: Sea level to 1,000 m.
Capital: Accra.
Head of State: General I. K. Acheampong.
Government: Military government, composed of a Supreme Military Council and a Cabinet of Commissioners.
Date of independence: 6 March 1957.
Languages: English (official), Twi, Fanti, Ga, Ewe, Dagbeni, Hausa and Nzima are among the principal Ghanaian languages.
Religions: Christianity of various sects, Islam and animism.
Currency: The Cedi ($\mathcal{C}$)divided into 100 pesewas. £1=$\mathcal{C}$1.97. $1=$\mathcal{C}$1.15.
Time: GMT
Electricity: 230/250V.

HOW TO GET THERE
By air: Kotoka International Airport, 10 km. from the centre of Accra, is served by Ghana Airways from London, Paris, Rome, Beirut and other West African capitals. British Caledonian, Air Afrique, Air Mali, Aeroflot, Alitalia, Ethiopian Airlines, KLM, Lufthansa, MEA, Nigeria Airways, Pan Am and Swissair also make regular calls, linking Ghana to Europe, America, the Middle East and African capitals.

Taxis are available at the airport.

An airport tax of $\mathcal{C}$3 is payable on departure from Ghana.

By Road: A good coast road links Lagos, Cotonou and Lome to Accra. The present road from Abidjan runs inland through Kumasi. A rough road enters the country from Upper Volta at Navrongo. Long-distance taxis operate between Ghana and its three immediate neighbours, though they become less frequent farther away from the busy coast.

Visas, currency and health regulations

A valid passport is required by all persons entering Ghana, though nationals of West African countries can enter with special travel certificates. Visas are also required by all non-Commonwealth visitors, while Commonwealth nationals need Entry Permits. Visas or Entry Permits should be applied for from a Ghanaian diplomatic mission well in advance of a visit.

All intending visitors must buy 'Cedi Vouchers' from the Ghanaian diplomatic mission issuing their visas or entry permits. The Vouchers for one day are for a minimum of ₵70. For each additional day you need vouchers of ₵20. These can be exchanged for cedis on arrival in Ghana. They are intended to reduce 'black market' currency dealings in Ghana—which tend to give the cedi a very low value compared with the dollar, franc or pound. Every foreign exchange transaction must be entered on the Exchange Control Form T5 issued to all visitors to Ghana and surrendered at the end of a visit.

International certificates of vaccination against smallpox, yellow fever and cholera are required by all visitors.

Dutiable goods: Personal effects, 400 cigarettes and half a bottle of alcohol or perfume are admitted free of duty. A special permit is required for arms and ammunition. All baggage is liable to examination.

CLIMATE

Taking the country as a whole, the temperature is hot and humidity is high, but there are local variations. It is cooler and wetter in the forest regions around Kumasi than on the coastal plain, while the climate in the north is dry and hot, even at night.

The rainy months are June and July, but the length of the rains varies from year to year. They can sometimes begin as early as April and go on until half-way through September. The only other climatic break is the *harmattan*, a dusty wind which blows south from the Sahara and dries the air for a few weeks in the early part of each year. The sudden drop in humidity cracks lips, wooden furniture and leather suitcases, and produces in the population a kind of euphoria, like a carnival.

On the coast there is no special 'season'. The whole year has excellent holiday weather.

What to wear: Clothing should be light, preferably of cotton. There is little formality, and a light suit is sufficient for evening functions. Women should take a number of light and easily washable dresses. Around August a thin sweater or wrap may ward off the occasional evening chill.

Health precautions: It is essential to take prophylactics against malaria for at least two weeks before a visit to West Africa as well as throughout one's stay and for another two weeks afterwards. Inoculation against typhoid and paratyphoid is recommended. Drinking water in Ghana's main towns is perfectly safe, but farther afield it should be boiled or filtered. Precautions against stomach upsets are advisable.

ACCOMMODATION AND FOOD

The international hotels are generally of a high standard but are rather expensive. There is a wide range of more reasonably priced hotels in the city. Accra also has a YMCA and a YWCA. A number of Government resthouses exist up and down the country.

Ghanaians are proud of their local dishes and many restaurants serve a range of traditional soups (palmnut, groundnut, etc.), stews (kontomere, okro, etc.), and their starchy accompaniments (fufu, kenkey or gari).

Tipping: This is called 'dash' in Ghana. Small children surround the stranger shouting with the greatest good humour 'dash me pesewa'—but their good humour is not a wit diminished if you don't. The usual rate of tipping is 10%. Taxi drivers do not expect a tip.

TRANSPORT
Air: Ghana Airways has daily internal services between Accra, Kumasi, Takoradi, Tamale and Sunyani.

Lake: There is a boat service between Akosombo and Yapei.

Rail: Regular passenger services operate between Accra, Kumasi and Takoradi, but they are very slow.

Road: A modern road system, which is kept in reasonable repair, connects all the main towns. A motorway runs between Accra and Tema. There are two roads to Kumasi from Accra, one goes through Aburi—where Dr Nkrumah's former country residence is a sprawling landmark—the other through Kibi, capital town of the Akim Abuakwa State. The main road to the Volta Region passes close to the great Volta Dam at Akosombo.

The main form of public transport is the 'mammy wagon', or 'tro-tro' which carries people and their assortment of possessions and market wares over any distance. Taxis are plentiful in towns. Painted predominantly bright yellow, they have no meters, so it's as well to fix the fare before beginning your journey.

For long distances one has the choice of state-run buses, which are comfortable and safe, mini-buses or taxis which are cheaper and faster but less reliable. The rates are remarkably similar for all three. Driving is on the right.

Car hire
Allways Travel Agency (Hertz), P.O. Box 1638, tel: 24590.
Speedway (Avis), P.O. Box 214, tel: 27744. **De Luxe Car Rentals,** Tunisia House, Accra, tel: 66158.

BANKS
The main commercial banks with branches throughout the country are Standard Bank of Ghana, Barclays Bank of Ghana and Ghana Commercial Bank.

Business hours: Shops: 0800 to 1200 and 1400 to 1730 Monday, Tuesday, Thursday, Friday. 0800 to 1300 Wednesday and Saturday.

Banks: 0830 to 1400 Monday to Thursday. 0830 to 1500 Friday.

Yapei Queen
ferry boat

Government offices: 0800 to 1230 and 1330 to 1700 Monday to Friday.

PUBLIC HOLIDAYS

New Year's Day; National Redemption day, 13 January; Independence Day, 6 March; Good Friday; Holy Saturday; Easter Monday; Republic Day, 1 July; First Monday in August; Christmas Day; Boxing Day.

FOREIGN EMBASSIES

Algeria—tel: Accra 76719; **Austria**—tel: 65928/9; **Australia**—tel: 77972; **Belgium**—tel: 76781; **Benin**—tel: 25701; **Britain**—tel: 64651; **Canada**—tel: 28555; **Denmark**—tel: 21369; **Egypt**—tel: 76701; **Ethiopia**—tel: 76807; **France**—tel: 28571; **Germany (West)**—tel: 21311; **Guinea**—tel: 65551; **India**—tel: 75601; **Italy**—tel: 75622; **Ivory Coast**—tel: 74611; **Japan**—tel: 75616; **Lebanon**—tel: 76727; **Liberia**—tel: 75641; **Mali**—tel: 66421; **Netherlands**—tel: 21655; **Niger**—tel: 24962; **Nigeria**—tel: 76158/9; **Senegal**—tel: 77737; **Sierra Leone**—tel: 26062; **Switzerland**—tel: 28215; **Togo**—tel: 77950; **Uganda**—tel: 28268; **USA**—tel: 66811; **Upper Volta**—tel: 21988; **Zaire**—tel: 75837.

ACCRA

Arriving from the airport, one's first impression of Accra is of trees and spaciousness. It becomes more densely packed towards its ancient core, the area around the harbour called Jamestown, seat of the Queen Mother of the Ga people. To the east of it, but still close to the sea, are the public buildings, the business and shopping areas, the colourful Makola market and beyond these the museums, the various hotels, the cinemas and the richer residential areas. The city is a mixture of architectural styles likely to dismay any planner, but the luxuriant vegetation and the friendly charm of its citizens transforms the chaos into a colourful and exciting place to visit.

The seat of government is Osu Castle (formerly Christiansborg) built overlooking the sea in 1662. Also at the sea's edge is the impressive Black Star Square where all major public ceremonies are staged. Another mark of Ghana's role as herald of the political independence of Africa is State House, a vast modern block with extensive conference facilities. Striking monuments to African unity and liberation stand at major traffic intersections, all dating from the Nkrumah era.

The National Museum presents works of ancient and modern Ghanaian art, and there is a small public zoo at Flagstaff House. At Legon, 13 km. north of the city, is the University of Ghana.

A pleasant drive along the coast past beaches and beach clubs takes one to the modern part of Tema, 30 km. to the east, with its great factories, and well-planned housing areas. It boasts a large luxury hotel, exactly on the Greenwich Meridian.

Hotels

Ambassador Hotel, P.O. Box 3044, tel: 64646, Ghana's most prestigious accommodation, centrally situated, with pleasant open air bars and restaurants, 152 rooms.

Continental Hotel, P.O. Box 5252, tel: 75361, equally luxurious and popular for music and dancing at weekends, 155 rooms, 5 suites.

Meridian Hotel, P.O. Box 330, Tema, tel: Tema 2878, Ghana's biggest and most modern hotel, 30 km. from Accra with views over the Atlantic and the new Tema port, 179 rooms.

Star Hotel, P.O. Box 652, tel: 77728, quietly situated and a popular evening rendezvous, with dancing, 60 rooms, 20 chalets.

Avenida Hotel, P.O. Box 756, tel: 23121, centrally situated with pleasant gardens, with luxury accommodation and cheaper non air-conditioned rooms in an annex.

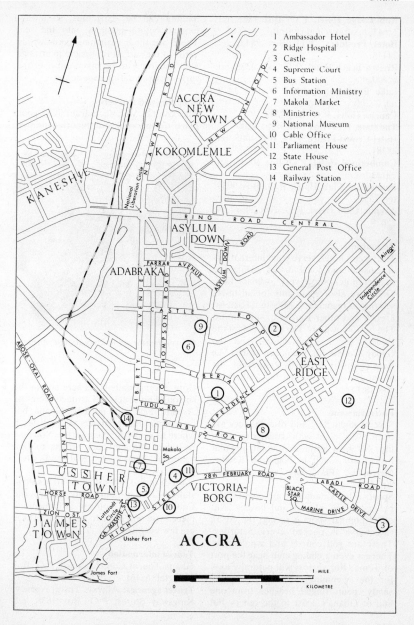

1 Ambassador Hotel
2 Ridge Hospital
3 Castle
4 Supreme Court
5 Bus Station
6 Information Ministry
7 Makola Market
8 Ministries
9 National Museum
10 Cable Office
11 Parliament House
12 State House
13 General Post Office
14 Railway Station

ACCRA

Kob Lodge Hotel, P.O. Box 1191, tel: 27647, luxurious and central.
Hotel President, P.O. Box 7842, tel: 24475.
Riviera Beach Hotel, P.O. Box 4226, tel: 62400.
Lake Bosumtwi Hotel, P.O. Box 1419, tel: 27200.
Caprice Hotel, P.O. Box 2499.
The Date, P.O. Box 3401, tel: 28200.
Hotel Crown Prince, P.O. Box 4005, tel: 25381.
Cumberland Hotel, P.O. Box 10845, tel: 29123.
Panoramic Club Hotel, P.O. Box 9039, tel: 75356.
Avenue Club Hotel, P.O. Box 2968, tel: 22679.

Restaurants

The largest hotels serve good international cuisine and local dishes, while the smaller hotels serve very ordinary fare. There are also restaurants for all tastes serving Ghanaian, Middle Eastern, French and other European specialities. The best known are **The Black Pot** (at the Riviera Beach Club Hotel) and the **Goody Goodie** for Ghanaian dishes, **Le Reve** (French), **Edwards Restaurant**, the **Mandarin** (Chinese) and the **Maharajah** (Indian).

Entertainments

Several nightclubs and discotheques are open every night with dancing to High-life, Afrobeat, or internationally popular rock music, such as **Napoleon Keteke**, **Metropole**, **Play Boy** and **Tip Toe Gardens**.
Sport: The Ghanaians are great footballers, tennis players and boxers. Another popular sport is racing; the Accra racecourse is packed every Saturday. There are golf courses and a polo club. There is even a gliding club near the port of Tema. But visitors will naturally look for the swimming, available along the sandy, palm-fringed beaches from one end of Ghana's coast to the other—but

bathing can be dangerous, so always inquire before plunging into the sea. There are three swimming pools within yards of the surf. It is possible to arrange with fishermen to be taken out over the surf—an exhilarating experience.

Shopping and markets

The central Makola market is a good place to buy local and imported printed

Souvenirs arrayed in Bolgatanga market

cloth. Occasionally stalls here and in the surrounding streets sell artifacts from the Ashanti region and northern Ghana, but by asking among friends you will learn where to get what you are after. You may be taken through back streets to find beautiful hand-made gold and silver jewellery.

Modern and older African art is sold at stalls near the Community Centre and Cable Office. If you are after genuine pieces you will have to pay a lot. There are few bargains.

Tourist information

Ghana Tourist Control Board, P.O. Box 3106, tel: 65461.
Travel agencies: Allways Travel Agency, Kingsway Stores, P.O. Box 1638, tel:

24590. Atlantic Travel Bureau, P.O. Box 3474, tel: 64171. Black Beauty Tours, P.O. Box 2189, tel: 76542. Overseas Travel Agency, P.O. Box 1163, tel: 25189. Tarzan Travel Agency, P.O. Box 396, tel: 66289. Speedway Travel, P.O. Box 214, tel: 28799. Scantravel, P.O. Box 4960, tel: 63134. Intertours, P.O. Box 6704, tel: 76230. State Shipping Travel Agency, P.O. Box 2760, tel: 64951. Frequency Travel and Tours, P.O. Box 4353, tel: 25026. Jet-Age Travel and Tours, P.O. Box 4676, tel: 64646.

THE COAST

The coast road to the west of Accra takes you through **Winneba** to Cape Coast and the twin city of Sekondi-Takoradi. The main feature of this coastline is the large number of castles and forts built by Portuguese, Dutch and British traders, mainly in the 17th century. At that time the open coastal plains were less forbidding than farther west and there were abundant supplies of gold, ivory and, later, slaves to be bought from the coastal peoples. The early Europeans rarely ventured inland from their fortresses. Not until the 19th century did the British conquer the Ashanti Kingdom—aided and abetted by the coastal people.

In many of the forts the dungeons still have chains attached to floor and walls, a sight to bring sadness and bitterness to the heart.

At Senya Beraku, 50 km. west of Accra, is a partially ruined Dutch fort of a much later date than the others—late 18th century. Beyond Winneba is **Fort Leydsaamheid** (1700), another Dutch construction at one time in the hands of the British. Bastions, with gun ports, project at the western and eastern angles. Three cannons still stand near the entrance. It is now used as a police station, but visitors are admitted.

The greatest concentration of forts is around **Cape Coast**. Fort Amsterdam at Kormantin is an English fort of 1638,

though it was later captured by the Dutch, changing hands a number of times until it was surrendered to the Ashanti in 1806. At Anomabu is **Fort William**, originally English, but bombarded by the French. It was also taken by the Ashanti in 1806. At Morwe is **Fort Nassau** dating from 1624, one of the earliest Dutch settlements, with a chequered history: captured by the English in 1664, by the Dutch in 1665, by the English in 1782, restored to the Dutch in 1785 and abandoned in 1816—now used as a public lavatory.

At Cape Coast itself is a castle built by the English in 1662, although it became Dutch in the following year, then English, until attacked by the townspeople in 1681. In 1703 and 1757 it was bombarded by the French. Part of it is now a prison.

Cape Coast is the cradle of Ghana's educational system, the earliest and best secondary schools are here and the town also has a university.

A few kilometres beyond Cape Coast on the main road is the best-known castle in Ghana, at **Elmina**, built by the Portuguese in 1482. The Dutch ended Portuguese domination of the area in 1637, and held on to the castle despite English bombardments, eventually selling it to Britain in 1872. It has a high courtyard with tall round towers at opposite corners. Nearby is Fort St. Jago. The area is now designated as the site of a new tourist complex.

Pressing on to **Komenda** one finds two forts, one English and the other, a more impressive structure, Dutch. Approaching Sekondi-Takoradi at Shama is another early Portuguese fort of impressive dimensions. The Dutch added to its fortifications.

Sekondi-Takoradi, 220 km. west of Accra, is a lively port and business centre and the favourite city of many Ghanaians. There is much of interest in the neighbourhood, not least the village of Nkroful, where Dr Kwame Nkrumah was born and is now buried.

The coastal forts beyond Sekondi-Takoradi include **Dixcove** (English), **Princes Town** (Dutch), **Axim** (Portuguese) and **Beyin**. Ghana's southernmost point, Cape Three Points, is flanked by two beautiful bays which have a reputation for excellent surfing—only to be attempted by experts.

Hotels
Atlantic Hotel, Takoradi, P.O. Box 273, tel: 3301, a modern luxury establishment overlooking the sea, 62 rooms, 8 suites.
Mid Wood Hotel, Takoradi, tel: 3028.
Catering Rest House, Cape Coast, P.O. Box 305, tel: 2594.
Elmina Motel, Elmina, P.O. Box 100, tel: 20.
Busua Pleasure Beach, Dixcove, P.O. Box 7, tel: 6.

EASTERN AND VOLTA REGIONS
A short drive inland from Accra takes you up to the Akwapim range, where the tropical forest begins in earnest. Aburi was a favourite spot for early colonisers and missionaries in the 19th century because the climate cools noticeably as one climbs the escarpment. In Aburi are the

Ghanaian limbo dancers

Botanical Gardens and nearby the Peduase Presidential Lodge.

The great Volta Dam at Akosombo generates enough electricity to supply not only southern Ghana but the needs of adjacent countries. Above it is the world's largest artificial inland sea, the Volta Lake. *The Akosombo Queen* takes passengers from here all the way to Yapei near Tamale in northern Ghana. Akosombo has a yacht club, a filtered swimming pool and on the hill above it, a modern hotel with a breathtaking view of the lake, the dam and the surrounding country.

A favourite weekend occupation for people living in Accra is a drive to Lome in neighbouring (ex-French) Togo. You can either cross the bridge over the Volta or take the more northerly route through Ho and cross by the Adomi suspension bridge. It takes about three hours to reach the border by the coastal route.

For those in search of sailing, water skiing, swimming and excellent fishing there is Ada, at the mouth of the Volta, about 90 minutes' drive from the capital along a good road but, in spirit, a world away. The river is salt water for several kilometres up and it is safe to swim without fear of bilharzia.

Hotels
Volta Hotel, Akosombo, P.O. Box 25, tel: 731, perched on a hilltop overlooking the lake, with breathtaking views, specialising in barbecues and fish dishes, 40 rooms.
Restaurant 'May', Abrui, Box 25, tel: 25.

KUMASI AND CENTRAL GHANA
At the heart of Ghana's wealth and culture, Kumasi is a bright and energetic city among attractive wooded valleys. Known alternatively as the 'Garden City' and the 'City of the Golden Stool' it has been the headquarters of the wealthy Ashanti Kingdom since the 17th century.

According to legend King Osei Tutu chose the site on the advice of his fetish-priest Okomfo Anokye, who planted seeds of the Kum tree at different sites. Only here did the seed sprout.

Kumasi is now an important centre of business (with Ghana's largest market) and education, and also houses the National Cultural Centre—a combination of museum, open air theatre, crafts workshop, art gallery, model farm and zoo. The Ashanti king, the Asantehene, has his court at Manhyia Palace. Kumasi Fort is also an historical museum.

Not far outside the city is another crafts centre at Bonwire, the home of woodcarving and the beautiful *kente* cloth. To the south east is Ghana's largest natural lake, Bosumtwi. To the south is the gold mine of Obuasi. The whole area is scattered with small cocoa farms.

Hotels
City Hotel, Kumasi, P.O. Box 1980, tel: 3298, set in beautiful grounds with view over the city, 75 rooms.
Catering Rest House, Kumasi, P.O. Box 3179, tel: 6500.
Hotel de Kingsway, Kumasi, P.O. Box 178, tel: 2441.
Tourist Cottage Hotel, Kumasi, P.O. Box 4649, tel: 5219.

THE NORTH

Northwards from Kumasi the tarmac road continues across the Volta Lake ferry and through the grassy savannah to Tamale, the largest town in these parts, with its fascinating markets, cultural centre and mosque. The main road then continues north to Bolgatanga (almost on the Upper Volta border) and into Upper Volta to Ouagadougou and, less smoothly, to Timbuktu.

Alternatively, from Tamale you can branch off west to the Mole National Park at Damongo—with its modern hotel high above a water hole for good game-viewing—then on north to Wa, where the chief's dazzling white palace is reminiscent of Gaudi's architecture. There is also a fine mosque. The road continues to Lawra, then back eastwards through the desolate and remote Tumu country of the so-called Fra-Fra, who will show you around their interesting houses, to Navrongo and Bolgatanga. The Bolgatanga baskets and hats are made in the market—the baskets are found as pots and closely woven from multi-coloured raffia. There are also earthenware pots, some so small they will fit into a handbag, others too big to transport. In all the northern markets you will find leatherwork and locally woven traditional shirts—heavy but cool.

The round trip from Accra to Bolgatanga and back again to Accra takes less than a week—if the river Lanyung, a few miles outside Navrongo, is not swollen into a torrent by the rains. There are few alternative routes.

Hotels
Mole National Park Motel, Damongo, P.O. Box 8, bookings must be made in advance, guides available for the reserve, 5 double chalets, 5 single rooms, 9 double rooms, more being added.
Lovi Rest Camp, Mole Reserve, grass huts and a dormitory, no food.
Catering Rest House, Tamale, P.O. Box 247, tel: 2978.
Catering Rest House, Bolgatanga, P.O. Box 50.
Black Star Hotel, Bolgatanga, P.O. Box 18, tel: 346.

HISTORY

It is probable that the forests and coastlands of modern Ghana were very thinly populated until the 12th century, when different groups of peoples began to enter the country from the east and north, as pressure on land in the savannah belt of West Africa forced people to exploit the potential of the forest. Throughout this period all the peoples of this region looked to the north for their contacts with the outside world. Two major trade routes linked the country with the Western Sudan: one from the central forest to Timbuktu and the other from around Tamale to Hausaland (in modern Nigeria).

By the time the Portuguese arrived on the coast (the Gold Coast) in the 15th century the people of the interior were already organised into quite powerful kingdoms.

The traditions of the Ga and Ewe peoples of the south-east indicate that they arrived from the area of Yorubaland. The Ga kingdom, established in the 16th century, had its capital at Great Accra (Ayawaso), about 18 km. from the coast, but it was conquered by the Ashanti in 1742, and remained under Ashanti hegemony until the battle of Dodowa in 1826, when the Ga won their independence again. Farther east and inland, the Ewe people were divided into a large number of autonomous states ruled by chiefs and elders.

Among the earliest inhabitants of northern Ghana were the Sissala, the Guan, the Konkomba, the Koma and the Chamba peoples. They had no states, kingdoms or forms of central government, but towards the end of the 13th century the invading Mamprusi and Dagomba peoples (from the east of Lake Chad) began to impose their authority. The founders of the Gonja kingdom arrived from Mandeland (to the west) at the end of the 16th century. All three of these invading groups had similar administrative systems, with strong central rulers.

The Portuguese dominated the coast trade, through their newly constructed forts, until ousted by the Dutch in 1642. For nearly 200 years the British, Danish and Dutch were rivals for the lucrative trade in gold, ivory and slaves. But by the mid-19th century Britain had signed treaties with many coastal and inland chiefs and was extending its influence beyond the confines of the forts and settlements. The only effective resistance to British penetration was put up by the Ashanti in a series of fierce wars.

In 1901 Britain started to administer the Gold Coast and its hinterland as a colony, absorbing part of German Togoland in 1922. National politics were more advanced than in many colonies and by 1957 the Gold Coast was granted independence after a successful political struggle under the leadership of Kwame Nkrumah.

The Gold Coast was the first African colony to achieve independence. Changing its name to Ghana to emphasise Africa's proud pre-colonial history, Dr Nkrumah declared that the country's independence was 'meaningless unless it is linked with the liberation of Africa'. One of the architects of modern Pan-Africanism, he remained primarily committed to the ideal of African unity by helping other countries to obtain their independence, and by becoming deeply involved in the Congo crisis of the early 1960s and in other African affairs. But his policies at home became increasingly out of touch with reality and oppressive, corrupted by sham-ideologists.

Faced with economic difficulties, political violence and bitter external enemies, Nkrumah saw his power slip away from his fingers at a time when he was still in the ascendant as an international figure. While on a visit to Peking in 1966 he was removed from power by the army. The whole trend of his policies was reversed. The army invited support from the West rather than the East, and handed back power to an elected civilian regime in 1969. The new Prime Minister, Dr Kofi Busia, faced great economic pressures and mounting social unrest in his two years in power; so the army stepped in once again in 1972 under Col. I. K. Acheampong, with an austere policy of self-reliance. Its most well-known policy has been 'Operation Feed Yourself'.

GUINEA

Guinea has been a revolutionary state since its independence in 1958, with no interest in developing its tourism potential. It remains a fascinating country—physically and politically—and those persistent enough to obtain visitors' permits will find a country proud of its indigenous culture and determined to move forward on its own lines. Its political thought for over a quarter of a century has been dominated by its President, Sekou Toure, who has described his policies as 'Marxism dressed in African clothes'.

THE LAND AND THE PEOPLE

A beautiful and hilly land, Guinea supplies water to much of West Africa through the rivers which rise there. The Niger begins its long journey (first north, then east and finally south) in Guinea's southern highlands.

The coastal plain is made up of mangrove swamps, but a short distance inland from Conakry are the Fouta Djallon hills, rolling on in several distinct ranges and plateaux over the whole of western Guinea. Rivers, streams and waterfalls water

C. HENNEGHIEN

Guinean dancers

GUINEA | 250 mls

Senegal

Guinea Bissau

Mali

316

Boke · Siguiri

Dabola · Kankan

Mamou

Kindia

CONAKRY

Sierra Leone

Beyla

Atlantic

Ivory Coast

Liberia

149

the trenched valleys that are used for fruit plantations. In the north east, savannah plains of the Sahelian region stretch into Mali.

To the south are mountains, known as the Guinea Highlands, producing coffee, once an important export.

The people of lower Guinea are mainly Susu, while those of the east belong to the Tenda group. Fulani pastoralists and Malinke traders are spread throughout central Guinea. The southern forest region is the home of the Kissi and related peoples.

The Government encourages Guineans to learn all the languages of the country. There is no one dominant people, culture or language.

Guinea's rich wildlife includes many species of birds, insects and butterflies as well as monkeys, gazelle, wild boar, hippo, elephant and leopard. There are no national parks.

GENERAL INFORMATION

Area: 245,857 sq. km.
Population: 5 million.
Altitude: Sea level to 1,515m.
Capital: Conakry.
Head of State: President Ahmed Sekou Toure.
Government: A seven-member political Bureau handles important policy decisions. Beneath this is the Government and the Central Committee of the sole party, the PDG (Guinea Democratic Party).
Date of independence: 2 October 1958.
Languages: French, Susu, Malinke and other local languages.
Religions: Islam (c. 65%), traditional and Christianity.
Currency: The syli, divided into 100 cauris. £1 = 38 sylis. $1 = 22 sylis.
Weights and measures: Metric.
Time: GMT.
Electricity: 220V.

HOW TO GET THERE

By air: UTA and Air Afrique serve Conakry from Paris and African capitals, several times a week. Other airlines operating regular flights are Air Guinee, Air Mali, Interflug and Sabena. Flying is the practical method of entry from Senegal. Gbessia airport is 15km from the town centre, and only taxis provide transport into town.

By sea: Various cargo ships with passenger accommodation call at Conakry. The principal lines are Lloyd Triestino, Slosna Plovba (Yugoslavia) and Polish Ocean Lines.

By road: If you are allowed to enter overland you will find that the roads in Guinea generally are in a very poor condition, and the same applies to those connecting with neighbouring countries. From Ganta at the Liberian frontier the road is tortuous and rough as far as Kankan. The tracks from Bandu and Falaba in Sierra Leone are little used. There is a ferry at Kambia (north west Sierra Leone) connecting with a more passable road direct to Conakry.

The road from Mali to Siguiri and Kankan is in a terrible condition, but from Kankan on to Conakry it is quite reasonable. Buses occasionally operate from Tambacounda (Senegal) and Bamako (Mali).

Visas and health regulations

Some recent visitors have fallen foul of a regulation limiting their trip to flying into Conakry and flying out again, without being able to travel outside the city. Other visitors have reported little trouble in travelling freely, once they had obtained a visa and entered the country. Getting a visa is a difficult procedure, partly because of a fear of conspiracies from abroad and partly because of the small number of Guinean diplomatic missions abroad.

Valid international certificates of vaccination against smallpox, yellow fever and cholera are essential.

Dutiable goods
Personal belongings are admitted free of duty but must be declared. 400 cigarettes and two bottles of spirits may be taken into Guinea duty-free. If you take a camera note that prior permission must be obtained from the Ministry of Information and Tourism before you can take any photographs.

Currency regulations
The import or export of Guinea currency is strictly forbidden. Foreign currency can be freely taken in or out, but must be declared.

The black market rate for foreign currency gives as much as five times the amount of sylis as the official rate, but penalties for illicit currency transactions have recently been stepped up.

CLIMATE
The climate is tropical with a long dry season and a rainy season which varies in length according to the altitude and location. In general the dry season lasts from November to May and the rains continue intermittently from June to October. Conakry has a very high rainfall in the summer months. Inland the rain is less persistent. The best time to visit is from November to April.

Health precautions: A prophylactic against malaria should be taken before, during and after your visit. The tap water in Conakry is drinkable, but it is advisable to drink filtered or boiled water.

ACCOMMODATION, FOOD
Conakry has a number of hotels catering for different tastes. In general they are cheaper than in neighbouring countries. Kankan also has a few hotels. Elsewhere there are small rest houses.

Restaurants generally serve Guinean dishes, including jollof rice, stuffed chicken with groundnuts and fish dishes. The staples are cassava, yams and maize. Guineans are partial to a very hot maize soup, served out of calabashes.

TRANSPORT
Air: Air Guinee operates regular flights from Conakry to Boke, Labe, Kankan, Kissidougou, Macenta, Nzerekore and Siguiri.
Rail: A railway connects Conakry and Kankan with occasional passenger trains.
Road: The road network is little used and in poor condition. The main Conakry to Kankan road is the only major thoroughfare in a reasonable state of repair. Many minor roads have become overgrown with bush and forest.

There are buses and taxis within Conakry and to a lesser extent the whole country. Taxis are very cheap and buses even more so. Traffic drives on the right.

BANKS
The main banks in Conakry are the *Banque Centrale* and the *Banque Guineene du Commerce Exterieur.*
Business hours: Banks: 0800-1230, Monday to Saturday. Shops and offices open at variable hours.

PUBLIC HOLIDAYS
Both Christian and Muslim holidays are observed. Plus:— 1 January; Labour Day, 1 May; 14 May; 15 August; Independence Day, 2 October; Army Day, 1 November; 22 November.

CONAKRY
Founded on Tumbo island in 1889, Conakry is named after a Susu settlement on the island. Extensive suburbs have grown up on the mainland at Kaloum, linked to Conakry by causeway.

The island is the centre of administration and commerce, and is the site of the harbour and the railway station. It is laid out in straight streets and avenues. The large Roman Catholic cathedral dates from 1930. On the mainland side is the city's main market. There is a fine view of the outer islands from the Blvd. des Iles de Los. On the mainland are the People's Palace (the National Assembly) and the smart residential area, with villas and schools. One suburb, Camayenne, has a botanic garden. In Landreah is the 28 September Stadium, the scene of political rallies, cultural festivals and sports events.

The residential area dates from colonial days and still stands in stark contrast to the huddled houses in the poorer parts of the city.

Hotels
Hotel Camayenne, B.P. 578, tel: 611.39, by the sea, 4km from town centre and 11km from the airport, 120 rooms.
Hotel de France B.P. 287, tel: 434.91, by the sea but near the town centre, 15km from the airport, 80 rooms.
Hotel Gbessia, B.P. 743, tel: 611.45, at the airport, 15km from the town centre, 60 rooms.

Entertainments
Austerity has made Guineans inventive and they spend little on Western-style entertainment, preferring to gather in the streets in the evening to dance, sing and play traditional musical instruments or home-made guitars. Conakry is a dynamic centre of music, and the singing of the Kindia people is particularly beautiful. Locally produced records are very cheap.

There are also nightclubs, including that at the **Gbessia Hotel** and the **Eldorado.** Dancing regularly at the **Jardin de Guinee, La Paillotte** and **La Miniere**. There are several cinemas.

There are one or two beaches on the mainland and on the Los Islands but one should not venture out of one's depth as the currents can be strong.

Shopping and markets
Conakry is not a place to buy imported goods. The few department stores are often almost empty of goods. The local markets however flourish and display goods quite unlike those in neighbouring countries. Guinean dress is both distinctive and brightly coloured and can be cheaply tailored for you on the spot. Look out for some unusual artifacts, wood carvings, leather rugs (in bold black and white designs), skins and metal jewellery.

Tourist information
Secretariat d'Etat de l'Information et du Tourisme, B.P. 617. *Office du Tourisme*, Sq. des Martyrs.

In the Ave. de la Republique are the offices of Air Guinee (B.P. 12, tel: 429.81), Air Afrique (B.P. 77, tel: 434.95) and UTA (B.P. 590, tel: 436.57).

INLAND
Guinea has some of the most beautiful scenery in West Africa, with much mountainous country like the Kakoulima range rising directly behind Conakry—a picturesque forest region reaching a height of 1,000m.

Further inland around **Kindia** the mountains have numerous streams and waterfalls, especially the Santa falls 22km east of the town. Travelling farther inland along the main road you reach **Mamou**, again an area of forest and waterfalls. The road north of Mamou leads to **Labe** in the Fouta Djallon range and eventually on to Tambacounda in Senegal. Labe was popular as a resort in colonial times, for its cooler, drier climate and fine scenery.

Guinea's second city, **Kankan**, is the main centre of Upper Guinea, built on the Milo tributary of the Niger river. There is a Presidential palace (with hippos in the grounds) and an attractive market enclosed by walls, selling everything from silver and gold to local medicine, from carpets to stools and calabashes. The Seer of Kankan is widely renowned for his prophetic prowess.

The dry savannah land around Kankan extends north east towards **Siguiri** and Bamako (Mali), but south of Dabola and Kankan the country is once again wooded and hilly, with beautiful valleys around Faranah and along the Sierra Leone border. This is where the Niger starts on its long journey east. The forest thickens as one approaches the southern town of Nzerekore, and the Nimba mountain range.

HISTORY

Inhabited by small groups of people since 'Iron Age' times, the area of modern Guinea came under the influence of the great empires of the southern Sahara, Ghana (700-1200 AD) and Mali (1100-1500 AD). Around 1400 the indigenous Susa people formed a new state in the Fouta Djallon hills, but this came to be dominated politically and commercially by the Fulani-Mandinka alliance that held sway over much of the region at the time. In the 18th century the 'Imamate' of Fouta Djallon was the source of the Fulani Muslim revival that swept throughout West Africa as far as Cameroon, reaching its peak in the mid-19th century.

An alliance of Mandinka states in Guinea in 1870 came under the control of a leader called Samory Toure, who proceeded to establish a large, if short-lived, empire, with a strong political, religious and military authority. He was dedicated to Islam and did much to destroy the corrupt practices of the traditional chiefly class. He founded a large number of schools. But he came into conflict with the spread of French colonial interests; he hoped to gain British support through Sierra Leone against the French but Britain merely bargained away his empire for French concessions elsewhere in Africa. Samory thus had to fight the French

alone and a fierce war broke out in 1891; he used modern warfaring techniques but he lost territory, moving his capital from Bisandugu, near Kankan, to Dabakala (Ivory Coast) on the edge of Ashanti territory. Finally Samory was encircled by the French and surrendered in 1898. The population of his empire had been reduced to a third of its original size and the land was devastated. Thereafter Guinea became a French West African colony.

France's constitutional referendum in 1958 offered all its overseas territories the choice of a gradual movement towards self-determination under the new constitution or immediate independence. Guinea voted for the latter and has ever since had a struggle to survive. France immediately withdrew all its aid and personnel and destroyed all files, equipment, machinery and communications, causing severe disruption.

The architect of present-day Guinea is Ahmed Sekou Toure, a former trade union leader who has followed principles of self-reliance and socialism in guiding his country through its tribulations, building up commercial institutions throughout the country, reducing the power of traditional chiefs in favour of local revolutionary committees, giving the country's women and youth an important say in national affairs, and vesting important decisions in the sole political party, the PDG.

President Sekou Toure's rule has been unbroken despite the exposure of successive plots to overthrow the regime, generally hatched by Guineans in exile. The nearest any of these came to succeeding was the Portuguese-backed seaborne invasion of Conakry in 1970. The Government subsequently instigated a large-scale purge of 'enemies of the revolution'.

Guinea has now undertaken a rapprochement with France, but relations with Ivory Coast and Senegal are very bad—hindering their communications.

GUINEA-BISSAU

Although only recently emerged from the horrors of war, Guinea-Bissau is a pleasant and friendly country to visit. Unfortunately there is only a handful of small hotels, and communications are very bad, but travellers based in Gambia or Senegal can sometimes arrange day trips to Bissau or the Bijagos islands.

THE LAND AND THE PEOPLE

The country is low-lying coastal plain broken up by numerous inlets. There are many islands. The surface area varies from 28,000sq km at high tide to 36,125sq km at low tide. Thick forest and mangrove swamp cover the area nearest the sea. Savannah woodland covers the inland areas.

The population is perhaps 800,000. The main ethnic groups are the Balante, Manjako, Fula, Mandinka, Pepel and Bijagos (out of a total of 15 groups). Some of these peoples also live over the Senegalese and Guinean borders, particularly the Fula and Mandinka who form the main Muslim presence in the country. Most of the other peoples practise traditional African religions, Christianity being limited to a small urban community.

The urban population is extremely small. The capital, Bissau, had a population of only 30,000 before the war. War-induced migration swelled the Bissau population to over 100,000, but since 1974 the PAIGC has been able to relocate some of these (often unemployed) city-dwellers in the countryside as part of its campaign to boost agricultural production. Bissau's present population is about 80,000.

Traditionally, the Muslim Fula and Mandinka had centralised political structures, while the non-Muslim groups, like the Balante (the largest group) tended to be more disparate 'stateless' societies based on age-grades and village lineage loyalties.

For 11 years, from 1963 to 1974, Guinea-Bissau (then an 'overseas province' of Portugal) was engulfed in war. Militants of the African Party for the Indepen-

dence of Guinea-Bissau and the Cape Verde Islands (PAIGC), the nationalist movement founded by Amilcar Cabral in 1956, fought an increasingly successful guerrilla war, liberating most of the countryside and driving Portugal's occupation army into isolated encampments and towns.

In the months following the April 1974 Lisbon coup, the Portuguese authorities finally decided to cut their losses and end the conflict.

By mid-September of that year, they had recognised Guinea-Bissau's independence and withdrawn their last troops.

Since then, the PAIGC regime has had to tackle huge social and economic problems. Upwards of 100,000 refugees, who had fled from the fighting into neighbouring Senegal and Guinea-Conakry, have had to be resettled. Pre-war production levels have still to be attained in the war-ravaged agricultural sector. Mines are still being cleared from roads. And woodlands, potentially rich timber sources which were hard hit by Portuguese bombing and tree-clearing operations, have to be reconstituted. Guinea-Bissau is now in a period of national reconstruction.

Guinea-Bissau is one of the poorest countries in Africa—the Portuguese, who first arrived in the 1450s, having done virtually nothing to develop it. There is almost no industry, there is as yet no mining sector and the import bill is up to six times greater than export earnings (which come mainly from peanuts).

There are plans for the eventual unification of Guinea-Bissau with the Cape Verde Islands, some 500 km west of Dakar. The Cape Verdian population is descended primarily from slaves shipped from present-day Guinea-Bissau and Senegal and there is a historic sense of identity between the two countries.

GENERAL INFORMATION
Area: 36,125 sq km.
Population: 800,000.

Altitude: Coastal plain rising to 300 m near the Guinea-Conakry border.
Capital: Bissau. Population: 80,000.
Head of State: Luis Cabral.
Government: Civilian, administered by the African Party for the Independence of Guinea-Bissau and the Cape Verde Islands (PAIGC). Guinea-Bissau is a one-party state, so the key political decisions are made by the party, especially its leadership body, the 85-member Supreme Council. The legislature is the National People's Assembly.
Languages: Portuguese, Crioulo,

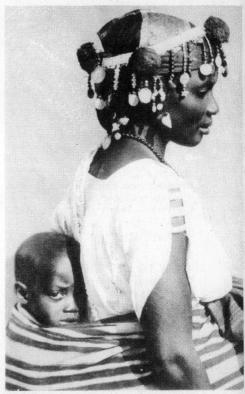

Biafada mother and child

Local carving

Balante, Fulani, etc.
Religions: Islam (30%), Roman Catholic (5%) and traditional beliefs.
Currency: Peso. £1=66.56 pesos. $1=32.95 pesos.
Time: GMT−1.

HOW TO GET THERE
The following airlines run scheduled flights to Bissau: TAP, Air Algerie, Aeroflot and TACV (Cape Verde Airline). Some tour operators in Gambia and Senegal run light aircraft into Bissau for one-day or two-day visits. These planes also fly to the Bijagos islands.

Visas and health regulations
Visas can be obtained on arrival or from representatives in Dakar (Senegal) or Lisbon. Certificates of vaccination against smallpox and yellow fever are required and cholera immunisation is recommended.

ACCOMMODATION, FOOD
Bissau has a couple of small hotels which provide clean, cheap and comfortable accommodation and excellent food.

TOURIST IMFORMATION
Centro de Informação e Turismo, CP 294, Bissau.

EMBASSIES
Argentina, China, Cuba, German Democratic Republic, Portugal and Sweden.

BISSAU
Whatever else they did, the Portuguese built nice towns in Africa and Bissau still has the echoes of fake colonial splendour amid its tree-lined avenues and large public buildings. It is a pleasant and easy town to walk around, with pavement cafes, a busy central market, some modern shops and a seaside promenade. Here and there are buildings dating from the earliest Portuguese presence hundreds of years ago. There is an excellent museum collection of early African carvings and artifacts (housed in the PAIGC headquarters).

OTHER TOWNS
The beaches and islands of Guinea-Bissau will probably be developed in years to come as the latest in a line of 'unspoilt' tourist paradises. As yet there are no facilities, except in the delightful town of Bolama and on the exquisitely beautiful island of Bubaque (and there only for the occasional visitor).

IVORY COAST

Unlike the arid lands fringing the Sahara, where the traveller can satisfy his curiosity about the past in an atmosphere where nothing very much has changed for hundreds of years, the Ivory Coast projects a vivid image of a new Africa thrusting forward into a future crammed with expectations.

A model of liberal capitalist development, President Houphouet-Boigny has led his country to achieve a rapid economic growth rate. This boom has made the country a bustling and hectic crossroads of informal commerce and trading between the coast and the dry, landlocked Sahel, as well as an increasingly modern and industrial State.

The country's main tourist asset is the chain of shining coastal lagoons. Here the Club Mediterrannee has its village, Assinie; and the State Hotel Corporation has another resort nearby at Assouinde. At either place you can lounge beside a sparkling swimming pool, with the Atlantic surf murmuring a few yards away, and sip *pastis*, before lunching on *fruits de mer* prepared by an imported French chef.

Among the lagoons lies the modern capital of Abidjan, with a number of excellent hotels, as well as French, Caribbean and Vietnamese restaurants, cinemas showing the latest French releases, and sophisticated night-clubs. Within 20 minutes drive of the city centre stretch the long sandy palm-fringed beaches, characteristic of West Africa, with beachside restaurants and swimming pools.

The Ivory Coast has more kilometres of tarmac road than anywhere in French-speaking West Africa, and the unsurfaced roads are usually reasonably good in the dry season. The State Hotels Corporation has a network of hotels across the country, complete with swimming pools. There is a choice of locally organised package tours to whisk you on a lightning tour of the country.

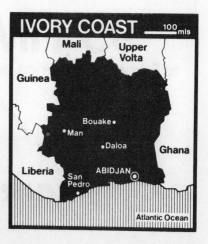

157

THE LAND AND THE PEOPLE

The Ivory Coast is a land of plains and plateaux. Along the north-west frontier with Guinea runs a ridge of uplands, part of the great chain that terminates in the Fouta Djallon; but the country is composed for the most part of flat plains covered in dense tropical forest.

Three rivers—the Sassandra, Bandama and Komoe—run directly north-south, and on their approach to the coast flow into a series of lagoons. Separated from the turbulent Atlantic Ocean by a narrow strip of land, the calm silky waters shelter the Ebrie people who build villages on stilts and glide about in slender dugout canoes.

Wrapped in the dim mystery of its dense tropical forests, the Ivory Coast remained in isolation from both the Arab and European civilisations until as late as the 15th century. Today Ivorians have not lost the sensitivity and secretiveness of a forest people. Despite the skyscrapers and brash modern villas of the capital, and their headlong dash into the consumer society, the Ivorian bourgeoisie still regularly return to their small villages, where ethnic ties remain strong, and where the man walking the narrow forest trail from the next village is a stranger, even though he is no longer an enemy.

President Houphouet-Boigny's most challenging task has been to draw together the many different ethnic groups living in this land of forests and savannah, and to forge them into a single nation.

Since the first Dioula tradesmen penetrated the north-eastern corner of the country 500 years ago to develop a major trading route from Bondoukou in the north to the Niger River, the country has been settled in successive waves. From the east came the brothers of today's Ghanaians.

Both the Agni—whose kingdom was centred in Agnibilekrou and Bondoukou—and President Houphouet-Boigny's Baoule—who crossed the Komoe River and settled in the centre of the country—are related to the Akan group.

The dense forests of the west are the home of the Krou, the Bete, the Wobe and the Dan, who also dwell across the border in Liberia. North, in the savannah lands, are hunters and cattle-raisers, the Senoufo. There is also an enclave of Malinke in the north-west, whose kingdom once extended far into Guinea and Mali.

The turning point in Ivory Coast's history came in the 1880s when the French planter, Verdier, sowed the seeds at Elima, near Grand Bassam, of the country's future agricultural revolution. His first plantation has been overtaken by miles of neat rows of pineapples, fresh green banana trees and the darker, coarser foliage of squat rows of oil palms. Between the Bandama River and the Ghana border there will soon be little of the land left to its natural green wilderness.

Most of the great Baoule cocoa and coffee plantations are in the centre of the country, around President Houphouet-Boigny's huge model farm at Yamoussoukro.

Abidjan scene

Further north, the land dries into savannah, but even here rice, cotton, sugar cane, kenaf and teak plantations are being developed.

The great forests only remain almost uninhabited west of the Bandama. Diseases—bilharzia, malaria and trypanosomiasis—discouraged settlement between the Sassandra and Bandama Rivers and this central strip remains the most sparsely populated region of the country. Further west still, towards Liberia, there is little in the way of agricultural development, but the vast forests are exploited by the timber industry—a major export earner—and a new port was recently opened at San Pedro. The great timber trucks that forge down Ivorian highways are a feature of the land. On the lagoons around Abidjan the huge logs are stocked and sorted.

Thousands of Mossi leave their homes in Upper Volta every year to come south in search of jobs; the Ivorians themselves are less hard working than the Voltaics from the arid north who have had to fight for food and water from their earliest days. There are also large colonies of Guineans, Malians and Ghanaians, and many clerks and artisans from Togo and Dahomey. It is not difficult to detect a degree of xenophobia against these immigrants and the Government controls the work they may perform.

The large French and Lebanese colonies are a striking feature. The European population is now estimated at four times its size before independence. Abidjan housewives will shop at the French butcher and baker and in Lebanese-owned supermarkets. French investment continues to grow and French technical assistants work in ministries and state corporations.

Even in the interior, if you visit the rolling hill country around Man or the dry savannah region along the border with Upper Volta, you will find a small French-run restaurant or a Lebanese hotel.

CULTURE

The Ivory Coast is traditionally one of the most important and prolific woodcarving centres of Africa. Its cultural heritage can be glimpsed in the rich storehouse of the Ifan museum in Abidjan. Similarities exist between the Baoule culture and ancient Egyptian legends: the ram, associated with heavens, is of great significance; the President's name—Boigny—signifies the ram.

Resort at Assinie

Baoule craftsmen are particularly gifted and well organised, and Baoule homes are often decorated with carved doors, splendidly carved furniture, and bas reliefs depicting sacrifices made to the gods. The most famous such legend concerns the Baoule Queen Pokou who, upon reaching the great Komoe River—symbolic of death because of disease endemic to the water—halted the tribe and sacrificed her child to the river, thus enabling her people to cross in safety.

The Senoufo, too, have a rich cultural tradition built around the Poro religion. The Poro initiation mask—a tall helmet with wide side panels—is easily distinguishable. There is also the twin-featured hieratic mask. The wonderfully peaceful 'mother of masks', intended to pacify quarrels and protect new-born babies, is often mounted on stilts and wrapped in robes. The most famous stilt masks come from Man where masks still play an important part in everyday life. They reflect the belief in the duality of body and soul; after death, the soul is reincarnated in the mask, giving it its own life.

The Dan people, who also live in the west, seek to protect themselves from the evil power of witch-doctors by forming secret societies, or animal brotherhoods named after beasts, such as the elephant, the leopard, the boar. Members of such societies claim they can be transformed into the animal and so escape the evil witch-doctors. The Dan mask is the only true human portrait mask in the country; most other masks usually portray a stylised creature with animal attributes. One theory is that the Dan mask, which often depicts an anguished or sorrowful expression, was taken by slaves to Rome where it inspired the original harlequin mask of the *Commedia dell' Arte* figure.

Genuine antique masks and sculptures are very difficult to buy. The Government's flourishing crafts industry provides most of the objects you will find on sale; but some of the modern carving is still remarkably true to the original, and should by no means be despised. A modern textile industry produces printed fabrics, while the more ancient tradition of weaving cloth in strips is encouraged.

As in Ghana, the Akan groups—the Baoule and the Agni—prized gold highly, and there is a fine tradition of goldsmiths. Like the Ashanti, the Baoule craftsmen decorated the copper-weights for weighing gold dust with intricate designs. They are known as *dia yabwe*. But there is no great tradition of jewellery craftsmen outside of the Baoule. The Government has created a national school to train Ivorian goldsmiths and silversmiths.

Pottery-making is centred in Katiola, where the renowned russet-coloured earthenware is made.

Music and dancing still occupy an important place in village life, and even in the suburbs of the capital groups of dancers perform regularly in the streets on Saturday nights.

WILDLIFE

Elephants still roam the dense forests around Grand Lahou and further north near Man. But the ivory trade which gave the country its name—it was also known for a time as the Cote des Dents—is now strictly controlled.

The Government is establishing a number of reserves to protect wildlife. So far only one is fully operational. Sited in the north-east, it is named after the Komoe River which flows through it. The park has buffalo, a variety of the antelope species, from the great horse antelope (bubale) to the small black antelope, the most common being the Buffon's kob. Lions are a rare sight. Many varieties of wild boar of the *phacochere* species roam the savannah lands. The most commonly sighted animals are dog-faced baboons (*cynocephali*) swinging through the tall grass; but many other types of monkey can also be seen.

Birdlife is plentiful but difficult to spot in the forests. Flights of migrating birds can often be seen near the coast.

Snakes are sacred to some ethnic groups, like the We, who keep them in their villages.

Hunting safaris may be organised through Abidjan travel agencies from January to May.

GENERAL INFORMATION

Area: 322,463 sq km.
Population: 6 million.
Altitude: Most of the country lies below 600 m rising to 1,200 m in the north-west.
Capital: Abidjan.
Head of State: President Felix Houphouet-Boigny.
Government: The President elected every five years by universal direct vote, is also Head of the Government and appoints the Council of Ministers. The National Assembly consists of 100 deputies all

belonging to the sole legal party—*Parti Democratique de la Cote d'Ivoire*.

Date of independence: 7 August 1960.

Language: French (official). The five main African language groups are those of: the Akan (including Agni and Baoule), Krou (in the west); the Lagoon peoples; and in the north Voltaic (including Senoufo) and Malinke (including Dioula and Dan).

Religions: Over 60% remain traditional; 24% are Muslim; 14% Christian (both Roman Catholic and Protestant).

Currency: CFA franc. £1 = 428 CFA francs. $1 = 249 CFA francs.

Time: GMT.

Electricity: 220/230V.

HOW TO GET THERE

By air: UTA and Air Afrique fly daily from Paris to Abidjan (the latter via Geneva and Rome) and there are regular services by Pan Am, KLM, Swissair, Middle East Airlines, Sabena, Alitalia, Egypt Air, Air Zaire; and from other countries of West Africa by Air Mali, Ghana Airways and Nigeria Airways.

The airport of Port Bouet lies 16 km from Abidjan. Taxis are readily available and some hotels provide free transport for their guests.

By road: The road from Kumasi in Ghana is good apart from the frontier region (a new coast road is planned) and there are roads (mostly good laterite, some tarred) from Upper Volta, Guinea and Liberia. The motorist needs a tryptique or a customs pass-sheet issed by the Automobile Club of the country of the vehicle's registration; insurance is compulsory; an international driving licence is advisable. Traffic drives on the right.

By rail: There is a railway from Upper Volta (see Transport below).

By sea: There are no regular passenger sailings but cargo liners ply to and from Europe with limited passenger accommodation.

Visas and health regulations: Nationals of France, Luxembourg and francophone African States require only a passport or national identity card. Nationals of the Federal Republic of Germany, UK, Denmark, Norway, Sweden, Finland, Tunisia, Italy and Nigeria require a passport and do not need a visa unless they wish to stay more than three months. All others must obtain a visa. All must have an onward or return ticket or repatriation guarantee.

All visitors must have valid certificates of vaccination against smallpox, yellow fever and cholera.

Dutiable goods: In addition to personal effects, each adult may bring in duty free: 200 cigarettes (or 400 gms of tobacco), 1 bottle of liquor, as well as a camera, movie camera, portable typewriter, binoculars, tape recorder, etc, proved to be more than six months old.

Currency regulations: There are no restrictions on foreign currency provided it is declared on arrival, nor on the importation of CFA francs but not more than 125,000 CFA francs per person may be taken outside the franc zone.

CLIMATE

The best season for a visit is October to May. There are two distinct climate regions: south of Bouake, the temperature remains much the same during the year (around 27°C) and rainfall is very high (1,500-2,000 mm per year). There are four seasons—the long dry season from December to April; long rains from May to July; a short dry season from August to September and short rains in October and November.

In the north the climate is more extreme (temperatures varying from 21°-35°C) and drier (rainfall averages 1,200mm) and there are only two seasons—rains from May to October and dry from November to April.

What to wear: Tropical lightweight clothes of cotton or linen are essential. Take plenty of shirts or dresses, a light raincoat in season and a hat for protection against the sun. Lightweight cardigan or wrap may be useful in the evening, especially in air-conditioned restaurants.

Health precautions: Malaria prophylactics are strongly advised. They should be taken for a fortnight before, during, and for a fortnight after the visit. Water is drinkable in Abidjan and Bouake but elsewhere it is advisable to drink the readily available bottled water.

Abidjan craftsman

ACCOMMODATION, FOOD

Hotel accommodation is excellent in Abidjan and elsewhere along the lagoons and there are fairly good hotels in most towns as well as small hotels and indeed restaurants in more remote areas. In Abidjan and resorts accommodation may be difficult to obtain and rooms should be reserved well in advance. Prices tend to be high.

Restaurants serve a wide variety of French, Italian, Caribbean, Lebanese, Vietnamese and Chinese food but prices are high. A number also serve local African dishes made of millet, yams, cassava or plantains, such as the national dish, *foutou*, basically plantains or yams accompanied by groundnut sauce or palm-seeds, or *atieke* made from cassava flour. There are several such reasonably priced restaurants in the Treichville area of Abidjan. *Bangui* (palm wine) or *tchapalo* (millet beer) are typical Ivorian drinks.

Tipping: Tipping is customary but to no set amount. Generally a service charge of 10-15% is added to restaurant bills.

TRANSPORT

Air: Air Ivoire operates regular flights from Abidjan to Bouake, Dalou, Man, Korhogo, Sassandra, San Pedro, Berebi and Tabou.

Road: The Ivory Coast has a good network of roads between all towns. There are about 15,000 km of good laterite and earth roads and 2,000 km of tarred surfaces. Filling stations are numerous (except in the north) and all towns of any size have at least one repair garage. Small private buses run throughout the country.

Rail: The railway passes from Abidjan to Bouake and Ferkessedougou and thence to Ouagadougou (Upper Volta). Four express trains with first and second class sleeping cars and dining-car run each week in both directions. Abidjan to Bouake takes 7½ ho urs. For information apply to *Compagnie des Wagons-Lits* (B.P. 699 Abidjan, tel: 32-20-66).

Car hire: Cars may be hired in Abidjan, Bouake, Daloa, Gagnoa, Man or Sassandra. Cars may be picked up at the airport.
Hertz (B.P. 4091, Abidjan, tel: 34-93-94)

also has offices in Ivoire, Parc, Relais and Grand Hotels. Other companies are **Air Service Ivorien,** airport lobby, Abidjan, tel: 36-80-14, and hotel reception desks, **Locauto, Auto Ivoire** and **Abidjan Location Auto,** all in Abidjan.

Note that for the same cost as hiring a car you can take a taxi for a few hours or even the whole day. The orange taxis with meters, however, work out more expensive, since (unusually for Africa) the meters work.

BANKS

The main commercial banks in Abidjan and throughout the country are the Banque Internationale pour le Commerce et l'Industrie de la Cote d'Ivoire, the Societe Ivoirienne de Banque, and the Societe Generale de Banques en Cote d'Ivoire. All of them have links with French banks.

Business hours: Banks: 0800-1130; 1430-1630 Monday to Friday. Government and commerce: 0800-1200; 1430-1700 Monday-Friday and 0800-1200 Saturday.
Shops: 0800-1200; 1600-1900 every day except Sunday.

PUBLIC HOLIDAYS

New Year's Day; Easter Monday; Labour Day; Ascension Day; Whit Monday; National Day, 7 August; Assumption of the Virgin Mary, 15 August; All Saints' Day, 1 November; Christmas Day. Variable dates: the Festival of Tabaski; the end of Ramadan.

In addition there are fetes such as the Carnival de Bouake in March; carnival de Bassam (in Abissa), November, and fete des Ignames (in Agni), December.

FOREIGN EMBASSIES

ABIDJAN. (Telephone numbers in brackets).
Algeria (31-23-40), **Belgium** (32-20-88), **Canada** (32-20-09), **Denmark** (32-33-63), **Ethiopia** (32-33-65), **Egypt** (31-10-86), **France** (22-62-62), **Gabon** (22-86-12), **West Germany** (32-47-27), **Ghana** (22-71-24), **Italy** (31-13-61), **Lebanon** (22-66-74), **Liberia** (22-23-59), **Mali** (32-31-47), **Mauritania** (35-60-68), **Morocco** (22-23-69), **Netherlands** (32-31-10), **Nigeria** (22-30-82), **Spain** (22-55-27), **Sweden** (22-22-34), **Switzerland** (32-17-21), **Tunisia** (22-50-53), **Upper Volta** (32-13-13), **UK** (22-66-15), **US** (32-25-81), **Zaire** (22-53-81), **Zambia** (22-76-78).

ABIDJAN

The site of the capital was originally chosen by French officers in 1898 as the junction for two railway lines—one running along the Atlantic coast, the other penetrating the interior towards the Niger River. But it took some 30 years for Abidjan to outgrow Grand Bassam, the region's most important trading centre, and Bingerville, the first seat of colonial government.

The Plateau, with its shining skyscrapers and bright lights, forms the city's commercial centre. On its western edge stands the Presidency surrounded by elaborate gardens and facing across the Baie du Banco with a fine view over the timber yards and the mist-shrouded forests and lagoons stretching as far as Grand Lahou. North-west of the city lies the exclusively African suburb of Adjame. Further out still, past the Banco National Park, the new town of Youpougon is rising. It is designed for a future population of 100,000.

East of the Plateau, across another arm of the lagoon, lies the largely residential suburb of Cocody, dominated by the Hotel Ivoire complex. Beyond the new Embassy Quarter lies the African Riviera project: a new garden city and tourist development with villas, apartment blocks, hotels and leisure facilities that will eventually stretch along the lagoon front as far as Bingerville.

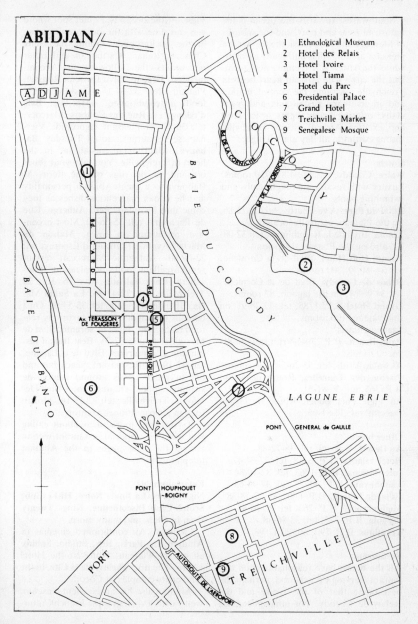

ABIDJAN

1 Ethnological Museum
2 Hotel des Relais
3 Hotel Ivoire
4 Hotel Tiama
5 Hotel du Parc
6 Presidential Palace
7 Grand Hotel
8 Treichville Market
9 Senegalese Mosque

ADJAME

BAIE DU COCODY

RUE DE LA CORNICHE

COCODY

BAIE DU BANCO

Bd CARDE

Bd DE LA REPUBLIQUE

Av. TERASSON DE FOUGERES

LAGUNE EBRIE

PONT GENERAL de GAULLE

PONT HOUPHOUET-BOIGNY

PORT

AUTOROUTE DE L'AEROPORT

TREICHVILLE

Southwards, towards the ocean is the industrial zone and port, and the suburbs of Marcory and Koumassi; the former is a pleasant area of villas and shady gardens, while the latter is a teeming new town. But the city's true African heart beats in Treichville. Around the central market and in its many restaurants and night clubs, offering bright lights, spicy food and exciting African music, Treichville throngs with life all day and all night.

Hotels

Ivoire, Cocody, tel: 34-94-81, 750 rooms. Luxury with restaurants, night clubs and swimming pools.

Hôtel du Parc, Ave Chardy, tel: 22-23-86, on the Plateau, centrally located.

Tiama, Blvd de la Republique, tel: 32-08-22, also on the Plateau, 145 rooms.

Forum Golf Hôtel, Blvd de la Corniche, tel: 34-94-80, 300 rooms.

Relais de Cocody, Blvd de la Corniche, tel: 34-96-61, on the lagoon, 82 rooms.

Grand Hôtel B.P. 1785, tel: 22-28-91, on the Plateau, 100 rooms.

Seafront hotels

Palm Beach, B.P.2704, Vridi, tel: 36-81-16, 60 rooms.

Akwaba, Vridi, tel: 35-26-58, 136 rooms.

Piscine des Tourelles, Route de Vridi, B.P. 365, tel: 36-81-51.

La Vigie Port Bouet, Route de Grand Bassam, tel: 36-81-05.

Other hotels

Au Desert, B.P. 89, tel: 35-72-88.

Hôtel Atlanta, B.P. 6318, tel: 22-34-47.

International, B.P. 1763, tel: 32-10-86.

Flamboyant, B.P. 30978, tel: 37-44-65.

Hôtel de France, B.P. 690, tel: 22-78-38.

Méditerranée, B.P. 263, tel: 22-20-88.

Pergola, B.P. 772, tel: 35-56-58.

Terminus, B.P. 790, tel: 32-11-98.

Restaurants

All the hotels have reasonably good restaurants serving French food, perhaps the best being that of the Ivoire and the Relais de Cocody. For atmosphere, **La**

Vigie on the ocean is a quiet spot where you can dine with the ocean murmuring in the background. Among the many Chinese, Italian, Caribbean and other restaurants the following are recommended: **Dragon**, Blvd Botreau Roussel, Plateau, tel: 32-34-15. Good Chinese food, air-conditioned, open late. **Baie d'Along**, 11, Rue des Colibris, Marcory, tel: 35-77-79. Pleasant lagoonside Vietnamese restaurant, closed Tuesday. **Babouya**, Mauritanian restaurant in the heart of Treichville. You take your shoes off and sit on rugs on the floor. M Babouya is a great Abidjan personality and he cooks marvellous dishes as they come into his mind. **Petit Auberge**, Rue de Pecheurs, tel: 35-66-00. Most expensive restaurant in town. **Maison du Maroc**, Avenue Franchet d'Esperey, tel: 22-69-60. Authentic Moroccan restaurant, excellent food and pleasant atmosphere. **Chez Valentin**, Ave 16, Rue 23 Treichville, tel: 32-47-16. **La Santa Maria**, Blvd de Marseille, tel: 35-54-66. On a boat in the lagoon, most luxurious seafood restaurant. **Pizza di Sorento**, Blvd de Marseille, tel: 35-57-75. Best Italian restaurant. **L'Aquarium**, Blvd de la Lagune, tel: 32-19-95. Restaurant, snack bar and bar in green lawns around lagoonside swimming pool. **Attoungblan**, 4 Blvd Delafosse, Treichville, tel: 22-37-14. African food in air-conditioned comfort.

If you want more ideas about eating you will find a special restaurant section among the blue pages in the Abidjan telephone book.

Entertainments

Night clubs: **La Boule Noire, Hi-Fi Club, Scotch-Club Discotheque, King, Twenty One, In Club**, and many more.

Cinemas: Air-conditioned cinemas in Abidjan are **Paris, Rex, Studio, Sphinx** all on the Plateau; **Ivoire** at the Hotel Ivoire. Theatre: **Theatre de la Cite**, in the University complex at Cocody.

Abidjan also has an excellent museum, well worth a visit, as is the French Cultural Centre, Plateau. The centre presents films and plays, sometimes free, and has a reference and lending library.

Sports: Riding at L'Eperon on the road to Bingerville; Saint Hubert: in Banco National Park, on Route du Banco. Sailing at Marina, Hotel Ivoire. Tennis at Hotel Ivoire, Aquarium on Blvd de la Lagune Seamen's Club in the port, and many of the hotels listed above. Golf at Hotel Ivoire course, in the Riviera. Swimming: inside Abidjan the best pools are at the Ivoire and the Aquarium, on the Blvd de la Lagune. On the coast, there are pools at Palm beach, le Cabanon, Les Tourelles, La Taverne Bassamoise (Grand Bassam) and Atlantic Hotel (Grand Bassam). All along this part of the coast there is a dangerous undertow and strong surf; all but the strongest swimmers are well advised not to venture further than knee-level. Water-skiing, ice-skating, and bowling at Hotel Ivoire.

Fishing may be enjoyed along the shores of the lagoons where there are red carp weighing more than 100 kg, barracuda, mullet and sole. Trips out to sea may also be organised through any travel agency to find sharks, swordfish, dolphin, bonito, marlin.

Shopping and markets
The Treichville market is highly disorganised, abundant and fun; but you will need to do some hard bargaining to get prices down to reasonable levels. On the second floor of the market building is a huge fabrics market where you can buy wax prints, Ghanaian kente cloth, indigo fabric and woven cloth brought down from the interior. A fairly small section is devoted to sculpture; but there is a good selection of bead necklaces and basketware. The food market on the ground floor is colourful and exciting. But take great care of your handbag and money. Even your wristwatch can vanish right off your wrist.

At Adjame there is also a large food and cloth market, but less in the way of artifacts. The best market for these is on the Plateau, opposite the Hotel du Parc, and further into the Plateau the food market on Avenue Franchet d'Esperey.

Tourist information
Office National du Tourisme, 9 Ave Barthe, B.P. 1173, Abidjan, tel: 22-60-35. Syndicat d'Initiative, 8 Ave Lamblin, B.P. 1561, Abidjan, tel: 22-29-48. Ministere d'Etat Charge du Tourisme, Immeuble La Corniche, Plateau, B.P. 20 949, tel: 32-51-97. The Ministry publish a small tourist guide which gives useful addresses and telephone numbers, and a number of ideas for tourism into the interior.

Travel Agents: ICTA, 9 Ave Barthe, Plateau, tel: 22-26-75; Express Voyages, Ave Delafosse, Plateau, tel: 32-49-44; ETTA Voyages, Blvd de la Republique, Plateau, tel: 22-25-29; ATA, 6 Rue Gourgas, Plateau, tel: 22-82-82; Kuhn and Nagel, Ave Chardy, Plateau, tel: 22-39-51.

GRAND BASSAM

Half an hour's drive from Abidjan, eastwards along the coast, Grand Bassam, the first French headquarters, is now an attractive but almost ghost town. Today, the old town centre is a nostalgic ruin, although some of the magnificent ·old brick buildings are being restored, the life of the place is concentrated around the beach, where many Abidjannais rent beach huts, and where a number of restaurants have sprung up for the weekend clientele.

The Government-sponsored craft Centre, the Office Nationale de l'Art et de l'Artisanat (ONAA) is well worth a visit. You can see fabric being dyed and dye-stamped, and watch craftsmen carve wood statuettes and masks.

Hotels
Atlantic Hôtel. Small hotel on the beach,

with bar, restaurant and swimming pool.

Restaurants
La Taverne Bassamoise, tel: 30-10-62.
Beachside swimming pool, hotel bar and
one of the two best restaurants in Grand
Bassam. The other is at **La Paillotte**, tel:
30-10-76.

ASSOUINDE

Two and a half hours' drive from the
capital, Assouinde is the latest Government beach resort, built on a strip of land
between the lagoon and the ocean, near
the Club Méditerrannée at Assinie. The
resort is reached by boat and has been
built in imitation of an African village.
Thatched bungalows cluster around a
central courtyard with swimming pool,
sun-deck, bar, restaurant, night club and
shops. The hotel has 300 bedrooms. The
restaurant menu includes African dishes.

Assouinde has facilities for water-skiing, tennis, volley-ball, table tennis, pe-
tanque and riding. Visitors can also join
organised excursions in dugout canoes to
tour neighbouring lagoon villages and to
see folk-dancing.

TIEGBA

About an hour and a half's drive from
Abidjan westwards beyond Dabou, the
lake village of Tiegba is built high on stilts
and is being developed as a tourist attraction. At Dabou, on the way, are several
reasonable French-run restaurants. Jac-
queville, nearby, is another old town, and
the home of the Ivorian Democratic Party Secretary, M. Philippe Yace. The old
slave market still stands in the town
centre.

BINGERVILLE

The former capital—named after Louis
Binger, the first French governor of the
Ivory Coast—Bingerville is only 15km
from Abidjan. Set on a plateau overlooking the Ebric lagoon, it is a charming
town with many graceful old houses set in
shady gardens and a pleasant botanical
garden dating back to 1912. Bingerville is
today a centre of agricultural research
and of secondary education. The old
governor's palace set on the hill is now an
orphanage.

The Atelier d'Art is worth a visit.

BOUAKE

The second largest city in the Ivory
Coast, 380km from Abidjan, Bouake is a
thriving provincial town and centre of a
modern textile industry. Gonfreville, the
oldest textile concern, was established
here in 1919. The city is the seat of local
government for the Centre-East Department. The market is colourful and well
stocked. Long a centre for Dioula traders, there is a famous mosque, 6km from
the town centre. Also worth a trip is the
sacred forest of Foro-Foro 26km outside
Bouake

L'Harmattan, tel: 63-21-31. 115 rooms.
Luxury.
Hôtel le Provencal, B.P. 105, tel: 63-34-
59. 32 bedrooms.
Hôtel du Lac, 18 bedrooms, tel: 63-26-29.
Hôtel du Centre, 18 bedrooms, tel: 63-32-
78.
Hôtel de la Gare, tel: 63-20-16.
Tropic Hôtel, tel: 63-21-31.

YAMOUSSOUKRO

Home town of President Felix Houphouet-Boigny, Yamoussoukro has rapidly grown to become a model town, and
favourite weekend resort for Ivorians.
The President's residence is set behind a
lake filled with sacred caymans (of the
crocodile family) in shaded, wooded
grounds. But of far greater importance is
his model plantation, reputed to be the
largest in West Africa, upon which all the
country's main crops are grown—coffee,
cocoa, yams, market gardening of all
kinds, avocados and rubber trees, all are

carefully tended and grown according to experimental, new methods. The President has thus cultivated a living laboratory for the Ivorian agricultural revolution.

Yamoussoukro is also the headquarters of the ruling National Democratic Party. As you approach the town from Abidjan the square Party Headquarters building can be seen high on a hill. Further down the slope is the luxurious Hotel President with a swimming pool, bars and restaurants overlooking the valley and the town.

A short drive through the President's plantations takes you to the huge Kossou dam and hydro-electric station. The dam is the focal point of an agricultural development project along the Bandama River.

The Yamoussoukro market is held every Wednesday.

Hôtel President, 150 bedrooms, tel: 64-01-59.

La Résidence Mobil.

Môtel Agip, 12 air-conditioned rooms.

Môtel Esso, 8 air-conditioned rooms.

Môtel Shell, 7 air-conditioned rooms.

Môtel Relais

Môtel du Lac

FERKESSEDOUGOU

Directly north of Bouake, near the border with Upper Volta, Ferkessedougou is the centre of a number of new agricultural development projects, notably sugarcane and rice plantations. The market and mosque are both witness to the region's overwhelmingly Muslim population.

This is one of the rare towns in the north where petrol is always available.

Relais Senoufo, 9 air-conditioned bedrooms, restaurant.

KORHOGO

Capital of the north and main town of the Senoufo, the second largest ethnic group on the Ivory Coast. Set in savannah land,

Korhogo is also the centre of a great hunting district and there is good fishing in the river.

Hôtel du Mont-Korhogo, 22 rooms, B.P. 263. Tel: 66-01-04.

BONDOUKOU

One of the oldest cities in the country, it was most probably founded by Doula tradesmen in 1466 although according to legend a hunter, Lorho Bontougou, first settled there in 1043. The town grew in importance as the caravan trade increased with the Niger River north. After the introduction of cocoa by the French in 1914, it became a rich agricultural plantation region.

Bondoukou is at the heart of the Agni kingdom, whose current chief still holds ceremonies seated on a solid gold throne surrounded by gilded ceremonial objects and robes.

Hôtel du Mont Zanzan, state hotel of pleasant design overlooking town, B.P. 132. Tel: 14.

MAN

Nestling in a green hollow high in the mist-shrouded mountains, Man is probably the most attractive of all Ivorian towns. It is best to fly there; several types of package tours are available. This is the only part of the country where the unbroken plains rise into densely forested uplands and peaks, the most famous being the Dent, a jagged out-crop of rock. The people of the region, Guere and Bete, are forest people par excellence; they are particularly isolated and mistrustful of authority. The region was long an area of turbulent uprisings. Here the religions hold almost unchallenged sway. The masks of Man region are famous.

Hôtel des Cascades, 49 rooms, B.P. 485. Tel: 79-02-52.

Aside from the Cascades, there is a Catholic monastery hidden in the hills, and the Gouessesso village hotel.

Short trips nearby take in the famous waterfalls and the Mont Tonkoui (1,200m), the mountain caves, and the new liana bridge at Danane. The most impressive trip is to Gouessesso, 50km north of Man, where a copy of an authentic African village has been developed as an hotel with 100 beds. Craftsmen and villagers practise traditional arts such as weaving, pottery and forging. There is dancing and folk music. The hotel has a swimming pool, restaurant and bar.

GAGNOA

In hilly country, on the way to the Man mountains, Gagnoa is a pleasant country town.

Hôtel Le Fromager, B.P. 317. Tel: 77-20-37.

Le Cottage, B.P. 557. Tel: 77-21-73.

KOMOE NATIONAL PARK

Package tours will fly you up to the north and take you round the park by minibus, but it is not accessible in the rainy season. Otherwise you must drive. The best route is via Abengourou, across to Kakpin, south of the reserve, where there is a resthouse with six rooms but no restaurant. From Kakpin you drive into the park, along the Komoe River where most of the animals gather, northwards to Bawe. Hippo can generally be seen at the ford 45km south of Bawe. From Bawe it is a short drive eastwards to the resthouse at Ouango-Fitini, which has a restaurant. Or you can turn west and travel to Ferkessedougou and return via the main road to Bouake.

Those wishing to combine the park with a trip to the Agni country around Bondoukou can drive on from Ouango-Fitini to Bouna, which used to be the French garrison town for this part of West Africa. At Bouna there is a small resthouse with four air-conditioned bedrooms and a restaurant. The Bouna market, which takes place every five days, provides an opportunity to see the Lobi people, one of the proudest and most independent in the Ivory Coast. All along the road from Ouango-Fitini to Bouna are Lobi villages, small two-storeyed fortified houses built in the local sunbaked red earth.

HISTORY

In the past thousand years the area of modern Ivory Coast has been peopled as a result of two main historic trends: the expansion of the Sudanic trading empires (Ancient Ghana, Mali and Songhai) and the growth of the Akan states in the east (from their centre in modern Ghana).

Some important trading centres were established in the north and north-east in the 14th century. These included Djangbanaso, Tininguera and Kong, and were dominated by Dioula traders of Mandinka origin. In 1705 Sekou Watara, the Dioula ruler of Kong, overthrew the traditional dynasty of the Lassiri and founded the Muslim dynasty of Watara.

Portuguese and other merchants arrived on the coast in the 15th and 16th centuries but did not establish very extensive commerce, as the Akan forest peoples prevented direct contact between the Europeans and the Muslim traders of the north. The French presence on the coast was dominant after the 1830s. One by one the lagoon and forest states surrendered their sovereignty. The French conducted several military campaigns, concluding with the long war against Samory Toure's Mandinka empire in the 1890s.

French plantation agriculture was introduced in the 1880s. Forced labour was still used until its abolition in 1946. Felix Houphouet-Boigny fought for the interests of Ivorian farmers and became the natural leader of the country at independence. He had already served as a Minister in France itself and has acted as a bridge between outright colonialism and a type of independence in which the French still play a very large part.

KENYA

Kenya has wildlife in staggering diversity and profusion; endless scenery of majestic proportions, forests, deserts, mountains, lakes and an exquisite tropical coastline; a wealth of lively traditional cultures, and (to make tourism possible) an efficient network of roads, air services to resorts with hotels and restaurants to suit all tastes. With so many attractive assets it is hardly surprising that Kenya is by far the most-visited country in Black Africa.

Every type of holiday is possible in Kenya. The very simplest is a week or two on the coastal beaches, swimming, sunbathing, fishing and goggling on the reefs. It is more usual to take in at least one game park, with short excursions from Nairobi or Mombasa. A large number of tour operators and travel agents organise a variety of game park, coastal and other scenic combinations. But it is also quite possible to be your own tour operator, by hiring a vehicle or by taking local transport. The more adventurous trips to Lake Turkana and the far north have to be tackled this way (unless you cheat and fly there).

The game park trips require proper organisation, whether by a tour operator or in private groups. The wildlife does not just materialise for your benefit. You need to learn something about the animals' habits in each park from wardens and other experts, or else you waste considerable energy. Accommodation has to be booked, sometimes even in the camp sites. The preparation is always rewarding, for Kenya has almost the entire range of East African animals, birds, reptiles, fish and insects.

Big game hunting was banned in 1977 after a long campaign by conservation groups. The ban limits hunters to photographic safaris for which they need a licence.

Kenya uniquely combines the utterly

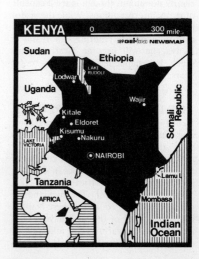

171

ancient with the utterly modern. Wherever you go in Kenya there are stark contrasts between the primeval world, where man had his earliest origins (and the same wildlife roamed free), and the impact of subsequent societies, whether in the subtle ways of nomadic herders, village agriculturalists and Arab traders, or the more obvious recent invasions of European planters, Asian shopkeepers, modern globe-trotting businessmen, and of tourists themselves. All these interacting elements have shaped and are shaping the direction in which Kenya is developing as a kind of microcosm world history.

Until very recently there were two distinct Kenyas: *Key*-nya for the whites, a land of make-believe, the world of Tarzan and white hunters, a country of luxury and romance amid the coffee plantations and the palm trees; and *Ken*-ya for blacks, a mix of traditional cultures that took on a new identity suddenly at independence, developing at breakneck speed, eager to be accepted in the modern world. Nowadays the divisions are much more complex. The *Key*-nya of the books is not quite dead, but it is scarcely relevant in the face of *Ken*-ya, which is clearly dominant, though in itself capable of many interpretations. While the visitor is unlikely to notice all the shades of cultural complexity during a short stay in Kenya, he will become aware of how much has happened so fast in recent years.

THE LAND AND THE PEOPLE

Kenya has a wide range of geographic and climatic conditions. Its 582,644 sq km area stretches from arid deserts in the north to the rolling savannah country of the southern plains; from ocean shores in the east to those of Africa's largest lake, Victoria, in the west. The highlands in the centre of the country, where Nairobi is situated, and of the west have a temperate climate, warm by day and cool, or even cold, by night.

The Great Rift Valley slices through the country from north to south, while right on the equator stands Mount Kenya with its snow-capped peaks. The semi-deserts of the north are populated by nomadic peoples like the Turkana, the Samburu and the Somali, with their herds of cattle, goats and camels. This area, occupying more than one-third of the country, has two major lakes, Turkana and Baringo, and contains only small towns and villages. Apart from the new Nairobi-Addis Ababa highway the region has few good roads.

The highlands are among the most productive areas of Africa. In addition to food grown for local consumption, the main crops—tea, coffee, maize, sisal and pyrethrum—are largely for export. The inhabitants are mainly Bantu-speaking, such as the Kikuyu, Kenya's largest tribe, who are well represented in the business community as well as dominant in politics.

Farther west, in the Rift Valley Province, are Kalenjin-speaking tribes such as the Kipsigi and the Nandi. Traditionally their economy was based upon cattle, but they are increasingly turning to agriculture. Also around the Rift Valley are the Masai. Although numerically not significant, their splendid physique, colourful dress and their attachment to their traditional way of life makes them one of the country's best-known tribes.

One of the largest groups in Kenya are the Nilotic Luo who live mainly on the shores of Lake Victoria. The Luo travel widely in search of paid employment and play a prominent role in the political and trade union life of the country. Also in the west are the Kisii and the Abaluhya who farm the rich but densely populated higher land near Lake Victoria.

Over to the east, between the highlands and the coast, the Kamba herd their cattle on the open plains and farm in the hills. They are famous for their carvings and their acrobatic dancing. Traditionally they are great travellers and fighters.

Early foreign explorers and traders—Arabs and Europeans—made use of the Kamba as guides, porters and soldiers.

The coastal region differs from the rest of Kenya in having been cosmopolitan for centuries. The dominant element is Islam, of which the most immediately visible aspects apparent to the visitor are the mosques and the black veils (bui-bui) of the women. Over the centuries Islamic traditions have fused with other African elements to produce a Swahili culture with its own distinctive language—KiSwahili, the lingua franca of East Africa.

On the northern coast are the seafaring Islamic Bajun of Lamu and the other islands. Close to Malindi are the Giriama, who have largely resisted alien cultures.

Apart from these well-defined regions, much of Kenya is savannah country, with vast, rolling, tree-dotted plains and tall grasses. This is many people's idea of the real Africa, and it is in these regions that one finds the large game parks, such as Tsavo, Amboseli and Meru.

CULTURE

Like many other African nations, Kenya has an ambivalent attitude towards its traditional culture, especially its external

Cheetah

manifestations. It is difficult to maintain the obligations of, say, the extended family in a money-based economy where advancement is supposed to be on merit and not according to kinship.

Even more of a problem is how to maintain traditional arts and crafts at a time when modern developments have made them less relevant in everyday life. Most dancing displays still preserve the traditional steps, movement and tunes, but the dress, regalia and often the instruments of the dancers are of foreign origin. A further complication is that Kenya's modernising elite wants visitors to see their country as a modern and progressive society; some feel that traditional dancing preserves the stereotype of 'primitive Africa'.

Visitors wishing to judge for themselves should make sure they are taken to a display in a coastal village or in one of the remoter areas, as well as seeing one of the more refined performances given in the hotels. For good measure they would be advised to visit one of the nightclubs where the ordinary people congregate and dance, to listen to the music and see the dancing of modern, urban Africa.

Other traditional art forms are woodcarving, particularly by the Kamba, and the shaping of soapstone by Kisii artists. At the coast more elaborate works—stools, chests and doors—are carved and inlaid with ivory and metals. In many parts of the country beads and sisal are strung and woven into decorations and ornaments.

While the literary traditions, especially of the KiSwahili, flourish in a modern form, Kenyans are also making an important contribution to poetry, novels and academic writing, especially history.

WILDLIFE

East Africa is the part of the world where the largest number of big mammals still roam over vast areas, and Kenya has a long experience of arranging for the game to be viewed in reasonable comfort with the least interference to the natural habitat.

Although lions have been killed in many areas because of their threat to livestock, they are still fairly common in the parks, and there is a good chance of seeing lions hunting their prey—usually antelope—even in the Nairobi National Park. Elephants are extremely common in suitable habitats both on the plains or in the hills. They are so numerous that there is a continuing debate as to whether or not they should be culled. You can sometimes see numbers of them if you drive along the main road from Nairobi to Mombasa.

Great herds of buffalo, considered by many to by the most dangerous of the large animals in Kenya, roam over the plains, and are also seen in the mountains. There are about a dozen common species of antelope as well as many of the rarer breeds, from the tiny and graceful dikdik to the massive eland. Other animals one can expect to see include zebra, wild dog, jackal, giraffe, hyenas, monkeys and baboons. Cheetah and leopard are less common, but a safari to the areas they are known to inhabit will normally prove rewarding.

Kenya also has a huge variety of birdlife. Lake Nakuru, where millions of flamingos assemble, is one of the world's wonders.

GENERAL INFORMATION
Area: 582,644 sq km.
Population: 12.9 million.
Altitude: Sea-level to over 1,300 m. on the inland plateau, rising to Mount Kenya (5,200 m.).
Capital: Nairobi.
Head of State: The President, Mzee Jomo Kenyatta.
Government: Republic within the Commonwealth with the President heading the Executive and a National Assembly forming the Legislature; elections held every four years; one-party State; the ruling party is the Kenya African National Union (KANU).
Date of Independence: 12 December 1963.
Languages: Swahili is the national language, English the official language of communication.
Religions: Protestant and Roman Catholic churches flourish; so do traditional religions among older people and nomads; Islam on the coast and the Somalia frontier; most Asians are Hindus.
Currency: Kenya shilling. £1 sterling=14.31 shillings. $1=8.37 shillings.
Time: GMT+3.
Electricity: 240V AC, 50 cycles.

HOW TO GET THERE
By air: Nairobi has a large international airport capable of taking Jumbo jets. There are regular daily services from Europe, Asia, America and other parts of Africa and connecting flights go on to Mombasa. Tour operators in many European countries and in America organise all-inclusive tours.

Kenya Airways, launched in 1977, now flies from London, Paris, Frankfurt, Zurich, Copenhagen, Cairo, Karachi, Bombay, Mauritius, Seychelles, Mogadishu and Addis Ababa. An airport tax of 20/- is payable on departure from Nairobi.

By sea: Occasional passenger ships come to Mombasa from Europe and America. A regular passenger service operates between Mombasa, the Seychelles and Bombay. Short-distance ships ply between Mombasa and Dar es Salaam and Zanzibar.

By road: Roads enter Kenya from Uganda, Tanzania and Ethiopia. A valid driving licence from the visitor's own country is acceptable for up to 90 days but it should be endorsed for Kenya at a local police station. Visitors bringing in vehicles with other than Ugandan or Tanzanian registration must, within seven days of arrival in Kenya, acquire an international circulation permit from the Licensing Officer, Nairobi. This will be issued free of-charge on production of (a) an international certificate of motor vehicles; (b) a fiscal permit of customs duty receipt; and (c) a certificate of insurance (third party). For further information, apply to the Registrar of Motor Vehicles, Gill House, Government Road, Nairobi (P.O. Box 30440), or from any District Commissioner's office.

Visas and health regulations

Visas are required by all visitors except British and Commonwealth citizens, nationals of Australia, Barbados, Botswana, Canada, Ceylon, Cyprus, Denmark, Eire, Ethiopia, Gambia, Fed. Rep. of Germany, Ghana, Guyana, India, Italy, Jamaica, Lesotho, Malawi, Malaysia, Maldive Is., Mauritius, New Zealand, Nigeria, Norway, W. Samoa, San Marino, Sierra Leone, Singapore, Spain, Swaziland, Sweden, Tanzania, Trinidad, Turkey, Uganda, Uruguay and Zambia. Admission is refused to residents of Rhodesia, regardless of nationality. A visitor's pass is required, obtainable free on arrival.

Smallpox vaccination is obligatory; a yellow fever vaccination certificate will be required on departure and cholera and yellow fever certificates for those travelling via infected areas.

Dutiable goods

Duty-free articles are: used personal effects, cameras, unexposed films, 250 kg of tobacco or the equivalent in cigarettes, and limited quantities of alcohol and perfume. Firearms and ammunition require a police permit before they are released from customs. Export permits, obtainable at shops or from the Game Department, are needed for game trophies or articles made from game skins, such as handbags.

Currency regulations

There is no restriction on imported foreign currency but it should be declared on arrival. A record must be kept of all foreign currency exchanged during a visit; this may be required on departure. No tourist may take out more than the amount of foreign currency brought in. It is illegal to take any Kenyan currency out of the country. There have been prosecutions following incidents at the airport, so make sure you are aware of current regulations.

Visitors should check on the interchangeability of the various East African notes; coins are not interchangeable.

CLIMATE

The coast is tropical and hot (21 C-32 C) but the humidity is relieved by monsoon winds from January to November. The hottest months are February-March and the coolest June-July. The best season for visitors is September-October. Rain can fall at any time but the wettest months are April, May and November. The lowland belt behind the coast is hot but dry.

The highlands, despite being on the equator, enjoy a temperate, invigorating climate. In Nairobi, for example, temperatures vary from 10 C-28 C. There are four seasons: January-March—a warm, sunny dry season; March-June—the long rains; June-September—cool, cloudy, dry season; October-December—the short rains. Near Lake Victoria the temperature is hotter (16 C-30 C) and rainfall can be high.

What to wear: On the coast—beach clothes, cool cottons and linens. Synthetic fabrics should be avoided. A woollen sweater may be useful in the early morning. An umbrella is more convenient than a raincoat.

In the highlands summer clothes are also worn all the year round. A warm jacket and light raincoat are advisable.

Dress is generally informal but some of the larger city hotels may require a suit and tie for evening wear.

Health precautions: Kenya has in general a very healthy climate. Malaria has been largely eradicated but it is wise to take prophylactic tablets. Tap water may be safely drunk in the main centres. Swimming is, of course, popular in the sea—the reef keeps out the sharks—but should be avoided in rivers and lakes because of bilharzia.

The East African Flying Doctor Services have introduced a special Tourist Membership which guarantees that any member injured or taken seriously ill while on safari in East Africa can call on the Flying Doctor for free air transport to a medical centre (Flying Doctors' Society headquarters, P.O. Box 30125, tel: 27281, Nairobi). There are public and private hospitals in Mombasa and Nairobi. Elsewhere health facilities are limited.

ACCOMMODATION AND FOOD

A full range of accommodation is available, from small 'up country' hotels to international-standard hotels. The popular resorts all have modern luxury hotels mostly with their own swimming pools. There are also smaller beachside hotels. Private houses and chalets (service included) can be rented. All the game parks have comfortable safari lodges as well as permanent tented camps. Privately owned camping sites have been established in some parts of the country.

Hotels are classified by the Ministry of Tourism and Wildlife according to elaborate guidelines. They are first divided into three different groups: town hotels, vacation hotels, lodges and country hotels. Within each category they are graded according to amenities, variety of facilities, etc. The rating award is subject to the fulfilment of severe requirements

covering technical equipment, comfort, services, sanitation and security. The awards are as follows: Class A☆, A, B☆, B, C, D, with the star denoting additional luxury or special comfort. In early 1977 approximate average rates were as follows: Class A over 200 shs. bed and breakfast; Class B 130 shs., Class C 100 shs., Class D 50 shs.

Kenya's national dishes appear on most hotel menus although for modern tastes meat has been added to the traditional grain and milk diet. The country's beef, chicken, lamb and pork are outstandingly good, as are the wide variety of tropical fruits: pawpaws, mangoes, avocados, bananas, oranges and grapefruit. Local trout, Nile perch and, on the coast, lobster, shrimps and Mombasa oysters are delicious.

The larger towns have restaurants serving continental and oriental dishes. Some of the more enterprising game park lodges serve gazelle, impala, eland, kudu and buffalo steaks marinaded in local liqueurs and berries and garnished with wild honey and cream. Of the local spirits, try Mount Kenya Liqueur, made to a secret formula from the country's finest coffee.

Tipping: Usually about 10% except when there is already a service charge, then an additional small tip can be made at the visitor's discretion.

LANGUAGES

There are three main African language groups: Bantu, Nilotic and Hamitic (from the Horn of Africa). Of the Bantu groups Swahili is the lingua franca, readily understood by most people in addition to their mother tongues of Kikuyu, Embu, Meru, Luhya, Kamba, Kisii and Nijikenda. The Nilotic peoples are divided into the highland groups on the Uganda border who speak Nandi and Kipsigi, and the river-lake group around the Kavirondo Gulf who speak Luo. The nomadic

Nilo-Hamitic groups of the central Kenya plains speak Masai, Samburu and Turkana. Their languages have borrowed widely from the Hamitic. The Hamitic peoples living in the north-west are mostly nomadic Somali.

Useful phrases in Swahili are:

Greeting	Jambo
Thank you	Asante
Please	Tafadhali
Yes	Ndiyo
No	Hapana
Goodbye	Kwa heri
How much?	Bei gani?
Excuse me	Samahani
Friend	Rafiki
Mister	Bwana
Madam	Bi
Child	Mtoto
I want	Ninataka
Where is the hotel?	Hoteli iko wapi?
Today	Leo
Tomorrow	Kesho

TRANSPORT

Air: Kenya Airways operates an extensive internal service, including scheduled flights to Mombasa, Malindi, Kisumu and all-inclusive tours to the game parks and the coast from Nairobi. There are private airlines (e.g. Caspair) operating light aircraft to small airstrips. Planes can also be chartered (**Air Kenya**, Box 30357, Nairobi; **Kenya Air Charters**, P.O. Box 30603, Nairobi; **Africair**, P.O. Box 45646, **Ticair**, P.O. Box 146, Malindi).

Rail: There are daily passenger trains between Nairobi and Mombasa and regular connections to Kisumu and through to Uganda; and along branch lines to Nyeri, Nanyuki and through Voi into Tanzania. Modern first- and second-class rolling stock provide comfortable accommodation convertible for night travel.

Road: All major roads are now tarred and many of the other murram surfaces have been improved, but vast areas of the north still have little means of communication. Care should be taken when leaving trunk roads as the surfaces of the lesser roads vary in quality, especially in the rainy season. Petrol stations are fairly frequent on the highways. There are regular, rather crowded bus services between towns and long-distance coaches go to Uganda and Tanzania.

Kenya is very well served by long-distance taxis (carrying seven passengers). The most efficient of these services are between Nairobi and Nakuru (**Rift Valley Peugeot Service**) and Nairobi and Mombasa (**Mombasa Peugeot Service**). Taxis and mini-buses are an easy method of travel on the coast.

Hitch-hiking is possible, but not recommended.

Car hire: Self-drive and chauffeur-driven cars may be hired from a number of travel agents in Nairobi, Mombasa and Malindi.

Tours and safaris

Many tour companies in Nairobi offer package arrangements for visits to the game parks and other attractions. Before booking it is important to know what the 'all-in' prices do *not* cover. Since early 1977 all package tours from Nairobi into the Tanzanian game parks (e.g. Serengeti and Ngorongoro) can only be undertaken by flying into Arusha, and not by bus or Land-Rover direct. Tanzanian tour operators are based in Arusha. Apart from regular photographic safaris the larger operators offer special tours for groups of 15 or more with common interest whether ornithology, mineralogy, trout fishing, archaeology or gambling.

BUSINESS HOURS

Banks: 0900-1300 (Saturday 0900-1100); **Shops:** 0830-1230 and 1400-1630; **Government offices:** 0830-1230 and 1400-1630; **Bar-licensing hours:** 1100-1400 and 1700-2300.

PUBLIC HOLIDAYS

New Year's Day; Good Friday; Easter Monday; Labour Day, 1 May; Madaraka (date of self-government), 1 June; Kenyatta Day, 20 October; Independence Day, 12 December; Christmas Day; Boxing Day. In addition Id-el-Fitr and Id-el-Azha are observed by Muslims.

Also of interest are the Mombasa Agricultural Show at the end of August, the Nairobi International Show in late September, the Malindi Sea Festival in November and the Kenya Safari Rally at Easter.

FOREIGN EMBASSIES
In Nairobi:

Australia, P.O. Box 30360; **Austria**, P.O. Box 30560; **Belgium**, P.O. Box 30461; **Canada**, P.O. Box 30481; **Denmark**, P.O. Box 40412; **Egypt**, P.O. Box 30285; **Ethiopia**, P.O. Box 45198; **France**, P.O. Box 41784; **Germany (F.R.)**, P.O. Box 30180; **Ghana**, P.O. Box 48534; **India**, P.O. Box 30074; **Italy**, P.O. Box 30107; **Japan**, P.O. Box 20202; **Lesotho**, P.O. Box 44096; **Liberia**, P.O. Box 30546; **Malawi**, P.O. Box 30453; **Netherlands**, P.O. Box 41537; **Nigeria**, P.O. Box 30516; **Norway**, P.O. Box 46363; **Pakistan**, P.O. Box 30045; **Rwanda**, P.O. Box 48759; **Somalia**, P.O. Box 30769; **Spain**, P.O. Box 45503; **Sri Lanka**, P.O. Box 49145; **Sudan**, P.O. Box 48784; **Swaziland**, P.O. Box 41887; **Sweden**, P.O. Box 30600; **Switzerland**, P.O. Box 20008; **U.K.**, P.O. Box 30465; **U.S.A.**, P.O. Box 30137; **Zaire**, P.O. Box 48106; **Zambia**, P.O. Box 48741;

NAIROBI

Nairobi—a Masai word meaning 'place of cool waters'—is the largest city in East and Central Africa and one of the most beautiful 'international' cities in the world. Rightly called the 'City of Flowers', its high altitude, healthy climate, fertile soil and sunshine all favour the growth of tropical and temperate flowers and plants. Graceful jacaranda trees and bright bougainvillea line the main streets.

An international commercial and communications centre, it is the only city in the world which can boast of a National Park, teeming with its original wildlife, just 8 km from the city centre. It is the headquarters of the United Nations Environment Programme secretariat. With its hotels and new conference centre and numerous direct, daily flights to and from all parts of the world Nairobi is a popular venue for major international meetings. It is a place to combine business with pleasure; the exhilarating climate is suitable for both.

Large areas of Nairobi are taken up by spacious parks and gardens. The city area covers 700 sq. km, most of it beautiful stretches of open countryside, forest areas and small cultivated farms. A drive through the outer suburbs like Langata, Karen and Limuru will show you fine houses set among exotic trees in large gardens with sweeping lawns and colourful flowerbeds. The main thoroughfares are crowded only for brief rush-hour periods. The traffic is orderly, the main shopping streets and places of interest are within walking distance of the central hotels and it is easy to find your way around. You can sit in open-air cafes and watch the city's unhurried cosmopolitan life.

The most favoured spot is The Thorn Tree at the New Stanley Hotel. At night you can wine, dine and dance in exotic and, if you choose, luxurious surroundings.

The visitor rarely sees the 'other side' of Nairobi, where there is poor housing, overcrowding, massive unemployment and occasional violence, but a short trip down River Road in daylight gives a flavour of the area where most of Nairobi's people live—in a constant struggle for survival.

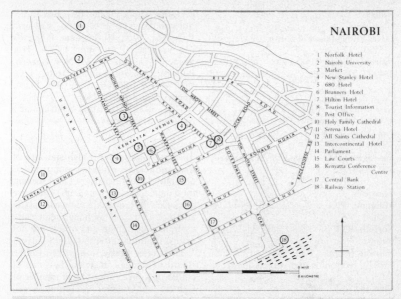

NAIROBI

1 Norfolk Hotel
2 Nairobi University
3 Market
4 New Stanley Hotel
5 680 Hotel
6 Brunners Hotel
7 Hilton Hotel
8 Tourist Information
9 Post Office
10 Holy Family Cathedral
11 Serena Hotel
12 All Saints Cathedral
13 Intercontinental Hotel
14 Parliament
15 Law Courts
16 Kenyatta Conference
                          Centre
17 Central Bank
18 Railway Station

Building a new house

179

Hotels

Class A ☆

Intercontinental, P.O. Box 30353, tel: 335550, 217 rooms;
Nairobi Hilton, P.O. Box 30624, tel: 234000, 335 rooms;

Class A

New Stanley, P.O. Box 40075, tel: 333233, 280 rooms;
Pan-Afric, P.O. Box 30486, tel: 335166, 160 rooms;
Six-Eighty, P.O. Box 43436, tel: 332680, 340 rooms;

Class B ☆

Milimani, P.O. Box 30715, tel: 29461, 75 rooms;
Norfolk, P.O. Box 40064, tel: 335422, 150 rooms;
Nairobi Serena, P.O. Box 46302, tel: 337979, 193 rooms (not yet classified).

Class B

Boulevard, P.O. Box 42831, tel: 27567, 70 rooms;
Ambassadeur, P.O. Box 30399, tel: 336803, 84 rooms;
Jacaranda, P.O. Box 14287, tel: 45272, 135 rooms;
Mayfair, P.O. Box 42680, 118 rooms;
New Avenue, P.O. Box 42382, tel: 28711, 64 rooms;

Class C

Chiromo, P.O. Box 44677. **College Inn**, P.O. Box 30471. **Brunners**, P.O. Box 40949. **Grosvenor**, P.O. Box 41038. **Fairview**, P.O. Box 40842. **Devon**, P.O. Box 41123. **New Continental**, P.O. Box 14301. **New Ainsworth**, P.O. Box 40469. **Safariland**, P.O. Box 48119. **Westview**, P.O. Box 14680. **Omar Khayyam**, P.O. Box 41998.

Class D

Plums, P.O. Box 40747. **Equator Inn**, P.O. Box 49279. **Impala**, P.O. Box 14144. **Embassy**, P.O. Box 47247. **Esperia**, P.O. Box 44658. **Azee House**, P.O. Box 45678. **Pigalle**, P.O. Box 10293. **Normandie**, P.O. Box 49985. **Gaylord**, P.O. Box 30208. **Hurlingham**, P.O. Box 43. **Fransae**, P.O. Box 43229. **Tree Shade**, P.O. Box 41793. **New Garden**, P.O. Box 46376. **Zambezi Motel**, P.O. Box 44018. **Hillcrest**, P.O. Box 14284. **Roma**, P.O. Box 21431.

There is a YMCA and YWCA and a campsite in City Park.

Restaurants
The best hotels offer a high standard of food and service, while the country hotels around Nairobi specialise in excellent food in beautiful surroundings. There are numerous restaurants and snack bars in and around the city, although some close early in the evening and others are not open on Saturday afternoons or Sundays.

The Coffee House, run by the Coffee Board of Kenya, offers the best cup of coffee in Kenya. There are a number of Chinese and Oriental restaurants as well as Italian and French-style restaurants. Some are expensive, while others are very reasonably priced for excellent food.

Entertainments
Cinemas: Kenya Cinema, 20th Century, Globe, Drive-in, Belle View (drive-in), Metropole, Cameo, Odeon, Embassy, Liberty, The Nairobi, Casino and Shan. Mainly 'B-quality' American, British and European films are shown. Some cinemas specialise in Indian films.

Theatre: The Donovan Maule Theatre (Parliament Road) has a resident professional repertory company with actors from all over the world. The Kenya National Theatre is used by a variety of groups for plays, dancing, music and other cultural activities.

National Museum and Snake Park: Situated together on Museum Hill, these two regular items on the Nairobi agenda are well worth a morning or afternoon. The Museum has a fascinating pre-history section and fine wildlife pictures. The Snake Park has 200 species of snakes.

Public Parks: Recommended are the Arboretum and the City Park.

Night-life: Most of the major hotels have dancing with live bands or discotheques each evening. The Casino has a restaurant, bars, floor shows, dancing and gaming rooms. There are a few nightclubs with an African flavour—but unfortunately some of the best from a few years back have degenerated, with not even good music to recommend them. Kenyan popular music has not flourished—the best bands still come from Zaire.

Short safaris: Tour operators organise visits to local villages, displays of Kenyan culture and traditional dancing. The best displays are those given by the Bomas of Kenya at their theatre near the Nairobi National Park.

Sport: Kenya has splendid sports facilities. The country has produced more Olympic medallists than any other African State. The Kenya Golf Union has 30 affiliated clubs. The Muthaiga Golf Club and the Royal Nairobi have resident professionals. Others include Karen Golf Club, Limuru Country Club, Railway Golf Club and Sigona Golf Club. A municipal golf range on the Langata Road hires clubs and balls as well as providing tuition.

Ngong, Langata and Karura forests provide outstanding horse rides through tea and coffee plantations or across open country, often close to giraffe and other game. Polo is played in Nairobi and elsewhere. Racing at Ngong Road provides an enjoyable day's outing, and should not be missed—even if you only go to see the cosmopolitan fashions of modern Kenya.

Trout-fishing in mountain streams and angling for black bass and tilapia on the lakes can all be arranged from a Nairobi

A 17-ft python at the Snake Park

base. Sailing and water-skiing are available on Nairobi dam, although the visitor might prefer the more open and warmer waters of the Indian Ocean. There are a number of swimming pools in Nairobi.

Most sports clubs accept visitors on a reciprocal or temporary membership basis.

Shopping

Foreign goods are expensive, but local produce and services are reasonably priced. Tailors make up suits and clothing items quickly. The popular *kanga* and other brightly coloured local cottons can be bought and made up into day, evening dresses, or shirts at reasonable prices.

Near to Biashara Street, originally the Indian Bazaar area, is the Municipal Market in Market Street. The ground floor has fruit, vegetables and flowers, while the upper gallery has stalls selling African curios. Buying everything in one place usually means a better discount. Always bargain. Goods can be made to order, and most shops will pack and despatch items to overseas addresses.

Three distinctive types of carvings are worth shopping for: those made locally are the work of the Kamba who live

181

Nairobi city skyline

between Nairobi and Tsavo Park; more expensive and original is the work of the Makonde from Mozambique; stone carving is a Kisii craft, usual items being bases and bowls with engraved flower and animal motifs. There are useful bowls and utensils carved in wood as well as traditional three-legged and four-legged stools, often inlaid with beadwork.

Glass beads, originally imported as a form of currency, are incorporated in jewellery and trinkets to make cheap but attractive, easy-to-carry gifts from Kenya. More difficult to carry is the decorated gourd, sometimes cut in half to form a ladle. Traditional pottery follows the shape of gourds and the genuine items are rough, but rarely attractive. They are shaped by hand without the use of a wheel. Bark cloth, made from tree bark, was a traditional form of dress but is mainly used now for decorative purposes such as table mats, often with a raffia design.

The many shapes and sizes and designs of baskets make them a popular and cheap item for visitors. There are also well-made handbags, coats, jackets and rugs made from animal and reptile skins. Skin items require export licences which should be obtained at the place of purchase. This is one of the ways animals are protected against poaching.

Gold, silver and other jewellery, mostly from India or the Middle East, are other suitable souvenirs. Two traditional imports are rugs from Persia or India, and superb carved Arab chests from Zanzibar.

Tourist information

The Visitors' Information Bureau in the city centre (tel: 23285) is open Monday to Friday 0830-1245 and 1400-1700. Saturday 0830-1230. The bureau has a wide range of guide books, including their Nairobi Handbook, pamphlets and maps, hotel lists and brochures.

NAIVASHA

Just an hour's drive from Nairobi on a scenically beautiful road, with particularly magnificent views from the top of the Limuru Escarpment, Lake Naivasha is rapidly becoming a recreational centre, with sailing, fishing, water-skiing, boats for hire, and bird-watching. More than 300 varieties of birds have been noted on the islands of this beautiful freshwater lake, including egrets, spoonbills, herons, fish eagles, crested grebes and cormorants.

Accommodation is available at the **Lake Naivasha Hotel**, the **Safariland Lodge** and at the **Naivasha Marina Club** (All Class B) in simple lodge-type style. Camping sites are at the Naivasha Marina, reached by taking the left turn towards the Lake Hotel on the Nairobi-Naivasha road—the Marina is a further two miles along this road. Club membership for visitors is available at the Marina for sporting facilities.

NYERI

At an altitude of 2,000m Nyeri is the capital of the rich agricultural Central Province. The town lies in the trough between Mount Kenya and the Aberdares, and provides an ideal centre for a holiday. A few kilometres from Nyeri are the famous game-viewing hotels Treetops and the Ark. Trips to Mount Kenya National Park and Aberdare National Park can be arranged from the Outspan Hotel.

Treetops, P.O. Box 24, tel: Nyeri 9, game outlook lodge, 37 rooms.

The Ark, P.O. Box 449, Nyeri, tel: Mweiga 17 & 25, game outlook lodge, 33 rooms.

Outspan Hotel, P.O. Box 24, tel: Nyeri 9, 42 rooms, swimming pool, riding, tennis. (Class B*.)

White Rhino Hotel, P.O. Box 30, tel: Nyeri 189, 24 rooms, golf, sports. (Class D.)

Naro Moru River Lodge, P.O. Box 18, tel: Naro Moru 23, 19 rooms, bunkhouses, camping facilities. Usual base for climbing Mount Kenya. Expeditions organised. (Class C.)

NANYUKI

Nanyuki is a busy farming centre at the foot of Mount Kenya and the starting-off point for excursions to the North Eastern Province. Nearby are the famous Mount Kenya Safari Club and Game Ranch, Mountain Lodge (similar to Treetops) and Secret Valley where black rhino, buffalo, sometimes elephant, and forest birds can be glimpsed from observation posts among the trees.

Mount Kenya Safari Club, P.O. Box 35, tel: Nanyuki 55, residential club, 61 rooms. Own game park, swimming pool, golf, tennis, riding, fishing, sports and sauna. (Class A*).

The Sportsman's Arms, P.O. Box 3, tel: Nanyuki 25, 32 rooms. Fishing. (Class C).

Secret Valley, P.O. Box 3, tel: Nanyuki 67, game outlook lodge, 21 rooms. Game and bird-watching.

THE RIFT VALLEY

Nakuru is in the Rift Valley, about 1160km west of Nairobi, with which it is connected by a first-class highway, and the main railway line. Lying in the heart of the old White Highlands, it still has the air of a frontier town. Many of the buildings along the main street are single-storeyed, with a covered walkway, and the side streets often peter out very suddenly into the open grasslands of the Rift Valley. Lake Nakuru National Park just outside the town is renowned for its flamingos (see National Park).

Above the town is the Menengai Crater, a fine example of an extinct volcano. The 'caldera' or cone is 11km across and although the road is steep you can drive to the top in a car. The wooded crater is 400m deep and descent is only for the adventurous. There are magnificent views of the Solai Valley, the town and the lake, and within the crater you can see steam jets and some wildlife, including giraffe and several kinds of buck.

Hotels
Stag's Head Hotel, P.O. Box 143, tel:

Nakuru 2516, 65 rooms. (Class B).
Midland Hotel, P.O. Box 257, tel:
Nakuru 2543, 51 rooms. (Class B).

WEST RIFT VALLEY

Kisumu

Kisumu is the commercial centre of the
expanding Nyanza province, an important grain-producing area. It is linked
with Nairobi by a tarmac highway, passing through Kericho, the important tea
centre. The section of the road through
the lovely rolling Kipsigi hills is being
resurfaced and is rough in places, but still
provides one of the most scenically beautiful drives in the country. The luxury **Tea
Hotel** at Kericho is a good place to break
your journey. The road from Kericho
passes through the highly cultivated Kipsigi countryside and then drops down into
the Luo country.

Kisumu stands on Lake Victoria, the
second largest freshwater lake in the
world. Lake steamers provide a comfortable twice-weekly service to and from the
various ports of Kisumu, Mwanza (Tanzania), Entebbe and Port Bell in Uganda.
From Kisumu you can also visit the
Olambwe Valley and Mount Elgon Game
Parks.

Hotels

New Kisumu Hotel, P.O. Box 1690, tel:
Kisumu 2520, 2652, 64 rooms. (Class C).
Lake View Hotel, P.O. Box 1216 (Class
C).
Embassy Lodge, P.O. Box 440, tel:
Kisumu 2909, 19 rooms. (Class D).

There is one good restaurant specialising in Indian dishes. The local dish of
lake fish (tilapia) and *ugali* can be had in
any local eating-house.

Eldoret

Eldoret lies at an altitude of over 3,000m
on the main road and rail route to Uganda. It is the centre of Uasin Gishu, a
farming district and an important educa-

tional centre. It has a thriving grain-
milling industry. The name of the **New
Wagon Wheel Hotel** (Class D) is one of
the few remaining signs that this was once
an area settled by Afrikaners from South
Africa. Only a few of them are left, most
having trekked south at the time of
independence. There is also the **Highlands Inn** (Class C).

Kitale

To the east of Mount Elgon in the rich
farmland of the Trans-Nzoia, Kitale is
linked by rail to Eldoret and the main
Nairobi-Kampala railway line, and by
roads leading to Kapenguria and the
Turkana region and into Uganda. The
district produces coffee, milk, butter,
pyrethrum, maize, wheat and some tea.
Kitale Hotel, P.O. Box 41, tel: Kitale 41,
34 rooms (Class C).

THE KENYA COAST

Mombasa is Kenya's second biggest city
and chief port. Combining ancient and
modern, this colourful island contains
two harbours and two towns. The old
harbour is still used by Arab dhows,
while the commercial harbour at Kilindini is one of the most highly mechanised
in Africa. The Old Town has many reminders of its stormy history, when
Mombasa was named by the Arabs the
'Island of War'. But the Old Town is now
an oasis of calm in an otherwise noisy and
hectic city. Its labyrinth of tiny streets
evokes some of the mystery and magic of
the Orient. This is the original Mombasa
with its numerous mosques and village
atmosphere, where children play freely
without danger from traffic. Modern
Mombasa town is a bustling, thriving
community of many different peoples and
a popular resort with good hotels and
splendid beaches and coral reefs nearby.

Many people regard Mombasa, rather
than Nairobi, as the most interesting and

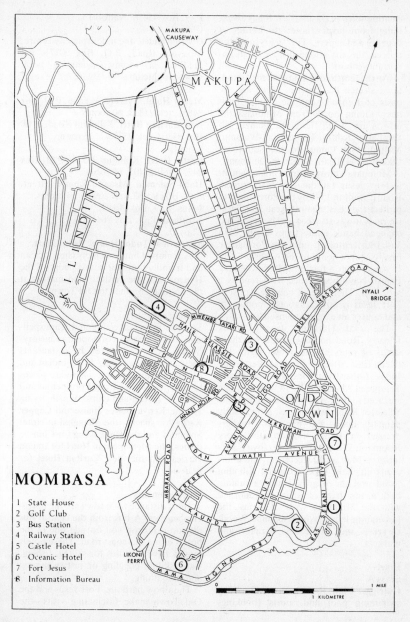

MOMBASA

1 State House
2 Golf Club
3 Bus Station
4 Railway Station
5 Castle Hotel
6 Oceanic Hotel
7 Fort Jesus
8 Information Bureau

exciting town in East Africa. It has everything from luxury hotels to hordes of beggars and lepers. The sleazy nightlife reflects the city's long history as an important seaport!

To the north and south of the island-town stretch the beaches which are the basis of Kenya's sunshine holiday business. Going north from Mombasa the resorts are Nyali, Bamburi, Shanzu, Kikambala, Kilifi, Turtle Bay-Watamu, Malindi and Lamu; to the south are Likoni, Tiwi, Diani Beach and Shimoni.

Mombasa's most prominent monument is Fort Jesus (at the end of Nkrumah Road). Built in 1593 by the Portuguese to protect the coast against Arab and Turkish raids it was attacked and besieged and changed hands many times in the 17th and 18th centuries, until the Portuguese finally abandoned it to the Arabs in 1729. It was used as a fort until 1875 when the British Navy bombarded it to repress a rebellion. Thereafter it became a prison. Fort Jesus is now a national monument and houses an excellent museum.

The Old Harbour down Mbarak Hinawy Road has been used for thousands of years by the dhows plying between East Africa and Arabia, Persia and India. Other sights include: the Hindu Temple at Mwagogo Road with its dome surfaced in pure gold and the one in Haile Selassie Road which has a brilliantly painted door showing two soldiers dressed in Indian fashion; the Ivory Room off Treasury Square (ivory auctions in May and December); the enormous elephant tusks spanning Kilindini Road and the nearby Uhuru Fountain built in the shape of Africa and adorned with the Mombasa Coat of Arms; the fascinating industry of Wakamba Woodcarvers; and numerous bazaars and markets.

Hotels

Class A

Outrigger Club, Ras Liwatoni, 42 rooms, swimming pool and sports (bookings P.O. Box 45456, Nairobi)

Class B*

Oceanic Hotel, one mile from city centre, Mbuyuni Road, P.O. Box 90371, tel: 311191, 84 rooms, swimming pool, sports, nightclub.

Class B

Manor Hotel, Nyerere Avenue, P.O. Box 84851, tel: 21822, 60 rooms.

New Carlton Hotel, Kilindini Road, P.O. Box 84804, tel: 23776/7, 25 rooms.

Class C

Castle Hotel, Kilindini Road, P.O. Box 84231, tel: 23403, 60 rooms.

Hotel Splendid, Msanifu Kombo Street, P.O. Box 90482, tel: 20967, 50 rooms.

Lotus, P.O. Box 90193.

Excellent, P.O. Box 98419.

Class D

Sportsview, Tudor House, Palm Court.

A cramped but extremely cheap, clean and friendly hotel for young people is the **Hydro**, near the central food market at the original entrance to Old Town.

Restaurants

Seafood is the speciality and is inexpensive. Reflecting its cosmopolitan history, Mombasa is well served by restaurants specialising in seafood, Arab, Indian and Middle Eastern dishes, There are places to suit most tastes from Continental and Chinese to fish-and-chips. Worth trying are the **Kenya Coffee House** and **Copper Kettle** for snacks, the **Shanghai** in Hotel Splendid and the **Hong Kong** for Chinese dishes, the **Metropolitan Hotel** for Indian curries and the **New Carlton Hotel** for seafood.

Entertainments

A short distance from town are the northern beaches. A bus from the central Bus Station can drop you outside one of the hotels along the coast road. These hotels mostly have facilities for sailing, fishing, water-skiing, goggling or just swimming and sunbathing.

The dhow harbour, Fort Jesus and the Old Town make fascinating visits—the latter for shopping as well as sightseeing.

The four cinemas tend to concentrate on westerns and other adventure movies when they are not showing Indian films.

The nightlife is mainly centred on the Kilindini Road, leading from the port. Apart from the numerous bars there are half a dozen lively night-clubs.

Shopping and markets

For craft goods and tailoring the Old Town is best. Silver and goldsmiths, tailors, carvers, cabinet-makers and many other have their shop-cum-workshops here. There is a covered municipal food market and an open-air market for general merchandise. Parallel to Jomo Kenyatta Avenue is Biashara Street, the best shopping area for *Kikori*, *Kanga*, *Kitenge* and other cloth, basketwork and local crafts—at prices lower than the craft stalls outside hotels.

Carvings and other curios can be bought in many of the shops or from pavement vendors. To quench your thirst there are itinerant sellers of coffee and of fresh coconut milk *(maduf)*.

Tourist information

The Information Centre is in Kilindini Road, close to the archway of tusks which span the road. Many of the tour operators, travel companies, airways and car-hire firms have their offices in the vicinity.

MALINDI AND THE NORTH COAST

Malindi is the site of one of the most ancient towns on the coast, 125 km north of Mombasa, to which it is linked by a good tarmac road. There is, however, a ferry crossing at Kilifi which can mean long delays. The resort area consists of a string of hotels spread along a sandy beach, adjacent to the old town which has interesting bazaar and market areas.

The Malindi and Watamu Marine National Parks are a unique form of environmental protection, offering the visitor a wonderful chance to see the colours of an undisturbed reef.

Driving along the road from Mombasa to Malindi the coastal scenery ranges through palm groves, citrus orchards, sisal and cotton plantations, sheep and cattle farms. All kinds of tropical fruits grow by the roadside such as pineapples, and bananas.

9-ft long black marlin caught off the Kenya coast

Beyond the Kilifi creek is the Arabuko-Sokoki forest where valuable timbers like ebony grow under natural conditions and birdlife flourishes.

The picturesque beach resorts north of Mombasa are **Nyali, Kenyatta Beach** (Bamburi). **Shanzu, Kikambala, Kilifi, Turtle Bay-Watamu.** The coral barrier makes the Turtle Bay-Watamu beaches safe for swimming and encloses some of the finest fishing areas in the Indian Ocean. Nearly all the hotels listed below

187

have facilities for fishing and other watersports.

Hotels

Nyali Beach Hotel, Nyali Estate, P.O. Box 90581, Mombasa, tel: 471551, 180 rooms, golf, watersports. (Class A).

Mombasa Beach Hotel, Nyali Estate, P.O. Box 90414 Mombasa, tel: Mombasa 471861, 100 rooms, water sports. (Class A).

Bahari Beach Hotel, P.O. Box 81443, Mombasa, tel: 471603, 92 rooms (Class A).

Reef Hotel, P.O. Box 82234, Mombasa, tel: 471771, 105 rooms (Class A).

Silver Beach, P.O. Box 81443, Mombasa,tel: 471471, 103 rooms (Class A).

Bamburi (Kenyatta Beach)

Kenya Beach, P.O. Box 80443, Mombasa, 68 rooms (Class A).

Sererin Sea Lodge, P.O. Box 82169, Mombasa, tel: 485215, 50 rooms (Class A).

Coral Beach, P.O. Box 81443, Mombasa, 42 rooms (Class B).

Whitesands, P.O. Box 90173, Mombasa, tel: 485252 (Class B).

Bamburi Beach, P.O. Box 83966, Mombasa (Class C).

Ocean View Beach, P.O. Box 81127, Mombasa (Class C).

Coraldene, P.O. Box 80940, Mombasa (Class D).

Shanzu

Dolphin, P.O. Box 81443, Mombasa, 108 rooms (Class A). Watersports centre.

Serena Beach, P.O. Box 90352, Mombasa, 121 rooms (Class A).

Casuarina Beach, P.O. Box 82792, Mombasa (Class C).

Kikambala

Whispering Palms, P.O. Box 81294, Mombasa. 100 rooms (Class B*).

Sun'n Sand Beach, P.O. Box 2, Kikambala, 37 rooms (Class D).

Kilifi

Mnarani Club, P.O. Box 14, Kilifi, tel: Kilifi 18, 50 rooms (Class B*).

Turtle Bay-Watamu

Turtle Bay Hotel, P.O. Box 457, Malindi, 75 rooms (Class B).

Watama Beach Hotel, P.O. Box 300, Malindi, tel: Malindi 101, 125 rooms. (Class B).

Seafarers, P.O. Box 274, Malindi (Class C).

Ocean Sports, P.O. Box 340, Malindi (Class D).

Malindi

Eden Roc Hotel, P.O. Box 350, Malindi, tel: Malindi 8, 150 rooms (Class B*).

Hotel Sindbad, P.O. Box 30, tel: Malindi 7, 63 rooms (Class B*).

Lawfords Hotel, P.O. Box 20, tel: Malindi 6, 136 rooms (Class C).

Blue Marlin Hotel, P.O. Box 54, tel: Malindi 4, 74 rooms (Class C).

Driftwood Beach Club, P.O. Box 63, Malindi (Class D).

Restaurants

All the hotels have à la carte restaurants and open air bars. Beach barbecues and dances are frequently held. Seafood is the speciality and the lobsters, prawns and fish you eat will certainly have been bought absolutely fresh only a few hours before. There is an abundance of fresh fruit and pineapples, pawpaws, bananas and mangoes will tempt you at every meal.

Entertainments

The beach and the Indian Ocean dominate Malindi's amusement attractions. There is excellent surfing, goggling, sailing, water-skiing and fishing. These and deep sea fishing can be arranged through the hotels and the modern boats are fully equipped with the necessary tackle and trained crews. Although there is fishing all the year round, the best game fishing is from November to March when catches of marlin, sailfish, tuna, barracuda and kingfish abound. The Malindi Sea Festival is held in November and the International Bill-Fish Competition takes place in late January.

Temporary membership is also available at the Malindi Golf Club which in addition to a nine-hole course offers tennis, squash, bowls, obstacle golf, water-skiing, sailing and horse riding. At night the hotels have dancing and beach barbecues in a friendly and informal atmosphere.

There are many interesting places to visit in and around Malindi. Near to Watamu is the Gedi National Park and an extremely well preserved ruined city, believed to have been founded in the 13th century. The first archaeological excavation was started in 1948 but the mystery of its desertion is unsolved. The excavated buildings include the Jamaa mosque, the palace pillar tombs and a number of large private residences. Excavations have unearthed blue and white porcelain bowls, brown and black flasks and beads from China, glass flasks from Persia, and cornelians from India, besides local cooking pots, eating bowls and utensils, all of which are on display at the site.

A few miles north of Malindi is the little coastal village of Mambrui where a huge ornate mosque towers above the little thatched houses.

LAMU

Away to the north is another ancient city, Lamu, which can only be reached by ferry. It is the island of the legendary Sindbad the Sailor. Normally the traveller arrives at the adjacent island of Manda by air from Mombasa, Malindi or Nairobi. At most times of the year it is accessible by road from Malindi via Garsen and Witu; there are taxis and mimibuses. Lamu is unique. By its very remoteness this island town has preserved

both physically and socially the Swahili culture that flowered in the 18th century. But it also quietly prospers now, in its functions as port, district capital and tourist resort. These functions have not yet required the motor car or disfigured the town's alleyways and impressive old mansions. Traditional crafts of building, wood carving, and boat construction persist as does the only means of transport, the small local dhow.

Lamu is also a centre of Islamic learning, with its twenty-two mosques (each with its own calls to prayer at regular intervals of the day and night) and with the continued festivals of *medrassa* music.

A look around Lamu Museum is an essential part of any visit. There are displays of Swahili costumes, furniture and some beautiful model dhows. The long contact with Arabia is very evident, and there is ancient pottery from India, the Persian Gulf and China.

The surrounding islands of Pate and Faza are accessible for those who have a few days to spare. Nearby, and taking only a few hours there and back, are the 16th century Takwa ruins on Manda island. These ruins are contemporary with Gedi and feature a mosque and a pillar tomb. To reach the islands dhow transport can be negotiated on the Lamu seafront. You can walk to the beaches beyond Shela, a distance of 2 km, or else walk through the cultivated area behind Lamu town for a view of the local vegetation and coconut palms.

Hotels
Peponi, on the beach at Shela, P.O. Box 24, Lamu, tel: 29, 17 rooms (Class B).
Petley's Inn, central seafront, Lamu, P.O. Box 4, tel: 48, 13 rooms (Class B).
Ras Kitau, isolated on beach at southern end of Manda island, P.O. Box 76, Lamu (and P.O. Box 40254, Nairobi, tel: 29467) 15 rooms (Class B).
Small hotels in Lamu town include **Mahrus** (P.O. Box 25), **Castle Lodge, Ka-**

dara's Lodging. Good cheap restaurant at **Libya Hotel**.

THE SOUTH COAST

South from Mombasa, across the Likoni ferry and accessible by an excellent new road are some of the most beautiful beaches of East Africa. A coral reef extends all the way down the coast, creating clear blue lagoons with safe bathing. Most of the beaches are fringed with trees.

The resorts on the south coast from Mombasa are at Likoni, Tiwi, Diani Beach and Shimoni.

Hotels
Likoni,
Shelly Beach Hotel, P.O. Box 96030, Mombasa, tel: Mombasa 451221, 70 rooms (Class B).
New Sea Breezes, on mainland near Likoni ferry, P.O. Box 96022, Mombasa (Class D).

Diani Beach
Leopard Beach, P.O. Box 34, Ukunda, tel: Mombasa 82235, 87 rooms (Class A*).
Leisure Lodge, P.O. Box 84383, Mombasa, tel: 82211, 119 rooms (Class A).
Robinson's Baobab, P.O. Box 84792, Mombasa, tel: 82281, 150 rooms (Class A).
Jadini Beach, P.O. Box 84616, Mombasa, tel: 82225, 117 rooms (Class B*).
Two Fishes, P.O. Box 8, Ukunda, 70 rooms (Class B).
Trade Winds, P.O. Box 8, Ukunda (Class C).

Shimoni
Pemba Channel Fishing Club (Class D).

NATIONAL PARKS, GAME RESERVES

Kenya has set aside certain areas for wildlife conservation. The present system of twenty main sanctuaries, totalling over 34,000 sq km, covers the entire geographic range of Africa and contains nearly all species of life native to Africa.

At the coast are three Marine Parks, protecting ancient coral gardens off the beaches at Malindi, Watamu and Shimoni, and acting as aquaria for the wealth of reef fish and underwater lifeforms.

The inland National Parks and Reserves are areas set aside for exclusive, or, occasionally, quasi-exclusive use by wild animals to roam at will and to lead a natural life unmolested by man. They often adjoin large areas where wild animals wander just as freely in places only sparsely populated by human beings. Most parks can be visited in your own vehicle and normally you can drive where you wish along a network of murram and dirt tracks during daylight hours. In most cases you may only get out of your car at appointed viewing places or at lodges. In certain parks, for example when visiting Treetops or The Ark in the Aberdare National Park, you must use the special transport provided. Most parks have a reasonable entrance fee.

Booking for all lodges should be made through a travel agent in Nairobi.

NAIROBI NATIONAL PARK

Only 8 km from the city centre Nairobi National Park is a mere 115 sq km in area, yet you can see more game there within two or three hours than in many of the larger parks. Behind it to the south lies the Ngong National Reserve and the animals roam between Park and Reserve at will. Thus the Park itself is a display of a much larger stock of wildlife. Thus there are occasional lions, leopards and cheetahs, as well as herds of giraffe and zebra.

All the roads in the park are accessible by ordinary saloon car, although you can hire Land-Rovers from touring companies. Among the advantages of a Land-

Rover are that you can see more easily into the long grass and the space is less confined when taking photographs.

Most of the park consists of open grassy plains, where you can see herds of buck, gazelle and zebra. There are wooded ravines and a small forest area where giraffe, monkeys and baboons can be found in large numbers and where rhino and buffalo can be seen. The elephant is the only large animal not found in Nairobi Park. There are numerous birds, from the large, ungainly ostrich and the unusual secretary bird to the tiny, brightly coloured sunbird and the African kingfisher. Altogether there are over 100 species of animals and 400 species of birds in the Park.

At the entrance to the Park is the famous Animal Orphanage which resembles a zoo with a large variety of animals.

AMBOSELI NATIONAL PARK
Only 40 km north of Mount Kilimanjaro this Park has the most photogenic backdrop of any wildlife sanctuary in Africa. The Park consists mainly of a dried lakebed, but Mount Kilimanjaro provides a subterranean run-off of fresh water to the springs and swamps at the park's centre.

The Masai used to control this game reserve but alternative water is being provided for their cattle so that the central 'Ol Tukai' water source is free for game viewing. There is an extremely delicate ecological balance in the Amboseli Park and visitors should not drive off the tracks or raise too much dust, which kills the grasses. There are herds of wildebeeste, zebra, buffalo, gazelle, impala and some lion, cheetah and leopard.

Accommodation
Amboseli Lodge, 54 rooms (Class B).
Amboseli Safari Camp, luxury tented accommodation.
Amboseli Serena Lodge, 50 rooms (Class A).

At Ol Tukai are self-service cottages and there are camp sites in the vicinity.

TSAVO NATIONAL PARK
Covering an area of 20,000 sq. km Tsavo is the biggest national park in the world. It offers many contrasts in scenery and contains the largest variety of game species to be found in Kenya. The park is divided into two parts (west and east) by the Nairobi-Mombasa road. The main entrances are on this road at Voi and Mtito Andei. There are more than 20,000 elephant, and numbers of black rhino, hippo (best seen at Mzima Springs), crocodile (at Lugard's Falls), lion, cheetah, leopard and different species of monkeys.

Below; Taita Hills Lodge
Right; Salt Lick Lodge in Tsavo National Park

Treetops' observation roof

Tsavo West

Kilaguni Lodge, 53 rooms, (Class B).
Ngulia Safari Lodge, 52 rooms (Class A).

There is a self-service lodge at Kitani and camping at Mtito Andei Gate.

Tsavo East

Voi Safari Lodge, 50 rooms (Class A).
Tsavo Tsafaris, tented camp with full service.

Self-service lodge at Aruba, and camping at Aruba and Voi Gate.

Near Park Boundaries

Hunters Lodge, 23 rooms, on Mombasa road north of Kibwezi (Class B).
Tsavo Inn, Mtito Andei, 32 rooms (Class B).
Taita Hills Lodge, 60 rooms (Class A*).
Salt Lick Lodge, 64 rooms (Class B).

MERU NATIONAL PARK

Situated to the north east of Mount Kenya some 110 km from Meru, it covers an area of 820 sq. km. Animals in this park include lion, buffalo, elephant, leopard and rhino. It is the only national park offering fishing facilities.

Accommodation
Mulika Lodge, 53 rooms (Class A).

There is a self-service lodge at Leopard Rock and a campsite at Bwatherongi River, 3 km from the Park headquarters.

MASAI—MARA GAME RESERVE

Covering an area of 1,800 sq. km it lies on the Kenya-Tanzania border and adjoins the Serengeti National Park in Tanzania. The wide variety of game includes rhino, buffalo, lion, elephant and antelope.

The reserve is particularly famous for the annual mass migration of zebra and wildebeeste.

Accommodation
Keekorok Lodge, one of the best in Kenya, 69 rooms (Class A).
Mara Serena Lodge, 50 rooms (Class A).
Governor's Camp, luxury tented accommodation.

There are several campsites, but with no facilities.

MARSABIT NATIONAL PARK AND SAMBURU GAME RESERVE

Marsabit Park lies in the remote northern part of Kenya and covers an area of 592 sq. km—a freak forest in the middle of desert, with huge elephant, lion, leopard, kudu, giraffe, hyena and aardwolf. The Game Reserves of Samburu, Isiolo and Shaba, north of Mount Kenya and more accessible than Marsabit, have thick riverine forest and dry bush landscapes. There are elephant, hippo, crocodile, Beisa oryx, ostrich, gerenuk and Grevy's zebra.

The modern and comfortable **Samburu Lodge** is situated on the Ewaso Ngiro River and has a swimming pool, 56 rooms (Class A). **Marsabit Lodge** serves the Marsabit National Park, 24 rooms (Class B). There is also camping which can be organised at the main gates.

ABERDARE NATIONAL PARK

Situated in the Aberdare Mountains, most of the park is moorland lying above 3,000 m. It has a special floral interest and is a sanctuary for elephant, buffalo, rhino and many other game animals. Accommodation is available at **Treetops** and **The Ark**, and there are campsites (see under NYERI).

MOUNT KENYA NATIONAL PARK

The highest mountain in Kenya is situated about 160 km north east of Nairobi. The mountain slopes are clothed with amazing tropical mountain vegetation, including giant lobelia and giant groundsel, and the rivers provide excellent sport for anglers. The view from the twin snow-capped peaks—Batian (5,199 m) and Nelion (5,188 m)—may extend as far as Kilimanjaro 300 km away. The park comprises the whole of Mount Kenya above 3,200 m and covers an area of 480 sq km. Several tracks enable cars and jeeps to reach a high altitude. Climbing on the two highest peaks should only be attempted by experienced climbers with proper equipment. But vast areas below the peaks are ideal for mountain walking and scrambling. Accommodation at **Mountain Lodge, Secret Valley Lodge** and **Naro Mora River Lodge**; also campsites well marked. (See under NYERI and NANYUKI).

LAKE NAKURU NATIONAL PARK

The Park is situated 160 km from Nairobi, along a good tarmac road which passes Lake Naivasha and Lake Elmenteita. Many tour operators organize daytrips, including a picnic lunch, or you can hire a private car and have meals in the town. The whole lake is about 40 sq. km in extent, but the Park area has been extended to cover 200 sq. km. Known as the 'home of two million flamingos',

Lake Nakuru has been described as the world's greatest bird spectacle. The lesser flamingos gather there in masses, 250,000 to a flock, and surround the lake in a shimmering band of pink.

HISTORY

The Stone Age: The Rift Valley which runs between Tanzania, Kenya and Ethiopia to the west of Nairobi was probably the cradle of all mankind. In 1972 Richard Leakey found a skull with large brain capacity, dated at 2.6 million years, at a site east of Lake Turkana.

The Growth of the Swahili Towns: (to AD1600): From Mogadishu (Somalia) to Sofala (Mozambique) a series of rival city-States grew up between the 10th and 15th centuries as an integral part of the Indian Ocean trading network, visited by ships from Arabia, Persia, India and even China.

By the 2nd century AD, when merchants from the Roman Empire frequented the coast, there were already trading villages where some Arabs had settled and inter-married with the local Africans, but it was not until the 9th and 10th centuries that major towns were built. All the towns have Chronicles, mostly written in KiSwahili (the Arabic word for coast) in Arabic script several hundreds of years ago. They record traditional stories about the foundation of the towns by Arabs and Persians who then mixed with the coastal Africans to form the Swahili ruling class.

They built houses of stone and mud and, of course, mosques for they brought Islam with them and lived in comparative luxury with silks and porcelain from the east. The towns were usually sited on islands like Mombasa, Lamu, Manda and Pate. Lamu's narrow streets still retain something of the atmosphere the town must then have had, and the vast acres of ruins at Gedi show the extent of its founders' wealth.

Meanwhile, on the mainland, Bantu

speaking peoples were entering Kenya from the south and Nilotic peoples came in from Sudan in the north. A unique group was the so-called 'Nilo-Hamites' (Masai, Samburu, Turkana and Kalenjin), who arrived in successive waves from the north. The coastal traders did not travel far inland but depended upon the people of the interior to bring them ivory, the main export item.

During the 15th century Mombasa took over from Kilwa (Tanzania) and Mogadishu as the most powerful city, so it was here that Vasco da Gama, the Portuguese explorer, came to find a pilot to guide him to India in 1498. The arrival of the Portuguese in the Indian Ocean disrupted established trade patterns and some of the Swahili towns were reduced to subsistence agriculture. Mombasa, however, did not finally succumb to Portuguese rule until 1589 when a Portuguese attack coincided with turmoil inland caused by the fierce Zimba who had stormed up from the Zambezi region to face their final defeat by the Segeju near Mombasa. The Portuguese took Mombasa and to defend their garrison they built Fort Jesus. Today the Fort is a comprehensive museum where relics of their rule are preserved.

The Middle Era (1600-1900): In addition to Portuguese threats from the sea, Kenya's coastal cities in the 16th and 17th centuries faced danger from the formidable Galla who overran southern Ethiopia and large areas of Somalia and north east Kenya. The people of the northern towns like Malindi abandoned their homes and fled to Tanzania or congregated in the safety of Mombasa. Others from the Shungwaya region (probably in southern Somalia) fled to the inhospitable Nyika territory behind Mombasa and established the Mijikenda ('nine tribes') community. The repercussions were also felt inland—here lived the Kamba and, beyond them, the Kikuyu cultivated the fertile slopes of Mount Kenya.

In the highlands of the far west the Kalenjin were being hard-pressed from the west by the Luo coming in to the lakeshore region from Uganda, and from the east by the fast-expanding Masai who were spreading during the 17th century from the lands of the related Turkana and Samburu far south into Tanzania. These were pastoral rather than agricultural people, moving their dwellings to follow the pasture. The Masai believed that at the Creation God had given all cattle to them and the *moran* (youth) had to prove their worth by capturing cattle belonging to anyone else.

The Portuguese were driven out of Mombasa in 1698 after a three-year siege by Arabs from Oman. For the next century the town enjoyed a resurgence of power under the Mazrui dynasty, ruling the coast from Malindi to Pemba Island. In 1837 it was taken over by the famous Seyyid Said, Sultan of Oman and Zanzibar and became an outpost of the flourishing Zanzibari trading system. The inland people were suspicious of traders' motives. The Kikuyu, for example, would only allow them to wait on their borders to buy ivory. The general indifference to the temptations of trade kept Kenya largely free of the slave trade.

The first 19th century European to enter Kenya—Joseph Thompson—accompanied an Arab caravan across Masailand in 1883-4 and thus mapped one of the last significant 'unknown' regions of Africa.

Colonialism and Independence (1895 to the present): Kenya did not at first attract foreign powers but was declared a British protectorate because it straddled the proposed railway route to Uganda. Only a few hundred of the Indian labourers brought in to work on the railway remained after their contracts expired but many traders followed the line inland and secured a monopoly of trade there.

In the early 20th century Europeans were attracted by Kenya's healthy climate and came either under their own steam or on Government-sponsored schemes. The main political struggle was for a time between the Indian and European residents, but the Europeans managed to get the upper hand by having 16,700 sq. miles of the highlands reserved for whites, where they became successful farmers producing most of the exports.

Kenyan Africans, in marked contrast with Ugandans, were not encouraged to grow cash crops and the colonial Government actively helped white settlers in the unpopular recruitment of contract workers who were paid only in kind.

Kenyans served against the Germans in Tanzania during the First World War and against the Italians in Somalia and the Japanese in Burma during the Second World War. The soldiers, returning with wider horizons, faced unemployment, rocketing prices and a shortage of land for the growing population in eroded African 'reserves'.

In 1946 Jomo Kenyatta, a highly-educated man who in London had been first President of the Pan-African Federation, returned after 15 years abroad and became leader of the Kenya African Union. Eventually Kikuyu land-hunger on the edge of the 'white' highlands erupted in the Mau Mau revolt (1953)—an expression of desperate fury rather than of a concerted plot—in which atrocities were commited on both sides. Yet, however unco-ordinated, it did break the power and nerve of those settlers who might have favoured Rhodesian-style white rule and it did persuade the British Government that Africans must be given more legitimate means of expression.

After brief experiments with multi-racial constitutions, Kenya in 1961 became African-ruled, led by Jomo Kenyatta who had been imprisoned by the authorities since the Mau Mau Emergency but who was respected as *Mzee* (the Elder) by all Africans. By his statements he soon allayed European and Asian fears and has led his country since independence in 1963 along a deliberately moderate path, encouraging foreign investment and links with the West.

Mount Kenya from Karatina, near Njori

196

LESOTHO

The rugged mountain kingdom of Lesotho is an island within the Republic of South Africa, on whom it is largely dependent for employment, trade and tourism. It is in many ways a traveller's delight with rugged mountains to be explored on horse or on foot, good trout-fishing, Bushman cave paintings and, everywhere, the colourful Basotho on their sturdy mountain ponies.

The Holiday Inn complex in the capital, Maseru, with its casino and other facilities, attracts many tourists from the Republic across the Caledon River.

Three South African rivers—the Orange, the Caledon and the Tugela—have their sources in Lesotho: a great irony, for although Lesotho has enough water and to spare, there is not sufficient cultivable land to sustain half its million people. Even with improved methods, less than a third of the total 30,344 sq. km. could be put to agriculture; and a third of that is being rapidly eroded. Nearly half the men and many of the women have therefore to leave as migrant workers to South Africa. Those

THE LAND AND THE PEOPLE

A note on nomenclature: the country is called Lesotho; the people are the Basotho; a single person is a Masotho; and the language is Sesotho.

Travel writers through the years have called Lesotho 'the Switzerland of Southern Africa'. However, the term is too glib: its mountain beauty is stark and uncompromisingly rugged, with few trees. From Thabana-Ntlenyana, the highest peak on the sub-continent, the Maluti limb of the Drakensberg (Dragon's Mountain) falls in dramatic steps to eroded foothills in the west, where two-thirds of the population live. Grey rock and unpeopled summits are the main features of the mountain terrain.

LESOTHO 0 — 60 miles

AFRICA

South Africa

Pitseng
MASERU Mokhotlong
Ntaotes
Mafeteng
Qacha's Nek
Quthing

136

who remain at home have to struggle to scratch a living from the depleted earth.

Basotho horsemen have a distinctive dress—grass-woven, conical hats and colourful blankets.

The Basotho have a strong literary tradition. With the help of a mission press at Morija they produced their own books at the end of the last century. They are writers of prose, poetry and drama, both in the vernacular and in English.

Since independence, the Lesotho National Development Corporation has established some home industries such as carpet- and tapestry-weaving and pottery.

GENERAL INFORMATION
Area: 30,344 sq. km.
Population: 1 million.
Altitude: The lowlands of the west average 1,600 m, rising to the highest mountain in the east at over 3,400 m.
Capital: Maseru.
Head of State: King Moshoeshoe II; Prime Minister: Chief Leabua Jonathan.
Government: Lesotho is a monarchy, but executive power lies with the Prime Minister and his Cabinet.
Date of independence: 4 October 1966.
Languages: English and Sesotho.
Religions: 70% of the population are Christian (over half Roman Catholic), and the rest retain their traditional beliefs.
Currency: South African Rand (R), divided into 100 cents. £1 = R1.49. $1 = R0.89.
Time: GMT + 2.

HOW TO GET THERE
By air: There are regular services three times a week from Johannesburg to Maseru, operated jointly by Lesotho National Airways and South African Airways.
By road: Several roads lead into the west and south of Lesotho from South Africa.

By rail: The South African railway system links up with the capital, Maseru.

Visas and health regulations
South African, UK, Commonwealth and US citizens can enter Lesotho with a valid passport and do not require a visa. Nationals of other countries should apply for a visa from a Lesotho or UK diplomatic mission abroad.

Since it is impossible to enter Lesotho without going through South Africa, one must conform to SA health regulations. At Lesotho entry points one must display a valid certificate of vaccination against smallpox.

Lesotho is a member of the South African Customs Union so that there are no extra customs formalities at its borders. Similarly there are no exchange controls.

CLIMATE
This is a land of extremes. In the summer (December-February) the temperature rises to 32°C in the lowlands (less in the mountains) and the rain can turn to hail. Most of the rain falls in short storms between October and April. No month is completely free of rain but the low total and uneven distribution make drought a common hazard.

In the winter (May-September) the temperature can drop to −7°C even in the lowlands, and below −18°C in the snow-capped mountains, with frost throughout the country.
What to wear: In summer light cotton clothes are needed during the day, but it can be chilly in the evening, and the essential raincoat. In winter plenty of warm woollen clothing is needed.

ACCOMMODATION AND FOOD
The Maseru Holiday Inn is of high international standard. There are several other hotels of varying quality, and

mountain lodges from which Lesotho's rugged scenery can be explored. New hotels have been built at Masionokang and Leribe.

TRANSPORT
Air: Considerable use is made of the airstrips at main centres for charter, tourist and mail flights.
Road: The system is rudimentary, most of the country being covered only by bridle paths, but the main road through the towns along the western and southern borders is tarred for over 100 km. of its length and a good scenic route leads into the mountains from Maseru.

BANKS
Standard Bank, Lesotho Bank, Barclays Bank International. Hours: 0830-1300 Monday to Friday; 0830-1100 Saturday.

PUBLIC HOLIDAYS
New Year's Day; Moshoeshoe Day Monday in mid-March; Good Friday; Easter Monday; King's Birthday 2 May; Ascension Day; Commonwealth Day 24 May; Family Day, Monday early July; National Tree Planting Day, Monday in early August; Independence Day 4 October; National Sports Day, Monday in early October; Christmas and Boxing Days.

FOREIGN EMBASSIES
Switzerland; UK (Box 521, Maseru) and USA.

MASERU
Despite its increasing population, Maseru still has the peaceful atmosphere of a village on the banks of the Caledon River, the frontier with South Africa.
Hotels
Holiday Inn, Box 868, tel: 2434, cable INNVITE, 238 rooms.

Lancers Inn, Box 30, tel: 2114.
Lakeside Hotel, Box 602, tel: 3646.
Stadium Hotel.

Entertainments
The **Royal Casino**, within the Holiday Inn complex, offers a comprehensive range of table games, including French and American roulette.

The **Holiday Inn** has a swimming pool. Visitors are allowed to use the bowling greens, tennis courts and golf course at the nearby **Maseru Country Club**. Horses may be hired at an hourly rate through the hotels. The **Basuto Hat**, on the edge of town, is the official shop of the Lesotho National Development Corporation. Pottery, basketware, rugs and blankets are on sale here.

Lesotho mountain village

Tourist information
The Government Information Office in the main street provides details of tours, places of interest, etc. The Holiday Inn also has an information counter.
Travel agencies: Lesotho Airways Corporation, P.O. Box 861, Maseru. **Maluti Treks and Travel**, P.O. Box 294, Maseru.

Excursions from Maseru

Day excursions from Maseru may be arranged through the Holiday Inn. These include trips up Lesotho's **Mountain Road**, an 80 km. journey which offers breathtaking views of the Maluti escarpment, and a visit to Bushman rock paintings. Another excursion takes in two of Lesotho's weaving and pottery factories.

A 40-minute trip to **Thabo Bosigo**—the Mountain of Darkness—is both scenically and historically interesting. This flat-topped mountain, scaleable only by one route, was the fortress retreat of the Basotho from which they were never dislodged by foreign invaders.

The royal capital at **Mafeteng** has little to offer the visitor, but the route is interesting. A stop is recommended at **Morija**, a thriving early missionary settlement with an old printing establishment and a craft centre.

Hotels
North:

Blue Mountain Inn, Box 7, Teyateyaneng, tel:231, 50 km. from Maseru on the new road to Butha Buthe, with perhaps the best restaurant in Lesotho (fresh trout a speciality) and nearby Bushman paintings, 15 rooms.

Crocodile Inn, Box 72, Butha Buthe, tel: 223, horse-riding to nearby Bushman paintings, fishing, 10 rooms.

Mountain View Hotel, Box 14, Leribe, tel: 242, horse-riding, Bushman paintings nearby, 22 rooms.

South:

Hotel Mafeteng, Box 109, Mafeteng, tel: 236, 9 rooms.

Hotel Mount Maluti, Box 10, Mohale's Hoek, tel: 224, horse-riding, mountaineering, 18 rooms.

Orange River Hotel (Moyeni), Box 37, Quthing, tel: 228, 6 rooms.

Maluti Hotel, Qacha's Nek, tel: 24, horse-riding, tennis, mountaineering, fishing, 6 rooms.

Mountain Lodges: The Government runs two small lodges—one near Sehlabathebe in the east of the country and one at Makoae's near Quthing (dry weather only); they provide accommodation but not food.

The Fraser Group has recently built three lodges offering bungalow accommodation with bathrooms and cooking facilities. Although access is difficult, they are situated in some of the most

Lesotho's capital, Maseru

I. FRANK

beautiful parts of the country. **Qaba Lodge** (for 12) is 80 km. from Maseru. **Semonkong Lodge** (for 8) is only accessible by air form Maseru; **Marakabei Lodge** (102 km. from Maseru). Booking office: The Manager, Fraser Lodge System, P.O. Box 5, Maseru, tel: 2601.

For the more adventurous who want to get right into the mountains the Holiday Inn runs the Maluti chalet camp at Oxbow which can only be reached by four-wheel-drive vehicle but provides accommodation and food, fishing, horseriding, swimming and even skiing in winter.

HISTORY

The mountains of Lesotho have always served as a refuge: first for the San (Bushman) rock-painters who were either eliminated or absorbed by invaders; later those fleeing from the Zulu King Shaka sought sanctuary on the high mountains. Later still, the young Sotho nation clung to the top of Thabo Bosigo to repel the Boers.

The birth of the Sotho nation dates from 1818 when Moshoeshoe the Great (d. 1870) gathered together the remnants of diverse southern Sotho Nguni-speaking peoples who had fled from Shaka's armies. They entrenched themselves in the fertile Caledon valley and along the natural mountain fortification where, with boulders as much as spears, they successfully repelled the raiders. They clung tenaciously to a political system centred in a unifying monarchy: all adult males had the right to attend the *pitso* (national council) and a chief was only a chief by the consent of the people.

The Boer trekkers posed an even more formidable problem than Shaka. Moshoeshoe built up an impressive army of at least 7,000 horsemen armed with guns, but failed to prevent the newcomers from occupying most of the Caledon valley. From 1833 French and British missionaries began arriving; their labours

gave the Sotho their lead in literacy over all other Africans in the region. Basotho women and men achieved over 80% literacy before independence.

When Moshoeshoe feared that neither his horsemen nor his diplomacy could save the Basotho from Boer conquerors he invited Queen Victoria to extend her protection over the country, but it was not made a protectorate. In 1868 the British annexed it as a part of the Cape Colony, making the Boers give up some of the country's fertile land.

British rule did not sit easily on the Basotho, who especially resented the ban on their carrying or buying guns, made under pressure from the Boers on their frontiers. The Gun War (1880-81) was lost by the Basotho but they were able to prevent the alienation of their land and were allowed to keep their guns for a fee. In the 1870s the Basotho were among the first migrants to work in the Kimberley diamond mines.

Continuing internal unrest led Britain to take the territory over from the Cape Colony and to make it a colony. The protectorates of Bechuanaland (Botswana), Swaziland and Basutoland formed the High Commission Territories, administered separately from South Africa.

On 4 October 1966 Lesotho became independent as a constitutional monarchy under Moshoeshoe II. In 1970 the first elections since independence were suddenly cancelled by the Prime Minister, Chief Leabua Jonathan, whose Basotho National Party stayed in power while the radical Basotho Congress Party and the royalist Marematlou Freedom Party were banned.

The King went into voluntary exile for a time when the Prime Minister proclaimed a 'holiday from politics' for a few years to allow the country to settle down again.

The Prime Minister and the King were subsequently reconciled and in 1972 political detainees were released, but opposition is still repressed.

LIBERIA

A stopping-off place for businessmen rather than tourists, Liberia has modern comforts in the capital city, Monrovia, but is almost untouched by the 20th Century in many inland areas. The road network is gradually being extended with the opening-up of new mining areas, plantations and agricultural schemes.

Liberia is American-orientated and uses the dollar as its currency. Ship-owners all over the world register their tankers and freighters in Liberia—but this merely provides a 'flag of convenience' for there is little shipping to Monrovia itself.

Liberia shares many of the geographical and cultural features of this part of Africa, including beaches, lagoons, forests and mountains.

THE LAND AND THE PEOPLE

On the western bulge of Africa, Liberia is bounded on the west by Sierra Leone, on the north by Guinea, on the south by the Atlantic Ocean and on the east by the Ivory Coast. The 560 km Atlantic coastline includes over 320 km of sandy beaches. Lying parallel to the shore there are three distinct belts. The low coastal belt, about 80 km wide, is well watered by shallow lagoons, tidal creeks and mangrove marshes. Behind it lies an undulating plateau, 500-800 m high, partly covered with grass and dense primaeval forests. Inland and to the north is the mountain area, rich in iron ore and other minerals, which includes Mount Nimba (1,300 m) and the Waulo Mountain (1,400 m).

A large number of islands and islets are scattered close to the coast. Lake Piso in the west is a large, picturesque expanse of water teeming with tropical fish and bordered by beautiful sandy beaches and belts of palm trees.

Ethnically, the population consists of

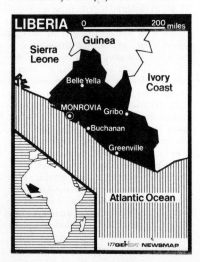

descendants of black settlers from the United States and the West Indies and members of about 30 local ethnic groups, of which the most populous are the Kpelle (250,000) and the Bassa (200,000). Government policy and inter-marriage between members of the various communities over a period of 150 years has resulted in the development of a national consciousness and of a unified segment of society whose members can no longer trace their origin.

CULTURE

Liberian handicrafts include the making of masks, heads, figurines, fetishes and other objects used mainly by priests and dancers for ritual purposes, and decorated household articles, game boards, musical instruments and weapons. The most noted in the first category are the Dan/Gio initiation and ancestor masks which, although found more commonly in the Ivory Coast, reach a higher degree of style and sophistication in eastern Liberia.

The favourite material of the Liberian carver is sapwood, though hardwoods (camwood, ebony and mahogany) are also used, as well as stone and ivory. Soapstone carvings, such as fertility symbols, come mainly from the Kissi tribe. Clay modelling is the speciality of the Cleboes of south-eastern Liberia, while the Dan artists of the same area are the authors of intricate metalwork, especially figurines and jewellery cast in bronze or brass by the lost-wax process. Other artistic objects include the reed dolls made by craftsmen of the Loma tribe.

As elsewhere in black Africa, dancing has a ritual character and is the most common form of artistic and emotional expression. Throughout Liberia people often dance until the early hours of the morning, even after a hard day's work in the fields. Major events in the life of villages and tribal communities prompt various dances, according to the occasion, and the greatest rhythmic activity takes place when the moon is full.

The 'forest symphony' is a form of highly rhythmic musical expression. The sound of reed rattles and bells is occasionally added to those of the 'talking drums', while horns and even stringed instruments, fashioned from gourds, forked sticks and piassava fibres, are used to contribute an element of melody. Vocal music ranges from the choirs of the Kru tribe, rich in harmony and feeling, to the ritual chants of Muslim groups and the antiphonal songs, full of lively rhythm, of the central and northern peoples.

Fables, myths and legends handed down by word-of-mouth from generation to generation constitute the literary legacy of tribal Liberians. Most of these point a moral or illustrate philosophical, ethical, political or medical precepts. Others are in the nature of satirical sketches or narratives relating to the history of the tribe. Traditional cultural values used to be transmitted mainly through powerful secret societies which provided the only form of organized education for the young. Two of Liberia's peoples—the Vai and the Bassa—developed their own alphabets and written languages before the arrival of the first settlers from the United States.

Urban culture is still partly inspired by 19th century America, as expressed in colonial-style architecture and square dancing, especially the quadrille. However, this influence is being rapidly overshadowed by the cultural impact of contemporary America and Western Europe and the rediscovery of traditional African values.

WILDLIFE

The forests of Liberia have a variety of animals and birds, some of which, like the elephant, are becoming rarer in accessible areas. The most famous among those which can still be seen is the dwarf or pygmy hippopotamus, found only in Liberia. There is a wide variety of carnivorous animals of the feline group, buffaloes, baboons, olive, red and black colobus monkeys, white spotted-nose monkeys, boars and porcupines.

Species of birds, some of them rare, include hornbills, pepper birds, African crows, guinea-fowl, jacanas or leaf-walkers, spur-winged wattle plovers, curlews, eagles, vultures, weavers, woodpeckers, flamingos, doves and the red phalarope.

GENERAL INFORMATION
Area: 113,370 sq km.
Population: 1.5 million.
Altitude: Sea-level to 800 m.
Capital: Monrovia.
Head of State: The President, Dr. William R. Tolbert, Jr.
Government: Republic with constitution and system of administration modelled on that of the United States. Two-chamber legislature—Senate and House of Representatives.
Date of Independence 26 July 1847.
Languages: English (the official language) and several African dialects.
Religions: The major Christian denominations are Baptist, Methodist, Presbyterian, Protestant Episcopal, Lutheran, Roman Catholic and Seventh Day Adventist. Islam also has many followers, especially in the north of the country and traditional religions are practised in some hinterland areas.
Currency: Liberian dollar, at par with the US dollar. US notes and coins and Liberian coins are all in circulation.
Time: GMT.

HOW TO GET THERE
By air: There are direct flights to Robertsfield International Airport from Europe and from the United States, also several flights to and from many African capitals. Airlines serving Liberia include Air Afrique, Air Guinea, Air Mali, British Caledonian, Ghana Airways, Middle East Airlines, Nigerian Airways, Pan Am, KLM, Sabena, SAS, Sierra Leone Airways, Swissair and UTA.

Robertsfield is a long way from Monrovia, but buses meet international flights. Some of the West African airlines land at Spriggs Payne airport in Monrovia itself.

By road: Laterite roads link Liberia with Guinea, Sierra Leone and the Ivory Coast, but it is not advisable to use them during the rainy season (May-October).

By sea: Unscheduled freighter services with passenger accommodation from various European ports.

Visas and health regulations:
Visitors must have a visa, which can easily be obtained from Liberian consulates. Application forms must be ac-

Liberian forest—preparing for logging

companied by two passport-size photographs. Visitors' visas are granted for up to 60 days but foreign nationals remaining in the country longer than 15 days are required to register at the Bureau of Immigration in Monrovia and must obtain an exit permit before departure. A passport must be valid for at least six months beyond the intended stay in Liberia.

Visitors must have an international health certificate showing inoculation against smallpox, yellow fever and cholera. Tourist visas cannot be automatically granted to nationals or residents of South Africa and Rhodesia.

Dutiable goods:
Visitors may bring into the country personal effects, as well as 200 cigarettes and one bottle of alcoholic beverage. Licences are required for the importation of firearms, ammunition and some pharamaceuticals. Export taxes are applied to diamonds and precious metals bought in Liberia.

CLIMATE
Liberia has a tropical climate with average temperatures ranging between 21°C and 28°C. There are relatively small variations between day and night and between seasons, with the temperature never exceeding 37°C or dropping below 16°C.

There are two seasons of approximately six months each—wet from May to October and dry from November to April. It seldom rains during the dry season, though there are dry periods during the so-called rainy season, including a dry spell in July or August lasting about two weeks. The annual rainfall averages 4,320 mm in Monrovia and 1,778 mm inland. The average humidity on the coastal belt is 78% during the dry season and 82% during the wet season, but it can drop to 30% from December to March when the Harmattan wind blows from the Sahara.

The best season for tourists is from early November to the end of April when the weather is dry and sunny.

Health precautions
Malaria is endemic and it is advisable to take prophylactic anti-malarial tablets, though many residents ignore this precaution. Most forms of malaria are mild. Swimming in the ocean and lagoons (like Lake Piso) is safe, but rivers and inland lakes should generally be avoided because of bilharzia. Most European and American medicines are available from chemists, and there are good private physicians as well as clinics and hospitals.

ACCOMMODATION AND FOOD
Liberia has some luxurious hotels and motels, small, but often with swimming pools, mini-golf courses and restaurants serving a variety of American, European, Asian and African dishes. One can also buy rice and traditional dishes at the 'cook shops' in the towns.

TRANSPORT
Road: The country is served by a road network totalling nearly 8,000 km, of which some 800 km are tarred. A further 800 km are primary, all-weather gravel or improved laterite roads.

Most parts of the country are now accessible by road from Monrovia, though the lack of a road parallel to the coast (due to the difficulty of bypassing large lagoons and bridging the river estuaries) involves long detours in travel between some coastal towns. The three neighbouring States—Sierra Leone, Guinea and the Ivory Coast—can be reached by road from Monrovia.

The Lamco iron ore mining company operates a daily 400 km passenger and goods motor-rail service between the port of Buchanan (linked with Monrovia by a 200 km tarred road) and Yekepa, in the north-east of the country, near the Guinea border.

Air: The Liberian National Airway (LNA) operates regular services between Monrovia and major towns, including Harper, near the Ivory Coast border. There are also several air-taxi companies which offer small aircraft for charter at short notice for internal flights. There are some 60 small airfields.

Car hire:
There are virtually no inter-city bus services. Cars, both chauffeur-driven and self-drive, can be hired in Monrovia. The main car and bus hire firms are: **Mensah Travel Bureau,** P.O. Box 86, tel: 22807; **WATCO,** at Bushrod Island, tel: 22016; **The Yes Taxi Co,** Camp Johnson Road, P.O. Box 49, tel: 22970; **International Automobile Co,** Sao Bosoe Street and Randall Street, tel: 22486.

BANKS AND COMMERCE

The major bank is the Bank of Monrovia, an affiliate of the First City Bank of New York. Other banks are The Bank of Liberia, The Chase Manhattan Bank, Commercial Bank of Liberia, International Trust Company of Liberia and Tradevco.

Business hours: Government offices: 0800 to 1600 Monday to Friday. Banks: 0800 to 1200 Monday to Thursday; 0800 to 1400 Friday. The International Trust Co. operates also on Saturdays 0800 to 1100. Major business houses: 0800 to 1200 Monday to Saturday; 1400 to 1600 Monday to Friday. Small businesses, shops, etc: generally 0800 to 1900 Monday to Saturday.

PUBLIC HOLIDAYS

New Year's Day; Pioneers' Day 7 January; Armed Forces Day 11 February; Decoration Day second Wednesday in March; J. J. Roberts Birthday 15 March; Fast and Prayer Day second Friday in April; Independence Day 26 July; National Flag Day 24 August; Christmas, Palm Sunday, Good Friday and Easter Monday.

FOREIGN EMBASSIES IN MONROVIA

Cameroon, P.O. Box 616; **CAE,** P.O. Box 545; **Egypt,** P.O. Box 462; **Ethiopia,** P.O. Box 640; **France,** P.O. Box 279; **West Germany,** P.O. Box 34; **Ghana,** P.O. Box 471; **Guinea,** P.O. Box 416; **Italy,** P.O. Box 225; **Ivory Coast,** P.O. Box 126; **Japan,** P.O. Box 2053; **Lebanon,** P.O. Box 134; **Netherlands,** P.O. Box 284; **Nigeria,** P.O. Box 366; **Sierra Leone,** P.O. Box 575; **Sweden,** Box 335; **Switzerland,** P.O. Box 283; **UK,** P.O. Box 120; **USA,** P.O. Box 98; **Zaire,** P.O. Box 1038.

MONROVIA

Monrovia, the capital, is a sprawling city situated on the Atlantic coast at the mouth of the Mesurado River which almost circles the inhabited area. The city, founded in 1822 as Christopolis, was later renamed after President James Monroe of the United States. Originally built on a reef of rocks, the city has now expanded over an area of sand. The adjoining inhabited areas are split up by beach lagoons into rugged headlands, peninsulas and islands.

The port and the industrial area are on Bushrod Island, linked to the rest of the city by a bridge.

Monrovia is a city of contrasts with up-to-date office and residental blocks next to shacks, traditional African huts with television aerials and gleaming American cars parked outside shanty town dwellings. Commodious stone houses, built in the graceful colonial style of the American Deep South, date back to the period of consolidation when the settlers had acquired the time and resources to build at leisure the type of dwellings with which they were familiar.

Luxurious restaurants offering the highest standards of French cuisine can be seen side by side with the 'cook shops' where rice and traditional African dishes are served.

Night-life is extensive with dozens of crowded night-clubs, discotheques and bars entertaining customers until the early hours of the morning.

Places of interest

Providence Island where the first US, settlers landed in 1822 has a National Museum, recently transferred to the island, containing documents and objects relating to the establishment of Liberia at the beginning of the last century, as well as samples of indigenous arts and crafts, including ebony, stone and ivory carvings. Providence Island also has an amphitheatre where performances of African dancing and music are staged, a band stand, huts, a restaurant and facilities for games.

Along the coast outside the city are several clean sandy beaches, some providing boating, swimming and refreshments. The more popular ones at which a small entrance fee is charged are: **Bernard's beach; Elwa beach; Kenema beach; Kendaje beach; Sugar beach; Cedar beach; Cooper's beach and Caesar's beach.**

The Firestone Plantation, the world's largest and most modern rubber plantation, lies 50 km from Monrovia. Conducted tours of the plantation and its research and processing facilities can be arranged.

Totota (120 km from Monrova) has a zoo where animals, including the pygmy hippopotamus, can be seen in their natural habitat. **Lake Piso** (76 km from Monrovia) is a shallow sea-water lake, ideal for swimming, fishing and water sports, girdled by a wide sandy beach behind which lies a belt of thick evergreen forest and a range of mountains. **Massating**, a large island in the lake, teems with wildlife. Fishing villages, rich in local tradition, are found along the shores of the lake.

Hotels

Ducor Intercontinental, P.O. Box 86, tel: 22200, 209 rooms and suites. **Traveller's Roost**, P.O. Box 1439, tel: 22522, centrally situated, 2-3 room service apartments with modern fully equipped kitchens. **Carlton Hotel**, P.O. Box 285, tel: 21245, centrally situated in the main business area, 60 rooms.

Bernard Motel, P.O. Box 49, tel: 26705, facing one of the safest beaches. **Ambassador Hotel**, P.O. Box 889, tel: 21058, facing the beach. **Panam Hotel**, near Roberts International Airport. **Palm Hotel**, P.O. Box 132, tel: 22964, 15 rooms.

There are several other small hotels in Monrovia and the main towns.

Street in Monrovia

Restaurants: There are several first-class restaurants offering high standards of cuisine. French-owned and operated **Julia's** in Gurley Street imports three times a week high quality products direct from France. **Salvatore's** has American and Italian specialities; **Oscar's** has Swiss and French; **Atlantic Restaurant**, French, German and Russian; **Roseline's Restaurant**, Liberian dishes in an African atmosphere; **Diana's**, American, Middle East and Indian dishes. There is also a good Chinese restaurant.

Shopping and markets

Elegant shops and boutiques, as well as

modern air-conditioned supermarkets compete with old-fashioned stores. A gift shop featuring Liberian handicrafts is open daily at the National Cultural Centre.

Tourist information
There is a Tourist Information Centre at the Ministry of Information, Cultural Affairs and Tourism.
Travel agencies: Morgan Travel Agency, Broad Street, P.O. Box 1260, tel: 22149; **Scantravel (Liberia) Inc.**, Chase Manhattan Plaza, Randall Street, P.O. Box 163, tel: 21634, 21635 and 22620; **Mensah Travel Bureau**, at the Ducor Intercontinental Hotel, P.O. Box 86, tel: 22200; **Brasilia Travel Bureau**, Broad Street, P.O. Box 54, tel: 22378.

OTHER TOWNS

Buchanan is the main centre of Grand Bassa county, lying east of the St. John River mouth; it is the port of export for Liberia's iron ore **(Hotel Louisa)**. Further to the south-east, near the Ivory Coast border, is **Harper**, an outlet for the vast rubber plantations. **Robertsport**, near the Sierra Leone border, has good bathing, fishing and diving, as well as exhibitions of local arts and crafts. **Sanniquellie** is the trading centre of northern Liberia and lies at the foot of the iron-producing Nimba Mountain. The most northern town in Liberia is **Voinjama**; to its south-west is the Wologisi range, the site of a projected national park.

HISTORY

Liberia's present inhabitants are believed to have migrated from the north and the east between the 12th and the 17th centuries. Some, like the Kru, are said to originate from western Sudan, probably from the Gao and Timbuktu areas of the present Mali Republic. These people brought with them elements of Berber culture, such as cotton spinning, cloth weaving and iron smelting, as well as some south-east Asian plants, including rice, and social and political institutions modelled on those of the Mali empire. The earlier inhabitants either disappeared or were assimilated by the new migrants.

Modern Liberia came into existence as a result of treaties concluded in 1821 between local tribal kings and representatives of black groups from the United States who, under the auspices of the American Colonisation Society, decided to resettle in and to evangelise the continent of their ancestors.

The first party stopped at Freetown, Sierra Leone, but later sailed along the Atlantic coast until they sighted the Mesurado Bay, now called the Mesurado River. They anchored offshore on 11 December 1821, and five days later, on Bushrod Island, at the town of Gahulong, they signed a treaty with six local chiefs, thereby obtaining the entire cape, the island at the mouth of the river and land extending into the interior. On 7 January 1822, they occupied the little island at the mouth of the river and named it Perseverence Island, later changed to Providence Island, a name it has retained until this day. The settlers then moved to the mainland—where Monrovia now stands—on 25 April 1822.

The early settlers suffered many hardships, both from tropical diseases and from periodic conflicts with some hostile inhabitants. However, they persevered and through various treaties their territory was extended to include all of what is now Liberia, as well as sizeable parts of what is now Sierra Leone, Guinea and the Ivory Coast.

Several other colonisation societies were active during that period, including those from the US States of Maryland and Mississippi. As the colonists acquired new territories, settlements were formed along the coast and in the interior. In 1838 these settlements, excluding those of Maryland, decided to unite within a

Kapatewe Falls, Bong County

self-governing 'Commonwealth of Liberia'.

However, the colonial powers refused to recognise its status, and Britain and France advised their nationals who were conducting trade along the African coast not to pay taxes or customs duties to Liberia. When the properties of the traders were seized by Liberian officials, the colonial powers sent gunboats to shell the settlements and mounted punitive expeditions.

The settlers, encouraged by the American societies, resolved to declare themselves an independent nation. They called a Constitutional Convention which opened in Monrovia on 25 June 1847, and ended on 26 July. On that day representatives from the various settler communities formally signed the Declaration of Independence. The first election was held in October 1847, when Governor Joseph Jenkins Roberts was elected President of the Republic and inaugurated on the first Monday in January, 1848. The State of Maryland (now Maryland County) which had remained outside the original Com-

monwealth, joined the Republic in April 1857. Thus, Liberia became the first independent black republic in Africa. To preserve its independence Liberia was forced to cede territories to France and Britain.

In the late 1920s Spanish agents, operating with the agreement of the Liberian Government, recruited Liberian labourers for their plantations in the island of Fernando Po where working conditions amounted to slavery. Though Spain was never blamed for condoning slavery, and though most of the labour force in the island had been recruited in the French-administered Cameroon and in Nigeria, the League of Nations accused Liberia of acquiescing in the activities of the Spanish recruiting agents. Attempts to impose trusteeship status on Liberia did not materialise, but the Government was forced to accept a number of humiliating conditions limiting the country's sovereignty.

President William R. Tolbert, Jr., inaugurated on 3 January 1972, is the 19th President of the Republic.

MADAGASCAR

A country with a unique culture dating from Malayo-Polynesians perhaps 2,000 years ago, Madagascar is a combination of Africa and Indonesia. As an island it has developed independently with unusual traditions, customs and religions, although it came under French influence in the colonial period. Now Madagascar is reasserting its own social and political traditions, and the Malagasy language, while the Government is also attempting to forge a modern socialist state.

Madagascar is well adapted for small-scale tourism and for the adventurous traveller, but with its beautiful coasts, interesting wildlife and mountain scenery it has potential for a bigger travel industry.

THE LAND AND THE PEOPLE

Madagascar's five major ecological regions have their own climate, vegetation and scenery. The capital, Antananarivo (Tananarive) is set among the twelve sacred hills near the centre of the mountain massif called the Hauts Plateaux—a landscape of bare rounded hills between 1,500 and 2,000m high.

The east coast, a narrow strip between the central mountains and the Indian Ocean, is partly covered with tropical rainforests, despite the ravages of a shifting cultivation. The west coast has large areas of dry deciduous forest but much of this has been destroyed leaving great expanses of grassland savannah dotted with Borassu palms and other secondary vegetation where huge herds of zebu cattle graze.

The southern region, south of a line drawn from Tulear to Farafangana, has the most striking vegetation. Cactus-like plants that have adapted to the semi-arid climate form great expanses of forest. Nearly all of them are indigenous to Madagascar.

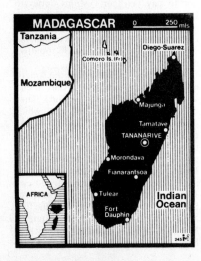

210

The small Sambirano area, lying west of the highest mountain, Tsaratanana, forms a separate sub-region in the north. It has a high regular rainfall, but a lot of sunshine. Here cocoa, coffee, pepper and perfume plants such as ylang-ylang are grown. The island of Nossi-Be lies off-shore from Sambirano.

Madagascar has many great rivers, the longest being the Ikopa which runs north from Antananarivo to Majunga. Many of those running east have spectacular falls: Namorona and Sakoleona. There are a number of large lakes: Itasy lies in a recent volcanic zone about 120 km west of Antananarivo; Alaotra lies in a "rift valley" parallel to the east coast; Kinkony and Ihotry are on the west coast. They are the breeding grounds of water-fowl and wild duck, and teem with many species of fish.

The Malagasy are of the same stock as the Malayo-Polynesians, with possible Melanesian elements. The African element is more recent, derived from slaves imported from the mainland (1700-1870). The 'proto-Malagasy' sailed from somewhere in Indonesia, using the type of large double canoe known to have been used by the Maoris in their migrations. The immigrants came equipped with useful plants—taro, sugar-cane, bananas, coconuts—which retain their Malay names. The likely route taken by these early travellers meant an astonishing voyage across the Indian Ocean, using the equatorial currents and south-east trade winds.

There were many migrations over several centuries; resulting in a number of physical types among the people. There is, however, only one language—Malagasy—spoken in different dialects. There is also unity of custom and way of life. It is more correct to speak of 'clans' rather than 'tribes' in describing the 18 ethnic divisions.

Of the 18 clans, the Sakalava are the most widespread and occupy the western part of the island from Majunga to Mor-

andavo. The Antankarana inhabit the northern part and along the east coast are the Betsimisaraka and the Antaimoro. In the south-east are the Antasaka and the Antanosy. The Antadroy live in the south and the Bara inland. The Mahafaly live in the south-west. Along the west coast are Vezo fishermen, who travel great distances up and down the coast and into the Mozambique channel. In the central region are the Tanala, Betsileo, Merina (around Antananarivo), the Bezanozana, Sihanaka and Tsimehety.

Madagascar is an agricultural country. Rice is grown all over the island except in the arid south. Coffee, vanilla, pepper, cloves and perfume products are grown for export. Sisal, sugar-cane, maize, groundnuts and tobacco are grown for home consumption.

CULTURE

The Malagasy language, which is closely related to Malay, was first written in Arabic script. Early books, called the *sora be*, were inscribed on ox-hide and contain mainly magical formulae Some of them dating probably from the 18th century, can be seen in the library of the *Academie Malgache*. In 1820 missionaries translated the Bible and wrote the Malagasy language in Latin Script, which is still used today.

The Malagasy are a musically gifted people. Each clan has its characteristic style in dances and songs. A large number of instruments are found in the different regions, many of them closely related to similar instruments in Indonesia, others showing an African origin.

Death and ancestral spirits play a significant role in Madagascar and the funerary theme is reflected in many of the handicrafts, such as the Vezo erotic statues which are placed on tombs in the Morundava region, and the remarkable *bibi-olona*, (animal-man) of the west, or the *aloalo*, the tall carved posts surmounted by figures of zebu cattle which are placed on tombs in the south.

Among the interesting souvenirs to be found are turtle shells, large mounted butterflies in frames, detailed model boats (Majunga, Morondava and Tulear), coral objects and along the west coast large and beautiful sea-shells. The Antaimoro hand-made paper—incorporating real flowers and grasses—is obtainable in Ambalavao or in Antananarivo. Fine marquetry furniture is made in Ambositra. Weaving of raffia, baskets and straw hats is widespread. Many Malagasy work in silver, minerals and semi-precious stones and the visitor will find ornaments made of rock crystal, obsidian, petrified wood and jewels.

WILDLIFE

Madagascar's mammals and birds evolved before the separation of the island from the mainland of Africa some 20 million years ago but there are many species unique to the island. The best-known animals are the lemurs with their fox-like heads. They climb trees and swing from the branches like monkeys and vary in size from one metre high— the babakoto—to a small nocturnal creature the size of a mouse. They are found all over the island and they are protected.

The fosa is the only wild beast and related to the weasel; it is the size of a large dog. It inhabits the forests and feeds on poultry. There are a number of small mammals of interest to zoologists. The "African" animals found on the island are crocodile, bush-pig, and guinea-fowl.

The prehistoric fish, the coelacanth, is found in waters off Nossi-Be. The Scientific Research Aquarium on the island has many interesting species of underwater life. Madagascar is poor in freshwater fish but carp, tilapia and black bass have been used to stock the lakes and rivers, and good line-fishing is available.

The birds of Madagascar are distinctive. Out of about 300 species, 67 are indigenous. About 1,200 years ago the biggest bird in the world lumbered through the tropical forests. *Aepyornis maximus* (literally 'largest tall bird') was three metres tall and weighed half a ton. The Academie Malgache has a museum of fossils and sub-fossils including the extinct giant bird.

GENERAL INFORMATION

Area: 590,000 sq. km.
Population: 8 million.
Altitude: Sea level to 1,500 m.-2,000 m. on the Central plateau; the highest point is in the Massif de Tsaratanana, 2,876 m.
Capital: Antananarivo.
Head of State: Lt. Cdr. Didier Ratsiraka.
Government: Military alliance with progressive political parties.
Date of independence: 26 June 1960.
Official languages: French and Malagasy.
Religion: Christianity, traditional, Islam.
Currency: The Malagasy franc (FMG). £1=425 FMG. $1=247 FMG.
Time: GMT+3.

HOW TO GET THERE

By Air: Direct and regular flights from Europe. From Paris by Air France and Air Madagascar; from Rome by Alitalia and Air Madagascar. Regional flights from Nairobi, Dar es Salaam, Djibouti, Maputo, Reunion, Mauritius and Comoro Islands.

By Sea: There are 18 ports, including four for long-distance calls: Tamatave, Diego Suarez, Majunga and Tulear.

Visas and health regulations

Visitors require a valid passport and visa. The latter can be obtained from the consular section of the Malagasy Embassy, 7 Boulevard Suchet, Paris 16, France, tel: 504.18.16. Early application is advised. No visitor without a visa will be permitted to land.

Visitors require international certificate of vaccination against smallpox and, if coming from endemic areas, cholera and yellow fever. Enquiries as to current regulations should be made before travelling.

Currency regulations
Any amount of foreign currency may be taken into the country, but visitors are advised not to cash more travellers' cheques than they need, as reconversion of Malagasy currency into sterling or dollars is impossible.

CLIMATE
A hot and rainy season from November to March and a cooler dry season from April to October. On the west coast the dry season lasts for about seven months; the south-west is hot, dry and semi-arid. By contrast, the monsoon brings violent storms and often cyclones to the north-east between December and March.

Around Antananarivo the weather is warm and sunny with frequent thunderstorms from November to April. For the rest of the year it is cool, windy and sunny with almost no rain.

What to wear: Clothing depends very much on the area. On the high central tableland in summer lightweight clothing, with something warmer for the evenings, is recommended. The weather can turn quite chilly, so a warm overcoat is useful. Dress is normally informal, although one may be expected to look reasonably smart in the evening in the bigger hotels.

On the coast and in the north and south light clothing is required all the year round. Because of the climatic variations, raincoats and umbrellas should not be forgotten.

Health precautions
On the central highlands there are very few mosquitoes, but they exist elsewhere in the island so it is wise to take a prophylactic. Mosquito nets are usually

provided in the big hotels along the coast but, if camping, bring your own.

Care should be taken to sterilize drinking water, except in the main town where it is treated. Many lakes and paddy fields are infected with bilharzia.

ACCOMMODATION AND FOOD
In most towns you will find hotels and restaurants of varying degrees of quality serving French, Italian, Indian, Indonesian, Chinese, Vietnamese and Arab food.

It is practically impossible to sample good Malagasy cooking unless invited to a private house. Malagasy will invite a foreigner if they are quite sure their food will be appreciated but such a degree of acquaintance takes time.

Hotely Gasy—which means both hotel and restaurant—are to be found almost everywhere. They are usually small and cheap, providing a rice and meat dish. These establishments are esentially Malagasy and are not tourist-orientated, although the proprietor will be happy to welcome foreigners. But don't be fooled by the name—very often there is no sleeping accommodation.

Tipping: In the European-style hotels and restaurants the French custom of tipping is followed. One should also tip in Chinese and Vietnamese establishments, but in the *Hotely Gasy* tips are not usually expected.

TRANSPORT
Road: In Antananarivo transport is fairly plentiful. Taxis will go anywhere in town—they have no meters and prices are fixed below a certain mileage, and above that you will have to haggle with the driver. After 8pm double tariff is charged. It is not customary to tip taxi drivers. There are also bus services in Antananarivo, but these can sometimes

be confusing. Air Route Services/ATO operates buses between Avato airport and Antananarivo.

In Tamatave, Majunga, Diego Suarez and other towns the *pousse-pousse*—a kind of rickshaw—is common. These are very cheap and the driver usually expects a tip.

Road transport between towns exists in a number of forms. The most common is the *taxi-brousse* (bush taxi). These travel the main roads between Antananarivo and the provinces and link main towns. Fares are usually reasonable, but do not expect great comfort.

Rail: The railway system is not extensive but does provide services between Antananarivo and Tamatave, stopping at the towns along the line. There are also rail links between Antananarivo and Ambatondrazaka, Antananarivo and Antsirabe, and Fianarantsoa and Manakara. These journeys are slow, but are usually through picturesque country, particularly so between Manakara and Fianarantsoa.

Air: Internal flights by Air Madagascar cover the whole country. There are 119 airfields, including 86 private airstrips, so planes can be taken almost everywhere, and certainly to all the main towns on the island.

Car hire: **Hertz**, 31 Avenue de l'Independance, B.P. 4152, Antananarivo. Tel: 233-36. **Avis**, Madagascar Hilton, Antananarivo.

Cactus-like vegetation of the south

BANKS AND COMMERCE
Banque Centrale de Madagascar; Banque Commerciale de Madagascar; Banque Financière et Commerciale Malagasy; Banque Malgache d'Escompte et de Credit; Banque Nationale Malagasy de Developpement; Banque pour le Commerce et l'Industrie de Madagascar.

Business hours: Offices and banks usually open from 0800 to 1100 and 1400 to 1600, Monday to Friday. Shops open from 0800 to 1200 and 1400 to 1800, Monday to Saturday. Supermarche is open on Sunday mornings, as are many local grocers.

PUBLIC HOLIDAYS
New Year's Day: Memorial Day 29 March; Good Friday: Easter Monday: Whitsun: Labour Day 1 May: Ascension: Independence Day 26 June: All Saints' Day 1 November: Christmas Day: Anniversary of the Democratic Republic 30 December.

FOREIGN EMBASSIES

(In Antananarivo unless otherwise stated)
Egypt, 47 Ave. Lenin, B.P. 4082; **France**, 3 Rue Jean Jaures; **West Germany**, 101 Route Circulaire, Ambodirotra; **India**, 77 Lalana Andriamaromanana, Tsiazotofo; **Italy**, 22 Rue Pasteur Rabary, Ankadivato; **Japan**, 20 Rue Clemenceau; **Switzerland**, B.P. 118; **USA**, 14 Lalana Rainitovo, Antsahavola.

TOURIST OFFICES

Office National du Tourisme de Madagascar, B.P. 610, Place d'Ambohij-Atovo, Antananarivo.

ANTANANARIVO

Tananarive has now reverted to its original name. Antananarivo means the 'town of a thousand men' but if it were named for the number of steps and stairways it would be more apt—there are certainly more than a thousand of them. The tall, balconied brick houses closely pack the steep sides of a horseshoe-shaped hill, and most are only approachable by narrow stone staircases and a maze of footpaths.

The capital is built on three levels. At the highest point is the sacred hill, graced by the Queen's Palace which commands a view over the city and dominates the scenery for miles around. On the lowest level, between the two arms of the horseshoe, lies Lake Anosy with its park of tropical flora, the large central *Place* and the great market of Analakely. The *Zoma*, the main market, is held every day, but on Fridays the stalls multiply and spill over most of the town centre. *Zoma* means Friday and has become synonymous with the market. Everything is sold here from poultry, fruit and vegetables to a great variety of handicrafts.

Other parts of the town have their markets, too—Andravoahangy on Wednesdays, Mahamasina on Thursdays and Isotry on Saturdays.

Places of Interest
The Queen's Palace is now a national monument and well worth a visit. Centuries before the French colonized Madagascar the Merina monarchs created the Rova, the royal village, on the sacred peak. The Palace is a fantastic network of wood and stone with beautiful panelling inside. Other palaces in the Rova closely resemble Indonesian architecture. Near the King's Palace is an Italian-style temple, designed by Willian Pool, an English architect, for Queen Ranavalona II who was a staunch Anglican. Madagascar Airtours offer tours of the *Zoma*, the Queen's Palace, Botanical Gardens and Antananarivo by night.

The countryside for 200 km around Antananarivo is varied and beautiful. Accessible by moderately good roads, there are several places worth a visit, such as the former royal residence of Ambohimanga (20 km) and Lake Itasy (120 km), the falls of Tsinjoarivo (120 km), and Lake Mantasoa (40 km). In the sub-tropical climate, walking is pleasant and the surrounding hills and villages are easily reached on foot.

Hotels
Madagascar Hilton, B.P. 959, tel: 260.60, telex: 2261. 5 minutes from main shopping centre, 189 rooms.
Hotel Colbert, Rue Carayon, B.P. 341, tel: 202.02, telex: 22248, 80 rooms. Old fashioned but comfortable and the service is good. High quality French cuisine in the restaurant.
Select Hotel, Avenue du 18 juin, tel: 210.01.
Motel Agip, Anosy, B.P. 3850, tel: 250.40, cable: Motelagip, 32 rooms.
Hotel Acropole, tel: 233.80, 15 rooms.
Hotel de France and **Hotel Terminus** in the centre of town are clean and adequate.

Entertainments: There are perhaps 10 nightclubs in Antananarivo mostly patronised at the weekends.

Tourist information
Madagascar Airtours, Galerie Marchande Hilton, tel: 265.15; **Transcontinents**, 10 Avenue de l'Indépendance, tel: 223.98.

ANTSIRABE

Built in 1923 when the railway was extended south from Antananarivo (167 km), Antsirabe was intended partly as a rest centre for French army and civilian personnel from the tropical coastline. At about 1,600 m above sea level, frosts are common in June and July. It is situated near to the second highest mountain in Madagascar (2,600 m) and has a distinctly European appearance, with many villas on the outskirts which might be in Normandy or a Paris suburb.

Antsirabe is especially famed for its thermal springs, earning it the name of the 'Malagasy Vichy'. Not far from the centre of town is the Swiss-like Lake Andraikiba.

Hotels
Hotel des Thermes, built in 1924 with huge overhanging roofs and a half-timbered façade. Some modernisation has taken place.
Hotel Truchet, Avenue de l'Indépendance, B.P. 47, tel: 480.36, 58 rooms, clean and adequate, French-style cuisine.

FIANARANTSOA

South on the tarred road to Tulear, Fianarantsoa is 407 km from Antananarivo and 1,370 m above sea level. The hill on which the town was built gave it its original name: Ivoanenana, but Queen Ranavalona I ordered a new city to be built and gave it the name it has borne ever since. Fianarantsoa means 'the city where one learns the good life', or just 'happiness'. It is the centre of a rich agricultural region in which rice and coffee are the principal crops. The hotel is **Chez Papillon**.

TULEAR

Tulear, the 'White City', is one of the more attractive towns in Madagascar. It has a Mediterranean climate with sunshine for most of the year. The esplanade is planted with palms and the broad streets are shaded with *kily* or tamarind trees.

The inhabitants, mainly of Vezo descent, are fishermen and sailors who have preserved the Polynesian outrigger canoe of their ancestors. They live in villages along the shore or sleep under sails rigged as tents on their boats when travelling up and down the coast.

Tulear has white sandy beaches, safe for swimming and water sports. There are no sharks on the landward side of a large coral reef 10 km offshore where there is sailing, skin-diving and fishing. There is no organised night-life but frequent dances are held in the town.

Many local jewellers work in silver, making the characteristic bracelets—*vanga-vanga*—for men, and smaller bracelets and necklaces for women. There is a colourful market held in the town centre near a large tamarind tree.

Hotels
Hotel le Capricorne, Avenue de Belemboka, B.P. 158, tel: 295, 14 rooms (simple but comfortable), seafood a speciality.
Hotel le Coquillage, tel: 125, 16 rooms.
Hotel le Tropical, tel: 69, 22 rooms.

There is a State-sponsored village of detached bungalows available to tourists.

TAMATAVE

The well laid out town of Tamatave is the chief port. The straight, broad streets are shaded with royal palms and flame trees and the sea-front is lined with casuarinas. It is an eight-hour drive from Antananarivo through beautiful mountainous country of forests and coffee plantations. Tamatave is the centre for cloves, vanilla, raffia, coffee, groundnuts, graphite and mica.

The town has a large well-stocked market with many handicrafts. Tamatave has some night-life and dances. The sea around Tamatave is shark-infested and it is not advisable to bathe off any of the beaches.

Hotels
Hotel les Flamboyants, Avenue de la Liberation, tel: 323.50, 25 rooms.
Hotel Joffre, tel: 323.90, 17 rooms.

FORT-DAUPHIN
The two routes to Fort-Dauphin (500 km from Ihosy and 630 km from Tulear) are worth travelling for the magnificent scenery through the semi-arid south, with its vast expanses of grassland which support huge cattle herds, the thorny cactus-like forest, mountains and great rivers.

The old city was the site of the first French settlement in the 17th century and remains of the fort may be seen on the Malagasy army barracks. Scenically, Fort-Dauphin is very beautiful, set along semi-circular beaches under high forest-clad mountains. Fort-Dauphin is famous for its excellent lobsters and oysters.

Hotels
Hotel le Dauphin, B.P. 54, tel: 138, 15 rooms.
Hotel de France, B.P. 8, 15 rooms.
Motel Libanoana, Libanoana, tel: 136, 6 rooms.

MAJUNGA
On the west coast, Majunga is the second largest port of Madagascar but it is rapidly silting up with red soil brought down from the deforested Hauts Plateaux by the Ikopa. Ships have to lie offshore and unload into lighters. Japanese and Le-

banese shrimp-fishing fleets operate from the port.

The weather is hot for most of the year, especially from November to May when temperatures of 35°C are common. A pleasant breeze blows in from the sea after sunset, when much of the population frequents the palm-shaded sea front. About 10 km north of the town, near the airport, is La Grand Plage—a fine beach with clean white sand and quite safe from sharks.

Hotels
Les Roches Rouges, Blvd. Marcoz, B.P. 481, tel: 21.61, 15 rooms.
Hotel de France, B.P. 45, tel: 26.07.

DIEGO SUAREZ
Situated in the extreme north, Diego Suarez (sometimes called Antsirana) has one of the most beautiful harbours in the world. This cosmopolitan town has Malagasy, Arabs, Indians, Reunionnais and French.

By road, Diego Suarez is about 1,200 km from Antananarivo. Only 700 km has been tarred and much of the road is impassable from November to June. The best way to reach it is by air or sea.

The province of Diego Suarez is rich in legends, folklore and ceremonial rituals such as the sacrifices in the sacred lake of Anivorano North. Much of the tradition is reflected in the local handicrafts. The province also produces most of Madagascar's vanilla for export.

Hotels
Hotel de la Poste, B.P. 121, tel: 44, 28 rooms.
Nouvel Hotel, tel: 162, 14 rooms.
Hotel le Tropical, tel: 323, 17 rooms.
Entertainments: There is a nightclub in **Hotel le Tropical**, and there are many bars and 'dancing'. There is one fine beach, Ramena, near the town which is safe for bathing.

NOSSI-BE

'Nossi' means Island and 'Be' is Great. The largest of Madagascar's satellite islands, it is also called Perfume Island because of the numerous plants such as

Tananarive's 15-storey Hilton hotel

ylang-ylang (from which is extracted macassar oil which is essential on the perfume industry), patchouli, vetiver and lemon grass, and the scent of vanilla pods drying in the sun.

Situated about 150 km south-west of Diego Suarez, the island can be reached by boat at the port of Hell-Ville, or, more easily, by air. Air Madagascar operates daily flights from Antananarivo (two hours), Majunga and Diego Suarez.

The hills are of volcanic origin, and contain deep crater lakes, the largest being that of Amparihibe, inhabited by crocodiles renowned for the quality of the skins. Of the beaches, the finest is the palm-fringed Andilana. At Palm Beach (Ambondro) there is the **Palm Beach** hotel with a casino and nightclub, water-skiing, skin-diving and goggle fishing. The beaches are safe for bathing.

The Madagascar Airtours agency, Marine Service, is based at the Palm Beach hotel and arrangements can be made through them for boat excursions to the neighbouring islands of Nosy Komba, Nosy Sakatia and Nosy Tanikely. Cars can also be hired with or without a driver for visits around the island.

Other interesting sights are the Scientific Research Aquarium (which has many interesting species of underwater life, including the celebrated coelacanth); the Indian cemetery of Ambabanoro; and Dzamandzar, a small village of balloon-shaped houses.

NATIONAL PARKS

Isalo

Lying to the north of the road from Antananarivo to Tulear, just after Ranohira (about 800 km), Isalo is situated in a spectacular chain of sandstone mountains. Camping is possible, but access should be by four-wheel-drive or on foot, with a guide from Ranohira.

The park contains some extensive caves, including the **Grottes des Portugais** where shipwrecked Portuguese sailors apparently live and died some time in the 17th century.

Montagne d'Ambre

This is a rainforest park around the summit of the 1,475 m tertiary volcano in the region of Diego Suarez. The peak receives about 5,000 mm of rain per annum. The forest contains many orchids and lemurs. Access is by forest paths or on foot from Joffreville, 32 km west of Diego Suarez.

HISTORY

Although Madagascar has only one language and basically one culture, the diversity of racial features points to a fascinating mixture of origins.

The Indonesian element is assumed to stem from parties of adventurers crossing the sea between 200 BC and AD 800 in huge outrigger canoes, each capable of holding 200 people.

They brought their language (an archaic form of Malayo-Polynesian), crops such as paddy rice, the coconut and banana; and customs such as the building of the large square family tombs still found all round Antananarivo.

The northern tip of Madagascar was always an extreme limb of the Arab-dominated Indian Ocean trade, where alluvial gold and mined silver from the interior was bought and a small-scale two-way traffic in slaves grew up with East Africa.

Arabs and Swahili built towns, such as Vohemar, dating back to the 11th century, where Chinese porcelain and Persian glass have been found.

Some settled along the east coast where the Antaimoro have preserved what are called 'the great writings' in Arabic-script Malagasy.

In the 16th century the Portuguese established themselves on Mozambique Island and introduced maize to western Madagascar and sold slaves to the island.

When the first Europeans rounded the Cape of Good Hope at the end of the 15th century, the south and east coasts of Madagascar attained a new importance as victualling posts, which could supply cattle and rice, for ships on their way to India.

The high, wealthy rice plain around Antananarivo became the centre of a unified Merina kingdom, which also extended over the Betsileo, under the autocratic King Andrianampoinimerina (1787-1810) who even claimed 'the sea is the limit of my paddy field'. The Merina were a caste society which used slaves to till the fields for the *hova* (freemen) and *andriana* (nobility). The latter were the craftsmen and soon monopolised trade with the coast.

The main ambition of Andrianampoinimerina's successor, Radama I, was to have a European-type army. In his drive to control the Betsimisaraka of the east coast he was abetted by the British who had wrested Mauritius from France in the Napoleonic wars. Radama succeeded in conquering the whole of Madagascar. Radama's wife, who became Queen Ranavalona I (1818-61), led a conservative swing against the Europeans, driving them out violently and persecuting Christians.

At the same time she encouraged an interesting attempt to make European goods rather than import them. But it was impossible for the island to remain isolated and in the next period the problem was to play off English against French.

The years 1883-85 saw a war which ended in the Merina's expulsion of the French, but in 1890 Britain traded its interest in Madagascar for French recognition of its Zanzibar protectorate.

As early as 1915 there was considerable nationalist fervour among intellectuals and the Merina nobility who resented their inferior position as 'subjects' liable to arbitrary law and forced labour. After World War II constitutional development speeded up with elections won by the MDRM party but the masses rose in 1947 in a violent rebellion, equally harshly suppressed, in which 60,000-80,000 were killed, mostly Malagasy.

A passive, shocked lull followed for more than a decade until the country proceeded to French-inspired 'independence' in 1960.

MALAWI

The Republic of Malawi (formerly Nyasaland) is a country of great beauty, with towering mountains, high plateaux, vast plains and the inland sea of Lake Malawi with its sandy beaches, tideless, sparkling waters and lakeside resorts.

There are several versions of how Malawi came to its name. Its meaning is roughly 'the lake where the sun-haze is reflected in the water like fire'. The early people were known as the aMaravi—'the people of the flames'. When David Livingstone came to the country in the middle 1850s he asked the name of the great stretch of inland water, not of the Chewa people who lived by the lake but of the Yao who come from what is now Tanzania, and they told him it was 'nyassa' which literally means 'lake'. Hence the lake came to be known as Lake Nyasa (Lake Lake!) and the country Nyasaland. When Malawi became independent on July 6, 1964 the new Republic chose the name of Malawi.

Although the lake is undoubtedly Malawi's dominant tourist feature, its majestic wooded mountains, vast plains and tropical forests give this relatively unspoilt country a tremendous attraction for sightseers and holidaymakers.

THE LAND AND THE PEOPLE
The surface area of Lake Malawi covers nearly 24,000 sq km, about one-fifth of the total territory. The lake lies 473 m

above sea level in the deep, trough-like rift valley which stretches the length of the country. High plateaux rise on either side of the trough with wide, rolling, grassy plains with an elevation of around 1,000 m to the west rising as high as 2,600 m in the Nyika Uplands in the north. In the south there is the rugged 3,000 m

MALAWI

Tanzania

150 miles

Livingstonia
Mzuzu

Zambia

Lake Malawi

Salima

Mozambique

Lilongwe

Mangoche

ZOMBA

Blantyre-Limbe

Mulanje
Thyolo

Nsanje

Mount Mulanje, set in the heart of emerald-green tea plantations, and Zomba Mountain, with the old capital city of Zomba nestling in its foothills.

Unlike adjacent territories, Malawi has little mineral wealth but has some of the most fertile soil in south-central Africa. Although just over half the land area is arable, only about a third of it is as yet under cultivation.

Malawi is one of the more densely populated countries in africa with an average of 51 people per sq km, although one is hardly aware of this density when travelling through the countryside, particularly in the Northern Region, which has only 12% of the population. The Southern Region, by contrast, is the most developed and carries 52%. The great majority of the African population are rural dwellers. Along the roadside the traveller will come across the village markets displaying the fruits of their labours—mounds of maize and groundnuts, tropical fruits, beautifully woven baskets and mats, wood carvings and beadwork.

The Malawians are a friendly, colourful people who stem from a number of ethnic stocks and whose culture is marked by a wide range of dance forms. Along the southern lakeshore, in the Mangochi district, the Yao culture groups predominate. These are mostly followers of Islam, speaking ChiYao, and are found in considerable numbers at Salima and Nkhotakota in the Central Region, with a sprinkling as far north as Karonga.

Intermingled with the Yao in the Mangochi, Salima and Nkhotakota districts, and predominating along the lakeshore, are the Chewa, the country's largest single ethnic group. They speak ChiChewa, the national language.

Around Ntakataka near Chipoka in the Central Region are the Ngoni of Chief Kachindamoto. They are an offshoot of the Maseko Ngoni of Nicheu and descendants of one of several Zulu warrior groups who broke away from Shaka's iron control and trekked north to Central and East Africa. The *ingoma* is their spectacular war dance.

The Tonga are found mainly betweeen Bandawe and Chinteche in the Northern Region as far as Usisya, although some also live as far south as Nkhotakota. They speak ChiTonga. They have no connection with people of the same name who live in adjacent territories.

The Tumbuka-Henga are found mostly between Nkhata Bay and Karonga. They speak ChiTumbuka, a tongue very different from the national language. From Karonga northwards the predominant people are the Ngonde. Mostly Christian, they have their own language, ChiNgonde.

WILDLIFE

Each of Malawi's three regions has its own game park with a wide variety of animals, but it is not unusual to come across elephant, eland and zebra when motoring through the countryside. Birdlife is particularly prolific, and over 900 species have been recorded.

In the Central Region around Dedza Mountain there are great upland plains. One of the principal attractions is the Kasungu National Park where elephant, buffalo, kudu, sable, lion, oribi, zebra and numerous smaller antelope roam. In the Northern Region the country is less populated and large herds of zebra and eland move freely in the rolling plains. The best time to see this area is between August and November when the wild flowers are at their best and the wildlife is more easily spotted. Most of the 880 sq km Nyika National Park lies at an altitude of 2,300 m with occasional peaks rising to over 2,600 m. It comprises ridge after ridge of undulating grassland with deep valleys and patches of evergreen forests.

Lake Malawi, its tributaries and fringing swamps contain over 240 varieties of fish. Over 220 species are to be found in the lake itself and the majority of these are not found anywhere else in the world. Nearly all make good eating when freshly cooked. The main lake types are varieties of catfish, perch and carp.

GENERAL INFORMATION

Area: 94,100 sq km of land and 24,400 sq km of water.
Population: 4.9 million.
Altitude: 500 to 3,300 m above sea level.
Capital: Lilongwe. Blantyre is the commercial centre.
Head of State: The Life President, Dr H. Kamuzu Banda.
Government: National Assembly of 81 elected members and 15 nominated by the President. One political party, the Malawi Congress Party (MCP). Republican status. Member of the Commonwealth.
Date of independence: July 6, 1964.
Languages: ChiChewa (national); English (official).
Religions: Christianity and Islam.
Currency: 100 tambala = 1 kwacha (K). £1 sterling = K1.56. $1 = KO.90.
Time: GMT + 2.

HOW TO GET THERE

By air: From the United Kingdom: Air Malawi and British Airways.

From the United States: direct flight to Nairobi in Kenya to connect with stopover flights.

From southern Africa: Air Malawi, South African Airways, and Deta Mozambique Airways have frequent flights to Blantyre.

Flights also operate to and from Dar es Salaam, Entebbe, Nicosia, Nairobi, Lusaka, Addis Ababa, Aden, Bombay and Beira.

Chileka International Airport is 17 km from Blantyre; buses and taxis operate.

By road: Malawi is connected to Rhodesia by a road running from Blantyre

Doing handicraft work for sale along the Lilongwe-Zomba road

through Tete in Mozambique to Mtoko; to Zambia by a road linking Lilongwe and Chipata; to Tanzania by a road linking Chitipa and Mbeya (via Nakonde in Zambia); and to the Mozambique coast by a road running from Mulanje to Quelimane. Driving licences issued in most countries of the world are valid in Malawi. Visitors are nevertheless advised to obtain a valid International Driving Permit. Motor vehicles, caravans and trailers may be imported temporarily by tourists visiting or in transit through Malawi provided they are currently licensed in their home countries and bear appropriate registration and nationality plates. A vehicle so imported requires a triptyque or a carnet de passage. If neither can be obtained, a temporary importation permit, valid initially for up to four months, will be issued at the border.

By rail: The cities of Blantyre and Beira in Mozambique are connected by rail, and diesel railcars operate on regular weekly daytime schedules.

Visas and health regulations

Nationals of the following countries do not need visas: Britain, Commonwealth countries, Denmark, Eire, Finland, Federal Republic of Germany, Iceland, Luxembourg, Madagascar, Netherlands, Norway, Portugal, Rhodesia, San Marino, South Africa, Sweden and the US. All others must have visas but can obtain transit visas covering a period of five days' travel in the country.

Visas can be obtained from Malawi embassies or honorary consuls. In Commonwealth countries with no Malawi mission, visas can be obtained from local immigration authorities. In all other countries visitors should apply to the British diplomatic mission. Travellers must be prepared to show they have adequate funds to support themselves during their stay and the means to leave the country.

Vaccination certificates required for smallpox and cholera—and yellow fever if arriving from endemic areas.

Dutiable goods

Duty is not normally charged on visitors' personal effects, when they are definitely intended for re-export. Visitors may not import firearms without a valid Tourist Firearms Permit, which should be obtained well in advance from the Registrar of firearms, P.O. Box 41, Zomba. Such permits are issued only in respect of sporting rifles (including air rifles) and shotguns; revolvers and pistols are specifically excluded.

Currency regulations

There is no limit to the amount of foreign currency brought into Malawi, but visitors are required to obtain a receipt from the customs officer at the point of entry as they will be asked to declare the balance on departure. Visitors may not import or export Malawi currency in excess of K20 and are therefore advised to keep the amount of Malawi money they export to the absolute minimum as it is not convertible abroad.

Travellers' cheques in dollars, sterling and other acceptable currencies are freely convertible. When travelling in the remoter regions travellers' cheques can be cashed at the Treasury Cashier's section of the local District Commissioner's office between the hours of 0730-1200 and 1300-1500, Mondays to Fridays; 0730-1300 on Saturdays. PTL stores and Oilcom petrol stations throughout Malawi, and Kandolo stores at Blantyre, Zomba and Lilongwe also accept travellers' cheques.

CLIMATE

Malawi's climate varies from the bracing air of the highlands to the relaxing, languorous atmosphere of the beaches of Lake Malawi. The dry winter season lasts from May to October (July: $20°C$); nights can be chilly, especially on high ground. The rainy season is from November to March (December: $27°C$) though intermittent showers occur during the rest of the year. At any time of the year the *chiperone*, a cold wind from the southeast, may blow up bringing cloud and drizzle, particularly on high ground. The area around the shores of Lake Malawi has a particularly low annual rainfall and the lakeshore is cooled by breezes throughout the year.

What to wear—N.B. Visitors must observe certain conventions pertaining to dress. There is a restriction on wearing dresses and skirts in public that do not fully cover the knee-cap when the wearer is standing upright. Women should not wear shorts and trousers in public. These limitations do not apply at any holiday resort on Lake Malawi, on the mountains of Zomba, Mulanje, Dedza, Vipya and Nyika, in the National Parks at Lengwe, Kasungu and Nyika, and at any hotel, airport or railway station if the visitor or wearer is in direct transit to a Malawi holiday resort or to other destinations outside the country. They also do not apply when the wearer is engaged in any form of sport for which short skirts and dresses or shorts or trousers are customary, or if it is part of a national dress. Men must not wear long hair or 'bellbottom' trousers.

Health precautions: There is no bilharzia in Lake Malawi, so the bathing there is safe. All stagnant or slow-moving waters are, however, infected. Piped water supplies, except where labelled to the contrary, are safe for drinking; otherwise water should be boiled. Hotels supply mosquito nets where required and visitors are advised to take prophylactic drugs against malaria.

ACCOMMODATION AND FOOD

In the main centres there are good hotels. Most hotels require booking deposits. There are several Government rest houses which provide adequate accommodation at reasonable rates. All rest houses have bathrooms and cooking facilities, but guests must provide their own food.

Rest houses are sited in the following areas: Central Region—Ncheu, Dedza, Kasungu and Nkhotakota. Northern Region—Mzimba, Nkhata Bay, Mzuzu, Rjumpi, Chisenga, Chitipa and Karonga. Southern Region—Ngabu.

Hotel, rest house and game camp bookings should be made well in advance. All hotels are fully licensed. Camping is permitted in the grounds of most rest houses, and in Zomba, Mkapola, Monkey Bay, Cape Maclear and Salima.

Fresh fish from Lake Malawi is the country's speciality. There are trout from streams on the Zomba, Mulanje and Nyika plateaux. Meat, poultry and dairy produce are plentiful and tropical fruits are abundant in season. The locally brewed beer is very good.

Tipping is not necessary in hotels where a 10% service charge is levied, except for extra attention.

TRANSPORT

Road: there are over 2,700 km of main road and 2,200 km of secondary road connecting Blantyre with all the places of interest in Malawi. Many of the major roads are tarred and the motorist might experience difficult driving conditions only at the height of the rainy season.

The lakeshore road from Mangochi to Monkey Bay is tarred, together with the access road between Liwonde and Mangochi. Just south of Monkey Bay a new link road has been constructed to join the highway between Balaka and Salima, which provides a more direct route to Mangochi, Monkey Bay, Cape Maclear and Salima lakeshore resorts.

Border posts are open from 0600 to 1800 on weekdays and Saturdays. A small charge is levied for services outside these hours and on public holidays.

Air: Air Malawi, the national airline, operates between Lilongwe and Zomba, Mangochi, Salima, Nkhotakota, Kasungu and Chilumba. Air Malawi and two private firms, Capital Air Services Ltd and Leopard Air Ltd, offer charter services. Air Malawi also operates the popular all-inclusive 'Skylake' package tours from adjacent territories.

Rail: Blantyre is connected by rail to Beira and Nacala in Mozambique. There are regular services from Blantyre to Salima, the railhead for Lilongwe and one of Malawi's main lake holiday centres.

Car hire
Automotive Products Ltd, P.O. Box 1222, Blantyre, tel: Blantyre 30161. **Hall's Garage Ltd,** P.O. Box 368, Blantyre, tel: Blantyre 2356. Mandala Motors Ltd, P.O. Box 467, Blantyre, tel: Blantyre 2011. **United Touring Company,** Car hire and Conducted Tours, P.O. Box

176, Blantyre, tel: Blantyre 30122/8251.
Central African Transport Co. Blantyre:
Central Motors Limbe and Zomba.

For taxi services in Blantyre telephone:
2604, 8929, 8046, 50025, 30812

BUSINESS HOURS
Banks: open 0800 Monday-Saturday.
Close 1230 Monday, Tuesday, Thursday,
Friday; 1130 Wednesday; 1030 Saturday.

Government Offices and Commerce: 0730
or 0800 to 1200 or 1230; 1300 or 1330 to
1630 Monday-Friday, 0730 or 0800 to
1200 or 1230 Saturday.

PUBLIC HOLIDAYS
New Year's Day; Martyrs' Day 3 March;
Good Friday; Easter Saturday; Easter
Monday; Kamuzu Day 14 May; Republic
Day 6 July; August Holiday, variable;
Mothers Day 17 October; Christmas
Day; Boxing Day.

FOREIGN EMBASSIES
UK: P.O. Box 30042 Lilongwe. Tel: Li-
longwe 31544.
US: P.O. Box 380, Blantyre. Tel: Blan-
tyre 2437.
France: P.O. Box 90, Blantyre. Tel:
Blantyre 30255.
West Germany: P.O. Box 5695, Blantyre.

Tel: Blantyre 50322.
South Africa: P.O. Box 30043 Lilongwe.
Tel: Lilongwe 30888.
Sweden: P.O. Box 5136, Limbe. Tel:
Blantyre 50403.
Belgium: P.O. Box 327, Blantyre. Tel:
Blantyre 2723/4.
Denmark: P.O. Box 22, Blantyre. Tel:
Blantyre 2700.
Austria: P.O. Box 5222, Limbe. Tel:
Blantyre 51143.

TOURIST OFFICES
Malawi: The Department of Tourism.
P.O. Box 402, Blantyre. Tel: 36811.
UK: Marketing Services Ltd, 52, High
Holborn, London, WC1V 6RL.
East Africa: Air Malawi, P.O. Box
20117, Nairobi, Kenya.

BLANTYRE
Named by missionaries after Livingstone's birthplace in Scotland, the city of
Blantyre was established in 1895. It is
cradled by impressive hills and mountains, and is the country's main commercial, industrial and communications centre. The city covers an area of 190 sq km
and comprises the neighbouring centres
of Blantyre (1,098 m above sea level) and
Limbe which are 8 km apart. Between
them lies the industrial area with its many
new factories and enterprises, and the

Ploughing a tobacco patch

modern complex of Government offices at Chichiri. Nearby are the 50,000-seat Kamuzu Stadium, the Museum of Malawi and the Independence Arch.

Places of interest
St. Michael's Church on the Chileka Road is a reminder of the part played by the Scottish Missions in the more recent history of Malawi.

Other places of interest are the tobacco auctions in Limbe which generally operate between April and October each year; Independence Arch and the Museum of Malawi at Chirichiri. Within easy motoring distance from Blantyre is Mulanje, Malawi's highest mountain, 3,350 m, with tea and coffee plantations spreading for miles across its lower slopes.

Mwalawolemba (rock of writing) Rock Shelter on Mikolongwe Hill off the Limbe-Midima road is interesting for its rock paintings and for the spectacular views of Mulanje Mountain. Other scenic attractions are, the Mpatamanga Gorge on the main Salisbury road, Mfunda Falls (60 km distant at Matope), the Nkula Falls and Kholombidzo Falls on the Shire River about 16 km from Chileka Airport.

Hotels
Mount Soche Hotel, Glyn Jones Road, P.O. Box 284, Blantyre. Tel: 35588, 100 bedrooms.
Ryall's Hotel, Hanover Avenue, P.O. Box 21, Blantyre. Tel: 35955, 65 bedrooms.
Shire Highlands Hotel, Churchill Road, P.O. Box 5204, Limbe. Tel: Blantyre 50055, 65 bedrooms.
Hotel Continental, P.O. Box 5249, Limbe. Tel: Blantyre 50670, 24 bedrooms.

Restaurants
The following restaurants are popular: **Ndirande** at Mount Soche Hotel (international cuisine, dancing nightly); **21 Room** at Ryall's Hotel (continental); **Balmoral** at Shire Highlands (continental); **China Bar and Restaurant** (Chinese); **Maxim's** (continental); **Cafe Capri** (Portuguése); **Riviera** in Limbe (Indian). **Hong Kong** (Chinese).

Entertainments
There are four cinemas as well as a well-equipped drive-in on Chikawa Road. The climax of Malawi's festival calendar is the annual display of traditional dancing held at Kamuzu Stadium on Republic Day (6 July).

Shopping and markets
Victoria Avenue is the main shopping area where there are well-stocked shops as well as street vendors displaying locally made curios. Off Victoria Avenue is the Curio and Handicraft Centre.

Another feature of the local scene is Limbe Market—a bargaining bustle of brightly dressed people and colourful merchandise. Exotic cotton and skirt lengths in brilliant prints called *chirundu* are popular buys; so also are the mats, baskets and hats woven in swamp reeds and raffia in traditional patterns.

ZOMBA

On the lower slopes of the Zomba Plateau lies Zomba (970 m), the former capital city of Malawi, now the University centre. In addition to State House, whose foundations were laid in 1901, there is the historic Old Residency, commissioned in 1886.

Spectacular panoramic views, mountain streams and waterfalls, brilliant birdlife and wild flowers distinguish the beautiful 2,000 m Zomba Plateau, a forest reserve planted with the stately Mulanje Cedar, a unique species of conifer, and with pines and cypresses

One takes different one-way routes to and from the plateau and there is an extensive network of forest roads on it leading to a number of splendid picnic spots.

Crowded countryside bus stop

Hotel
Ku Chawe Inn, P.O. Box 71. Tel: 403.
Thirty-six beds, beautiful views across the
plains 1,000 m below to Mount Mulanje.

LILONGWE

Lilongwe is the second largest town and
the new capital of Malawi. From Lilongwe the visitor can easily reach the
nearby Salima lakeshore which is one of
the more popular holiday spots on the
lake. North of Lilongwe is Malawi's main
tobacco growing area where burley leaf is
grown and air-cured on small plots and
farms around the villages. 90 km from
Lilongwe is Dedza. Scenically this area
has few rivals in Africa. Dedza Mountain
rises 2,000 m and offers some challenge
to the climber. On the lower slopes there
are splendid wooded walks and fine views
over the lake.

Hotels
Lilongwe Hotel, P.O. Box 44, Lilongwe,
83 beds, recently modernised.
Capital Hotel, 216 beds, new luxury
hotel.

LAKE MALAWI

Lake Malawi is the heart of Malawi and
the cradle of its culture. Its shores provide the visitor with a fascinating mixture
of scenic beauty, golden beaches, holiday
amenities, historic sites and picturesque
dwellings. The water is fresh and free
from bilharzia, the scourge of other African lakes. There are no tides or currents,
and the crocodile has been effectively
banished from the resort areas, making
the lake one of the safest water sports
venues in Africa.

Lake Malawi has a constantly changing
character depending on the time of the
day, the weather and the season—one
moment the water may be as smooth as
silk and then suddenly waves seven
metres high can thrash the shores. It is
generally calmest from March to May,
and the year-round temperature never
drops below 21.1°C.

One of the best ways of seeing Lake
Malawi is to cruise in the 620-ton *Illala
II,* the lake's mini-liner which starts and
finishes at Monkey Bay. The present
Illala has accommodation for nine cabin-
class passengers in three double and three
single cabins.

Leaving every Friday, the vessel calls
at Chipoka Nkhotakota, Likoma Island,
Nkhata Bay, Usisya, Ruarwe, Mlowe,
Chitimba, Chilumba and Kambwe, taking seven days for the 1,000 km round-

the-lake voyage. The cruise enables the visitor to sample in comfort some of Africa's finest lake and mountain scenery. It visits several interesting ports and historic sites such as Likoma Island, whose mission station, established in 1885, has a cathedral rivalling Westminster Abbey in size. It houses carvings from Oberammergau, earth from Jerusalem, and stone from Canterbury, and the wood for its crucifix was taken from a tree near Serenje in Zambia underneath which the heart of David Livingstone is buried.

Lakeside hotels

Nkopola Lodge, the newest and most up-to-date holiday hotel, reservations through Mount Soche Hotel, Blantyre; 52 beds, marina, goggling equipment available.

Club Makokola, P.O. Box 59, Mangochi; thatched cottage complex, 50 beds, boats water-ski and goggling equipment available, own airstrip, golf.

Monkey Bay Hotel, P.O. Box 30, Monkey Bay; block and chalet accommodation with 32 beds.

Fish Eagle Inn, P.O. Box 16, Salima; 60 beds, safe swimming, boats, water-ski and fishing tackle available for hire.

Grand Beach Hotel, P.O. Box 11, Salima; 113 beds, boats and fishing tackle for hire.

There are rest houses at Nkhotakota, Nkhata Bay, and Karonga.

NATIONAL PARKS

National park animals are not tame, and drivers should therefore exercise caution when approaching game, particularly potentially dangerous animals such as elephant. Visitors should arrive before dark and should return to camp before dark each day during their stay. Fires of any description are forbidden in the parks outside the game camps and great care should be taken in the disposal of cigarette ends and matches. Firearms, dogs and other pets are not allowed inside the parks.

Camp accommodation in each park can be booked through local agents (see details below). Besides the accommodation charges, a park entrance fee is levied on each vehicle.

Nyika National Park

This park is situated in the northern part of the Northern Region and is open to visitors throughout the year. It covers 880 sq km and lies at an altitude of 2,300 m with occasional peaks rising to over 2,600 m. The rolling grassland is broken by deep valleys and patches of evergreen forest. Large herds of eland and zebra roam the plains and groups of roan antelope may be seen, together with the smaller species such as reedbuck, bushbuck, duiker and klipspringer. Warthog are relatively common. Lion and leopard follow the herds and may be seen lurking in the wake of their prey. The three dams near Chilinda Game Camp offer fine bird-watching, and the Wattle Crane and Stanley's Bustard are two of the larger varieties often spotted.

Accommodation at **Chilinda Game Camp** is provided for 18 persons in four self-contained chalets and, in addition, 12 people can be accommodated in a block of six double bedrooms adjacent to the central lounge/dining room. Sole booking for the Chilinda Game Camp is at present through the Chief Game Warden. P.O. Box 30151, Lilongwe.

Kasungu National Park

The park is situated in the north-west corner of the Central Region and is usually open from 1 May to 31 December. The range of game to be seen is the most extensive in Malawi. Elephant occur in some numbers, together with an occasional rhinoceros. There are buffalo, Zebra and many species of antelope, including the stately kudu, sable and roan. Lion, leopard and cheetah may be sighted from time to time

Lifupa Game Camp has its own swimming pool and electricity supply. Up to 27 persons can be accommodated in the camp's nine chalets. There is a centrally situated lounge, dining room and bar.

The sole booking agent for Lifupa Game Camp is at present the Mount Soche Hotel, Box 284, Blantyre.

Lengwe National Park
Situated in the south-west corner of the Southern Region, it is only 130 sq km in extent. The park is unique in that it is the farthest place north where the rare, shy nyala antelope is found. This beautiful animal may be seen, often in large numbers, together with bushbuck, kudu, hartebeest; impala and duiker. Other rarities are the Blue or Samango Monkey and Livingstone's Suni. Lion, leopard and buffalo are often spotted. Bird life is varied and interesting. Visitors may view game at very close quarters from carefully concealed, shaded hides. The best viewing time at these hides is generally the morning.

Accommodation at **Lengwe Game Camp** is provided for eight persons. There is a fully equipped kitchen and the services of a cook are available, but visitors must bring their own food. No provisions or petrol are available at the camp, but soft drinks are on sale.

The sole booking agent is the United Touring Company. P.O. Box 176, Blantyre.

HISTORY
The tribes migrating to the Nyasa region in early times were those belonging to the pre-Luba Malawi group whom the Portuguese called Maravi. Coming down either the east or west side of Lake Tanganyika from the northern lakes, they reached the Nyasa-Tanganyika plateau towards the end of the 15th century.

Prior to the arrival of David Livingstone in 1859, small bands of Jesuit missionaries had traversed the country. It was Livingstone's early journeys which first drew the attention of Britain to the horrors and cruelty of the Arab slave trade, but it was not until the 1890s that this practice was brought to an end.

Following the arrival of Scottish missionaries in the mid-1870s, a Glasgow merchant started the Livingstone Central Africa Trading Company, later known as the African Lakes Corporation.

By this time the European scramble for Africa was in full swing. The Germans were busy in the north and east; Portugal was intent on joining Mozambique with Angola and on annexing the intervening territory; Cecil Rhodes was pushing upwards from the south. Alarmed at the Portuguese claims of sovereignty over the Shire Highlands the missionaries in 1880 appealed to the Foreign Office for protection. This was ignored until 1890 when the Foreign Office sent Portugal an ultimatum to withdraw.

Many Malawians had first-hand knowledge of living in white-dominated Rhodesia and South Africa and were completely against the imposition of similar rule in their country, but although opposition was widespread, they lacked effective local leadership. An appeal was made to Dr Hastings Kamuzu Banda to return home after 41 years abroad in South Africa, the U.S., Britain and Ghana.

He quickly rallied the Nyasaland African Congress Party, and vowed to bring his country to independence—something he accomplished exactly six years to the day after his return home.

Under his powerful and paternalistic rule, Malawi has achieved a somewhat repressive kind of stability. Dr Banda has concentrated on two priorities: to turn his country from a 'rural slum' into a profitable agricultural society; and to maintain cordial relations with his white-ruled neighbours, especially South Africa. He was the first black President ever to visit South Africa. Many white South Africans visit Malawi for their holidays.

MALI

Mali has a very special appeal to visitors interested in the ancient history of West Africa, and to those waiting to witness the living African traditions of the Bambara and Dogan peoples where once flourished the powerful empires of Ghana, Mali and Songhai. At the height of Mali's influence Timbuktu was a centre of learning that attracted scholars from all over the Islamic world.

THE LAND AND THE PEOPLE

Mali is a vast land covering over 1.2 million sq km but with a sparse population of only 5 million. It is a land of flat plains. Two major rivers give it life—the Senegal on its western edge, and the more important Niger. On its journey north the Niger forms a vast inland delta stretching for 450 km of the river's length, and 200 km wide. At Timbuktu the river reaches the desert and turns east, then south-east at Bourem, where it heads for the ocean. The Niger is navigable most of the way towards Mali's eastern neighbour, the Republic of Niger. The stretch from Bamako to Mopti is particularly busy and fairly large river boats steam along it. Some stretches are not always navigable, either because of flooding, or for lack of water, remote places in the west and south must transport their supplies when the water level is

just right, after which they are cut off from the world for up to five months.

In the desert and near the Algeria and Niger borders in the north-east, the Adrar des Iforas Massif rises to 800 m. Here, and particularly in the fossil valley of Tilmesi, archaeologists and anthropologists have found evidence of early human occupation. At Asselar, Professor Monod discovered the *homo sapiens* considered to be closest to the present negroid type and also a cousin of *cro-magnon* man.

The north is true desert, empty save for

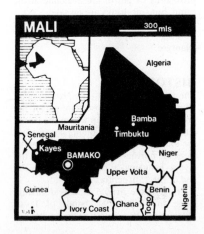

the Tuaregs living around the oases and along the ancient trans-Sahara camel routes. The Tuareg and Fulani cattle-raising nomads further south are thin and tall people, and their features are Arab more than Negro.

The arid grazing land at the centre of Mali is called the Sahel, and here the effects of droughts have been the most damaging. Nomads have had their herds decimated as the Sahara has advanced relentlessly southwards.

Mali's most populated area is the southern savannah region, bordering the states of Upper Volta, Ivory Coast and Guinea. The peoples of this area, the Songhai, Malinke, Senoufou, Dogon and the Bambara (Mali's largest ethnic group), can also be found in the neighbouring states, but they have their origins in Mali.

Proud of their glorious past, Malians find it hard to accept a secondary position in West Africa and their dependence for communications on the southern states. These tall, dignified and reserved people may be aloof and distant, but they are never hostile or petty. They consider their poverty less important than their rich traditions, and will gracefully welcome you into their modest homes.

CULTURE

Mali has two distinctive and rich areas of art—Bambara and Dogon. Bambara sculpture—fashioned mainly from softwood and occasionally from iron—includes masks, musical instruments, head-dresses, ancestral figures and marionettes. The best-known are the rhythmic, semi-naturalistic carved antelope head-dresses or headpieces used in the ritualistic dance. Bambara art is still closely related to their religious life and social organization which is based on fraternal societies, the *komo*, whose cosmology and traditions infuse all religious thought and social behaviour.

The industrious Dogon—who live on the rocky plateau around Bandiagara and the Hombori hills on the bend of the Niger River—are known by their Muslim neighbours as *Habbe* (the unbelievers) because of their ancient resistance to Islam. Their villages, often perched spectacularly below massive rock cliffs, have produced not only an interesting variety of art but also a fertile mythology.

Originally, and even now in the remoter Dogon villages, a full-scale festival would be held only every 60 years in each locality. In recent years coach-loads of tourists have been known to bribe the villagers to put on a show for their convenience. The thrilling dances thus inevitably lose their spontaneity and ancient ritual significance.

The materials used in Mali's rich and varied crafts range from wood and ivory to copper and gold. In the side streets off Bamako's Place de la Mosquée are hundreds of skilled craftsmen, jewellers and weavers, representative of all the country's traditions. Also on sale in Bamako are the striking masks of the Bambara, Dogon and Malinke peoples, and wood and ivory carvings. Excellent pottery is made in Segou region, while Timbuktu is a good centre for iron and copper articles, including swords, daggers and traditional household utensils.

WILDLIFE

The best concentration of wildlife in Mali is in the National Park of La Boucle du Baoulé. It contains examples of all the southern Sahelian species: elephant, lion, leopard, giraffe, buffalo, hippo and numerous types of antelope. The reserve is only 120 km from Bamako and has a number of *campements* in its vicinity.

GENERAL INFORMATION

Area: 1,240,000 sq km.
Population: 5 million.
Altitude: Plateau of 300 m with scattered mountains.

Capital: Bamako.
Head of State: Col. Moussa Traore.
Government: Military.
Date of independence: 22 September, 1960.
Languages: French (official). Bambara understood almost everywhere. Arabic in the north.
Religions: Islam (75%), traditional and Christianity.
Currency: Mali France (FM). 1 French Franc=FM 100. £1 sterling=FM850. US$1=FM495.
Time: GMT.

HOW TO GET THERE
By air: There are flights from France, Eastern Europe, North Africa and West Africa, by the following airlines: Air Mali, Air Afrique, UTA, Interflug, Aeroflot and Air Guinée.

Bamako airport is 3 km from the town. Cheap bus transport into town is available.

By rail: There is a twice-weekly passenger service from Dakar in Senegal—a tedious 26-hour journey, alleviated by the comfort of sleeping and dining cars.

By road: The best road connections are from the Ivory Coast and Upper Volta, but the surfaces are not all good. The road from Senegal via Kayes is very rough. The remote and desolate trans-Saharan route, from Algeria is considerably more hazardous than the Tamanrasset route, for reasons of scarce water and petrol supplies, and lack of clear marker beacons, though in places the surface is good. The 600 km Mali stretch is nevertheless less troublesome than the preceding 600 km in Algeria. Petrol is occasionally available in Tessalit and Bourem. The first completely reliable supply and rest point is Gao. The all-weather road then follows the Niger as far as Niamey.

Bus services operate from Kankan (Guinea) to Bamako, as well as from Bobo Dioulasso (Upper Volta) to Segou and Mopti, and Niamey (Niger) to Gao.

Visa and health regulations
Visas are not required by citizens of France or former French territories. Other visitors must obtain a visa before attempting to enter Mali. There are Malian diplomatic missions in Paris and several West African capitals. A return ticket (or proof of intended departure) is required of all visitors. On arrival you must apply for a 'tourist card' and photography permit.

International certificates of vaccination against smallpox, yellow fever and cholera are required.

Dutiable goods
Personal effects and 50 cigarettes (or equivalent tobacco) are admitted free of duty. Cameras, films, record players and records should be declared on entry.

Currency regulations
All currency taken into Mali must be declared on entry. If this is not done visitors run the risk of being forbidden to take any currency out of the country again.

CLIMATE
There are three main seasons, varying according to latitude, with diminishing rainy seasons as one travels north. The rainy season in the south lasts from June to September or October. In Bamako the average temperature for August is 25°C. The cooler dry season lasts from October to February, followed by an extremely hot dry season until June; the average temperature for April in Bamako is 35°C.

What to wear: Lightweight clothing is essential, but between November and February warm outer clothing is needed at night.

Health precautions: A prophylactic against malaria is essential and should be taken before and after, as well as during, your stay. It is advisable to boil or filter all drinking water, or buy bottled water.

ACCOMMODATION AND FOOD

Only Bamako has hotels approaching international standard, but the other main towns have hotels with varying degrees of comfort, usually with some form of air-conditioning and a restaurant. Prices tend to be quite high. In every town there are small restaurants serving local and north African dishes.

Although bars in Bamako and other towns are open late into the night and all drinks are available, most of the people seated around the small tables will be sipping fruit juice rather than whisky. Malian tamarind and guava juices, when drunk in tall glasses full of ice, are delicious.

A 10% tip is customary in restaurants and bars. Taxi drivers expect about 10%.

TRANSPORT

Air: Air Mali flies regularly from Bamako to Gao, Goundam, Kayes, Kenieba, Mopti, Nara, Nioro, Segou and Timbuktu.

Rail: There are two rail-car services daily from Bamako to its river port of Koulikoro. Six trains a week run from Bamako to Kayes, a journey of 8 to 10 hours.

River: Between July and December there are regular weekly services between Koulikoro (for Bamako) and Gao via Timbuktu—a distance of 1,300 km. The journey takes five or six days, depending on the direction of travel. Between December and March the river trip is only possible between Mopti and Gao (3 days).

Road: The main road in the country runs from Sikasso in the south to Bamako, and then on to Mopti and Gao in the east. The Mopti-Gao stretch is occasionally difficult during the rains. Sturdy vehicles are recommended. Off the main roads one should travel in convoy and take a complete set of spares. Petrol stations are few and far between.

Buses run between the main centres. In Bamako taxis and buses are the usual means of transport, though the taxis are very expensive.

BANKS

The main bank in Bamako, Kayes and Mopti is the Banque Centrale du Mali. Banks are open 0800-1100.

PUBLIC HOLIDAYS

Muslim feast days are observed, as well as the following on the Christian calendar: New Year's Day; Army Day 20 January; Easter; Labour Day; Africa Day 25 May; Independence Day 22 September; Revolution Day 19 November; Christmas Day.

FOREIGN EMBASSIES IN BAMAKO

Algeria, Egypt, France (B.P. 17), West Germany, Ghana, Guinea, India, Libya, Morocco (B.P. 78), Senegal, Sierra Leone, USA (B.P. 34), Upper Volta.

BAMAKO

A predominantly modern town built around a straight central road running parallel to the river Niger, Bamako is the administrative, educational and cultural capital of Mali. It boasts some impressive modern buildings and hotels, and a crafts centre. The streets are shaded with flamboyant and other flowering trees. The main places of interest are the markets,

Great mosque at Bamako

the botanical gardens and the zoo. The wooded Manding mountains, only 50 km away, have a variety of game. The **Boucle de Baoulé National Park** is 120 km away.

Hotels:
Hotel de l'Amitié, newly-opened tourist complex by the river, 200 rooms.
Grand Hotel, B.P. 104, tel: 225.81, central, 59 rooms.
Le Motel, B.P. 911, tel: 236.22; 52 rooms.
Les Hirondelles, B.P. 1026, tel: 244.34, 36 rooms.
Majestic, B.P. 153, tel: 229.20, central, 17 rooms.
Le Lido, B.P. 133, tel: 221.88.
Buffet-hotel, tel: 220.15, central, 15 rooms.

Restaurants:
Le Berry, Les Trois Caïmans (with night club), **l'Aquarium, la Gondole, Bar-Mali, Restaurant Central.**

Tourist information:
Commissariat au tourisme, Hôtel de l'Amitié, B.P. 191, tel: 246.73.
Société Malienne d'exploitation des ressources touristiques (SMERT), Place de la République, tel: 239.41. SMERT organises tours to principal sites.

MOPTI
At the confluence of the Bani and the Niger, the 'Venice of Mali' is built on three islands joined by dykes. Its fine mosque resembles the one at Djenne.

Motel de Sévaré, tel: 45, 15 rooms.
Campement de Mopti, tel: 45, 12 rooms.
Campement de Sangha, 12 rooms.

DJENNE
The 'jewel of the Niger' was founded in 1250. Its beautiful mosque was built this century but is utterly faithful to the age-old architectural styles and replaces an almost identical structure destroyed in 1830.

TIMBUKTU

Undeniably in a state of decay, this historic city still retains something of its ancient mystery. The oldest mosque is the Djinguereber (13th century). The Sankore and Sidi Yahya mosques date from the 14th and 15th centuries respectively. There are ancient, beautifully carved and decorated doors. The tombs of Sheikh El Moktar and Sidi Ahmed Ben Amar still survive. The houses inhabited briefly by the first European explorers, Gordon Laing (1825), Réné Caillé (1827) and Karl Barth (1853) are an essential part of the tourist circuit.

Every year a magnificent camel caravan from the Taoudeni salt mines enters Timbuktu. Here the salt is sold and distributed throughout the Sahelian region.

Hotel de Tombouctou, tel: 07, 29 rooms.

GAO

Once the capital of the Songhai empire, Gao houses the mosque of Kankan Moussa and the curious tomb of the Askia dynasty. Much of this sprawling city's ancient and proud past has, however, disappeared under the impact of recent urban development, but it continues to throb vitality, especially in the market.

Hôtel Atlantide, B.P. 29, tel: 03, 25 rooms.

HISTORY

The Empire of Ghana's influence began in the 6th century AD, at a time when a complex and valuable trade was growing in the Western Sahara between the Berbers of Morocco and the blacks of the Sahel. Camel caravans linked Fez, Tlemcen and Tunis with Aoudaghost, Koumbi-Saleh, Oualata, Timbuktu and Gao. The king of Ghana was described by an Arab geographer as 'the richest king in the world' on account of his vast stocks of gold.

The Empire of Mali developed the trans-Saharan trade even further, and reached its peak of influence under King Kankan Moussa in the early 14th century. Its dominant people were the ancestors of the present-day Manding (or Malinke) peoples.

They have been a dynamic force in politics, commerce and the spread of Islam throughout the western Sahel even into the 20th century.

As an Empire, Mali began to crumble under the impact of the Tuaregs around 1430, while its eastern territories developed independently to become the Empire of Songhai, with its capital in Gao.

The frontier between Mali and Songhai ran through Segou, until Songhai's influence was extended, first under King Ali Ber (or Shi) in the 1460s, and then by his successor Mohamed Toure (who took the name of Askia the Great). Songhai was a cohesive state until 1591, when an invading military force from Morocco defeated its troops in battle.

The states that followed built their power on the demands of the European slave-traders at the coast, and the area went into sad decline. In the early 19th century the Fulanis founded the Islamic state of Macina, with its capital at Hamdallaye (30 km from Mopti). This was succeeded by El Haj Omar's reform movement—which led to the brief establishment of a Tukolor Empire in the 1860s, but this fell to the French in the 1880s. France captured city after city, Segou in 1890, Djenne in 1893, Timbuktu in 1894. The country became known as French Sudan until independence in 1960.

A federation of Senegal and Mali was proposed but conflicting aims of the two leaders, Senghor and Modibo Keita, made this impossible.

In the early 1970s the long drought played havoc with the precarious agricultural economy and with the livelihood of farmers and nomads.

MAURITANIA

Mauritania is a country for travellers fascinated by the Sahara desert and with a sense of adventure. Vast arid landscapes of drifting dunes contrast with rocky plateaux intersected by wide canyons sheltering occasional palm groves and mountain oases.

The coastline, from the Senegal River to the Bay of Levrier, offers endless sandy beaches fringed by the Atlantic surf, where bathing and fishing are possible all the year round. There is abundant wildlife in the Senegal River valley.

Mauritania is a link between the Maghreb and Black Africa. Its history is illustrated by neolithic remains, rock paintings, Berber architecture and medieval towns half buried in sand, while a way of life virtually unchanged for a thousand years is perpetuated by the nomads.

THE LAND AND THE PEOPLE

The most clearly defined frontier is the line of the Senegal River which divides Mauritania from Senegal. All the other frontiers are imaginary lines separating Mauritania from Algeria, Mali and the disputed Western Sahara (which Morocco and Mauritania aim to divide between them). Within these borders lies a territory of over 1m km but with little over one million people.

Mauritania consists mainly of a vast Sahelian and Saharan plain of sand and scrub, shifting and stationary sand dunes, but in certain regions the land rises in rocky plateaux with deep ravines formed by erosion leaving isolated peaks called *kedia* when large and *guelb* when small. The Adrar plateaux in the west-central

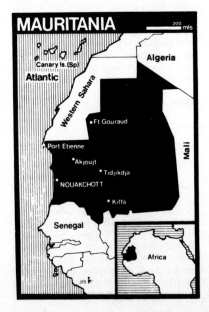

region rise to 500m and the Tagant farther south to 600m.

Three-quarters of the Mauritanian people are Moors (or Maures) of Arabo-Berber stock, who speak Hassiniyya dialects of Arabic. They are divided into the Bidan or 'white' Moors (55%) and the Harattin or 'black' Moors, descended from slaves. This division is based on social factors rather than on skin colour. Moors are nearly all nomadic pastoralists, leading a patriarchal life similar to the Arab Bedouins.

The country's Negro peoples (Toucouleurs, Sarakoles, Wolofs) comprise 20% of the population and are sedentary cultivators, concentrated in the Senegal River area. There is a small group of light-skinned nomads called Peulh (or Fulani), Despite these wide ethnic and cultural differences, all Mauritanians are bound by a common Muslim attachment to the Malekite sect.

CULTURE

Mauritania's prehistoric civilisations are to be glimpsed in neolithic tools and weapons and rock paintings, especially in the Adrar; those at Bir Mogrein near F'Derik in the north show wheeled vehicles, proof that the trans-Saharan routes were travelled far back in history.

Medieval towns, once important caravan ports, preserve fine examples of Berber architecture. Forts and mosques stand as reminders of the great power and the spiritual ideals of the Almoravids, who in the 11th and 12th centuries ruled what is now Mauritania and moved northwards to conquer Morocco and southern Spain. Archaeologists are uncovering towns long abandoned and buried under sand, such as Koumbi Saleh, in the south east, once capital of the Ghana Empire, and Aoudaghost, an ancient Berber capital. Efforts are being made to rescue towns like Chinguetti in the Adrar which are still inhabited but are slowly disappearing under the sand of the encroaching desert.

Islam has been the cornerstone of learning since the 7th and 8th centuries. Oualata, an ancient centre for scholars, has a valuable library of old manuscripts. Ouadane is the seat of an old Islamic university. Other important Arab libraries are found at Boutilimit, Kaedi, Mederdra, Tidjikdja and Chinguetti (which also contains pre-Islamic manuscripts). The scholarly tradition is continued at Boutilimit, where an Institute for High Islamic Studies was founded in 1961.

Crafts are based on traditional designs, and belong to the everyday life of nomads and cultivators: carved wood and silver chests from Mederdra, in which the camel driver locks his precious tea and sugar, brightly coloured rugs of camel and goat hair from Boutilimit, hand-woven carpets with traditional designs, hand-dyed leatherwork, cushions and saddles, silver daggers, palm-cane mats, traditional instruments, and, in the south, African woodcarving, especially of ebony. Perhaps the finest handicrafts in Mauritania are the jewellery and caskets of incised gold and silver.

GENERAL INFORMATION

Area: 1,030,700sq km.
Population: 1,120,000.
Altitude: The highest point in the Adrar massif is 732m at Tanaou Adjari; and 600m in the Affolle massif.
Capital: Nouakchott.
Head of State: President Mokhtar Ould Daddah.
Government: Mauritania is an Islamic Republic with a President and a National Assembly of 70 members, all belonging to the single ruling party, the Mauritanian People's Party (PPM).
Date of independence: 28 November 1960.
Languages: Official languages are Arabic and French. The Moors speak a Berber-Arabic dialect called Hassiniyya, re-

garded as the national language, although the Negro peoples of the Senegal valley have their own languages.

Religion: Islam, of the Malekite sect.
Currency: Ouguiya. £1=85 ouguiya. $1=49 ouguiya.
Time: GMT.

HOW TO GET THERE

By air: There are flights from Paris to Nouakchott and Nouadhibou, operated by Air Afrique and UTA. From Dakar, Air Afrique operates four flights a week to Nouakchott and there are three flights a week to Nouadhibou operated by either Air Mauritanie or Air Afrique.

From Las Palmas, Air Afrique, Air Mauritanie and Iberia fly to Nouadhibou. Several African capitals are linked by Air

Fisherman

Mauritanie, Air Maroc, Air Afrique and UTA.

There are taxis at the airports.

By road: From Dakar it is easy to reach Nouakchott along a road tarred the whole way. The distance is 575km. The River Senegal is crossed at Rosso by a ferry which operates daily between 0700 and 1230 and 1500 and 1800 hours.

With the present trouble in Western Sahara it is not advisable to attempt entry to Mauritania from the north (either from

Algeria or Morocco).

Visas and health regulations
A valid pasport and visa are necessary except for nationals of France, Italy, Liberia and former French territories in Africa who need only a passport or identity card.

Certificates of vaccination against yellow fever, smallpox and cholera are required. TAB vaccination is advisable.

Currency regulations
Foreign currency may be imported and exported freely, provided that it is declared on entry and that the amount taken out does not exceed the amount taken in.

CLIMATE

About two-thirds of the country can be described as Saharan—hot and dry with practically no rainfall—but in the south annual rainfall can reach 500mm. The rainy season is from July to September and the dry season from October to June. The coastal area, influenced by ocean and trade winds, has mild temperatures except for the hotter Nouakchott region, whose rainy season is in August and September. Strong desert winds blow sand in March and April. The best season for other areas and for touring is November-May.

Visitors should bring lightweight cotton clothes, a raincoat in season and something warm for the cool evenings.

Health precautions
Precautions against malaria are advisable, particularly for visiting the south, and anti-malarial tablets should be taken before, during and after the visit.

From Nouakchott northwards and at Boutilimit the water can be drunk, but in Ayoun and in the Senegal area water should be boiled or treated with purifying tablets.

ACCOMMODATION AND FOOD

Hotel accommodation is very limited and it is advisable to book in advance. Bills normally include service charges and local tax. The larger hotels in Nouakchott have air-conditioning.

European food and alcoholic drinks are available in hotels, but few restaurants outside the hotels cater for tourists. Traditional Mauritanian food includes dates, *zrig* (camel's milk), *mechoui* (whole roast lamb), *couscous*, sweet mint tea, spiced fish and rice with vegetables, fish balls, dried fish, dried meat.

Tipping is left to the discretion of the client but is generally 10%.

TRANSPORT

Air: Air Mauritanie operates domestic flights between Nouakchott and the main towns. It is possible to hire light aircraft at the Nouakchott aeroclub.
Road: Apart from the roads linking Nouakchott with Rosso and Akjoujt all other routes are sand tracks which can usually be negotiated with a four-wheel-drive vehicle, except in some cases during or immediately after the rainy season. Some of these tracks are frequently obliterated by drifting sand; and on the worst of these a guide is necessary. Never attempt a desert journey without a full set of spare parts and essential safety equipment.

The **Secretariat Generale a l'Artinasat et au Tourisme** in Nouakchott supplies information and advice about road travel.
Car hire: Available in Nouakchott, Nouadhibou and Atar. **Taxis** are very expensive in the towns (Nouakchott and Nouadhibou).

BUSINESS HOURS

Shops are open Monday to Saturday, 0800-1200 and 1430-1800 (during June-November, in some cases 1530 or 1600-1900). However, these times may vary and some shops are open on Sunday and closed on Monday. Banks are open Monday to Friday 0800-1115 and 1430-1630. Government offices are open Monday to Friday, 0800-1200 and 1430-1800. During the period of Ramadan some Government offices work 0730-1430.

PUBLIC HOLIDAYS

1 January; 1 May; 25 May (Africa Day); 28 November (Independence Day); Muslim feasts are observed.

FOREIGN EMBASSIES

Egypt, France, Gabon, West Germany, Guinea, Libya, Morocco, Senegal, Spain, USA and Zaire.

NOUAKCHOTT

The capital of Mauritania is a new city created in 1960. It lies near the sea in a flat landscape of low dunes scattered with thorn bushes, on a site adjoining an old moorish settlement, the Ksar. The modern buildings are in traditional Berber style. The port is being developed to handle copper from Akjoujt.

Worth visiting are the Plage du Wharf, the mosque, the Ksar and its market, the African market and the camel market, the crafts centre, the National Museum, and the carpet factory. There are facilities for deep-sea fishing.

Hotels
Marahaba, Ave de la Dune, B.P. 135, tel: 20.94, 45 rooms.
Hôtel el Ahmedi, B.P. 596, 5 minutes from centre of Nouakchott and by the sea.
El Amane, B.P. 13, tel: 21.78.
Parc, B.P. 150, tel: 21.44.
Oasis, B.P. 4, tel: 20.11.

Restaurants: Diama, l'Atlantide, Chantal, Nezha, Café Oriental.

Shopping

Handicrafts such as dyed leather cushions and some incised silver articles, rugs and wood carvings can be bought in the open market, but for the finest selection of silver jewellery and daggers, wood and silver chests and carpets, go to the crafts centre.

Tourist information

Direction du Tourisme, B.P. 246, tel: 20.20. **Société Mauritanienne** de Tourism (SMTH), B.P. 552, tel: 23.53.

NOUADHIBOU

A growing port and centre of the fishing industry, Nouadhibou is situated on a peninsula at the northern end of the Bay of Levrier. Inland is empty desert, devoid of vegetation.

The waters of this coast abound in fish and Nouadhibou has commercial refrigeration and processing plants. The port is served by several shipping companies and there is a new quay for tankers and ore carriers. Across the Cap Blanc peninsula is La Guera, formerly in Spanish Sahara but now administered by Mauritania.

Hotels: Hotel des Imraguen, B.P. 90, tel: 22.72.

Entertainments: Canary Island fishermen from the Spanish fishing village rent out sailing boats for fishing. Information about inclusive organised fishing trips, with accommodation at the Hotel des Imraguen for six or nine days, can be obtained from Air Afrique or UTA agents. Most common species of fish are bar, red and silver dorado, dogfish, cod, skate, mackerel, scad, bonito, and carp.

ADRAR REGION

The Adrar is a spectacular massif of pink and brown plateaux gilded with dunes and intersected by deep canyons sheltering palm groves. It lies in the north central part of the country, and begins about 320 km north east of Nouakchott.

Atar, capital of the region, is an oasis lying on the route of salt caravans. It is the market centre for the nomads of northern Mauritania and has an old quarter, the Ksar, with flat-roofed houses and a fine palm grove. Half-day excursions can be made southwards to the mountain oasis of Tergit, dramatically sited between step rock faces and watered by thermal and cold springs; and northwards to the Ksar-Torchange palm grove. The oasis of Azoughui was the Almoravid capital in the 11th and 12th centuries. Remains of fortified buildings from this period can be seen.

A whole-day excursion from Atar leads over the breathtaking mountain pass of Hamogjar, through deep ravines and up rock-strewn tracks—an unforgettable experience. At the summit of the pass, where the plateau begins, there are rock paintings on the left, below overhanging rocks. They represent suns and hunters and, though semi-obliterated, are of great beauty. This track continues as far as Chinguetti, 120 km from Atar. A Land-Rover is necessary, or it may be possible to travel on the local food lorry which makes the trip twice a week from Atar.

Chinguetti is a holy city of Islam and was founded in the 13th century. It has a medieval mosque and a library housing ancient manuscripts. Much of the old town is disappearing under the encroaching drifts of sand.

There are hotels or rest-houses in Atar, Chinguetti and Ouadane.

TAGANT REGION

This area in the centre of Mauritania, south of the Adrar, is still undeveloped and visitors must use four-wheel-drive vehicles and be prepared to camp. However, the adventurous will find much to reward them in this region rich in still largely unexplored archaeological treasures. The capital, Tidjikdja, has a fort built in the Saharan style by the French official, Coppolani, who was assassinated here in 1905. It has a busy market. Nearby one can find neolithic arrowheads, awls and pottery.

Tichitt lies 200 km along a desert track from Tidjikdja. It is a medieval fortress town perched high on a rock in an area rich in historic sites and prehistoric rock paintings. Founded in the 13th century as a halting place for caravans en route for Morocco to the Sahel, it is now largely decayed. The houses are built of hewn slabs of rock in Berber style; the mosque and many other buildings are decorated with multi-coloured stones and recessed motifs.

AFFOLE AND ASSABA

It is worth making a tour of the Affole and Assaba regions, south and south east of the Tagant, via Kiffa, Tamchakett and Ayoun el Atrous, to the wild plateaux of El Agher. There is a rest house at Ayoun el Atrous which was founded in 1945 as the administrative centre of the Hodh region. The interesting archaeological sites include Koumbi Saleh, once capital of the Ghana Empire, 70 km from Timbedra along a good track. Near Tamchakett is Tagdawst, which has been identi-

fied as Aoudaghost, ancient capital of a Berber empire, conquered by the Almoravids in 1054. The town has been repeatedly rebuilt as it has sunk into the sand, further storeys being added to the houses. Archaeologists have uncovered eight distinct levels.

Reached by a desert track, 100 km from Nema, is Oualata, once one of the greatest caravan entrepots of the Sahara. A fortified medieval town built in terraces up a rocky peak, it has for centuries been a place of refuge for scholars and has a fine library. Nearby is the Muslim cemetery of Tirzet.

THE SOUTH

Boutilimit is 168 km south-east of Nouakchott and is reached by a very poor desert track, passable only by a four-wheel-drive vehicle. The journey can take five hours, but there is a weekly flight. It is a marabout centre where fine carpets of goat and camel hair are made. There are rest house which can be booked through the **Secretariat Generale a l'Artinasat et au Tourisme** at Nouakchott. Mederdra is famous for its richly inlaid wooden chests in which the nomads keep their precious possessions.

The Chemama is the fertile region in

Drawing water.

the Senegal basin. Here there is bathing, boating and hunting—lion, wart-hog and guinea fowl—from November to June. Gazelle can be hunted in the interior. Kaedi is situated on the Senegal River and has a colourful market and a rest house. Rosso is a river port on the Senegal, rebuilt after floods in 1950.

There is the **Hotel Trarza** at Rosso and a hunting camp at Keur Massene.

THE NORTH

F'Derik was once a stage on the western trans-Saharan route from Agadir in Morocco to Dakar. Its importance now is due to the iron ore deposits mined in the Kedia Idjil range. It has a State-owned rest house.

At Zouerate there is a modern mining settlement with hotel, school and hospital. Bir Mogrein once also a stage on the trans-Saharan route, is 400 km north-east of F'Derik and has a rest house. It has some interesting rock paintings.

HISTORY

Mauritania was once inhabited by cultivators and hunters. It was well watered and covered with vegetation capable of sustaining giraffe, horses, rhinoceros and elephant. The desert, however, advanced southwards and the Berbers moved down from North Africa, pushing the black indigenous population before them. The introduction of the camel into the Sahara desert in the 3rd and 4th centuries enabled the Berbers to cover long distances, and they established regular trading patterns throughout the Western Sahara region.

A powerful confederation of Sanhadja nomads assured the protection of salt caravans from the Aouilil salt pans, as well as the subsequent trade in slaves and gold that gave rise to the Empire of Ghana, thought to have been centred on Koumbi-Saleh, in south-east Mauritania. The Empire of Ghana flourished in the 9th and 10th centuries.

In the 11th century a reforming Islamic group, known as the Almoravids, established its hold over the Sanhadja Berbers, whereupon they travelled north to found their capital at Marrakesh. The Almoravids ruled the whole of North West Africa and Andalusia in Spain, but they did not forget their origins, for they repeatedly raided the black states to the south, seizing the capital of Ghana in the 11th century. But while the later Empires of Mali and Songhai flourished on the River Niger, and the Almohads and Merinids controlled Morocco to the north, there was no central authority among Mauritania's nomads. They merely continued their wandering existence, obeying the tenets of Islam, and gradually absorbed a greater degree of Arab influence.

Portuguese navigators established a first foothold on the coast in the middle of the 15th century. There were limited contacts between them and the Mauritanian nomads. The Dutch and then the French in the 17th century took over the island of Arguin, where the Portuguese had made their base, but it was not until the 19th century that the first contacts were made between the Moors and the French, by then installed in Senegal.

The French negotiated treaties with the Moorish emirs for trade in gum arabic, and colonization came about as a result of their desire to impose their own terms. The real process of colonization was, however, begun in 1901 by Coppolani and continued by Gouraud. With the defeat of the Regueibat tribes at Mijik in 1933 this process was completed, though the colonial territory of Mauritania had been created in 1904. From 1920 onwards the colony was administered by Saint-Louis in Senegal, as part of French West Africa.

It achieved its independence on 28 November 1960, despite initial opposition from Morocco which had claimed Mauritania as one of its provinces.

MAURITIUS

Lying 2,000km from the south-eastern African coast, Mauritius is a small, independent island-state whose predominantly Asian population lives largely off the proceeds of sugar-cane.

Tourism has been on the increase in recent years so that now more than 50,000 visitors from Britain, South Africa and France take advantage of Mauritius' beautiful tropical beaches.

THE LAND AND THE PEOPLE

Mauritius stands on what was once a land bridge between Asia and Africa—the Mascarene archipelago. From the coast the land rises to form a broad, fertile plateau on which flourish rows and rows of sugar-cane, broken only by a few towns and a much larger number of shanty villages where most of the cane-workers live.

Some 500km to the east is Rodrigues Island which is subject to intense heat and frequent hurricanes. The 25,000 Rodrigues farmers and villagers are Creoles of African, Malagasy and French stock. To the north-east of Mariritius lie the lonely Cargados Carajos Shoals (Saint Brandon), and 900km to the north is solitary Agalega, all inhabited by small crews of fishermen, copra plantation workers and guano

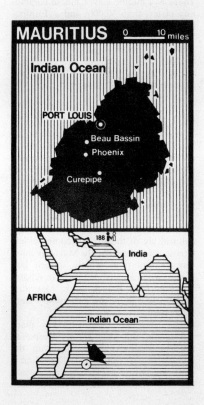

diggers, birds, turtles and marine life. The westernmost Mascarene is Reunion.

An awareness of 'being Mauritian' has only recently begun to spread among the separate communities of Mauritius. The majority of them are Hindu, descended from indentured field labour transported from India after the liberation of African, Malagasy and Creole slaves in 1835. The emancipated bondsmen gravitated towards towns and coastal villages, where 250,000 Creoles now occupy economic, professional and cultural positions. Muslims from the Indian sub-continent number 150,000, many of them artisans and tradesmen. There is a middle-class Chinese community of less than 30,000, and a 'European' (Franco-Mauritian) plutocracy of 10,000.

There has been great political activity in Mauritius in recent years, with a strong attack from the left on the island's established interests.

CULTURE

It is now 200 years since Bernardin de Saint Pierre evoked images of a tropical paradise when he used the island as an idyllic setting for *Paul et Virginie*. Since then Mauritius has produced artists of its own, some of whom have gained world-wide recognition.

The British presence would appear to have exerted very little influence on the cultural life of the various communities. Creole (a French-Bantu-Malagasy mixture) is the most widely spoken language, while English is taught in schools and used (with French) in the Mauritian Parliament but is not otherwise extensively used.

The festivals which take place throughout the year are as diverse as the communities which make up the population of Mauritius. The Hindus celebrate Divalee in October or November and Maha Shivaratree in February

or March. The Chinese maintain their own traditions while the Muslims celebrate New Year (Muharram) with a good deal of ceremony and colour.

WILDLIFE

Mauritius's mountain slopes retain a small herd of deer, carefully protected but open to hunting in the June-August season. The indigenous dodo and giant land tortoise can now only be seen in natural history museums, but there are still monkeys, rabbits and fish in large numbers on and around the island.

GENERAL INFORMATION

Area: 1,856 sq km.
Population: 900,000.
Altitude: Sea level to plateau of 580m; peaks up to 820m.
Capital: Port Louis.
Head of State: Her Majesty Queen Elizabeth II.
Government: Independent member of the Commonwealth. Parliamentary coalition government headed by Prime Minister Sir Seewoosagur Ramgoolam.
Independence: March 12, 1968.
Languages: English and French (official) and Creole.
Religions: Hinduism, Islam and Christianity (Roman Catholic and Protestant).
Currency: Mauritius Rupee (Rs) divided into 100 cents. £1 sterling=Rs11.44; US$=Rs6.63.
Time: GMT+4.

HOW TO GET THERE

By air: From UK: British Airways (3 times weekly) via Addis Ababa and the Seychelles. From Paris: Air France (5 times weekly). From Australia and South Africa: Qantas and South African Airways (4 times weekly). From Bombay: Air India (2 times weekly) and Air France (8 times weekly) from Paris via

Marseilles, Athens, Djibouti, Entebbe and Nairobi. From Rome: Alitalia (1 weekly) via Nairobi and Antananarive. From Nairobi: East African Airways (1 weekly) via Dar es Salaam and Antananarivo. From Frankfurt: Lufthansa (1 weekly) via Cairo, Entebbe, Dar es Salaam. From Lusaka: Zambia Airways (1 weekly) via Blantyre.

By sea: Messageries Maritimes monthly from Marseilles via Cape Town, Madagascar, Reunion and occasionally the Comoro Islands. British, French, American and many other lines connect Mauritius with all continents.

Visas and health regulations

All visitors require valid passports, return tickets and international certificates of vaccination against smallpox (vaccination against yellow fever and cholera if arriving after travel through an infected area).

Visas are not required by citizens of the UK and Commonwealth countries, South Africa and most West European countries except for visits exceeding six months (three months for West Germans and Israelis). British consulates issue visas wherever Mauritius is not represented diplomatically.

Currency regulations

Foreign currencies and travellers' cheques may be taken into and out of Mauritius at liberty. A maximum of Rs700 can be imported and Rs350 exported in Mauritian bank notes. Rupees are virtually worthless outside the island, so sterling or travellers' cheques should be used as often as possible. The major international and sterling credit cards are acceptable.

CLIMATE

Mauritius' coasts are warm the year round, averaging 25°C between January and April, around 19°C at other times: they are coolest and driest from June to October. Humidity and rainfall increase with altitude: temperatures drop about 5°C from the coast to the residential plateau around Curepipe. January to March is cyclone season: travellers may encounter a succession of tropical storms during this period, but with a bit of luck the island offers abundant sunshine and maritime breezes all year (the south coast is the breeziest). Good off-season periods for visiting are May-June and October-December. Deep-sea fishing is best in the period from October to March.

What to wear

Visitors on business or vacation may dress informally except in fashionable European circles and in a few of the older hotels.

Jackets, sweaters and raincoats are all essential for evenings in the Curepipe plateau area.

One of Mauritius' fine beaches

Health precautions

Normal prudence satisfies most needs on Mauritius.

Malaria and other endemic tropical diseases are virtually non-existent, water and foodstuffs generally safe, the sun benign and insects seldom troublesome.

ACCOMMODATION, FOOD

The number of hotels (half of which are beach establishments) available to date is 35, providing between them some 3,000 beds of more than moderate comfort. Six more hotel projects of international de luxe standard should bring the bed capacity to 4,245. As hotels increase, the number of family pensions and modest beach bungalows diminishes, but those that exist provide reasonable accommodation for families. The Mauritius Youth House in Port Louis and the Port Louis Diocese (for Roman Catholics) have camping and other accommodation for young people.

Reservations should be made for all hotels during the June-September high season, although one seldom has difficulty finding adequate lodgings somewhere on the island.

A few restaurants offer authentic French, Chinese or Indian cuisine, and many try to combine all three styles. Fruit, meat, vegetables and even fresh seafood are often in short supply, and depend on imports. Venison in season, *camarons* (fresh-water crayfish) in hot sauces, creole fish, rice and curry are among the island's specialities. While motoring around the villages, travellers can depend on the refrigerator stocks at Chinese groceries. Rum and beer are staple beverages for Mauritians, but there is good local milk, imported wine and mineral water as well.

Tipping: A tip of 10% is usual in most hotels and restaurants. Taxi drivers do not expect a tip.

TRANSPORT

There is a good network of tarred roads to all parts of the island. Taxis are numerous, conspicuous and often adventurous. Buses connect major towns conveniently and comfortably.

Air Mauritius connects Plaisance Airport and Rodrigues Island four times weekly. A monthly passenger steamer also goes to Rodrigues (36 hours, with minimum adequate comfort). Private fishing boats link the main island with the other islands.

Car hire

Hertz concessionaire, Royal Road, Curepipe, tel: 6-1455. Mautourco, Royal Road, Curepipe, tel: 6-1455. Avis, Brabant Street, Port Louis, tel: 2-1624. ERC, Pailles, tel: 2-1946. Europcars, Evenor Mamet Street, Rose Hill, tel: 4-3447. Concorde, Weal House, Port Louis, tel: 2-4194.

BANKS AND COMMERCE

Barclays Bank International, the Mauritius Commercial Bank and the Mercantile Bank all have branches in various parts of the island. The Habib Bank and the Bank of Baroda have offices in Port Louis.

Business hours: 9am-4pm Mondays to Fridays; 9am-noon Saturdays. **Banks:** 10am-2pm Mondays to Fridays; 9.30am-11.30am Saturdays. **Shops—Port Louis:** 8am-5pm Mondays to Fridays; 8am-12 Saturdays. **Curepipe and Rose Hill:** 8am-7pm Mondays-Fridays; 8am-1pm Thursdays and Sundays.

FOREIGN EMBASSIES

Central African Empire: 50 Rémy Ollier Street, P.O. Box 688, Port Louis, tel: 2-4861. **France:** Rue St. George, Port Louis, tel: 2-3755. **India:** Baroda Building, Port Louis, tel: 2-3775. **Madagascar:** Sir William Newton Street, Port Louis, tel: 2-2843. **Pakistan:** Anglo-Mauritius House, Intendance Street, tel: 2-1862. **UK:** Cerné House, Port Louis, tel: 2-0201. **US:** Anglo-Mauritius House, Port Louis, tel: 2-3218.

PUBLIC HOLIDAYS

The fixed holidays are New Year's Day; Independence Day, 12 March; Labour

Day; All Saints Day, 1 November; Christmas Day. Variable Hindu, Muslim and Christian holidays are also observed, including Cavadee, Maha Shivaratree, Divalee, Id-el-Adha, Id-al-Fitr, Easter, as well as the Chinese Spring Festival.

PORT LOUIS

Most of the activity of Port Louis is concentrated around the bustling port and the neighbouring commercial area. On Pope Hennessy and other streets there are pretty wooden Creole houses with iron balustrades and bamboo shutters. The Indian and Chinese bourgeoisie live on the slopes of Signal Hill.

. Government House, built by the illustrious 18th-century Governor Mahe de Labourdonnais, presides over an esplanade (Place d'Armes) leading between tall palm trees to the port. The avenues behind it contain banks and major office buildings. Nearby is the handsome Mauritius Institute building, housing the excellent National Archives and Natural History Museum, both dedicated to Indian Ocean history, flora and fauna.

The Hippodrome at the Champ de Mars (built in 1812) has horse racing on weekends between May and October. Other places of interest include the Anglican and Roman Catholic cathedrals, the Jummah Mosque, the Chinese Pagoda (on the outskirts of town near the Hippodrome), the Old Theatre, the Town Hall, and an abundance of statues and monuments.

Most visitors stay at the beach hotels or on the residential plateau, but Port Louis itself has a number of adequate hotels, the majority having air-conditioning.

Hotels

Ambassador Hotel, 96 rooms, Desforges Street, tel: 2-4105. **Hotel des Touristes,** 13 rooms, Jummah Mosque Street, tel: 2-2774. **National Hotel**, 12 rooms, Pope Hennessy, tel: 2-0453. **Bourbon Tourist Hotel**, 18 rooms, Jummah Mosque Street, tel: 2-4407. **France Tourist Hotel**, 8 rooms, J. Riviere Street, tel: 2-22087. **President Tourist Hotel**, 12 rooms, Rémy Ollier Street, tel: 2-4518. **Palais d'or Tourist Hotel**, 12 rooms, Jummah Mosque Street, tel: 2-5231. **Rossignol Hotel**, 13 rooms, 36 Pope Hennessy, tel: 2-1983.

Restaurants

Among several good restaurants are **La Flore Mauricienne** and **Cafe de la Cite**. Several small Chinese and Indian bars with food and atmosphere include **Lai Min**, **Carri Poule**, and the **Bonne Marmite**.

Shopping

Port Louis's Central Market, *soukhs* and Chinese wholesale emporia are fascinating for the browser, but most systematic shopping takes place at Curepipe on the plateau. For souvenirs try the Mauritius boutique and the Cottage Industries Show Room in Port Louis.

Tourist information

Mauritius Government Tourist Centre, Cerne House, La Chaussee, tel: 2-1846/7. Mauritius Travel and Tourist Bureau, Ltd (semi-official), Sir William Newton Street. Automobile Association of Mauritius, 2 Queen Street, tel: 2-1104. Alliance Touristique de l'Ocean Indien (ATOI) Galerie Rémy Ollier, Place Foch, Port Louis.

Travel agencies: Air Maurice, Place Labourdonnais; Seven Seas Travel and Tourist Agency, 57 Royal Street; Rogers and Co. (for overseas travel), Sir William Newton Street.

CUREPIPE AND THE PLATEAU

Private gardens, monumental schools and other public buildings, shopping arcades and theatres, down-at-heel business districts and busy traffic mark the island's central residential zone. In spite of frequent afternoon rains Curepipe, 600m. in altitude, is a good base for operations. Other central towns—Beau Bassin, Rose Hill, Vacoas—serve mainly as dormitories for the sugar industry and Port Louis.

Places of interest include the Curepipe botanical gardens, the French colonial-style City Hall, and a scenic drive along the rim of the Trou aux Cerfs crater above the town.

At Moka there are waterfalls, and opportunities for mountain climbing. The Reduit, near Moka, the Governor General's residence has splendid lawns and a fine view of cliffs and the sea. Saint Pierre and other sugar mills near Moka are especially interesting to visit during October and November.

Hotels
Hong Kong Hotel, 20 rooms, tel: 6-1613, Chateauneuf Street. **Continental Hotel**, 52 rooms (air conditioned), tel: 6-2036, Currimje Arcade. **Relais Isle de France**, 26 rooms, tel: 6-4944, Royal Road. **Belle Vue Hotel**, 52 rooms + 4 suites, tel: 6-2046/6-2044, Eau Coulée.

Shopping
Jewellery, Chinese and Indian ivory work, jade, teak and silks, tortoise shells, basketry, pottery and sea shells are available at numerous shops in Curepipe, including Handicrafts Ltd; and Corinne, and at Commercial Centre in Rose Hill.

THE COASTS
Villages, beaches, lagoons and inlets, cliffs, bamboo and banana palm forests, canefields and fishing grounds all form part of the Mauritian coast. Every visitor should undertake at least one day-long circuit along the island's roadways. Starting from Plaisance Airport in the south-east, visit Mahebourg, the

beautifully situated old colonial capital with mementoes of the Napoleonic Wars and an interesting historical museum nearby; then proceed along the coast, coming first to Blue Bay, then to Souillac with the Rochester Falls and a little museum in the coral house of the poet, the late Robert Edward Hart. The rugged cliffs of Moren Brabant overlook an exceedingly fine beach. Grande Case and Le Chamarel are below the wild forests and ravines of the Riviere Noire mountains, with strange rock configurations, waterfalls and wildlife.

Riviere Noire is a Creole fishermen's district, where *sega* dancing is especially lively on Saturday nights. Trou aux Biches in the north-west, just south of the new Club Mediterrannee vacation village at Pointe aux Canonniers, is excellent for surfing. Grand Baie, north of Pamplemousses Gardens, is a favourite beach area for Mauritian residents, with excellent fishing and skin-diving at Pointe aux Piments and swimming in the Cove of Péyrebère. The yacht club stages sailing regattas from July to October. Cap Malheureux is the site of the British occupation force landing in 1810, after months of siege at Mahebourg, and where Bernadin de Saint-Pierre's Virginia was shipwrecked. Fishermen at Grand Gaube have boats for hire on the lagoon. Flacq is another fishermen's district, north of Trou d'Eau Douce.

Hotels
Beach hotels and bungalows:
Isle de France, Grand'Baie, 34 rooms, tel: 38-543/5.
Troux aux Biches Hotel, Trou aux Biches, 145 rooms, including family units (i.e. 23 suites), tel: 36-574.
Merville Hotel, Grand'Baie, 74 rooms, tel: 38-621.
Paul et Virginie, Grand'Gaube, 15 rooms, tel: 39-511.
Franconem, Peyrebere, 37 rooms, tel: 38-641/2 or 2-2811.

Touessrok, Trou d'Eau Douce, 14 rooms, tel: 51-533.

Villa Caroline, Flic-en-Flac, 6 rooms, tel: 58-511.

Le Chaland, Blue Bay, 90 rooms, tel: 73-511/2.

Le Morne Brabant, Le Morne, 85 rooms including 4 suites, tel: 4-4778.

Dinarobin Pierre Desmarais, Le Morne, 139 rooms, including 6 suites, tel: 56-531.

Relais de Lamivoire, La Preneuse, 15 rooms, tel: 56-522.

Le St. Giran, Belle Mare, 170 rooms, tel: 4-1076.

La Pirogue, Flic-en-Flac, 200 rooms, tel: 4-7041.

Tamarin Bay Hotel, Tamarin, 32 rooms, tel: 56-581.

Blue Lagoon, Pointe d'Esny, 14 rooms, including 3 suites, tel: 71-529.

Pearle Beach, Volmar, 13 rooms, tel: 58-528.

Arc-en-Ciel, Tombea Bay, 20 rooms, tel: 37-616/7.

Coin-de-Mire Hotel, Butte à l'Herbe, Grand'Gaube, 14 rooms, tel: 4-2782.

Bungalows

Villa Caroline, Flic-en-Flac, 5 bungalows of 2 rooms, 7 of 1 room, tel: 58-511.

Paul et Virginie, Grand'Gaube, 11 bungalows of 2 rooms, tel: 39-511.

Etiole de Mer, Trou aux Biches, 10 air-conditioned bungalows of 2 rooms, 4 of 1 room, tel: 36-561.

Merville, Grand'Baie, 14 bungalows of 2 rooms, tel: 38-531.

Little Acorn Holiday Centre, Flic-en-Flac, 8 family units (2 adults and 2 children), bathroom and kitchenette, tel: 58-531.

Kuxville, Cap Malheureux, 10 bungalows (various sizes), tel: 2-4040.

Mocambo, Tamarin Bay, 4 bungalows of 3 rooms, tel: 56-538.

Palm Beach, Poste Lafayette, 16 bungalows of 2 rooms, tel: 4-7603.

Relais de Lamivoire, La Preneuse Rivière Noire, 8 air-conditioned bungalows of 2 rooms, tel: 56-522.

Franconem, Peyrebere, 6 bungalows of 2 rooms, tel: 38-641/2.

Beach Hotel, Pointe aux Sable, 4 bungalows of 2 rooms, tel: 34-505.

Tamarin Bay Hotel, Tamarin Bay, 5 bungalows of 3 rooms, 5 of 2 rooms, tel: 56-581.

Le Morne Brabant, 13 bungalows (superior categories) tel: 4-4778.

Peyrebere Guest House, 7 flats, tel: 38-679.

Casuarina Village Hotel, Trou aux Biches, 20 bungalows (various sizes), tel: 36-552.

HISTORY

Lying south of the monsoon belt, Mauritius was little known in Europe until it became a station between the Cape of Good Hope and the East Indies in the 16th Century. Dutch merchantmen occupied it for a few years, but left in 1710. From 1721, France developed a colonial society there of planters, traders, naval forces and corsairs, using slaves from southern Africa and Madagascar.

Governor Mahe de Labourdonnais (1735-47) was responsible for Mauritius' prosperity, in conjunction with nearby Reunion (then called Bourbon) and other tiny islands in a sea that was disputed by all major European powers.

Intensive sugar cane cultivation required new sources of labour and several waves of indentured workers came from India, many of them remaining after the expiration of their contracts.

In more recent years, high birth rates, advances in public health and limited opportunities for emigration have combined to produce serious overpopulation on the island. Declining living standards, rising unemployment and stagnating investment during the 1950s heightened tensions between the communities, bringing turbulent politics.

MOZAMBIQUE

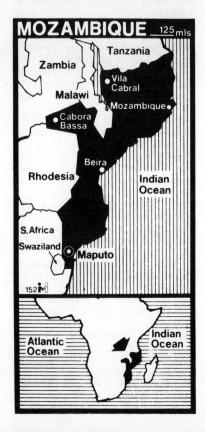

Mozambique has been a sovereign and independent country since 25 June 1975. From the tourists' viewpoint it has two different attractions: its coastline, bathed by the Indian Ocean, offers beautiful beaches and islands with safe bathing, sailing, skin-diving and excellent game fishing while in the interior of the country there is rich fauna in the National Parks. The tourist industry is, however, restricted by the political situation in Rhodesia.

THE LAND AND THE PEOPLE

Nearly half Mozambique consists of low-lying sedimentary rock and marshland, since the coastal plain here, much wider than elsewhere in southern Africa, is formed by the biggest rivers: the Limpopo, the Save and the Zambezi.

The Indian Ocean shore is peppered with excellent harbours in the estuaries near river mouths, and elsewhere long sandy beaches are intersected by lagoons. Nearby are coral reefs and islands such as Inhaca, Bazaruto and Mozambique Island. Inland the escarpments of the Central African plateau rise behind Beira to the hills of Manica and again north of Quelimane.

Throughout the lowland the rainfall is unreliable, causing unexpected droughts. Far more rain falls on the hills where the off-sea winds are forced upwards.

Along the coast, especially on the estuaries and delta of the Zambezi, mangrove and marsh-type vegetation is common and near some of the beaches are the largest palm-groves in the world. the western and northern highlands are patched with moist, montane forest, sometimes of needle-leaf trees. The remainder of the landscape of Mozambique is dominated by savannah, more or less dry and open woodlands with occasional tracts of short-grass steppe.

The population of Mozambique is made up of black and white, *pardo* (mixed race) and Asian peoples. Religious beliefs and practices are extremely diverse and include those of traditional Africa, Islam, Buddhism and Christianity, both Catholic and Protestant.

The Africans are most densely settled in the more productive Zambezia, Mozambique and coastal districts, while elsewhere large tracts of country are little used. The government is developing a system of communal villages in the whole country. The average density is 10.6 people per sq.km. Non-Africans are largely concentrated in the coastal towns.

North of the Zambezi Valley, Africans are matrilineal by descent, traditionally organised in very small units; most are Muslims. In the far north, one-third of the Makonde live in Mozambique, the rest in Tanzania. In the middle of the country are the Shona (e.g. Teve, Ndau and Manyika), closely related to the people of eastern Rhodesia, and in the wide lowlands of the south are the Thonga (Shangana, Ronga, Tswa and Hlengwe).

On the Inhambane coast the Chopi, famous for their traditional music, throng the coastal towns.

CULTURE

Mozambique has its own culture and the government is engaged in reconstructing what was lost during the colonial period. Much of the traditional culture can be seen in the dances, songs and music of the people. The best-known wood carving is that of the Makonde, although in a number of regions these are sculptors in wood, marble, ivory and bone as well as artisans engaged in ceramics and basketwork.

WILDLIFE

Mozambique possesses a rich fauna which is protected in National Parks, the principal being Gorongosa, and in other Reserves. However, there are in the south and centre of the country—Province of Maputo, Gaza, Inhambane and Sofala—several areas where you can go on safaris.

Deep-sea fishermen find game fish such as marlin and swordfish, especially off the Bazaruto archipelago.

GENERAL INFORMATION

Area: 785,000 sq.km.
Population: 9.2 million.
Altitude: Half the country lies under 1,000 m, rising in the west to Monte Binga (2,436 m).
Capital city: Maputo.
Head of State: President Samora Moisés Machel.
Government: The Council of Ministers is presided over by the President of the Republic. It comprises Ministers and Vice-Ministers of the People's Republic of Mozambique.
Languages: In general these coincide with ethnic divisions. Portuguese is the official language.
Currency: Decimal, based on the escudo, divided into 100 centavos. Esc.1,000=1 conto. £1=57.08 escudos. $1=33.13 escudos.
Time: GMT+2.

HOW TO GET THERE

By air: Regular flights to the international airport of Mavalane (8km from Maputo centre); from Luanda by DETA

(Mozambique Airlines); Johannesburg and Durban by DETA and SAA; Manzini (Swaziland) by DETA and Air Swazi; Madagascar by DETA and Air Malgache; Lusaka by DETA and Zambia Airways; Mtwara, Dar es Salaam and Nairobi by DETA; Lusaka by DETA and Zambia Airways; Moscow by Aeroflot.

The majority of these flights make intermediate landings at the Beira Airport to which there are also flights from Blantyre (Malawi) by DETA and Air Malawi.

There is an airport tax on departure of Esc.50.

By sea: Portuguese, Dutch, British, Japanese, Italian, American, French, South African and many other liners arrive at Maputo and Beira.

By road: There are reasonably good roads from and to South Africa, Swaziland, Rhodesia, Malawi, Zambia and Tanzania.

Insurance is obligatory and traffic drives on the left.

By rail: Passenger services in air-conditioned coaches with sleeping and restaurant facilities run from Johannesburg to Maputo and from Blantyre to Beira.

Visas and health regulations

Any foreign citizens may enter and travel throughout Mozambique provided they comply with the following requirements: forward their visa applications to their countries' embassies, consulates or other representative offices in Mozambique;— foreigners may also send their applications directly to the Ministry of Foreign Affairs of the Government of Mozambique;—cost of reply to be borne by the applicant.

Applications may also be made by telex indicating besides the name of the applicant, the nationality, passport number and other information establishing the identity of the applicant.

Visitors should have valid international certificates of vaccination against small-

pox and yellow fever, and it is advisable to be protected against typhoid and cholera.

Dutiable goods

Tobacco (up to 100 gm), personal clothing, sporting and camping equipment, cameras, radios, typewriters, etc., for personal use are exempt from duty.

Currency regulations (adapted from Official Tourist Guide)

Entry into Mozambique of bank-notes and coins which are legal tender in foreign countries is permitted when carried by travellers in reasonable amounts for tourist expenses provided it is in compliance with the regulations in force in countries where such bank-notes and coins are legal tender.

Travellers when entering Mozambique are required to declare in writing on a proper form, in duplicate, the amounts of all currencies in their possession in banknotes, travellers' cheques and coins specifying the respective monetary units.

The declaration should be handed over at Exchange Counters found in the Customs Precincts at ports, airports and territorial boundaries.

After being stamped at the Exchange Counters, the duplicate copy of the declaration will be returned to the traveller in whose possession it must remain during his stay in Mozambique.

The original copies of the declaration will be retained at the Exchange Counters for 90 days after which they are forwarded to the Exchange Control Board.

It is important that the declaration should be entirely accurate as in cases of doubt Exchange officials may call in the police to investigate further. The entry of bank-notes and coins which are legal tender in Mozambique is strictly forbidden, except when imported by the Bank of Issue. Foreign bank-notes and coins which do not satisfy the conditions laid down in Article 1. No.1 and also bank-notes and coins which are legal tender in Mozambique, entry of which is forbidden in terms of Article 2, shall be deposited in the custody of the Immigration Authorities and shall only be returned to the owners of such currency on their return journey.

All travellers except those holding passports issued in Mozambique or those living in Mozambique under residential permits must change the equivalent of Esc.1,000 per person.

CLIMATE

The interior is always cooler than the coast and the rainfall, too, is greater as the land rises. There are two seasons. From April to September the coast has a temperate climate, sunny and pleasantly warm (average 19°C in Maputo in June/July) and mainly dry. The best season for a visit is May to July.

The hot, wet season lasts from October to March. Most of the rain falls between January and March but it is extremely variable from one year to the next, averaging 750 mm in the south, more in the north and rising inland even to 1.7 m per year. Temperatures on the coast average 27°C-29°C and humidity can be 80% when there is no wind from the sea. Inland the temperature averages about 21°C.

What to wear: In the hot season light, tropical clothing, preferably of pure cotton rather than synthetic materials because of the humidity, will suffice; but take some kind of wrap for the evening. A light raincoat will also be needed. In the cool season wear lightweight clothing and woollens, especially inland.

Health precautions: Precautions should be taken against malaria.

ACCOMMODATION AND FOOD

Hotels of international standard are to be found in Maputo and Beira, and accommodation is adequate in smaller towns. There are camp sites along the beaches and one rest camp with a restaurant in Gorongosa Game Park.

The cuisine is basically Portuguese, enriched by Far East recipes. Specialities are piri-piri chicken and shellfish such as the famous Delagoa Bay prawns which are grilled and served with piri-piri sauce.

Tipping: Tip waiters 10% of the bill and taxis at least that proportion; railway porters Esc.10.

TRANSPORT

Road: Much progress has been made with road-building. The tarred roads connecting Maputo with Beira and Beira with Tete are now complete and roads in the northern half of the country are being improved.

Rail: The country is well served by railway lines, all running east-west from Maputo, Beira and Nacala.

Air: In addition to air-taxi services operated by private firms, DETA operates flights linking Maputo with Vilanculos, Inhambane, Beira, Nacala, Cuamba, Quelimane, Tete, Vila Coutinho, Angoche, Lichinga, Nampula, Lumbo, Pemba and Mocimboa da Praia.

Car hire: There are several car-hire firms, among which are: *Agência Navetur*, Av. da República, 1502 tel: 24098—Maputo, *Agência Albatroz*, Av. Fernão Magalhães 267, Maputo, tel: 91366. Prices range from Esc.200 per day and Esc.4 per km for a large car. It is usually necessary to book a car about ten days in advance.

BANKS AND COMMERCE

The main banks in Mozambique are the Banco de Moçambique (Bank of Issue) Banco Standard Totta de Moçambique, Banco Comercial e Industrial, Banco Comercial de Angola and Banco Pinto & Sotto Mayor with the head offices in Maputo and branches in the principal

villages and cities.
Business hours: Banks: 0800-1100 from Monday to Friday. Closed on Saturday. Shops: 0800-1200 and 14.00 to 1800. Government departments: 0800-11.30 and 14.00 to 17.00

PUBLIC HOLIDAYS
New Year's Day, 1 January; Heroes' Day, 3 February; Mozambican Women's Day, 7 April; Labour Day, 1 May; Independence and Foundation of Frelimo Day, 25 June.

EMBASSIES IN MAPUTO:
Cambodia, China (PR), Congo, Denmark, Egypt, Finland, East Germany, Guinea-Bissau, Guyana, India, North Korea, Nigeria, Norway, Portugal, Romania, Somalia, Sweden, Tanzania, UK, USSR, Zaire, Zambia.

TOURIST OFFICES
Centro de Informação e Turismo, C.P. 614, Maputo, tel: 5011, Cable: CITMO; Telex: 6-436 CINAT MO.

MAPUTO
Hotels
Hotel Polana, Av. Julius Nyerere CP 1151, tel: 741001.
Polana-Mar, Av. Julius Nyerere CP 1151, tel: 744151.
Hotel Cardoso, Av. Brito Camacho, CP 35, tel: 741071.
Hotel Tivoli, Av. 25 de Setembro, CP 340, tel: 22005.
Hotel Turismo, Av. 25 de Setembro, CP 1393, tel: 26153.

Restaurants
The following are worth a visit: **Cave** and **Alta Roda** (typical cuisine) **Oiha-Oiha, Kalifa, Bocage, Macau, Abadia, Marialva, Shaik** and **Telavive.**

Street in Maputo, before independence

Shopping and markets
The main curios a visitor may like to buy in Mozambique are goods made of game skins and the interesting local wood, marble and bone-work. The picturesque Municipal Market, set amid 19th-century buildings, attracts many visitors.

Tourist Information
Centro de Informação e Turismo, CP 614 tel: 5011; Telex: 6-436 CINAT MO

COASTAL RESORTS
Ponta do Ouro lies at the southern frontier and the motel and camp sites serve those wanting to swim, relax and fish from the rocks. **Inhaca Island** near Maputo is a haven for same fishing and underwater sport. It has an airstrip, hotel and camp sites and an important marine biology station. **San Martinho do Bilene** has a crystal-clear lagoon of safe water for swimming, dinghy sailing and aquatic sports. **Xai-Xai** and **Chongoene** both have pools formed by an offshore coral reef. **Quissico's** camp site is popular with fish-

ermen. **Zavora's** coral reef provides a fascinating world for skin divers to explore. There is a camp site.

The Bazaruto Archipelago of four islands is the country's most famous game-fishing area. Large and plentiful marlin, barracuda, sailfish and swordfish provide the sport for international competitions as well as holidaymakers. There is good accommodation on **Santa Carolina** where the life-style is carefree and informal. There is a camp site at **Inhassoro** on the mainland opposite. North of Beira (see below) is **Zalala** (Quelimane area) where the beach is bordered by one of the largest palm groves in the world.

BEIRA

The bustling modern port of Beira has excellent beaches and is the base for game-viewing and hunting trips in the Gorongosa.

To the south, **Nova Sofala** has a beautiful beach surrounded by tropical scenery near the site of the famous Arab and Portuguese gold-trading town of Sofala, which has since been destroyed by the sea.

Far inland are the interesting ruins of the Vila de Manica area and of Sena.

Hotels
Hotel Moçambique, CP 1690
Hotel Beira, CP 1242, tel: 3045
Hotel Embaixador, CP 1249, tel:3121
Hotel Don Carlos, CP 139, tel: 711158
Motel Estoril is on the beach.

Others are the **Savoy, Safari** and **Miramar.**

There are camping facilities near the beach.

Restaurants
There are several gourmet restaurants serving seafood, piri-piri chicken and Portuguese dishes, e.g. Campino, Arcadia, Jockey-Bar, Kanimambo, Piqueni-que, Luso and Veleiro.

MOZAMBIQUE ISLAND

Mozambique was for many years the capital of the province, but was replaced in 1898 by Lourenço Marques, now Maputo, and has now lost importance to Nampula and the new port of Nacala. The coral island is joined by a 3.5 km-long bridge to the mainland where there is a good beach at **Chocas.** The Fortress of **São Sebastião** was built in the 16th century. Most of the island's churches, mosques, residences and palaces date from the flourishing 17th and 18th centuries.

Especially interesting are the Fort of São Lourenço and the Chapel of Nossa Senhora do Baluarte. There is good fishing on the island.

The one hotel is being improved and extended. Work has started on renovating one of the old public buildings to become a traditional-style inn.

NATIONAL PARKS
Gorongosa National Park

This is one of the finest game parks in southern Africa. The scenery varies from wide grassland to forest, savannah to marsh and river, all occupied by large herds of buffalo, lion, elephant, hippopotamus, kudu and many other species.

It is open from 1 May to 31 October. One arrives by car from the Beira-Umtali road or at the airstrip at Chitengo (by airtaxi from Beira). Special guides and cars are available within the park and trails are well marked.

Comfortable accommodation is to be found at both the main camp at Chitengo where there are bungalows, a restaurant and swimming pool and at the less luxurious Bela Vista, which does not have a restaurant.

Other reserves
The **Maputo Elephant Park** lies on the right bank of the Maputo River, south of Maputo. **Marromeu** at the mouth of the Zambezi River has great herds of buffalo.

There are two partial reserves at **Gile** (Zambezia) and **Niassa** (near Vila Cabral).

Safaris

Mozambique is one of the few remaining areas still sufficiently well-stocked with game to allow extensive hunting concessions covering millions of sq.km.

Hunting seasons and numbers of animals killed are regulated, as are the type and number of arms. Licences are obtainable from the Veterinary Services on Form H (10 days), or Form 1 (30 days).

HISTORY

Arab and Indian traders were visiting Sofala by the 10th century to buy gold which was brought (by Africans) down to the coast from the Manica hills and the goldfields beyond Great Zimbabwe.

In 1498 the Portuguese seafarer Vasco da Gama arrived, seeking a new route to the riches of India. He missed Sofala but found at Quelimane and Mozambique Island a black Muslim community of traders.

During the next century the Portuguese took over most of these ports, replacing the Arabs in the Indian Ocean trading system and sending the ivory and gold home or to Goa in India, which became the administrative centre of their eastern empire.

Explorers like António Fernandes (1516) travelled to the kingdom of Mwene Mutapa (Monomotapa) on the Zambezi escarpment in what is now Rhodesia. They settled at Sena and Tete and sought constantly, but in vain, the source of the valuable metals in the interior. They weathered attacks such as that of the Zimba who swept down the Zambezi and right up the east coast in the 1580s.

Missionaries, too, established seminaries, educating some of the 17th-century Mwene Mutapa's sons and assisting in the partial domination of that kingdom.

Soldiers and traders, some Portuguese and many Goans, set up large estates *(prazos)* run on feudal lines with large private armies of slaves.

In the late 18th century the slave trade took over. The Portuguese raided what is now Zambia, and the Yao operated around Lake Malawi. They sold slaves to Kilwa, on the coast of Tanganyika, where terms of trade were more favourable.

At the same time, explorers such as Lacerda (1798) sought the way across Africa from Tete to Angola. Lourenço Marques became an important source of ivory.

The *prazeros* continued to be powerful into the 19th century. The most famous was a Goan known as Gouveia, whose estate was in the Gorongosa hills. He ruled the whole area from the Zambezi to the Pungur and inland to Manica. His main rival was Soshangane's Gaza empire among the Thonga.

During the scramble for Africa, Portugal's aim of joining Angola to Mozambique was dashed by Britain's Cape to Cairo schemes.

The Portuguese began promoting an *assimilado* (assimilationist) philosophy—elitist rather than racist—by which other races were acceptable if they conformed to Portugueses culture and religion. Opportunities, however, were so limited that by 1951 only 0.08% of Africans in Mozambique had attained that status.

In 1964, the Front for the Liberation of Mozambique (Frelimo), launched a guerrilla struggle in the northern Cabo Delgado province under the leadership of Dr Eduardo Mondlane, who was assassinated in 1969. Under his successor, Samora Machel, the war was extended considerably, until the 'Lusaka Agreement' was drawn up on 7 September 1974. Next there was a Transition Government made up of Portuguese and Mozambicans and finally, on 25 June 1975, Mozambique gained complete independence. In February 1977 Mozambique became a Marxist state under the leadership of the Frelimo Party.

NAMIBIA

Namibia is a land in limbo. Its international status has been disputed at the United Nations for 30 years; the present ruling regime—South Africa—has been declared 'illegal' by the UN and by the World Court; even the country's name is in dispute. While the UN formally renamed it Namibia in response to black Namibian representations, South Africa still officially calls it by its old name 'South West Africa', first conferred on the country by the German colonizers in the 19th century.

Namibia is a vast, rugged country with clear, sunny skies and clean, dry air. By day it is baking hot in summer, and often also in winter; by night it is cool or even bitterly cold. Drought is endemic, and the land has aptly been described as having been 'made by God in anger.'

THE LAND AND THE PEOPLE
Namibia stretches along 1,280 km of the most desolate and lonely coastline in the world. Along its whole length, the vast, constantly shifting sand dunes of the Namib Desert spread inland for distances of 80 to 130 km. The coast is bisected by the closely situated towns of Walvis Bay, the country's major port (legally part of South Africa) and Swakopmund, the major seaside and summer resort.

Inland, along the escarpment of the high central plateau, rainfall increases slightly. The plateau slopes down to the Kalahari Desert, on the Botswana border, and can generally support little more than yellow grass and 'bush' vegetation. The country's highest rainfall, about 600 mm, is in the swamplands of eastern Ovamboland and the Okavango, but this tails off to only about 150 mm in the south west near the Namib. Rainfall is unreliable, and droughts can last for as long as seven years.

In the far north-west, in the largely unmapped 66,000 sq. km of the 2,500 m Kaokoveld Mountains live 10,000 pasto-

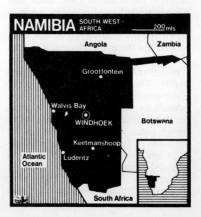

ral Ovahimba, Ovajimba and Herero. To the east of the Kaokoveld lie the plains of Ovamboland. Its northern border with Angola is a military fence dividing the Ovambo on both sides of the frontier.

Further to the east, the Ovambo plains give way to swamps of the great Okavango, a river which carries more water than all the rivers of South Africa combined and yet does not flow into the sea. To the south of it live the 40,000 Kavango. The last part of Namibia's northern border, leading from the Okavango to the Zambezi, is also fenced in. It contains the strategically important Caprivi Strip, separating Namibia from Zambia and Botswana, where South Africa maintains its northernmost air defence systems. It was unilaterally annexed by South Africa during World War Two. This far north eastern corner is Bushman country; about 14,000 of these ancient people still lead their traditional lives, although they and other Caprivian dwellers have been moved entirely out of the Eastern Caprivi, which is now a noman's land for South African security forces and insurgent guerrillas.

The second largest indigenous group are the 65,000 Damara, a negroid people who mostly speak the Nama language. Both they and the Nama themselves live largely in the so-called 'Police Zone' (the white-inhabited area) providing a part of the black labour force.

Perhaps the best-known of the black peoples are the proud Herero, who were decimated under German rule before World War One; they now number only 60,000. Their main reserve is in the Waterberg region south of Tsumeb.

South of the capital, Windhoek, lies the Rehoboth Gebiet, home of the Rehobother (once known as the Basters, or 'Bastards'). They are an intensely religious and conservative mixed race who migrated from the Cape Colony in the 18th century.

Namibia's ruling whites number about 100,000. They are predominantly engaged in ranching, mining and commerce. Two-thirds are Afrikaans-speaking, a quarter German, and the rest English-speaking.

CULTURE

Despite increasing South Africanisation in the post-war years, Namibia retains a strong cultural character of its own. Its indigenous peoples have preserved their distinctive identities to a much more marked degree than have those in the Republic. Although much of the country is closed or inaccessible, visitors can get some fascinating insights into the society. The most colourful and moving festival is the annual ceremony at the time of the full moon in August of the Herero who gather to mourn their departed chiefs at Okahandja, about 70km from Windhoek.

Some of the finest Bushman paintings are in the Brandberg—scene of the famous 'White Lady'—to the north of Windhoek and at Bushman's Paradise, near Usakos on the road to Walvis Bay. The Bushmen, who still live in the Kalahari, were painting in the country until about 60 or 70 years ago.

Ovambo culture and history are well illustrated by the linocuts and etchings of John Muafangejo, with their graphic descriptions of Ovambo Kraals, husbandry and great Ovambo events; they can be obtained through the Anglican Mission in Windhoek.

The whites tend still to lead the 'great outdoors' life, with good strong local German beer, barbecues, camping and hunting playing a major role in keeping alive a distinct frontier spirit.

Religion, and in particular Christianity, plays an important role in the lives of all the communities, and the Church takes an active part in political events.

WILDLIFE

With its sparse population and vast open spaces, Namibia is an ideal haven for wild animals. It has some of the last great migratory herds remaining in Africa, and several rare and unique species. Although all game is protected by a 'close' hunting season, proclaimed game reserves account for roughly one-seventh of the total land surface and, with closed mining areas and almost uninhabited 'native reserves', game is, in effect, totally protected in a fifth of the country.

The animals most commonly seen are kudu (a menace to drivers at night), springbok and warthog, particularly in the Etosha Pan, which is also the home of great herds of common zebra, gemsbok (or oryx), blue wildebeeste, impala, hartebeeste and eland. There are cheetah, leopard, lion, giraffe, elephant (a unique sub-species), and, rather less plentiful, black rhino and the tiny Damara dik-dik.

GENERAL INFORMATION

Area: 824,269 sq. km.

Population: 852,000.

Altitude: Up a steep escarpment from the Namib desert, the central plateau lies at 1-2,000m above sea-level descending again towards the east.

Capital: Windhoek.

Government: Administered from South Africa, Namibia may soon be achieving a limited form of multi-racial autonomy.

Languages: Afrikaans and English are the official languages. German is widely spoken. The Herero, Ovambo and Nama peoples have their own languages.

Religions: Christianity (Lutheran, Anglican, Dutch Reformed, Roman Catholic, etc.), and traditional beliefs.

Currency: South African Rand. R1=100 cents. R1.50=£1 sterling. R0.87= US$1.00.

Time: GMT+2.

Electricity: 220/230V.

HOW TO GET THERE

By air: South African Airways run regular flights to the international airport at Windhoek from Johannesburg and Cape Town and to Keetmansdorp from Kimberley. One can also fly direct from Salisbury (Rhodesia), London and Frankfurt.

By rail: Passenger trains, running each way twice a week, connect Namibia to South Africa, and there are daily goods/passenger services. Rail travel, however, is not recommended for the visitor; it is neither quick nor particularly comfortable.

By road: The road from Luanda in Angola, through Namibia to South Africa is now completely tarred. The route from Maun in Botswana is far more difficult. Visitors wishing to drive between Luanda and Windhoek should check with their nearest South African Tourist Office for regulations regarding passage through Ovamboland, which is under a state of emergency.

By sea: Walvis Bay and Luderitz are the only ports.

Visas and health regulations

South African regulations apply to Namibia. See under South Africa: General Information, in this guide.

What to wear

Cool summer clothes are needed most of the year, but warmer clothes are sometimes needed for chilly evenings

Health precautions

Take malaria prophylactics if you plan to visit a game park. Do not swim in inland water as it may contain bilharzia snails. Those going on long safaris should beware of snakes and scorpions, and would therefore be wise to carry anti-bite serum.

ACCOMMODATION AND FOOD

Most towns have modest hotels, while Windhoek and the seaside resort of Swakopmund have several of a more luxurious standard. Many towns still have shops and cafes selling *wurst,* German bread and pure German coffee, and bars selling the excellent local German beer. Meat, too, is generally of high quality.

Camping grounds are scattered throughout the country but some have few amenities.

TRANSPORT

Air: Because of distances, flying is not only the quickest but also often the most economical means of transport. Daily scheduled flights within the country connect Windhoek, Walvis Bay, Swakopmund, Okahandja, Otjiwarongo, Outjo, Tsumeb, Grootfontein, and Keetmanshoop. Charter flights can also be arranged to other airstrips.

TOURIST INFORMATION

The Director, Dept of Nature Conservation and Tourism, P.B. 13186, Windhoek. South Africa Tourist Corporation offices in South Africa and abroad.
Banks, business hours, public holidays and diplomatic representation: see under South Africa: General Information, in this guide.

WINDHOEK

Founded in 1890 by a German officer, Windhoek is situated in the rugged Khomas-Hochland Mountains at the centre of the country. Like all southern African cities, the capital is socially segregated with black Namibians entering the white area only as daytime workers. At night they return to their less salubrious townships on the outskirts and to the depressing compounds of Katatura. The white part of the city is tri-lingual, with German cafes, fashion shops, delicatessens, restaurants and hotels setting the tone. The German colonial-style buildings—the Alte Feste (Old Fort), which houses the Cultural History Museum, the three German castles at Klein Windhoek, and the Tintenpalast—are the major tourist attractions.

Hotels
(A selection.)
Thuringerhof, Kaiser St, tel: 6031, 44 rooms.
Continental, Kaiser St, tel: 2681, 74 rooms.
Kalahari Sands, Fuerstenhof.

SWAKOPMUND, WALVIS BAY

The German legacy can best be seen at Swakopmund. Perhaps the country's most attractive town, this seaside resort on the edge of the Namib used to be the German administrative capital during the hot summer months. It has a fine Lutheran church, an excellent museum, an Olympic swimming pool and other tourist facilities.

Not far south is the main port of Walvis Bay whose main tourist attraction is the flamingo-filled lagoon. There are extensive fishing possibilites, but otherwise it is an unattractive, fish-smelling town.

The coast around Cape Cross, 130km north of Swakopmund, is a paradise for fishermen, particularly the desolate Skeleton Coast further north.

Hotels
(A selection.)
SWAKOPMUND
Strand, Strand St, tel: 2605, 24 rooms.
Panorama, P.O. Box 630, tel: 336, 21 rooms.
WALVIS BAY
Mermaid, 6th St, tel: 2541, 24 rooms.
Flamingo, 7th St, tel: 3011, 38 rooms.

THE NORTH

Okahandja, 72km north of Windhoek, is the spot where the Herero gather every August to mourn their departed chiefs.

I. FRANK

Herero family

The town has a picturesque mission house and church and a private zoo. Near Karibib, 114km west on the Swakopmund road, is the vast extinct volcano of Erongo, whose surroundings are particularly rich in Bushmen paintings. The famous Bushman painting 'White Lady of the Brandberg' is, however, much less accessible, lying about 210km north west of Karibib on a rough dirt road. In this area, too, are Bushman rock engravings at Twyfelfontein; the Burnt Mountain, completely bare of plantlife and composed of rainbow-coloured lava rock; and the Petrified Forest, 45km from Welwitschia on the road to Torra Bay. Further east, near Kalkfeld, are the footprints of a dinosaur. North west of Usakos, rising out of the Namib, is the 2,000m. Spitzkoppe, the country's 'Matterhorn', known for its rock paintings and popular for mountaineering.

THE SOUTH

South of Windhoek the main road passes through Rehoboth to Mariental. Nearby is the Hardap Dam Park, and to the west, 72km from Maltahohe in the Namib, is the remarkable Schloss Duwisib, a German-built castle, immaculately preserved and housing a fine collection of 17th and 18th century furniture, portraits and weapons. Also in the west is the Nauklauft Mountain Zebra Park. Between

Mariental and Keetmanshoop is Mukaros—'The Finger of God'—a 30m weathered stone tower near Asab, and to the south, Brukkaros, a 1,500m high extinct volcano.

At Keetmanshoop, the centre of the country's major karakul farming area, there are hotels, shops and an airport. The Kokerboom Forest is nearby.

The main places of interest towards the South African border are the hot springs at Ai-Ais and the dramatic Fish River Canyon, which some claim is an even finer sight than the American Grand Canyon. In the midst of a desolate mountain landscape the earth suddenly falls away dizzyingly to the sandy river bed winding 600m below, over a distance of 110km. Approach the Canyon with care—it is difficult to see the lip until you are within only a few metres of it. It can be visited at any time of the year, but walking tours of the Canyon only take place in winter because of the danger of summer flooding. Visitors to the Canyon can stay at Keetmanshoop; there are also camping facilites at Ai-Ais. A permit to visit the springs there must be obtained from the Magistrate at Karasburg.

Part of the area surrounding the Canyon has been declared a national park—the home of leopard, zebra, kudu, ostrich and several species of antelope.

NATIONAL PARKS

About one-seventh of the country comes under the Department of Tourism and Nature Conservation, and there are now ten national parks.

Some 400km north of Windhoek by tarred road, the **Etosha Pan Game Reserve,** is the country's most outstanding tourist attraction. It has well-equipped rest camps, each with furnished rooms.

HISTORY

Namibia's earliest inhabitants—the Khoi Khoi cattle-keepers (progenitors of the modern Nama) and the San (Bushmen)—were very largely decimated by the later waves of Bantu, Damara and European invaders. Later, in their turn, the Herero became the victims of near genocide under German rule. The first European explorer, the Portuguese Diego Cao, found Bushmen who gathered fruit, hunted game with poison arrows and who left a record of their life in the rock art of the hills. There were also copper and iron-smiths selling their wares to their neighbours. The Bantu-speaking peoples such as the Herero and Ovambo came from Central Africa and brought more cattle with them. They drove both game and the San hunters off the better pasture lands.

From the late 18th century groups of Coloured people, such as the Rehobother, came to seek land in Namibia. They were closely followed by white hunters, traders and missionaries. In 1878 the British annexed the best harbour on the coast, Walvis Bay (officially still a part of South Africa). The British were followed five years later by the Germans who claimed the whole territory. Their castles testify to the fierce opposition from the Nama and Herero people from 1904 to 1907. In 1904, after Herero resistance had been crushed, General von Trotha issued his notorious 'Extermination Order': 65,000 Herero were killed or perished in the desert into which they were driven; only 15,000 survived. To this day their population is still below what it was before German rule. Ovamboland, on the other hand, was never effectively ruled by the Germans.

During World War One, South African military forces drove out the Germans. When the League of Nations Permanent Mandate Commission was established in 1920 to supervise the former German colonies, Namibia was given in trust to South Africa to rule 'in the interests of the indigenous inhabitants'. The condition of the Africans in fact showed remarkably little improvement, while the area administered for white occupation crept further north as ranching and mining developed. By 1949 the white settlers had gained six representatives in the Cape Town Parliament, and the territory was virtually treated as a fifth province of South Africa.

An attempt was made to achieve the territory's formal incorporation in 1947 when General Smuts' regime stage-managed a referendum which was intended to demonstrate majority support for a request to the new United Nations Trusteeship Council to terminate the mandate in favour of South African rule. But African counter-petitions from leaders like the Herero Chief Hosea Kutako frustrated this plan, and the country was brought under UN Trusteeship.

Namibia has become the longest drawn-out international controversy at the UN; it has never been off its annual agenda since 1946. Finally, in 1970, the UN terminated the mandate and declared South Africa to be in illegal occupation of the country—but it has not yet found a way of enforcing its decision despite a World Court opinion giving it legal sanction.

South Africa's first response to these developments was to divide the country into separate Homelands (as in the Republic) for each of the peoples to whom 39% of the land in all had been allocated, while 61% was retained for the small white community.

In the mid-1970s the mineral wealth of Namibia had become of sufficient strategic interest to the Western countries (especially Britain and the US) to make some kind of internationally acceptable political solution appear desirable. South Africa even appeared willing to grant some kind of independence, but it still refused in 1977 to discuss Namibia's future with the main nationalist organisation, the South West African People's Organisation (SWAPO).

SWAPO has been recognised by the UN as the legitimate voice of the Namibian people.

NIGER

The River Niger flows through the southwest corner of this vast country, which stretches through savannah into the most desolate area of the Sahara, bordering Algeria and Libya. Many people cross Niger on their way between North Africa and West Africa, and the country's key position on the proposed Trans-Sahara Highway will make it a very popular tourist destination in the years to come, with its beautiful Sudanic cities and oases and the exquisite scenery of the Aïr Mountains. The scorching heat of summer is not always relieved by the seasonal rains. Millions of animals have died and many nomadic Tuareg and Fulani herders have seen their centuries-old way of life altered, perhaps beyond recovery by the drought of the early 1970s.

Niger's economic future is, however, less bleak than it might have been, with the exploitation of valuable uranium reserves from the Aïr region.

THE LAND AND THE PEOPLE

The Niger River flows from 500 km through the country that bears its name. Several large rivers such as the Tapoa and Mekrou flow into it. Their seasonal flooding provides the only real hope for agriculture, notably rice. The south-east corner, hardly accessible by road, also has some arable land on the banks of

Lake Chad. The remainder of the southern border strip is sandy, but receives just enough rain (560 mm a year) to grow millet and groundnuts, the main export. This sandy strip quickly gives way in the north to thin Sahel grassland and thorn scrub on a wide plateau where large herds of cattle, sheep, goats and camels are moved seasonally in search of well-water. The past five years of drought have driven the nomads from their traditional lands to the towns. Further north again, covering half the country, is the true desert, while north of Agadez the land rises to the impressive, partly volcanic Aïr Massif, 300 km by 200 km across, reaching a height of 2,310 m on Mont

Greboun. Its humid valleys sheltered the work of the ancient rock artists as the Sahara dried up.

The Songhai and Djerma people, living in the Niger valley and making up one-quarter of the population, are mainly farmers and fishermen. Along the border with Nigeria live the Hausa-speaking peoples. They are closely akin to the Hausa of Nigeria and make up half the population. Most of them are farmers and stock-raisers, but they also possess a strong commercial tradition which takes them to markets all over the country. The nomadic Fulani (known in French as Peulh) are a tall, fine-featured, brown people, who have spread all over the West African parts of the Sahel.

The robed and veiled Tuareg, whose mounted legions based on Agadez once dominated the southern cities, had a highly-stratified society with the Sultan at the top and the black slave caste at the bottom. They also developed their own script, Tifinar. Still camel-herders and caravaneers on the Saharan routes, they come frequently to the markets to exchange their stock and leather goods for the farmer's millet and tea but it is the Tuareg who have suffered most from the drought. Many of them now live as beggars in the cities of Nigeria.

Near Lake Chad, live the Manga (or Kanuri) once part of the Kanem empire which controlled eastern Niger.

WILDLIFE

One corner of the excellent 'W' game park juts into Niger and can be visited from the rest camp at La Tapao. Here, in mountain and savannah country, are herds of elephant, buffalo and antelope as well as lion and leopard. Birds, fish, hippos and crocodiles can be seen all along the Niger valley. North of Niamey live large groups of giraffe, often seen casually crossing the road. After the tragic decimation of game in this south-western area by hunters, big game hunt-

ing has been suspended to allow stocks to replenish. However, poaching is still a considerable threat to game.

GENERAL INFORMATION

Area: 1,187,000 sq. km.
Population: 4 million.
Altitude: The plateau averages 300 m rising in the heights of the Aïr massif to 2,000 m.
Capital: Niamey.
Head of State: Lt-Colonel Seyni Kountchi.
Government: Supreme Military Council. Cabinet consists of both soldiers and civilians.
Date of independence: 3 August 1960.
Languages: French is the official language but it is hardly spoken outside the towns. The principal African languages are Hausa and Songhai, while in much of the east Kanuri (Manga) is spoken, and Arabic in the north.
Religion: 85% of the people are Muslim; the rest are traditional with some Christians in the Niamey area.
Currency: CFA franc; £1 sterling=427 CFA francs; US$1=249 CFA francs.
Time: GMT+1.
Electricity: 220/380V.

HOW TO GET THERE

By air: Air Afrique and UTA fly regularly from Paris and Sabena from Brussels. There are also links by these and lines such as Air Mali and British Caledonian with other West African capitals. Air Libya operates a flight from Tripoli allowing a stop-over in Agadez en route to Niamey.

The airport lies 10 km out of the capital. No taxis are allowed but the hotels provide free transport for their guests and Agence Transcap (B.P. 522, tel: 32.34) will arrange for a car to meet flights.

By road: Visitors arriving by road need a

registration book or carnet de passage for their car, and a national or international driving licence (preferably with a photograph).

There is a good tarred road from Kano (Nigeria) to Zinder, fair laterite ones from Upper Volta and Benin and a sandy track from Mali. The route from Algiers to Agadez is one of the major trans-Saharan routes but involves tough desert-driving.

At In Guezzam on the border with Algeria there is normally water but no petrol. The following section is extremely sandy and desolate and the kilometre marker beacons are not always easy to see. (Many of them have disappeared.) At Tegguiddan-Tessoum one enters semi-desert; the track divides, south to In Gall and Tahoua and south east towards Agadez.

Bus services run from Mali, Upper Volta and Benin.

Visas and health regulations

Nationals of Belgium, France, Italy, Luxembourg, Netherlands, French-speaking African states and Madagascar, Federal Republic of Germany, Andorra and Monaco require only an identity card or passport. Visitors to Niger carrying a British passport do not require a visa. All others must have a visa obtained in advance at an embassy of Niger or France. An onward or return ticket, or a repatriation guarantee, may be required.

Visitors must have certificates of vaccination against smallpox, yellow fever and cholera.

Dutiable goods

Personal effects are allowed in duty free and include a camera, movie camera, portable musical instrument and typewriter, a carton of cigarettes, 25 cigars of 50 gm of tobacco.

Currency regulations

There is no limit to the amount of local or foreign currency which may be taken into the country, but exports outside the franc zone are rigidly controlled. The maximum amount a visitor may take out in local currency is 50,000 CFA francs.

CLIMATE

It is extremely hot in summer. December to April is the best time to visit. The dry season lasts from October to May. It is hot in the day (average 28°C) but cools off towards evening, dropping to 12°C—in the north it occasionally freezes. From November to January a dry and cooling but dusty *harmattan* blows from the east.

In July and August heavy rain falls with tornadoes in the south; temperatures can rise above 40°C. The south receives an average of 600 mm of rain but the north may have only 10-20 mm and sometimes none at all.

What to wear: Plenty of lightweight cotton or linen shirts or dresses, and cotton, not nylon, underwear. Since most of the inhabitants wear long national dress it is polite when travelling in the countryside for women to avoid wearing short skirts.

Health precautions: Smallpox, yellow fever and cholera immunisation is required. A prophylactic against malaria should be taken; TAB vaccination against typhoid is recommended. Tap water should not generally be drunk—bottled water is plentiful. Do not swim in lakes or rivers as there is schistosomiasis.

ACCOMMODATION AND FOOD

There are good hotels in Niamey and less good ones at Zinder, Maradi and Agadez. **Tipping**: c. 10%. Most hotels add a 10-15% service charge to the bill.

TRANSPORT

Air: Air Niger flies twice a week to Agadez and Tahoua, and three times a week to Maradi and Zinder.

Road: The only tarred road is the road from Niamey to Zinder. Other roads are of laterite or sand, the major ones rutted and difficult. Heat and rains make long journeys inadvisable except from December to March. Even on the main west-east road petrol stations can be up to 170 km apart (elsewhere 500 km). Garages are also infrequent, and in Niamey repair prices are high. A daily coach runs between Niamey and Zinder. North and east of the main road (e.g. for those going to Agadez) desert conditions prevail, although ordinary cars can be used.

Travel in convoy if possible; always notify the authorities of your plans, and be sure your vehicle is in sound condition. Take plenty of water, petrol, spare parts, tools for the car, a shovel, metal tracks for the wheels and at least two spare wheels and a first aid kit.

Aïr, Lake Chad and Bilma regions require a four-wheel drive vehicle.

BANKS AND COMMERCE

The main banks have branches only at Niamey, Maradi and Zinder.

Business hours: Banks: 0800-1200; weekdays. Government and commerce: 0800-1200; 1500-1830 Mondays to Saturdays. Government offices close on Saturday afternoons and every afternoon during Ramadan. Shops: 0800-1200; 1600-1900; closed Saturday afternoons and Sundays.

PUBLIC HOLIDAYS

New Year's Day; Good Friday; Easter Monday; Labour Day; Whit Monday; Independence Day 3 August; The Assumption of the Virgin; All Saints' Day; Christmas Day.

The following Muslim feasts are observed: Id-al-Fitr (the end of Ramadan); Tabaski (the Fete du Mouton commemorating Abraham's sacrifice); Mouloud (a feast retracing Mohammed's life).

The Tuareg in the north celebrate the Salt Cure to mark the end of the rains (usually in September).

FOREIGN EMBASSIES

Algeria; Benin, B.P. 944; **China PR**, B.P. 732; **France**, B.P. 240; **West Germany**, B.P. 629; **Libya**, B.P. 633; **Nigeria**, B.P. 617; **Saudi Arabia**, B.P. 339; **USSR**, B.P. 723; **USA**, B.P. 201.

TOURIST INFORMATION

Office Nationale du Tourisme, B.P. 612, Niamey.

NIAMEY

The capital is a growing modern city of c. 102,000 people. Until recently it was a small fishing village and Say, nearby, was of more importance. It lies on the Niger River, a bustling highway thronged by dug-out canoes bringing fish and vegeta-

Old man in Agadez

C HENNEGHIEN

bles from the green belt on the opposite bank.

The Small Market, at the hub of the commercial centre sells mainly food, while the picturesque Great Market specializes in cloth made in Niger or Mali, such as indigo tie-dye and leather, iron and copper craftwork, much of it made around the market place. Nearby is the Great Mosque, a white modern building built in traditional style.

Along the river the fascinating, well-arranged National Museum is a park with a zoo and a display of Niger's musical and artistic heritage, rock paintings from Aïr as well as typical huts and tents of the different areas. Craftwork is also displayed for sale.

Hotels
Grand Hotel du Niger, B.P. 471, tel: 26.41. **Le Sahel**, B.P. 627, tel: 30.31. **Les Roniers**, B.P. 795, tel: 31.38. **Terminus**, B.P. 882, tel: 22.52. **Rivoli**, B.P. 87, tel: 25.09.

Restaurants: Baie d'Along; Pagode; Saigon; Flotille; Kasbah; Epi d'Or.

Shopping
Street vendors sell craftwork in the Great Market. Highly-priced but high quality artifacts are sold at the Museum. Courteous bargaining is expected in markets. Nigerien craftsmen make fine multi-coloured blankets, leather-goods, engraved calabashes, silver jewellery, swords and knives.

Tourist information
Office du Tourisme du Niger, near the city centre.

AGADEZ
A beautifully preserved caravan trading city in semi-desert surroundings, Agadez was host to a huge Tuareg refugee camp during the worst years of the drought, 1972 and 1973. But it now has a thriving, if small, tourist trade. Excellent silversmiths and leatherworkers still work with artistry and enthusiasm in the quiet backstreets, while the busy little matting-stall market sells a host of traditional artifacts in use over the whole region.

This old Tuareg capital is a perfect example of Sudanic mud architecture, with clean sandy streets. All the modern buildings conform perfectly to the traditional style. The famous landmark is the mosque with its spiky tower, which should be climbed at sunset for a colourful view of the town.

Hotels
Hotel de l'Aïr, B.P. 109. tel: 330, by the old mosque, 8 rooms. **Family House**, 8 rooms. Restaurants at the hotels, and **L'Auberge Gabriel** and **Big Boy.**

EXCURSIONS FROM AGADEZ
The Aïr Massif north of Agadez is an impressive range of stark jagged peaks, the most exciting landscape in Niger, sheltering the occasional humid valley with gardens irrigated by springs often containing mineral salts. One can sometimes see wild sheep, antelope, fox and ostrich on the tracks through the massif.

ZINDER
Zinder is set in agricultural country on an important trade route to Kano (Nigeria), 920 km from Niamey along the rather monotonous main highway along the south. The colourful *birni* (old town), founded in the 18th century, is a typical Hausa town with a compact maze of alleyways. Near the centre is the Sultan's Palace (1860) and the mosque, which offers a good view from the minaret. The old fort is still in use. The important market, where some of the best leatherwork may be found, takes place on Thursdays.

Hotels
Central Hotel, 22 rooms, good restaurant.

Fulani herders with their cattle

MARADI

This rapidly growing commercial centre on the main highway moved to its present site only 30 years ago when the old one was flooded. Several of the houses have cupola-shaped roofs and attractive geometric designs on the walls.

Hotels

Niger Hotel, B.P. 18, tel: 02.12, 7 rooms.

A campement also provides accommodation.

HISTORY

The area now called Niger has not always been as arid as it is today. Some 6,000 years ago it was well-watered and archaeologists have found evidence of a flourishing civilization there. The last 1,000 years have seen the rise of the great Borno and Songhai empires as well as the intrusion of the Hausa peoples. The Borno dominated the east of Niger, in particular the area around Lake Chad, from around the 8th century until the end of the 19th century when they were finally overthrown. The Songhai originated in the south-west of the country, near the border with Mali and their history is marked by constant conflicts with the forces of the powerful empire which existed among their neighbours.

The Hausa are descended from a number of different ethnic groups, and were responsible for the establishment of fortified cities which became prosperous commercial and intellectual centres from the 13th century onwards. In the early 19th century Islam among the Hausa was revived by the Fulani Osman Dan Fodio who united the Hausa states.

French colonisation of Niger began in 1899. The fiercest opposition came from the nomadic Tuareg in the north of the country. Niger was declared a French colony in 1921 and effectively remained so until independence in 1960.

NIGERIA

For the first-time visitor, travel in Nigeria is far from being an easy or straightforward business. There are frequent delays, hold-ups and inconveniences in getting from place to place. Telephones rarely work. Taxis are expensive. Buses are overcrowded. Traffic jams abound, while power cuts have a habit of bringing city life to a complete standstill. Hotels and food are expensive while many essential commodities are difficult to obtain.

Such are the growing pains of a populous and oil-rich third world nation. The expansion of the population in the cities and the mushrooming of business activities have not been matched by a growth in basic facilities. And although much is being spent on improving services of all kinds, it is never enough. These day-to-day problems, confronting the resident and visitor in Nigeria alike will inevitably remain for some years to come.

But for those who have a genuine interest in Africa, Nigeria should not be missed. It has a powerful human interest combined with strong cultural traditions and a fascinating history. Moreover its large size embraces an incredible variety of people, types of society, terrain and scenery. On closer acquaintance Nigeria's bustle and confusion becomes not tedious or enervating but actually invigorating and compelling. The inter-ested visitor will always be welcomed and entertained.

THE LAND AND THE PEOPLE

The Federal Republic of Nigeria has the largest population in any country in Africa and possibly the greatest diversity of cultures, ways of life, types of city and terrain.

The low-lying coastal area is a network of lagoons and rivers of the Niger delta, with an almost unbroken line of sandy beaches. Between the creeks and mangrove swamps runs an intricate system of

NIGERIA   250 mls

UBA

The Bank that Covers the World

Linked with a global network of financial expertise, United Bank for Africa
Limited through their overseas partners in France, Italy, U. S. A., United Kingdom
and in 70 other countries with UBA correspondents are at your service.

United Bank for Africa Limited

Head Office,
97/105, Broad Street.
P. O. Box 2406, Lagos, Nigeria
Cables: Mindobank, Lagos
Tel: 20311/2/3/4
Telex 21241 & 21580

Overseas Shareholders

Banque Nationale de Paris Ltd.
(Formerly known as
British & French Bank Ltd.)
Plantation House
10 – 15, Mincing Lane,
P. O. Box 416,
London, EC3P 3ER
United Kingdom.

Banque Nationale de Paris,
16, Boulevard des Italiens
Paris, France

Banca Nazionale del Lavoro,
Via Vittorio Veneto,
119, Rome, Italy.

Bankers Trust Company,
16, Wall Street,
New York, U.S.A.

Monte dei Paschi di Siena,
Piazza Salimbeni
Siena, Italy.

35 BRANCHES THROUGHOUT NIGERIA

inland waterways. Inland the country rises in hills and valleys covered with luxuriant vegetation, a productive area where forest trees, oil palms, rubber and cocoa grow. About 160km inland the forest gives way to savannah parkland, and the land rises to an average of 700m with high mountains in the central Jos Plateau and the Cameroon Highlands of the east. Farther north the savannah turns to Sahelian plains which suffered from the drought of the early 1970s.

Two great rivers merge at the country's centre: the Niger, which rises in Guinea and flows into the Sahara before turning southwards; and the Benue from Cameroon. The Jos Plateau, to the north of this juncture, is the source of numerous streams flowing into both rivers and others flowing north on the Sahara's edge about 300m. above sea level and subject to continuous evaporation.

Nigeria has about 70 million people, belonging to 250 ethnic groups, but with three peoples numerically stronger than the rest—the Hausa of the north, the Ibo of the south east, and the Yoruba of the south west. Between the 'heartlands' of the three dominant peoples are numbers of related but distinct groups. Bendel State is a good example of harmonious ethnic variety—with offshoots of both Yoruba and Ibo. The larger 'minor' groups are the Fulani, Tiv, Kanuri, Igala, Idoma, Igbirra and Nupe in the north; the Ibibio, Efik, Ekoi and Ijaw in the east; and the Edo, Urhobo, Itsekiri and Ijaw in the west.

Nigeria's new states

In 1976 Nigeria was reconstituted from a Federation of 12 States to one of 19 States, and it was announced that the Federal Capital would be moved eventually from Lagos to a new location in the centre of Nigeria, south of Abuja. An area of some 12,000 sq km was designated for development as the capital. Lagos will of course remain the dominant commercial centre.

The new States and their capitals are:

STATE	CAPITAL
ANAMBRA	ENUGU
BAUCHI	BAUCHI
BENDEL	BENIN CITY
BENUE	MAKURDI
BORNO	MAIDUGURI
CROSS RIVER	CALABAR
GONGOLA	YOLA
IMO	OWERRI
KADUNA	KADUNA
KANO	KANO
KWARA	ILORIN
LAGOS	LAGOS
NIGER	MINNA
OGUN	ABEOKUTA
ONDO	AKURE
OYO	IBADAN
PLATEAU	JOS
RIVERS	PORT HARCOURT
SOKOTO	SOKOTO

CULTURE

Nigerian art goes back well over 2,000 years, and beyond the mysterious terracotta heads of the Nok culture, found in the plateau region. Other artifacts and sculptures of even earlier origins have been found.

The famous Ife terracotta and brass sculptures, dating from around AD1000, provide a vivid insight into Ife's ancient civilisation. Somewhat later, the Benin kingdom—ceded by Ife—established a long-lasting and prolific tradition of bronze casting, wood and iron carving and sculpture. Much of the best work was seized by the British Punitive Expedition of 1897 and is now dispersed all over Europe and North America, but there are still some good examples in Nigeria's museums. The earliest surviving wooden carvings from Oron, Cross River State, are between 200 and 300 years old.

Nigeria's museums are all well worth visiting for the tremendous display of historic treasures and contemporary artifacts on show. The National museum in Lagos is the most comprehensive, but any opportunity to see the museums at Ife, Jos, Esie and Owo should not be missed.

Nigeria is a treasure hoard of beautiful hand-made objects, for the visitor to

*Pottery at Badagry Market,
near Lagos*

marvel at or buy—wood carvings, decorated calabashes, leatherwork, metal work, jewellery and traditional clothes, which can be made at little cost in a matter of hours.

The tremendous variety of Nigeria's dances is matched by its innumerable musical instruments—stringed, wind or percussion. The drums are as popular as ever and are often incorporated into modern Juju, Highlife or Afrobeat, while the stringed and wind instruments have tended to give way to the guitar and brass.

As many Nigerian languages are tonal, their percussion instruments can be made to talk intelligibly. The variety of the drums used is immense; with four or five distinct groups of drums. The talking variety used by the Yoruba belong to the *dundun* group, the most popular drums being known as the *bata*, the *gangan* and the *koso*.

The music of the Kanuri of the north east is distinctive in its use of reed pipes as well as large drums. The dancing is often slow and stately with men and women both taking part.

Durbars are a feature of Northern communities—long lines of horsemen led by a band, horses in quilted armour with metal face pieces, tassels, dyed sheepskins over the saddles, the riders wearing quilted coats with sashes holding swords. The Sallah festivals of the north (especially in Katsina, Kano and Zaria) celebrate the end of Ramadan, when Muslims throng together in their best regalia to hear the local emir announce the event. It is an occasion for pomp and confusion, with processions of nobles on horseback, musicians, acrobats and dancers.

Festivals are now less frequent because of the expenses required of the participants, but they are still widespread. The Nigerian Tourist Association publishes a comprehensive guide to traditional festivals.

One of the world's greatest cultural festivals was held in Nigeria in 1977—the 2nd Festival of Black and African Arts and Culture (FESTAC)—brought black artists and intellectuals from all over the world to Lagos to meet, give displays and to discuss new ideas and trends.

Nigeria also holds annual art festivals at States level, as well as all-Nigerian Festivals held in different State capitals.

WILDLIFE

Nigeria cannot boast of game parks to match other countries in Africa, but it has a wealth of birds, butterflies, monkeys and larger animals in every corner of the country. A particularly rare river mammal, the manatee, lives in the Benue river and tributaries.

There are two official game parks but more are planned. The one at Borgu in the north west is at present rather inaccessible but rewards the visitor with a wealth of game unusual in West Africa; the other, Yankari National Park near Bauchi, is small, but contains a remarkable cross-section of West African wildlife, from lions to elephants and giraffes to marabou storks.

Jos and Ibadan zoos have excellent collections of West African animals.

GENERAL INFORMATION

Area: 923,773 sq km.
Population: 72 million.
Altitude: Sea level, rising to central plateau of 1,200m.
Capital: Lagos.
Head of State: Lt-Gen. Olusegun Obasanjo.
Government: Federal and Military. The Supreme Military Council rules by decree in conjunction with a Federal Executive Council, consisting of civilian commissioners.
State Governments: Each of the 19 States has its own government and institutions.
Date of Independence: 1 October, 1960.
Languages: English is the official and commercial language and is widely spoken. The predominant Nigerian languages are: Yoruba and Edo in the west; Hausa in the north; Ibo and Efik in the east.
Religions: Islam is the principal religion of the north and west, while Christianity is strong in the south. About 20% of the population follow traditional beliefs.
Currency: The Naira (N) is divided into 100 kobo. £1 sterling = N1.13; US$1.00 = N0.6310.
Time: GMT+1.

HOW TO GET THERE

By air: The main international airports are Murtala Mohammed Airport at Ikeja (about 25 km from Lagos) and Kano. Direct flights to and from London (Gatwick) are provided by British Caledonian three times a week, and by Nigerian Airways from London (Heathrow) five times a week. There are services from European airports: Amsterdam, Brussels, Frankfurt, Paris, Rome and Zurich, in conjunction with Sabena, KLM, Lufthansa, UTA, Alitalia and Swissair, as well as with New York and Beirut, in conjunction with PanAm and MEA. Within Africa there are direct connections with Abidjan, Accra, Banjul, Dakar, Douala, Freetown, Monrovia and Kinshasa.

There are taxis available at Murtala Mohammed Airport but one should agree the fare in advance—the journey into Lagos should not exceed N8 (mainland destination) or N10 (Lagos Island), although the visitor will invariably be asked to pay much more. Your introduction to Lagos immediately puts your bargaining skills to the severest test, and gives you a taste of prices to come during your stay!

There are occasional Nigeria Airways bus services to and from the main hotels.

By sea: There are passenger and cargo vessels plying from London, Liverpool and other European ports to Lagos and West African ports

By road: There are roads connecting Nigeria with its immediate neighbours— Benin, Niger, Chad and Cameroon. The principal link with Benin is via the Idiroko border point, from where the road to Lagos is excellent. The two main trans-Saharan routes enter Nigeria from Niger, one from Niamey and the other from Agadez. Two good roads converge on Kano, one via Maradi and Katsina, and the other from Zinder.

Maiduguri, in north east Nigeria, is accessible by all-weather roads from Ndjamena in Chad and Maroua in Cameroon. Farther south there is a road from Mamfe, in Cameroon, to Enugu; when this eventually becomes part of the Trans-African Highway it will be considerably improved.

Visas and health regulations
UK and British Commonwealth citizens

require an entry permit which can be obtained from a Nigerian diplomatic mission abroad. Application should be made a month in advance. An entry permit cannot be obtained on arrival in Nigeria. Citizens of other countries require a visa, which should be applied for well in advance.

Visitors require valid international certificates of vaccination against smallpox, yellow fever and cholera. TAB vaccination is recommended.

Dutiable goods

Personal baggage, a camera, a typewriter and similar personal articles for the use of bona fide visitors are admitted free of duty. In addition 200 cigarettes or 50 cigars are allowed. Arms and ammunition, drugs and narcotics are prohibited. A customs declaration has to be completed and handed to the examining officer at the point of entry.

Currency regulations

A currency declaration in duplicate is required on arrival and departure. All declared currency should be changed only at banks and this should be registered on the declaration form. The import or export of Nigerian currency in excess of N50 is prohibited.

CLIMATE

The climate of the southern coast, on the Bight of Benin, is quite different to that of the north, which borders the Sahara desert. Lagos and the areas around the Niger delta are generally hot and humid, with a long rainy season stretching from March to November. In the north the rainy season lasts from April to September. Rainfall varies from over 2,000mm per annum in the south to under 250mm per annum in the north.

Temperatures in the north may reach 43°C in the daytime, but can rapidly drop below 4°C at night in December and January. The average temperature in the

south is 29°C. During the dry season, especially around December and January, the *harmattan* wind blows fine dust from the Sahara; this brings the temperatures and humidity down.

What to wear: Clothes should be lightweight and washable. A sweater is advisable for visitors to the north. A light raincoat and/or umbrella are essential for the rainy season. Take light shoes or sandals. Only in a few places (ie some Lagos restaurants) are men expected to wear jackets, though a long-sleeved shirt and tie are regarded as proper in other 'smart' establishments. Colourful Nigerian shirts are very popular with local Europeans.

Dry-cleaning facilities are available in the larger cities.

Health precautions: Tap water is generally safe in large towns. Elsewhere (and in Kano) avoid drinking tap water and eating uncooked fruit and vegetables. Antimalarial tablets should be taken before, during and after visit. In the south especially mosquito nets are advisable. The best hospital in Lagos is the Teaching Hospital.

ACCOMMODATION AND FOOD

There are first-class hotels in Lagos and in the major towns but they are frequently heavily booked. One should therefore make reservations well in advance. Otherwise there are facilities for less comfortable but cheaper accommodation, though hard to come by in Lagos.

In most big towns it is often worth joining the local sporting club, where temporary membership is available, for the chance to eat cheaply and well, to meet people, and for sports and entertainment.

There are restaurants of all varieties in Lagos and the major towns. European and oriental food is available as well as

Nigerian dishes—groundnut stew, pepper soup, *egusi*, *dodo* (fried plantain), *akara* (fried bean-flour cake), fried yam or sweet potatoes.

Tipping: Ten per cent of the bill is usual for hotel and restaurant staff unless it is provided for in the service charge.

TRANSPORT

There is regular transport to all parts of the Federation. The main centres can be reached by air, road or rail. For all comfortable forms of public transport it is advisable to book in advance.

In the north of Nigeria travelling is difficult during the annual pilgrimage to Mecca (the Hajj) when hotels and planes are always fully booked.

Air: Nigeria Airways operates a sometimes unreliable domestic service between Lagos and the main towns: Ibadan, Benin, Port Harcourt, Enugu, Calabar, Kaduna, Kano, Jos, Sokoto, Maiduguri, Yola and between these towns. Advance booking is advisable.

Air charter facilities within Nigeria are available from: Aero Contractors, 8-10 Broad Street, P.O. Box 2519, Lagos (tel: 24347); Pan-African Airlines, P.M.B. 1054, Ikeja (tel: 33098) and Delta Air Charter, P.M.B. 1067, Ikeja (tel: 33579).

Roads: Good all-weather roads connect major centres. Much are in bad repair but new roads are being constructed in most parts of the country. Traffic travels on the right hand side.

Taxi and minibuses ply regularly between the main towns, generally filled to overflowing. There are motor parks in all main towns, often a separate one for each principal direction. The location of these can be ascertained easily on the spot. This form of transport is less easily available in the north than in the south.

Modern and air-conditioned bus services operate between main centres. Being fast and comfortable they have become very popular.

Transport within the main towns is variable but taxis are usually available. These are expensive in Lagos and slightly less so in other towns. Buses within towns are very cheap and ply along fixed routes which can easily be discovered by asking.

Car hire: Information can be obtained from the main hotels, but it is often difficult to arrange satisfactory car hire.

Rail: A slow but generally safe method of travel. There are two main routes: Lagos to Kano, with branches to Jos and Maiduguri; and Port Harcourt to Kano.

For first and second class you need to book a week in advance. There is food on trains and there are long stops at every station for provisions.

BANKS

Every significant town has branches of Nigerian banks or locally-incorporated international banks.

Business hours:

Government offices: Usual hours for Federal Government and State Governments, 0730-1530 Monday to Friday and 0730-1300 Saturday;

Commercial offices: 0800-1230 and 1400-1630 Monday to Friday (approximately), 0800-1230 Saturday (Northern States only);

Banks: 0800-1500 Monday and 0800-1300 Tuesday to Friday;

Shops: 0800-1700 Monday to Friday and 0800-1630 Saturday.

FOREIGN EMBASSIES IN LAGOS

Algeria: 26 Maitama Sule Street, S.W. Ikoyi, P.O. Box 7228.

Australia: 21-25 Broad Street, P.O. Box 2427.

Austria: 8-10 Broad Street, P.O. Box 1914.

Belgium: 8-10 Broad Street, P.O. Box 149.

Benin: 36 Breadfruit Street, P.O. Box 5705.

Brazil: 84 Norman Williams Street, Ikoyi, P.O. Box 1931.

Cameroon: 5 Femi Pearse Street, Victoria Island, P.M.B. 2476.

Canada: New Niger House, Tinubu Street, P.O. Box 851.

Central African Empire: 108 Awolowo Road, Ikoyi, P.O. Box 2642.

Chad: 2 Goriola Street, Victoria Island, P.M.B. 2801.

Denmark: 4 Eleke Crescent, Victoria Island, P.O. Box 2390.

Egypt: 81 Awolowo Road, Ikoyi, P.O. Box 538.

Equatorial Guinea: 20 St. Gregory's Road, Obalende, P.O. Box 4162.

Ethiopia: 14 Ademola Street, Ikoyi, P.M.B. 2488.

Finland: 8-10 Broad Street, P.O. Box 4433.

France: 161 Taslim Elias Close, Victoria Island, P.O. Box 567.

Gabon: 74 Awolowo Road, Ikoyi, P.O. Box 5989.

West Germany: 15 Eleke Crescent, Victoria Island, P.O. Box 728.

Ghana: 21-23 King George V Road, P.O. Box 889.

Greece: 7 Thompson Avenue, Ikoyi, P.O. Box 1199.

Guinea: 8 Abudu Smith Street, Victoria Island, P.O. Box 2826.

India: 107 Awolowo Road, Ikoyi, P.O. Box 2322.

Iran: 20 Apartment Building, Adeola Odeku Street, Victoria Island.

Iraq: 7 Keffi Street, Ikoyi, P.O. Box 2859.

Ireland: 31 Marina, P.O. Box 2421.

Italy: Eleke Crescent, Victoria Island, P.O. Box 2161.

Ivory Coast: 5 Abudu Smith Street, Victoria Island, P.O. Box 7786.

Japan: 24-25 Apese Street, Victoria Island, P.M.B. 2111.

Kenya: 52 Queen's Drive, Ikoyi, P.O. Box 6464.

Lebanon: 57 Raymond Njoku Road, S.W. Ikoyi, P.O. Box 651.

Liberia: 19 Alhaji Bashorun Street,

Ikoyi, P.O. Box 3007.

Libya: 46 Raymond Njoku Road, Ikoyi, P.O. Box 2860.

Netherlands: 24 Ozumba Mbadiwe Avenue, Victoria Island, P.O. Box 2426.

Niger: 15 Adeola Odeku Street, Victoria Island, P.M.B. 2739.

Norway: 8-10 Broad Street, P.M.B. 2431.

Pakistan: 20 Keffi Street, Ikoyi, P.O. Box 2450.

Saudi Arabia: 182 Awolowo Road, Ikoyi, P.O. Box 2836.

Senegal: 12-14 Kofo Abayomi Road, Victoria Island, P.M.B. 2197.

Sierra Leone: 192 Awolowo Road, Ikoyi,

Tinubu Square, Lagos

P.O. Box 2821.

Somalia: 114 Norman Williams Street, S.W. Ikoyi, P.O. Box 6355.

Spain: 9 Queen's Drive, P.M.B. 2738.

Sudan: 40 Awolowo Road, Ikoyi, P.O. Box 2428.

Sweden: 8-10 Broad Street, P.O. Box 1097.

Switzerland: 11 Anifowoshe Street, Victoria Island, P.O. Box 536.

Syria: 4 Raymond Njoku Road, S.W. Ikoyi, P.O. Box 3088.

Tanzania: 45 Ademola Street, Ikoyi, P.O. Box 6417.

Togo: 96 Awolowo Road, S.W. Ikoyi, P.O. Box 1435.

UK: 62-64 Campbell Street, P.M.B. 12136.

USA: 1 King's College Road.

Venezuela: 10 Ikoyi Crescent, Ikoyi, P.O. Box 3727.
Yugoslavia: 7 Maitama Sule Street, S.W. Ikoyi, P.M.B. 978.
Zaire: 23A Kofo Abayomi Road, Victoria Island, P.O. Box 1216.
Zambia: 11 Keffi Street, S.W. Ikoyi.

PUBLIC HOLIDAYS
Both Christian and Muslim holidays are observed throughout Nigeria. The only other fixed holidays are New Year's Day and National Day (1 October).

TOURIST INFORMATION
The Nigerian Tourist Association (47 Marina, P.O. Box 2944, Lagos) publishes some leaflets on aspects of travel. The Federal Ministry of Information publishes a *Nigeria Handbook* available at Nigerian Embassies and High Commissions abroad. The *Daily Times* (Lagos) also publishes a *Nigeria Year Book*, and there is a *Guide to Lagos* in the bookshops.

LAGOS
There has been a settlement on Lagos Island since the 15th century, when Yoruba groups used it as a refuge from outside attacks. It subsequently became a trading post between the Benin Kingdom and the Portuguese until the arrival of British traders in the 19th century, presaging the colonisation of the interior.

Lagos today is very different. Probably the most congested city of Africa, it is a seething conglomeration of people, vehicles and every type of dwelling place, from hovels to skyscrapers. Lagos never sleeps; the bustle continues through the sultry night into the torrid day. It is somehow symbolic of the restless energy that characterises Nigeria as the modern 'giant of Africa'.

The overcrowding of Lagos makes relaxation difficult, but there are always spots where one can find peace and quiet. The high cost of living is another negative factor even for those who have a knack of finding the cheapest places to stay and means of travel, but with experience you can find your way around.

Lagos is divided into several parts, each with its distinctive character. The heart of the city is Lagos Island, containing most of Nigeria's commercial and administrative headquarters, with large shops and offices; it is linked to the mainland by two road bridges that can take ages to cross during rush hours, and also to Ikoyi Island and Victoria Island by road. These latter are residential areas, with palatial houses, expansive gardens and smart hotels amid beautiful trees.

The National Museum at Onikan on Lagos Island is well worth a long visit. The Oba's Palace consists of a wing over 200 years old, to which a modern extension was added in 1960. The National Hall is a conference centre with finely carved doors depicting Nigerian culture.

The Brazilian Quarter of Lagos is fascinating historically and architecturally. It was originally a settlement for freed slaves from South America following the abolition of the slave trade.

For relaxation by the sea visit Bar Beach, on Victoria Island, and, by ferry from the Federal Palace Hotel, Tarkwa Bay and Lighthouse Beach.

Hotels
Eko Holiday Inn, Victoria Island, P.M.B. 12724. Tel: 52365, telex 22650. International standard.
Federal Palace Hotel and **Federal Palace Suites Hotel**, Victoria Island, P.O. Box 1000, Lagos. Tel: 26691.
Ikoyi Hotel, Kingsway, Ikoyi, Lagos. Tels: 22181, 24075/6/7, 24053, 25375.
Bristol Hotel, 8 Martins Street, Lagos. Tel: 25901.
Mainland Hotel, Denton Street, P.O. Box 2158, Lagos. Tels: 41101, 46191.
Excelsior Hotel, Ede Street, Apapa. Tel: 41694.

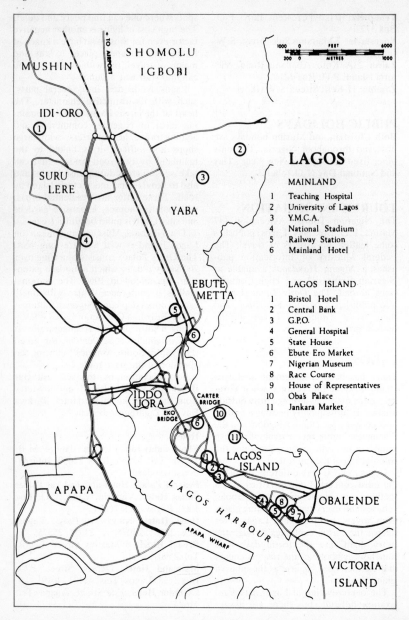

LAGOS

MAINLAND

1 Teaching Hospital
2 University of Lagos
3 Y.M.C.A.
4 National Stadium
5 Railway Station
6 Mainland Hotel

LAGOS ISLAND

1 Bristol Hotel
2 Central Bank
3 G.P.O.
4 General Hospital
5 State House
6 Ebute Ero Market
7 Nigerian Museum
8 Race Course
9 House of Representatives
10 Oba's Palace
11 Jankara Market

Airport Hotel, Ikeja. Tel: 32051.
Niger Palace, Yaba. Tel: 44699.

There are many more, including **Regent, Domo, Geralco, Maryland, International, Ebenezer, Caban Bamboo, Bobby's, Oasis, Tip Top.** Cheaper hotels include: **The Majestic, Angel's Lodge, Pension Smith, Wayfarer, Victoria House, Lagos Hostel for Ladies, SIM Hostel, YMCA** and **YWCA.**

Restaurants
The large hotels have good restaurants, but are fairly expensive. In the same class are the **Cathay** Chinese restaurant, **Maharini** Indian restaurant, **Chez Antoine, Tam Tam** and the **Phoenicia.** There is a growing number of restaurants serving a wide range of Nigerian and international specialities. For less expensive meals try the cafeterias at the big stores, **UTC, Kingsway** and **Leventis.** Nigerian dishes at **Central Hotel.**

For a night out with good food and dancing try the **Bagatelle, Le Paon Rouge, El Morocco** (at the Excelsior Hotel) and the **Federal Palace Hotel.**

Entertainments
Lagos nightlife is explosive. With new nightclubs all the time there are more varied musical talents than ever before. The big names of Nigerian Highlife, Juju and Afrobeat include Ebenezer Obey, Victor Uwaifo, Segun Bucknor, Monomono and Sunny Ade.

The famous **Shrine** of Fela Ransome-Kuti has been closed down by the Army but Fela has now been allowed to play at other nightclubs. Most clubs are open-air with awnings against the rain. All of them have live bands every night. To name just a few: **Caban Bamboo, Central Hotel, El Morocco, Gondola, Crystal Gardens, Kakadu, Lido, Mexico, Ritz Hotel, Bacchus, Barakoto.**

Cinemas include the **Metro, Plaza, Roxy, Glover**. (See *Daily Times* entertainments page for what's on).

Sports: There is great scope for sportsmen, with swimming clubs at some large hotels, beaches at Tarkwa Bay and Bar Beach. English-style social and sports clubs have facilities for tennis, squash, golf, polo, fishing and sailing (**Island Club, Ikoyi Club, Ebute Metta Club, Apapa Club, Yacht Club**).

Shopping and markets
The large department stores on Lagos Island sell a wide range of quality imported goods. At the biggest hotels are boutiques for trendy clothes and jewellery shops selling excellent filigree silver.

The Craft Centre at the museum sells a variety of craftwork at fixed prices. In the Jankara Market on Lagos Island you can get, by bargaining, locally-dyed cotton and handwoven cloth, herbs and leather goods.

The Oyinbo Market, near the Mainland Hotel, and Agege Market outside the city, sell fruit and other merchandise.

Travel agents
Alex Travel Agencies, 37 Martins Street; Daboul Travel Service, 94 McEwen Street; Elder Dempster Travel Bureau, 47 Marina; Holts Shipping Services, 149 Broad Street; Mandilas, 96 Broad Street; Scan Travel, 6 Broad Street; Transcap, Travel Bureau, 21/23 Marina; West African Travel Agency, 9a Martins Street; Umarco Travel Bureau, 170 Broad Street; Metropolitan Travel Services, Airport Hotel, Ikeja.

IBADAN
With over a million inhabitants Ibadan is as crowded and noisy as Lagos, with more gaiety. It sprawls over hills in every direction. A modern city, with hotels, shops, cinemas and electricity, Ibadan is a convenient place to stay as a base for trips to the other, more traditional, old towns of the Western State.

Ibadan is famous for its University, which has made the city the intellectual

279

capital of the country. The population is mainly Yoruba, though a considerable number of Hausa people live in the Sabo quarter. Both Christianity and Islam are very strong, and seem to give the city an excess of religious festivals and holidays.

Hotels

Premier Hotel, P.O. Box 1206, tel: 62340, 87 rooms.

Catering Rest House, tel: 24537, 18 rooms.

Greenspring Hotel, tel: 24275, 40 rooms.

Lafia Hotel, tel: 24275, 52 rooms.

Esco Hotel, 2 Felele Layout, tel: 23665, 7 rooms.

Atico Rest House, 5 Owo-eye Way, tel: 25213, 7 rooms.

Bodija Guest House, Bodija Housing Estate, tel: 24331, 6 rooms.

Restaurants

Lebanese food at reasonable prices is available at **Yasmina Restaurant** and **West End Restaurant**. Other restaurants include **Koko-Dome**, the **Catholic Hostel**, and **Paradise Club.**

Entertainments

Nightclubs include the **Gongon** (at the Lafia Hotel), and the **Central Hotel.**

The Mbari Group of artists and writers put on art exhibitions, plays, poetry readings, jazz and juju music.

Shopping and markets

In Lebanon Street every conceivable kind of cloth is on sale; including the locally-made Adire cloth. Thorn carvings are available from numerous local traders. The Dugbe Market is good for most goods and artifacts. King's Market is good for beads.

OYO, OGUN AND ONDO STATES

Oyo is a large and traditional town, with some old Portuguese-style houses. It is the replacement of Old Oyo, the ancient

capital of the Yoruba Empire, and has an interesting Oba's palace. The local calabash carvers produce some fine work and there are some fascinating festivals: masquerades in June; the Oro Festival when women are forbidden to go out at night, in July; the Shango Festival in August.

Old Oyo on the Kwara State border is inaccessible without a cross-country vehicle. Only a handful of foreigners have penetrated to this ancient Yoruba capital, which was abandoned during Jihad riots in 1837.

North of Oyo is **Ogbomosho**, a large town but little developed until the return of 40,000 traders expelled from Ghana in 1970.

The market is large and very lively in the evening; it sells good Yoruba cloth (Aso Ofi) much of it woven on the spot. In February is the Ebo Oba Ijeru festival; in July the Egungun festival; in August the Ashun festival.

Igbetti is a useful stopping point between Ibadan and Kainji Dam. It is dominated by the hill of Oke Iyamapo (Mother of the Mapo people), where an old woman recently lived in a cave, claiming to be the Mother of Mapo herself. By tradition no one may climb the hill on the day after market day (every five days). A guide is necessary to climb it as there is only one route—it proved impregnable against Fulani invaders during the Jihad. There are ruins and magic wells on the hill.

Oshogbo is a unique cultural centre, famous for its dyed cloth and the spectacular shrine to the giver goddess Oshuno. The Mbari group of artists produce beautiful paintings on panels of cloth. The Oshun festival is held in July/August, accompanied by sacrifices, dancing and drumming. There is a museum on the Offa road out of town.

Ile-Ife, or Ife, dating from about the 8th century is the legendary home of the Oduduwa, the founder of the Yoruba people, and the burial place of the Oduduwa's son Oranmyan. The town also has its University, which has a museum of its own. The Oba's Palace is said to contain over 300 shrines. The well-known Ife Museum contains objects from the 13th century, including many of the famous bronze Ife heads. The carved monolith known as 'Oranmyan's Staff' is of great archaeological interest. There are a number of private art galleries. In October is the Olojo festival and in November the Edi festival.

Akure is a good base to explore the seven Olumirin waterfalls in the gorge at Erinoke-Ijesha—a pleasant and cool spot. Some fascinating festivals in July and September.

Abeokuta has the Olumo Rock as its main attraction; it used to be used for defence and has now become a shrine. Also see the palace of the Alake. Festivals: May, Akogun; November, Giriwo: December, Gelede.

Hotels
Catering Rest House, Abeokuta, 8 rooms.
Catering Rest House, Akure, 6 rooms.
Afunbiowo Hotel, Akure.
Catering Rest House, Ijebu-Ode, 11 rooms.
Boye Guest House, Ikare, 10 rooms.
Mayflower Hotel, Ile-Ife.
Highway Hotel, Ilesha, 16 rooms.
Catering Rest House, Ogbomosho, 13 rooms.
Catering Rest House, Oshogbo, 8 rooms.
Rasco Motel, Oshogbo, 16 rooms.
Merrytime Hotel, Oyo.
Rest House, Oyo.

BENIN CITY

The modern Benin bears little relation to its glorious past history, dating back to the 10th century. The Binis were great warriors with one of the most powerful states in West Africa until the British conquest of Benin City in 1897. Relics of the past include the moat and wall built round the city as a defensive measure,

and one or two old houses. Do not miss the Oba's Palace—more fascinating from the inside than the exterior would suggest—and Ogiamen's Compound. The museum is in the centre of the city.

Modern Benin is rapidly developing as an administrative and educational centre. It is also a friendly city (if the children chant rhymes at you in the street it is not mockery but a sign of welcome). The people are predominantly Bini (or Edo) but there is great mixture of groups, with English as the common language.

Hotels
Bendel Hotel, P.M.B. 1126, tel: 1001, 48 rooms.
Motel Benin-Plaza, P.M.B. 1126, tel: 1090, 40 rooms.
Midwest Hotel, 19 rooms.
Airport Hotel, Akenzua Street, 20 rooms.
Green Garden, Ozuola Street or Commercial Avenue, 18 rooms.
Chrisbo Hotel and **Edo Guest House** provide cheaper accommodation.

Entertainments
Nightlife: The best clubs are **City Belles, Joromi Hotel, Brodericks** and the **Bamboo Garden** (Bendel Hotel).
Sport: There is swimming at the **Motel Benin Plaza** and at the **Ogbe Stadium**. The **Benin Club** provides tennis, golf and snooker.

BENDEL STATE

The State is full of villages of interest for their handicrafts and magic, but many of them are only accessible on foot or by canoe. Those accessible by road include **Sapoba** (off Sapele road), and **Abaraka.** One can swim at both in bilharzia-free rivers.

Sapele is quite a prosperous town with shops and timber yards, on the way to **Warri,** a booming oil town. The expatriate oil-men with their clubs and bars are a set apart from the locals. There are some good restaurants. You can hire canoes to explore the creeks in the area.

Near **Auchi** (north) the scenery changes rapidly from tropical rain forest to open savannah. The Auchi weavers' co-operative is good for cloth. Ososo is on the Kwara State border where the scenery is hilly, rocky and very striking.

Hotels
Eluko Lodge, Sapele, tel: 211, 7 rooms.
Uviesa Inn, Ughelli, 31 rooms.
Catering Rest House, Uromi.
River Valley Hotel, Warri, tel: 223, 48 rooms.
Peju Guest House, Warri, tel: 204, 6 rooms.
Catering Rest House, Warri, tel: 67, 8 rooms.
Palm Grove Motel, Warri, tel: 172, 60 rooms.
Mid-West Inn, Warri, tel: 350, 25 rooms.

ENUGU
Enugu owes its existence to the discovery of coal by a geological expedition looking for silver in 1909. A railway to Port Harcourt for the exploitation of the deposits was completed in 1916. In 1939 Enugu became the headquarters of the Eastern Region, and retains its large government buildings, including the Old House of Assembly. The town was one of the least damaged in the East Central State by the civil war (1967-1970) but was for a time deserted. It is now recovering its former vitality and prosperity.

Hotels
Presidential Hotel, Independence Layout, P.M.B. 1096, tel: 3511, 100 rooms.
Phoenix Hotel, tel: 2074, 120 rooms.
New Haven Resort, Bassey Duke Street, 35 rooms.

Panafric Hotel
Cheaper accommodation is provided by: **Palm Beach Hotel, Greens Hotel, Atlantic Hotel, Day Spring Hotel, Queens Hotel, Metro Hotel, Hotel de Placia, Ambima**

Enterprises, Enugu Gurst House.

Shopping and markets
The huge market is interesting for its beads, pottery and carvings, and juju crafts. there is a local handicraft centre for filigree silver and Akwete cloth. Ekulu pottery can be seen being made just outside the town off the Onitsha road.

ANAMBRA AND IMO STATES
Onitsha, on the left bank of the Niger, was badly damaged in the war but is recovering steadily. The Niger bridge is in action again and the famous market, the largest in West Africa, has now been rebuilt and reopened.

Umuahia is also thriving once again as a commercial centre and is a good stopping-place between Enugu and Port Harcourt.

Owerri, 175 kms south of Enugu, was once a graveyard of Federal and rebel soldiers. Now it is once more a quiet town with a good market selling pots and pitchers.

Aba was always famous for its flourishing market; this is still the case; local people come once more from as far afield as Port Harcourt and Uyo for their trading. It has good road and rail links with the rest of Nigeria.

Nsukka is a university town and the campus has some excellent facilities.

Hotels
Aba: **Enta Guest House, Hotel Florida, Phoenix Hotel, Sorrento** and **Stella**.
Abakaliki: **Phoenix Hotel, Mayor's Hotel** and **Premier Hotel**.
Onitsha: **Phoenix Hotel,** 31 rooms.
Owerri: **Progress Hotel** and **Golf Course Motel**.
Umuahia: **Phoenix Hotel. Green Spot, Tourist Inn** and **Maryland Hotel**.

PORT HARCOURT AND RIVERS STATE

A large, modern, well planned town, Port Harcourt has grown rapidly in wealth and importance with the development of oil production in the area. Oil flares can be seen all around the town and there are extensive residential areas for the world's oil-men.

The town is a good base to explore the local creek villages and towns. The local people are varied—Efik, Kalabari, Rivers and Ibos, not to mention British, French, American and Dutch. There is no one dominant culture.

Hotels
Presidential Hotel, Aba Road, tel: 8371, 100 rooms.
Catering Rest House, Harley Street, tel: 8333, 20 rooms.
Cedar Palace, Harbour Road, tel: 275, 47 rooms.
Dond's Tourist Hotel, Nchia-Eleme, 33 rooms.

Shopping and markets
The Diobu Market is good for printed and Akwete cloth; also at Greek Road, Market and Mile Three Market. The local sea-food (fish, shrimps, periwinkles) is cheap and delicious.

CALABAR

Calabar was in a state of isolation and sleepy decay until the civil war, but it is now recovering a former commercial and administrative importance. It is in a beautiful setting, high on a hill on a bend of the Calabar River, the first piece of firm and hilly land inshore. It commands fine views over the water. The spot was visited by the Portuguese as long ago as the 15th century. A centre of the slave trade until the 19th century, it became an important port for palm oil and rubber.

Calabar is pleasant to walk around; it is compact and undulating and gives good views. The people are extremely friendly and helpful. At the waterside you can see fishermen mending their nets. From the ferry you can make an interesting excursion to Greek Town, and old colonial-style place, which fills on Sunday with church-goers in Victorian-style dress.

Hotels
Catering Rest House, 28 Marian Road, 12 rooms.
Government Guest House, tel: 113, 8 rooms.
Metropolitan Hotel, Calabar Road, tel: 490, 28 rooms.
Cheaper accommodation is available at: **Corner deLuxe Hotel, Hotel Manilla** and the **Taj Mahal Hotel.**

CROSS RIVER STATE

Ikot Ekpene is a centre for beautiful baskets and carvings. The traditional Ekpo and Ekpe masks are particularly fascinating, but if you meet people wearing them do not photograph them without permission (which may not be granted). A unique sight is the huge Ikoro slit-drums, which are regarded as treasured possessions of the local people, though only half a dozen remain in good condition.

Oron, accessible by ferry from Calabar (every two hours, 0630 to 1630), is famous for its museum with hundreds of hardwood figures depicting the ancestors of the Ibibio and Efik peoples. The museum is a tribute to a carving skill that has now died out.

Ikom, on the road to Cameroon, has curious carved monoliths, set in circles within groves, representing human figures.

Hotels
Obudu Cattle Ranch, a remarkable spot, with a cool fresh climate, cows in green fields, gently rolling hills, set up as an agricultural centre cum holiday hotel. Booking is essential. Address: Obudu Cattle Ranch, P.O. Box 37, Obudu-Ogoja. The Ranch is 70 km by hairpin

bend road from Obudu town.

Catering Rest Houses at Eket, Ikom, Ogoja and Uyo.

Anchor Inn, Ikot Ekpene.

Iket Inyamagun Guest House, Isitibori-Ogoja.

Rainbow Catering, Oron.

Helena Hotel, Palace Hotel and **Tevoli Hotel** provide accommodation in Uyo.

Chief Apollo's Rest House and **Ikpi's Hotel**, Ugep.

ILORIN

Ilorin has some of the character of both north and south, but with a predominance of Islamic culture, as indicated by the Mosque, the Emir's Palace and the Sallah festivals. The dominant group is nevertheless Yoruba. There are government craft shops along Jebba Road and in the Kwara Hotel.

Hotels

Kwara Hotel, international standard, but mediocre food.

Unity Hotel.

Nasara Guest House, Niger Hotel, and the **SIM Guest House** provide cheap accommodation.

Restaurants

Unity Hotel, Catering Guest House and **Ilorin Club.** There are some good Nigerian-style chop-bars, such as the **Adekola Inn.**

Shopping and markets

There is a market selling pots by the Mosque and another one near the Emir's Palace which is good for woven Aso Ofi cloth. One can visit basket-makers and weavers working on horizontal looms. Benin silver is available at the SIM Bookshop. Excellent thorn carvings can be ordered from the carver near the Niger Hotel. There is a plentiful supply of artifacts from farther north.

KWARA STATE

Jebba is the crossing point on the Niger river and there are some fine views. Do not attempt to photograph the bridge or your film will be removed by soldiers.

Kainji Dam was completed in 1969 to supply hydro-electric power for Nigeria (and Niger), as well as to allow passage for large vessels (by means of large locks and a canal). The flooding of the area behind the dam made it necessary to re-house 47,000 people in resettlement villages. The town of **New Bussa** replaced old Bussa.

Due west of the Kainji reservoir is the **Borgu Game Reserve**, approximately 4,000 sq kms bounded by the river on the east and the Benin Republique border on the west. **Wawa** is the nearest town of access, 14 kms from New Bussa. There are elephant, buffalo, antelopes, bush pig, baboons, monkeys and hippos and occasional lion, leopard and cheetah.

Esie has the largest collection of stone carvings in Africa—about 1,000 human figures a metre high. They are probably about 200 years old. (To get there take the road out of Ilorin to Ajasse, continue 9 kms to Oro, where you turn right; continue until you reach Esie church, where you turn right again; continue for 3 kms.)

Hotels

Kainji Motel, P.O. Box 4, New Bussa.

Catering Rest House, Lokoja 8 rooms.

Offa Hotel, Offa, 20 rooms.

SOKOTO

On the edge of the desert the climate is hot and dry with a short rainy season from June to August and a chilly *harmattan*. The old town was founded by Sultan Bello during the lifetime of his father Usman Dan Fodio. Sokoto is also the home of Sarkin Musulmi—the spiritual head of Nigerian muslins. The population is Hausa/Fulani.

Despite its ancient history Sokoto is not of great tourist interest. There are some lively festivals in the neighbourhood, notably the Fishing Festival at Argungu 100 km west in February, the Sallah Festivals and Independence Day.

Hotels
Sokoto Hotel, international standard.
Catering Rest House, tel: 31, 10 rooms.
The **SIM Hostel** and the **Cement Club** both provide accommodation.

Shopping and markets
The market is most interesting on Friday, when camel trains arrive from the north. The leatherwork is good and locally made, available from the Leather Shop in

Bakura, a small town near Sokoto

the main street. One can also buy camel-hair blankets, lengths of dyed blue cloth and beads.

SOKOTO AND NIGER STATES
Yelwa is a pleasant small town on the Niger, trading chiefly in fish and onions. The Emir's palace houses Mungo Park's stick—he died just outside Yelwa. There are interesting boatyards and remnants of the old Emirs Palace.

Bida is the centre of the Nupe people, whose traditional head is the Etsu Nupe.

The architecture and occupations of its inhabitants are predominantly traditional, including the brassworkers, glassworkers and blacksmiths. The history of the Nupe is well covered in Paul Nadel's book *Black Byzantium*. One should visit the Emir's Palace. The best objects to buy in the town are local cloth, brass figures, glass beads and bangles, carved stools. The surrounding villages are a treasure-horde of local crafts; mats, baskets, wooden floor panels, stools, etc.

Hotels
The Abuja, Abuja, 5 rooms.
Catering Rest House, Bida, 6 rooms.
Ab Waziri's Home, Bida.
Catering Rest House, Gusau, 12 rooms.
Catering Rest House, Kontagora, 16 rooms.
Catering Rest House, Minna, 12 rooms.

KADUNA CITY AND STATE
Once the capital of the entire north of Nigeria, Kaduna is an artificial Government town laid out by the British. It retains its fine buildings and gardens and has modern amenities and entertainments, but there is little of lasting interest.

From Kaduna you can visit interesting villages with markets, such as Kujama (33 kms west) or Turunku, amid some beautiful scenery, scattered with 'inselbergs' (rocky outcrops). Some of Nigeria's best scenery and most picturesque villages are found along the base of the Jos Plateau; near Kagoro and Manchok there are excellent hill climbs and splendid views in completely unspoilt surroundings.

The ancient walled city of **Zaria** (80 kms north of Kaduna) was formerly named Zazzau after the Queen who founded it. It is the headquarters of one of the seven Hausa emirates and at one time was a centre for the slave trade. The walls are now crumbling but the city retains its character with its decorated mud walls clustered along rambling streets. The Friday Mosque has been restored, But from outside is unimpressive. The interior vaulting is magnificent. The Emir's Palace is worth a visit.

Zaria has some good restaurants such as the Kongo Club, Solt and Pepe and at its clubs.

Katsina (nearly 400 kms north of Kaduna, accessible via Kano) has perhaps the most spectacular Sallah festivals in the north though it is a small town. Perhaps because of its isolation on the edge of the desert it has preserved its traditions and way of life more than most northern towns. The City Walls make a good walk or drive in the late afternoon. The Minaret at Gobir should be visited. There are old Hausa burial mounds outside the town.

Daura (also accessible via Kano) is a fine old city of mud architecture with a remarkable Emir's Palace.

Hotels in Kaduna
Durbar Hotel, Independence Way, P.M.B. 2218, tel: 42660, telex 71134, cable Durbar. Opened for FESTAC 1977, international standard, 302 rooms.
Hamadah Hotel, another brand new hotel, P.O. Box 772, tel: 22673.
Hamdala Hotel, tel: 2505, 72 rooms

The **YMCA Hostel** and the **SIM Mission** provide cheap accommodation.

Hotels elsewhere
Catering Rest House, Daura.
Victory Hotel, Funtua.
Catering Rest House, Katsina, 5 rooms.
Catering Rest House, Samaru, 8 rooms.
Catering Rest House, Zaria, 17 rooms.
Conference Centre, Zaria.

KANO CITY AND STATE
The largest of the ancient Housa cities, Kano in also modern Nigeria's third city after Lagos and Ibadan, and an important industrial area. South and east of the old city the new commercial districts sprawl along tree-lined avenues, until they blend with the neighbouring farmlands. The mass of the working population is crammed into the Sabon Gari district, where the majority of Nigerian-owned hotels and restaurants are located. Despite its disorganised tourist facilities, Kano offers many facets to the visitor, from the medieval atmosphere of the old market to the colonial-style sporting clubs and the carefree nightlife of the new Nigeria. The universal language is Hausa.

Founded before AD1000, Kano was a major terminus of trans-Saharan trade for many centuries. At the Kurmi market traders from the Sahara and North Africa still sell their wares alongside the local crafts of weaving, basketwork, dyeing, leatherwork, jewellery, and the modern imported goods now common in every corner of Africa. Also centrally situated is the huge mosque with its green dome and twin minarets, which can be climbed for an extensive view of the city. The Friday prayers attract around 50,000 people to the Mosque and the surrounding prayer area.

The Emir's Palace is not open to the public, but the ancient Gidon Makama museum opposite illustrates the early architecture of the city.

The walls of the old city measure 17 km in circumference and contain 16 gates, the principal being Kofar Motta, where the dye-pits are situated. Still inside the walls is Dala Hill, the legendary starting place of Kano's history and once a souce of iron ore. A good way of seeing the old city is by hired bicycle in the company of a Hausa-speaking guide.

Other sights of Kano are the new zoo and (from December to April) the huge groundnut pyramids to the west of the Zaria road.

The **Danbatta Market** (50 kms north) is the largest cattle market in the north. **Kazaure** (80 kms north) is a beauty spot with hills and a lake, a good place to walk in utterly peaceful surroundings. At **Birnin Kudu** (120 kms east) are prehistoric rock paintings.

Hotels
Central Hotel, tel: 5141, 200 rooms.
Daula Hotel, P.M.B. 3228, tel: 5311, double rooms only.
Bagauda Lake Hotel, 50 kms towards Zaria, 150 rooms.
Kano Guest Inn, Zungeru Road, tel: 2717, 150 rooms.
Cheaper establishments include **Kandara Palace**, **International**, **Akija**, **Shehu Usman Memorial**, and **SIM Guest House** (for cheap if rigorous mission-style accommodation).

Restaurants
The big hotels serve meals. Also **Kano Club**, **Megwan Water Restaurant** (excellent oriental dishes) **Danbatta** (Nigerian), and the **Pink Peacock** (Chinese).

Entertainments
Nightlife: **Moulin Rouge**, **Campari**, **Casino**, and many other small clubs. Sports: **Kano Club** (temporary membership available), swimming, squash, tennis, cinema.

JOS

The gentle climate of Jos makes it a favourite holiday centre. At 1,200 m above sea level its air is crisp and invigorating, in contrast with the heat and humidity of other parts. The town is well laid-out and pleasantly situated amid the surrounding rocky hills. To add to its atmosphere there are locally grown European vegetables and fresh milk in the main shops. It is also the centre of Nigeria's mining area.

The museum, established by Bernard Fagg, is famous for its remarkable collection of antiquities; it is devoted primarily to the archaeology and ethnography of the plateau region and displays relics of the highly sophisticated Nok culture of 2,000 years ago, notably the well-known terra cotta figures. It also houses a cross-section of cultural achievements throughout Nigeria, has a pottery workshop and runs courses for students from all over Africa.

There is also a small zoo. Otherwise the attraction of staying in Jos is the easy access to the surrounding countryside which offers such sights as Assob Falls (50 kms south) on the escarpment, Kurrah Falls hydro-electric scheme, Vom dairy farm and the Bukuru modern tin mines. A day's drive will take you to Panakshin and back through some beautiful but rugged scenery.

Hotels
Hill Station, 24 rooms. Luxury accommodation, good food, good service.
Plateau Hotel, 100 rooms.
Naraguta Country Club, nearly five kms along Bauchi road, beautifully situated, with restaurant and bar.
Cheap accommodation is available at the **Ambassador Hotel**, **Jubilee Hotel**, **Plateau Pax Hotel**, **Terminus Hotel** and **Herwa Motel** as well as at the **Museum chalets**, the **SIM** and **SUM Rest Houses**.

Restaurants
Good food at reasonable prices at the big hotels. Others: **Plateau Club**, **Madam Fulanis**, **Domino** and **Rugby Club**.
The main night clubs are the **Havana**, **CC Night Club** and **Gondola Nite Spot**.

PLATEAU AND BENUE STATES

There is a very scenic tarred road connecting Jos to Barakin Ladi, Panyam, Pankshin, Langtang, Garkawa, Yelwa to Shendam or to the Benue river at Ibi (from where one can reach Katsina-Ala and Cross River State). It joins the Jos-Makurdi road at Lafia Beriberi. From the echoing rocks of Pankshin this road leads round an extremely attractive hilly circuit, descending to Kabwir.

Makurdi, 320 kms south of Jos by scenic road, is the second largest town in the state. Attractively sited on the River Benue, amid hills, it is the centre of the

Tiv and Songi peoples, whose dynamic music and dancing are legendary.

Hotels
Viewpoint Hotel, Gboko, **Viewpoint Hotel**, Makurdi, and **Catering Rest Houses** at Keffi, Makurdi and Vom, as well as at all divisional headquarters.

MAIDUGURI
Maiduguri is an attractive, well laid out town with wide streets, avenues and many trees. It has strong traditions and culture, but is also a rapidly expanding commercial and administrative centre.

The Sallah festival in November or December provides a magnificent display of the skill of the Borno horsemen, led by the Shehu of Borno himself. Maiduguri is a good centre for encountering the Kanuri people, with their fine tribal markings, and the Shuwa women, with their plaited hairstyles and flowing gowns. The daily market is large and colourful, but at its best on Mondays. Other attractions are the Sheh's Palace and the city park, containing a zoo and museum.

From March to May it is dry but very hot indeed. The rains from June to September, though intermittent, can be very heavy and hazardous to drivers. The best time to visit is from October to February, but it can be cold at night around Christmas.

Hotels
Lake Chad Hotel, Sir Kashim Road.
Catering Rest House, 12 rooms.
Cheap accommodation is available at: **Racecourse Hotel**, **Beach Guest Hotel**, **SUM Mission**, **West End Club Hotel** and **Galadima Hotel/Club**. The free camp site beside the zoo provides showers, toilets, firewood and a night guard and is certainly the best of its kind in Africa, even if its location makes one feel like a caged hyena!
Restaurants: the hotels serve rather mediocre food, as do the restaurants: The best are **Leventis** and **Alheri Brothers**.
Entertainments: Nightlife—There are two cinemas. Dancing on Saturdays at **Yerwa Club**, **Galadima** and **West End**, with local or Sudanese groups.

BORNO, GONGOLA AND BAUCHI STATES
The Borno region around Maiduguri is one of the most fascinating in Nigeria. Along the northern borders of the country it is Sahel-savannah country-rolling sand dunes punctuated by oases in the dry season, but during the rains covered with vegetation. Southern Borno is generally green savannah land, full of hills and rocks. The best mountain scenery is around Biu and towards the Cameroon frontier.

In contrast the **Lake Chad** area is flat, much of it being flooded during and after the rains. The Lake is shallow and of a very variable shape. It is covered with large floating papyrus islands and sandbanks used by fishermen. It is an ornithologist's paradise and the home of the largest elephants in Africa.

An interesting market 64 kms from Maiduguri is at **Ladi Bida** on Sundays. It is typical of Bornu rural markets in many ways, selling local food, clothes, saddlery, jewellery, etc. Every town or village in the region has its weekly market; the signs are crowds on the roads, horsemen, women carrying bowls of food, donkeys with bales of goods, etc. Any of these markets are well worth a visit.

The **Mambila** plateau area south of Yola and Jalingo consists of beautiful hills and valleys with cattle grazing for dairy produce.

Halfway along the Yola to Bauchi road is **Kaltungo**, set in hilly scenery. There is a lively Friday market with Fulani dancing.

Bauchi, 460 kms south west of Maiduguri by good road, is a traditional mud-walled Huasa town, with an old mosque and Emir's Palace, developing as a modern centre. Seventeen kms out of Bauchi, off the Jos road, are the **Geji** paintings. Further in the same direction is the dramatic Panshanu Pass through the mountains.

Hotels: There are **Catering Rest Houses** at Bauchi, Gombe, Jimeta, Mubi, Potiskum and Yola. Bauchi also has the **Horizontal Hotel**.

YANKARI NATIONAL PARK

The park is 60 km south west of Bauchi, off the road to Yola at Dindima. Covering 2,000 sq km the park is the home of elephant, hippo, buffalo, various antelope, lion, giraffe, ostrich, marabou stork and a wide range of birdlife.

There is a small charge on entry to the reserve. The visitors' camp at **Wikki Warm Springs** is beautifully situated in a grove of trees overlooking the Gaji valley and plains. There is accommodation for 105 and there are catering facilities. It is essential to book for accommodation.

HISTORY

In the past thousand years the dominant civilisations in the south of Nigeria have been Yoruba (whose culture centred on Ife before AD1000), Benin (also connected with Ife culture) and Ibo (whose legends indicate struggles with invaders from the north and east). In the north of the country strong political systems emerged, following the establishment of the Kanem-Borno empire around Lake Chad in the 10th and 11th centuries. Until the 15th century only the northern states had direct links with the outside world. But the arrival of the Portuguese on the swampy Nigerian coasts heralded a new phase in the history of the region, although for four hundred years the European contact with the south was predominantly coastal, while the existing African states controlled the slave trade in the hinterland. But the slave trade was a destructive and destabilising influence and the authority of the old Yoruba kingdoms crumbled in the 19th century.

Lagos was constituted a British Crown Colony in 1862. The Berlin Conference of 1885 designated the Niger region as a 'British sphere of influence' and the area from Lagos to Calabar was proclaimed the Oil Rivers Protectorate, while the Royal Niger Company was given a charter to trade in the interior. In 1900 The British Crown took over the powers of the Company and divided the territories it controlled into Southern Nigeria and Northern Nigeria. In 1914 the Colony and Protectorate of Nigeria was declared.

Military coups took place in January 1966 and again in July 1966. This was felt to be northern-inspired and anti-Ibo, a feeling that was aggravated by widespread massacres of Ibos in northern cities and towns. A mass Ibo exodus from the north took place and precipitated on attempt at eastern secession from Nigeria. Colonel Ojukwu declared the region the 'Republic of Biafra', but he was not able to hold more than a small portion of the proposed territory. Nevertheless civil war raged in Nigeria between 1967 and 1970.

The Federal forces were finally victorious and reconciliation was achieved under the leadership of General Gowon. In the years following the civil war Nigeria's new-found oil-wealth created economic euphoria which appeared to blind the Gowon government to the continuing political difficulties. In July 1975 Gowon was deposed. A more dynamic military regime was installed under General Murtala Muhammed. It promised to return the country to civilian rule by 1979 and clean up corruption in the country. Despite General Murtala's assassination in February 1976 his government's programme is still being followed.

REUNION

A spectacular, far-flung French possession, Reunion lies between Madagascar and Mauritius. Its landscape is volcanic, its climate tropical, its *lingua franca* is Creole, and most of its people are of mixed race. Fine beaches and good fishing lies close to magnificent hill country with trout streams on the slopes and volcanoes in its heart.

THE LAND AND THE PEOPLE

Running diagonally across Reunion is a chain of volcanic peaks, separating it into a green, humid eastern zone (called Le Vent) and a dry, sheltered south and west (Sous le Vent).

Most of the population lives along the coast. The majority are Roman Catholic but there is also a large community of Hindus, descendants of indentured workers brought here from India after the emancipation of slaves in 1848, as well as a smaller minority of Muslims from Pakistan and the Comoro Islands, and some 20,000 Chinese. The unassimilated Asians and the Europeans comprise about a quarter of the otherwise *metis* (mixed race) population.

CULTURE

Traditional Creole *sega* dancing is popular. Hindus and Muslims have preserved some of their rituals, including the so-called Malabar dancing and ordeals of fire-walking. Craftsmanship on the island includes some fine lace and embroidery from the hills around Cilaos.

GENERAL INFORMATION

Area: 2,150 sq. km.
Population: 475,000.
Altitude: From sea level to 3,000 m., often in abrupt ascents.
Capital: Saint-Denis.
Head of State: The French President.
Government: Departmental status in Metropolitan France, administered by an

292

appointed Prefect, with elected local council and deputies to the French Parliament.

Language: French and Creole.

Religion: Primarily Roman Catholic, with Hindu, Muslim and Buddhist minorities.

Currency: French Franc. $1=4.95FF. £1=8.50FF.

Time: GMT+4.

HOW TO GET THERE

By air: Air France, in conjunction with Air Madagascar, call seven times a week en route Paris-Athens-Cairo-Djibouti-Nairobi-Dar es Salaam-Antananarivo-Reunion-Mauritius. From Mauritius: Air France and Air Mauritius (daily) connecting in Mauritius with flights from UK, Western Europe, East Africa, India, South Africa and Australia.

By sea: From Europe: Messageries Maritimes passenger liners call fortnightly, and passenger-freighters of the Nouvelle Compagnie Havraise Péninsulaire and other French lines from Marseilles via South Africa and Madagascar call at regular intervals, as do British, Scandinavian and South African lines.

Visas and health regulations

Basic regulations conform to those of France. Visas are not required for visits of up to three months by holders of most West European, American or African passports.

An international certificate of vaccination against smallpox is required, as are yellow fever and cholera vaccinations for travellers arriving from infected areas.

Dutiable goods

Personal effects and limited amounts of alcohol and tobacco may be taken into Reunion. The importation of sugar cane is prohibited and other live plants are subject to strict controls.

CLIMATE

The island is at its best from May to October when temperatures average from $18°C$ to $30°C$ on the coasts, while the hills are considerably cooler (dropping to freezing on certain nights in the highlands). It turns hot and wet during the cyclone season (January to March). The eastern half of the island (Le Vent) and the mountain slopes are subject to substantial rainfall most of the year.

What to wear: Dress is informal. Be prepared for considerable temperature contrast between coasts and mountains, and for wet weather, especially in the east. A mountain hike requires sturdy shoes and a hat.

Health precautions: Reunion's climate is relatively benign, particularly in the bracing air of the hills. Water is safe to drink and sanitation facilities normal. There is malaria on the coasts and anti-malarial drugs should be taken 14 days before, during, and 14 days after the visit. The sun can be deceptively vicious and sun-bathing should be done in moderation.

ACCOMMODATION AND FOOD

There is a good network of small hotels, provincial inns, family lodges and pensions. The prices are high but the food is often excellent, even when plumbing and other conveniences leave something to be desired. There are shelters (called *gîtes*) for hikers at La Roche Ecrite, Cilaos and Pas de Bellecombe.

A variety of restaurants caters for French and exotic tastes fairly well. Reunion's Creole specialities include seafood with sauces (often called *rougail*), curries, rice and dried fish, a good rum and Arabic coffee (*Cafe Bourbon*).

Hotel tariffs usually include bed and breakfast, taxes and service charges. Tipping is sporadic but is all the more welcome when service has proved its merit.

TRANSPORT

There are paved highways around the island, and two zig-zag roads across the centre. These can be covered on public buses, by taxi or hired vehicle.

Hertz rentals are located at 40 rue Victor MacAuliffe; you can also hire cars at Air France's **Relais Aeriens** at La Montagne outside Saint-Denis and at **Transcontinents**, 5 rue du Mat de Pavillon in the capital.

Private boats can be hired in the fishing ports and at Saint-Gilles.

Two aero-clubs at Gillot Airport hire planes for flights over the craters and contours of the island—an experience worth the price. Energetic travellers should come prepared to hike, climb, and even to hitch-hike.

BANKS AND COMMERCE

There are three main banks: Banque de la Réunion, 15 Rue Jean-Chatel, Saint-Denis (Crĕdit Lyonnais), Banque National pour le Commerce et l'Industrie, rue Juliette Dodu, Saint-Denis and Caisse d'Epargne et de Prevoyance, Rond-Point du Jardin, Saint-Denis.

Business hours: Normal hours of business are 0800 to 1200 and 1400 to 1800.

PUBLIC HOLIDAYS

New Year's Day; Easter Monday; Labour Day; Ascension Day; Whit Monday; National Day 14 July; Assumption Day; All Saints' Day; Armistice Day 11 November; Christmas Day.

CONSULATES

UK: Rue de Paris, B.P. 99, Saint-Denis, tel: 21.06.19; **Norway:** 2 rue Renaudière de Vaux, Le Port, tel: 22.00.85; **West Germany:** Rue Rontaunay, Saint-Denis, tel: 21.33.04; **Belgium and the Netherlands:** B.P. 785, Saint-Denis, tels: 21.10.85-21.38.01; **Madagascar:** 13 rue Labourdonnais, Saint-Denis.

The nearest European and US diplomatic missions are at Port Louis (Mauritius) and Antananarivo (Madagascar).

TOURIST INFORMATION

In Reunion: Syndicat d'Initiative—Office du Tourisme, rue Rontaunay, Saint-Denis. Abroad: Any French diplomatic mission or Air France office.

SAINT-DENIS

A fast-growing city of 100,000 people, Saint-Denis stands on the north coast between Gillot Airport and the island's seaport, Pointe des Galets. The capital possesses a number of dignified old French buildings (especially the Prefecture, former residence of the great 18-century Governor Mahe de La Bourdonnais), several white-verandahed Creole houses (particularly on rue de Paris), a Hippodrome, a handsome Museum of Natural History in the Botanical Gardens, the Dierx Museum of Art, and abundant statues and fountains. Its markets are lively just after sunrise, and the sea promenade (Le Barachois), once a functioning port, is popular in the evening. You can drive part of the way up La Roche Ecrite and clamber the rest of the way (2,000 m.) without great difficulty; the view is superb.

Hotels

Relais Aeriens (or *La Residence de Bourbon*) four star, B.P. 1 La Montagne, Saint-Denis, tel: 21.12.03, 26 rooms.

St François, three star, Rampes de St François, B.P. 1197, tel: 21.27.14, 75 rooms.

Labourdonnais, two star, Pl de la Prefecture, tel: 21.37.10, 40 rooms.

Others

Touring Hotel, 6 rue Juliette Dodu, tel: 21.22.48, 17 rooms.

Les Mascareignes, 3 rue Lafferiere, tel:

21.15.28, 12 rooms.
Central Hotel, 27 rue de la Compagnie, 24 rooms.

Restaurants
La Ferme, **Cafe de Paris**, **Le Bosquet** (out of town), **Le Rallye** for Creole and Malagasy food. The hotel restaurants serve excellent French cuisine.

THE COASTS
To the south-west is the old East India Company capital of Saint-Paul, full of literary and historical reminiscences and set against a fine natural hinterland of lakes and woods. South of Saint-Paul, along the Sous le Vent coasts, lie the largest and most popular of Reunion's beaches, Saint-Gilles-des-Bains, with a reef-protected lagoon, fine coral sand edged by filao trees, several lively bars and restaurants, and sailing at the Club Nautique.

Farther along the coast are Saint-Leu, a small fishing village with a good beach, and Etang-Sale-les-Bains, with black lava sand. For more solitary beachcombing and water-sports (but be careful to inquire about sharks) try Saint-Philippe.

Hotels
Saint-Benoit: La Confiance, 3 rooms;
Saint-Gilles-des-Bains: Loulou, 20 rooms, Creole and Indian food. La Souris Chaude, at Saline-les-Bains, 10 rooms, (5 bungalows).
Saint-Philippe: Le Baril, 8 rooms, extensive sporting facilities and good food.
Saint-Pierre: Les Horizons, 23 rooms.
Restaurants: Apart from the hotels, the good restaurants along the coast are **La Taverne,** at Saint Pierre and **L'Arche de Noé, Etang salé les hauts.**

MOUNTAINS
Reunion's Plaines, peaks and Cirques (high volcanic basins) offer rest cures and mountaineering. There is excellent trout fishing at the Takamaka Falls on the Riviére des Marsouins in the north east. The Cirque de Cilaos can be reached from St. Louis. The town of Cilaos itself is a mountain spa with curative waters, set in the midst of rocky volcanic scenery.

In the Cirque de Salazie on the other side of the 3,000 m. Piton des Neiges stands Hell-Bourg, a pretty town with a bracing climate. One can walk between Hell-Bourg and Cilaos in as little as six hours.

Crossing the island in the south-east permits a two- or three-day trek from the arid, bracing Plaine des Cafres east to the Pas de Bellecombe (an overnight shelter, farthest point of the traversable road) into the Piton de la Fournaise, a broad, smoking crater 8 km. in diameter, 2,336 m. at its highest point. The volcano is in steady activity; it last erupted in 1961.

Hotels
Cilaos: Grand Hotel, 21 rooms.
Hell-Bourg: Hotel des Salazes, 11 rooms. Good French provincial cooking.
Plaine des Cafres: Hotel Lalemand, 23rd km., 17 rooms. **Auberge du Volcan,** 27th km., 5 rooms.
Tampon: La Paille en Queue, 10 rooms. **Metro Hotel,** 20 rooms.

HISTORY
Governed until 1767 by the French East India Company, Reunion produced spices and Arabic coffee and served as a station for French shipping around the Cape of Good Hope. Occupied by British forces from 1810 to 1815, the island was returned to France at the Congress of Vienna, although its twin Mascarene, Ile de France, was retained by England, as Mauritius.

Reunion is now governed as an Overseas Department of France and administered by a Prefect delegated from Paris, 11,000 km. away. This status entitles it to a share of French national taxes, budget allocations and Parliamentary seats.

RHODESIA

On 11 November, 1965, the Ian Smith regime rebelled against the British Government and issued a Unilateral Declaration of Independence for this British colony. Since then white settler rule has survived despite economic sanctions and almost total diplomatic isolation. Although the economy has not collapsed, it has been severely hit and the pressures have annually increased. More recently the country's security has also come under attack from armed guerrillas and in 1977 the entire country was threatened with warfare, although the main towns were still not directly affected. Anglo-American diplomacy was engaged in a last-ditch attempt to bring about a peaceful transition to black rule.

Tourism has more or less collapsed and will not now recover until a lasting solution is found to the political problems.

THE LAND AND THE PEOPLE

Rhodesia is a beautiful country covering 390,620 sq. km., about three times the size of England or nearly as big as California. Situated in south-central Africa between the Limpopo and Zambezi Rivers, the country is land-locked, lying astride the great African plateau. Features are granite outcrops or *kopjes* that stud the landscape. Caves found in some of these kopjes contain evidence of early human habitation and many examples of rock art.

Over six million people live in Rhodesia; about 270,000 of them are of European origin, mainly British, Portuguese, Greek and South African. The African population comprises Mashona peoples—Kalanga, Karanga, Zezuru, Ndau, Korekore and Manyika—and the Ndebele (500,000) also known as the Matabele. There are smaller tribal groups such as the Tonga of the Zambezi Valley, the

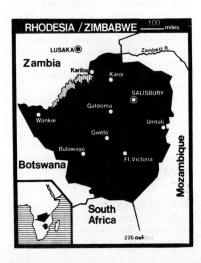

Sena, Hlengwe, Venda and Sotho.

Shona-speaking people are thought to have come to Rhodesia about AD 850 and occupied all the land between the Limpopo and Zambezi Rivers, establishing the great Empire of Monomatapa (Mwene Mutapa) and the Rozwi Mambos. They dominated the area until the 1830s. Then there were stirrings in the south and in Zululand, destined to shatter the Rozwi power. The Khumalo clan in the south, under their chief, Mzilikazi, broke away from the rule of Shaka, the Zulu king, and moved north across the Limpopo where they occupied new lands: the Khumalo created a new nation and became the AmaNdebele.

The first whites to come to Rhodesia were missionaries and hunters seeking ivory and skins. When Henry Hartley was hunting elephant he came across a place where gold had been mined; this led to a minor gold rush. In the wake of the prospectors came the traders, followed at the end of the last century by the Pioneer Column of some 200 men raised by Cecil Rhodes.

Although many of the old pioneers stayed to develop the modern Rhodesia, the white Rhodesian population has tended to be transient, with as many leaving as entering the country. A minority of white Rhodesians were born in the country. In 1976 there were the beginnings of a white exodus from Rhodesia.

GENERAL INFORMATION

Area 390,620 sq. km.

Population Total: 6,650,000 of whom 6,340,000 are Africans; 273,000 are Europeans; 21,900 are Coloureds, and 10,200 are Asians.

Altitude 300-1,500m above sea level.

Capital Salisbury.

Head of State John James Wrathall.

Government Status—an illegal regime in rebellion against the British Crown.

Languages English (official), Ndebele, Chishona and Chimanyika are the three main languages.

Religion Christianity.

Currency Rhodesian Dollar (R$) divided into 100 cents.

Time GMT + 2.

MEANS OF ACCESS

Most world airlines maintain a ban on flights to Rhodesia, but South African Airways operate a total of five flights a week direct from Britain, and there are a number of daily flights from Johannesburg. Air Rhodesia operates from Durban and Johannesburg.

Since the closure of the border with Zambia in 1973 road travel has not been possible through the border posts at Chirundu, Kariba Dam and Victoria Falls. The routes through Mozambique and Botswana are also closed.

The road from South Africa (at Beit Bridge) is heavily used. Express Motorways operate a coach service from Johannesburg.

Rhodesia Railway links the main centres of Rhodesia and connects with South Africa (through Botswana).

Since January, 1973, the line from Zambia has been closed to passenger traffic.

CLIMATE

Temperatures are moderated by the altitude and Rhodesia's inland position keeps the humidity comfortably low. Mean monthly temperatures during October, the hottest month, range from 22°C on the high central plateau to 30°C in the low-lying Zambezi valley, whereas mid-winter (July) temperatures are around 13°C on the highveld and 20°C in the Zambezi valley. The climate is warm without being oppressive with bright sunny days averaging seven hours of sunlight the year round.

Health precautions

Although all water in towns is safe for

drinking and swimming pools for swimming, bilharzia parasites infect all lakes, dams and rivers. The malarial mosquito is present in the lower altitude areas such as Kariba, Wankie National Park and Victoria Falls, and drugs should be taken before, during and after visits to these areas.

ACCOMMODATION

A full range of accommodation is available in the main centres, while at the tourist resorts there are hotels or chalets. The Rhodesia National Tourist Board publishes a guide giving details of all hotels and tourist establishments.

BANKS

Barclays Bank DCO, National and Grindlays, Rhodesian Banking Corporation and the Standard Bank have branches throughout Rhodesia.

FOREIGN EMBASSIES

No country has recognised Rhodesia although South Africa has an accredited diplomatic mission in Salisbury.

SALISBURY

Salisbury is a spacious modern city with wide streets. The Rhodes National Gallery is an impressive building which stages exhibitions of paintings, sculpture and ceramics by local and overseas artists. The Workshop School encourages artists of all races and the Gallery has sales rooms where their works are sold. An impressive feature of the new Queen Victoria Museum is its frontage of giant sculptures of Rhodesian animals which are floodlit at night. The theme of the museum is 'The Story of Man and Animal in Mashonaland'. Among the exhibits are some exceptionally good examples of rock paintings.

BULAWAYO

The National Museum houses more than 20,000 specimens of birds and a collection of over 10,000 minerals. The Mzilikazi Art and Craft Centre is situated in the Mzilikazi village near Mpilo hospital and is well known for its pottery. Another centre of African crafts is the African Village about 27km from Bulawayo where the Matabele, Kalanga, Sotho and Tonga are represented in natural settings. There is also a museum on the site. The Khami Ruins about 19km from the city are archaeologically interesting and the buildings are said to date from the 17th century. The ruin of the Church of the Cross is thought to be a site of a church run by the Portuguese Dominican Order in the 16th century.

From Bulawayo one can visit the Matopos Hills which have been a place of retreat for centuries and Bushman paintings can be found in many caves. The most accessible is the Nswatugi Cave which has paintings of people, antelope, giraffe and elephant. Much of the Matopos area has been turned into a game park.

ZIMBABWE RUINS

The Zimbabwe Ruins, 30km from Fort Victoria, have intrigued archaeologists since they were discovered in 1898. The ruins comprise a 100m wide walled enclosure (The Temple), a granite hill supporting extensive building (The Acropolis), and, lying between, an expanse of less spectacular ruins in what is called the Valley of Ruins (which inspired the Dead City in Rider Haggard's *She*). Zimbabwe's walls are made from hand-trimmed granite blocks standing as much as 10m high and 6m wide, without the aid of mortar of any description. The Temple is irregularly elliptical in shape. Its exterior wall is more than 250m in circumference, and for some 70m runs roughly parallel with an interior wall to form the

Parallel Passage. Within these walls stands the Conical Tower. The oldest part of Zimbabwe is on Acropolis Hill which is thought to have been a special and important religious centre, possibly connected with rain-making or fertility rites, and may also have been the burial place of great chiefs. The Temple was probably the royal palace.

The ruins are in a national park of some 1,786 acres and are protected by the Historical Monuments Commission of Rhodesia. Near them is a museum which displays many fascinating objects recovered from diggings in the vicinity.

Another attraction near the ruins is a modern reconstruction of a 19th century Karanga village where everything from the huts to the utensils authentically depicts how the Karanga people lived.

VICTORIA FALLS

Few can fail to be overwhelmed by the fantastic beauty of this massive curtain of water plunging more than 75m and the great clouds of spray. The 1,950 metre crest of the Falls is divided into five separate waterfalls: the Devil's Cataract, Main Falls (the most impressive stretch), Horseshoe Falls, the Rainbow Falls and Eastern Cataract. In mid-April, when the Zambezi River is swelled by the summer rains, 345m litres of water cascade over the brink of the Falls and plunge through eight narrow gorges below.

The Victoria Falls National Park spreads 60 km along the Rhodesian bank of the Zambezi. It is well populated with Rhodesia's national animal, the Sable antelope, which is relatively rare in other parts of Africa, and with buffalo, kudu, waterbuck, bushbuck, impala and warthog. Elephant and other animals can be seen on the banks of the Zambezi by taking a cruise upstream.

Near the hotels is a replica of a 19th century Matabele village which is open to visitors throughout the week. Craftsmen can be seen making various instruments

and curios which are for sale.

NATIONAL PARKS

Kyle National Park: Lying to the south east of Fort Victoria, the Kyle National Park offers boating and fishing in Lake Kyle, mountain scenery and some of the most concentrated game-viewing in Rhodesia. The wide selection of antelope

Zimbabwe ruins

includes many rare species such as blesbok, Lichtenstein's hartebeest, nyala and oribi.

WANKIE NATIONAL PARK

Situated in the north-west corner of Rhodesia, Wankie National Park contains some of the largest concentrations of wildlife on the African continent. Air Rhodesia operates services to the park airport. The park is a short distance from the Bulawayo-Victoria Falls road with the southern entrance near Dett, 296 km from Bulawayo. There is also a tarred road via Panda-ma-Tenga from Botswana. The northern entrance is through Matetsi, 120 km from the Victoria Falls. The new **Sinametella Camp** can be reached from Wankie via Lukosi. Because of the gravel roads within the park, not more than 350 cars a day are allowed. Platforms overlooking pans afford the opportunity of viewing large herds of animals at close quarters. The park abounds with elephant, and herds of 150 are not uncommon. Other animals include giraffe, lion, rhino, wildebeest, buffalo, crocodile, numerous species of antelope, cheetah, leopard, hyena, jackal, wild dog and monkey. Bird life is both colourful and prolific.

HISTORY

By AD 1000 there were Bantu settlements from the Zambezi to the Limpopo Rivers. Metal and gold workers traded through Arab settlements on the coast. In the 16th century the Portuguese reported that Arab states were trading with Africans along the east coast. By that time the Zulus had established settlements throughout southern Africa. In 1870 Lobengula succeeded Mzilikazi as king of the Matabele.

The discovery of gold in Mashonaland led to increased European interest, resulting in a minor gold rush involving, among others, Boers from the Transvaal, Germans, British and Belgian prospectors. Cecil Rhodes sent emissaries to Lobengula to negotiate a concession and, by what is now accepted by many historians as a trick, they got the king to sign a treaty supposedly giving Rhodes a concession to all the mineral rights.

When the king heard that Rhodes had assembled a column of 200 men to occupy Mashonaland and a further force of British South Africa Company Police to protect the advancing column he was dismayed, but he refrained from openly attacking the column. In September, 1890, the Union Jack was ceremoniously hoisted in what was to become Salisbury, the capital of Rhodesia. The Pioneers carved out farms of great acreages for themselves and began prospecting for gold. An uneasy truce prevailed between the settlers and the Matabele and there was a constant fear of Matabele warriors attacking small European settlements. There was also friction between Rhodes' Charter Company and Lobengula over numerous incidents involving the rustling of the king's cattle, until Dr Leander

Starr Jameson, the Company's administrator, decided to crush Lobengula and obtain most of the Matabele land. A punitive raid by Matabele warriors on the Mashona in the Fort Victoria area provided the *causus belli* and led to the outbreak of the Matabele war in 1893. The Matabele were defeated and the Company occupied Matabeleland.

In 1919 the settlers petitioned Britain for 'responsible government' in preference to continual company rule. A referendum, held in 1922, offered the white voters a choice between 'responsible government' or amalgamation with South Africa. The majority opted for 'responsible government'. On 12 September, 1923, Rhodesia was formally annexed to the British Crown and it became a self-governing colony within the British Empire.

After World War Two there was a tremendous influx of immigrants from Britain and Europe—in the five years between 1946 and 1951 the white population increased by 65.1% (from 82,000 to 135,000). In other words, more immigrants entered Rhodesia in those five years than in the previous 30 years. In 1951 and again in 1953 conferences were held on the question of a Central African Federation amalgamating Rhodesia with Northern Rhodesia (Zambia) and Nyasaland (Malawi), which envisaged rapid economic development in combining the vast copper reserves of the north with the agricultural resources of the south. The Federation came into being on 3 September, 1953, regardless of strong African opposition.

Despite considerable economic expansion, the Federation lasted for only 10 years. Northern Rhodesia (Zambia) and Nyasaland (Malawi) were allowed first to secede, then to become independent. This right was withheld from Southern Rhodesia because of the failure to get constitutional agreement between white and black Rhodesians. In 1965 the whites declared independence.

RWANDA

To the traveller undaunted by Rwanda's physical isolation, the country offers rich dramatic scenery and a sense of peace. In the midst of seemingly endless hills and mountains cultivation is unusually intense with subsistence farmers using every available square metre of land whether valley or hilltop.

THE LAND AND THE PEOPLE

Rwanda lies in the dramatic, remote centre of Africa, split by the Rift Valley. Lake Kivu, one of the chain of lakes running from Lake Tanganyika to Ethiopia, forms the western border with Zaire. Steep, forest-clad slopes rise above it to the Nile-Zaire watershed; great peaks of up to 3,000 m run through the country from north to south.

From the great Nile-Zaire divide the land falls eastwards in distinctive hills, separated by rivers, lakes and swamps. The landscape of eucalyptus trees, banana groves and fields alternating with luxuriant pasture shows that although Rwanda is financially poor it is still a wealthy country in terms of sustenance, culture and security. The traditional way of life continues to be based on agriculture and cattle.

The Rwandese, densely settled in scattered homesteads in the fertile areas, do not form villages. Each family is surrounded by its own fields. Every hill was a traditional unit where pasture rights were controlled by local Tutsi, once the ruling caste, but now forming only 9% of the populaion. Many fled as refugees in the uprising of the Hutu peasant majority in 1959 and in subsequent disturbances, but the country has succeeded in establishing a degree of ethnic tolerance in the last decade. Tutsis still herd their cattle and live freely in the towns.

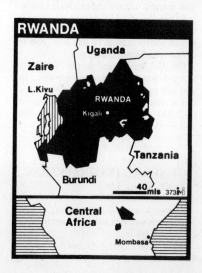

301

CULTURE

Music and dance are important in home and village life. The Rwanda National Ballet is famous for its traditional dancing and singing and displays can be seen either at national ceremonies or, perhaps more satisfactorily, on request in the villages. Stringed instruments, xylophones and drums are made by the musicians themselves.

The pygmy Twa are the traditional potters. Their work is simple and fine, and uses no artificial colours or mechanical devices. Rwanda's basketwork is the most beautiful of the inherited crafts. There are official museums and shops at Butare, Nyundo and Nyabisindu (Nyanza), where prices are fixed and quality excellent.

WILDLIFE

In the Kagera National Park, lion and jackal prey on herds of buck, zebra and the rarest species of buffalo in Africa *(syncerus caffer)* which, in March and April, gather in vast herds on the plain. The marshy valleys and the Kagera River itself are thronged by water birds, snakes, fish and insects. When the waters dry up the stranded masses of fish are food for cormorant, heron and crane.

On the volcanoes in the north-west there are a few remaining gorillas. Shy and not aggressive unless provoked, they live in the thick forest above an altitude of 2,800 m and browse on leaves, fruit and roots.

GENERAL INFORMATION

Area 26,338 sq. km.

Population 4,160,439.

Altitude Average 1,500 m rising to 4,507 m in north western volcanic region.

Capital Kigali.

Head of State: General Juvenal Habyalimana.

Government Military, headed by Committee for Peace and National Unity semi-political National Revolutionary Development Movement (MRND) set up in 1976.

Date of independence 1 July 1962.

Languages Official languages are Kinya-Rwanda and French. KiSwahili is used by some traders and townspeople.

Religion 50% traditional, the remainder are predominantly Roman Catholic.

Currency: Rwanda Franc (RF); £1 = RF159; US$1 = RF93.

Time GMT + 2.

HOW TO GET THERE

By air: There are flights by Sabena, Air France or Air Zaire to the international airport of Kanombe, 12 km from Kigali. There are also flights from Bujumbura (Burundi). Taxis from the airport are few. The Rwanda Travel Service runs a bus from the airport to the main hotels.

By road: There are main roads from Burundi, Uganda, Tanzania and Zaire.

Visas and health regulations

Visitors to Rwanda must have a valid passport and visa. Visas of up to three months' duration are obtainable from Rwandan embassies abroad. They should be applied for at least six weeks in advance. A visa may be obtained at Kigali airport on arrival for those countries where there is no Rwanda representative, or can be applied for directly from Ministere de l'Interieur, Service de l'Immigration, B.P. 63, Kigali, Rwanda.

Visitors must possess a valid international certificate of vaccination against smallpox and yellow fever. Inoculation against cholera is also advisable.

Dutiable goods

Customs formalities are not strict for short-stay visitors. Usual amounts of tobacco and spirits can be taken in duty-free. Personal effects are not subject to duty.

CLIMATE

Close to the equator but very high, Rwanda has a delightful, equable and healthy climate. The average temperature is 23°C over most of the country but in the mountains it can fall to 15°C. There are two rainy seasons: mid-January to mid—May and mid-October to mid-December when rainfall is generally heavy, especially on mountain slopes.

Health precautions

Malaria prophylactics should be taken, although at Lake Kivu itself there are no mosquitos and allegedly no bilharzia. Tap water should not be drunk.

ACCOMMODATION AND FOOD

Hotels in Kigali tend to be expensive. More reasonably priced are those at Butare, Gisenyi and Ruhengeri (the Muhabura). Camping is now forbidden.

TRANSPORT

Air: Internal services are operated by Air Rwanda, B.P. 177, Kigali, between Kigali, Kamembe and Butare. There are non-commercial airports at Ruhengeri, Nemba, Gisenyi and Gabiro which can be reached by chartered two-engine planes for up to seven passengers, but the cost is high.

Road: Roads are very poor and the terrain difficult; these should be attempted only by adventurous and experienced drivers. The main north-south road is being tarred.

Bus services are being introduced slowly by **Autobus**, B.P. 619, Kigali, tel: 5404-5411. Hitchhiking is more reliable but one is usually expected to pay a reasonable fare.

Car hire: Rwanda Links, B.P. 573;

Agence Solliard, B.P. 335, tel: 5660; and Rwanda Motor, B.P. 448, tel: 5294.

BANKS AND COMMERCE

The Banque Commerciale du Rwanda, B.P. 354, Kigali, Bd de la Revolution, tel: 5591 (largely foreign-owned) has branches at Cyangugu and Gisenyi. The Banque de Kigali, rue des Republicains, B.P. 575, tel: 5493-5371 has branches at Kigali and Ruhengeri. **Business hours:** Banks: 0830 to 1200 Monday to Friday for cash transactions; 1400 to 1500 for other business. Government and commerce: 0800 to 1200 and 1400 to 1700, Monday to Friday; Shops are open from dawn to dusk. Kigali post office and airline offices are also open on Saturday mornings.

PUBLIC HOLIDAYS

New Year's Day; Holy Thursday; Good Friday; Easter Monday; Labour Day; Whit Monday; National Holiday 1 July; Assumption; Government Holiday 26 October; All Saints' Day; Justice's Holiday 24 November; Christmas Day.

FOREIGN EMBASSIES

Belgium: B.P. 81, Kigali; **France:** B.P. 53, Kigali; **West Germany:** B.P. 335, Kigali; **US:** B.P. 28, Kigali; **Switzerland,** B.P. 597, Kigali; **Uganda,** B.P. 656, Kigali; **Zaire,** B.P. 169, Kigali.

KIGALI

An administrative and commerical centre, the tiny capital has little to offer in the way of tourist attractions.

Hotels
Hotel des Mille Collines, B.P. 1322, tel: 6530, 66 rooms.
Hotel des Diplomates, B.P. 269, tel: 5579, 16 rooms.
Hotel Kiyovu, B.P. 1331, tel: 5106, 42

rooms, 2 suites.

Motel, B.P. 276, tel: 5673, 23 rooms.

Restaurants at the main hotels. Others in town include **Chez John, La Sierra, Le Picket.** There are many small bars such as **Aux Delices, Cafe de Kigali, La Bonne Source, Lumiere, Terminus, Panorama, Come Back, Venus.**

Tourist information

Office Rwandais du Tourism et des Parcs Nationaux B.P. 905, Kigali, tel: 6512.

Travel agencies: AMI (tours) B.P. 262, tel: 5395; **RTS** (Rwanda Travel Service, public transport) B.P. 140, tel: 6512. **Sabena,** B.P. 96, tel: 5294. **Agence Solliard** (tours and car hire), B.P. 335, tel: 5660. **Star** (air taxis) B.P. 177, tel: 5238. **Transintra-Transafricair,** B.P. 383, tel: 5287. **Taxis Aeriens de Bry** (air taxis) B.P. 352, tel: 5318.

GISENYI

Gisenyi, the attractive town on Lake Kivu, has an avenue of flowering trees and a sandy beach on one of the most beautiful lakes of Africa. Swimming is safe (no crocodiles or hippos) and one may water-ski. The lake itself is lined with banana plantations rising steeply to high hills, making access difficult. The road from Kigali is high and winding but in fair condition. The road down the lake to Cyangugu gives beautiful views of the lake but is very rough. This is the centre, too, for expeditions to the national park of the Virunga Volcanoes (see below).

Hotel Edelweiss, B.P. 82, Ave du Progès, tel: 7082, 9 rooms. **Hotel Palm Beach,** B.P. 142, 25 rooms. **Hotel Regina,** B.P. 63, tel: 7063, 14 rooms.

BUTARE

Butare, on the main north-south road, is the university town and centre of scientific research. There is an interesting craft museum and shop. The forest of Nyungwe lies between Butare and Cyangugu on a very rough road, which passes through the forest of exotic trees and shrubs. Troops of monkeys can be seen from the road, and a small elephant herd inhabits the forest. **Hotel Faucon** and **Hotel Ibis.**

NATIONAL PARKS

Kagera: The north-east of Rwanda is covered by 2,500 sq. km. of savannah and hilly plains beside the great Kagera River and is devoted to game preservation—mostly lion, zebra, antelope, hippo, the biggest species of buffalo in Africa, as well as impala, tapir, warthog, water-

Rwandan cattle-herder

C. HENNEGHIEN

buck, eland, leopard, crocodile, monkeys and a fascinating varied waterbird population of crested crane, heron, fish eagle and cormorant.

One passes through plains and marshy valleys to reach the series of lakes along the river by a 150 km. track. For some days or even weeks (especially in December, March and April) the route may be impassable because of rains.

The visitor arrives at the entrance to the park at Gabiro by air or road and buys a permit at the office of the Conservateur there, picking up a Rwandan guide. No accommodation facilities exist within the park but there is a guest house on the edge of the reserve—**Gabiro Hotel,** Byumba. Accommodation should be booked in advance.

The Virunga Volcanoes: Between Ruhengeri and Gisenyi lies a range of volcanoes that is of special interest to both geologists and photographers. The Zaire border runs along the peaks of the mountains on the other side of which stretches the great Virunga National Park of Zaire. Fair roads lead from Gisenyi into the beautiful mountain regions of the Zaire-Uganda frontier.

Of the volcanoes, Karisimbi (4,507m) is the most imposing. Mahabura (4,127m) above Ruhengeri is the main haunt of gorillas. The still active Myiragongo in Zaire (3,470m) is the most commonly climbed from Gisenyi.

The visitor can take special air trips from Gisenyi to view the craters. No real climbing is involved and assisted by Rwandan guides the expedition takes two or three days. Rest huts are provided.

HISTORY

The history of the old Kingdom of Rwanda can be traced back through remembered king-lists to about 1386, but it became powerful only with Ruganza Bwimba (15th century) and did not expand to its present size until the con-

quests of the ruthless absolute monarch Kigeri Rwabugiri (1860-1895) who, at the same time, centralized his kingdom under non-hereditary bureaucrats appointed by him. Then as before, however, all power was with the Tutsi aristocracy which formed a segregated ruling caste controlling the only source of wealth—cattle. As in similar kingdoms set up in Uganda and Burundi by the pastoral Tutsi and Hima from southern Ethiopia, the local Hutu became clients in a semi-feudal relationship whereby they performed services for their patron in exchange for protection, the use of some cattle and pasture rights. The pygmy Twa were used as the chattels by both Tutsis and Hutu.

Swamp, mountains and their fearsome reputation kept the Rwandese isolated from the Zanzibari slave and ivory trade of the 19th century. It was not until the late 1890s that German explorers from the East Coast entered and annexed the country. The Germans, like the Belgians who took over in 1916, left the country largely to its traditional rulers. The joint country of Ruanda-Urundi had its capital at Bujumbura and, although held under League of Nations mandate, was administered together with the Belgian Congo (Zaire).

A peasant revolt in 1959, led by educated Hutu who feared the entrenchment of Tutsi power at independence, resulted in the violent overthrow of Tutsi rule and the abolition of the monarchy. Rwanda became independent in 1962, and separated itself from the still Tutsi-dominated Burundi. Frontier tensions grew up between the two countries due to attempts by Tutsi guerrilla bands (known as *inyenzi*—cockroaches) to restore the former monarchy. Rwanda, however, succeeded in establishing a degree of political stability under the cautious leadership of its first President, Gregoire Kayibanda, until an ominous revival of tension provoked the coup d'etat of July 1973, bringing the army to power. There is at present a fairly calm atmosphere.

SAO TOME & PRINCIPE

The islands of Sao Tome and Principe lie 360 km to the west of Gabon in the Gulf of Guinea. Under the Portuguese there was widespread poverty and malnutrition among the local population, most of whom worked as agricultural labourers on the large cocoa plantations. In July 1975 the islands gained independence after some 500 years of foreign rule.

THE LAND AND THE PEOPLE

Sao Tome, 857 sq km in area, is by far the bigger of the two islands. Principe is only 139 sq. km in area. The population is likewise concentrated primarily in Sao Tome.

The islands were uninhabited before the Portuguese seamen arrived in 1471. Most of the islanders are first- or second-generation migrants from other Portuguese territories or are the descendants of slaves and *serviçais* shipped from various parts of the mainland over the centuries.

GENERAL INFORMATION

Area996 sq. km.

PopulationApprox 80,000.

CapitalSao Tome, which has an approximate population of 6,000.

GovernmentThe islands are ruled by a civilian administration, headed by the MLSTP, which is the sole legal party. The country's legislature is the 18-member People's Assembly.

PresidentDr Manuel Pinto da Costa.

Prime Minister Miguel Trovoada.

Languages:Portuguese (official) and Crioulo.

ReligionRoman Catholic.

Currency: Escudo (=100 centavos). £1=66 escudos. $1=39 escudos.

TRAVEL TO SAO TOME

There is an international airport on Sao Tome island. Airlines serving the country include TAP and Air Gabon.

Entry and Health requirements

All visitors must possess valid visas, which should be requested prior to arrival direct from Sao Tome. Immunisation against yellow fever, smallpox and cholera is required. Water should be boiled before drinking.

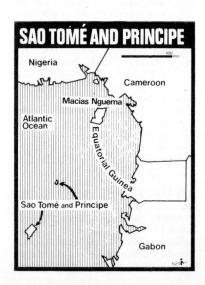

SENEGAL

Senegal has natural advantages which make it very attractive: sunshine all year round and pleasant breezes during the good season, which lasts eight months during Europe's winter; miles of magnificent sandy beaches; villages where traditional culture flourishes; the gaiety and friendliness of its people.

Long contact with the outside world has left the country with a cosmopolitan atmosphere and a mixed and varied population.

THE LAND AND THE PEOPLE

A flat, sandy country on the most westerly point of Africa, Senegal lies between Guinea to the south, Mali to the east and Mauritania to the north. Most of the land is less than 100 m above sea level, except for the Fouta Djallon foothills in the south-east and the Bambouk mountains on the Mali border.

The country has four main rivers. The Senegal has its source in the Fouta Djallon and flows 1,600 km into the Atlantic at Saint-Louis. The Saloum flows through the central region and is joined by the Sine almost at its estuary. The Gambia and the Casamance water the south.

On the coast between Dakar and Saint-Louis is a wide belt of shifting dunes. Cape Verde was formed by volcanic activity and the prevailing south-westerly

winds make it verdant. South of Dakar the coast consists of shallow estuaries where palm trees and coconut palms grow. Much of the southern part of the country is forested. The northern part of the country, below the Senegal basin, consists of the Ferlo desert, a hot, dry Sahelian plain with little vegetation.

The total population is estimated at about four million. The Wolof are the largest ethnic group, followed by the Serer, Toucouleur (especially in the north and north-east), Fulani in the south, the Diola and the Malinke. There are also smaller groups such as the Bain-

ouk, Manjak and Balante. Of the non-African population the majority are French.

Senegal's cultural history has been strongly influenced by the earliest contacts with Europeans, dating to the 15th century, and by the rapid spread of Islam. However, an unbroken line of tradition still continues in the great variety of handicrafts produced by different ethnic groups, and in the rich repertoire of music and dance which are part of innumerable feasts and rituals, both Muslim and Christian. There are two national dance companies which perform traditional Senegalese dances.

WILDLIFE

The variety of wildlife is limited, but in Casamance in particular there are warthogs, monkeys and baboons, and all kinds of birds: francolins, guinea-fowl, snipe, pheasants, duck and bustards. The National Park of Niokolo-Koba has antelope, monkeys, baboons, hippos, leopards, hyenas, lions, elephants and buffaloes.

Birdlife, is abundant in the Senegal River area and especially around the Lac de Guiers; herons, scoter-ducks, rails, marabous and teal can be seen. The Djoudj Bird Park near the Senegal River is a sanctuary for hundreds of African and migratory European varieties, particularly waders.

The coastal waters abound in fish, especially off Cape Verde. Hunting is strictly regulated and a permit is necessary. The hunting season is from December 14 to April 30.

GENERAL INFORMATION

Area: 196,192 sq. km.

Population: 4 million.

Altitude: The highest point is 498 m in the Fouta Djallon foothills in the south-east corner of the country.

Capital: Dakar.

Head of State: President Léopold Sédar Senghor.

Government: The President is elected every five years. The National Assembly, also elected every five years, has 100 members.

Date of independence: August 20, 1960.

Languages: French (official). Wolof is the most widely spoken language.

Religions: 80% Muslim, 10% traditional and 10% Christian.

Currency: CFA franc. £1 sterling=429 CFA francs. US$=249 CFA francs.

Time: GMT.

HOW TO GET THERE

By air: There are direct services between Gatwick (UK) and Dakar (Senegal) by British Caledonian Airways once weekly in each direction, as well as regular services from London, changing at Frankfurt, Paris, Rome, Brussels or Geneva and Las Palmas. Flights from New York are operated by Pan Am and Air Afrique; from Santiago (Chile) by Air France, Lufthansa and Swissair; from Rio de Janeiro by Lufthansa and Swissair. Dakar is linked with other African capitals by Air Afrique, Royal Air Maroc, Air Mauritanie, Air Liban, Air Mali, Air Guinée, Air Zaire, Ghana Airways and Nigerian Airways. PAA, Air Canada, Alitalia, Aeroflot, CSA, also fly to Dakar.

Dakar airport is situated at Yoff, 15 km from the city. There is a bus service and taxis are always available.

By road: The distance from Nouakchott in Mauritania to Dakar is 575 km and the road is tarred all the way.

Senegal can also be reached from Europe via the Tenezrouft route crossing the Sahara and Mali. The route to Dakar passes through Reggane, Gao, Bamako, Nioro, Kayes, Tambacounda and Kaolack. From Bechar in Algeria the distance is about 5,500 km.

By sea: A number of French lines call at Dakar, linking it with Europe and South

America and with other West African ports.

By rail: From Bamako (Mali) there is a twice-weekly passenger train to Dakar with couchettes, restaurant and air-conditioned carriages. **Fer Tourisme,** 38 Bd. de la Republique, B.P. 2099, tel: 317.47 and 347.83.

Visas and health regulations

Nationals of European or francophone African countries require only an identity card. Those from other countries must have a valid passport and visa. Collective visas are obtainable for tourists travelling in organised groups. A return or onward travel ticket must be held, otherwise a deposit must be made.

Valid international certificates of vaccination against smallpox, yellow fever and cholera are necessary. TAB is advisable. Malaria is prevalent in many regions and visitors are advised to carry a supply of one of the anti-malaria drugs.

Dutiable goods

The following are allowed in free of duty, per person: two different types of camera, one cine-camera, one portable radio, one record-player, one tape-recorder, 20 records, one portable typewriter, one pair of field-glasses, two sporting guns or rifles of different calibre and 250 cartridges for each.

Tourists arriving in their own cars must have a carnet de passage; otherwise they are issued with a temporary pass by the customs authorities, valid for three or four days. After this period has elapsed an extension must be requested from the Touring Club de Senegal and a deposit must be lodged with the Ministry of Finance, Avenue Carde, Dakar.

Currency regulations

There is no limit on the amount of foreign currency taken into or out of Senegal but the amount taken out must not exceed the amount taken in. Not more than 25,000 CFA francs may be imported or exported. Travellers' cheques can be cashed at banks and large hotels.

CLIMATE

The best season for visiting Senegal is the dry season, December to May, when maximum temperatures are between $18°C$ and $29°C$. This good season is shorter in Casamance, and much shorter in the east of the country. The coast, particularly Cape Verde, has cool trade winds from the north during this dry period. During the rest of the year a hot monsoon wind blows from the south, bringing the rainy season of hot, humid weather, known as *l'hivernage*. Inland, temperatures and rainfall are higher. Rainfall is heavy in Casamance and in the south-east; it is very slight in the Sahelian region in the north-east and east.

What to wear

Lightweight clothing may be worn all the year round, but a raincoat is necessary from May to November. Slightly warmer clothes are needed for evenings and for the cooler season.

Health precautions

A prophylactic against malaria should be taken daily from 14 days before departure, throughout the stay and for 14 days afterwards. Outside Dakar, drinking water should be boiled. There are two hospitals and several clinics in Dakar, and medical facilities in the main towns. Medical treatment and pharmaceutical goods are very expensive.

ACCOMMODATION AND FOOD

The country has a number of luxury hotels and there is an extensive programme for more hotel building. Accommodation should be reserved in advance. Most hotels have air-conditioned rooms. Elsewhere there are resthouses, *campements* with bungalows or grass huts, and in some places camping sites.

The classification of hotels was fixed by the Delegation Generale du Tourism. International cuisine is available in the main hotels and larger restaurants. Dakar, in particular, has a wide variety of restaurants: African, European, Lebanese and Vietnamese. Specialities on the coast are lobster, crayfish and fish chowder; other Senegalese specialities are *thieboudiene* (fish and rice), mutton or chicken *mafe* (in peanut sauce), *gombos* (spiced fish-balls in a hot sauce) and *yassa* (chicken with lemon, pimentoes and onions). The national drinks are palm wine and ginger ale. Fruit and vegetables are plentiful.

A service charge of 10-15% is included in practically all hotel and restaurant bills. Other tipping is left to discretion, but is not necessary for taxi drivers.

TRANSPORT

Road: Senegal has a good road network, with 2,517 km of asphalted roads (linking Dakar with Saint-Louis, Rosso, Diourbel, Joal, Kaolack, Ziguinchor and with Banjul, capital of The Gambia), and 466 km of other roads and 10,288 km of earth tracks (although some of these are impassable in the rainy season). There are numerous bus services within the city of Dakar and taxis are easy to find. Fares are doubled between midnight and 0500 hours. *Taxis de brousse* and *cars rapide* travel between main towns. There are plenty of filling stations and repair garages in the Cape Verde region but they are infrequent in the interior.

Air: Air Senegal links Dakar with all the main towns of Senegal. Private aircraft can be chartered.

Sea: The USIMA steamer *Cap Skirring* makes the trip from Dakar to Ziguinchor once a week (see under Ziguinchor and Casamance).

Car hire

There are a number of car hire firms in Dakar and in the main towns.

BANKS AND COMMERCE

Among the banks operating in Senegal are: Banque Internationale pour l'Afrique Occidentale (BIAO), B.P. 129, Place de l'Independance, Dakar; Banque Internationale pour le Commerce et l'Industrie Sénégalaise (BICIS), B.P. 392, 2, avenue Roume, Dakar; Société Générale de Banques au Sénégal (SGBS), B.P. 323, 19 avenue Roume, Dakar; Union Sénégalaise de Banques (USB), B.P. 56, 17 blvd. Pinet-Laprade, Dakar; Banque Centrale des Etats de l'Afrique de l'Ouest (BCEANO), B.P. 1398, 3 avenue W-Ponty, Dakar.

Business hours: Shops: Monday to Saturday 0800-1200 and 1430-1800. These hours may vary, and some shops are open on Sunday morning and closed on Monday morning. Government offices: Monday to Friday 0800-1200 and 1430-1800. Banks: Monday to Friday 0800-1115 and 1430-1630. During the month of Ramadan some offices work 0730-1430 continuously.

PUBLIC HOLIDAYS

All the Muslim feasts (variable dates) and the Christian feasts are celebrated, in addition to January 1, April 4 (Senegal's National Day) and May 1.

FOREIGN EMBASSIES

(in Dakar)

Austria: 24 blvd. Pinet-Laprade, B.P. 3247; **Belgium:** route de la Corniche, B.P. 524; **Brazil:** Imm. BIAO, 2eme etage, Place de l'Independance, B.P. 136; **Canada:** Imm. Daniel Sorano, blvd. de la République; **France:** 1 rue Thiers, B.P. 4035; **West Germany:** 43 avenue A; Sarraut, B.P. 2100; **Italy:** 26 avenue Roume, B.P. 348; **Japan:** Imm. BIAO, Place de l'Indépendance, B.P. 3140; **Netherlands:** 5 avenue Carde, B.P. 3262; **Spain:** Imm. Daniel Sorano, 45 blvd. de la République, B.P. 2091; **Sweden:** 43 avenue Albert-Sarraut, B.P. 2052; **Switzerland:** 1

rue Victor Hugo, B.P. 1772; **UK:** 20 rue du Dr Guillet, B.P. 6025; **USA:** Imm. BIAO, Place de l'Indépendance, B.P. 49.

DAKAR

The capital of Senegal lies on the Cape Verde peninsula, on a rocky spur jutting into the Atlantic Ocean. Founded in 1857 on the site of a fishing village, it became the capital of French West Africa in 1902 and since 1958 has been capital of Senegal.

Built on a plateau exposed to cool sea breezes, the city is surrounded on three sides by a coastal road. The modern centre is Place de l'Independance, but for the bustle and colour of an African town, go to the markets: the Kermel, near the port, for flowers and basketwork; the Sandaga for exotic fruit, spices and dried fish; the Medina market, in Avenue Blaise Diagne for food, textiles and pottery; and the market in Place des Maures, where Moors from the north sell exquisite jewellery. In Place Tascher there is the IFAN Ethnographical Museum with treasures from Senegal, the Ivory Coast, Upper Volta and Benin (open every day except Monday and Friday).

There is a superb view of the peninsula from the top of the minaret of the Great Mosque (67 m).

Dakar craftsman

C. HENNEGHIEN

Excursions from Dakar
Island of Goree: The boat leaves from the port, and does the trip in 25 minutes. The island became known to Europe through Portuguese sailors in 1444. It later became a Dutch naval base and then a major centre for the slave trade. It has three museums: the 'Maison des Esclaves', the Historical Museum and the Marine Museum. Goree has many other reminders of its past: 18th century houses with wrought-iron balconies; the Governor's palace; the Admiral's house; dungeons where slaves where kept before being shipped to the New World; and the ruins of Fort Nassau and Fort Orange.
Cape Verde: There are many fine sandy beaches, such as those at Anse Bernard, Hann, Almadies, N'Gor, Yoff and Camberene. The Route de la Corniche Ouest leads to the reconstructed village of Soumbedioune, the Musee Dynamique, built for the first Festival of Negro Art in 1966, the University, the monument commemorating the first successful flight across the south Atlantic by Jean Mermoz, the two hills called Les Mammelles, from where there is a fine view and the Pointe des Almadies, the most westerly point on the African continent. It continues to the village and beach of N'Gor, and to the airport at Yoff.
Kayar: a typical fishing village north-west of Dakar, where at around 5pm the visitor can watch the return of the pirogues filled with fish. It is reached via Hann (beach, zoo and botanical garden); Rufisque (industrial town with a fish market); and Sangalkam (a botanical park containing many tropical plants). Farther north-east is the village of M'Boro on a lake inhabited by many birds.

Hotels
Hotel Teranga, Place de l'Independance, B.P. 3380, tel: 205.75.
Hotel Diarama, Rte de N'Gor, B.P. 8092, tel: 455.35.
Hotel de N'Gor, Rte de N'Gor, B.P.

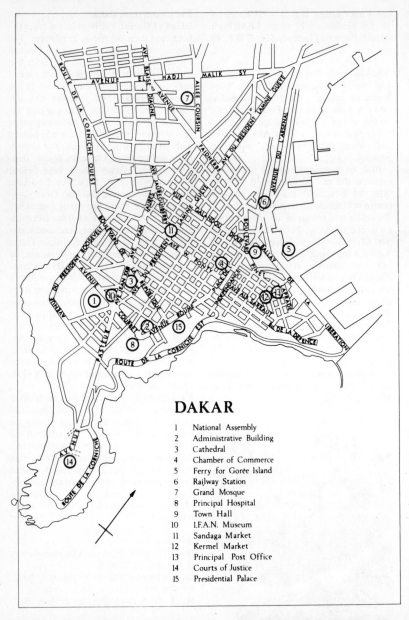

DAKAR

1. National Assembly
2. Administrative Building
3. Cathedral
4. Chamber of Commerce
5. Ferry for Gorée Island
6. Railway Station
7. Grand Mosque
8. Principal Hospital
9. Town Hall
10. I.F.A.N. Museum
11. Sandaga Market
12. Kermel Market
13. Principal Post Office
14. Courts of Justice
15. Presidential Palace

8114, tel: 455.35.

Hotel Meridian, Rte de N'Gor, B.P. 8092, tel: 501.22.

Hotel Croix du Sud, 20 Avenue A; Sarraut, B.P 232, tel: 229.17.

Village de N'Gor, Rte de N'Gor, B.P. 8114, tel: 456.15.

Hotel du Plateau, 62 Rue Jules Ferry, B.P. 2906, tel: 337.74.

Hotel Massata Samb, Rte Plage de N'Gor, B.P. 8140, tel: 455.53.

Hotel Village Sunugul, Rte de N'Gor, B.P. 8066, tel: 456.30.

Hotel de la Paix, 38 Rue Thiers, tel: 260.44.

Hotel Jaama, 7 Rue Paul Holle, B.P. 1642, tel: 327.34.

Hotel le Globe, 44 Rue Vincens, tel: 336.13.

Hotel le Farid, 51 Rue Vincens, B.P. 1514, tel: 167.65.

Hotel Clarice, Avenue Jean Jaures Sandiniery, tel: 320.90.

Relais de l'Espadon, Goree Island, tel: 209.53.

Touring Hotel, 42 Avenue Lamine Gueye, B.P. 924, tel: 363.55.

Hotel Atlantic, 52 Rue du Dr; Thèze, tel: 223.24.

Hotel Vichy, 26 Rue Felix Faure, B.P. 2082, tel: 236.66.

Hotel Central, 16 Avenue W; Ponty, B.P. 679, tel: 232.32.

Hotel Metropole, 8 Blvd. Pinet-Laprade, tel: 220.38.

Hotel de Relais, Rte de Ouakam, Km. 5, B.P. 5011, tel: 339.35.

Hotel Oceanic, 9 Rue de Thann, B.P. 219, tel: 220.78.

Hotel des Princes, 49 Rue Raffenel, tel: 331.06.

Hotel du Marche, 3 Rue Parent, B.P. 232, tel: 222.84.

Hotel Provençal, 17 Rue Malenfant, tel: 226.40.

Club Aldiana, Nianing/M'Bour, tel: 830.84. (Reservations Dakar 325.34).

Hotel de Thiès, Thiès.

Village de Somone, M'Bour, tel: (Dakar) 268.17.

Domaine de Nianing, M'Bour, tel: 830.85.

Centre Touristique de la Petite Côte, M'Bour, tel: 830.04.

Hotel de M'Boro, M'Boro.

Hotel Rex, Thiès, tel: 81.08.

Motel de Sebissou, Sebikotane, tel: 69.308.

Restaurants

The following is a small selection from the many restaurants in and around Dakar. For Senegalese specialities; **Le Baobab, Le Tam Tam, Le Ramatou, Le Saint-Louis.** European: **Le Lagon, L'Esterel, Le Virage.** Vietnamese: **Kim Son.** Lebanese: **Le Farid.**

On the Island of Goree: **Le Chevalier de Boufflers** and **Taverne des Boucaniers.**

Entertainments

Cape Verde and the Petite Cote have miles of white sandy beaches where it is possible to swim, skin-dive, sail and water-ski. Hire of equipment at: **Le Lagon**, route de la Petite Cornish; **Le Marinas**, route de Bel-Air; **Cercle de la Voile**, plage de Hann; **Hotel de N'Gor.** Swimming pools at: **Le Lido**, route de la Corniche; **L'Ocean**, Domaine de Ouarar, route de Yoff; **Sub-nu-gab**, route de N'Gor. Riding at: the **Cercle de l'Etrier**, plage de Hann; **Hotel de N'Gor; Cercle Hippique Sportif,** route de Rufisque; **Ranch du Sagittaire**, route de Rufisque (all-day rides in the forest of Malika). Tennis at the **Tennis Club Dakarois, Le Marinas, Hotel de N'Gor, Union Tennis Club** and the **University.** There is a 9-hole golf course on the route de Camberene.

Trips by air round Cape Verde can be arranged through the **Aeroclub Iba Gueye** at Dakar-Yoff. (Reservations must be made 24 hours in advance.)

Cape Verde is a fisherman's paradise. From November to May there is fishing for mackerel, grouper, bonito, bluefish, etc. The big fish—from June to October—are tuna, barracuda, sailfish, blue marlin, etc. On the Island of Goree there is a **Centre de Péche Sportive** which rents out boats and equipment. Dakar has an angling centre run by Air Afrique.

Night-clubs: the **Niani, Kings, Hugo, L'Oeil, Miami, Taverne du Port.** There is the **Casino** on the route de N'Gor. There are many cinemas showing the latest French films.

Shopping and markets

At Soumbedioune, on the Corniche de Fann, a craft village provides the opportunity of watching craftsmen at work and of buying their wares: woodcarving, fabrics, gold and silver jewellery, musical instruments, carved ivory, leatherwork, pottery and basketwork.

Dakar has several markets: Kermel, Sandaga, the marché de l'or, marché des poteries and the marché des bijoutiers Maures.

Tourist information

Office du Tourisme, Place de l'Indépendance, B.P.2018, tel: 230.61, open every day 0845-1215 and 1430-1830 except Sunday and Monday morning. **Air Afrique/UTA**, Place de l'Indépendance, tel: 203.70.

Travel agents: Afric Turim, 9 Blvd. Pinet-Laprade, tel: 238.95; **Havas Voyages**, 15 bis Blvd. Pinet-Laprade, tel: 262.52; **ATVT**, 43 Rue Vincens, tel: 232.90; **Agence E,** Haroun, 15 Rue Sandiniery, tel: 234.19; **Fer Tourisme**, 38 Blvd. de la République, tel: 317.47; **Voyages Labery**, 71 Avenue Peytavin, tel: 330.19; **Senegal International Tourisme**, 31 Rue Felix Faure, tel: 261.96; **SCTTAO**, 67 Avenue W. Ponty, tel: 318.33; **SOCOPAO**, 1 Place de l'Indépendance, tel: 267.88; **TRANSCAP**, 27 Avenue W. Ponty, tel: 228.35; **USIMA**, 5 Place de l'Indépendance, tel: 267.88; **Voyages Nassar**, 101 Rue Mohamed V; **Vacances et Loisirs**, 2 Place de l'Indépendance, tel: 200.91.

SAINT-LOUIS AND THE SENEGAL RIVER

The French founded a settlement in 1659 on the island of N'Dar at the mouth of the Senegal River. After Senegal became a colony in 1864 Saint-Louis was made the administrative capital of both Senegal and Mauritania. The town retains memories of its past in its 18th century houses with wrought-iron and wooden balconies. The river delta has silted up and the harbour's importance has consequently diminished; there are, however, plans for comprehensive development of the river basin.

Excursions from Saint-Louis

A cruise lasting several days can be made up the Senegal River. Calls are made at towns such as Richard Toll, named after a gardener called Richard (Toll means garden) who created an experimental garden here in 1830. The atmosphere of the valley is one of complete peace. There is fishing on the Lac de Guiers, which is the home of a wide variety of birds, particularly waders.

Hotels

Hotel de la Residence, 254 Avenue Blaise Daigne, B.P. 254, tel: 712:60;
Hotel de la Poste, B.P.48, tel: 711.18.
At Richard Toll there is a resthouse, the **Gite d'Etape du Fleuve**, tel: 30.

SINE-SALOUM

The area round the source of the River Saloum is rich in archaeological remains. High megaliths, blocks of hewn stone (often arranged in circles), pottery, skeletons, iron spears and leather bracelets have been discovered—relics of a very ancient civilisation about which little is known. The delta of the Saloum should be seen from the air for a spectacular view of dozens of little islands covered with mangroves and village huts half-hidden under palm trees.

Village on the banks of the Senegal River

Hotels
Hotel de Paris, Kaolack, tel: 87.019;
Centre Touristique de Kahorne, Kaolack, tel: 87.116;
Centre Touristique du Baobab, Diourbel, ·tel: 86.007;

There are *campements* at N'Dangane and Missirah and a hotel/restaurant at Toubacouta.

CASAMANCE

The chief town of this most southerly region of Senegal is **Ziguinchor,** founded in the 16th century by the Portuguese who exported skins, ivory, rice, cotton textiles, gold and slaves from there. An attractive town with long, low houses roofed with straw, and wide tree-lined avenues, it lies on the south bank of the River Casamance. It has a handicrafts centre and a colourful market. Zinguinchor is reached from Dakar either by air (one hour) or by road, crossing the Rivers Saloum, Gambia and Casamance. An alternative journey is by boat; the *Cap Skirring* departs from Dakar, calls at Carabane, and allows for excursions into the forest of Bissine and to Cape Skirring before returning to Dakar four days later. Reservations should be made at USIMA, 5 Place de l'Indépendance, Dakar.

Excursions from Ziguinchor include a drive through Diola villages to Cape Skirring, near Guinea-Bissau, where

there is a good beach. It is also a good starting point for journeys into the bush, to villages of mud and staw houses.

Hotels
Club Mediterranee, Cape Skirring, B.P. 9, Zinguinchor;
Hotel Aubert, Zinguinchor, B.P. 55, tel: 91.379.
Cheaper accommodation in Zinguinchor is available at the **Centre Touristique Nema**, **Hotel-Restaurant du Tourisme**, **Hotel-Restaurant de l'Escale** and the **Campement du Cap Skirring**; at Badioure at the **Motel du Relais Fleuri**.

There are rest houses at Kolda and Oussoye and a *campement* at the Loer Caramance National Park.

Tourist information
USIMA-Senegal Tours, B.P. 22, Zinguinchor. The Co-ordinateur du Tourisme en Casamance, Chambre de Commerce, Zinguinchor, tel: 913.10.

NATIONAL PARKS
Niokolo-Koba Wildlife Park. This vast park of 813,000 hectares lies on the upper Gambia in the southern part of the eastern region, the least populated part of Senegal, and it is an immense territory of forest and savannah. The park, 600 km from Dakar, is reached by road, via Kaolack and Tambacounda (450 km from

Dakar, 280 km tarred); by rail to Tambacounda (there is a train from Dakar several times a week), and then by hired car or by coach, which connect with the various *campements* in the park. The alternative is to fly to Tambacounda or Simenti on the park border.

Visit permits are obtainable from the Direction or at the various entrances. The park is open from late December to mid-May. At least three days should be allowed for a visit.

The landscape consists of savannah and dense forests, waterholes and rivers. Over 70 species of mammals exist in the park and 300 species of birds, several types of reptiles and more than 60 species of fish and turtles. At least 1,500 types of plant life have been identified.

Hotels
Relais de Simenti, northern edge of park;
Hotel Asta Kebe, Tambacounda, B.P. 119, tel: 328.29;
Campement-Hotel de Niokolo Koba (eastern edge of park);
Campement de Badi at the main entrance to park.
Apply to Direction des Parcs Nationaux at Tambacounda (tel: 120).

There is a *campement* at Bakel, and camp sites with amenities at Koba, l'Eland, near Gue de Vorouli, M'Badoye, Malapa, Banhare.

Djourd Bird Park
This 10,000-hectare park lies between the Senegal River and the Gorom stream, and can be visited by Land-Rover or by pirogue. It was opened in 1971 with the backing of Air Afrique, which organises visits to the park. More than 100 bird species have been counted. Accommodation is in a *campement*.

HISTORY
Traces of prehistoric civilisations have been found around Dakar. Early and middle palaeolithic remains include dou-

ble-edged weapons, arrowheads and tools, and among neolithic and late neolithic objects are mill-stones, hoes and spears. The territory was divided in the 11th century into a number of kingdoms—the Walo in the north, the Djolof and Bambouk in the east, the Dimar in the north-east, the Kayor and the Baol in the west, and those of the Sin and the Saloum in the central west area.

Senegal became one of the first African countries to be visited by Europeans. In 1444 the Portuguese Dinis Dias arrived, followed the next year by the Italian Gadamosto. The Portuguese installed themselves first on the island which they named Palma and which is now Goree. They then settled in The Gambia and the Casamance. The Dutch took Goree (Goede Reede) in 1588. In 1659 the French built a fort at the mouth of the Senegal River, which they called Fort Saint-Louis. They acquired Goree, Rufisque and Joal from the Dutch; ceded their settlements to the English in 1783, who returned them to France under the terms of the 1814 treaty.

The French continued their colonisation in the interior of Senegal during the 19th century, meeting considerable opposition throughout the country. Resistance to French colonial rule built up during the period between the two world wars. Finally in 1956 the *loi cadre* gave Senegal semi-autonomy, creating the *Conseil de Gouvernement* presided over by the Governor. Senegal became a member of the Union Français, established in 1958, and in 1959 joined with the French Sudan to form a single State called the Federation of Mali. The Federation achieved its independence in June 1960 but broke up in August 1960. Senegal then became an independent republic with a new constitution. The poet-politician, Léopold Sédar Senghor, was elected President of the Republic, and has held the post continuously since then.

Senghor had served in the French Parliament since 1946.

SEYCHELLES

The completion of the first international airport in 1971 meant that the Seychelles became much more accessible to tourists than had previously been the case. The results have been dramatic, but not disastrous to this hitherto unspoiled corner of the world. The Seychellois remain charming and easy-going, and the islands' beauty is unimpaired.

The natural beauty of the countryside is matched by a rich and varied plant and animal life. Fortunately the Seychelles Government has a strict conservation policy—including establishing natural parks and introducing legislation to protect the flora and fauna.

Areas already designated as national parks include the most spectacular part of Mahé's mountain range; a marine park covering the offshore islands of St Anne, Moyenne, Round, Long and Cerf, and the coral reefs in between; the famous Vallée de Mai on Praslin, where the legendary coco-de-mer palms grow and black parrots live; much of La Digue island and the lovely, brooding island of Silhouette, with its indigenous forest

Other Special Reserve areas have been demarcated. The island of Cousin—already a bird sanctuary—falls into this category, as do several of the outlying islands.

THE LAND AND THE PEOPLE

Scattered over a large area in the western Indian Ocean, the Seychelles archipelago consists of 87 islands, of which 40 are granite and the rest coral. Mahé, the largest island, lies four degrees south of the equator; its hightes peak, Morne Seychellois, rises to nearly 1,000m above sea level. The other granite islands, including Praslin (the second largest) all lie within a radius of 50km of Mahé. Mountainous with lush, green tropical vegeta-

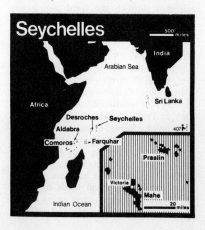

tion, these granite islands are about six million years old. The coral islands are mostly low-lying atolls and have no permanent population.

There were no indigenous inhabitants in the islands. The present population of about 60,000 is descended from the 18th-century French colonists and their African slaves. There are also a small number of Indian and Chinese traders, British officials and retired expatriates. While considerable racial mixing has occurred, the minorities—the big landowners (known as the *grands blanc*) the Indians and the Chinese—have maintained their ethnic identity.

Most of the population is Roman Catholic, the result of energetic French missionary activity in the 19th century. English and French are the official languages and widely spoken, but Creole is the lingua franca.

The imprint of France is still the strongest single cultural influence on the islands. It is expressed in the Creole language—pidgin French with many African, Indian and English words added—in religion, in law and in general outlook.

Among the traditonal crafts there is some fine basket weaving and tortoise-shell carving. Seychellois vitality is given full rein through the local pop bands which play in the night-clubs in Victoria.

WILDLIFE

The Seychelles are the home of dozens of the world's rarest birds. Individual islands like Cousin and Aldabra are already bird sanctuaries, and other places such as Praslin, where the black parrot lives, and La Digue, home of the paradise flycatcher, are specially protected. These birds and other rare species attract ornithologists and scientists from all over the world. There are also huge numbers of more common tropical birds including the lovely fairy tern—as many as 10,000 live in Cousin alone—egrets and the fruit-

eating flying fox (which is a large bat).

Big game fish abound in the deeper waters—barracuda, tuna, kingfish, marlin, sailfish and bonito. Bottom fishing is also excellent, the most common local fish being bourgeois, job, vieille and parrot fish—the first two making the best eating. The Government has banned spearguns but encourages goggling and scuba diving.

The coral reefs and underwater plateaux around the granite island group are truly spectacular and unspoiled. Sharks do not venture inside the reefs or in the coastal waters and lagoons. The swimmer can spend hour after hour wandering through intricate and ever-changing subterranean scenery watching a thousand varieties of tropical fish flit and dart in the darkening depths of the coral canyons.

The prolific plant life is as much of an attraction as the birds, fish and giant land tortoises—some of which have been known to live for century and a half. There is a broad range of tropical fruits and vegetables, including delicious mangoes, guavas, coconuts and *fruit-a-pain*. The coco-de-mer grows only on the islands of Praslin and Curieuse. The tall palm trees can live up to 800 years, the nuts take 25 years to mature and the fruit seven years to ripen.

It is an offence under the Protection of Shells Regulations not only to collect shells from protected areas but also to disturb them on their natural environment. The damage which has recently come to light includes turning over live coral, causing it to die. Any offence under the regulations is punishable by a fine of Rs 1,000 and one year's imprisonment. The areas protected under the Protection of Shells Regulations are as follows: on Mahé, from Rat Island southwards to Pointe au Sel and from North East Point northwards to the northern boundary of the Carana Beach Hotel site; the islands of Cousin, Curieuse, St Anne, Cerf, Cashée, Long, Moyenne and

Round; on Praslin, from and including Anse Boudin eastwards to Pointe Zanguilles; on La Digue, from the lighthouse at La Passe northwards to Grosse Roche.

The protected areas are not only the foreshores and the reefs but also the sea for a distance of 400 metres from the nearest point on the low-water line.

GENERAL INFORMATION

Area 376 sq km (total).
Population 60,000.
Altitude Sea level, with a few scattered peaks, the highest being Morne Seychellois (1,000m).
Capital Victoria (on Mahé Island).
Head of State Albert René.
Language English and French (official); Creole used by majority.
Religion Roman Catholic (90%), Anglican (7%).
Currency Seychelles Rupee (Rs), divided into 100 cents. 13.33 rupees=£1 sterling; 7.75 rupees=US$1.
Time GMT + 4.

HOW TO GET THERE

By air: British Airways fly from London, via Nairobi, Addis Ababa or Dar-es-Salaam, five times a week; from the Far East twice weekly; from Johannesburg and from Mauritius weekly. South African Airways fly from Johannesburg and from the Far East weekly. Air India has a weekly flight from Bombay and one from Mauritius. Air France operates a weekly service from Paris and Djibouti and from Reunion and Mauritius. Air Malawi flies once a week from Blantyre.
By sea: There are no regular passenger services to Seychelles, although a number of passenger-carrying cargo ships stop in Seychelles.

Visas and health regulations
A valid passport is necessary. Visas are not required by UK and Commonwealth citizens and nationals of Belgium, Den-

mark, Finland, Iceland, Italy, Liechtenstein, Luxembourg, Monaco, Turkey and Uruguay. Austrian, French and US citizens do not require a visa if their stay is less than three months. Citizens of other countries must have a visa, which may be obtained from The Immigration Office, Victoria, Mahé. Visitors must produce valid onward or return travel documents.

Valid international certificates of vaccination against smallpox, cholera and yellow fever.

Dutiable goods
Personal effects (including cameras, binoculars, typewriter and sporting equipment) are allowed in free of duty, but

Local fishermen with pirogue

must be declared. Firearms may not be taken into the Seychelles. A litre of spirits, a litre of wine, 200 cigarettes (or 50 cigars or 250gm of tobacco) and a small amount of perfume may be taken in free of duty.

Currency regulations
There is no restriction on the amount of foreign currency taken into the country. On departure visitors may take out Seychelles currency notes to the value of Rs 100.

CLIMATE
The most pleasant months of the year are

May to October, during the south-east trade winds. These winds are cool and dry but sometimes bring overcast skies and choppy seas. The coolest months are July and August, but throughout the year there is only slight variation in the temperature from 24°C to 30°C. The average annual sunshine rate is seven hours a day.

The hottest months are March and April, during the north-west trade winds, which are calmer but hot and wet. The greatest rainfall is between December and February but the amounts are variable throughout the islands. Even on Mahé total annual rainfall varies from 175 to 335cm in different parts. The coral islands have considerably less. After a heavy rain shower the air clears and the skies become a brilliant blue.

What to wear: The Seychelles are very informal and clothes should be light and comfortable. It is advisable to take something warmer for the evenings.

Health precautions: The islands have few of the diseases common in tropical countries. Malaria is non-existent and the water is uncontaminated. There is no need for special health precautions.

ACCOMMODATION, FOOD

Most of the hotels in the Seychelles are very new and nearly all are on Mahé, the main island. The facilities are modern but prices are inevitably high. Camping is not allowed at present. Some of the hotels have very good restaurants. In Victoria there are Chinese, Italian, Swiss, German, French, Austrian, and Seychellois restaurants (the Tourism Office publishes a comprehensive restaurant guide).

TRANSPORT

Road: Mahé has nearly 160km of mostly tarred roads. Taxis are available from hotels and within Victoria. Buses offer cheap transport to all parts of the island.

Motor coaches run sight-seeing tours.

Sea: The 'Lady Esme' runs a ferry service to the islands of Praslin and La Digue, leaving Victoria at 0800 every Monday, Wednesday, Friday and Saturday and returning in the evening. There are a number of excursions from Victoria to St Anne Island (cruising around Cerf, Round and Long Islands) as well as to Praslin, La Digue, Cousin and Bird Island.

Air: Air Mahé and Inter Island Airways have quick and frequent flights (several a day) from Mahé to Praslin. The flight takes 15 minutes and nine seats are available on each trip. There are daily 30-minute flights to Bird Island.

Car hire: Cars are available for hire from approximately Rs 120 per day. Car hire firms: Avis, tel: 22711; Holiday car hire, tel: 22860; Victoria car hire, tel: 76314; Petit car hire, tel: 22353; Parcou self-drive car hire, tel: 23317; Leisure car hire, tel: 22447; Nelson car hire, tel: 22923; Kojak car hire, tel: 76535; Union Vale car hire, tel: 23252; Phoenix car hire, tel: 23446; Equatoria car hire, tel: 23901; Praslin car rentals, tel: 33219.

BANKS

Barclays Bank International, PO Box 167, Victoria, Mahé and the Standard Bank, PO Box 241, Victoria, Mahé, are the only commercial banks on the islands. Barclays have offices in Beau Vallon on Mahé and in Grand Anse on Praslin.

TOURIST OFFICES

The Seychelles Tourist Board has an office at Kingsgate House Victoria (PO Box 92) open Monday-Friday 0800-1200 and 1330-1600, Saturday 0800-1200. Overseas representation is through Seychelles Tourist Information with the following offices:

London: tel: 01-580 7765;

Paris: 7ème étage, 53 rue Francois ler, Paris 75008, France, tel: 256-39-53;

Frankfurt: Goethestrasse 11, 6 Frankfurt 1, tel: 0611/285428;
Johannesburg: 703 Pan Africa House, Bree/Troye Streets, Johannesburg 2001, tel: 23-3062;
Nairobi: PO Box 30702, Nairobi, Kenya, tel: 25103/26744.

MAHÉ

The largest island, where 90% of the population lives, Mahé is the centre of the tourist industry. Much of it is surrounded by a coral reef and the warm, blue waters are both safe for swimming and clean. Skin-diving, deep-sea fishing, sailing, water-skiing and the less demanding pursuits of sun-bathing and picnicking are all available in one of the world's most spectacular and lovely tropical settings.

Victoria, the capital and port, on the north east side of Mahé, is the only town of any size. It is a quaint, rather ramshackle place, the central point of which is a statue of Queen Victoria and a miniature Big Ben. The clock chimes twice, once on the hour and again a few minutes later in case the sleepy islanders missed the first strike. Indian and Chinese shops with wide verandahs and tin roofs line the main streets. Local handcrafts such as baskets, straw hats, carved fishbone, tortoise-shell and exotic sea-shells can be bought at reasonable prices.

Victoria is the business centre of the islands, and possesses all the normal services like banks, a tourist information office, travel agents and airline offices and a post office.

A little out of town on rising ground with the magnificent mountains of Morne Seychellois and the Trois Frères soaring above, is State House—a classic white-painted colonial mansion with wide verandahs, green lawns and cool colonnaded interiors. Botanical gardens and a museum are on view to the public.

Hotels

Beau Vallon Bay Hotel, Beau Vallon. 184 rooms, tel: 22141. Cable: Beautel. 4km from Victoria. All rooms have private balcony or patio. Swimming pool.
Mahé Beach Hotel, Port Glaud. 177 rooms, tel: 78451. Cable: Mahsey. 16km from Victoria. Several restaurants and bars as well as a night-club. Tennis, squash, croquet, bowls and putting-green available. Swimming pool.
Reef Hotel, Anse aux Pins. 150 rooms, tel: 76254. Cable: Reefotel. Tennis and golf available. Swimming pool.
Coral Strand Hotel, Beau Vallon. 103 rooms, tel: 22036. Cable: Colstrand. 5km from Victoria. Scuba diving can be arranged and equipment hired on the premises. Swimming pool.
Fisherman's Cove Hotel, Bel Ombre. 38 rooms, tel: 22552. Cable: Fisherman. 5km from Victoria. Guests can swim from Beqau Vallon Beach. Swimming pool.
Vista do Mar, Glacis. 24 rooms, tel: 23351. Cable: Visdomar. 8km from Victoria. Swimming pool.
Pirates Arms Hotel, Victoria. 24 rooms, tel: 22202. Cable: Pirate. Swimming pool.
Residence Danzilles, Bel Ombre. 21 rooms, tel: 23901. Cable: Danzilles 7km from Victoria. Pleasant gardens with seawater pool built into the granite rocks.
Casuarina Beach Guest House. 12 rooms, tel: 76211. Cable: Casuarina. 14km from Victoria. Sandy beach and nearby coral reef provide excellent snorkeling.
Bougainville Hotel, Anse Royale. 13 rooms, tel: 76334. Cable: Bougainville. 21km from Victoria.
Sunset Hotel, Glacis. 15 rooms, tel: 23227. Cable: Sunset 7km from Victoria. Creole cuisine is a speciality.
Auberge Louis XVII, La Louise. 9 rooms, tel: 22611. Cable: Dauphin. Swimming pool.
Bel Air Hotel, Bel Air, Victoria. 8 rooms, tel: 22616. Cable: Hotel Belair. 1km from Victoria. Overlooks the harbour.

Victoria town centre

Glacis Hotel, Glacis. 8 rooms, tel: 23213. Cable: Glacishotel. 7km from Victoria.

Northolme Hotel, Glacis. 9 rooms, tel: 23222. Cable: Northholme. 6km from Victoria.

Le Niol Guest House, Le Niol. 7 rooms, tel: 23262. Cable: Powerhouse.

Abbeville Hotel, La Misère. 6 rooms, tel: 78338. Cable: Abbeville. 8km from Victoria. Creole and Chinese cuisine available.

La Charrette, La Misère. 8 rooms, tel: 78334. 8km from Victoria. European and Creole cuisine.

Mountain Rise Hotel, Sans Souci. 5 rooms, tel: 22605. Cable: Hunt. 3km from Victoria. Panoramic view of Victoria Harbour.

Harbour View Guest House. 8 rooms, tel: 22473. Cable: Seyharbour. 2km from Victoria.

Villa Carol, Machabee. 4 rooms, tel: 23445. 9km from Victoria.

Belle Vue Guest House, Pointe Conan. 2 rooms, tel: 22926. Cable: Adam. 2km north of Victoria. Swimming pool.

Carefree Guest House, Anse aux Pins. Tel: 6237. Cable: Leon Monthy. 2km from Airport, 12km from Victoria.

Palm Grove Guest House, Mare Anglaise. 2 rooms, tel: 22624. Close to Beau Vallon Beach.

Turtle Bay Apartments, Anse aux Pins.

12 self-catering apartments, with maid and caretaking services available. Tel: 76212. Cable: Castle. A safe swimming beach is within easy walking distance and a self drive car per apartment is included in the weekly tariff.

OTHER ISLANDS

Praslin, about 50km from Mahé is like a wild tropical garden. At its centre is the beautiful Valle de Mai, where the coco-de-mer palms grow to a height of 30m.

La Digue is considered by many to be the most beautiful island of all. There are no tarred roads and no cars; transport is by ox-cart.

The other more accessible islands all have their own spectacular features and fascinating birdlife, among them Cousin, Fregate and Bird Island. Except for Praslin none of the outer islands have airstrips—they can only be reached by boat.

Hotels
Moyenne Island
Maison Moyenne. 2 rooms. Cable: Moyenne. Set on small island 20 minutes by boat from Port Victoria. Self-catering although Creole cuisine can be arranged.

Praslin
Paradise Hotel, Cote d'Or. 32 rooms, tel:

33355/33356. Cable: Paradiseotel. Palm thatched chalets.

Chateau de Feuilles, Pointe Cabris. 9 rooms, tel: 33316. Cable: Chateau. Swimming pool.

Indian Ocean Fishing Club, Grand 'Anse. 10 rooms, tel: 33324. Cable: Marlin. On the beachfront.

Village du Pecheur, Anse Volbert. 4 rooms, tel: 33342. On the beach.

La Digue

Gregoire's Island Lodge, La Reunion. 10 rooms, tel: 34233. Cable: Gregoires. Creole cuisine is a speciality.

Chabanes des Anges, La Reunion. 9 rooms, tel: 34237. Cable: Stange. Faces the beach. Creole cuisine and regular beach barbecues.

Choppy's Bungalow, La Reunion. 4 rooms, tel: 34244. Cable: Coppys. Exclusively Creole food. Beside sandy beach.

Fregate Island

Plantation House. 4 rooms. Tel: 22717. Cable: Sursav. Creole cuisine.

Bird Island

Bird Island Lodge. 17 rooms, tel: 22768. Creole cuisine.

HISTORY

The first reliable record of the Seychelles dates from 1609 when a British naval expedition landed there. There was no settlement until the 18th century, but it seems likely that the islands were known to Persian, Arab and Indian sailors from the 12th century, and to Portuguese navigators from the 16th century. The French explored the islands in 1742 and 1744 and set up a 'Stone of Possession' on Mahé in 1756. The first French settlers with their African slaves arrived in 1777. They named the islands after Vicomte Moreau de Séchelles, Minister of Finance in the Louis XV Government. Mahé was named in honour of the French Governor of Mauritius and Réunion.

The early settlers lived off a lucrative trade from the islands' timber and the giant tortoises. When this was stopped by the authorities in 1789, the colonists turned to agriculture. On the eve of the French Revolution the islands' population was still only 69 French, 32 Coloured (of mixed race) and 487 slaves.

During the Napoleonic Wars the Seychelles changed hands several times, but were finally taken by the British in 1810. They were ceded, with Mauritius, to Britain by the Treaty of Paris in 1814, and were administered as a single British colony for nearly a century.

Slavery was abolished in 1834 and later in the 19th century there was an influx of Chinese and Indian traders. Some degree of internal autonomy was granted to the Seychelles in 1872, and separation from Mauritius began in 1888 when an administrator (he became Governor in 1897) was appointed. Executive and Administrative Councils were established the following year, and in 1903 Seychelles became a separate Crown colony.

General elections, for four seats in the Legislative Council, were first held in 1948. A new constitution with a single Governing Council, consisting of eight elected, four nominated and three ex officio members, was introduced in 1967 and the first elections with full adult suffrage were held in December of that year. The first election and the next one in 1970 were both won by James Mancham, and his Seychelles Democratic Party (SDP) who favoured integration with Britain. The opposition, the Seychelles People's United Party (SPUP), led by Albert René, advocated independence. Subsequently Mr Mancham accepted the principle of independence and formed a coalition with SPUP. Independence came on 29 June 1976, with Mr Mancham as President and Mr René as Prime Minister. In 1977 a coup d'état brought Mr René the leadership of the country.

SIERRA LEONE

Sierra Leone's tourist potential has only just begun to be exploited, although the palm-fringed sandy bays along the Freetown peninsula are among the finest beaches in the world, the fishing and water-skiing are good, and there is a casino.

A country of 72,000 sq km and about the size of Austria, Sierra Leone's northern borders with Guinea follow the Great Scarcies River, and its southern borders with Liberia are the Mano and Moro Rivers. The country has three different types of terrain. A flat belt of lowland up to 112km wide stretches along the coast. Behind it is the central forest, drained by eight principal rivers, with much of the land cleared for agriculture, rising to a mountainous plateau near the eastern frontier.

The most fertile part of the country is the forest around Bo, Kenema and Koidu, where palm kernels, coffee and cocoa are grown mainly in smallholdings. More economically profitable are the diamond diggings in this area.

The two main ethnic groups are the Mende and the Temne, each comprising 30% of the population. The Mende live in the south and speak a similar language to the Lokko and the Sherbro, two smaller groups who live in the same region. The Temne live in the north and have close contacts with the Limba, Susu,

Fulani and other smaller groups in that part. The Kono who occupy the richest part of the country, represent about 5% of the population.

The settlers in Freetown and the descendants of resident traders formed the basis of Krio (or Creole) society—a group that accounts for only 2% of the population, but which has provided many of its intellectuals and professional men.

The Krios have been par excellence the

upholders of Western traditions and Christianity. The older generation is still strongly traditional and there is often a mid-Victorian flavour to their style. Villages around Freetown are named Hastings, Sussex, Wellington and Waterloo.

However, the majority of Sierra Leoneans follow a more typically African culture. Internal rule by chiefs is backed up by the traditional religions. Secret societies still flourish, particularly the Poro society. These have always fulfilled useful social and political functions, educating the youth in local customs, hygiene and self-discipline; they have also played a major part in maintaining social stability and in keeping traditional culture alive despite the extensive penetration of both Christian and Muslim ideas. Many of the dances—which are performed by the internationally known Sierra Leone Dance Troupe—stem from the traditions of these secret societies.

Although English is the official language, most people speak their local languages and all speak Krio (or pidgin) which has been developed into a rich colourful language with a literature of its own.

WILDLIFE

Monkeys and baboons are common and crocodiles inhabit the rivers. There are also plenty of snakes, not all dangerous, and scorpions. Game is rare, although there are some duiker, bush-cow and civet cats. In the far north-east, pigmy hippo and elephant are occasionally seen.

Sporting sealine and underwater fishermen can catch jack, large mackerel, barracuda and shark. There are few instances of barracuda or shark attacking humans in these waters.

GENERAL INFORMATION

Area: 71,740 sq km.
Population: 3 million.

Altitude: The coastal half of the country average 120m; the highlands 480m.
Capital: Freetown.
Head of State: President Siaka Stevens.
Government: The country became a republic in 1971. the President is the Head of State and the Head of the Government, assisted by a Prime Minister who is also Vice-President. The House of Representatives consists of 85 elected Members and 12 Chiefs. The governing party is the All People's Congress.
Date of independence: 27 April 1961.
Languages: English is the official language. Krio (or pidgin) is widely spoken. There are about 12 main African languages of which the most important are Mende (in the south) and Temne (in the north).
Religions: The majority remains traditional; 25% of the population is Muslim, particularly in Northern Province; the remainder are Christian, concentrated on the Freetown Peninsula.
Currency: The Leone (Le) divides into 100 cents. Le2 = £1 sterling; Le1.16 = US$1.
Time: GMT.

HOW TO GET THERE

By air: Sierra Leone Airways, in conjunction with British Caledonian, operates several flights a week from London. Other international airlines flying to Sierra Leone are: Egypt Air, Ghana Airways, Nigeria Airways, MEA, Air Afrique, UTA, KLM, Lufthansa, Interflug, CSA, Air Guinée, Air Mali.

The international airport is at Lungi which lies across the harbour from Freetown so that the journey, by road and ferry, to the town or the Cape Sierra Hotel takes two hours.

Visas and health regulations: All travellers require a valid passport; nationals of Commonwealth countries need an entry permit; all others need a visa. These should be applied for well in advance at a Sierra Leone diplomatic mission. An entry permit or visa is normally given for a period not exceeding one month, although on application the period may be extended up to a maximum of three months. Travel regulations are liable to change at short notice and intending visitors should consult their travel agents before leaving. International certificates of vaccination against smallpox and yellow fever are required and against cholera for those arriving from infected areas. Cholera and TAB vaccinations are, however, recommended.

Dutiable goods
Personal baggage is normally admitted free of duty. This includes one camera, one portable typewriter, one bottle of spirits and one bottle of wine, half-pint of perfume, and 200 cigarettes or the equivalent in cigars or tobacco. A special permit is required for arms or ammunition.

Currency regulations
Visitors may take in unlimited foreign currency provided they declare it on arrival; any unused balance may be taken out on departure. Visitors are not allowed to acquire currency other than

Leones during their stay.

CLIMATE
The best time to go to Sierra Leone is during the dry season, November to April, when temperatures in Freetown vary from 24° to 30°C. There is usually a pleasant sea breeze on the coast and sometimes, especially in December and January, the dry, cool, dust-filled harmattan wind blows from the Sahara. During the rainy season from May to October torrential downpours bring as much as 325cm of rain to the Freetown area, diminishing to 316cm a year in the interior near Kabala.
What to wear: Plenty of lightweight clothes and cotton underwear are essential. In the rainy season an umbrella or lightweight raincoat is needed.
Health precautions: Malaria has been virtually eradicated from the Freetown-Peninsula but prophylactics should still be taken. Cholera appeared in the country in 1970 so it is advisable for all visitors to be vaccinated against this and against typhoid (TAB). Only filtered and boiled water should be drunk. Raw fruit and vegetables should be well washed before eating.

ACCOMMODATION, FOOD
Accommodation in Sierra Leone is limited and reservations should be made well in advance. In the interior, hotels are rare: they exist at Bo and Koidu and one at Magburaka which is now little used. There are some very plain rest-houses; guests must bring their own supplies and linen. Apply to the Hotels and Tourist Board for information.

Various restaurants in the capital serve English, French, Armenian and Lebanese food while one can sample African dishes at the Cape Sierra Hotel.
Tipping: All hotels add a 10% service charge to their bills. It is not customary to tip taxi drivers.

Street scene, Freetown

TRANSPORT

Air: Sierra Leone Airways operate flights from Hastings airport (14 miles from Freetown) every day except Sunday to Kenema, Yengema, Bo, Bonthe, Gbangbatoke and by request to Marampa and Port Loko.

Road: There are some good all-weather roads. the remainder are laterite, often very poor, pot-holed and dusty or, in the rainy season, muddy and impassable. The two main arteries are Freetown to Kenema and Lungi to Kabala. A fleet of 60 buses serves the whole country.

In the capital taxis are readily available but carry no meters so the price must be fixed in advance. It is possible to hire a taxi for a whole day.

BANKS

Standard Bank, 9 Wallace Johnson Street, P.O. Box 1155, Freetown, and Barclays International, P.O. Box 12, Freetown, have main offices in Freetown and branches elsewhere in the country. The Sierra Leone Commercial Bank, 30 Walpole Street, Freetown, opened in 1973.

Business hours:
Banks: 0800-1300 Monday to Friday; 0800-1100 Saturday.
Government: 0800-1230; 1400-1545 Monday to Friday. 0800-1200 on alternate Saturdays. Shops: 0800-1200 or 1230, 1400-1630 or 1700 Monday to Friday; 0800-1230 Saturday.

PUBLIC HOLIDAYS

New Year's Day; Good Friday; Easter Monday; Republic Day, 19 April; Independence Day, 27 April; Whit Monday; Bank Holiday; Christmas Day; Boxing Day. Muslim holidays which vary in date are also observed: Eid-ul-Adha; Moulidun-Nabi; and Eid-ul-Fitr. The President's birthday, 24 August, is also celebrated.

FOREIGN EMBASSIES IN FREETOWN

Egypt, 20 Pultney Street; France, 2 Pademba Road; The Gambia, 3 George Street; West Germany, 18 Siaka Stevens Street; Ghana, 18 Pultney Street; Guinea, 4 Liverpool Street; Lebanon, Leone House, Siaka Stevens Street; Liberia, 30 Brookfield Road; Nigeria, 21 Charlotte Street; UK, Standard Bank Building, Wallace Johnson Street; USA, Walpole Street.

FREETOWN

Freetown retains much of its old-world charm, slow-moving and decorous, with the people variously dressed in staid European suits or in colourful local costume or gay locally made shirts and slacks.

The 18th-century timber-framed houses still to be found between Kroo and Susan's Bay are rapidly giving way to modern architecture. The famous Cotton Tree, half way down Siaka Stevens Street, near the Law Court, is reputed to be 300 years old. In the hills behind the city is the new campus of Fourah Bay, West Africa's oldest university, established as a school in 1827.

Hotels and restaurants are springing up along the beautiful, shark-free Lumley beach, 5km from Freetown, and glorious sands stretch southward some 50km down the coast. There are numerous sightseeing attractions in the vicinity worth visiting such as Bureh Town and Bunce Island—an old slave fort.

Hotels
Paramount Hotel, P.O. Box 574, tel: 24531, modern hotel in the centre of town, 68 air-conditioned rooms with bathroom or shower, international cuisine or local specialities.
Cape Sierra Hotel, P.O. Box 610, tel: 024-266, new modern hotel on Lumley Beach, 75 air-conditioned rooms with bathrooms, international cuisine and

local specialities, night-club, swimming pool.

Brookfields Hotel, New England, tel: 40875, just outside the centre of town, 72 rooms with shower, some in chalets in garden.

Bintumani Hotel, Aberdeen, Freetown, brand new tourist hotel on the beach.

Restaurants

In addition to the hotels the **Atlantic** specialises in French and Lebanese food, with dancing. The **Cape Club** is recommended for grills, snacks and dancing (open weekday evenings only). The **Lighthouse Restaurant** specialises in Armenian food. All three are at Lumley. In town is **La Tropicana** with dancing.

Shopping and markets

Freetown has a wide range of shops. Visit the covered market at King Jimmy Wharf and the markets at East Street. Sierra Leone offers a range of curios and is particularly noted for its *gara* materials.

Tourist information

Ministry of Tourism Arts and Crafts Centre, Government Wharf, and Tourist and Hotel Board, 28 Siaka Stevens Street, Freetown.

HISTORY

The early inhabitants of the interior seem to have lived in small kingdoms dependent on subsistence agriculture. An account of this period can be found in Christopher Fyfe's *History of Sierra Leone.*

Sierra Leone's modern history begins with the arrival of the Portuguese traders in the 18th century. The main attraction for European traders was the slave trade. When the British gained ascendancy, control of the area was vested in the Sierra Leone Company until 1808 when Britain declared the peninsula a colony.

In the 19th century increasing use was made of the new educated elite in Free-

town. Krios dominated the professions and they were appointed to senior posts in the civil service; many came to play a prominent role in other capitals of British West Africa. Things began to change at the turn of the century with the building of the railway, the opening of the Hill Station reservation for Europeans, the arrival of the first Syrian shopkeepers (always referred to as 'Lebanese'), and with greater pressures from London for the colony to pay its way.

In 1924 some elected Members were admitted to the Legislative Council under a strictly limited franchise and a new constitution was proposed in 1948 which gave the majority on the Executive and Legislative Councils to the people. This liberal reform moved the political power to the majority group—who were the people of the interior.

Having lost ascendancy, most of the Krios grouped into the Sierra Leone People's Party, led by the country's first Prime Minister, Sir Milton Margai. On his death, in 1964, he was succeeded by his brother, Sir Albert, until the closely contested elections of 1967, the results of which were controversial, but victory was claimed by the All People's Congress (APC) party, dominant in the north, led by Dr. Siaka Stevens. When he tried to form a Government, the army commander, Brigadier Lansana, proclaimed martial law but was himself immediately ousted by a group of senior officers who formed the National Reformation Council.

Two mutinies in 1968 brought chaos, out of which the army called back Siaka Stevens who was sworn in as Prime Minister. In 1971 he had to rely on help from neighbouring Guinea after an attempted coup. In April, 1971, Sierra Leone became a republic. A general election in 1973 resulted in an outright victory for the APC. Disturbances by students and workers in 1977 were followed by another general election, but the APC retained its majority.

SOMALIA

Somalia, officially known as the Somali Democratic Republic since the 1969 military coup, has so far remained virtually untouched by the tourist wave spreading over Africa. Although it has the second largest coastline on the African continent—stretching for nearly 3,200km along the shores of the Indian Ocean, around the Horn of Africa and along the Gulf of Aden—facilities for the tourist are largely lacking. The National Agency for Tourism has recently, however, embarked on a hotel programme and on improving facilities in the game parks.

Those who do visit the country will find people who are warm and friendly, beaches which are unspoilt and wildlife which is colourful and varied.

THE LAND AND THE PEOPLE

Somalia is a hot, arid country, with a nomadic population, and scenery ranging from mountains in the north, through flat semi-desert plains, to the sub-tropical region of the south. Separated from the sea by a narrow coastal plain, the mountains gradually slope south and west to the central, largely waterless, plateau which occupies most of the country. While there are some ports, notably Mogadishu, Kismayu and Marka, good natural harbours are rare. The beaches are protected from sharks by a coral reef that runs from north of Mogadishu to the Kenyan border in the south. They are among the longest beaches in the world, with many rare shells, including the Marginalis cowrie.

The only two perennial rivers, the Juba and the Shebelle, both rise in the Ogaden region of Ethiopia. Most of the agricultural land lies on the banks of these two rivers. Much of the interior—waterless

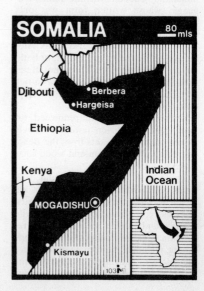

329

and with little vegetation—is of little use and remains isolated, although an ambitious road programme will open up the remoter regions.

Somalia experiences little change in the seasons, except in the areas above 1,600m. Most of the country is uniformly hot, with temperatures in the northern coastal towns rising to 42°C between June and September. The coastal regions are generally hot and humid while the interior is hot and dry. Rainfall is generally higher in the south, varying from 30 to 50cm a year.

The population is concentrated in the coastal towns, in the northern areas with the highest rainfall and in the south near the two rivers. A large nomadic population is lightly scattered throughout the interior. Since the 1974 drought the Government has persuaded many nomads to settle as farmers or fishermen in new communities.

A tall, lithe people, the Somalis form a cultural, linguistic and religious unit, with Islam the dominant religion for over a millenium. The idiosyncratic Somali language, whose written form was only finally decided in 1972, has now become the national language.

All educated Somalis also speak Arabic and either Italian or English, or both. Possibly because Somali was not traditionally a written language, it has a rich literature of narrative poetry of exceptional quality.

Somali craftsmen are renowned for their gold and silver jewellery, finely woven cloth and baskets from the Benadir region. Meerschaum and wood carvings are also produced.

Traditional dance, music and folk songs still flourish. Ritualistic dances are meant to placate evil forces and spirits, diseases, crop failures, marauding wild animals and foreign invaders, while recreational dances celebrate the happy events, including the coming of the rains, the harvest, marriages and births, the arrival of important visitors and the many and frequent traditional feasts.

Poetry and drama have both seen considerable revival since independence and performances are given regularly in Mogadishu's National Theatre.

WILDLIFE

Lying astride the division between the near-desert and the bush territory of East Africa, Somalia has a wide selection of wildlife. The fauna has remained relatively undisturbed by development. The greatest profusion of wildlife is in the south near the two rivers, and includes elephant, rhino, hippo, giraffe, zebra, hartebeeste, gazelle, the greater and lesser kudu and the smaller antelope species. Animals in the northern and drier areas include the rare oryx and the wild ass.

GENERAL INFORMATION

Area: 637,657 sq.km.

Population: 4 million.

Altitude: Rising from sea level to mountains over 2,600 m in the north.

Capital: Mogadishu.

Head of State: Major-General Mohamed Siad Barre.

Government: One-party socialist state under Somali Revolutionary Party.

Date of independence: 1 July 1960.

Languages: Somali, Arabic, English and Italian; the latter three were the official languages until October 1972 when Somali was adopted.

Religion: Islam.

Currency: Somali shilling. 10.81 Somali shillings=£1 sterling; 6.29 Somali shillings=US$1.00.

Time: GMT+3

HOW TO GET THERE

By Air

Somalia can be reached directly from Rome, Cairo, Moscow, Khartoum, Addis Ababa, Asmara, Jeddah, Aden or Nairobi by air, and is served by five international airlines: Alitalia, Egyptair, Aeroflot, Alyemda, and the Republic's own Somali Airlines which also connects the principal cities inside the country in a network of regular flights.

Visas and health regulations

A visa is necessary for the visitor to Somalia and this is obtainable at Somali Embassies in Washington, Paris, Rome, London, Bonn, Brussels, Addis Ababa, Cairo, Khartoum, Jeddah, Dar es Salaam and Lusaka; from the Somali Consul-General in Aden; or from the Italian Embassy in other cities. It is important that a visa be obtained *before* entering Somalia.

Certificates of vaccination against smallpox and inoculation against yellow fever and cholera are essential. Vaccinations against typhus, typhoid and tetanus are advisable, but not essential.

Dutiable goods

No customs duty is exacted for normal personal effects. Duty will be charged on any commercial items.

Cars may be imported duty-free for a period of three months on presentation of a carnet de passage or on personal surety by a resident of the Republic. Extension beyond three months can be obtained by application to the customs authorities. If the car is subsequently sold in the Republic its value will be assessed and the appropriate duty charged.

Currency regulations

Visitors staying in the country for three months or less may import or export any amount of foreign currency. Import and export of East African shilling and Somali shillings is restricted. On arrival one has to pay 2s. for a foreign currency declaration form and 2s. for a counter-declaration form on departure.

Visitors should note that exchange of currency except through a bank or authorised hotel is prohibited in the Republic. An exchange control form is issued to visitors on arrival and should be filled in each time foreign currency is exchanged during the visitor's stay.

CLIMATE

The nomadic cycle of movements follows the climatic pattern of four seasons: the *jilal* starts around January and is the harshest time, when vegetation dries up and the search for water begins in earnest. *Gu*, the first rainy season, generally lasts from March to June. August is the start of the dry season of *hagaa* when dust clouds are everywhere and the heavier monsoon winds blow. The second rainy season starts around September. This is called *dayr* and lasts till December.

What to wear: Dress is informal and lightweight. There is no objection to bikinis on the beach.

Health precautions: Somalia is virtually free of such diseases as yellow fever, smallpox and sleeping sickness but malaria is endemic and a prophylactic should be taken for a fortnight before the visit, during the visit and for a fortnight after.

ACCOMMODATION AND FOOD

Hotels of European standard exist in Mogadishu and Hargeysa. Other accommodation facilities are in Berbera, Borama, Burao, Afgoi, Marka and Kismayu, usually at least one reasonable commercial hotel. There is also a system of Government rest houses in many places which provide four to ten beds. Accommodation facilities are provided in the national park south west of Kismayu and the one north of Hargeysa.

There are good restaurants in the larger towns, particularly in the capital, which serve Somali, European and Chinese food. The lobsters, prawns, squid and other fish are excellent.

TRANSPORT

There are restrictions on travel outside Mogadishu. It is advisable to check with the authorities on arrival. Roads connect all the Republic's towns. Road communications do not yet cover the entire country.

Travellers wishing to see more than the main towns, and their surroundings within a 150 km radius, will probably need to use the Somali Airlines internal services.

Improvements to roads to the Game Parks in Lac Badana and Gedka-Dabley, as well as the construction of suitable landing strips, are being undertaken.

Car hire: In the larger cities there are taxi services. In Mogadishu, in addition to the regular saloon-car taxis there are little 'Bee-taxis' constructed around a motor-scooter which do a brisk trade in the city. In Mogadishu, the visitor with an international driving licence can hire a drive-yourself car at reasonable cost. Taxis can also be hired by the hour. It is advisable to fix the tariff beforehand.

BANKS

National Commercial Bank, P.O. Box 203, Mogadishu; branches in principal towns and cities.

PUBLIC HOLIDAYS

Labour Day 1 May, Independence of Somaliland 26 June; Republic's Independence Day 1 July; Revolution Anniversary 21-22 October; first day of the month of Sciaual, after Ramadan Id-El-Fitr and the two following days; 10th day in the month of Dul-Hija-Arafa, and the two following days; first day in the month of Muharram—Muslim New Year's Day; 12th day in the month of Rabi-Al-Wal, Anniversary of the Prophet's birth.

The *Stoon-ka* festival is a stick fight between groups of gaily dressed men

from opposite banks of the Shebelle River at Afgoi, 32 km from Mogadishu, which commemorates the traditional contest used to decide which group would get the best part of the river's water during the dry season.

The International Somali Trade Fair and African film festival is held from 29 September to 12 October (this is a biennial event).

FOREIGN EMBASSIES IN MOGADISHU

Egypt, P.O. Box 74; Ethiopia, Via Benedetti; France, Corso i Luglio, P.O. Box 13; West Germany, Via Muhammed Habi, P.O. Box 17; India, Via Balad, P.O.Box 955; Italy, Via Trevis, P.O. Box 6; Kenya, P.O.Box 618; Pakistan, P.O. Box 339; Sudan, Via Cavour; UK, Via Londra, P.O.Box 1036; USA, Via Primo Luglio; Yemen Arab Republic, Via Primo Luglio; Yemen, People's Democratic Republic, Mnobolyou Street.

MOGADISHU

Lying alongside the Indian Ocean, Mogadishu offers a mixture of Somali and Italian influences. The old quarter of the capital, Hammar Wein, retains signs of the city's former status as a major trading port for the region with an Arabic influence visible in the buildings. One major mosque, Fakhr-Din, dates from the 13th century, and another, Sheikh Abdul Aziz, is of unknown age.

Narrow alleys bustle with traditional craftworkers in gold, silver and cloth. Tourists can order their own jewellery designs in gold and silver in the smith's shops, where the prices remain relatively low.

The National Museum of Somalia, in the former palace of the Sultan of Zanzibar, is worth a visit. The building has beautifully carved doors and inside is some fine silverwork and a maritime room. The Museum is generally open

Literacy campaign for nomads

from 0900 to 1300.

Four hotels are of international standard: the new **Juba Hotel** (swimming pool); the **Croce del Sud**; the **Shebelli**; and **Hotel Rugta Taleh** (motel suites). The **Shebelli** is also the centre of the National Agency for Tourism.

Eating out is not luxurious, but cheap and fairly good. There are a number of Italian restaurants, as well as places offering local specialities. The restaurant **Azan's** of the Shebelli Hotel, with views over the city, is popular, particularly during the month of Ramadan when only restaurants in tourist hotels are allowed to open in daylight hours. The open-air restaurant, the **Trocadero**, of the Croce del Sud is worth experiencing. The **Cappuccetto Nero** near the Croce del Sud, and the Chinese restaurant the **Ming Sing**. At these places seafood, especially the lobsters and prawns, are good and cheap. Somali mangoes and grapefruit are marvellous.

By day, the city's greatest attraction is the shark-free beach. Visitors may join the American Club which offers swimming and inexpensive food. The Golf Club is a popular social rendezvous. Night-clubs with local bands playing European and African music include the **Lido** and **Azan's**.

OTHER TOWNS

Capital of the former British Protectorate, **Hargeysa** (population 100,000) is situated in the highlands of the north. It is the only city other than Mogadishu with a modern airport and hotels of European standard. Some international flights stop at Hargeysa, which is a livestock trading centre.

Tourists should make their arrangements with the National Agency for Tourism for visits to the city and the smaller towns of **Afgoi**, an agricultural centre, and the old seaport of **Marka**, both near the capital, and **Berbera**, the seaport on the northern coast, and **Kismayu** on the southern coast near the Kenyan border.

An expansion programme for Kismayu airport has begun and the Government hopes to make it into a major centre for the national parks in the south. Kismayu's architecture displays evidence of both Portuguese and Arab styles.

NATIONAL PARKS

Somalia has three game parks and ten game reserves. The game reserves fall into three categories: absolute reserves (Lac Badana, Gedka-Dabley, Mogadishu and Mandere); controlled game reserves (Borama, Bush-Bush and the Juba left bank areas) and partial game reserves (Jowhar, Beled Weyne and Bulo-Burti areas). The Kismayu National Park in the south west contains the widest variety of animals, including all the species common to East Africa and also many rarer species such as the Soemmering gazelle, the Speke gazelle and the Somali dibtag.

The game park north of Hargeysa in the mountainous area bordering the Gulf of Aden has such rare animals as the wild ass and klipspringer. A new national park was recently opened within easy reach of the capital.

Roads are passable to the absolute reserves of Lac Badana and Gedka-Dabley. A number of parks and reserves can be reached from Kismayu and Mogadishu. Tourist and hunting lodges are being constructed at Lac Badana and Bush-Bush—a controlled game reserve—as well as in other areas.

HISTORY

Rock paintings and cave inscriptions in the northern region, such as those at Gaanlibah and Gelweita, near Las Khoreh, date from the early Stone Age. As early as 1500 BC, the port of Mogadishu was known to the Egytians, who called the country the 'Land of Punt'. Mogadishu also traded with the Phoenicians and supplied most of the frankincense and myrrh to the pre-Muslim kingdoms of the of the Arabian peninsula. In the 12th and 13th centuries Mogadishu's trading links extended to Thailand and China, as well as East Africa and the Middle East; while Berbera, on the north coast, Marka, a small seaport south of Mogadishu, and Zeila, now a ruined city near the Djibouti border, were also major trading centres.

Islam reached Somalia in the 7th century from Saudi Arabia across the Gulf of Aden. By the 13th century, Zeila was not only the capital of a powerful city-State but also one of the acknowledged centres of Islam. The ruler of Zeila in the mid-16th century beat back joint Portuguese-Ethiopian attacks, capturing the Abyssinian highlands.

The Sultanate of Oman—which had extended its control over Zanzibar and the East African coast and as far east as Pakistan—took control of southern Somalia. Britain, having established a base in Aden early in the 19th century, announced a protectorate over northern Somalia in 1927, while the French later occupied the port of Djibouti, which they controlled. The Omani-Zanzibari dynasty, which had occupied Mogadishu in 1871, sold its area to Italy in 1889. In the same decade, between 1881 and 1886, Britain extended its control in the north by more treaties with local chieftains. In 1898, Italy occupied its colony.

A major rebellion against colonial rule broke out in the south east corner of the British Protectorate in 1899, led by a famous religious leader whom the Europeans called 'Mad Mullah of Somaliland', Mohammed Abdille Hassan; it lasted until the Mullah's death in 1921. Joint operations by Ethiopian, British and Italian troops—which included the first use of aircraft for military purposes in Africa—eventually penned him up in a remote area, but failed to destroy his movement. It eventually disintegrated shortly before his death under the impact of a smallpox epidemic.

The Italian colony was occupied during World War II by British and South African troops; but the United Nations handed the territory back to Italy in 1949 on a ten-year trusteeship basis. With the preparation for independence of the Italian trusteeship territory, the British came under pressure in the northern territory. The two territories bacame independent within five days of each other in June and July 1960 and immediately united to form the Somalia Republic.

A series of multi-party Governments succeeded each other until the army, led by Major-General Mohammed Siad Barre, took power in October 1969 in a bloodless coup. In 1974 Somalia joined the Arab League. The Government pursues policies of socialism and self-reliance.

In 1977 Somalia made a major bid to annex the Ogaden region of Ethiopia, which is peopled by Somali-speaking nomads.

SOUTH AFRICA

South Africa is a land of great and often stunning contrasts; of fertile green valleys and harsh near-desert conditions; of rugged mountains and endless silver beaches along two oceans; of hot summers and cold winter conditions; of bustling 20th century cities and settlements of hovels; of great wealth and bitter poverty; of dynamic growth and artificial restrictions to growth; of freedom for some and denial of basic human rights for the majority.

It is a country of surging confidence and of deep fears—a land in which millions of people are being forcibly uprooted to create a more rigidly, racially, divided society in pursuit of the country's official policy of *apartheid*. This quite simply means separation: physically separating whites, blacks, Coloureds (people of mixed race) and Asians. Both socially and politically it is a unique country.

The sharp contrasts will affect visitors differently—a black traveller, if he could secure a visa, would find himself seriously restricted in his freedom of movement; the white traveller, by contrast, will find an open welcome from a hospitable country: neither will find it easy to see what lies behind the economic dynamism of the society, or beyond the unsurpassed physical splendour. The inviting travel posters are misleading only in what they don't tell.

THE LAND AND THE PEOPLE

South Africa has three major natural regions; the plateau, the mountains and the coastal belt. The high plateau has sharp escarpments which rise above the flat plains, or *veld,* broken up only by the characteristic flat-topped hills. These are some of the oldest hills on earth, flattened by constant weathering. Occasional outcrops of granite are sometimes associated with immensely rich mineral deposits, particularly gold, of which the most famous is the ridge rising gently from the plateau known as the Witwatersrand (the Ridge of the White Waters). The vegetation is open grassland, changing to bush in the northern Transvaal and to thornveld in the arid south west which receives only 5cm of rain a

335

year, or in poor years none at all.

Despite two main river systems, the Limpopo and the Orange, most of the plateau lacks surface water. On the eastern rim of the plateau soar the Drakensberg range (the Dragon Mountains) whose highest peak, the Mont-aux-Sources, rises to 3,482m. Rainfall is abundant in these mountains but the soil is thin and often eroded.

The coast is lined with fine sandy beaches and rocky coves. The Mediterranean climate gives Cape Town and the south western Cape Province dry summers (October to March) and wet winters with shrub-type vegetation such as the pink protea—the national wild plant. The Cape Range, which includes the famous landmark of Table Mountain, runs along the sea.

Inland is the arid Karoo which rises to the high plateau. Further north, the dramatic Wild Coast of the Eastern Province, the Ciskei and Transkei softens into lusher sub-tropical forests of palm and wild banana on the coast of Natal and Zululand.

South Africa is the most highly urbanised and industrialised country in the continent, a development it owes mainly to its rich mineral resources, its pool of cheap black labour and its extensive network of communications and power. The major conurbation is the string of towns along the golden Reef, or Rand, which centres on Johannesburg. The Reef forms one side of the Vaal Triangle, the industrial-mining 'Ruhr' of South Africa. The administrative capital, Pretoria, is by contrast quiet and spacious, but industry is developing rapidly in nearby towns like Rosslyn.

The country's other major industrial centres are in and around its ports—Cape Town, Port Elizabeth, East London and Durban.

Of the 25 million people in South Africa some 4 million are officially classified as 'whites', of whom one third are English-speaking and nearly two thirds are Afrikaans-speaking. The Afrikaners (or Boers, meaning farmers), are a mixture of Dutch, French Huguenots, Germans and English.

The bulk of the population is officially classified 'non-white'—comprising Africans, Coloureds and Asians. The two million Coloureds evolved in the early colonial society of the Cape Province from the Dutch settlers, the brown-skinned San (Bushmen) and Khoikhoi (Hottentots), who were the original inhabitants of that area, and from the Malay slaves of Indonesia. Most of the Coloureds live in the Western Cape. Predominantly Afrikaans-speaking, their culture is largely European.

The Asian community of 700,000 consists mainly if Indians, found mostly in Natal where they were brought to work on the sugar plantations in the 1870s. Many subsequently turned to trade, market-gardening and to skilled and semi-skilled labour. The majority are Hindu.

Two out of every three South Africans are black (about 18 million). Officially designated as Bantu (which simply means 'the people') the blacks themselves prefer the term 'Africans' or 'blacks', they regard 'natives' as a term of opprobrium and 'Bantu' as meaningless and politically offensive.

Under the policy of apartheid—also known as 'Separate Development'—the entire country has been divided into racially exclusive areas to keep the people socially apart. Over 87% of the land is designated for white occupation—and is known as the 'white area'; the other c. 13% is for black occupation: these are the reserves which have been divided into eight 'Bantu Homelands' or 'Bantustans' which, in the ripeness of time, are supposed to achieve their separate independence. There is no land exclusively reserved for Coloureds or Asians. However, every village, town and city is sub-divided into separate areas reserved exclusively for one of the four racial groups. It is a crime for a member of one group to live in a different racial area.

Africans are deemed to be citizens of their own Homeland and have no rights in the 'white areas' where they are officially treated as temporary sojourners under the Government policy of making all black workers into migrants—moving between the work-starved Homelands and the worker-starved 'white areas'. The black workers may stay there only as long as they are 'deemed' to be of useful service to the whites. If they are no longer of use they are declared 'surplus labour appendages' (an offical designation) and are 'endorsed out', that is, forcibly repatriated to the Homelands where they must go through the process of finding new employment. Only a privileged minority of black urban dwellers are partially exempt from this migratory system.

Since the adoption of apartheid as a policy in 1948, over two million blacks, Coloureds and Asians have been uprooted from their former homes to achieve racially exclusive neighbourhoods. Official policy is to allow only African males to come and work for contract periods in the towns leaving their families behind; or, in the case of women, they may not be accompanied by their children. This policy makes migrants of the black workers and furthers the breakdown of African family life. Special privileges are, however, issued to wives to visit their husbands in the 'white areas' for a strictly limited period of 72 hours for the purpose of conception—a phenomenon possibly unique in history.

The Homelands are scattered around the periphery of the 'white areas'. With the partial exception of the Transkei all the others are made up of fragmented areas of land—sometimes, as in the case of the Zulus, over 80 in number; or, as in the case of the Tswana, three areas separated from each other by up to 300 miles. Attempts to reduce this degree of fragmentation have not, so far, proved

successful except in minor areas. Half the Africans live in 'white areas' and others commute daily from the Homelands to work in the white 'border industries'.

The Homelands stretch along the east coast and the northern borders with Botswana, Rhodesia and Mozambique, where the African population is densest. Travelling up the east coat from Grahamstown, one finds the Xhosa people in the Ciskei and Transkei; the Zulu in Kwazulu (in Natal); and the Swazi on the borders of Swaziland. All these speak closely related Nguni languages, some of which have 'click' sounds absorbed from their Khoikhoi and San neighbours long ago. Most of the other black groups in South Africa are related to the Sotho, the Tswana along the Botswana border (in Boputhatswana), the Northern Sotho of Lebowa in the Transvaal, and the Southern Sotho of Basothoqwaqwa in the Orange Free State near Lesotho. Other groups in the Transvaal are the Venda and, near the Rhodesia border, the Tsonga who are joined with the Shangaan in the Gazankulu Homeland. The Ndebele are joined to Lebowa

CULTURE

South Africa is as diverse culturally as it is racially. Its cultural history can be traced on the African side to the San (Bushmen), and on the European side to the early Dutch settlers. Bushman art—mainly realistic portrayals of animals and people painted in reddish, yellow and black tints on cave walls—was prolific. In contrast to the hunters the pastoral Africans traditionally made polychrome pottery, blankets of sheep's wool, elaborate ornaments out of tiny, coloured beads whose patterns had distinct meanings, as well as weapons and tools. Their art still survives. While attempts are being made to foster beadwork industries in the Homelands, modern handicraft centres have already been set up at Papatso, north of Pretoria, and near the Numbi

Gate of the Kruger National Park. North west of Pretoria there is also a fine Ndebele village whose inhabitants wear traditional costumes and sell their craftwork.

On the European cultural side, the principal, and perhaps the most original, flowerings of culture were the simple, but elegant, 18th and 19th century Cape Silver of immigrant German and English smiths, whose work can be seen in collections of Cape Town's Cultural History Museum and Johannesburg's Africana Museum, and in the superb Cape Dutch architectural style and furniture.

South African art has been vigorously sustained both by the European immigrant painters and sculptors and local talent. There are many fine white and black painters whose work is well described in David Lewis' *The Naked Eye*. Permanent collections of modern art are on view at the National Gallery in Cape Town, the City Art Centre in Durban and the Johannesburg Art Gallery.

Afrikaans literature has been created in under a century. It is vigorous, experimental and richly redolent of the local atmosphere, owing very little to its Dutch origins, and has been a crucial element in the nurturing of Afrikaner nationalism.

The South African English writers have produced a number of outstanding poets and novelists from Olive Schreiner, whose *Story of an African Farm* is a minor classic, to Nadine Gordimer, Dan Jacobson and Alan Paton (author of *Cry, the Beloved Country*). Two poets, William Plomer and Roy Campbell, have won universal recognition.

All the major cities have flourishing theatres, which produce mostly imported plays.

The African Music and Theatre Trust has been largely responsible for enabling the country's black talent to break out of the limits imposed by the rigid system of segregation which affects the arts as it does every other aspect of the country's life.

WILDLIFE

Most wild animals of any size have long since been hunted out, except in the national parks. The Kruger National Park, which can be explored from rest camps at all times of the year, has most of the larger species including lion, leopard, elephant and giraffe. The Kwazulu game reserves are noted for different kinds of white and black rhino and in St Lucia and Umfolozi one can go on Wilderness Trails by boat and on foot. On nearby ranches Zululand Safaris organise hunting safaris as well as the more usual photographic expeditions.

The Gemsbok Kalahari National Park provides more adventurous holidays, giving a real insight into the wild, lonely desert, inhabited only by gemsbok, springbok, lion and ostrich. By contrast, the Drakensberg reserves (Giant's Castle and the Royal Natal National Park) are set in magnificent mountain scenery where one can ride or walk amid fascinating wild flowers, bird and baboons.

The best season for flowers is the southern spring (September and October) when the Cape blossoms with arum lilies, red aloes, wild geranium, Namaqualand daisies and the pink protea bushes. Altogether 16,000 species of plant are found in South Africa. The Kirstenbosch National Botanic Gardens in Cape Town are well worth visiting at any time of the year.

South Africa's reptiles range from friendly chameleons and geckoes to the venomous Cape cobra, the shy, but deadly, *boomslang* (tree snake) and the more vicious mamba. Visitors who intend to go trekking in the wilds should keep their eyes open for the lazy, and highly venomous, puff-adder and for scorpions, particularly where it's rocky.

GENERAL INFORMATION

Area: 1,221,042sq km.

Population: 25 million (18 million Africans, 4 million whites, 2.3 million

Coloureds, 700,000 Asians).

Altitude: Apart from the coastal belt most of the country is plateau over 1,000m high, rising to 2,150m in the mountains.

Capitals: Pretoria (Administrative), Cape Town (Legislative), Bloemfontein (Judiciary).

Head of State: State President: Nicolaas D. Diederichs; Prime Minister: Balthazar J. Vorster.

Government: South Africa is a Republic with executive power vested in the State President; the Parliament has a House of Assembly elected by all adult whites and a Senate partly elected by the different provinces and partly nominated. There is a Coloured People's Representative Council with very limited legislative and administrative powers. There are eight Homeland Territorial Authorities with Legislative Assemblies composed partly of elected members and partly of chiefs. Each of the four provinces—Natal, Cape Province, Orange Free State and Transvaal—has an all-white elected Provincial Council and Executive Council with responsibility for roads, hospitals, local government, etc.

In 1969 South West Africa (Namibia) was incorporated into South Africa for administrative purposes. In 1977 an administrator-general was appointed.

Religion: Christian, with Muslim, Jewish and Hindu minorities.

Official languages: English and Afrikaans.

Currency: The Rand, divided into 100 cents. £1=R1.50, $1=R0.87.

Time: GMT +2.

HOW TO GET THERE

By air: South African Airways and a number of other international airlines operate frequent services to and from Europe, North and South America and Australia. Flights direct to South Africa from other countries within Africa are at present available only from Rhodesia, Malawi, Kenya, Lesotho, Botswana, Swaziland and Mauritius.

The main airport for Pretoria and Johannesburg is Jan Smuts Airport about 15 miles from Johannesburg. Services go to Cape Town, Durban, Port Elizabeth, East London, Kimberley and Bloemfontein.

By sea: There are regular services to most overseas countries and also connections between the ports of South Africa. Many shipping companies reduce their fares from February to July.

By rail: There is transport from Mozambique, Botswana, Rhodesia and Malawi.

By road: There is a twice weekly coach service from Salisbury to Johannesburg. If one is travelling by car, a triptyche (or carnet), South African third party insurance (available at border posts) and a valid driver's licence incorporating a photograph are required. Opening hours of border posts vary but all posts are open at least from 0800 to 1600. For further information contact The Automobile Association of South Africa, AA House, 42 de Villiers St., Johannesburg.

Visas and health regulations

Most visitors to South Africa require visas in addition to valid passports. These are obtainable at the local office of the South African diplomatic representative.

Cape Town docks and Table Mountain

R. WATTS

In countries having no representative, apply to the nearest South African representative or direct to the Secretary for the Interior, Private Bag 114, Pretoria. (Teleg. INTERIOR PRETORIA). Apply well in advance, on the correct form, sending your passport. Non-white tourists are advised to make careful enquiries before embarking. Some visas are valid for one entry only; if so, a re-entry visa must be obtained if the visitor wants to make a trip to an adjacent country such as Swaziland and then to return.

All visitors must satisfy the officials on arrival that they have sufficient means to maintain themselves for the period of their visit and either a return ticket or funds to obtain one.

Valid international certificates of vaccination against smallpox are required. Anyone arriving from places in Africa or Asia where cholera and yellow fever are endemic should be vaccinated also against those diseases.

Dutiable goods

Travellers may import personal effects, used cameras, radios, firearms, camping equipment etc., restricted amounts of spirits, wines, cigarettes etc., but all other articles are dutiable. For a firearm a permit is necessary, issued by customs officials at the point of entry. The firearm must have a number stamped in the metal.

Currency regulations

There is no limit to the amount of foreign exchange a visitor may take into South Africa.

On arrival visitors must complete special customs forms listing all their holdings of currency, and a stamped copy is retained by them. On departure from the country visitors are allowed to take out as much foreign exchange as is shown on the customs form.

Up to R50 per person may be taken into or out of the country in bank notes. Visitors arriving from Zambia, Rhodesia, Malawi or Mozambique may be allowed to bring R100 in bank notes.

CLIMATE

South Africa has a sunny, pleasant climate. The Western Cape has a Mediterranean climate with dry summers (October to March) when the temperature averages around 20°C. Most of the rain falls in winter. The rest of the country lies in the temperate zone. Along the coast of Natal, February may be extremely humid with temperatures over 38°C, but elsewhere it is seldom too hot. On the plateau in summer a little rain may fall in an afternoon shower and in winter the nights are cold and crisp. Snow falls in the Drakensberg. In Johannesburg in June the temperature averages 15.5°C. The best time to visit is between September and May.

What to wear

In summer (October to March) lightweight clothes are essential, with a light sweater sometimes for evenings. Take a raincoat and umbrella for the short sharp showers. In resorts, casual clothes are normal but in cities in the more exclusive hotels—and often in those that are not—ties and jackets are worn. From April to September cool clothes are also needed but it is advisable to take warmer ones for the Cape or the mountains.

Health precautions

Water is drinkable throughout South Africa but many rivers and lakes are not suitable for bathing as they may be contaminated with bilharzia. When swimming in the sea, great care should be taken to read notices on safety and one should always swim within the shark nets. Precautions against malaria are necessary in the Kruger National Park and St Lucia Game Reserve. Much of the ground may be infested with hook worm, so do not go barefoot and keep your eyes open for snakes and scorpions.

LANGUAGES

Afrikaans and English rank equally as official languages. Most South Africans are bilingual. The main Bantu languages are Xhosa, Zulu, and Sotho.

ACCOMMODATION

There is a large number of hotels for whites in South Africa graded by the Hotel Board on an exacting one- to five-star formula. They range from the modern international hotels in the large cities, through medium-sized, and priced, tourist hotels to unpretentious but comfortable hotels in country towns. We have given a brief selection of hotels in the different towns: the visitor should refer to the Guide produced by the South African Hotel Board for fuller information.

Black travellers must make special arrangements for accommodation.

There are many first-class motels along main highways, on the outskirts of the Kruger National Park and along the Garden Route. The game and nature reserves are well provided with rest camps of rondavels (round huts). South Africa is also well organised for the caravan and camping holidaymaker. Complete lists of camp-sites may be obtained from the South African Touring Corporation. For the young, there are also some youth hostels.

It is normal to tip railway porters, taxi drivers, waiters, room servants and petrol pump attendants, between 7-10%.

TRANSPORT

Air: South African Airways fly several flights a day linking Cape Town, Johannesburg, Durban, Port Elizabeth, East London, Kimberley and Bloemfontein. Other services are operated by Air Cape, Commercial Airways and Namakwaland Air Services.

Rail: Except for express trains, most others are slow. The Blue Train is a luxury express running from Johannesburg/Pretoria to Cape Town, offering air-conditioned comfort, excellent cuisine and shower baths at surprisingly low cost. Reservations should be made well in advance.

Road: Modern freeway systems take the traveller out of the major cities, and 25,000 km of tarred roads lead to almost all places of tourist interest. A wide variety of coach tours is available. The major operators are South African Railways, Atlas Tours, Grosvenor Tours, and Springbok Safaris. Bookings can be made through travel agents outside the country, as well as on arrival.

Visitors who decide to drive themselves are advised to take extra care—South Africa has among the highest road accident rates in the world. They should watch their speed, particularly on the many rural dirt roads, and on fast tarmac roads with soft gravel edges. Maximum speed limits of 60 kph in urban areas and 80 kph elsewhere are in force. All limits are enforced by provincial traffic police who have the power to make spot fines. Visitors hiring cars should not underestimate fuel costs and distance charges—in South Africa, these soon mount up. Filling stations are closed on Sundays. As elsewhere, hitch-hiking is the cheapest way of travelling—but women should beware of hiking on their own.

Car hire: South African Airways arranges car hire to connect with flights. There is also a large number of car hire firms operating from all cities.

BANKS

There are many branches of Barclays National Bank, Standard Bank of SA, Volkskas, Nedbank and Trust Bank.

BUSINESS HOURS

Shops generally open from 0800-1700 Monday to Friday and close at 12.30 on Saturdays. Most Government offices are closed on Saturdays.

Banks: In cities 0900-1530 Monday, Tuesday, Thursday, Friday. 0900-1300 Wednesday. 0830-1100 Saturday.

Licensing hours vary in different Provinces but are generally 1000-2300.

PUBLIC HOLIDAYS

Public holidays: New Year's Day; Good Friday; Easter Monday; Ascension Day, May; Republic Day, 31 May; Settlers' Day, first Monday in September; Kruger Day, 10 October; Day of the Covenant, 16 December; Christmas Day; Boxing Day.

FOREIGN EMBASSIES

All in Pretoria:

UK: Greystoke, 6 Hill Street. Tel 74-3121.

USA: Thibault House, Pretorius St.

France: 807 George Ave, Arcadia.

Federal Republic of Germany: 180 Blackwood St, Arcadia.

Sweden: 521 Pretorius St. Box 1664.

Belgium: 275 Pomana St, Muckleneuk.

Netherlands: 1st floor, Netherlands Bank Bldgs, cnr Church and Andries Street, Box 117.

Canada: Netherlands Bank Centre, cnr Church and Beatrix Street.

Australia: Standard Bank Bldgs, Church Square.

Argentina: 1059 Church St, Hatfield.

Austria: 405 Church St.

Brazil: 2243 Poynton Centre, Church St West.

Finland: 310 Sunnyside Galleries, Sunnyside.

Greece: 995 Pretorius St.

Israel: 496 Walter Lanham St.

Italy: 796 George Avenue.

Malawi: 99 Burns St.

Portugal: 261 Devenish St.

Spain: 286 Bosman St.

Switzerland: 818 George Avenue, P.O. Box 2289.

TOURIST OFFICES

South African Tourist Corporation (SATOUR) has offices in London, Frankfurt, Paris, Amsterdam, New York, Zurich, Toronto, Sydney and Buenos Aires. Satour provides travel information on every aspect of travel to and from. It does not handle hotels or other reservations.

If none of these is convenient, write to The Director, South African Tourist Corporation, 10th floor, Arcadia Centre, 130 Beatrix St, P.B. 164, Pretoria. Tel: 25201/5.

RULES TO REMEMBER

While whites love talking politics, they frequently equate the mildest dissenting or 'liberal' view with communism, so it's as well to be careful what you say, and to whom you say it. Visitors should avoid taking political books, magazines or leaflets into the country with them. They should also leave behind any form of erotica or pornography. There's a long list of banned books and publications.

Under the Immorality Laws, it is an offence to commit, or conspire to commit, sexual acts with a member of another racial group. Under the numerous residential and 'influx control' laws it can be an offence to stay overnight in another race's 'group area'. It is an offence to use any amenities (eg. park benches, railway entrances and public service counters) reserved for a different colour group.

Other offences include the carrying of liquor in unwrapped containers, and the buying and selling of liquor on Sundays. Under the Sunday Observance Laws, hotel visitors can generally drink only when they buy a meal as well; cinemas, theatres and nightclubs are closed, and all organised sports are forbidden on Sundays. Most bars are reserved for white men only. 'Pot', known locally as 'dagga', is in plentiful supply, but the use of this drug carries penalties of up to 25 years' imprisonment.

Anyone may travel freely along the through roads and the tourist routes of the Homelands, but if visitors wish to digress they must obtain permits three months in advance from the Secretary for Bantu Administration and Development, Bantu Affairs Building, cnr Paul Kruger and Jacob Mare Street, Pretoria.

Organised bus tours are run around Soweto (South Western Townships) by Johannesburg's Non-European Affairs Department at 81 Albert Street. To enter other black locations (townships), applications must be made to the local magistrate who may in turn refer the visitor back to Pretoria. For reasons of political sensitivity, permits are increasingly difficult to obtain.

For the black tourist visas are needed. There are African hotels in some towns and some for Coloureds, and some international class hotels are allowed to take black tourists if special arrangements are made.

Beaches are strictly segregated.

CAPE TOWN

Founded in 1652, Cape Town is the country's oldest white settlement. A port with a sheltered bay, beaches, fishing grounds, old trees and beautiful gardens, it nestles below the craggy Table Mountain and Lion's Head. As the seat of South Africa's Legislature, it is home for Members of Parliament from November/ December to June/July.

Although there is still plenty to remind the traveller of the city's Dutch period, much of its most attractive architecture has been demolished to make way for high-rise buildings serving the needs of modern business and trade.

On fine days Robben Island is clearly visible from Cape Town. It has had an interesting history, but today it is once again a prison island where many of the Republic's non-white political prisoners serving life or long-term sentences are confined. They include prominent black nationalists like Nelson Mandela, Walter Sisulu and Govan Mbeke.

The Cape Town Castle dates back to 1666, and its State Rooms house period furniture and paintings. There are many fine examples of Cape Dutch architecture, notably the Koopmans-De Wet Museum and the Old Town House, built in 1755. The Malay Quarter is still the home of descendants of Malay slaves. On New Year's Day the Coloured population parade with both traditional and modern singing and dancing in the 'Coon Carnival'.

In Newlands, on the slopes of Table Mountain, are the world-famous Kirstenbosch National Botanic Gardens, open daily from sunrise to sunset. Table Mountain itself may be ascended by cable car from the station off Kloof Nek. It affords superb views of Table Bay and the country around.

Further examples of fine architecture are Groot Constantia, an old Cape farmhouse, and, further inland, Paarl, a typical Western Province town set in orchards and vineyards with a backdrop of the Hottentots Holland Mountains.

All round the Cape Peninsula coast are beaches, fishing villages and popular resorts like Muizenberg, St James, Kalk Bay and Simonstown on the warm Indian Ocean side, or Clifton and Llandudno on the cold Atlantic coast, where one can swim, surf, sunbathe, or enjoy excellent fishing.

Hotels
A selection: for details of cheaper hotels see the Guide prepared by the South African Hotel Board.

Heerengracht, Box 2936, on the Foreshore, 210 rooms.

The Alphen, Peter Cloete Avenue, Constantia, 29 rooms.

President, Beach Road, Sea Point, 152 rooms.

Mount Nelson, Orange St, 144 rooms.

Arthur's Seat, Arthur's Road, Sea Point,

120 rooms.
Carlton Heights, 88 Queen Victoria St, 64 rooms.
Surfcrest, 327 Beach Road, 61 rooms.

OUTSIDE CAPE TOWN

Two beautiful towns within easy reach of Cape Town are **Paarl** and **Stellenbosch**, seat of the foremost Afrikaans university. Lanzerac, in Stellenbosch, is an hotel converted from a Cape Dutch winery which offers first class accommodation and food. Reasonably priced wine and cheese lunches are available on weekdays.

Further away from Cape Town lie three picturesque mission stations. **Genadendal** (near Caledon), **Elim** (near Bredasdorp) and **Wuppertal** (near Clanwilliam). **Hermanus** is a famous seaside resort, and **Caledon** is the main centre for the Cape's spectacular wild flowers.

The Eastern Cape Province still retains something of its early 19th century flavour. **Grahamstown**, a cathedral town, is also the seat of Rhodes University. Nearby is **Alice**, a wooded area below the Hogsback. Here, too, is the oldest African university in the country, Fort Hare.

Further north is the old Dutch frontier capital of **Graaff-Reinet**—known for its architecture and its period museum.

THE TRANSKEI

The Transkei became politically 'independent' in South African eyes in 1976. But it has yet to be recognised as such by any foreign country. It was the first of the Homelands established under the Separate Development policy, and its creation necessitated the declaration 10 years ago of a state of emergency, which has never been lifted. The Transkei's capital is Umtata.

In the Transkei one drives through attractive undulating downland. Some of the Xhosa people keep their elaborate traditional costumes and ornaments, and the Tourist Corporation lays on highly artificial dances for visitors. The rocky seashore here is called the Wild Coast and is intersected by broad, unbridged rivers. Angling in the rivers and sea is particularly good.

Port St Johns, with its high, wooded hills and rocky enclosed bays is a place of extraordinary natural beauty.

NATAL COAST

The Natal coast is the most popular holiday area among white South Africans. It offers a wide choice of resorts with warm all-year-round swimming and surfing.

The coast south of Durban is the more developed, especially the Hibiscus Coast around Margate. Sugar fields, which in places run almost into the sea, give the coast an incredible lushness when the cane is growing. Most beaches are reasonably well protected from sharks, and it's wise to avoid any which are not.

Hotels
AMANZIMTOTI
Beach, Box 24, 54 rooms.
MARGATE
Marina, Box 27, 42 rooms.
UVONGO
La Crete, Box 1, 103 rooms.
TONGAAT BEACH
Tongaat Beach, Box 48, 29 rooms.
SALT ROCK
Salt Rock, 79 rooms.

There are also numerous camping and caravan sites.

DURBAN

As the centre of the Natal coast and the country's major port, Durban is a vast sub-tropical resort: very humid in summer and warm in winter. It is the main town of the only predominantly English-speaking province of the Republic.

The Eastern influence on Durban is everywhere—Hindu temples and mosques, the Indian market full of Oriental curios, tropical fruit and spices. The fantastic dress and ornaments of the *ricksha* pullers brighten the streets. The city dwelling Zulu perform Ngoma Dances most weekends in the African recreation grounds off Somtseu Road.

Two interesting rural festivals occur nearby: the Festival of First Fruits at the March new moon in Mafunza, near Elandskop, 40 km from Pietermaritzburg, and the Shembe Festival, a mixture of traditional and Christian ideas, in the week before full moon at the end of July at East Kupakumein, near Inanda, 32 km

H. F. Verwoerd Dam on the Orange River

from Durban. The Durban Visitors' Bureau arranges tours to the latter, but a permit is needed if you wish to use private transport because it lies in the restricted area of a Homeland.

Entertainments

Safe bathing and excellent surfing: all kinds of sport, theatres, cinemas, amusement parks, nightclubs. It is an important horseracing centre—the country's classic horse race, the July Handicap, is run there on the first Saturday of July.

Hotels

A selection: for further details see the Guide prepared by the South African Hotel Board.

Edward, Box 105, 101 rooms.
Beverley Hills, Umhlanga Rocks, 16 km north of Durban, Box 71, 87 rooms.
Four Seasons, Box 1379, 195 rooms.
Oyster Box, Umhlanga Rocks, Box 22, 845 rooms.
Lonsdale International, Box 345, 330 rooms.
Pavilion, Box 1366, 75 rooms.

KWAZULU

The Zulu Homeland, unlike the Transkei, is scattered all over Natal, interspersed by large 'white' areas. Like the Transkei, however, it is generally dry, eroded, and overpopulated. The most solid concentration of land is in northern Natal, with the administrative centre at Nongoma, but even here are 'white spots' like the developing port of Richard's Bay—a point of conflict between the Homeland and the Government since it would provide the only natural seaport for the Zulus if ever they became independent.

The Zulus' Chief Minister is Chief Gatsha Buthelezi, one of the most influential of the black leaders in the country. He is a strong believer in a multi-racial future for the country and has little faith in the Homelands policy succeeding.

The visitor may travel on main roads through some beautiful scenery, but a permit is required to leave the road. The area is famous for its game reserves.

There are five game reserves. Hluhluwe is one of the most popular, noted particularly for its large numbers of black and white rhino. There are also a variety of buck, zebra, wart-hog, buffalo, baboons and some lions, leopards and cheetah. The Umfolozi Game Reserve is famous for its square-lipped rhinoceros, saved from extinction in this area from where it was reintroduced into other parts of Africa. Wilderness trails may be followed on foot in the reserve, as well as at Ndumu in the far north, and at the St

Lucia Lake Reserve.

Accommodation: Each game reserve has a comfortable camp of rest huts, but the traveller must bring his own food. At Hluhluwe (pronounced 'Shushluwey'), there are two hotels. **Hluhluwe Holiday Inn**, Box 92, 605 rooms. **Zululand Safari Lodge**, Box 116, 42 rooms.

THE DRAKENSBERG

The 'Dragon Mountain', snow-covered in winter, spreads from Lesotho (where it is known as the Malutis) along the border of the Orange Free State and Natal, to the Lebombo range which, in places, divides the Transvaal from Mozambique. The mountains provide walks, riding, climbing, fishing, flowers and some game as well as superb scenery. The hotels also have swimming, tennis and bowling facilities.

Mont-aux-Sources, at 3,482m, is the highest peak in the Republic. It is the source of the Orange, Caledon and Tugela rivers—hence its name. There are countless streams and waterfalls, wild flowers, small buck and baboons. The Giant's Castle reserve organisers riding tours around the magnificent mountain drives full of flowers with some game, notably the rare Cape eland. There are fine Bushman paintings in the caves.

A chain of hotels stretches along the border between South Africa and Lesotho, and there are also rest huts in the nature reserves, where the visitor must bring his own food.

Cathedral Peak, P.O. Winterton, 100 rooms.

Royal Natal National Park, P.O. Mont-aux-Sources, 56 rooms.

PIETERMARITZBURG

Generally shortened to Maritzburg, this is the old capital of Natal, the seat of the Natal Provincial Council, the High Court and a branch of the Natal University. It is an attractive, sleepy town with marvellous surrounding areas.

Hotels

Camden, 99 Pietermaritzburg St, tel: 2-8921.

Imperial, 224 Loop St, tel: 2-6551, P.O. Box 140.

Crossways, P.O. Box 16, Hilton, tel: 3-1143.

JOHANNESBURG

The country's wealth is based mainly on the golden Reef which forms the Witwatersrand (Ridge of White Waters) of which Johannesburg (pop.1,446,000) is the centre.

The Witwatersrand, known mostly as the Rand, has two radials—the East Rand with the mining and industrial towns of Germiston, Boksburg, Benoni, Brakpan, Springs and Nigel; and the West Rand with Florida, Roodepoort, Krugersdorp and Randfontein. It has extended with the discovery of newer goldfields to the Far West Rand town of Klerksdorp—where the gold reef submerges to appear again in the Free State goldfields. To the south of Johannesburg are the coalfields and industries of Vereeniging and the steel and oil processing complex of Sasolburg. Nearby is the huge steel complex of Iscor (the Iron and Steel Corporation). Together this area forms the Vaal Triangle, the South African Ruhr, always starved for more water and power.

The Rand is traversed by enormous mine dumps, the man-made range of hills dug up from some of the deepest mines in the world. Lying at 2,000m above sea-level Johannesburg has an invigorating climate—hot in the summer, cold when the sun goes down in the early dusk of winter. It is a city of extremes—of political reaction and of progressive ideas; of a vibrant culture and of brash philistinism; of white affluence and of black poverty; of violence and lawlessness which take their toll indiscriminately among whites and blacks.

The city is strictly segregated. The western, eastern, and southern suburbs are mostly occupied by white artisans or middle-classes; the northern suburbs have among the finest and richest homes and gardens in the world. The million or so Africans are mostly concentrated in the great black city of Soweto on the southern periphery, or in the vast complex of bachelor compounds in Alexandra township—the home of many of the migrant workers, which has no parallel in the world. The Asians have been uprooted from their old homes and resettled in the segregated town of Lenasia on the southern outskirts.

Conducted tours of the gold mines take place three times a week, and the strenuous tour gives a fascinating insight into the surface and underground workings. Protective clothing is provided. It is necessary to book such a trip three months in advance, either direct through the Public Relations Department, Chamber of Mines, 5 Holland St, P.O. Box 809, Johannesburg, or through the Tourist Bureau.

Hotels
A selection: cheaper hotels may be found listed in the Guide prepared by the South African Hotel Board.
President, P.O. Box 7702, 242 rooms.
Tollman Towers, P.O. Box 535, 150 rooms.
Casa Mia, 37 Soper Road, Berea, 150 rooms.
Kyalami Ranch, P.O. Box 19, Kyalami, Bergvlei, 1201 rooms.
Kelvin Grove, P.O. Box 52004, Rosebank, 34 rooms.
White Horse Inn, P.O. Box 9, Fontainebleau, 40 rooms.

PRETORIA

The administrative capital of South Africa is only 48 km from Johannesburg, but still retains its old-world atmosphere. The Union Buildings dominate the city, which is also the seat of the Transvaal Provincial Council and of one of the Afrikaner universities.

Pretoria holds many reminders of both Afrikaner and English history. The Boer military victories are commemorated in the massive Voortrekker Monument, 40m high and visible for miles around, and a national shrine for Afrikaners. President Paul Kruger's house in Church Street is now a museum. The Transvaal Museum has a notable collection of geological, archaeological and natural history specimens from the Stone Age period and ealier. The Old Museum, next to the zoo, contains a rare exhibition of San (Bushman) art, as well as the art of the other African peoples of South Africa and relics of the Voortrekkers.

Hotels
Boulevard, 186 Struben St, 75 rooms.
Union, P.O. Box 1739, 62 rooms.
Assembly, van der Walt/Visagie Sts, 84 rooms.
Continental, 152 Visagie St, 70 rooms.

Miners at the headgear of gold mine

R. WATTS

Wooden sledge as transport in the Transkei

Culemborg, P.O. Box 2323, 70 rooms.

BLOEMFONTEIN

The capital of the Orange Free State, Bloemfontein, is a city of some architectural charm, and stolid Calvinist character. North west of the city are the new Free State gold fields, centred on Welkom, and developed over the last few decades. They are now even more important than those on the Rand, and are the richest in the world.

Bloemfontein is a good starting-point to visit the mountain splendours of Lesotho, or to approach Kimberley.

Hotels
President, P.O. Box 1851, 89 rooms.
Cecil, P.O. Box 516, 52 rooms.

KIMBERLEY

The great diamond rush of the 1870s took place around Kimberley, whence the blue pipes of rock containing diamonds derive their name—kimberlite.

The famous 'Big Hole', 1,000m deep and 463m across, covering 38 acres, is now disused, but in its time it has yielded three tons of diamonds. The visitor can view it from a special observation point. The working diamond mines may be seen by conducted tours run by the De Beers Company. One can see the crushing and washing, the surface workings, the recovery process and the day's final haul.

The tour takes three to four hours and permits and information may be obtained from the Town Clerk's office.

Hotels
Savoy, P.O. Box 231, 50 rooms.
Grand, P.O. Box 197, 44 rooms.

NATIONAL PARKS

Kruger National Park is the largest and most popular game reserve in South Africa. The best time for visiting is from June to the end of September when the dryness drives the animals to waterholes where they can easily be seen. The southern part of the park is open all the year round, but the north is open only from May to mid-October.

The park contains a remarkable collection of animals with buffalo, elephant and lion predominating. There are plenty of giraffe, ostriches, crocodiles, all kinds of buck and a profusion of bird life including the grotesque hornbill, the eagle, the vulture and red-eyed oxpecker.

Accommodation: There are 11 rest camps. The largest ones have well-appointed restaurants and shops. Bookings should be made in advance through the National Parks Board of Trustees, Sanlam Bldgs, Andries and Pretorius Sts, Box 787, tel: 44-1194, cable NATPARK, Pretoria.

The Lion Inn complex is under construction and will provide hotel-motel and caravan park at the gate to the park,

$3\frac{1}{2}$ km from Phalaborwa. At Phalaborwa: **Impala Inn**, Box 139, 49 rooms.

Kalahari Gemsbok National Park: This northern Cape park has abundant game and is the home of vast herds of springbok, eland and red hartebeest. It is also the only place where the gemsbok, with its sword-like horns, is to be found in profusion. There are three rest camps and a small store selling some tinned food; anything else needed should be brought. The park is open all year round.

Other South African game parks include the **Addo Elephant Park**, on the Garden Route, and the **Hluhluwe Game Park** in KwaZulu.

HISTORY

South Africa has produced the most complete series of Stone Age remains in Africa, dating from a pre-Acheulian culture of about 1.8 million years ago. At that time an ape-man of the Australopithecine type—lightly built and about four feet tall—lived in the Transvaal, where bones and fossils have been found, notably in the Sterkfontein and Makapan caves. From these tool-users evolved Stone Age men who made their own tools of stone, wood and bone (from about 40,000 BC). Their sites have been found in the far south as well as in the Transvaal. The late Stone Age culture shows some affinities with that of the Khoisan peoples, who were later driven out or absorbed by Bantu-speaking iron-miners in the north or Europeans in the south.

The Khoisan were a brown-skinned people speaking a variety of 'click' languages. The name is an amalgam of Khoikhoi ('Hottentot') and San (the Khoikhoi name for Bushman). The main distinction between the two was that Khoikhoi were herders of sheep and cattle whereas the San were hunters.

San sometimes attached themselves as servants of Khoikhoi, scouting and hunting for them; sometimes they raided and stole from them. The Khoikhoi had sheep, but cattle were probably introduced from Bantu-speakers in about the 15th century. They used the cattle for riding as well as for dairy products.

The paintings found in caves all over South Africa but especially in the Drakensberg are attributed to the San and record their culture in lively detail. The caves themselves can still be visited, for example in the Royal Natal Park, and the Sederberg range north of Cape Town. The Old Museum in Pretoria has a rare collection of other San art.

From early times mining and barter added to the subsistence economy of the Transvaal but the metals mined were copper and iron rather than the gold for which the area has since become famous. Copper may have been mined at Phalaborwa (near the Kruger National Park) as early as the 8th century, and certainly from the 11th to the 14th centuries Mapungubwe (on the Limpopo above Beit Bridge) became an important centre where archaeologists have found copper and gold ornaments. Copper mining continued in the area (especially at Messina) under Venda chiefs who came perhaps in the 17th century from Rhodesia, so that the Limpopo came to be known to the Portuguese as the Copper River.

Much further inland in the Transvaal the Sotho also mined copper and iron and sold it to the Tswana in the west and, through Tsonga middlemen, to the Portuguese in the east. The Sotho and Venda have left many small stone ruins, huts as well as enclosure walls. They and the related Tswana lived under powerful chiefs in large villages.

The foothills of the Drakensberg were inhabited by cattle-keeping Nguni peoples certainly by the 16th century and probably by the 14th. These people also grew millet, made their huts of reeds and their sandals and shields of skin. Cattle were of vital significance for their religious ceremonies as well as their economy. Originally living in scattered groups they were united in the 19th century into the great Zulu nation by Shaka.

The Dutch at the Cape (1652-1795). In 1652 Jan van Riebeeck arrived at the Cape of Good Hope to set up a revictualling station for Dutch ships on their way to the East. He built a fort around which soldiers and servants of the Dutch East India Company, for which he acted, began to grow vegetables and fruit. This they sold to some 33 Dutch ships a year passing through. Later settlers were producing enough wheat for the whole Dutch Eastern empire and owned large cattle ranches.

As the Dutch spread, the Khoikhoi lost their grazing lands and many became servants of the whites, learned Dutch and eventually produced a Eurafrican (Coloured) population. The San, less amenable to the new order, were exterminated or fled to the desert.

More settlers were not encouraged at this time as the hinterland and transport were poor, but some Huguenot refugees from France settled in 1688. During the 18th century a number of slaves were imported from West Africa and Malaysia. The isolated white community became closely united, all speaking the new language, Afrikaans, and all members of the Calvinist Dutch Reformed Church.

In about 1770 began the long series of Xhosa Wars ('Kaffir Wars') when the Europeans and Xhosa, both expanding and in search of land, met and fought on the Great Fish River.

The Cape was a bone of contention in the Napoleonic Wars and in 1806 it finally became British so that the period of Dutch rule ended and British settlers and governors began to arrive.

The 19th century was a time of violent expansion by Xhosa, Zulu, Afrikaner and British to produce the triangular struggle between 'Boer, Briton and Bantu'. The Africans were defeated by superior fire-power and the Afrikaners were eventually subdued by the British in a war at the end of the century so bitter that the victors lost public support and soon afterwards made concessions.

Among the Northern Nguni in Natal, three great leaders had arisen one after the other—Dingiswayo, Shaka and Dingaan—to conquer a large kingdom and unite it to form the Zulu nation. With tough discipline, new tactics and weapons (like the short stabbing *assegai* instead of a throwing spear), they annihilated all opposition. The repercussions of Shaka's wars in Natal were felt right across the Highveld where refugees like the Ndebele conquered new kingdoms and much land was abandoned as its people hid: indeed some fled as far as Tanzania, Malawi, Zambia and Mozambique. Nearer home the Swazi and some Sotho united in mountain strongholds and successfully defended their independence against Zulu and Afrikaner, with the aid later on of British protection. They now form the independent countries of Swaziland and Lesotho.

Both Ndebele and Zulu were in their turn defeated (1837-40) by the Afrikaner *Voortrekkers*. The historic Great Trek in 1836 of many Afrikaners (then called Boers) away from the Cape was caused by the introduction of British rule. They set out in wagons to find new land where they could be independent, speak their own language and live according to their own customs. They sought farm land with access to the sea at either Lourenco Marques or the as yet unclaimed Natal coast. Malaria, tsetse fly and the Tsonga, however, barred their way to the first port and in the 1850s English settlers and their Indian labourers occupied Natal. The Boers did succeed in seizing large tracts of land and established the two independent Republics of the Orange Free State and the Transvaal.

Most of the Ndebele under Mzilikazi fled before them into present-day Rhodesia and at the Battle of Blood River (near Dundee) 3,000 Zulu, unable to adapt their tactics, were slaughtered with no white casualties. The survivors retired north of the Tugela to recuperate. By

Young black artisan

1879, strong again under Cetshwayo, the Zulu won a victory at Isandhlwana over the British; but then again were finally defeated.

Until 1870 South Africa had been a purely agricultural country, but during the last part of the century the economy was revolutionised by the discovery first of diamonds, then of gold.

In Hopetown someone picked up a diamond by chance in 1867 and adventurers rushed to the Kimberley area to exploit the biggest concentration of diamonds in the world. Gradually Cecil Rhodes's company, De Beers, bought out smaller miners and the Cape Colony quickly annexed Kimberley before the Afrikaners should claim it. In 1886 the Witwatersrand gold deposits were discovered. This resource was indisputably in the Transvaal but large numbers of foreigners *(uitlanders)*, many of them British, flooded in to seek their fortunes. Their complains against the Afrikaner government and the ambition of Cecil

Rhodes, then Prime Minister of the Cape Colony, led to the disastrous Jameson Raid of 1896 in which Jameson tried unsuccessfully to stir up rebellion in the Transvaal to give the Cape an excuse to annex it.

The final military conflict between Britain on one side and the two Boer Republics on the other came in the terrible South African War of 1899 to 1902 (known in Britain as the Boer War). The Afrikaners had no outside help and were subdued only with concentration camps and the burning of their farms. The War Museum at Bloemfontein vividly recalls the period. This struggle brought out a fierce Afrikaner national consciousness which still survives.

After the peace, Britain quickly made concessions and by 1910 had given self-government to the resulting Union of all the provinces. The Afrikaners, however, had their final revenge when in 1948 they won the general elections which ensured their political supremacy and enabled them to embark on their policy of apartheid.

This had a rigidly doctrinal objective of 'separate development' for each of the four main racial communities—white, black, Coloured and Asian—to ensure the preservation of white supremacy over two-thirds of the country, with the other one-third divided into eight black Homelands which have been promised some form of separate independence.

In 1961 South Africa's racial policies were so far out of step with the multiracial Commonwealth of Nations that it was forced to withdraw to avoid being voted out. It became a Republic on 31 May 1961.

South Africa stands alone politically, defended by an ultra modern defence system, but its present stability is still assured by its enormous economic importance to the West. However, the rumblings of black unrest, exemplified by the Soweto rising of 1976, are likely to gather momentum in the coming years.

SUDAN

The Sudan is the largest country in the whole of Africa and covers an area of 2,505,813sq km. Although it is almost as large as Western Europe its population is only 16.5 million. The country has great variety geographically and ethnologically. Much of the land is fairly flat, but there are ancient monuments, mosques and churches to see and exotic handicrafts to buy. Lovers of scenic hills, hunting and camping will find these at Imatong in East Equatoria, (3,500m) Jabal Marrah (3,430m) and the summer resort of Erkowit (1,000m) in the Red Sea Hills.

taries. In the centre lies the Sudd, an enormous marsh over 120,000 sq km. Mount Kinyeti rises 3,480m on the Sudan-Uganda border.

The White Nile enters the Sudan near the town of Nimule and flows northwards to 3,420km until it leaves at Wadi Halfa. In 1966 the Roseires Dam, supplying water to two million acres of land was completed across the Blue Nile at Damazin 576km south of Khartoum.

In the eastern Sudan lies the Red Sea coast with its beautiful marine gardens. The clear blue water and the coral reefs are a great tourist attraction. The ancient

THE LAND AND THE PEOPLE

The Sudan may be divided into four geographical regions. The desert region, covered by the Libyan and Nubian deserts, lies in the north and extends south to Khartoum. The Nile River Valley runs through the centre of this area and there is some vegetation at the scattered oases. The steppe region from Khartoum to El Obeid in central Sudan is covered by short, coarse grass and small bushes. The Kurdufan plateau lies 500m above most of the area. The savannah region is south of the steppe. The equatorial region stretching across the south of the country consists mainly of a shallow basin traversed by the Nile and its tribu-

city of Suakin 56km from Port Sudan, was once the capital of the Beja Kingdoms. Near Suakin is Erkowit, the Sudan's only developed summer resort, which lies on a high plateau surrounded on all sides by mountains.

The Sudanese are of Hamitic and Negro origin, though in the north there has been much intermingling with the Arabs and the people there are traditionally nomadic or semi-nomadic. In the south, the Nilotic peoples predominate. The highest population densities occur along the Nile and around Khartoum.

The Sudan has now largely recovered from its main political problem; the rebellion in the three southern provinces— Upper Nile, Equatoria and Bahr-al-Ghaza which lasted from 1956 until 1972. Unlike the north, which is largely Muslim and Arab these provinces are much more African in culture. British policy had not been one of promoting national unity and the conflict was long and bitter. The south's main problem, now that the struggle for autonomy has been resolved, is one of isolation, and this has not been helped by the troubles in Uganda.

Sudan's agricultural potential is being developed with massive food-crop and sugar schemes financed by Arab oil-money and often managed by large Western corporations.

CULTURE

The Sudanese like to think of their country as a meeting point for the Middle East and Africa and they often speak of it as being a bridge between Africa north and south. Whilst African dances and music can be seen or heard more in the three southern provinces, the north has its own tradition of Islamic music, which can be heard especially on Fridays in Omdurman (the largest of the three towns that make up Khartoum).

About 160km north of Khartoum is the Shendi area where monuments dating back to the ancient Meroe kingdom are found. They include the antiquities of Naga, Masawarat and Bajrawia as well as churches and monasteries from the period when the Sudan was a Christian country (343-1340 AD.)

North of Shendi, and half-way between the Egyptian border and Khartoum in the middle of the Nile loop, is the town of Kuraymah near the Barkal Mountain, site of the ancient Napata kingdom, centre of the first Sudanese Empire which ruled the whole of ancient Sudan and Egypt during the 24th Egyptian dynasty. The temple of the God Amun is well preserved. In the Kuru area, a few miles from Kuraymah, are the pyramids of the kings of Napata. Across the river are the pyramids of Nuri. All these areas can easily be reached by rail, air or road from Khartoum.

WILDLIFE

With peace restored to the southern region, it is now possible not only to visit Juba, Waw and Malakal, but also to travel freely into the bush where elephant wander in herds of up to 400 and buffalo are estimated to exceed 20,000. Giraffe and zebra are also plentiful. Hippo and crocodile are to be found in the reeds and swamps.

Darfur is another area rich in game. There are more addax and oryx here than in any other part of Africa. The ibex, which is rare almost everywhere else, can still be hunted in the Red Sea Hills area.

The Dinder National Park is the best developed of the tourist areas and can be reached by road from Khartoum.

GENERAL INFORMATION
Area: 2,505,815 sq km.
Population: About 16.5 million.
Altitude: Sea level 3,000m; mainly about 200m.
Capital: Khartoum taking in Omdurman and Khartoum North.
Head of State: Major-General Gaafar

Mohammed Numeiry.

Government: Military, controlled by the political bureau of the Sudan Socialist Union, the only legal political party.

Date of independence: 1 January 1956.

Languages: Arabic (official) and many local dialects. English is widely spoken and is the language of the government in the south.

Religions: Islam in the north, traditional African in the south, with Christian communities.

Currency: Sudan Pound (£S), divided into 100 piastres (PT) and 1,000 milliemes.

£S0.562 = £1 sterling; £S0.348 = US$1.00.

Time: GMT + 2.

HOW TO GET THERE

By air: Khartoum Airport is served internationally by Aeroflot, Alitalia, British Airways, BUA, Egypt Air, Ethiopian Airlines, Interflug, Lufthansa, MEA, SAS, Saudi Arabian Airlines, Sudan Airways, TWA. Sudan Airways connects Khartoum with Bahrain, Egypt, Ethiopia, W. Germany, Greece, Kenya, Italy, Iraq, Lebanon, Libya, Saudi Arabia and the UK.

All passengers embarking on international flights from Khartoum Airport must pay an airport charge of £S1. Taxis are available at the airport, about ten minutes by car from the centre of Khartoum, on the eastern outskirts of the city. On request airlines sometimes arrange for passenger transport from hotels to the airport.

By sea: Ships from various parts of the world dock at Port Sudan on the Red Sea, the country's only seaport.

By road: Motorists must apply for permission to drive through Sudan well in advance of the journey. Applications should be made to the Under Secretary, Ministry of Interior, P.O. Box 770, Khartoum, or any Sudanese Legation or Embassy, and should list names and nationalities of travellers; number, make and horsepower of vehicles, reason for journey; proposed route and ultimate destination. Motorists must have a tryptique of carnet de passage from a recognized automobile club, or must pay a deposit or provide a guarantee signed by a known resident of the Sudan, a bank or business firm. Vehicles must be insured.

Permission to motor in, or through, Sudan may not be granted for less than two vehicles travelling together, and drivers should enquire about the state of roads before starting the journey. In main towns and environs roads are surfaced but most outlying roads are rough tracks with sandy stretches, requiring

CAMERAPIX

Camel train passing Khartoum Hilton

strong vehicles.

Entry from Ethiopia has been impossible for some years because of the state of emergency in Eritrea.

By river and rail: From Egypt there is a train from Cairo to Aswan High Dam, by Aswan High Lake steamer, with rudimentary accommodation from Aswan High Dam to Wadi Halfa, and from there a train to Khartoum. Train reservations must be made in advance.

In normal circumstances road transport can be taken from Ethiopia to Kassala (proceeding from there by train to Khartoum) and river transport operates from Uganda to Nimule (thence by road to Juba, steamer to Kosti and by train to Khartoum).

Visas and health regulations

A visa is required by all visitors and should be obtained in advance from a Sudanese diplomatic mission abroad; they are not obtainable at Khartoum airport. Passports must be valid for at least two months beyond the period of intended stay.

Transit visas are available on arrival for visitors from countries with no Sudanese representation, provided they hold the required documents and have a confirmed reservation for a connecting flight within 24 hours. These visitors may not leave the Airport. Admission to Sudan and transit rights are refused to holders of Israeli passports, or passports containing a valid or expired visa for Israel, Rhodesia or South Africa.

Visitors staying in the Sudan longer than three days must report to the police. For travel to the southern regions—Bahr-al-Ghazal, Equatoria and Upper Nile, including Malakal, Waw and Juba airports—a special permit must be obtained from a Sudanese representative abroad, of from the Ministry of Interior in Khartoum (which takes five days).

Inoculation against smallpox, yellow fever and cholera is compulsory.

Dutiable goods

Customs may sometimes be levied on articles such as cameras, typewriters, firearms, etc., subject to refund if they are taken out again within six months. A guarantee signed by a bank or business firm or a known resident may be accepted in lieu of a deposit. Special permission from the Ministry of Interior is required for the import of firearms.

Currency regulations

Foreign currencies in unlimited sums may be imported, provided these amounts are allowed by the country of origin. All foreign currency, including travellers' cheques and letters of credit, must be declared upon entry and departure. Exchange should only be made at authorised exchange points—i.e. banks and certain hotels and travel agencies—and entered on the declaration form which needs to be shown to Customs on departure. Export of foreign currency by visitors is limited to the amount imported. Import and export of local currency is prohibited.

CLIMATE

There is little rain in the extreme north. In the central region rainfall averages about 15cm most of it confined to July and August. In the south the annual average is about 100cm and the rainy season lasts from May to October. Summers are hot throughout the country with temperatures ranging from $27°C$ to $46°C$. Winter temperatures are around $16°C$ in the north and $27°C$ in the south. Between April and October severe sandstorms *(haboobs)* sweep in from the Sahara desert, sometimes lasting three to four days. The best time to visit Sudan is in winter (November to March).

In Khartoum the coolest month is January and the hottest is June.

What to wear: Light-weight clothing is essential for most of the year. Dress is almost always informal.

Health precautions: Precautions against malaria are advisable, although Khartoum itself is free of the disease. The water supplies of major towns are safe to drink. Swimming in slow-moving fresh water is not advisable as bilharzia is endemic.

ACCOMMODATION, FOOD

There are a limited number of high-standard hotels in Khartoum and Port Sudan. Elsewhere there are rest houses, with variable standards, and permission must be obtained in advance to use their facilities. There are plenty of cheap hotels in the main towns, although proprietors may be unwilling to take foreigners unless you make it clear you do not mind sharing a room. The only youth hostel is in Khartoum; it has showers and cooking facilities.

The restaurants in the Khartoum and Port Sudan hotels serve international cuisine. There are a few Greek and Middle Eastern restaurants.

Sudanese dishes served in small restaurants usually consist of *fool*-beans and bread and meat, and *dura*-cooked millet or maize. If you are invited into a Sudanese home you will be regaled with much more exotic fare.

Tipping: Hotels, restaurants, 10% of the bill.

TRANSPORT

Official permits are required for all journeys in the Sudan; they can be obtained from the Registry Office, Khartoum. You must also register with the police in each town you spend the night.

By air: Sudan Airways operates regular flights to Atbara, Dongola, Al Fashir, Juba, Geneina, Kassala, Khashim al Girba, Kosti, Malakal, Marawi, Annuhud, Nyala, El Obeid, Port Sudan, Roseires, Wad Madani and Waw.

By rail: The railways are comfortable and clean (first class) and are a good way to see much of the country and its people. They are, however, extremely slow. There are trains to Port Sudan, Wadi Halfa, El Obeid, Nyala, Waw, Roseires and Kassala. Sleeping cars and catering services are available on the main routes. Students' reductions are available on applicatiuon to the Ministry of Youth.

By river: The main stretch of river transport is between Kosti and Juba. It is a long slow journey, taking up to 11 days; one needs to stock up with food in Kosti and Malakal.

By road: Motorists should make inquiries about road conditions and administrative restrictions in the places they intend to visit. Roads in the north are often closed during the rainy season (July-September). In the south a number of roads are open throughout the year although surfaces are poor. Sudan has virtually no tarred roads. A complete spare-part kit should be taken on any long journey.

Car hire facilities are available in the main towns. Traffic drives on the right.

The green-striped yellow taxis can be hailed in the street. They are not metered and fares should be arranged before the journey is undertaken. It is not necessary to tip the driver. There are also collective taxis which can be found in Khartoum market place.

Buses run between the main towns, and leave from the central market place (there is one in each of Khartoum's 'Three Towns'). Trucks travelling long distances also take passengers. Hitch-hiking is not recommended.

BANKS

El Nilein Bank (P.O. Box 466, Khartoum) has branches in Omdurman, Port Sudan, Adueim, Kuraymah and Wad Madani. Other banks are Bank of Khartoum, P.O. Box 1008, Khartoum (formerly State Bank for Foreign Trade); Unity Bank, P.O. Box 408, Khartoum (formerly Juba Commercial Bank); People's Co-operative Bank, P.O. Box 922, Khartoum (formerly Msr Bank); Sudan Commercial Bank, P.O. Box 1116, Khartoum.

Business hours

Weekly closing day: Friday. Opening hours: Banks 0830-1200; Government offices 0730-1430; Post offices 0830-1300 and 1730-1830; Central Telegraph Offices open 24 hours daily, including holidays; shops usually open 0800-1300 and 1700-2000 (Friday 0800-1130) and some shops close on Sundays.

PUBLIC HOLIDAYS

Independence Day 1 January; National Unity Day 3 March; 1969 Revolution Day 25 May; Christmas Day; Easter Day (for Christians only).

The following Muslim holidays are also observed: Ramadan Bairam, Kurban Bairam, Islamic New Year's Day, Birthday of the Prophet.

FOREIGN EMBASSIES IN KHARTOUM

Algeria: Junction Mek Nimr Street and 67th Street, P.O. Box 80; Austria: Slavos Building 29, 3rd Floor, P.O. Box 1860; Belgium: Sharia Al Mek Nimr, House No. 4, P.O. Box 969; Central African Empire: Africa Road, P.O. Box 1723; Chad: P.O. Box 1514; Egypt: Mogram Street; Ethiopia: P.O. Box 844; France: 6H East Plot 2, 19th Street, P.O. Box 377; West Germany: Baladiya Street, P.O. Box 970; Greece: Block 74, 31st Street, P.O. Box 1182; India: El Mek Nimr Street, P.O. Box 707; Iran: Baladiya Street; Italy: 39th Street, P.O. Box 793; Japan: P.O. Box 1649; Jordan: 25 7th Street, New Extension; Kuwait: 9th Street, New Extension; Libya: Africa Road 50, P.O. Box 2091; Morocco: 32, 19th Street; Netherlands: P.O. Box 391; Niger: P.O. Box 1283; Nigeria: P.O. Box 1538; Pakistan: P.O. Box 1178; Qatar: Street 15, New Extension; Saudi Arabia: Central Street, New Extension, P.O. Box 852; Somalia: Central Street, New Extension; Spain: Street 3, New Extension, P.O. Box 2621; Syria: 3rd Street, New Extension; Tanzania: P.O. Box 6080; Turkey: 71 Africa Road, P.O. Box 771; Uganda: Excelsior Hotel, Room 408/410; United Arab Emirates: Street 3, New Extension; UK: New Abulela Building, P.O. Box 801; USA: Gumhouria Avenue; Yemen Arab Republic: Street 35, New Extension; Yemen, People's Democratic Republic: Street 51, New Extension; Yugoslavia: Street, 31, 79-A Khartoum 1, P.O. Box 1180; Zaire: Gumhouria Avenue.

KHARTOUM

Khartoum is generally known as the 'Three Towns' capital, i.e. Khartoum, Omdurman and Khartoum North. Omdurman is considered to be the national capital; Khartoum the commercial and administrative capital; and Khartoum North the industrial capital. The three towns lie at the junction of the Blue Nile and the White Nile. Omdurman is joined to Khartoum by the White Nile bridge; the Shambat bridge joins Omdurman to Khartoum North and the Burri bridge joins the eastern extension of Khartoum to Khartoum North across the Blue Nile.

Rebuilt after its destruction in 1885, Khartoum is planned on modern and spacious lines with huge colonial buildings but old houses with shuttered windows, narrow streets and colourful market-places can still be found.

A few yards from the museum is the Zoo—a place to view animals or merely stroll on the lawns.

A tree-lined embankment leads to the People's Palace where there is a marvellous collection of antique field guns, swords and cutlasses, used by General Gordon before he was stabbed at the foot of the now famous staircase by a soldier of the Mahdi's National Army. A few years later Lord Kitchener perpetuated Gordon's name when he gave Sudan the Gordon Memorial College. This is now the University of Khartoum.

OMDURMAN

Omdurman is rich in traditional Sudanese architecture: flat-roofed, baked mud or clay houses, city walls, narrow streets of dark little shops where some of the finest Sudanese handcrafts can be found. Omdurman was built by the Mahdi when he began his siege against Gordon in Khartoum, and it became the capital of the Mahdi's empire. It was captured in 1898 when Lord Kitchener victoriously led the British and the Egyptians against the forces of the Khalifa. You can see the Mahdi's tomb and the Khalifa's museum next door to it.

Omdurman has long been the meeting place of all the peoples of the Sudan; the Jaaleen, Shaigiyya, Danagla, Rubatab and Mahas of the north live side by side with the Baggara and Fur of the west and the Shilluk and Dinka of the south.

In the bustling *souk*, the smell of incense fills the air as Arab and African traders conduct their business. Here you can buy carpets from Persia, ivory goods, silverware, beads and handcrafts of the Middle East, Central and Eastern Africa.

Hotels
Acropole, P.O. Box 48, central location, tel: 72860, cable: Hotelacrop.

Excelsior, P.O. Box 272, central location, tel: 81181, cable: Excelhotel.

Grand, P.O. Box 316, tel: 72782.

Oasis, P.O. Box 272, tel: 81101.

National, P.O. Box 1808, tel: 70246.

De Paris, P.O. Box 1808, tel: 44154.

Sahara, P.O. Box 2208, tel: 75240, cable: Sarotel.

Sudan, P.O. Box 1845, tel: 80811, cable: Sudatel.

Khartoum Meridien, P.O. Box 1716, tel: 73107.

Khartoum Hilton, at the junction of the White and Blue Niles.

Metro, P.O. Box 589, tel: 71166, cable: Lukmetro.

Restaurants
Acropole Hotel has a roof-garden restaurant with interesting cuisine. Other recommended places are St. James in Gamhouria Street and the Blue Nile Casino in Khartoum North.

Entertainments
National Theatre, Nile Avenue, Omdurman, tel: 51549—the season is 1 October to 30 June. Gordon Music Hall, Gamhouria Avenue, tel: 72045, for dinner, dance and cabaret nightly.

There is a sailing club, a nine-hole golf club, and the Cultural Centre has a good library and facilities for tennis and swimming. There are several cabarets and a number of cinemas.

There are also a number of interesting Nile cruises. Launches with capacity for 15 persons can be hired: 24 hours notice for booking is required.

Additional entertainments are Hamad Floating Casino, Nile Avenue, Khartoum; Blue Nile Cafeteria, Nile Avenue, Khartoum; Ali Abdel Latif Stadium, Omdurman and Youth Stadium, Omdurman; Khartoum Stadium, Khartoum; Jimmy's Night Club, Khartoum.

Shopping and markets
The best place for books is Khartoum Bookshop (P.O. Box 968). For ivory and skins go to Sudan Folklore House (67 New Abou Lela Building, tel: 71729); it also has a picture gallery. Souvenirs can be obtained at Sudan Crafts (3/9 New Abou Ela Building in El Kasr Avenue, P.O. Box 2207, tel: 77367). For hides and skins and excellent Sudanese chamois, go to the Khartoum Tannery (P.O. Box 134, Khartoum South). A recommended boutique is Salwa Boutique, with branches in Khartoum and Khartoum North.

The bazaar in Omdurman has hand-beaten silver and copper; gold and silver filigree—jewellery, ivory and ebony carvings; handbags, slippers, belts and wallets of lion, leopard and lizard skin, ostrich eggs, beaked coffee pots, etc.

Tourist information

Sudan Tourist Corporation, P.O. Box 2424, tel: 70230, cable: Hababkum, Khartoum. There are regional offices in Port Sudan and Nyala. Travel Agent: Sudan Travel and Tourism Agency, P.O. Box 769, tel: 72119.

THE RED SEA

Port Sudan has been the country's port since the beginning of the century, when it totally replaced the old-established city of Suakin 56km down the coast. The new port is now a bustling commercial centre with plenty of entertainment and interest. The 'marine gardens' with their exquisite coral and tiny fish can be visited in glass-bottom boats. There is sailing in the harbour, swimming in a choice of pools and tremendous scope for fishing (barracuda, grey cod, shark, etc.) The main hotels are the **Red Sea, Olympia Park, Sinkat** and **Haramein**.

A visit to the Red Sea is not complete unless it includes the deserted city of Suakin, with its crumbling but beautiful houses, many of them masterpieces of Islamic architecture. This is also a good spot for swimming, fishing and sailing. One comes away with a lingering smell of salt and seashells.

Erkowit is a summer resort in the Red Sea Hills, inland from Suakin and Port Sudan, offering peaceful relaxation among beautiful mountains which rise to 1,200m above sea level. It has a first-class hotel with easy access from the railway station.

OTHER PLACES OF INTEREST

Kassala is in the mountains near the border with Ethiopia. South of Khartoum by tarred road is Wad Madani, an important town with three hotels: **Continental,**

El Gezira and **El Khawad**.

West and south of Khartoum lie the Nuba mountains, an area rich in folklore. The main town is El Obeid, the largest market of gum arabic in the world. Further west is Jabal Marrah, a huge mountain rich in vegetation and natural beauty. There are waterfalls, volcanic lakes and springs (some cool, some warm, some hot). The rest houses in the region include that at Suni, near the summit.

The main town of the south is Juba, a centre for safaris and Nile cruises. It has the comfortable and pleasant **Juba Hotel**.

NATIONAL PARKS

There are three game parks and 17 game reserves and sanctuaries.

Dinder National Park (6,100sq km) is open to visitors annually from Christmas to the end of April. It is 512km south east of Khartoum and closer to Europe than any of the other more popular African big game reserves. Visitors can stay in a specially built village with an attractive restaurant and bar area under spreading trees.

The visitor can expect to see many different types of animals and birds and a spectacular range of rolling savannah grasslands, sandy palm groves and tropical forest.

The most abundant animal species are the many types of antelope—the magnificent roan antelope, quite rare in most African game parks, the spiral-horned greater kudu, waterbuck, reedbuck, singa gazelle, oribi and bushbuck. There are also lion, giraffe, buffalo, warthog, several types of monkey, mongoose, fox and wild cat. The bird species include ostrich, eagle, vulture, guinea-fowl, pelican, bustard, crowned crane and large numbers of colourful smaller birds.

In the south are Numule National Park (192km south of Juba) and the Southern National Park (Bahr-al-Ghazal Province—18,400sq km). In these two parks and in other parts of the Southern Sudan, amid gigantic trees and high waving grass, elephants roam in herds which occasionally number as many as 400. Among the swamp reeds hippo, crocodile and buffalo are plentiful, as well as giraffe, rhino, zebra, leopard, lion and various types of cat. There are many types of antelope as well as countless birds, butterflies and beetles.

Hunting and Photographic Safaris

With the 17-year war now over, the vast area of the Southern Sudan has become a paradise for the game hunter. Animals include the giant eland, bongo, nile lechwe (three of the rarest beasts in the world), white-eared cob, roan antelope, greater kudu and yellow-backed duiker. The white rhino, although completely protected, forms an excellent subject for photography.

Permits are required for making films and for hunting. Film permits are obtainable from the Sudan Tourist Corporation, P.O. Box 2424, Khartoum.

Safaris formalities may be arranged through the Sudan Tourist Corporation (P.O. Box 2424, Khartoum). They specialise in Red Sea Coast Safaris which combine ibex hunting, deep sea fishing and aqua-sports from December to May.

HISTORY

The history of the Sudan, especially the region north of Khartoum, was bound from ancient times with that of Egypt. In 750 BC the first Sudanese kingdom of Nafata flourished near the Barkal Mountain and its Cushitic kings also ruled over Egypt. Meroe, near present-day Shendi, was the second of these ancient kingdoms, famous for its iron works which exported iron to other parts of Africa. The medieval kingdoms of Nubia, Maqurra and Abodia—which flourished in the northern Sudan—were converted to Christianity during the 6th Century. The next important phase came with the

penetration of the Arabs and Islam. The 16th century saw the rise of the kingdoms of the Fung, Darfur, Tagali and other minor dynasties. During this period, Arabisation and Islamisation of the northern parts was completed, but the South has been largely unaffected.

In 1820 the country was conquered by Egypt and the Turko-Egyptian regime was established.

In 1881, Mohamed Ahmed Al-Mahdi led his successful revolt against the Turko-Egyptian rulers. General Gordon, who was employed by the Egyptian Government, failed to arrest the Mahdi's revolt. Khartoum was captured by the Mahdi and Gordon was killed. The Mahdi was succeeded by Khalifa Abd Ullahi. For 15 years the Khalifa attempted to resist the invasion from Egypt, and to establish a strong government, but he failed. In 1898, the armies of the Khalifa were defeated in the battle of Omdurman, and a year later the Khalifa himself was killed.

From then on until 1956 Sudan was ruled by the Condominium Administration—a supposedly joint Egyptian and British Administration but in reality British. The achievements of the colonial administration included the establishment of railways, a modern system of education, the important Gezira peasant cotton scheme, and a modern system of government.

The Sudan became independent in 1956 and a parliamentary system of government was established. But in 1958 the parliamentary regime was overthrown by a military government which was, in its turn, overthrown in 1964. In May 1969 the army came back to power, this time led by younger radical officers under Major-General Numeiry who was elected President in September 1971. Agreement with the Southern Sudanese rebels was reached in March 1972, at Addis Ababa, which gave the South regional autonomy and brought to an end the war which had sapped the country for 17 years.

SWAZILAND

Swaziland contains within its small area nearly every example of African landscape, with the exception of desert. In a 160 km. drive the road may pass through sugar cane plantations, rugged often mist-shrouded mountains, savannah and thornbush country, citrus orchards and pineapple groves.

Before its independence on 6 September 1968, Swaziland formed part of the British High Commission Territories with Basutoland (now Lesotho) and Bechuanaland (now Botswana). It is a member of the Commonwealth, the Organization of African Unity and the 14-nation East and Central African Regional Organization. Unlike most African States it emerged into independence under the firm guidance of its King, Sobhuza II, who began his rule in 1922. Known by the traditional title *Ngwenyama* (the Lion), he is Head of State. In his absence his place is taken by the Queen Mother, the *Ndlovukazi* (the She-Elephant).

THE LAND AND THE PEOPLE

Despite its smallness Swaziland has a rich variety of soils and vegetation and is one of the best-watered areas in southern Africa. Four major rivers—the Komati, Usutu, Mbuluzi and Ngwavuma—flow from west to east to the Indian Ocean. There are four well-defined topographi-

cal regions, extending longitudinally north and south in roughly parallel belts.

The 5,100 sq. km. Highveld (locally called *Inkangala*) is a wide ribbon of rugged country in which lie its two richest mines, the Havelock Asbestos Mine and the Ngwenya Iron Ore Mine. The original forest has long been destroyed, but in its place has been planted the 40,000

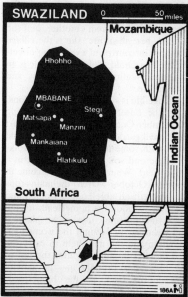

361

hectares of Usutu pine and eucalyptus forest. The 5,000 sq. km. Middleveld, rolling down from the Highveld through hilly country with well-watered valleys, is ideal for mixed farming, the main crops being rice and sub-tropical fruits (citrus and bananas) grown under irrigation, and maize, cotton, beans, tobacco and pine-apples cultivated on drylands. The rivers afford extensive irrigation schemes. The Lowveld (known as *Liblanze*) covers 5,100 sq. km. of gently undulating land-scape with hills rising from 170 m. to 350 m. Once cattle-ranching country, it is now an area of intensive cultivation of sugar-cane, rice and citrus fruits under irrigation. The 1,530 sq. km. Lubombo plateau is an escarpment along the eastern fringe of the Lowveld, mainly cattle country and good mixed farming land.

Nine-tenths of the population still live in villages where they raise cattle, hunt game and plant cereals, the families often working communally in the fields. Villages are divided into family homesteads (*umuti*) under control of a headman, the village patriarch. The most important woman is the headman's mother, or if she is dead, her substitute; she is the village 'mother' in control of everything affecting the household. This mother role is an important feature of Swazi family and national life.

Village life is strictly set by the seasons. With the onset of the rains in spring (September-October) the women start their small gardens along the river banks; later, with some help from the menfolk, they hoe and sow maize and millet in a larger field. When the full rains come in summer (October-March) the main crops are planted; all able-bodied women and children abandon the homesteads for the fields and the men join in the planting and weeding. In autumn the women cut the grain and the men help to carry the tied bundles home. In winter the last of the harvest is brought in—the activity now moves back to the homesteads where maize and corn is threshed. The best grain is stored in the grain pits and the inferior is consumed at once. Winter is a time for relaxing and of a plenitude of food; the men go hunting and entertain, and the women go on visits to their parents.

CULTURE

Swaziland is a constitutional monarchy. The present King, Sobhuza II, the *Ngwenyama*, is the longest-reigning mon-arch in the world. Tradition traces his descent through the Swazi royal family, the *Nkosi-Dlamini*, back to the 15th cen-tury. But he is much more than just a King to the Swazi people and tradition endows him with mystical characteristics.

Traditional ceremonies and music play an important part in Swazi social life. The main instruments are rattles tied to wrists and ankles. the shield is used for percus-sion; two types of horn, whistles and long reed flutes are the principal wind instruments.

The two major cultural events are the *Ncwala* ceremony (December-January) and the Reed Dance (*Umhlanga*) in June-July, both of which are held at the Lobamba Royal Village. The Ncwala, the most sacred of ceremonies, represents the King as the source of fertility and the symbol of power and unity. It lasts for six days and is a highly ritualised festival of song, dance, folklore and martial displays by the regiments. The Reed Dance, which lasts a whole week, is intended to encourage girls of the same age-group to work in harmony under discipline, and to preserve their virginity.

WILDLIFE

Once Swaziland was rich in wildlife but years of unchecked hunting ravaged the game population and many of the larger antelopes were in danger of becoming extinct. Animals still to be seen are zebra, hippo, kudu, water buck, impala, duiker and wildebeest. The establishment of large forestry concerns has led to a return of some of the smaller antelope to the sanctury of the trees. Crocodiles inhabit the lower reaches of the main rivers.

Birdlife is prolific and you will see the European stork, sacred ibis, blue crane, wattled crane and crested crane (the mating dance of cranes is a fantastic sight), hornbill, hammerhead, the lilac-breasted roller, bee-eaters, hoopoes and kingfishers. Guinea-fowl are common and you will come across flocks of them by the roadside. Several species of water-fowl including the spur-wing geese, congregate on the rivers and the Sand River Dam.

GENERAL INFORMATION

Area: 17,364 sq. km.
Population: 477,023.
Altitude: 170m. to 200m.
Capital: Mbabane.
Head of State: King Sobhuza II.
Government: The Government is Royal-ist, with all power and authority centred on the King since he staged his own Palace Revolution in 1973, sweeping away the multi-party democratic Parlia-ment established at independence on 6 September 1968. The only legal party is the *Imbokodvo* (Traditional Royalist) Party.
Languages: SiSwati and English.
Religion: 60% Christian (African Baptist, Roman Catholic and Protestant) and 40% traditional.
Currency: Lilangeni (plural: Emalan-geni); 1 Lilangeni=1 Rand (SA); US$1.00=L.0.87; £1 sterling=L.1.50.
Weight and measures: Metric.
Time: GMT+2 (South African Standard Time).
Electricity: 380-220V.

HOW TO GET THERE

By air: Matsapha Airport near Manzini is the main air entry point. Swazi Air and South African Airways flights connect at Jan Smuts (Johannesburg) and Durban airport. Daylight landings only at Matsa-pha. Weekday flights daily scheduled. DETA flights from Maputo, Mozam-bique. There are three Government-owned airstrips and 20 privately owned grass strips used by light aircraft. Charter planes are available.

By road: A week-end bus service oper-ates between Johannesburg and Mba-bane, and between Maputo and Manzini.

Numerous tourist buses visit Swaziland from Natal and the Transvaal in South Africa. The quickest road route to Swazi-land from Johannesburg is via Bronk-horstspruit, Witbank, Carolina (Oshoek border post), Mbabane—some 340 km. of tarred roads. From Durban there is a tarred road via Ladysmith, Volksrust, Ermelo, Oshoek, or a shorter but rough-er route, much of it on dirt roads, through northern Zululand and Lavumisa (border post). From Maputo motorists' entry point is Nomahasha to Mbabane, 130km. away, includes some 65 km. of dirt road. Check on border post opening times before starting a road journey to Swaziland. An upper speed limit of 95

On the road near Manzini

km. per hour applies throughout the country.

Visas and health regulations

All visitors to Swaziland require valid passports. They are required by law to report to an immigration officer within 72 hours of entering the country. There are immigration posts at Nomahasha and Goba on the Mozambique border but visitors entering from South Africa must register with the Immigration Office, Mbabane, or at any police station. Visitors staying more than 60 days require a temporary visitors permit.

Citizens of Britain, or Commonwealth countries do not require visas for Swaziland, nor do the nationals of the following countries: Belgium, Denmark, Finland, France, Greece, Iceland, Italy, Israel, Portugal, Liechtenstein, Luxembourg, Netherlands, Norway and its Colonies, San Marino, South Africa, Sweden, Switzerland, Uruguay and the United States.

Visitors must have sufficient resources to cover their stay and have a return ticket or the means to buy one.

Visitors who come from an endemic yellow fever area require a valid yellow fever inoculation certificate. Similarly those from smallpox areas require proof of vaccination against smallpox.

If you intend spending any time in the Swaziland Lowveld during the wet months (September-March) you should take malaria prophylactics before, during and after your stay. Bilharzia is a hazard in most rivers and dams.

Dutiable goods

With South Africa, Lesotho and Botswana, Swaziland is part of the southern African common customs area, and visitors from South Africa are not subject to customs formalities. Those arriving from Mozambique have to comply with certain regulations. Vehicles registered in Mozambique may enter for up to six months without payment of duty. Those from other countries (excluding South Africa, Lesotho or Botswana) may also remain for up to 12 months without payment of duty if a deposit is paid to cover the duty, by using carnets de passage or triptyques from recognised international motoring organisations, or through temporary customs importation permits.

Tourists from outside the common customs area may bring in tobacco and wines subject to the usual limitations. Arms and ammunition may not be brought in without advance permission from Police Headquarters, P.O. Box 49, Mbabane.

CLIMATE

Because of variations in altitude the weather is extremely changeable. Except in the Lowveld, it is seldom uncomfortably hot and no part of Swaziland is ever very cold although frosts occasionally occur in the Highveld.

The Highveld is near temperate but humid: temperatures can be as high as 32°C from October to February, with mid-year winter temperatures dropping to zero. Average rainfall varies between 1,000 and 2,000mm. The Middleveld and the Lubombo are sub-tropical and drier, with annual rainfall of 750-1,150mm. Most of the rain falls between October and March, but long periods of continuous rain are uncommon. In the Lowveld the terrain drops from 350m. to 170m. above sea level and the mean annual rainfall is 660mm., although in a drought year it can fall well below this. The Lowveld climate is particularly pleasant during the winter months (mid-year).

What to wear: Light, casual clothing is the norm, but the evenings can be cool, even in summer, and it is advisable to have something warmer. A light raincoat is necessary during the summer months (October-March).

More formal wear is customary at the casino and sophisticated hotels. Dinner jackets are sometimes worn but are not obligatory.

USEFUL PHRASES

	SiSwati
Hello, good day	*Sawubona*
Yes	*Yebo*
How are you?	*Unjani*
I am well	*Ngikhona*
Thank you ·	*Ngiyabonga*
Goodbye (Stay well)	*Sala Kahle*
Go well	*Hamba Kahle*

ACCOMMODATION, FOOD

Swaziland is very popular with tourists. Existing hotels are hard put to meet the growing demand, so accommodation bookings should be made well in advance—and confirmed. Peak holiday periods are week-ends, South African public holidays and school holidays (Easter, June, September and December-January). The Swazispa Holiday Inn, The Ezulwini Holiday Inn, and the Royal Swazi hotel with its casino, all near Mbabane, attract the most custom. All hotels are open to non-residents and some have a very high standard of cuisine, but to be sure of a table it is wise to book in advance.

Camping sites exist in Mbabane and Manzini and there are motels and caravan parks in the Ezulwini Valley. The Mlilwane Game Park and the Timbali Caravan Park in Ezulwini offer good facilities for campers.

Tipping should be 10% of the bill.

TRANSPORT

Public transport is still in its formative stage. While there is a fair, if erratic, bus service between Mbabane and Manzini, the visitor would be well advised to hire a car, or arrange for transport through an hotel. Bus services meet scheduled air flights.

Car hire: Hertz United, P.O. Box 360, Manzini, tel: 2404, Mbabane; **Swazi Safaris**, P.O. Box 680, Matsapha.

BANKS

Barclays Bank of Swaziland Ltd., P.O. Box 667, Allister Miller Street, Mbabane. The Standard Bank Swaziland Ltd., P.O. Box 68, 5 Swazi Plaza, Mbabane—3 branches. The Swaziland Development and Savings Bank, head office in Mbabane—5 branches.

Business hours

Banks: 0830 to 1300 Monday-Friday; 0830-1100 Saturday. Government offices: 0800 to 1700 with one hour lunch break. Immigration Office closes at 1500. Shops generally follow the Government office hours but cafes and restaurants in Mbabane and Manzini stay open until 2230 and the more expensive restaurants until midnight.

PUBLIC HOLIDAYS

New Year's Day; Good Friday; Easter Monday; National Flag Day 25 April; Ascension Day; Commonwealth Day 11 June; King's Birthday 22 July; Umhlanga (Reed Dance) Day; Somhlolo (Independence) Day 6 September; United Nations Day 24 October; Christmas Day; Boxing Day; Incwala (First Fruits) Day, in December or January.

FOREIGN EMBASSIES
(in Mbabane)

UK: Allister Miller Street; USA: Allister Miller Street.

TOURIST INFORMATION

Useful addresses are The Tourist Officer, P.O. Box 451, Mbabane; Swazi Air, P.O. Box 9, Mbabane.

MBABANE

A mixture of old and modern buildings, Mbabane (the largest town in Swaziland) is the administrative capital and an expanding commercial centre. Attractively situated among the Dalengi hills, it overlooks the beautiful Ezulwini Valley. In the valley, 20 km. from Mbabane, is the Royal Swazi Hotel and Casino, one of Swaziland's main tourist attractions.

The Tavern, P.O. Box 25, tel: 2361, Mbabane.

Swazi Inn, P.O. Box 121, tel: 2235.

Highland View Hotel, P.O. Box 223, tel:2464, Mbabane.

Jabula Inn, P.O. Box 15, tel: 2406, Mbabane, centrally situated, recently modernised.

EZULWINI VALLEY

Besides the restaurants in the hotels, which are open to non-residents, there are a number of others in the town itself. There is a particularly good Portuguese restaurant opposite the Tavern Hotel. There are two night-clubs: the **Penguin Nite Club** (adjacent to the Jabula Inn) and the **Highland View Night-Club** (adjacent to the Highland View Hotel).

Several hotels stage cabarets. The **Royal Swazi Hotel** has nightly dancing except Mondays. The **Casino** opens at 2000 from Monday to Friday; at 1400 on Saturdays, Sundays and public holidays. It closes when the last player leaves. French roulette, American roulette (one zero) and blackjack are played every night; also *chemin de fer* and stud poker at holiday periods.

Swazispa Holiday Inn, P.O. Box 412, Mbabane, adjacent to Royal Swazi Hotel and Casino (free admission to casino).

Royal Swazi Hotel, P.O. Box 412, tel: 2722, Mbabane.

Timbali Caravan Park, in Ezulwini Valley on Mbabane-Manzini road, 10 km. south of Mbabane.

Shopping and markets

The Government-sponsored Small Enterprises Development Co. (SEDCO) has opened an estate on the Mbabane-Manzini Road where you can watch Swazi craftsmen at work and buy their products. Items available include a wide variety of beadwork and basketwork, grass and sisal mats, copperware, leatherwork, wooden bowls, local gemstone jewellery, wooden and soapstone carvings, calabashes, knobkerries, battleaxes, walking sticks, drums, karosses (animal skin mats), python skins, handwoven fabrics, clothing using characteristic Swazi techniques, from batik to tie-and-die. Well worth a visit. There is also the Swazi Market in the main street on the corner before the road to Manzini.

MANZINI

Situated 40 km. south of Mbabane, Manzini is the industrial hub of Swaziland and an agricultural centre. The town itself offers comfortable hotels, well-stocked shops and a Swazi market where traditional handcrafts can be bought at modest prices.

The George Hotel, P.O. Box 51, tel: 2666, Manzini, dates from the Anglo-Boer War but has been extensively modernised and a new annexe built.

Manzini Arms, P.O. Box 48, tel: 2297, Manzini.

The Paramount, P.O. Box 28, tel: 2360, Manzini.

The Chaline, P.O. Box 645, tel: 6113, Manzini.

SITEKI

The only town on the Lubombo escarpment, Siteki is a convenient stopping place to or from Mozambique; the Mhlumeni border post is 28 km. away. The old-fashioned but comfortable **Stegi Hotel** is one of the oldest in the country.

BIG BEND

In the sugar growing area of the southern Lowveld, Big Bend is situated on a bend of the Great Usutu River. Besides the sugar estates which cover vast tracts, the surrounding countryside is very attractive, particularly in winter when the aloes are in bloom. The **Bend Inn** is the favourite resort of the local sugar planters—a speciality of the hotel is the Sunday night South African style *braaivleis* (barbecue).

SCENIC TOURS
Mbabane—Mhlambanyati—Bhunya— Malkerns Valley—Lobamba—Mbabane (101 km.). From Mbabane, this drive passes through the heart of the Usutu Forest, one of the largest man-made forests in the world. The road is gravel for the first 24 km. after which it is tarred. In the midst of the Usutu Forest is a very good hotel, the **Forester's Arms**, which has recently been enlarged and modernised. (P.O. Box 14, tel: 77 Mhlambanyati, good menu, trout fishing, 9-hole golf course.) After the gravel road the tarred road passes through the Usutu Pulp Mills from which about 100,000 tons of sulphate pulp are exported annually; it then follows the Usutu River into the Malkerns Valley, the centre of the country's pineapple industry and an important citrus-growing area. Turn left when you come to the trans-territorial highway and the road takes you past the King's Maize Field to Lobamba, the spiritual and legislative capital. It is the location of Parliament Building, the State Palace and the National Stadium, the latter financed on a self-help basis by the people of Swaziland. In the vicinity is the Queen Mother's Village—an intricately constructed complex of traditional 'beehive' houses where many of the King's wives live. The annual Reed Dance by Swazi maidens takes place in July-August. Visitors are welcome but photographs may only be taken with the permission of the Government Information Service (P.O. Box 338, Mbabane). From Lobamba the road winds through the Ezulwini Valley, past the Swazispa Hotel and the Casino, and then up the Malagwane Hill.

Mbabane—Pigg's Peak—Tshaneni— Mhlume—Siteki—Manzini—Mbabane (250 km). Pigg's Peak, named after an early prospector, William Pigg, is at the heart of some very beautiful country in north west Swaziland. About 16 km. away, at Nsangwini Shelter in the Komati Valley, are some remarkable rock paintings depicting 'bird-men'. Should you wish to spend a few days in this fascinating area there is the **Highlands Inn** in Pigg's Peak, a modernised and enlarged old farmhouse which offers good accommodation. Tshaneni is the headquarters of the Swaziland Irrigation Scheme, a Commonwealth Development Corporation project where sugar-cane, citrus and rice are cultivated. The Sand River Dam

Dancing at a Swazi celebration

is the largest stretch of water in Swaziland and provides excellent fishing, sailing and water ski-ing. On the edge of the dam there is a 600 hectare game sanctuary where you can see kudu, impala, zebra and duiker. There is an hotel at Tshaneni, the **Impala Arms**, with a good dining-room and a bar. From Tshaneni the drive continues to Mhlume (the name means 'good growth') which is the headquarters of the Mhlume (Swaziland) Sugar Co. Ltd. and from there to Siteki in the Lubombo Mountains. You will pass the Ehlane Game Reserve which is not yet open to the public.

A note to motorists: exercise extreme caution at narrow bridges on many of the country roads as approaches may be steep and warning signs are frequently absent. A blind rise is often followed by a deep descent. Herds of cattle using the roads are also a hazard.

NATIONAL PARKS
Mlilwane Wildlife Sanctuary

A small game sanctuary in the Ezulwini Valley, Mlilwane was started by a keen conservationist to protect and foster the country's wildlife and flora. Earth roads, along which visitors can travel in their own cars, cross the reserve but to get the best out of game viewing travel slowly, stay in your car and do not make much noise. The animals are remarkably tolerant of vehicles and allow you to approach quite close.

There is a wide variety of wildlife to be seen but no elephant or carnivores. Bird-life is prolific and colourful.

Also in the Mlilwane Game Sanctuary is the Gilbert Reynolds Memorial Garden, dedicated to Dr. Gilbert Reynolds, a well-known authority on aloes. The gardens contain a number of rare cycads and 230 aloe species collected throughout Africa and Madagascar. The gardens are particularly colourful in winter (mid-year). Accommodation at Mlilwane consists of chalets 'beehive' huts equipped with beds and mattresses and camping and caravan facilities. Baths and showers.

HISTORY

In the 16th century the Nguni people (a group which includes Zulu and Xhosa as well as Swazi) were living in small disunited chiefdoms on the good grazing land of eastern South Africa. When Shaka created the Zulu nation in the early 19th century dissidents fled and many different clans formed a stronghold in Swaziland taking the Dlamini royal clan as their leaders. The King was respected as a raingiver as well as the political head. All his family, and particularly his mother, had great prestige but his laws were promulgated in conjunction with the *Li-*bandla* (national council) which consisted of all heads of households.

King Mswati (1840-68) welded the Swazi nation together, extending his dominions to three times the size of modern Swaziland and building up a powerful army to rival that of the Zulu. After his death the Transvaal Republic's ambition of forging an outlet to the sea, perhaps building a railway along the Great Usutu with German help, began to threaten Swazi independence and also worry Britain. Yet in the 1880's King Mbandzeni appears to have been netting £12,000 per year, recklessly granting a myriad of over-lapping concessions to foreigners for the use of grazing land and prospecting rights. In 1894 Britain recognised—without consulting the Swazis—the Transvaal's control over Swaziland. After the South African War (1899-1902) Britain made Swaziland a protectorate while the Transvaal joined the Union of South Africa.

Swaziland was an economic and political backwater. Concessionaries—often absentee—remained in control of two-thirds of the land—one-third was reserved for the Swazi. The 10,000 or so whites had some political say through the European Advisory Council while Africans continued to be ruled by their chiefs and king under colonial officials. After brief attempts at a multi-racial constitution in the 1960s and considerable internal disturbance from strikers, Swaziland was the last directly-administered British colony in Africa to become independent, in 1968.

The King, Sobhuza II (born 1899, installed 1922) maintained considerable power in the independent State, especially through the ruling Imbokodvo party, and in 1973 took power entirely into his own hands. The country has taken a moderate, non-doctrinaire line, necessarily linked to surrounding white-ruled countries, but enjoying greater prosperity over the last decade than the similarly-placed Lesotho and Botswana.

TANZANIA

Tanzania is a beautiful country, rich in wildlife and the scene of mankind's earliest habitats. Its Government, under President Julius Nyerere, has two major priorities: building an egalitarian non-racial society, and protecting the natural environment. It is the only country in the world where the Government has set aside almost one-quarter of all the land as national parks, game reserves and forest reserves. At the time of independence in December 1961 there was only one national park—the Serengeti. Today there are 12.

THE LAND AND THE PEOPLE

Situated just south of the equator, Tanzania (which also includes the Indian Ocean islands of Pemba and Zanzibar) is East Africa's largest country—larger than France, West Germany, Austria and Switzerland combined. Over 53,000 sq km of the total area are covered by inland water. Most of the lakes were formed by the Rift Valley, which is one of the world's most remarkable geographic features.

There is still volcanic activity in the neighbourhood of the Rift Valley. Ol Donyo L'Engai, in the eastern Rift Valley, last erupted in 1966. Kilimanjaro, Africa's highest mountain at 5,895 m was once thought to be dormant but has had

recent rumblings. One of the best views of Kilimanjaro and the nearby Mount Meru can be gained while landing at Kilimanjaro International Airport, on the road between Arusha and Moshi, in the Sanya Juu Plains.

The Tanzania mainland is divided into several clearly defined regions. The coastal plain, which varies in width from 16 to 64 km, is hot and humid. In the north, the Masai Steppe, 213 to 1,067 m above sea level, is semi-arid with small hills and occasional mountains. The

MEMORABLE VACATIONS

An exciting adventure begins from the moment your plane lands at the new Kilimanjaro International Airport. Its 4 kilometer Airstrip and modern handling facilities serve the world's leading Airlines.

AN EXCITING SAFARI!

Magnificent Mount Kilimanjaro serves as a towering background to the airport. Africa's highest Mountain at 19,340 ft. above sea level, remains snow-capped throughout the year, even though it lies almost on the equator. Tanzania's Pride! It is a gate-way to the World's greatest wild animal sanctuaries . . . Serengeti. . . Ngorongoro. . . Manyara. Unique spectacles of wildlife in their natural, unspoiled habitat. They are all nearby!

BEACH AND SEA SPORTS

For tourists who want to combine a wildlife safari and a sunny beach holiday, Tanzania's coastal circuit is ideal.

Mile after mile of white sandy beaches fringed by waving palm trees. . . clean blue water with a sky that meets the vast Indian Ocean on the horizon. . . The dramatic sunsets are a spectacle of flaming re orange and purple! Bring along plenty colour films.

Nearby Mafia Island, offers deepsea fish men some of the most exciting sport in E Africa, not to mention the underwa beauties of the coral reef for those w prefer goggling or underwater photograp

ZANZIBAR . . . THE ISLAND OF SENSATIONS

Served daily by Air Tanzania, is the exc pearl of the Tanzania Coast. With its char teristic Arabic architecture, brass antiq and winding streets, it offers some wonder sightseeing.

The lush tropical surroundings and lov beaches make for a unique travel experien This "Spice Island" is much more than famous cloves.

ΛΝΙΑ
MANJARO

MFORTABLE HOTELS

re are many luxury and first class tourist
els and lodges all managed by Tanzania
rist Corporation.
ry visitor to our hotels is treated as an
oured guest throughout the entire stay.
Kilimanjaro is one of our many luxury
els which offers all modern comforts and
ditional Tanzanian hospitality against an
tic African background.

LKLORE ... SOUVENIRS

visit to Tanzania would be complete
hout some shopping for momentoes.
phies and animal skin articles like Purses,
ndbags and Sandals — made from
codile, leopard, lion, ostrich and
phant hide, may be purchased from most
rist Shops throughout TANZANIA.

Unique Makonde carvings of artistic merit,
decorative pieces carved in local ivory, and
jewellery fashioned in gold, silver and
copper are perfect souvenirs of a memorable
vacation in TANZANIA!

TANZANIA TOURIST CORPORATION

P.O. Box 2485, Telephone: 27572
Telex: 41062, Cable TANTOUR
DAR-ES-SALAAM, TANZANIA

371

southern area towards Zambia and Lake Malawi is a high plateau.

The high altitude of the greater part of Tanzania counteracts its tropical location. Its climate and vegetation are not 'tropical' in the usual sense, except along the lush coastal belt. Woodland and bush occupy more than half the country. Desert, semi-desert and arid lands account for the remainder.

Tanzania is the home of 120 different peoples, without any single dominant group; this has given the country a stability lacking in many neighbouring States. Most groups are Bantu-speaking, and are thought to have entered Tanzania from Zambia and Zaire around 100 BC, mixing with and absorbing the earlier inhabitants—the Hadzapi (Wakindiga) and Sandawe, an extension of the Xhosa peoples of southern Africa who speak a 'click' language. A second group, now living around Mbulu in the north, speak a similar language to the Cushitic group in Ethiopia. A third group (including the Masai) who migrated from the north, are Nilo-Hamitic.

The German colonial authorities encouraged Indian immigration to provide workers for the building of the railways. Many subsequently went into the construction business, or set up as traders.

The population of the Zanzibar islands is almost entirely Muslim. They are a mixture of peoples originating from the East African mainland—Shirazis, who are the descendants of the early settlers from Persia, Arabs from the Gulf States, and Comorians from the Comoro Islands.

GENERAL INFORMATION

Area: 945,087 sq km
Population: 15 million.
Altitude: Sea level to 5,895 m (Kilimanjaro); predominant high plateau of 914 m.
Capital: Dar es Salaam (moving to Dodoma, to be developed over the next 10 years).
Head of State: President Julius K. Nyerere.
Government: Single-party rule by the Chama Cha Mapinduzi (Revolutionary Party).
Date of independence: 9 December 1961.
Languages: Swahili is the official language; English is widely spoken.
Religions: Christianity, Islam and traditional.
Currency: 1 Tanzanian shilling=100 cents. 14.28 Tanzanian shillings=£1 sterling; 8.33 Tanzanian shillings=US$1.00.
Time: GMT +3.

HOW TO GET THERE

By air: Tanzania is served by numerous international airlines: British Airways, Deta, Air Comoros, Aeroflot, Air Zaire, Air France, Air India, Alitalia, Egypt Air, Ethiopian Airlines, KLM, Lufthansa, PanAm, PIA, SAS, Sabena, Swissair, TWA and Zambia Airways. International airports are Dar es Salaam and Kilimanjaro.

By road: Tarmac roads connect Tanzania with Kenya and Zambia. **In 1977 the**

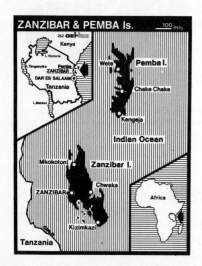

ZANZIBAR & PEMBA Is.

border with Kenya was closed to all traffic. From Lusaka in Zambia the Great North Road is tarmac all the way to Dar es Salaam. The main route from Rwanda is being improved and road links are being built from Mozambique. Many other all-weather roads are suitable for saloon cars except during the long rains in April and May. Inexpensive bus services are available throughout the country.

By rail: The railways offer first-class accommodation with connections to all major towns in East Africa. Further information is available from the District Traffic Superintendent, East African Railways, P.O. Box 9040, Dar es Salaam.

By sea: Dar es Salaam is served by ocean-going freighters and passenger liners. Both Lake Victoria and Lake Tanganyika have steamer services. For details contact: East African Harbours Corporation, P.O. Box 9184, Dar es Salaam, also National Shipping Agencies Co. Ltd. (NASACO), P.O. Box 9082, Dar es Salaam.

Visas and health regulations

Visitors to Tanzania, except for citizens of Commonwealth countries, require visas. In countries where Tanzania has no diplomatic representation visas may be obtained by writing directly to: The Principal Immigration Officer, P.O. Box 512, Dar es Salaam. All temporary visitors must hold a visitor's pass.

Visitors must have an international certificate of vaccination against smallpox and yellow fever. It is also advisable to have a certificate showing vaccination against cholera.

Dutiable goods

Tourists on a visit not exceeding six months' duration are granted duty-free baggage importation privileges in respect of all non-consumable goods for their own use.

Visitors over the age of 16 years are permitted one litre of alcoholic liquor and 250 gm of tobacco or equivalent cigars or 200 cigarettes, ½ litre of perfume or toilet water.

Currency regulations:

There is no limit on the amount of foreign currency one may bring into Tanzania. There are, however, strict exchange control laws. Visitors are required to declare the amount they have upon entering the country and are required to show receipts for money spent upon departure. Travellers' cheques may only be cashed at authorised dealers (banks, tourist hotels, etc.). At no time may they be cashed by a private individual. It is generally more advantageous to change foreign currency at hotels since banks charge high commission.

When leaving Tanzania the visitor may not take out more than shs. 100 in Tanzanian currency. It is therefore advisable to have small denomination travellers' cheques. (There is an airport departure tax of shs. 20.)

CLIMATE

Even though Tanzania lies in the tropics and is a land without winter, its climate is governed by its altitude.

Coastal strip: Temperatures vary from 24°C-27°C in the cool season (June-September) to 27°C-30°C during the hot months of December-March when the humidity is very high, though at night it drops considerably. Short rains in November last for three weeks. The long rains begin around April and last for six weeks, when there are periods of sunshine or just cloud cover; this is often a good time to visit Tanzania (April-May) as rates are reduced and hotels are less crowded.

The Central Plateau (800-1,200 m): The plateau covers much of the country, and is warm and dry (average 27°C) in the daytime and cool at night.

The Highlands: (1,600-2,200 m): This is a

semi-temperate zone, pleasant in the day-time and quite cool at night.

What to wear: Dress is generally informal. Warmer clothing is recommended for evenings, especially from June to September. It can be very cold at the higher altitudes, and you may need a warm jersey.

The strength of the direct sun can be deceptive at these higher altitudes. So whether you are coming to the parks or the beaches it is wise to bring sunglasses, suntan oil and a hat. Insect repellents are advisable, and are easily purchased locally.

Health precautions: Malaria is prevalent throughout Tanzania except at altitudes over 1,600 m. It is advisable to begin taking a prophylactic two weeks before arrival and for two weeks after departure. Most tourist hotels are either air-conditioned or furnished with mosquito nets, but if you intend camping nets are essential. They are readily available locally.

All urban centres have hospitals, while many rural areas have clinics and dispensaries.

Most inland watercourses and dams are infected with bilharzia, so it is not recommended to swim in lakes and rivers. The ocean is of course free of it. The majority of game lodges have treated swimming pools (see under individual parks). The water in all urban and tourist areas is chemically treated and safe. It is wiser, however, to bring some medication for dysentery.

For a modest fee visitors to East Africa can take out a limited membership of the Flying Doctor Service of East Africa. If injured or ill, the service will fly you out of the bush to an urban centre for treatment. For further information contact: The Flying Doctor Service, Kilimanjaro Christian Centre (KCMC), P.O. Box 3010, Moshi, Tanzania.

ACCOMMODATION AND FOOD

Tanzania has many excellent hotels. The cheaper establishments are not comfortable, but adequate.

The food served in most hotels tends to be roasts, steaks and seafood. It is generally good and in Dar es Salaam there are several excellent restaurants, including Indian and Pakistani, but in the major Government-operated tourist hotels the quality is variable.

To get good Tanzanian traditional dishes, one has to be invited to a Tanzanian home—the food then is superb.

Tanzania produces two wines—Dodoma Red is variable in quality, and Dodoma Rosé is usually quite pleasant. A good selection of imported wines, spirits and liquors are available, but no imported beer. Tanzania produces four types of beer, all very good.

There is a Government levy of 10-$12\frac{1}{2}\%$ on accommodation charges in all hotels.

Tipping: Though tipping is generally frowned upon in this socialist State, the waiter will also generally frown if you do not tip. However, many of the hotels in the game parks and some hotels in the cities make a service charge. Tips should NOT be offered in Zanzibar.

TRANSPORT

Road: Tanzania has a good network of tarmac and all-weather roads connecting all major points. Traffic drives on the left. The Automobile Association of East Africa, Cargen, Corporation House, Maktaba Street, P.O. Box 3004, Dar es Salaam, telephone 21965, has reciprocal facilities in East Africa with the AA and RAC in Britain.

Air: Air Tanzania, launched in 1977 to replace the defunct East African Airways, has introduced regular services to all main towns. All national parks have air strips and there are two charter companies operating single- and twin-engine aircraft to take you to any town or bush strip in the country. Contact Tanzania Air Services, P.O. Box 364, Dar es Salaam, tel: 22032 and 29974; Tim-Air Charters, P.O. Box 804, Dar es Salaam, tel: 27128.

Car hire
In Dar es Salaam: Tanzania Safari Tours Ltd., P.O. Box 20058, tel: 63546; Subzali Tours and Safaris, P.O. Box 3121, tel: 25907; Tanzania Tours Ltd., P.O. Box 9354, tel: 25586.

In Arusha: Tanzania Tours Ltd., P.O. Box 1369, tel: 3300; Subzali Tours and Safaris, P.O. Box 3061, tel: 3681; United Touring Co. Ltd., P.O. Box 3173, tel: 3727.

BUSINESS HOURS
Banks: Monday-Friday 0830-1200, Saturday 0830-1100; Government: Monday-Friday 0730-1430, Saturday 0730-1230; Business: Monday-Friday 0730-1430. Most diplomatic missions work Government hours.

PUBLIC HOLIDAYS
Zanzibar Revolution Day, 12 January; Idd-el-Haj, variable; Afro-Shirazi Day, 5 February; Good Friday; Easter Monday; Union Day, 26 April; Workers' Day, 1 May; Maulid Day, variable; Saba Saba Day, 7 July; Idd-el-Fitr, variable; Independence Day, 9 December; Christmas Day.

LANGUAGES
Swahili is the official language of Tanzania and is spoken throughout the country, but English is very widely used in all urban and tourist centres. There are, of course, many local dialects.

Radio Tanzania generally broadcasts in Swahili. There are several news and entertainment programmes broadcast in English.

Useful phrases
Hello	*Jambo*
Please	*Tafadhali*
Thank you	*Asante*
Goodbye	*Kwaheri*
Welcome	*Karibu*
Tea	*Chai*
Coffee	*Kahawa*
Milk	*Maziwa*
Good	*Nzuri*

Kilimanjaro Hotel, Dar es-Salaam

How much (does it cost)?	*Shillingi Ngapi?*
Where is the lavatory?	*Wapi Choo?*

FOREIGN EMBASSIES IN DAR ES SALAAM
Algeria: P.O. Box 2963, 34 Upanga Road; Australia: P.O. Box 2996, NIC Investment House, Independence Avenue; Belgium: Flat No. 7, NIC Building, Mirambo Street; Burundi: Lugalo Road, Upanga; Canada: P.O. Box 1022, NAFCO Building; Denmark: P.O. Box 9171, Bank House, Independence Avenue; Egypt: P.O. Box 1668, 24 Garden Avenue; Finland: P.O. Box 2455, NIC

Investment House, Independence Avenue; France: P.O. Box 2349, Bagamoyo Road; West Germany: P.O. Box 9541, NIC Building, Independence Avenue, Guinea: P.O. Box 2969, 35 Haile Selassie Road, Oyster Bay; India: P.O. Box 2684, NIC Investment House, Independence Avenue; Indonesia: P.O. Box 572, 299 Upanga Road; Italy: P.O. Box 2106, Plot 316, Lugalo Road; Japan: P.O. Box 2577, Bagamoyo Road; Madagascar: P.O. Box 5254, 14 Msasani Beach; Mexico: P.O. Box 571, Kimara Street, Plot 2052/5, Sea View; Netherlands: P.O. Box 9534, IPS Building, Independence Avenue; Nigeria: P.O. Box 9214, 3 Bagamoyo Road, Oyster Bay; Norway: P.O. Box 2646, IPS Building, Independence Avenue; Pakistan: P.O. Box 2925, Plot 149, Malik Road, Upanga; Rwanda: P.O. Box 2918, Plot 32, Upanga Road; Somalia: P.O. Box 2031, Plot 31, Upanga Road; Spain: P.O. Box 842, IPS Building, 7th floor; Sudan: P.O. Box 2266, "Albaraka," 64 Upanga Road; Sweden: P.O. Box 9274, IPS Building, 9th floor, Independence Avenue; Switzerland: P.O. Box 2454, 17 Kenyatta Drive; UK: P.O. Box 9200, Permanent House; USA: P.O. Box 9123, National Bank of Commerce House (4th floor) City Drive; Zaire: P.O. Box 975, 438 Malik Road, Upanga; Zambia: P.O. Box 2525, Plot 442, Malik Road, Upanga.

FOREIGN CONSULATES IN ZANZIBAR

USA: 83A Tuzungumzeni, P.O. Box 4, Zanzibar, tel: 218; India: Migombani, P.O. Box 871, tel: 2585; Egypt: 625 Nyerere Road, P.O. Box 669, tel: 2525.

DAR ES SALAAM

Dar es Salaam—meaning 'Haven of Peace'—nestles around one of the prettiest ports and harbours in the world, and the town stretches northward along the Indian Ocean coast. It is not at all a modern metropolis like Nairobi or Abidjan, though a few skyscrapers are starting to rise.

Most of the streets are narrow and winding with low buildings, many dating back to the Arab period. In German times, the architecture consisted of squat two-storey square buildings with very high ceilings and verandahs around the outside—very practical in the tropical heat. There are examples of these all along the harbour front.

The main street, Independence Avenue, is filled with curio shops, banks, airline offices, chemists, Government Ministry buildings, embassies and clothing stores. There are usually a dozen freighters and a few passenger ships in port, and occasionally an old Arab dhow from the Persian Gulf calls, following the downward monsoon. The fast and graceful *ngalawas* bring in their daily catch to a large open-air fish market just at the entrance to the harbour. *Ngalawas* are sail boats made of dugout canoes with outriggers.

Dar es Salaam has a profusion of rich tropical flora. Although December is one of the hottest months, it is the best time to appreciate the city's beauty. All the flame trees and frangipanis are in bloom, as well as the India laburnum, a spectacular flowering tree with cascades of yellow blossoms. Many of the plants only give off a scent at night.

Hotels
Kilimanjaro Hotel, P.O. Box 9574, tel: 21281;
Motel Agip, centrally situated, P.O. Box 529, tel: 23511;
The New Africa Hotel, P.O. Box 9314, tel: 29611;
The Oyster Bay Hotel, P.O. Box 1907, tel: 68631. A small hotel 8 km from the city centre in a lovely setting on the Indian Ocean;
Twiga Hotel, city centre, P.O. Box 1194, tel: 22561;
Mawenzi Hotel, city centre, P.O. Box

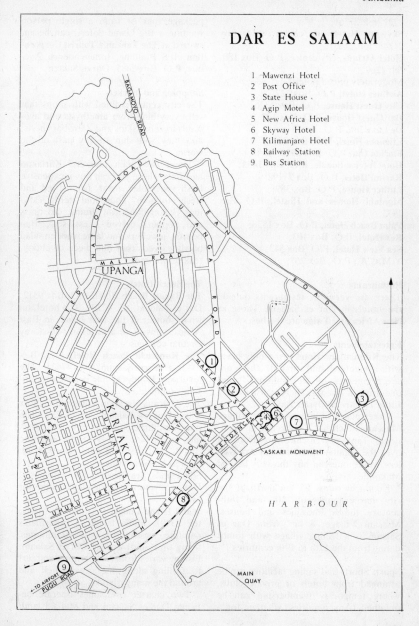

DAR ES SALAAM

1 Mawenzi Hotel
2 Post Office
3 State House
4 Agip Motel
5 New Africa Hotel
6 Skyway Hotel
7 Kilimanjaro Hotel
8 Railway Station
9 Bus Station

3222, tel: 27761;
Skyways Hotel, city centre, P.O. Box 21248, tel: 27601;
Hotel Afrique, city centre, P.O. Box 180, tel: 22695;
Moderately priced hotels:
Airlines Hotel, P.O. Box 227;
City Guest House, P.O. Box 1326;
Dar Guest House, P.O. Box 132;
De Luxe Inn, P.O. Box 84;
Etiennes Hotel, P.O. Box 2981;
Florida Inn, P.O. Box 2975;
Hotel Internationale, P.O. Box 1453;
Karimi Hotel, P.O. Box 21192;
Luther House, P.O. Box 389;
Mgulani Homes and Hostel, P.O. Box 1973;
Palm Beach Hotel, P.O. Box 1520;
Rex Hotel, P.O. Box 103;
Sea View Hotel, P.O. Box 542;
Y.M.C.A., P.O. Box 767;

Restaurants

There are very few restaurants outside the hotels in Dar es Salaam. Those at **New Africa** and **Twiga** are the best.

Entertainments

The **Kilimanjaro Hotel** is the only place with a nightclub and cabaret. There are seven cinemas, all air-conditioned; and one drive-in cinema. There is also a lively **Little Theatre** at Oyster Bay.

Other places of interest are the **Village Museum** which has a collection of traditional Tanzanian architecture from all over the country; the **National Art Gallery** where one can buy the very best of Makonde carvings.

Kunduchi ruins, 25 km north of the city, has examples of 15th- and 18th-century tombs, mosques and houses. Msasani Village, 8 km. from Dar es Salaam is a fishing village with tombs dating from the 17th to 19th centuries.

Sport: Sports and sailing facilities can be arranged from hotels or private clubs, where temporary membership can be obtained. Any inquiries, whether for a package tour or from a single person wanting a Big Game Safari, can be answered at **The Tanzania Tourist Corporation**, IPS Building, Independence Avenue, P.O. Box 2485, Dar es Salaam.

Shopping and markets

The city centre is lined with shops that sell everything from amethysts and avocados to zebra skins and Zanzibar chests, and they will ship to any part of the world.

There two main markets: Kariakoo and Ilala where you can buy inexpensive fresh vegetables, meat, fish—dried and fresh—tobacco, household items, carvings, *kitenge*, African drums, old brass and copper, carved chess sets, Bao boards, jewellery and large wooden salad bowls carved from one piece of ebony, teak or *mninga*.

The Beach Hotels

The Bahari Beach Hotel, P.O. Box 9312, Dar es Salaam, tel: 47101. The hotel, on what some call the best beach in East Africa, consists of a series of two-storey circular cottages.

The Kunduchi Beach Hotel, P.O. Box 9313, Dar es Salaam, tel: 47621. The luxurious Kunduchi has beautiful Arab-style architecture.

The Africana Vacation Village, P.O. Box 2802, Dar es Salaam, tel: 53257. The hotel had three-bedroom units and pleasant food. One can visit the offshore islands, and there are water sports, boating and tennis facilities.

Silversands Sea Resort, P.O. Box 901, Dar es Salaam, also provides facilities for camping.

Mafia Island Lodge, P.O. Box 2, Mafia, tel: 23491. Mafia Island, a fisherman's paradise, is situated only 40 minutes' flying time south-east of Dar es Salaam. Fishing varies from rock, bottom and surf to trolling along the ocean shelf and around the many islands.

Two charter companies operate between Dar es Salaam and Mafia Island.

The main fishing season is from September to March.

Kilwa Ruins

There are actually three settlements all bearing the name of Kilwa. The oldest, Kilwa Kisiwani—Kilwa on the Island—resisted the Portuguese until they finally gave up trying to take it from the Arabs in the 15th century. Kilwa Kivinje—Kilwa of the Casuarina Trees—is 27 km to the north, built on the mainland. It was probably founded about 1830 and has a fine market built by the Germans but in Arab style. The newest, and still very small, is Kilwa Masoko—Kilwa of the Markets—built as an administrative centre and situated on a peninsula.

Kilwa can be reached by road about five months in the year, but the best way to get there is by charter aircraft. There is no accommodation for tourists.

THE NORTHERN CIRCUIT

This circuit is the most popular with visitors. Here are the famous Serengeti plains, Kilimanjaro and the Ngorongoro crater. There are entry fees to all parks.

The snow-capped peak of Mount Kilimanjaro

TANZANIA TOURIST SERVICES

Points to remember: Firearms and domestic pets are prohibited in the parks. Leave radios behind. Blowing horns or chasing animals will only make them more timid, and if you drive fast you will also frighten the animals and see very little. The speed limit is 50 km per hour but you will see much more if you drive at 25 km per hour.

Remember that, of all the animals, the big cats can be the most dangerous because they can see you *in* the car. All other animals only see the vehicle.

ARUSHA

Arusha, a lovely city with an extravagant display of flowers and blooming trees, is the headquarters of the East African Community. Its altitude is 1,380 m on the slopes of Mount Meru. It is in an important area producing coffee, wheat, sisal, pyrethrum, sugar, textiles and dairy products. It also manufactures plastics, radios, the world-famous meerschaum and briar pipes.

Arusha is the starting place for safaris into the parks of northern Tanzania—Serengeti, Manyara, Ngorongoro Crater, Tarangire, Olduvai Gorge and Arusha National Park. There are many shops and services catering for photographic and hunting safaris.

The city is reached by tarmac road—680 km from Dar es Salaam, 272 km from Nairobi—or by rail.

Hotels:
Mount Meru Hotel, brand new tourist hotel.
The New Arusha Hotel, P.O. Box 88, tel: 3241, Arusha.
Safari Hotel, centrally situated, P.O. Box 303, tel: 3261, Arusha.
Hotel Equator, P.O. Box 3002, Arusha, tel: 3127.
Mount Meru Game Lodge, 22 km east of Arusha, P.O. Box 659, Arusha; tel: Usa River 43. The hotel accommodates only 12 people at a time, and is one of the

most enchanting hotels in Tanzania. It has a game sanctuary where tame young animals freely walk around the lawn. The larger animals are across a moat but still come near to your cabin door. Safaris for photography or big game hunting can easily be organised.

Tanzanite Hotel, 22 km from Arusha, P.O. Box 3063, Arusha, tel: Usa River 32. This is a fairly new hotel with a swimming pool and tennis court, overlooking the Mount Meru Game Sanctuary. Good food and pleasant gardens.

YMCA, centrally situated, P.O. Box 658, tel: 2765, Arusha, inexpensive accommodation.

Camping: Lake Duluti, 11 km from Arusha and one and a half km off the tarmac road to Moshi, has a camping/caravan site on the shore. Application for use of the site should be made to P.O. Box 602, Arusha.

MOSHI

The town is overshadowed by the imposing presence of Kilimanjaro. Situated at 900 m it is the heart of Tanzania's coffee growing region. This is very lush and fertile volcanic country and 40% of Tanzania's wheat is grown on the slopes of the mountain.

The new Kilimanjaro International Airport—capable of handling all types of aircraft, including jumbo jets—is on the Sanya Juu plains between Arusha and Moshi with a tarmac road connecting it to both towns. The area is being developed to take large package-tour groups on charter flights from Europe to East Africa's game parks.

Accommodation:

Coffee Tree Hostelry, P.O. Box 184, tel: 2787, Moshi, rooftop restaurant overlooking the mountain.

Livingstone Hotel, P.O. Box 501, tel: 3071, Moshi, centrally located.

YMCA, P.O. Box 865, Moshi, tel: 2362. Good standard and low prices.

NATIONAL PARKS

Mount Kilimanjaro

The climb up Kibo to Gillman's point on the crater rim generally takes five days—three up and and two down. No special equipment is needed but it is essential to have very warm clothing, gloves, boots, a sunproof hat, dark glasses or goggles and protective lotion for the face. For Uhuru Peak, a further 600 m, as well as for Mawenzi, the smaller peak, it is necessary to have alpine equipment.

The best months for climbing the mountain are January, February, September and October when there usually is no cloud cover. However, it can be climbed any other month except April and May during the long rains.

There are four huts on the mountain run by Tourism Division, namely Mandara Hut (formerly Dismark) at 3,000 m above Marangu; Horombo Hut (formerly Peters) at 4,100 m below Mawenzi; Kibo Hut at 5,000 m on the west side of Mawenzi. Mandara hut can accommodate 24 climbers; Horombo Hut 31 climbers; Kibo Hut 18 climbers and Mawenzi 4 climbers. Water is available at Mandara Hut and Horombo Hut but not Kibo Hut, the last water point being a mile above Horombo Hut. Firewood is available near Mandara Hut, but is scarce near Horombo Hut and unobtainable near Kibo Hut.

All intending climbers must reserve accommodation well in advance through one of the hotels in Marangu who organise safaris for climbers. Safaris up the mountain are organised by The Kilimanjaro Mountain Club, P.O. Box 66, Moshi. Guides and porters, food, cooking and lighting equipment are provided. Sleeping bags and other equipment can also be hired.

Accommodation: Marangu, on the eastern slopes of the mountain and 32 km east of Moshi, has two comfortable lodges. They are both able to organise mountain climbing safaris.

Marangu Hotel, P.O. Box 40, Moshi, tel: Himo 11Y1. Good food, camping sites.

Kibo Hotel, Private Bag, Moshi, tel: Himo 2.

Osirwa Safari Cottages: P.O. Box West Kilimanjaro, tel: West Kilimanjaro 542, or contact Osirwa Safari Cottages, 9 Upper Grosvenor Street, London W1, tel: 01-499 4850.

The cottages, situated 80 km from Moshi on the spectacular wheat farms on the north-west slopes of Kilimanjaro, are well equipped and at 1,950 m have sweeping views of Masailand and the Amboseli Game Reserve and Kilimanjaro.

Arusha National Park

The park is situated 32 km east of Arusha on the Arusha-Moshi road; within it are to be found three distinct areas—Ngurdoto Crater, the Momela lakes and the rugged Mount Meru. Altitudes range from 1,600 m at Momela to nearly 5,000 m at the summit of Meru.

This is a park with a difference—it has no lions. Neither are there tsetse flies nor mosquitoes, but there is a wealth of wildlife, including the colobus monkey, bushbuck, buffalo, red forest duiker, hippo, rhino, reedbuck, waterbuck, elephant, giraffe and leopard. Birdlife, especially waterfowl, is abundant and during October and May there are many northern migrants. The lush, green rain-forest contains ancient cedar and podocarpus trees.

Visitors may not go down into Ngurdoto Crater but may view the wildlife on the crater floor from lookout points on the crater rim. The area has been set aside as a reserve within a reserve, and it has been decided that here there should be no interference whatsoever from man.

The best times to visit the park are the months of July through March, with December as the best month of all.

Accommodation: There is no hotel in the park yet, but it can be easily visited from Arusha where there are several comfortable hotels. Just outside the park gate, comfortable accommodation is offered in thatched rondavels at the **Momela Lodge,** P.O. Box 535, tel: 4622.

Camping is allowed on Meru Mountain, where there are sites at 1,600 m, 2,200 m and 2,600 m. Clean, safe water may be drawn from nearby mountain streams and firewood can be gathered. All sites should be booked in advance through the Park Warden, Arusha National Park, P.O. Box 3134, Arusha.

Tarangire National Park

The Tarangire National Park in northern Tanzania forms the dry season retreat of much of the wildlife of southern Masailand and is therefore at its best during the months of June to October inclusive, with September probably the best month of all.

There are nine distinct vegetation zones in the park, of which the Acacia Tortilis parklands are the most attractive. Here one may spot the fringe-eared oryx, an imposing antelope which, when seen in profile, sometimes appears to have only one horn—which possibly gave rise to the myth of the unicorn.

The park is heavily infested with tsetse fly, but without them the area would in all probability not be a park at all—domestic cattle, goats, sheep and donkeys cannot survive in tsetse areas, but the wildlife is immune.

Accommodation: Tarangire Safari Camp, P.O. Box 1182, Arusha, tel: Arusha 3625. Each tent has a private toilet and shower.

Camping is permitted on application to the Park Warden. Campers must be completely self-sufficient, except for water and firewood. Contact Tanzania National Parks, P.O. Box 3134, Arusha.

Lake Manyara National Park

Lake Manyara is 128 km from Arusha on

a road part tarmac and part all-weather, but good all year round. The ride is through the stark landscape of the Masai Steppe.

The 325 sq km park and lake are in the Great Rift Valley. Within this comparatively small area lie five distinct vegetation zones: an area of delightful groundwater forest with towering fig and mahogany trees and open glades; an extensive stretch of marshland and reeds; plains of open grassland; parklands scattered with acacia trees; and finally the characteristic scrubland on the precipitous face of the Rift Wall.

For the adventurous this park offers a close-up view of animals that are rarely found in any other park. It is famous for great herds of buffalo, sometimes over 400 strong, and for lions. The birds of Manyara too are spectacular—the varied vegetation and the extensive mud-flats, reedbeds and marshlands provide ideal feeding grounds for countless resident and migratory species. The most profuse and lovely of these are the thousands of flamingos that, during certain times of the year, form a solid line of shimmering pink stretching many miles down the lake.

Accommodation: Lake Manyara Hotel, 100 rooms with private baths. The hotel is 10 km from the park gate on the very edge of the Rift Wall, 300 m above the park, and commands an incredible view. There is an airstrip for light aircraft. Information from Tanzania Tourist Corporation, P.O. Box 2485, Dar es Salaam.

Camping: Sites are available near the park entrance, but campers must bring their own food and drinking water, and must be completely self-sufficient. Mosquito nets are essential.

Ngorongoro Crater

Ngorongoro is the largest intact crater in the world (there are five damaged ones that are larger) and was an active volcano

some eight million years ago. Technically it is a caldera: the cone collapsed and slid back into the volcano, leaving a crater 17 kms in diameter. Its floor is 160 sq. km in extent, and the rim of the crater, where all the hotels are located, is 2,286 m above sea level. From the rim down to the crater floor is 610 m and only four-wheel-drive vehicles are allowed down. The crater rises high above the Serengeti plain, and from it six mountains over 3000 m are always in view.

Over 30,000 animals live in the crater, from the smallest gazelle—the dik-dik—to the elephant. During the spring months this is an important migratory point for flamingo, and the lake edge is covered with hundreds of thousands of them, giving the impression of pink foam. Ngorongoro has an invigorating climate, enabling hours of game viewing.

The Ngorongoro Crater burial mounds were the site for some of the earliest archaeological finds in East Africa.

Accommodation: Ngorongoro Wildlife Lodge, located on the rim of the crater. 75 rooms with private bathrooms. All rooms are heated.

For information and reservation: Northern Circuit Reservations, P.O. Box 3100, Arusha.

Ngorongoro Crater Lodge; for further information: Ngorongoro Crater Lodge Ltd., P.O. Box 751, Arusha.

The Ngorongoro Forest Lodge; provides more modest, but comfortable accommodation; for further information: Ngorongoro Forest Lodge, P.O Box 792, Arusha.

Camping: No camping is allowed inside the crater, but is permitted in the conservation area. Campers must be fully self-supporting, even with water. There is no tsetse fly at the higher levels and no mosquitoes.

Serengeti National Park

The Serengeti National Park contains over one and a half million animals—the

A pride of lions and cubs in the Serengeti National Park

largest and most spectacular concentration of plains animals anywhere in the world. Serengeti is also famous for the massive movement of animals known as 'the Migration'.

The country within the park varies from the vast treeless central Serengeti plains and savannah-type stretches to thick scrub and forest in the north and along the Mara River. The plains are dotted with flat-topped acacia trees, and interspersed with magnificent rock outcrops. Streams, rivers, small swamps and lakes all add to the fascinating variety of scenery.

The park is 14,700 sq. km in area, and Tanzania's largest. The altitudes range from 900 to 1,830 m. Seronera Lodge lies at 1,520 m. The driest months are June-December, and heavy storms may be encountered in April and May, though the roads usually dry quickly. Midday temperatures are around 27°C but drop to 16°C at night, so warm clothing is necessary.

The annual migration, usually in May or June, of wildebeeste and zebra from the central plains to permanent water in the west and north is a truly remarkable

sight. The wildebeeste—over 500,000 of them—with their unending grunting 'hee-haw' sound, mill around in the southern part of the park making the horizon hazy with dust. Suddenly two break away and start running, and the whole herd moves after them in single file. They might only move half a mile and then stop, or they might keep moving till they disappear from view. They mill about in this fashion for several months until suddenly they begin the migration, followed by thousands of zebra. Then the great herds move steadily westwards in a long stream, sometimes several miles long. The migration then breaks into two parts. One group goes west, often outside the park, where poaching is a problem, and then turns north east. The second group heads straight north and continues until it reaches the Mara Masai reserve in Kenya. The two groups join up there and turn around to head south again, back to the central plains. At the tail end of the processions come the cripples, and those too old to keep up, followed inevitably by lion and other carnivores.

There are two types of lion in the Serengeti—the sedentary lions who stay around Seronera in the centre of the park, and the migratory lions which follow the great herds on their trek.

The **Serengeti Research Institute** at Seronera is the most advanced centre for the study of the ecology in Africa. It was founded in 1966 by the trustees of the National Parks to conserve wildlife. Research there is providing information upon which to base sound management and conservation of the plants and animals of the Parks. Its findings are also being employed for the benefit of the peasants.

Olduvai Gorge lies just outside the park boundaries, about 40 km north-west of the Ngorongoro Crater. At Olduvai in 1959 Dr and Mrs Leakey, world-famous anthropologists from Kenya, unearthed a skull one and three-quarter million years old.

Accommodation:
Lobo Wildlife Lodge, 75 rooms with private bathrooms. This is a boldly designed lodge, 64 kms north of the park centre, built into the faults and contours of a massive kopje, with the swimming pool dug out of the rock and filled by a waterfall. For information: P.O. Box 3100, Arusha, Tanzania.

Fort Ikoma, lies about 72 kms west of the park centre. This charming hotel was built as a fort by the Germans in the First World War.

Ndutu Safari Lodge, on the shores of Lake Lgarya near the south eastern corner of Serengeti National Park has 12 double rooms with private bathrooms and 21 double tents with ample shower and toilet facilities. All rooms and tents have an unrestricted view of the lake and the vast plains beyond. In the evenings one can sit around a large bonfire, relax and listen to the African night.

For further information: George Dove Safaris, P.O. Box 284, Arusha.
Seronera Wildlife Lodge, 75 rooms.

Camping: There are nine camping sites within four kms of Seronera. No camping is allowed elsewhere in the park. Campers must provide entirely for themselves and may not use the lodge facilities.

For information and reservations contact: Tanzania National Parks, P.O. Box 3134, Arusha.

Lobo Wildlife Lodge

THE SOUTHERN AND COASTAL CIRCUIT

This circuit is not as well known as the northern, but there is a variety of scenery which the north does not offer—800 km of untouched white beaches on the Indian Ocean, exotic Zanzibar, the great Selous Game Reserve and very good parks.

BAGAMOYO

Once the capital of Tanganyika, Bagamoyo was the last mainland halt for the slaves before they left, first for the Zanzibar slave markets, then to be scattered around the world.

During the 19th century it was also the starting point on the mainland for many of the explorers from Europe. The chapel in which Livingstone's body rested for the last time on the African continent is still there, and so is the Old Customs House, the ruins where the slaves were kept, and a small German fort. Quaint gas-lamps still adorn the streets, and some of the houses have Zanzibar-carved doors, often over 100 years old.

Bagamoyo, 64 km north of Dar es Salaam can only be reached by road, unless you are adventurous and want to hire a *ngalawa* and sail up the coast to it.

TANGA

Tanga (population 89,000) is the country's second port. It is located in the north-east corner of the country near the Kenya border and is the centre of the sisal industry. There is an airport, and rail connections to all the major towns in Tanzania. The road to Dar es Salaam and Arusha is tarmac all the way, and an all-weather road connects the town with Mombasa in Kenya.

Tanga is off the visitor's path, and does not offer first-class accommodation:
Palm Court Hotel, P.O. Box 783; **Planter's Hotel,** P.O. Box 242; **Seaview Hotel,** P.O. Box 249; **Splendid Hotel,** P.O. Box 397; **Tanga Hotel,** P.O. Box 625.

Places of interest

Eight km north of Tanga are the Amboni caves, a vast maze of limestone caves, full of stalactites, stalagmites and crystal formations.

A few kms from the town are the Galanos sulphur springs, warm sulphur water baths with a large bath-house with separate rooms.

Twenty kilometres from Tanga on the Pangani road are the Tongoni Ruins of 13th-century mosques and some 40 graves—the remains of a Persian settlement.

In the Usumbara Mountains there are two pleasant hotels:
Lawns Hotel, P.O. Box 33, Lushoto;
Oaklands Hotel, P.O. Box 41, Lushoto.

MOROGORO

This important agricultural centre at the foot of the Uluguru mountains is 288 km west of the capital on an all-tarmac road. It can also easily be reached by railway. The town lies at 500 m and has a population of 39,000. It has an airport.
Acropol Hotel, P.O. Box 78,
Savoy Hotel, P.O. Box 35.

DODOMA

Dodoma, in the very centre of Tanzania, is harshly arid. The town lies 1,133 m above sea level, 512 km west of Dar es Salaam, which it is designated to replace as Tanzania's capital. It is on the central railway line. The 84,000-acre Kongwa ranch, a source of excellent beef and high quality breeding cattle, lies in this region. The very promising Dodoma wine industry started by the Fathers at Bihawana Mission is also located here.

In the neighbourhood of Dodoma are many *ujamaa* villages of the Wagogo peasants who broke away from their traditional life in the early 1970s. These villages show the beginnings of a vast agrarian revolution.

The Stone Age Kondoa Irangi rock paintings can be seen 176 km north of Dodoma on the Arusha road.
Dodoma Hotel, P.O. Box 239.

IRINGA

Iringa (population 46,000) is 502 km south-west of Dar es Salaam on the main Tanzania-Zambia road. Because of its altitude (1,635 m) it is relatively cool. It is within easy reach of the Ruaha National Park. It is a farming centre and tobacco is the important crop.
White Horse Inn, P.O. Box 48.

MBEYA

Mbeya (1,737 m, population 20,000) is 875 km from Dar es Salaam and only 114 km from the Zambian border. When the Tazara railway is finished it will be a convenient way of reaching the town.
Mbeya Guest House, P.O. Box 153.
Mbeya Hotel, P.O. Box 80.

NATIONAL PARKS

Mikumi National Park

The park lies in a horseshoe of towering mountains—the Uluguru range rises to 2,750 m—and forested foothills which almost enclose the flood plain of the Mkata River. This plain lies 550 m above sea level. The climate is influenced by the monsoons, so the days are hot and the evenings cool.

Mikumi has a large concentration of buffalo, elephant and lion. Giraffe can be seen in herds of over 50, and lions are often found in prides of 20 or more. One of their favourite resting places is the hangar at the airstrip, if not on the airstrip itself.

Elephants can be seen throughout the park. One of them learned how to turn on a water tap in the Park Headquarters, though he never learned how to turn it off again. They often gather around the lodge and tented camp and seem to enjoy the proximity of humans.

Mikumi Wildlife Lodge. The lodge is beautifully constructed from local *mninga*, *podo* and bamboo and is situated on a cliff overlooking a lake. Bookings through Coastal Holidays Circuit, P.O. Box 9500, Dar es Salaam.

Mikumi Wildlife Camp. The hut camp is 300 m off the main road and the accommodation is comfortable and pleasant. There is a spacious and cool thatched bar with an adjoining dining-room. Booking through Oyster Bay Hotel, P.O. Box 1907 Dar es Salaam.

Camping: The only camp site in the park is situated 4 km from the entrance gate. Camping is not permitted elsewhere and campers must be self-supporting except for water, which can be drawn free at the Wildlife Camp.

The Ruaha National Park

The Ruaha is the second largest national park (12,950 km) after Serengeti, and July to November are the best months to visit it. Elephant are probably its greatest single attraction. They may be seen congregating in huge herds along the bank of the Great Ruaha River. Apart from elephant and a wide variety of smaller animals, the park is best known for sighting and photographing greater and lesser kudu, sable and the rare roan antelope. The birdlife is rich and interesting too—over 300 species have been recorded.

130 km of good all-weather road connect the park headquarters with Iringa. Light aircraft take half an hour from Iringa, two hours from Dar es Salaam and about three hours from Nairobi.

Most of the park is undulating plateau country over 1,000 m high with many rocky hills and outcrops.

The Great Ruaha River flows along the entire eastern boundary eventually joining the Rufiji River many miles downstream. It changes from rocky rapids to deep pools to a shallow river of many channels which wander between the sandbanks. Hippo, crocodiles, turtles and many fish inhabit the river, while the birdlife contrasts sharply with that of the surrounding dry bush country.

Special facilities are available for the serious photographer or naturalist. Photographic blinds have been built at a number of strategic places where wildlife concentrates.

Accommodation: There is no lodge as yet in the park, but the town of Iringa offers a choice of two comfortable hotels.

Camping: Camping is permitted at a variety of unspoiled places. Parties must be completely self-supporting.

There is a do-it-yourself camping unit near the Park Headquarters at Msembe consisting of two rondavels on the bank of the Ruaha River. Piped water, firewood, beds and bedding are provided, but all other requirements must be brought by the campers.

Bookings should be made in advance to: Park Warden, Ruaha National Park, P.O. Box 369, Iringa.

Gombe National Park

Gombe National Park is located on the eastern shore of Lake Tanganyika, 16 km from Kigoma, and is famous for its population of wild chimpanzees.

The park's mountain slopes are deeply cut by densely forested ravines. Chimpanzees usually stay in these forests of tall trees, though they can sometimes be seen on the grasslands between the valleys. The chimpanzees in the north of the park are accustomed to people and do not run away, but the males can be dangerous. Chimpanzees are highly susceptible to human diseases, and a few years ago they suffered severely from an outbreak of poliomyelitis.

Because of the research still being carried out by scientists and the tameness of the chimpanzees, visitors are restricted in this park, and only five of six people are allowed in at a time.

For information on visits to the park, contact: The Director, Tanzania National Parks, P.O. Box 3134, Arusha, Tanzania.

Tanzania banned all big game hunting in 1973.

ZANZIBAR

Only 20 minutes' flight from Dar es Salaam, Zanzibar is one of the world's most beautiful islands. The gateway to Zanzibar—the airport—is surrounded by coconut plantations and the visitor can still see the house near the dhow harbour where Livingstone lived while fitting out his last expedition to the mainland. Another reminder of the past is the house of the notorious slave trader Tippu Tip.

The Anglican Cathedral Church of Christ stands on the site of the great Zanzibar slave market, while on the seafront the palace of the former Sultan and the towering Beit-el-ajaib (The House of Wonders), the largest building in Zanzibar, are vivid reminders of the island's long and colourful history. To enjoy the old town to the full the visitor should go on foot, to see the buildings with their handsome carved doors. Many of them have been allowed to deteriorate, but some are now being restored.

To see the island you can take a taxi, but the Government tours are recommended. The guides are very good and a two-hour ride around the island takes in a great deal.

Hotels

Africa House, Zanzibar Hotel, Amaan Hotel, as well as a new 200 room hotel the **Hoteli ya Bwawani.** The Government is attempting to develop tourism on the island.

Recent history of Zanzibar

The revolutionary regime which won power in 1964 virtually closed the island to tourism for several years, but under the more restrained leadership of the new President, Aboud Jumbe, some of the old tranquillity has returned.

When Shaikh Abeid Karume (who was assassinated in 1972) and his Revolutionary Council came to power they set about righting some of the injustices of the previous regime. The large Arab plantations were broken up, with 18,000 plots of three acres each going to peasant families. New housing schemes were undertaken for workers who previously lived in mud and wattle huts. They now receive free modern housing and pay very little for electricity and water.

The island depends upon cloves for foreign exchange and has one of the highest per capita incomes in Black Africa.

One note of caution. All visitors to the island must conform to Zanzibar's rules on dress, which are very strict, as the Zanzibaris are devout Muslims. Women must at all time wear dresses that do not expose the knees, even when sitting; shorts on men and women are strictly forbidden, as are tight-fitting trousers or any see-through clothing on both sexes. And advice to the men—if your hair is longer than 5 cm tie it up and wear a hat or, as the rules say, 'you will receive a free haircut'. Women visiting the island generally buy a few lengths of *kanga* in Dar es Salaam and wear them as full-length wrap-around skirts.

Visas

All visitors to Zanzibar must contact the Principal Immigration Officer, Zanzibar, or the Friendship Tourist Bureau of Zanzibar, P.O. Box 216, Zanzibar, directly.

HISTORY

Early times. In the Rift Valley between Kenya and Tanzania is the famous Olduvai Gorge where the remains of Nutcracker Man (Zinjanthropus) were found. Here his later descendants made some of the first stone hand-axes in the world. At that time there were more lakes along the valley and greater rainfall made it lusher than it is now, although it was still open grassland abounding in game. Stone Age hunters also occupied the highlands to the south, and in the Kondoa district there are over 1,000 of their rock paintings, vivid naturalistic portrayals of human and animal life.

During the first millenium AD, Bantu speakers began to come in from Zaire, south and north of Lake Tanganyika. They brought the knowledge of iron-working and pottery-making and absorbed the hunters and gatherers into more settled communities.

In Roman times, Rhapta (perhaps at the mouth of the Rufiji River) was already known at a trading village where ivory was sold. At Pemba Island men searched for turtle shells in boats sewn together and driven by matting sails. Soon the mixture of Arabs and Bantu-speaking Africans became known as Swahili, from the Arabic word for 'coast' and formed an aristocracy governing a number of separate city-States on islands and peninsulas along the seashore.

By the 10th century they had been joined by Persians and people from even farther east, bringing with them the Muslim religion. The Swahili began to build houses, mosques and palaces of stone, and their foundations can still be seen at Kilwa. By the 13th century Kilwa surpassed all the other towns, since it gained control of the gold trade from Zimbabwe in Rhodesia.

The arrival of the Portuguese in the Indian Ocean, although it did not lead to political domination, slowly strangled the commercial life of the Swahili cities, and many of the inhabitants eventually turned to subsistence farming on the nearby mainland.

In the interior, the poor soils and drainage supported only a sparse population, ruled for the most part by chiefs who exercised religious as much as political power over small groups of villages.

During this period, two Nilo-Hamitic groups moved in. The first, arriving perhaps about 1500 AD, were a Kalenjin people whose language is still spoken by the Pokot; then in the 18th century came the Masai. They were not interested in farming but settled on the pastures of the Masai steppe and raided their neighbours for cattle—they believed God had intended cattle only for the Masai.

The 19th century brought trade, with Arab and Swahili caravans dealing in ivory, rhinoceros horn and coconut oil. Later there was also gold and copper. The caravans widened their range as the demand abroad increased for ivory, and for slaves to work the new clove plantations introduced in Zanzibar by the Imam of Oman, Seyyid Sayed, and for export to Persia, Egypt, Turkey and even farther afield. After establishing trading centres at Unyanyembe (Tabora) and Ujiji they pressed on north into Uganda and by mid-century west into Zaire.

In the meantime Ngoni invaders had swept up from South Africa under their leader Zwangendaba, who died on the Fipa plateau in about 1845. His followers split up into small groups: some settled, for example in Songea, and others became mercenary bands (*ruga ruga*) who would fight for any chief. The lawlessness of these times and the advent of guns caused some societies to disintegrate, but others, like the Hehe or Mirambo's Nyamwezi, united in a combined defence.

German influence in the area began in 1884 when Dr Karl Peters negotiated with the tribal chiefs for their land. In 1890 the coastal strip was acquired by Germany on payment of £200,000 to the Sultan of Zanzibar. The mainland territory was declared a Protectorate of German East Africa and Zanzibar became a British Protectorate under the Anglo-German Agreements of 1886 and 1890.

The years from 1888 to 1898 were difficult for the Germans as they tried to establish themselves over the territory.

They built a railway and tried to encourage both settler plantations of sisal and rubber and peasant cash-cropping in cotton. The soil was unsuitable however and the attempt had disastrous results which led to a major trans-tribal rebellion against the Germans, known as the Maji Maji rising (1905-6), which is still vividly remembered for its bloodshed and the succeeding famine.

When the British defeated Germany in the First World War, German East Africa was allotted to Britain under a League of Nations mandate as a Trust Territory to be governed until deemed fit to rule itself. The name was changed to Tanganyika, with the present day countries of Rwanda and Burundi in the west being split from the colony and given to the Belgians to administer.

Independence came in 1961 after a peaceful and remarkably united campaign by TANU (Tanganyika African National Union), led since 1954 by President Julius Nyerere. Meanwhile Zanzibar had erupted into riots against the Arab sixth of the population who held great bureaucratic power. The conflicts ended in 1964 with the dispossession of the Arabs, 5,000 Arabs killed and the rise to power of an Afro-Shirazi alliance, led by Shaikh Karume and consisting of Shirazi, long resident on the island, and mainlanders. This radical Government joined in April 1964 with Tanganyika to form the United Republic of Tanzania. After Karume's assassination in 1972 President Aboud Jumbe was appointed to head the still largely autonomous Government.

President Nyerere is widely admired for his exposition of African Socialism.

TOGO

Togo's capital Lomé was a busy trading centre since the Slave Coast traffic began but is now a free port, and traditional trade in coconuts and fish has been overtaken by sales of cloth, cigarettes and alcoholic drinks, all of which can be bought cheaper here than anywhere else along the coast. Most of the trade is in the hands of Togo's women, or *revendeuses* as they are called.

If you are lucky enough to be in Lomé over one of the numerous public holidays, you will be drawn down to the marina, the wide palm-shaded avenue along the ocean front, to watch one of the colourful parades for which Togo is famous. There, the waves of singing and dancing *revendeuses* grouped according to their trades will far outnumber and outshine the men, army, civil service and trades unions combined.

THE LAND AND THE PEOPLE

Togo derives its name from Lake Togo, near the former capital of Aného. A narrow strip of a country, 600 km long and at times as little as 50 km wide, it rises behind the coastal lagoons and swampy plains to an undulating plateau, the last thrust of Benin's Atakora highlands. Northwards, towards Upper Volta, the plateau dips again into a wide plain irrigated by the river Oti.

The central part of the country is covered by deciduous forest and is the least inhabited, while north and south stretch savannah lands. To the east, near Benin, the river Mono descends to the sea and to the long sandy beaches shaded by palm trees characteristic of the coast from Lomé to Cotonou.

Togo's population of two million comes from over 30 different ethnic groups. Thrown together in the desperate

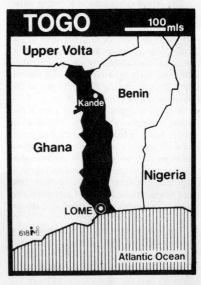

conditions of the Slave Coast this hetero-geneous people became united in the south of the country by the Voodoo cult which continues to play an important part in the lives of many Togolese.

The hard-working Ewes, who consti-tute the largest single ethnic group in Togo, work the cocoa and coffee planta-tions of the west while in the north the tall thin cattle raisers and huntsmen of the savannah, the Kabyé, the second largest group, are well known for their fighting qualities.

CULTURE

Because of their varied colonial heritage, many Togolese can still speak German and English as well as French, the official language.

Exposed to a variety of Christian de-nominations and to Islam from the north, the country is peppered with churches, chapels and mosques. Lomé has a famous German cathedral and even the smallest bush village has one Protestant and one Catholic place of worship.

The Voodoo religion is a strong influ-ence in the country. Differing from tradi-tional African religions by its emphasis on the role of the dead in the lives of the living, Voodoo plays an important part in modern Togo and many young girls, after fulfilling their novitiate, will still devote their lives to serving the religion and the Voodoo village priest.

African religions are at the root of the wood sculpture which is to be found in Togo. Some of the statuettes are connect-ed with services for the dead. In certain religions they are spiritually incarnated in such statuettes to which food and drink is regularly brought. The living both fear and respect these figures. Craftsmen also carve traditional wood chairs and stools, and work ivory into figures.

Traditional weaving of Kente cloth is mainly carried out in the coastal and savannah regions. The more decorative the cloth the more prestigious its wearer.

Music is easily Togo's most popular art, however. Wherever you go you will hear the warm lilting rhythms of West African music, played on a wide variety of traditional stringed and percussion instruments.

GENERAL INFORMATION

Area: 56,600 sq. km.
Population: 2,100,000.
Altitude: Sea level to plateau of 400m. Highest point 1,000m.
Capital: Lomé.
Head of State: Major-General Etienne Gnassingbé Eyadema.
Government: Military rule backed up by the single party, the Rassemblement du Peuple Togolais. Most Ministers are civilians.
Date of independence: 27 April 1960.
Languages: French (official), Ewe, Kabre and other local languages.
Religions: Traditional, Christianity and Islam.
Currency: CFA franc. £1 sterling=427 CFA francs; US $1.00=247 CFA francs.
Time: GMT.

HOW TO GET THERE

By air: There are direct flights from Paris, Marseilles and African capitals by Air Afrique and UTA. Local flights con-nect with Lagos and Accra international flights. Lomé airport is four km from the centre of town and transport by bus and taxi is available to the hotels.

By road: The well-surfaced coast road between Accra and Lagos runs through Lomé. There are regular buses and taxis from Accra, and taxis from Lagos and Cotonou (Benin). The road from Ouaga-dougou (Upper Volta) to Lomé running through the centre of Togo has recently been improved.

Visas and health regulations

Citizens of France, former French colonies in West Africa, Ghana and Nigeria require only a valid passport. West Germans, Italians and Gambians do not need a visa unless their stay is more than three months. All other visitors require a visa, which is best obtained from a Togolese or French consulate abroad, allowing plenty of time for issue. The official requirement is that a return ticket should be presented before a visa is issued, although this is rarely insisted upon.

Valid international certificates of vaccination against smallpox, yellow fever and cholera are required.

Dutiable goods
Personal effects including cameras and typewriter may be taken into Togo duty free, as are 400 cigarettes and 2 bottles of spirits. A special licence is required for firearms.

Currency regulations
Any amount of local or foreign currency can be taken into Togo. Foreign currency taken out of the country must not exceed the amount taken in.
One may not take out more than 75,000

Harvesting the fruit of the palm

CFA francs in local currency.

CLIMATE
Togo is not as hot as some parts of the West African coast. It has cooling breezes off the sea in summer and in December and January the harmattan wind blows from the north. The average temperature is between 27°C and 30°C. The main rainy season is from April to July. The short rains occur in October and November. The driest and hottest period is during February and March.

What to wear: Clothes should be lightweight and practicable. There is little need for formality. A raincoat and a light sweater may come in useful.

Health precautions: A prophylactic against malaria is essential. Tap water should be boiled or filtered before drinking.

ACCOMMODATION AND FOOD
There are hotels in all the main towns but only Lomé has international class accommodation. The restaurants catering for foreign visitors tend to be French orientated.

A tip of 10% of the bill is normal in hotels and restaurants.

TRANSPORT
Air: Air Togo, B.P. 1090, Lomé runs internal services between Lomé, Sokodé, Mango and Dapango.
Rail: There are rail services from Lomé to Palimé, Atakpame and Aného.
Road: The main roads have recently been improved, and even those with laterite surfaces are generally passable throughout the year, except in the far north.

Taxis are easy to find and cheap within Lomé. Long-distance taxis (sharing with other passengers) run from Lomé to all the main towns. Car hire is possible in Lomé.

BANKS

The main commercial banks are the Bank Togolaise pour le Commerce et l'Industrie, 9 rue du Commerce, B.P. 363, Lomé, the Union Togolaise de Banque, B.P. 359, Lomé, and the Banque Commerciale du Ghana, B.P.1321, Lomé.

Business hours: businesses, shops and Government offices generally open 0700-1200 and 1430-1730 Monday to Friday and shops only 0730-1230 on Saturday. Banks open 0730-1130 and 1430-1530 Monday to Friday.

PUBLIC HOLIDAYS

New Year's Day; Liberation Day 13 January; Easter Monday; Independence Day 27 April—Labour Day; Ascension; Whit Monday; Assumption; All Saints; Christmas. If a public holiday falls on a Sunday, the next day is usually observed as a holiday.

FOREIGN EMBASSIES

France: Rue du Colonel Derroux, Lomé, B.P. 91; **West Germany:** Rue d'Afllao, B.P. 289, Lomé; **Ghana:** Tokoin, Lomé; **USA:** 68 rue de la Victoire, Lomé; **Egypt:** Angle blvd. Circulaire et route d'Anèche, B.P. 8, Lomé; **Nigeria:** 311 Blvd Circulaire, Lomé.

LOME

The Togolese capital has a population of 200,000 and is easily the largest town in the country. An attractive place, it has something of a resort atmosphere with its long ocean-front marina lined with palm trees, and an increasing number of modern hotels and sea-front villas for rent.

It is at night that Lomé really comes to life. Most nightclubs also serve dinner and in all of them you can dance till the early hours of the morning to a mixture of West African rhythms and the latest sounds from America, Britain and France.

Hotels
Hôtel de la Paix, route d'Aného, B.P. 3452, Lomé, tel: 62-65;
Hotel le Benin, Avenue du Général de Gaulle, B.P.128, tel: 24-85, international class, near the sea and the centre of town;
Hotel du Golfe, 5 rue de Commerce, B.P. 36, tel: 51-41, typical of the colonial period, with an attractive layout and good restaurant, situated near the town centre;
Hotel et Casino Miramar, route d'Aného, B.P. 502, tel: 61-41, beside the sea 3 km from town centre and 4.5 km from the airport;
L'Auberge Provencale, Blvd. de la République, B.P. 1138, tel: 44-79, in the centre of town;
Hôtel de la Plage, tel: 44-59, on the seafront 800m from the Benin, with a very fine French restaurant;
Le Pussy-Cat, tel: 38-48, restaurant and nightclub;
Edith's Inn, B.P. 1703, near Hotel de Ville, old Peace Corps Hostel, restaurant.

Out of town
Village du Benin, villas for rent.
Hôtel Tropicana, B.P. 2724, tel: 34-04, 18 km east of Lomé, a joint German-Togolese complex of 200 bungalows, restaurant, nightclub, two swimming pools. Designed for German package tourists.
Hôtel du Lac, Porto-Seguro, 32 km from Lomé on Lake Togo, with water sports, 3 chalets.

Restaurants
The Golfe and **Hotel de la Plage** have the best restaurants among the hotels. The **Benin** poolside restaurant is pleasant for lunch. The **Auberge Provencale** and **Le Rêve** are both good, and there is a

German restaurant serving specialities like sauerkraut. The **Mini-Brasserie** stays open the latest. Several Vietnamese restaurants are also good, like the **4eme Zone**. Outside town, on the road towards Cotonou is the **Miramar** restaurant and nightclub. There are also small cafes serving local food.

Entertainment
Nightclubs: Le Rêve, La Maquina Loca, Edelweiss, Watusi, L'Abreuvoir and **Capri**.
Sports: Football is the great national game and the Togolese team is always well placed in the Africa Cup. If you go seabathing be extremely careful—the surf is very dangerous and all but the strongest swimmers are better advised to use the pools along the beach. The Benin Hotel has a tennis court and miniature golf course. The lakeside resort of Porto-Seguro, a short drive from Lomé offers water-sports such as water-skiing and sailing, as well as safe swimming.

Shopping and markets
Lomé's central two-storey market has the widest selection of cloth on the West African coast. After a look around the food market on the ground floor, go to the first floor for the fabrics. There you will find local waxprints, indigo cloth, Kente and dye-stamped Adinkra cloth from Ghana, and the Abomey designs as well as Dutch imported batiks, brocades, laces and velvets, all at remarkably cheap prices. A warning: the market is only open until 1400 every day.

Also watch for locally produced heavy marble ashtrays. Gold and silver jewellery are cheaper here than elsewhere in West Africa, although limited to traditional Senegalese designs. A good selection is on sale in the Golfe and Benin Hotels, and there are many small shops in town. Be careful to watch for the hallmark to ensure the quality has been controlled.

If you are shopping for masks, look for good copies and consult an art book to identify and explain them. Genuine antiques are virtually impossible to find these days. La Gazelle Noire is also well worth a visit, selling a variety of Togolese crafts and original fabrics designed by Lydie Kauffman, who also designs the men's and women's clothes you will see there.

Tourist information
Office National du Tourisme, B.P. 1177, Lomé; Haut commissariat au Tourisme, route d'Aného, B.P. 1289, tel: 64-10;

Travel agents: Suvato, 16 rue d'Alsace Lorraine. Chargeurs Reunis, rue Marechal Gallieni, B.P. 34, tel: 26-11.

ANEHO

Aného, 44 km east of Lomé, is an attractive old town dating back to the slave trade. Later it was the capital of Togo under both the Germans and the French. It is a pleasant hour's drive from Lomé, and on a walk through the town you will see the great thick-walled colonial houses built by the Germans to withstand the tropical heat and damp, and gather something of the atmosphere of 19th-century Togo.

PALIME

Togo's cocoa town, Palime is attractively situated in hill country dominated by Mount Agbou (1,000m). The famous Kolme waterfalls are near by, and ceramics enthusiasts will want to visit the Pottery Centre. Palime's most modern hotel, fully air conditioned and recently completed, is the **Hotel du 30 Aout.**

ATAKPAMÈ

Also located in rolling hills, Atakpamé is the centre of the cotton-growing belt and has a large textile factory.

There are three hotels: **Roc Hotel, 27**

rooms, **Hotel de Voyageurs** and **Hotel des Plateaux.**

SOKODE

With a population of 17,000 Sokodé is Togo's second largest town. It is at the heart of Togo's forest land and is a great centre for hunting and shooting. All Muslim holidays are celebrated here including the famous Adossa or Festival of Knives. There is a four bedroom *Campemènt*, and **Nouvel Hôtel Central.**

DAPANGO

Set on a hillside in the extreme north of Togo, Dapango is noted for its mild climate. The markets are festive occasions that draw people from all over Togo and Upper Volta. The local dances are representative of the culture of the region, especially the Muslim marriage and funeral dances. There is a *Campement* in the town, and **Relais de Sorad des Savanes.**

OTHER TÓWNS

Lama-Kara, Tsevie, Nuatja, Kandé, Bassari and Klouto each have a *Campement,* the French West African equivalent of a rest-house, although, thanks to the French influence, the restaurant is usually of good quality.

HISTORY

Little systematic research has yet been done on early Togolese history. It would appear that in the 17th or 18th centuries various peoples from regions in and around the Western Sudan established themselves in the north of Togo without destroying the culture and way of life of older established groups such as the Kabyé. During the 15th and 16th centuries the Ewes moved in successive waves from

Tado, a commercial centre near the border with Benin, throughout the south of the country where, with the Mina, they formed the largest and most influential group.

European interest in the coastal countries of West Africa was centred around the slave trade in the 18th century and palm oil in the 19th. By the middle of the 19th century a number of French and German companies had been established in Togo, and in 1884 the country became a German protectorate to be later divided up between Britain and France after the First World War. The western sector was then ceded to Ghana in 1957. What remains is a mere sliver of land, only 50 km across at the coast.

At independence in 1960 the party of Sylvanus Olympio was elected to rule the country. Dogged by internal opposition and unpopular with the French, Olympio was assassinated in 1963 and his Government overthrown by the army. The civilian Government that replaced him was headed by Nicolas Grunitzky who had to face even more discontent until a second coup in 1967 brought Lt-Col. Etienne Eyadema to power.

Now a General, Eyadema has instituted a strong regime modelled on that of General Mobutu in Zaire. A Government-sponsored single party, the Rassemblement du Peuple Togolais (RPT) has absorbed and even reconciled the warring factions that used to reflect tribal and social groupings.

Togo has always tended to be overshadowed by its neighbour Ghana and in President Nkrumah's days there was considerable bitterness between the two countries. Some Ewes of Ghana have recently been campaigning for secession so that they may return to the fold of a 'Greater Togo'.

Togo is also aligning itself economically with Nigeria with which it particularly instrumental in the formation of the West African Economic Community (ECOWAS).

UGANDA

It is possible to visit Uganda but the atmosphere of political and economic insecurity has made it a risky venture in recent years. Apart from anything else there are severe shortages of many essential commodities, but more to the point is the unpredictability of events. The large-scale killings of recent years have not claimed the lives of many tourists, but there is a high level of suspicion and paranoia in the ranks of the army.

In better days Uganda was a wonderful country to visit, being spectacularly beautiful, with its mountains, rivers, lakes and fine game parks, and having exceptionally friendly and hospitable people and temperate climate.

THE LAND AND THE PEOPLE

Uganda has almost every conceivable variety of scenery—lush tropical forest and tea plantations on the slopes of the Ruwenzori's snow-capped peaks; arid plains of the sparsely populated Karamoja; the lush, heavily populated Buganda; the rolling savannah of Acholi, Bunyoro, Tororo and Ankole; the fertile cotton area of Teso.

The heartland skirts Lake Victoria, which is the size of Ireland. The White Nile, flowing out of the lake, traverses much of the country. Few African countries are so well-watered; this makes survival comparatively easy for many of the eleven million inhabitants whose staple diet is the green banana (*matoke*), or in other areas, millet-bread, cassava and sweet potatoes. There is ample fish in the lake and Nile, and large herds in the cattle country.

The south is green and heavy with banana plantations fronting the hills. 500km north the harsher ribs of the land show through the thinner soil. Here the shorter grass burns off more easily in the harder dry season.

Lake Kyoga forms the northern bound-

397

ary for the Bantu-speaking peoples who cover much of East, Central and South Africa. In Uganda they formed powerful kingdoms, notably Buganda in the central area, west of Kampala; Bunyoro to the north as far as Lake Mobutu Sese Seko; Toro, around Fort Portal near the Ruwenzori mountains; and Ankole in the south west. These, together with Rwanda and Burundi, were the famous Interlacustrine Kingdoms, in existence for some 600 years, and isolated until the 18th century from all non-African influence. The people within each kingdom are typically stratified into a pastoral aristocracy (called the Hima or Tutsi, who may possibly have come originally from southern Ethiopia, speaking Cushitic languages) and a majority of peasants. There were smaller kingdoms too in Eastern Region, the main peoples there being the Bantu-speaking Basoga and Bagisu.

In the north live the Lango near Lake Kyoga, and the Acholi between them and the Sudan border. Both speak River-Lake Nilotic languages. East of them are the Teso and the desert-dwelling Karamojong who are Plains Nilotes, related to the Masai of Kenya and Tanzania. In the far north west of Uganda are the Central Sudanic Lugbara people. In the far south west in the Ituri forests are pygmies.

GENERAL INFORMATION
Area: 235,886 sq. km.
Population: 11,172,000 (1974 estimate).
Altitude: Mostly 1,000—1,500 m with the highest peak of the Ruwenzori rising to 5,110 m.
Capital: Kampala
Head of State: Field Marshal Idi Amin Dada, Life President.
Government: Uganda is a republic with a president as head of the executive. Since the military coup of January 1971, legislative power has also been in the President's hands with the assistance of a Council of Ministers nominated by him. The former National Assembly has been

dissolved and political parties suspended.
Date of independence: 9 October 1962
Languages: English is the official language but Swahili is also spoken
Religions: Strong Christian (mainly Catholic and Anglican)—and also Muslim communities. The Government has ordered the 'Ugandanisation' of the churches and has banned several religious sects.
Currency: The Uganda shilling. (Sh.1=100 cents). £1 sterling=13.61 Shs. US$1.00=8.38 Shs. There is a flourishing black market, since the Uganda shilling is one of the world's most worthless currencies.
Time: GMT+3.

HOW TO GET THERE
By air: A large number of international airlines including Air Zaire, Alitalia, British Airways, British Caledonian, Ethiopian Airlines, Lufthansa, Sabena, SAS, and Sudan Airways fly to Entebbe. On departure at Entebbe Airport there is an Airport Departure Tax of 40 Shs.
By road: The road approach to Uganda is from Kenya and the journey may be made in a tour company coach or by the air-conditioned buses of Akamba Bus Company which leave Nairobi at 20.00 every evening, arriving in Kampala the following morning.

In recent years overland travellers have made a point of avoiding the main Kampala-Jinja-Tororo road if their journey necessitated passing through Uganda from Kenya or Sudan. Army road-blocks are frequent on this stretch, and tourists have often been jailed on suspicion of being 'mercenaries'.
By rail: There is a rail service from Kenya.

Visas and health regulations
No visa is required by nationals of the UK and Commonwealth countries. Admission is refused to nationals of Israel, South Africa and holders of Rhodesian

passports issued on or after 11 November 1965. Visas are not issued on arrival but are obtainable from a Uganda diplomatic mission. All visitors should first make inquiries. Visitors not in possession of onward tickets may be required to leave a refundable cash deposit of Shs. 3,000 on arrival.

Smallpox, yellow fever and cholera vaccination certificates are required.

CLIMATE

Although Uganda lies on the Equator the temperature remains pleasant due to the altitude and low humidity level. Temperatures range from 26°C in the day to 15°C in the evening. The mountain areas become much cooler, and the top of Mount Elgon is often trimmed with snow. After the air-conditioning of Kampala's modern buildings it is refreshing to see the log fires and open grates in the Kabale area. Rain tends to fall more heavily in the March-May and October-November period.

A good catch from Lake Albert

Health precautions: Tap water is safe in cities. It is wise to take a malaria prophylactic and vaccination against yellow fever is essential because it is endemic in Uganda. There is bilharzia in most lakes, but Lake Nagubo in the Kigezi hills is free of it. Medical facilities are not readily available.

ACCOMMODATION AND FOOD

Kampala has several hotels, and throughout the country the Government-owned Uganda Hotel Limited (P.O. Box 7173, Kampala) run a network of hotels, but catering facilities have been disrupted by the shortages of sugar, salt, beer, soap, and many foods. East National Park is provided with lodges, groups of *banda* (cabins) and camping sites. Restaurants may be found in and around Kampala and all the State-owned hotels now serve local dishes. The most famous of these are *matoke*, a staple food made from bananas, maize bread and the chicken and beef stews which are eaten with it.

The national drink is Waragi, a banana gin, very popular among visitors as a cocktail base.

TRANSPORT

All the main towns are connected by bitumen roads. The main routes from Kampala radiate southwest to Masaka, Mbarara and Kabale; west to Fort Portal and Kasese; north to Masindi, Gulu and Kabalega Falls; east to Jinja, Tororo, Mbale and Soroti. Lira and Gulu can also be reached by heading north from Soroti; and Kasese can also be reached by travelling north from Labale. Entebbe is linked to Kampala by a tarmac road.

Bus services operate between most parts of Uganda, but they are generally very full and rather unreliable. Taxis operate between most townships, but they are also overcrowded and sometimes erratically driven.

BANKS

Uganda Commercial Bank, Libyan-Arab-Uganda Bank, Standard Bank, National and Grindlays, Bank of India, Bank of Baroda.

BUSINESS HOURS

Banks: 08.00-12.30 (Saturdays 08.00-11.00). Government offices: 08.15-12.45 and 14.00-16.00. Post Offices: 08.00-12.30 and 14.00-16.30. Shops: 08.30-12.30 and 14.00-17.00 (Fridays to 19.00).

PUBLIC HOLIDAYS

25 January, Revolutionary Day; 17 September, Victory Day; 9 October, Independence Anniversary; Christmas Day; Id al Fatr; Good Friday; Easter Monday; Id al Adha, and Muhammad's Birthday.

FOREIGN EMBASSIES IN KAMPALA

Burundi: P.O. Box 4379; Egypt: P.O. Box 4280; France: P.O. Box 7212; West Germany: P.O. Box 7016; Ghana: P.O. Box 4062; India: P.O. Box 7040; Italy: P.O. Box 4646; Libya: P.O. Box 6079; Nigeria: P.O. Box 4338; Rwanda: P.O. Box 2468; Somalia: P.O. Box 7113; Sudan: P.O. Box 3200; Zaire: P.O. Box 4972.

ENTEBBE

Entebbe is the gateway to Uganda for air travellers. Prior to independence in 1962 it was the seat of the Governor and most government departments were located there. The **Lake Victoria Hotel** has a swimming pool. Skirting the lakeside are the Botanical Gardens which offer a fine collection of tropical trees and plants. Although there is a fine beach it is most unwise to bathe in the lake because of bilharzia.

KAMPALA

Kampala, the capital is set among hills, each dominated by a particular feature—the Anglican and Roman Catholic cathedrals, a mosque, and the palatial complex of the Old Kingdom of Buganda. The tree-lined avenues, with colourful flowerbeds and waving palms, wind along valleys and up hillsides. Modern Kampala has a fine skyline dominated by the towering International Hotel and a fine mosque. Parliament Buildings and the National Theatre are fine architectural examples.

A view of the city can be had from the **Kampala International Hotel**. The **Imperial Hotel** is just across the park from the International. The **Speke Hotel** is located near both the other hotels. The ultra-modern **Uganda Conference Centre**, which contains the **Nile Mansion** is also operated by Uganda Hotels. It offers accommodation, but has limited facilities for food. The **Fairway Hotel** is one of Uganda's newest; as its name suggests it overlooks the scenic Uganda Golf Club. There is a number of smaller hotels such as the **Park**, the **Equatorial**, **The Antlers Inn**, and the **Tourist** and **Amber** hotels. The former Kampala Club, known as the Top Club because of its hilltop location, has been taken over by Uganda Hotels Ltd., and has now been renamed the **Standard Hotel**.

Kasubi Hill is the site of the Kabaka's Tombs; here are buried Mutesa I, Mwanga, and the late 'King Freddie', Sir Edward Mutesa II. They offer one of the finest examples of Buganda thatched buildings in the country. Strict observance of the customs of the tombs should be followed; it would be taken as a gross discourtesy if one entered the building without removing one's shoes.

Namugongo is the site of the Uganda Martyr shrine. The shrine is located 16 km out of Kampala on the Jinja road.

JINJA

Jinja is Uganda's second largest town and lies 80 km to the east of Kampala on the main route to Kenya. It is the country's main industrial area built around the Owen Falls dam and power station. **Crested Crane Hotel**.

TORORO

Tororo, a small township close to the Kenya border is an important road and rail link. The town nestles under a hill dominating the skyline. The main hotel is the **Rock**.

MBALE

Mbale, Uganda's third largest town, is at the hub of the Eastern Region. Mount Elgon provides a beautiful backdrop to the fertile and lush countryside. Nkokonjeru is a steep hill which looms out of the plains to protect the town. The **Mount Elgon Hotel** was once regarded as one of the best up-country hotels and made Mbale a popular tourist spot.

The hotel is an ideal base for an ascent of the mountain, which offers a steep walk rather than a climb. The mountain, an extinct volcano, is 4,600 m high. The round trip to the summit takes three days. It is recommended both for the easy climbing and for an interesting encounter with village life as you make your way up the slopes through coffee and matoke (cooking banana) plantations. In the rainy season the climb can be very difficult and local advice should be sought before you begin.

MOROTO

Moroto is the main centre of Karamoja—a dusty dry area. Its plains are rich with zebra, ostrich, eland, giraffe, gazelle and elephant. It has now become a vast army complex.

The Karamojong are turbulent, tall,

athletic people, very proud and still clinging stubbornly to their traditions. Only recently after a request from Field Marshal Amin, have they begun to wear clothes. They are cattle people and are frequently in dispute with Kenya border tribes over cattle raiding. These men still carry, and use, long spears; the women wear beautiful necklaces, bangles and bracelets. It would be foolish to roam around this area without a guide who knows and understands the people.

MBARARA

Mbarara is the headquarters of a large army camp. It is rather reminiscent of a Western movie set, an effect heightened by the large pair of Ankole cattle horns mounted on a plinth at the entrance to the town. It is the centre of a cattle ranching area, home of the famous Ankole cattle who have a hornspan of over one metre. The rolling hillside is a very direct contrast to the lush greenery of the Eastern Provinces. There is the **Agip Motel**. The town is a base for Lake Mburo Game Reserve with bushbuck, oribi, buffalo, lion and leopard.

KABALE

Kabale, at 2,000 m above sea level, is Uganda's highest town. The **White Horse Inn** is the local hotel. Trips to the lakes—Lake Bunyonyi, in particular—are worthwhile. The climate is naturally more variable at this height, and warm clothes will be necessary in the evenings.

KISORO

Kisoro, nearby, is the starting point for climbing expeditions to Mounts Muhavura and Mgahinga. Seven lakes in the vicinity offer fishing and possible duck and fowl shooting. From Kabale you can drive north to Lakes Idi Amin Dada and George and the Ruwenzori Park. The road sweeps down from the mountains alongside the Kazinga Channel which links the two lakes. The view of the Game Park from Kichwamba on the escarpment is a photographer's dream. Kasese and Kilembe are the starting points for the game parks in the area.

FORT PORTAL

Fort Portal is an ideal base for exploring the Ruwenzori Mountains. It lies 1,700m above sea level and is the centre of the tea estates. The local hotel is called the **Mountains of the Moon**.

The town is within easy reach of the Ituri Forest—home of the pygmies—the hot springs of Bundibugyo, and the Toro Game Reserve. For climbing enthusiasts the Ruwenzoris offer Mount Speke, Mount Stanley, and Mount Baker, all over 5,000 m high. The vegetation of this area, equatorial forests with giant lush vegetation, gives one a very realistic picture of the Uganda of earlier years. The women of this area are famous for their beauty, poise and dignity.

GAME PARKS

Uganda has three major parks and 16 game reserves. Many wildlife enthusiasts claim Uganda's natural beauty is the finest in the world.

Kabalega (formerly Murchison) Falls National Park

This well-known park takes its name from the magnificent falls on the Nile river. It is famous for the rare white rhino as well as other rhino, hippo, elephant and crocodile. It is also the habitat of over 400 bird species. Visitors stay at either **Paraa Safari Lodge** or **Chobe Safari Lodge**.

Ruwenzori (formerly Queen Elizabeth) National Park

This park is along the shores of Lake Idi Amin Dada and Lake George, which are joined by the Kazinga Channel, and provides breeding grounds for the hippo, elephant, buffalo, Uganda kob, waterbuck and topi, lion, leopard, giant forest hog, warthog, sitatunga antelope and chimpanzee. There is a vast array of waterbirds. **Mweya Safari Lodge** serves the park.

Kidepo National Park

This park covers about 1,200 sq. km on the borders of the Sudan in north east Uganda. It is not as well known as the other two and consequently is often overlooked by visitors. The park has a variety of big game, but is perhaps best known for several rare species—the greater kudu, Bright's gazelle and Chandler's reed buck.

HISTORY

From the late 15th century, the kingdoms of Bunyoro, Toro, Ankole, Kigezi, Rwanda, Burundi, Karagwe, Buganda, Busoga and Bugisu fought and allied with each other, their territory varying with their power. Buganda remained a very small kingdom until the 18th century when it began to expand dramatically, never losing any area it conquered. In this period developed its characteristic highly centralised political system. The Kabaka (king) had great autocratic power, based not on a belief on his divinity or his ritual function as in many African kingdoms but on his control of the administration, wealth and army of his country.

In the 19th century Swahili-speaking tribes and Zanzibari Arab traders made their way to Uganda. They used a route through Tanzania to Karagwe (the kingdom on the west of Lake Victoria) where they would settle for perhaps 12 years, trading until they had bought enough to make the journey back to the coast profitable. Other traders came from Sudan to northern Uganda. In the wake of both came European explorers.

Religious conflict and protection (1870-1900): Traders and explorers opened the country up for missionaries who for some time concentrated only on Buganda where the rivalry between Muslim, Anglican and Catholic (French) caused bitterness, martyrdom and civil war. Kabaka Mutese (1860-84) encouraged each in turn—Islam in the 1860s, Christianity in the 1870s (when he put to death 100 Muslim converts). In 1886, during the reign of Mwanga many young Christian converts who have since been made saints by the Catholic church, were martyred for their faith, for their criticism of Mwanga's homosexuality and because Mwanga suspected the foreign influence over them. This suspicion proved well-founded, for in the ensuing civil wars when the Anglican faction triumphed it was helped by the British representative, Lord Lugard, who made Buganda a British protectorate (1890). Later the deportation of Mwanga and a succession of minor chiefs helped to turn Buganda into an oligarchy rather than an autocratic state.

The colonial period and after: Despite the violent beginning, Uganda had a more trouble-free and prosperous time under colonialism than did many African countries. The old kingdom remained the unit of administration and similar forms of local government were introduced to the north, so that African rulers kept their powers and the British ruled indirectly through them. One less fortunate result of this was the intensification of regional differences dividing the country.

Africans were encouraged to grow cash crops. Uganda was all the time recognised as an essentially African country and its traditional leaders were listened to. For example, the efforts of its chiefs were partly responsible for the abandonment of schemes to federate East Africa which would probably have meant domination by Kenyan white settlers. Yet Asian and European traders did flood into Uganda and their monopoly of marketing and production and the low fixed prices for the farmers' products caused

periodic resentment among the people.

The traditional divisions within the country, fostered during colonialism, caused considerable inter-party strife on the road to independence but finally in 1962, Milton Obote emerged as Prime Minister heading a coalition of his own Uganda People's Congress and the Kabaka Yekka (Kabaka Alone) party. A year later the Kabaka, Sir Edward Mutesa, was elected President. The kingdoms retained their automomy in local matters. By 1966 this alliance had failed and Obote's army sacked the royal palace at Kampala, destroying all the regalia and causing casualties on both sides; the Kabaka escaped to England where he later died. A new constitution then abolished the kingdoms completely. Dr. Obote tried to introduce a political and economic system resembling that in neighbouring Tanzania.

In January 1971 an army coup brought General (now Field-Marshal) Idi Amin to power and Obote, who was in Singapore at the time, took refuge in Tanzania. Amin tried to reconcile the Baganda by retrieving the remains of the last Kabaka and burying them with the tombs of his ancestors at Kampala, but the kingdoms have not been revived. Under the Field Marshal's rule ethnic bitterness has in general been aggravated and consistent reports of massacres usually by the Army have discredited Amin and his claim to be universally popular.

After a period of friendship with Israel, Amin reversed his position and formed an Islamic alliance with Libya. His dealings with the Asian community embittered his erstwhile friendly relations with Britain. Amin ordered all non-citizen Asians to leave within the very short time of three months up to November 1972.

Many internal attempts to remove Amin have failed, largely because he relies on an extremely ruthless mercenary force recruited from Southern Sudan, which owes its dominant position entirely to Amin.

UPPER VOLTA

Upper Volta is about the poorest country in the world. In the arid, acacia-dotted plains the great swollen trunks of the baobab trees, with their refreshingly feathery leaves in the rainy season, rear up as friendly landmarks. Out in the fields men, women and children hoe and plant. This is one of the most densely populated countries in Africa despite the terrible hardships of the climate and eroded soils: the relentless march southwards of the great Sahara desert is stripping the savannah lands of trees and gradually turning the thin layer of cultivable soil into sun-blackened rock-hard laterite.

THE LAND AND THE PEOPLE

The southern part of the country, with its slightly better rainfall, is less arid than the north, and around the old capital of Bobo-Dioulasso are fertile fields, and gardens. The old city's thick-walled colonial houses and tree-lined streets contrast with the deserts to the north. There is a magnificent Sudanese mosque here. Nearby are the waterfalls of Banfora and the Volta River with its sacred caymans.

From the wooded savannah in the southern part of the country, the plains of Upper Volta dry out into sand and semi-desert. The country takes its name from the three great rivers which bring water

to the arid plains—the Black, the Red and the White Volta; these are also the three colours of its national flag. But the rivers also bring the dreaded diseases of river blindness, bilharzia and malaria—for this reason the most densely populated areas of the country are far from the infested river valleys. Yet the major hope of the country is gradually to eradicate the snails and flies that breed in the water, and then to resettle the valleys and develop the country's agriculture. An important step in this direction is the Kou Valley project, near Banfora, where Taiwan's aid has produced lush green rice paddies. Travellers must remember never to bathe in the fresh water here.

It is a strange feature of West African history that Upper Volta should boast the

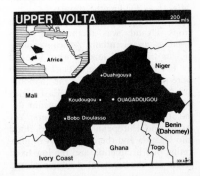

longest continuous royal dynasty and one of the strongest empires of old. It is the history of the great Mossi Kingdoms that marks out what is now Upper Volta from the rest of former French Soudan (now Mali). Today, the Mossi form about a half of the country's population. The rest is made up of Fulani, Gourmantche, Bobo (the farmers of the south), the remote Lobi in their fortress homes, the Senoufou and the Bissa.

Historically a war-mongering and fiercely individualistic people, the Mossi were divided among themselves into four kingdoms—Tenkodogo, Ouagadougou, Yatenga and Gourma, each with its own ruler, or Naba. Hostile to the Islam invaders, they constituted a major barrier to that religion's progress southwards. Today, the Mossi courage and determination has turned to his land which he obstinately continued to farm in the face of terrible odds.

The second most powerful kingdom was Yatenga, and its capital Ouahigouya. If you take the road out to Ouahigouya and on towards the Mali border, you will pass through wonderfully structured villages of baked earth and thatched roofs: round and square huts and houses, and grain stores set apart on stilts. Nothing here has changed very much for centuries. Yet all the time the acute poverty is with you.

WILDLIFE

There are three national parks. The nearest to Ouagadougou is the Po Park. In the east, on the border with Benin and Niger, is the three-country 'W' Park, and the Arly Park. A number of organised hunting safari trips are set up during the hunting season (December to April).

The savannah grasslands shelter a variety of wild boar, antelope, buffalo and monkeys, while in the forested areas near Benin there are also elephants. There are reserves at Pama, Kourtiagou, Deux Bales, Bontioli and Singou.

GENERAL INFORMATION

Area: 274,200sq. km.
Population: 5,900,000 (mid 1974).
Altitude: Mean altitude 200-300m. Highest point 733m.
Capital: Ouagadougou.
Head of State: General Sangoulé Lamizana.
Government: Military rule which may soon give way to civilian democracy.
Date of independence: 5 August 1960.
Languages: French (official). Indigenous languages include More (spoken by the Mossi), Dioula (spoken by the Bobo), and Gourmantche (spoken in the east).
Religions: About 80% follow traditional beliefs; about 15% are Muslims and 5% Roman Catholics.
Currency: CFA franc. £1 sterling=429 CFA francs; US$1.00=249 CFA francs.
Time: GMT.

HOW TO GET THERE

By air: Upper Volta has international airports, at Ouagadougou (2 km out of town at Borgo and Bobo-Dioulasso (16 km out of town). International services are provided by Air Ghana, Air Afrique, Air Mali and UTA.

By rail: From Abidjan a railway runs into Upper Volta, linking Bobo-Dioulasso and Ouagadougou with Ivory Coast. There is an express train with sleeping cars which although not luxurious is quite comfortable. The journey from Abidjan to Bobo takes 19½ hours and to Ouagadougou, 27 hours.

By road: Regular bus services are run during the dry season from Bobo to Bamako in Mali (14-hour journey) and from Ouagadougou to Niamey in Niger.

Passable roads enter Upper Volta from Ivory Coast, Ghana, Togo, Niger and Mali, though surfaces tend to be rough, and progress is slow. Traffic drives on the right.

Visas and health regulations

For nationals of France and former French colonies, a valid passport or national identity card is sufficient; in most other cases a visa is required obtainable from French embassies abroad. Visitors must hold a return ticket or other document guaranteeing repatriation.

Valid international certificates of vaccination against smallpox, yellow fever and cholera are required.

Dutiable goods

Personal effects and a limited amount of tobacco, alcohol and perfume is allowed in free of duty.

Currency regulations

There are no restrictions on the amount of foreign currency taken in or taken out.

CLIMATE

The best time to visit Upper Volta is December to March. Apart from the north which has a Saharan climate, Upper Volta is in the Sudanic climatic zone. From November to mid-February it is dry and relatively cool, although the dusty *harmattan* wind frequently blows from the east. In March and April there is also a short rainy season particularly in the south west. There is an intermediate warm and dry season between mid-February and the end of May. The rainy season is from June to October, with violent storms occurring in August. Annual rainfall is between 635 and 1,145mm. Rainfall is highest in the south west and lowest in the north east. The mean temperature is 27°C between December and March.

What to wear: Lightweight clothing. During the rainy season a light raincoat is needed. Hat and filter-lens sun-glasses are essential. Stout walking shoes are necessary in the bush.

Health precautions: A suitable prophylactic against malaria should be taken before arrival, during the stay and after departure. Typhoid vaccination is also recommended. Water is drinkable in major towns but elsewhere should be boiled.

ACCOMMODATION AND FOOD

Most hotels have some air-conditioned rooms. There are a few restaurants in Ouagadougou and in Bobo, in addition to those in the hotels. Specialities include *brochettes* (meat cooked on a skewer) and roast chicken.

Tipping: This is not customary; service is included in hotel bills.

TRANSPORT

Air: Air Volta operates regular flights between Ouagadougou and Bobo-Dioulasso and between Ouagadougou and Tambao in the north. A five- or six-seater Cherokee VI can be chartered from the Aero-Club.

Road: Upper Volta has 4,451 km of local roads and 8,100 km of tracks, passable in the dry season only. Regular bus services are operated in the dry season.

Car hire: Cars can be rented from **Volta Auto Location**, Ouagadougou, B.P. 1040 (tel: 27.20) and from **Location Desplat** (tel: 22.19). Cars can also be hired by the hour in the town.

BANKS

Banque Internationale des Voltas (BIV) B.P. 362, Ouagadougou and Banque Internationale pour le Commerce, l'Industrie et Agriculture de la Haute Volta, B.P. 8, Ouagadougou.

Business hours: Shops: Monday to Saturday 0800-1200 and 1500-1830; Banks: Monday to Friday 0800-1200; Government offices: 0800-1230 and 1500-1730.

PUBLIC HOLIDAYS

In addition to the main Muslim and Christian feast days, the following are observed: New Year's Day; Anniversary of the Revolution 3 January; May Day; Proclamation of the Republic 11 December.

FOREIGN EMBASSIES IN OUAGADOUGOU

France: B.P. 504: **West Germany:** B.P. 600; **Ghana:** B.P.212; **USA:** B.P. 35.

The diplomatic missions of other countries are in Abidjan (Ivory Coast).

OUAGADOUGOU

The capital has a population of 150,000. Although the modern city has grown up very recently, especially since being linked to Abidjan by railway in 1954, Ouagadougou was the capital of the Mossi Empire from the 15th century onwards. The centre of the city is an avenue known as the Champs Elysées. At one end is the former Governor's Palace and at the other the neo-romanesque cathedral. Nearby is the Palace of the Moro Naba, Emperor of the Mossi. The National Ethnographical Museum is worth visiting (closed Sundays).

Excursions from Ouagadougou include a trip to the nearby wooded area known locally as the Bois de Boulogne; the 'dam circuit', a drive round the reservoir north of the city; a visit to Pabre, a Mossi village beside another, smaller artificial lake 18 km to the north, where wild animals come to drink; and 50 km distant, Sabou, where crocodiles can be seen at close quarters.

Hotels

Hotel Indépendance, Avenue Ouezzin Coulibaly, B.P. 127, tel: 27.20;
Ran, B.P. 62, tel: 32.40, 34 rooms;
Central Hôtel, B.P. 56, tel: 34.18, 12 rooms;

Hôtel Ricardo, B.P. 349, tel: 21.75;
Les Ambassadeurs, 12 rooms;
Hôtel du Marché, 12 rooms;
Pavillon Vert, 19 rooms.

Restaurants

In addition to restaurants in the hotels, Ouagadougou has the following: **L'Eau Vive** (run be a lay Catholic order), **Escale,** and the **Volta Bar.**

Entertainments

Swimming **(Hotel Indépendance)**, tennis **(Hotel Indépendance** and, by invitation, the **Volta Club)** and riding **(Club Hippique).**

Ouagadougou has two open-air cinemas and the following night-clubs: **Chez Maurice, Le Cave, Volta Club.**

Shopping and markets

Visitors can bargain for souvenirs in the traditional market: wooden statuettes, bronze models, masks, worked skins, jewellery, leather goods, fabrics, handwoven blankets.

Ouagadougou has a unique tannery, Government-owned and run by both French and Voltaic experts. It produces remarkably original and well-finished leather stamped goods and crafts, ranging from chess sets to elephant's foot ashtrays.

Tourist information

Office du Tourisme de la Haute Volta, B.P. 624, tel: 28.01; Air Afrique, place d'Armes, B.P. 141, tel: 24.38; UTA, Avenue Binger, tel: 22.61; Air Volta, rue Binger, B.P. 116, Ouagadougou.

BOBO-DIOULASSO

Bobo, with 80,000 inhabitants, is the commercial and industrial centre. It has a lively market, an interesting mosque, a zoo and a botanical garden. It is a good centre for touring the Black Volta area and the south west, a region rich in folklore. Koulima is well known for its mask-making. So is Koumi (15 km) which also has many traditional dances. At Dinderesso (17 km) bathing is possible in the clear spring at Kou. Hippos can be seen at the Mare aux Hippos, 76 km to the north. Banfora is situated in a beautiful and well-watered region with cliffs, waterfalls and springs. Nearby are the Kartiguela Falls, the Comoe Falls and Lake Tengrela.

Hotels
Royan, B.P. 185, tel: 91.33, 24 rooms; **Ran Hôtel,** B.P. 50, tel: 96.84.

Restaurant: Le Perroquet.

HISTORY

The cave paintings found at Banfora as well as the many stone objects unearthed by archaeologists suggest that Upper Volta had a rich pre-history. Other recent investigation would seem to show that gold was being mined throughout the south of the country in the 13th and 14th century.

As far as we know the earliest inhabitants of Upper Volta were Voltaic-speaking peoples such as the Bwa and the Senoufo. From the 12th or 13th century onwards peoples from other parts of Africa established themselves in successive waves: the Bobo from the north-west, the Mossi and the Gourmantché from Central Sudan, the Lobi-Dugani who settled in the south-west and the Peulh who moved into the north-east. These various peoples formed a large number of separate kingdoms and chiefdoms, the most notable of which was that of the Mossi, ruled by an absolute monarch himself subject to rigid controls imposed by traditions. The numerous

kingdoms and chiefdoms knew periods of expansion and eclipse until the end of the 19th century when the French succeeded in exploiting the internal rivalries which had always existed and made the country into a French protectorate in 1897. Eventually Upper Volta became a French colony and in 1932, for purely commercial reasons, the country was divided up and over half of it attached to the Ivory Coast. It was not until 1947 that it regained administrative and territorial unity.

At independence, in 1960, the ruling *Union Démocratique Voltaique* (UDV) of Maurice Yameogo banned opposition parties and imposed austerity measures on the demoralised workers and civil servants. After mass demonstrations and protests the army took over in January 1966 and Lt.-Col. (now General) Sangoulé Lamizana became President.

The army remained in control until a new Constitiution was drawn up in 1970, allowing for semi-civilian rule for the next four years. Elections were held in December of that year—with the UDV winning 37 seats, the *Parti de Regroupement Africaine* (PRA) 12, and the radical *Mouvement de Liberation Nationale* (MLN) 6.

In February 1974 the army assumed power again and the Constitution of 21 June 1970 was suspended. Political activity was banned, but freedom of press, trade unions and worship were allowed. The National Assembly was dissolved and replaced by a National Consultative Council of Renewal. Power at both national and regional levels is in the hands of the army. In January 1976 the Government promised to introduce a constitution which would be 'a true instrument of dialogue'.

Most young Voltaics leave the country after the autumn harvest to migrate southwards to the plantations and cities of the coastal states, where they earn money to bring back home in time for the spring sowing. Few emigrate for ever.

ZAIRE

Not the easiest country in Africa for conventional tourism, Zaire has two facets: the international life-style of the expatriates and ruling elite in Kinshasa, the capital, and the Copperbelt towns; and the neglected rural areas, where travel is hazardous. The eastern border with its lakes, mountains and game parks is accessible from Rwanda, Burundi and Tanzania.

THE LAND AND THE PEOPLE

The Republic of Zaire, the largest black African State, covers an area of over two million sq. km—approximately three times the size of France. It is bounded to the west and north by the Zaire (formerly the Congo) and Oubangui rivers; to the east by the mountains and land rift containing Lakes Mobutu Sese Seko, Kivu and Tanganyika; and to the south-east by the waters of the Luapula, bordering the Shaba (formerly Katanga) region.

The various arms and tributaries of the Zaire River are wide, swift-flowing waterways fed by heavy rainfall. It has the second largest volume of water of any river in the world and has a remarkably even flow, being fed alternately by rains in the northern and southern hemisphere. Upstream from Kinshasa the Zaire River is over 15 km. wide.

The west and centre of the country are taken up with equatorial forests, with ample rainfall. In the eastern region of lakes and rift valley the land rises to cool highlands with fertile farmland. The southern Shaba region is savannah land with poor soil but rich mineral deposits which can easily be worked. On the Atlantic shore-line are coconut palms and mangroves.

Kivu region, in the east, has a mild climate which provides excellent conditions for agriculture: It is an area of great natural beauty with high mountains, lakes and valleys.

Zaire's 24 million people belong to a complex pattern of ethnic groups. The

409

Kongo people are divided territorially between Zaire, the Congo People's Republic and Angola, the Zande between Zaire and the Sudan and the Bemba between Zaire and Zambia. The majority groups are: the Kongo, around the Zaire estuary; the Kwangu-Kwilu people farther upstream; the Mongo, in the southern forest; the Luba and their cousins the the Lulua and the Songe in the south; and the Bwaka and the Zande on the northern borders. The Ngala people of the main stretch of river in the north-west have given the country a widely-used languge, Lingala.

The peaceable pygmies of the Ituri forest in the east of the country maintain their traditional way of life, hunting and gathering the fruits of the forest.

Zaire's population is unevenly distributed. The Great Forest has only three to four people per sq. km and vast areas are deserted. At the northern edge of the forest the density increases to 10-20 people per sq. km. The mining areas of Shaba are heavily populated as are the majority of Zaire's cities. The population of Kinshasa is well over two million. Lubumbashi, Kisangani, Mbuji-Mayi, Bukavu and Kanaga each have several hundred thousand inhabitants.

CULTURE

Zaire has had a strong artistic tradition and each region of the vast country formerly had distinctive styles of carving and decoration. The Government is now establishing a national museum at Mont Ngaliema (Kinshasa) and others around the country. Thousands of valuable objects have been saved for the nation in recent years. The Government also controls the outflow of examples of the traditional arts.

Wood sculpture continues in the tropical rain forests of the Zaire basin, and among peoples known for their carving are the Kongo, Pende, Kuba, and Tshokwe. Much of the traditional craftwork can only be found in museums, however, although traditional designs have been incorporated in the decoration of the presidential palace grounds in Kinshasa which are open at weekends to the public. Panels are modelled on genuine Tshokwe and Songe masks, and extensive use is made of the geometrical designs of the Kuba.

Modern Zairean music is the most popular in Africa. The songs have an urgent rhythm but a curiously sad and lilting melody. The instruments used are straightforward and familiar, drums and guitars, but more and more traditional instruments are being rediscovered and put to use.

WILDLIFE

Zaire has several climatic zones, but is richest in game in the east and north—Virunga and Garamba national parks, set in dramatic and beautiful surroundings. The country is bounded on the east by several of Africa's most important lakes, Tanganyika, Kivu, Idi Amin (formerly Edward), and Mobutu (formerly Albert). All, except for Kivu, are rich in fish, as are the rivers which cross the country. Fish include catfish, *mbenga* and tarpon in the Zaire estuary, and *tilapia* which are fished commercially in the lakes. The fish in Lake Idi Amin attract pelicans and marabou storks.

Virunga Park has buffalo, hippopotamus, antelope (including Zaire cob, topi and waterbuck), lion, leopard, elephant and the very rare okapi. Garamba, open from December to June, has white rhinoceros and giraffe. Kahuzi-Biega, near Bukavu, has mountain gorilla. Upemba National Park in Shaba region has zebra, eland, and roan and black antelope.

GENERAL INFORMATION

Area: 2,345,000 sq. km.
Population: 24 million.
Altitude: Sea level, rising to central basin

800 m. Shaba plateau 1,500 m eastern mountains 2,000 m.

Capital: Kinshasa.

Head of State: General Mobutu Sese Seko.

Government: Military/civilian rule. The single party, *Mouvement Populaire de la Revolution* (MPR) was founded in 1967 and has headquarters at N'Sele, near Kinshasa.

Date of independence: 30 June 1960.

Languages: The official and administrative language is French; the four national languages are Swahili, Tshiluba, Kikongo and Lingala.

Religions: Christian (Catholic, Protestant and Kimbanguist) and traditional.

Currency: The Zaire (Z)=100 makuta. US$1.00=Z0.86 £1 sterling=Z1.49.

Time: GMT + 2 in the centre and east; GMT + 1 in west.

HOW TO GET THERE

By air: Air Zaire serves 20 countries and the national airlines of foreign countries link up with Kinshasa: Sabena, UTA, Alitalia, PanAm, Iberia, Air Afrique, Swissair, Lufthansa, British Caledonian Airways, and Ethiopian Airlines.

Air Zaire has direct links with Brussels, Paris, Madrid, Geneva, Athens, Rome, London and Frankfurt. Within Africa there are direct links with main centres including Lagos, Entebbe, Nairobi, Dar es Salaam, Libreville, Bangui, Abidjan, Dakar, Kigali, Bujumbura, Yaunde, Luanda, Lome.

Kinshasa's airport is at Ndjili, 29 km out of the city. Air Zaire provides free transport. Taxis are expensive.

By sea: Direct shipping connections between Zaire and the outside world pass through Matadi port (388 km from Kinshasa by rail or road). The national shipping company operates regular services to and from Antwerp and the Americas and round Africa.

By road: The rivers Zaire and Oubangui which form the country's western and northern frontier can be crossed by rudimentary car-carrying ferries from Brazzaville to Kinshasa, Bangui to Zongo and Bangassou to Ndu. When you get to Zaire, however, be prepared for some of the worst road conditions in Africa, especially in the forest areas.

There are also roads, in varying states of disrepair, from Juba in Sudan, Fort Portal and Kabale in Uganda, Bujumbura in Burundi, the Copperbelt in Zambia and Kigali in Rwanda. The latter road is well-used and adequate at least as far as Lubumbashi.

Visas and health regulations

All visitors must produce a valid passport and visa, **which should be applied for from a Zaire diplomatic mission in or nearest to their own country of residence.** Visas will only be issued if there is proof of one's intention to leave the country after the visit (eg. a return ticket). Transit visas will be issued at the point of entry on presentation of a visa for the destination country. Sometimes internal flights have documentation checks.

Getting to Zaire and travelling within the country demands a lot of patience on the part of the intending visitor. Every trip, from the first step of obtaining a visa, until final departure requires forms in duplicate or triplicate. In 1976 some easing of entry regulations came about.

International certificates of vaccination against smallpox and yellow fever are compulsory. Inoculation against cholera for those coming from affected areas is required, and typhoid and paratyphoid is also recommended.

Dutiable goods

As well as personal effects, 200 cigarettes and an unopened bottle of spirits may be taken into the country free of duty. Customs men keep a sharp watch for precious stones, whether smuggled or not, and for rough ivory or authentic old sculptures.

Currency regulations

There is no restriction on the import or export of foreign currency, but it must be declared on entry and the balance on departure with official exchange proof for the difference. No local currency may be taken out of the country.

CLIMATE

Zaire is so huge that it is difficult to summarise the climate briefly. Roughly speaking, the dry seasons in the north correspond to the rainy seasons in the south. Thus around Kisangani the main dry season is from December to February, followed by a short rainy season in March and May, another short dry season in June and finally a long rainy season from July to November. But around Kinshasa and Lubumbashi the long dry season runs from May to October followed by short rains in November, another dry season in December and January and a long rainy season from February to April. In the eastern mountain area (on the equator) there are only two short dry seasons, in January and July.

On the whole the temperature varies between 20°C and 30°C in the tropical forest and between 15°C and 25°C on the high plateau. It is cooler in the tourist region of Kivu, which can be said to have an almost Mediterranean climate throughout the year.

What to wear: Lightweight clothing is essential. Take also a light sweater and light raincoat. In the cities one requires a lightweight suit for formal occasions.

Health precautions: Take precautions against malaria, before, during and after your stay. Other hazards to health are dysentery, typhoid, scrub typhus, yellow fever and bilharzia. Tap water should be boiled and filtered before drinking. Medical services are adequate but expensive. There are hospitals in the main towns.

ACCOMMODATION & FOOD

Hotels and restaurants that cater for Europeans are luxurious, but expensive and often heavily booked. It is advisable to make reservations in advance.

There are good restaurants in the main towns, serving both European and Zairean dishes (such as *moambe* chicken cooked in fresh palm oil, with rice and spinach).

TRANSPORT

(For precise details consult any travel agency in the main towns).

Air: Air Zaire links Ndjili Airport (Kinshasa) with about 40 airports in Zaire, including Lubumbashi, Bukavu, Goma, Mbuji-Mayi, Kisangani, Bandundu and all the important towns.

River and lake car-carrying ferries: Kinshasa to Kisangani takes seven days; Kinshasa to Ilebo takes five days. River services connect with rail services. There are fast boats connecting Bukavu and Goma, on Lake Kivu (5 hours).

Rail: The main internal route is from Lubumbashi to Ilebo, with a branch from Kamina to Kalemie (on Lake Tanganyika). Kinshasa is connected by rail to the port at Matadi.

Road: The roads in Zaire are in general of poor standard outside the main areas of population, except the stretches between Kinshasa and Matadi, between Lubumbashi and Ndola (Zambia), between Lubumbashi and Kolwezi (serving the Zairean copperbelt), and between Kisangani and Mambasa (eastern Zaire).

Bus services connect main towns, but the distances are great and the roads bad. Enquire on the spot. In the main towns buses and taxis are plentiful. For the latter you should agree on the fare before starting the journey.

Car hire: This is available in the main

towns but is expensive. Apply at **Autoloc,** Avenue des Aviateurs, Kinshasa, tel: 23.322, or **Hertz,** Hotel Inter-continental, B.P. 9535, Kinshasa, tel: 318.00 ext. 6.

BANKS
There are numerous banks. Union Zair-oise de Banques, 19 Avenue de la Na-tion, B.P. 197, Kinshasa, has connections with the Standard Bank. Barclays Inter-national, Banque de Paris it des Pays Bas and First National City Bank have offices in Kinshasa.

Business hours
Banks: 0800-1130 Monday to Friday. Shops: 0800-1200 and 1500-1800 Monday to Saturday. Offices: 0730-1200 and 1430-1700 Monday-Friday and 0730-1200 Sat-urdays. Government: 0730-1330 Monday to Friday, 0730-1200 Saturdays.

PUBLIC HOLIDAYS
New Year; Martyrs of Independence 4 January; Labour Day; MPR Day 20 May; Zaire Day 24 June; Independence Day 30 June; National Army Day 17 November; Anniversary of the Regime 24 November.

Every year between mid-June and mid-July is the Kinshasa International Fair (FIKIN) which attracts businessmen from all over the world.

FOREIGN EMBASSIES IN KINSHASA
Austria: B.P. 7797; Belgium: Building Le Cinquantenaire, Place du 27 Octobre, B.P. 899; Benin: B.P. 3265; Burundi: B.P. 1483; Cameroon: B.P. 10998; Can-ada: B.P. 8341; Central African Empire: B.P. 7769; Chad: B.P. 9097; Congo Peo-ple's Republic: B.P. 9516; Denmark: B.P. 1446; Egypt: B.P. 8838; Ethiopia: B.P. 8435; France: B.P. 3093; Gabon: B.P. 9592; Ghana: B.P. 8446; West Ger-many: B.P. 8400; Greece: B.P. 478; In-dia: B.P. 1026; Italy: B.P. 1000; Ivory Coast: B.P. 9514; Japan: B.P. 1810; Ke-nya: B.P. 9667; Liberia: B.P. 8940; Lib-ya: B.P. 9198; Mauritania: B.P. 16397; Morocco: B.P. 912; Netherlands: B.P. 10299; Nigeria: B.P. 1700; Rwanda: B.P. 967; Senegal: B.P. 7686; Spain: B.P. 8036; Sudan: B.P. 7347; Sweden: B.P. 3038; Switzerland: B.P. 8724; Tanzania: B.P. 1612; Togo: B.P. 10197; Tunisia: B.P. 1498; Uganda: B.P. 1086; UK: B.P. 8049; USA: B.P. 697; Zambia: B.P. 1144.

KINSHASA
Formerly Leopoldville, until the local name for the area was restored in May 1966, Kinshasa was developed as the centre of commerce and colonial adminis-tration. It has a population of 2 million and is administered as a series of com-munes, with clearly identifiable smart residential areas, a business centre, and a government centre. It remains, in effect, a divided city with the shops and airline offices on one side and with the Cité, a huge sprawling African township, on the

Tribal figure sculpture from the Baluba-Hemba tribe

THE BRITISH MUSEUM

other. Expatriate businessmen and the élite of Zairean Government circles live in the hilly residential area in large detached houses. In the township groups from various up-country areas live together in cramped conditions.

The city centre has the Boulevard du 30 Juin with luxury shops, pavement cafes, and banks. Mount Ngaliema (ex-Stanley) once had a statue of the explorer, but this was removed in the 'return to authenticity' campaign. The present government has developed an elaborate presidential park with formal gardens, extravagent but attractive, and open to the public at weekends. The Organisation of African Unity has its own village built on President Mobutu's orders for the summit meeting in 1967, with chalets for African leaders, a restaurant, a zoo and a recreation ground. N'Sele is the MPR party's town.

Other sights are the markets, the University, Kingole fishing village, Lake Vert, the Black River, the Kinsuka rapids.

Hotels
Intercontinental Hotel, B.P. 9535, tel: 318.00, outside the city in Gombe residential quarter, international luxury standard.

Hotel Okapi, B.P. 8697, tel: 596.22, in Binza quarter, perched on the side of a hill 10 km from centre.

Hotel Le Memling, Avenue de la République du Tchad, B.P. 68, tel: 232.60, in the centre of town.

Hotel Regina, Blvd du 30 Juin, B.P. 8902, tel: 236.91, centre of town, near the river.

Guest House, Avenue de Flambeau, B.P. 68, tel: 234.90.

Afrique Hotel, B.P. 1711. tel: 319.02, 27 rooms.

Restaurants
Hotels generally offer food of French/Belgian cuisine, with a wide choice of dishes but do not be surprised if the service tends to be slow: the result will usually be excellent.

Bapende dance mask

The main restaurants in the town are good but expensive. They draw their custom chiefly from businessmen. **Le Devinière**, in Binza, the **Zoo** in town and the **Grill** in the City are three among several first-rate restaurants. Others in town are **Mandarin** (Chinese), **Chez Nicola** (Italian), **Pergola**, **Carthage** (Tunisian), **Namouna**, **Café de la Paix** (Pub), the **New Pub** (Oriental) and **Coq Hardi** (quarter Joli Parc). There are also some cafes and snack bars.

Entertainment
There are occasional performances by visiting international entertainers, but the Zairean bands are hard to beat; they have a keen local following and move about from bar to bar depending on whether they are well or badly treated by proprietors. Kinshasa is a lively, late-night town so long as the pay packets have not run out; then it suddenly quietens down.

There are several air-conditioned and open-air cinemas, showing recently released films.

Nightclubs: **Les Anges Noirs**, **Baninga**, **l'Etoile**, **Jumbo**, **Kamalondo**, **la Rigola** (Limete), **Safari** (Binza) **V.I.P.**, **Capitale**, **Chez Cara**, **Une-deux-trois**, **Vatican**. Casinos: **Kin Casino**, **Olympic**, **Casino National**.

Sport: Tennis is very popular and can be played at the Cercle de Kin, Athenée, Elaeis, Familia Clubs, OUA and Funa sport centres. **Swimming**: at the Athenée, OUA, Funa N'Sele Pool. **Riding**: Centre Hippique of Kin, l'Etrier. **Sailing**: Nautic Club of Kin, Yacht Club.

Shopping and markets

There are ambitious curio shops in the main streets, and a small open-air souvenir market near the Memling Hotel. The central market is modern, spacious, and impressively clean and well kept, with controlled prices. One section sells produce from the presidential farm at N'Sele, and has a tiny cafe with delicious fresh fruit juice from the farm.

Large shops sell goods imported from Europe, but prices are high, and it is not a town in which to think casually of buying clothes.

Local craftwares on sale include ivory objects, ebony carvings, bracelets, crocodile and snakeskin bags and shoes, semiprecious stones and paintings.

Tourist information

National Office for Tourism, Blvd du 30 Juin (B.P. 9502), tel: 224.17.
Travel agencies: **Agetraf**, Avenue Equateur 87, B.P. 8834, tel: 269.21;
Amiza, Avenue des Aviateurs, B.P. 7597, tel: 246.02, 230.83;
Immo-Voyages, Blvd du 30 Juin 22A, B.P. 798, tel: 222.63;
Zaire Tours, Blvd du 30 Juin 11, B.P. 14795, tel: 22.38;
Zaire Travel Service, Blvd du 30 Juin 11, B.P. 15812, tel: 232.88.

LOWER ZAIRE, BANDUNDU, AND EQUATOR REGIONS

These regions are accessible for travellers staying in Kinshasa, though there are hotels in the main towns. The Lower Zaire region stretches to the Atlantic beaches at **Moanda**, a relaxing spot.

Boma, on the north bank, is also a good place to stay; visit the Mayumbe forest area with its caves, waterfalls and ancient tombs.

Matadi, on the southern river bank, is Zaire's major port. It is a bustling and colourful town built on terraces along rocky hillsides. There is a ferry for cars over the river.

Other sights in the Lower Zaire region are the Inga hydroelectric scheme, Kisantu botanical gardens and the massive Zongo Falls. A centre for this entire area is the town of **Ngungu** (formerly Thysville).

In Bandundu province is the low-lying lake that used to bear the name of King Leopold, now called Lake Mai-Ndombe. The pleasant town of Inongo on its shores is accessible by river transport from Kinshasa. It is the best centre for seeing the unrivalled Bayaka and Bapende dancers. In the far south of the region, on the Angolan frontier, are the Tembo and Kasongo-Lunda Falls.

The main town of Equator region is **Mbandaka**, set in the heart of Africa's deepest forests, and accessible only by river transport. About 100 km. away is the town of Bikoro on Lake Tumba, with the Eala botanical gardens.

Hotels:
Moanda
Hotel Mangrove, B.P. 51, 32 rooms.
Boma
Hotel Boma, B.P. 252, 17 rooms; **Hotel Mabuilu**, 40 rooms.
Matadi
Hotel Metropole, 63 rooms.
Ngungu
Hotel Cosmopolite, 22 rooms.
Mbandaka
Hotel Ancien, 40 rooms.

LUBUMBASHI

Formerly Elisabethville, this is the main town of the country's copperbelt, and the scene of the secession of the then Katanga Province, now Shaba Region.

Hotels
Hotel Karavia, tel: 3977, outside the city in golf residential quarter. International luxury standard.
Parkhotel, 837 Avenue du Kasai, B.P 112, tel: 3523, 92 rooms. Not all rooms have screens or air-conditioning, but the grill-room is still excellent.
Hotel Shaba, 486 Avenue Wangermee, B.P 733, tel: 3617, 46 rooms.
Hotel du Globe, 247 Avenue Meupu, B.P 716, tel: 3612, 34 rooms.
Hotel Wagenia, 535 Avenue Mobutu, B.P 1323, tel: 3484, 16 rooms.

SHABA AND KASAI REGIONS
The open, undulating land of Southern Zaire is dotted with lakes such as the Fwa and Munkamba in Kasai and waterfalls such as the Kiobo Falls (60 km. high, 250 m. wide) on the Lufira river, the Lofoi Falls (340 m. high, the highest in Africa) north of Lubumbashi, the Johnston Rapids and Falls near Kasenga on the Luapala.

An excursion can be made from Lubumbashi to **Kalemi**, on Lake Tanganyika, over either the Kundelungu plateau or the Marungu plateau near Lake Mweru. The region between the Lualaba river and Lake Tanganyika is picturesque, especially from the Portes d'Enfer ('Gates of Hell') near Kongolo to the Kyimbi Falls north of Kalemi, which is a beautifully situated town (**Hotel du Lac**, 27 rooms).

The towns of these two regions have a number of hotels suitable for travellers (Kolwezi: **Hotel Impala**, P.O. Box 209, tel: 2421, 25 rooms; **Hotel Bonne Auberge**, 30 Avenue Kajama, P.O. Box 209, tel: 2421, 21 rooms. Mbuji-Mayi: **Hotel Mukeba**, 22 Avenue Serpents, P.O. Box 590; Kananga: **Hotel Atlanta**, 700 Avenue Lumumba, P.O. Box 185, tel: 2828, 31 rooms; **Hotel Musube**, Avenue

Commerce, P.O. Box 1024, tel: 2438, 21 rooms).

BUKAVU
Remote from Kinshasa, Bukavu still has something of the air of an Edwardian watering place, with lakeside views and walks rather than mineral springs to refresh the visitor. Further information from Office National du Tourisme, Avenue President Mobutu, B.P 2468, tel: 3001.

Hotels
Hotel Belle-vue, 143 Avenue Mobutu, B.P. 278, tel: 2266, 13 rooms.
Hotel Residence, 88 Avenue Mobutu, B.P. 406, tel: 2131, 42 rooms.
Hotel Metropole, Avenue Mobutu, B.P. 662, tel: 2690, 18 rooms.
Hotel Riviera, Blvd Elisabeth, B.P. 1084, tel: 2326, 22 rooms.
Hotel la Fregate, Avenue Mobutu, B.P. 715, tel: 2823, 38 rooms.

KIVU REGION
Virunga National Park (ex-Albert)
About 350 km. from north to south, Virunga National Park is enclosed by natural boundaries of mountains to the west and Lakes Idi Amin (formerly Edward) and Kivu to north and south. With nearly two million acres, it is rich in lion, elephant, buffalo, antelope, and leopard. It has all-year tourism, currently on a modest scale.

The park is in an area of active volcanoes, and contains at Vitshumbi a fisheries co-operative for lake fish, which can be bought freshly caught and grilled. The park has a camping site, but visitors usually stay in the double-roomed chalets of the hotel at Rwindi.

The park is administered for the Presidence de la République, by the *Institut National Pour La Conservation De La Nature, Direction Générale et Scientifique*, Rumangabo, B.P. 18, Rutshuru, Kivu.

The park's address is Parc National des Virunga, B.P. 660 Rwindi par Goma, Kivu (cable address: PARCVIRUNGA RWINDI) and has in the country's capital the Bureau Administratif et de Contact, Kinshasa, B.P. 4019, tel: 592.89.

Lake Kivu is deservedly famous. It is also one of the few African lakes where one can swim without fear of bilharzia. To the north are the Virunga mountains with their two volcanic peaks, Nyiragongo (3,470 m) and Nyamuragira (3.056 m). Lake Idi Amin is excellent for fishing and its shores are a paradise of bird life. North of it are the Ruwenzori Mountains with their snow-capped peaks, of which the highest is the Marguerite (5,119 m).

Hotels
The main towns of the region provide good accommodation. Goma is the starting-point for tours of Virunga National Park (**Hotel des Grands Lac**, P.O. Box 253, 51 rooms; **Hotel Karibu**, 100 rooms, located on the shore of lake Kivu; **Hotel Kikyo-Butembo**, 50 rooms; **Hotel Ruwenzori-Mutwanga**, 50 rooms). Rwindi is in the centre of the park (**Hotel de la Rwindi**, 49 rooms) and Rutshuru to the east near the Uganda border (**Hotel du Parc**, 8 rooms). Tourist information available from Office National du Tourisme, Avenue Volcans, Rwindi, P.O. Box 242, tel: 440.

KISANGANI

Formerly Stanleyville, the town is the headquarters of Upper Zaire Region (ex-Eastern Province), and grew at a point on the river where major waterfalls interrupted navigation. It was a Lumumbist stronghold, and during the years of conflict fairly extensive damage was done, much of which has not been repaired. There is river sailing, and at the Wagenia fisheries a charming fishing community catch the *capitaine du Zaire*, a large tasty fish, in special long baskets placed at the falls. They organise the work and placing of nets through a complex social structure

which the village children will happily explain to visitors. The town has a busy central market.

Local tourist information can be obtained from Office National du Tourisme, Avenue de l'Eglise, P.O. Box 1658, tel: 2648.

Hotels
Hotel des Chutes, Avenue Mobutu, B.P. 242, tel: 3498, 40 rooms.
Hotel Zaire Palace, Avenue de l'Eglise, B.P. 501, tel: 2664, 100 rooms.

UPPER ZAIRE REGION

Garamba National Park
The park has nearly one million acres close to the Sudan border, and is specially known for the white rhinoceros, in addition to its plentiful giraffes, lions, leopards, cheetahs, antelopes and hyenas. The region has a centre for the taming of elephants at Gangala na Bodio.

Lake Mobutu (formerly Albert) is notable in that it contains more fish than any other lake in Africa. South of the lake is Mount Hoyo with its caves and waterfalls, and the forest region is the home of pygmies. Between Bunia and Kisangani at Epulu Station you can see the unique okapi in captivity.

Hotels
The best centre for this area is Bunia (**Auberge du Mont Hoyo, Hotel Semliki, Hotel Ngoto**).

HISTORY

The tropical forest which covers the whole central area of Zaire presented a formidable barrier to pre-Iron Age peoples who were unable to cut paths through it. Even now most habitation is confined to the river banks and the main mode of transport is the canoe. Along these rivers grew up small-scale kingdoms such as that of the Kuba people near

Ilebo on the tributaries of the Kasai. In the far interior in the Ituri forests near the Uganda border the pygmies still live by hunting and gathering the fruits of the forest.

The Kongo kingdom became powerful in the 14th century before the arrival of the Portuguese in 1482. It was highly centralised under an autocratic king who controlled the currency of the country which was a particular kind of shell—the *nzimbu*—found only on Luanda Island and collected only by his officials.

The great expansion of East African trade became important in the mid-19th century for most of eastern Zaire and this is why Swahili is widely understood there. Traders seeking slaves, ivory and Katangan copper normally stayed many years in the interior raiding and trading, some even establishing their own kingdoms.

In the 1870s Livingstone reached Nyangwe; Cameron crossed the continent from Bagamoyo, through Nyangwe and Katanga to Benguela; and Stanley finally travelled right down the Congo from Nyangwe (1874-77). He was so impressed with the economic potential of the country that he urged European countries to take over the area. Leopold II was the only one interested at the time, so from 1879 to 1885 Stanley made treaties with various peoples to establish a Belgian sphere of influence.

The country's present boundaries were established following the Berlin Conference of 1884-5 which brought together representatives of the European powers. The 'Congo Free State', as it was then known, was personally ruled until 1908 by King Leopold of Belgium (who never visited the territory); it then became a full colony of Belgium.

The establishment of plantations and the discovery of great mineral wealth led to large-scale recruitment of labour, in its scale and nature not far removed from the horrors of the slave trade that King Leopold claimed to have eliminated. In some districts there was a serious deple-tion of the population.

From the 1930s onwards the urban centres grew rapidly. Congolese town-dwellers were divorced from their traditional ways of life which found no substitute in the cities. It was the emergent class of European-educated urban Congolese, or *évolués*, that led the nationalist movement. The Belgian failure to recognise their aspirations until too late was responsible for much that followed.

Within a week of independence a mutiny occurred within the *Force Publique* (the combined army and gendarmerie) which still did not have a single Congolese officer. Subsequent events led to the temporary flight of most European residents, the collapse of the administration and the new Government's appeal for United Nations' intervention. The Province of Katanga, under Moise Tshombe (backed by Belgian financial interests and European mercenaries) seceded.

Crisis followed crisis for the next six years. The first Prime Minister, Patrice Lumumba, was early removed from office and then murdered. His supporters set up a rival government in Stanleyville (now Kisangani). The succession of Katanga was finally ended by UN military action at the beginning of 1963.

When the UN forces left in 1964 a nation-wide rebellion challenged the Government. Tshombe, switching roles, became the Prime Minister of the centre government—but he did not last long. A military coup brought a young General Mobutu to power in November 1965. Thereafter law and order was gradually restored, the foreign mercenaries were expelled, a new constitution set up, and President Mobutu began to consolidate his power through his single party *Mouvement Populaire de la Revolution*.

General Mobutu's search for new national objectives was responsible for the renaming of the country in 1971, followed by changes in the names of many regions, towns and institutions and even of Zairean citizens.

ZAMBIA

Zambia is a vast, thinly populated, tree-clad plateau at the heart of Africa, so high that the weather is perfect most of the year round, but especially so during the dry warm sunny days of May to September, the best season to go there.

The main attraction to visitors is without doubt the magnificent Victoria Falls. The Luangwa and Kafue Game Parks offer a fascinating variety of animals and birds. Luangwa has the most prolific animal population in Africa. In many parts of the country traditional ceremonies are still very much alive and there are displays of Zambian dancing to be seen, particularly in Livingstone.

Zambia is now famous as the world's third largest producer of copper, mined in the Copperbelt where modern towns like Kitwe and Ndola sprang up when Zambia was a British protectorate. In 1964 the country was led to independence by President Kenneth Kaunda.

THE LAND AND THE PEOPLE

The Zambezi River marks the western border of the country. It has a broad, fertile flood-plain, where the traditional seasonal movements for agriculture are still adhered to and where canoes and boats are the best means of transport. In the south it becomes the frontier with Rhodesia from the Victoria Falls to the

274 km long man-made lake of Kariba, formed when the dam was built for hydro-electric power in the 1950s. In the east and north east the country rises to pleasant hills, especially in the Mbala region.

The plateau—about 1,200 m high—is covered by deciduous savannah wood, small trees of no economic value, with occasional outlets of grassy plains or marshland alive with birds. Streams are fairly widespread and villages are sited near them, where the people grow one crop a year during the rainy season (No-

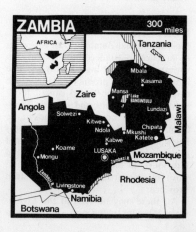

vember to April) and, in areas free from tsetse fly, keep cattle. Soils are on the whole sandy, acid and infertile, with pockets of better alluvial types.

In the Copperbelt region and elsewhere are mineral ores, producing copper, zinc and lead. The railway was first built (1906-10) to link the mines and almost all development since then has centred on this line of rail, from the industrial towns like Kitwe to the commercial farms of Southern Province. Altogether 4,750,000 people live in this country which is almost the size of France and West Germany combined. The non-African population totals about 60,000—Europeans, working mainly in mining and industry, Asians, mainly in commerce, and Coloureds (people of mixed race).

The country's motto is 'One Zambia, one nation', reflecting the aspiration to build a non-racial society, divided neither by race, colour nor tribe. There are six main African languages spoken: Bemba, Tonga, Lozi, Lunda, Luvale and Nyanja. While there is no lingua franca, Bemba is used on the Copperbelt, in the Northern and Luapula provinces; Nyanja is common in the Eastern Province and Lusaka. English is the official language and is widely spoken.

CULTURE

Most traditional Zambian craft is severely practicable—undecorated pottery, a variety of spears or ingenious traps. The most interesting products perhaps are elaborate basketwork and carved food-bowls from Western and Eastern Provinces; carefully moulded pipe-ends in the form of animals or mythical creatures from Southern Province; and masks and disguises made of bark and mud, painted ferociously in black, white and red and worn by dancers from North Western Province.

All these may be seen at the Livingstone Museum, along with a comprehensive collection of musical instruments and the tools of the old economy, including copper crosses formerly used as currency and long thin baskets used to drain salt from mud on the Kafue Flats. Most of the crafts are dying out in the villages, but professional craftsmen continue and may be seen at work in the Maramba Cultural Centre at Livingstone. For anyone wanting to buy genuine Zambian curios it is advisable to visit these two places first, as many of the street-seller's wares may come from East Africa or Zaire.

By contrast traditional dancing is very much alive and appreciated by Zambians in village, township and school. Visitors to the country can see a variety of different dances performed regularly at the Maramba Centre, Livingstone, and the cultural village in Lusaka. Some are pure entertainment, telling folk stories, gossip or jokes; others form part of a ceremony—a wedding, funeral, initiation rite, the beginning of the rains or a cure for the sick.

One very colourful ceremony in the west of the country is the *Ku-omboka* during February or March, when the Lozi chief (the *Litunga*) moves all his goods and family, and is paddled by his councillors in striped barges along man-made canals from the main capital of Leaului to another at Limulunga, near Mongu, where they remain for the duration of the flood. A similar, less elaborate move, more accessible to the visitor, is the *Kufulehela* in about July when the royal court moves back again. Other annual ceremonies include the *Shimunenga* of the Ba-Ila people at Maala, on the Kafue Flats, in September or October, and the *Mutomboka* of the Luando people in Luapula Province on 29 July. For details and information about visiting these ceremonies—contact the Zambia National Tourist Bureau.

WILDLIFE

Both the major game parks—Kafue and

Luangwa—lie along rivers abounding in hippos and crocodiles, and birds like the fish-eagle (Zambia's emblem) and the crested crane. The plains beside the rivers are thronged with different kinds of buck, from the regal Kudu to the enchanting Thompson's gazelle and the red lechwe, which is unique to Zambia. Luangwa has the Thornicroft giraffe, not found anywhere else. Sumbu National Park is situated by Lake Tanganyika.

These three parks contain elephant, rhino, lion and most other species of big game. For the more adventurous, walking safaris and hunting expeditions can be arranged. The Kafue River, Lake Kariba and Lake Tanganyika provide excellent fishing for bream, Nile perch, lake salmon and tiger fish. Altogether there are 18 gazetted National Parks in Zambia.

GENERAL INFORMATION

Area: 752,614 sq. km.
Population: 4,750,000
Altitude: 915 to 1,500 m. above sea level.
Capital: Lusaka.
Head of State: The President, Dr Kenneth David Kaunda.
Government: Zambia became a one party 'Participatory Democracy' in December 1972. The only legal party is the United National Independence Party. Parliament consists of the President and National Assembly which has 125 elected members, plus 10 members nominated by the President and the Speaker.
Currency: The Kwacha (K), divided into 100 ngwee. K1.36=£1 sterling; K0.79=US$1.00
Religions: Christianity and traditional.
Languages: English is the official language. The main African languages are Bemba, Nyanja and Tonga.
Time: GMT+2.

HOW TO GET THERE

By air: From the United Kingdom: Zambia Airways has three nonstop services a week to Lusaka, as does British Caledonian.

From Europe: Zambia Airways (twice weekly) from Rome; Alitalia from Rome and Athens; UTA from Paris (weekly). Zambia Airways also operates from Belgrade, Yugoslavia and has a partnership flight with Lufthansa from Frankfurt.

From the United States: Direct flight to Nairobi in Kenya to connect with stopover flights.

From southern Africa: Since the closure of the Zambian-Rhodesian border flights are only operative from South Africa via Malawi and Botswana. DETA of Mozambique also serves Lusaka Airport.

Zambia Airways flights also operate from Lusaka to Botswana, Malawi, Mozambique, Mauritius, Dar es Salaam (Tanzania) and Nairobi (Kenya).

Taxi service is available at the International Airport. There is an Airport Departure Tax of K3.00.

By road: Motorists enter Zambia through Kazungula (by ferry) from Botswana; through Lundazi and Mwami from Malawi; through Tunduma from Tanzania and through Kasumbalesa or Mokambo from Zaire. Entry into Zambia via Chirundu or the Victoria Falls from Rhodesia is no longer possible since the closure of the border.

A driver bringing a motor vehicle into Zambia must have a tryptique or carnet de passage issued by a recognised motoring organisation, or a Customs Importation Permit issued at the point of entry under certain conditions. Motorists should contact the Controller of Customs and Excise, Customs Headquarters, P.O. Box 500, Livingstone, Zambia, for information regarding these conditions.

By rail: The new Tazara railway, opened in 1975 two years ahead of schedule, gives access to the country from Tanzania. The journey from Kapiri Mposhi, north of Lusaka, to Dar es Salaam takes over 33 hours. The existing rail link from the south through Rhodesia ceased taking passenger traffic when the border between the two countries was closed. Zambia Railways operate daily trains with overnight sleeper accommodation from Livingstone through Lusaka to Zaire.

Visas and health regulations
Visas are not required by holders of valid UK or Commonwealth passports. The same applies to citizens of Scandinavian countries, Iceland, the Netherlands, Luxembourg, Liechtenstein and San Marino.

Citizens of the United States, France, West Germany, and most other nations of the world can get a special tourist visa when they enter Zambia if they are visiting the country solely as tourists and provided they satisfy the immigration authorities with regard to character, financial resources and ability to leave Zambia at the end of the visit. As passport and visa regulations are subject to changes from time to time, intending visitors are advised to consult their travel agents beforehand. Tourists' visas cannot be issued at the Zambian border to any national or resident of the Republic of South Africa, or Rhodesia. Intending visitors from these territories should apply directly to the Chief Immigration Officer, P.O. Box RW 300, Lusaka, allowing from four to six weeks for an application to be processed.

All visitors must have a valid international certificate of vaccination against smallpox. For people who have travelled through the yellow fever endemic zone of Africa (i.e. between the $15°N$ and $10°S$ parallels of latitude) an international certificate of vaccination against yellow fever is also required. Similarly, for persons travelling from or via an infected cholera area a certificate of immunity is necessary.

Airline passengers are advised to have these certificates in case the aircraft is unavoidably delayed in infected areas.

Dutiable goods
Free import is allowed of personal effects (including camping and sports equipment, cameras and binoculars), 200 cigarettes or 450 gm. of tobacco, and one open bottle of an alcoholic beverage. Hunters must obtain a Tourist's Import Permit at point of entry for firearms and ammunition. The permit is valid for six months and must be returned to the Customs Officer at the point of departure from Zambia.

Currency regulations
No Zambian currency may be taken into or out of Zambia, and there are absurdly rigorous searches of travellers' clothing and luggage on departure from Lusaka airport. Any stray *ngwee* have to be donated to the national wildlife fund. Visitors are advised to carry travellers' cheques in small denominations and cash only enough for their current needs.

Victoria Falls from the Zambian side

There is no limit to the amount of foreign currency which can be brought into Zambia, but visitors should obtain a receipt from the customs officer at point of entry as they will be asked to declare the balance on departure. All foreign money should be changed at a bank and receipt kept until the end of the visit. Not more than the equivalent of K20 in foreign exchange may be taken out of Zambia unless a receipt is produced to prove that the amount in excess was brought into the country on that particular visit.

Diner's Club cards are accepted by the Inter-Continental, Ridgeway and Lusaka Hotels; American Express cards by the Inter-Continental and Lusaka Hotels. Bank credit cards are not yet accepted by shops.

CLIMATE

Although Zambia lies in the tropics, the elevation of the plateau ensures that the climate is seldom unpleasantly hot. The dry winter season from May to September (July: 16°C) is the best time for touring, when the days are sunny but can be cold and windy. The hot months are October and November (24°C) when even the nights are oppressive, though the heat is occasionally relieved by thunderstorms, which become more frequent with the approach of the rainy season in November. Rains usually last a few hours before the freshened countryside returns to sunshine. The wet season continues until early April and then the country is dry for the next seven months.

What to wear: Dress is generally informal. A cardigan or pullover is often needed in the cool early mornings and after sunset, except during the hot months of October and November.

Health precautions: The climate is healthy if reasonable precautions are taken. Lusaka and the Copperbelt towns are practically free from malaria but outside these centres it is endemic and prophylactic drugs should be taken. It is safer to swim only in swimming pools as all water courses and dams are infected with bilharzia, which causes a troublesome and debilitating disease. All clothes washed and hung in the open air to dry should be ironed to kill the eggs of the *putsi* fly which it lays in damp clothing. Insect repellant is advised in the game parks and rural areas. There are hospitals and clinics in the main urban areas which are open to outpatients every day, including Sundays.

ACCOMMODATION AND FOOD

There is international-standard hotel accommodation in Lusaka and the Copperbelt towns.

Reasonably priced Government Rest Houses are available in the following areas:

Central Province: Kabwe (Bwacha Rest House), Serenje, Mkushi, Mumbwa and Feira.

Southern Province: Livingstone (Maramba Rest House), Namwala, Sinazongwe.

Northern Province: Kasama, Chinsali, Luwingu, Mbala, (Mpulungu Rest House), Isoka and Mporokoso.

Western Province: Mongu, Kalabo, Kaoma (formerly called Mankoya), and Sesheke.

North Western Province: Solwezi, Kasempa, Kabompo, Zambezi (formerly called Balovale), and Mwinilunga.

Eastern Province: Chipata (Kapata Rest House), Katete, Petaluke, Lundazi (Lundazi Castle and Nyika Rest House), and Kachalola.

Luapula Province: Kawamba, Samfya, Nchelenge, Mwense and Mausa.

As a result of Southern African political problems imported food is sometimes in short supply, but local food is always available. Bream from the Zambezi River, Nile perch, lake salmon and other freshwater fish are excellent. Zambian beer is very good.

Tipping: Tipping in hotels and restaurants is illegal and instead a service charge of 10% has been levied.

TRANSPORT

Road: Zambia is served by a network of tarred, gravel and earth roads which is being steadily improved. Tarmac roads run from the Rhodesian border (closed at present) to Chirundu, where the Otto Beit Bridge spans the Zanbezi River, and from the Victoria Falls northwards through Lusaka to the Copperbelt towns which are all linked by tarred roads. The Ndola-Kitwe road is, however, one of the worst accident runs in Africa. Take it easy and do not drive on pay-day.

The Great North Road to Tunduma on the Tanzanian border is fully tarred and joins the road systems of Tanzania and Malawi. The tarred highway from Lusaka, the Great East Road, through Chipata links Zambia with Malawi and the main access route to the South Luangwa Valley National Game Reserve. From Mpika a road runs to Mpulungu on Lake Tanganyika where a steamer operates to Kigoma in Tanzania.

Besides the main arterial roads there are all-weather gravel roads throughout the country, enabling the motorist to visit centres of scenic beauty and game parks, but the rains make January and March the least satisfactory time for motoring as many of the rural roads become impassable.

Air: Zambia Airways (P.O. Box 272, Haile Selassie Avenue, Lusaka) domestic service has eight flights weekly between Lusaka and Livingstone and two flights weekly between Lusaka and Kasaba Bay. From the middle of May to the end of October there are three flights weekly to Mafue Lodge in the Luangwa Valley which is open all year. A new airport has been completed 25 kilometres from Mafue Lodge. From mid-May to the end of December Kafue National Park has two flights weekly from Livingstone and two from Lusaka. Flights operate twice weekly between Lusaka and Ndola, including Sundays. The game-viewing flights from Lusaka may be of interest to the visitor with little time to spare.

Rail: An overnight sleeper service is run by Zambia Railways from Livingstone through Lusaka to the Zaire border. The Zambia National Tourist Bureau (P.O. Box 17 Lusaka; P.O. Box 342 Livingstone) conducts luxury coach tours to the Victoria Falls and Livingstone, Kariba Dam, and the National Parks, as well as sightseeing tours of Lusaka.

Car hire: Taxis are scarce but a number of car hire firms operate in the main centres. Visitors' driving licences are valid for 90 days. Lusaka: **Ridgeway Car Hire Service,** P.O Box 929, tel: 73968; **Central African Motors (CAMS),** P.O. Box 672, tel: 73181; **Streamline Car Hire Ltd.,** P.O Box 3189, tel: 75728. Ndola: **Corner Taxi and Car Hire,** P.O. Box 263, tel: 2469; **Central African Motors (CAMS),** P.O Box 105, tel: 3621. Kitwe: **Central African Motors (CAMS),** P.O. Box 2795, tel: 2390.

The Zambia National Tourist Bureau runs a bus and car hire service from Livingstone and Lusaka.

BUSINESS HOURS
Banks: Monday, Tuesday, Wednesday and Friday 08.15-12.45; Thursdays 08.15-12.00; Saturdays 08.15-11.00.
Government offices: 07.30-13.00 and 14.00-17.00 Monday-Friday. Shops: Monday to Friday 08.00-17.00; Saturdays 08.00-13.00.

PUBLIC HOLIDAYS
New Year's Day; Good Friday; Holy Saturday; Labour Day, 1 May; Africa Freedom Day, 25 May; Heroes Day, first Monday in July; Unity Day, first Tuesday in July; Youth Day, 8 August; Independence Anniversary, 24 October; Christmas Day; Boxing Day.

FOREIGN EMBASSIES IN LUSAKA
Austria: 4th Floor, Woodgate House,

Cairo Road, P.O Box 1094; Belgium: Plot 377A, Reedbuck Road, Kabulonga, P.O. Box 1204; Botswana: 2647 Haile Selassie Avenue, P.O. Box 1910; Canada: Barclays Bank Building, Cairo Road, P.O. Box 1313; Denmark: 352 Independence Avenue, P.O. Box RW 299; Egypt: Plot No 5206, United Nations Avenue, P.O. Box 2428; Finland: Kalima Tower, corner Chachacha Road/Katunjila Road, P.O. Box 937; France: Unity House, corner of Katunjila Road and Freedom Way, P.O. Box 62; West Germany: 350 Independence Avenue, P.O. Box RW120; India: 1st Floor, Anchor House, Lusaka Square, P.O. Box 2111; Italy: Woodgate House, Nairobi Place, Cairo Road, P.O. Box 1046; Japan: 342 Independence Avenue, P.O. Box 3390; Kenya: Kafue House, Nairobi Place, Cairo Road, P.O. Box 3651; Malawi: Woodgate House, Heroes Place, P.O. Box RW425; Netherlands: 5028 United Nations Avenue, P.O. Box 1905; Nigeria: Zambia Bible House, Freedom Way, P.O. Box 2598; Somalia: Farm 913:377A Kabulonga Road, P.O. Box 3251; Sweden: Kalima Tower, corner Chachacha Road/Katunjila Road, P.O. Box 788; Tanzania: Ujamaa House, Plot 5200 United Nations Avenue, P.O. Box 1219; UK: Stand No 5210, Independence Avenue, P.O. Box RW50; USA: corner of Independence and United Nations Avenue, P.O. Box 1617; Zaire: Plot 1124 Parirenyatwa Road, P.O. Box 1287.

TOURIST OFFICES

UK: ZNTB, Zimco House, 129/139 Finsbury Pavement, London EC2 1NA. Tel: 01-638 8333; 01-638 8882. Telex: 8811438.

West Germany: 6 Frankfurt, Kaiserstrasse 23, Frankfurt-am-Main, tel: (0611) 236-338-39. Telex: 0416526.

Italy: c/o Zambia Airways, Via Bissolati 84, Rome. Tel: 470-8440.

USA: 150E 58th Street, New York, NY 10022. Tel: (212) 758 9450. Telex: 62327.

Kenya: c/o Zambia Airways, Hilton Hotel, P.O. Box 42479, Nairobi. Tel: 24722.

Lusaka: Century House, Cairo Road, P.O. Box 17. Tel: 72891/5. Telex: ZA4178.

Livingstone: P.O. Box 342, Musi-O-Tunya Road. Tel: 3534/5.

Ndola: P.O. Box 1520. Tel: 3588 and 4441.

LUSAKA

Lusaka has been the country's capital since 1935. It is a city with no defined centre—the main administrative buildings are four to five km. away from the shops, which are strung out along the mile-long Cairo Road where all the banks, airline offices, the post office and the Lusaka Hotel also are. The University campus is on the airport road, as are the new copper-plated square-domed National Assembly building and international conference hall.

The Zambia National Tourist Bureau offers a sightseeing tour of the capital which includes the new National Assembly building; the President's residence, State House; the Anglican cathedral; an open-air market; the tobacco auction floor (open from April to August); the curio sellers; a copper boutique, where gemstones are polished, set and sold; and

In one of Zambia's national parks.

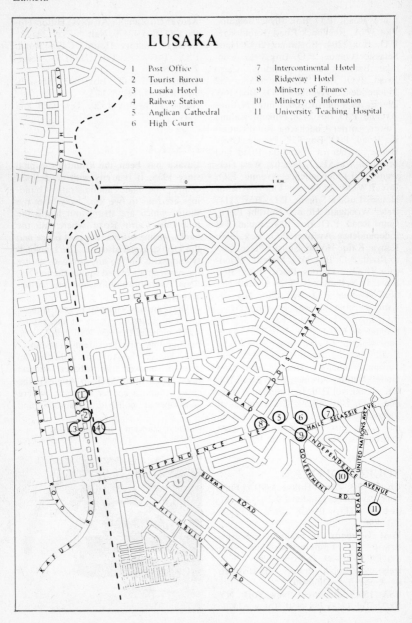

LUSAKA

1 Post Office
2 Tourist Bureau
3 Lusaka Hotel
4 Railway Station
5 Anglican Cathedral
6 High Court

7 Intercontinental Hotel
8 Ridgeway Hotel
9 Ministry of Finance
10 Ministry of Information
11 University Teaching Hospital

the Geological Survey Museum which has exhibits from the copper industry and local gemstones such as garnets, tourmalines, emeralds, amethysts and malachite.

On a separate tour the visitor can see the Munda Wanga Botanical Gardens and nearby the headquarters of the Zambian Wildlife, Fisheries and National Parks Department at Chilanga. The Tourist Bureau also offers game-viewing flights from Lusaka.

Hotels
Four Star
Inter-Continental Hotel, P.O. Box 2201. tel: 5100;
Pamodzi Hotel, near completion in 1977;
Three Star
Ridgeway Hotel, P.O. Box 666, tel: 51699.
Two Star
The Lusaka Hotel, just off Cairo Road, P.O. Box 44, tel: 73136/73830;
Andrews Motel, P.O. Box 475, tel: 75682/75688.

Restaurants
Besides the restaurants in the hotels the better eating places include the **Fresco Restaurant** and the **Kuku Inn**. Others are the **Woodpecker Inn** and the **Fimbano Night Club**. Prices are high everywhere and menus may be affected by food shortages.

Entertainments
Dancing and floor shows in the main hotels; modern cinemas, including a "drive-in"; theatre; art gallery; excellent library; sports and sailing facilities at private clubs where temporary membership is usually available to visitors. Casino at the Inter-Continental Hotel.

Shopping and markets
Lusaka has modern, well-stocked shops and supermarkets, and an open air market. African carvings, beadwork, pottery and copperware are readily available. A visit is recommended to Zambia's Gem-stones Polishing Works where local gemstones are sold.

Tourist information
The Zambia National Tourist Bureau, P.O. Box 17, Century House, Cairo Road, tel: 72891/5.

THE COPPERBELT
The seven mining towns of Kitwe, Ndola, Chililabombwe, Chingola, Kalulushi, Mufulira and Luanshya make up the copperbelt. Luanshya has the country's oldest mine which has the richest ores in Zambia, followed by Mufulira near the Zaire border with the second most extensive underground copper mining installations in the world.

United Bus Company of Zambia run a daily luxury coach service to the Copperbelt and the Zambia National Tourist Bureau also operates luxury coach tours, but on request only, to the Copperbelt centres, and itinerary includes a visit to the Dag Hammerskjold Memorial. Of interest outside Ndola are the Sunken Lake and Slave Tree. Visits to the copper mines should be arranged in advance from Lusaka; visitors to Ndola should see the Monkey Fountain Zoo.

Kitwe Hotels
Three Star
Hotel Edinburgh, P.O. Box 1800, tel: 3416.
One Star
Nkana Hotel, P.O. Box 664, tel: 2410/2358.
Ungraded
Bucchi Hotel

Ndola Hotels
Two Star
Savoy Hotel, P.O. Box 1800, tel: 3771.
One Star
Coppersmith Arms Hotel, P.O. Box 1063, tel: 2395;
Falcon Hotel, P.O. Box 127, tel: 2355;
Jacaranda Hotel, P.O. Box 43, tel: 3571.

Entertainments

Casino in the **Savoy Hotel**; dinner dances in the **Edinburgh** and **Savoy Hotels**; private clubs offer temporary membership to visitors, and their facilities include tennis, bowls, swimming pools, and golf (the course at **Chingola** being particularly good). Near Kitwe is the **Mindolo Dam** with swimming, speedboating and water sports (but boats and equipment cannot be rented at the dam); Kitwe is the major horse racing centre in Zambia.

LIVINGSTONE

Established in 1905, Livingstone was the capital of Zambia (Northern Rhodesia) until 1935. The old Government House is now a National Monument. The town is a tourist centre for the Victoria Falls, and there are excellent hotels, Rest Huts and camping sites and numerous excursions to interest the visitor.

Places of interest

The Victoria Falls have always been considered one of the natural wonders of the world. At the height of the floods, from March to May, more than five million litres of water surge over every second, causing clouds of vapour that can be seen 50 km. away.

The recently completed Knife Edge footbridge spanning a narrow ridge of rock between the mainland and an island downstream opposite the Eastern Cataract affords the best view of the Rainbow and Main Falls, the First Gorge and the Boiling Pot. The best view is from the Eastern Cataract between 20.30 and 21.30. Other main vantage points are the larger Falls Bridge, which is further away, the Boiling Pot, the Power Station and the various gorges. There are two major scenic approaches downriver as far as the Seventh and Songwe Gorges, on one of which is the Lookout Tree, a huge and ancient baobab in which a platform has been built to give an excellent view of the Falls.

The Livingstone Game Park just outside the town contains over 400 animals which include lion, giraffe, zebra, white rhino, a variety of antelope, warthog, bush pig and gnu. As the park is small the lions are confined to an acre enclosure. In the centre of the park is a fenced area where crocodiles, tortoises, snakes and leguans are housed in pits and cages. There are also aviaries for indigenous birds such as the Zambezi Lovebird, and enclosures for small mammals not normally seen in the main park.

Luxury river-boats cruise up the Zambezi where hippopotami and crocodiles can be seen in the water and a variety of animals and birds on the banks and islands. Elephants and monkeys are plentiful. Further up river, especially as far as Mambova and the Maramba River, there are good places for game fishing.

The Maramba Cultural Centre was established to preserve the arts and crafts of age-old Africa. It contains at least one dwelling typical of each of the main areas of Zambia, where blacksmiths, mask carvers, potters and craftsmen ply their trades as their ancestors did through the centuries. In the centre of the village is an arena where traditional dances are performed, including those of the Makishi dancers in basketweave costumes who used to perform during the Luvala circumcision rites in the North Western Province.

Inside Livingstone itself is Zambia's national museum which records the history of man in Zambia in traditional and anthropological exhibits. The museum is renowned for its collection of Livingstone's possessions and correspondence, including a notebook in which the explorer recorded the date he first set eyes on the Victoria Falls.

Four Star Hotels
Musi-o-Tunya Inter-Continental Hotel, P.O. Box 151, tel: 211, 300 yards from Eastern Cataract of the Falls;
Two Star

North Western Hotel, P.O. Box 69, tel: 2255/6.
New Fairmount Hotel, P.O. Box 46, tel: 2066.
One Star
The Chalets Hotel, P.O. Box 143, tel: 8655.
Ungraded
The Motel, P.O. Box 105, tel: 3060.

A camping site for tents and caravans is situated near the banks of the Zambezi River. Adjacent are the Falls Rest Huts where furnished huts may be rented with or without bedding. The Falls Restaurant overlooks the river and serves both the camping site and Rest Huts with meals and food. **Rest Camp** including restaurant catering, P.O. Box 86, tel: 2981 (ungraded).

MBALA

Mbala is set among lovely hills, and nearby are the Kalambo Falls (240 m. high), the nesting place of the maribou stork. At Mpulungu is a harbour for fishing boats on Lake Tanganyika.

Hotels
Ungraded
Grasshopper Inn, P.O. Box 93, N. Province, tel: 291.
The Arms Hotel, P.O. Mbala, N. Province, tel: 6427.

MONGU

This town is situated on the upper reaches of the Zambezi in the Western Province. The *Ku-omboka* in March when the Lozi chief moves all his goods and family to Limulunga for the duration of the rains, and the *Kufulehela* in July when they all move back to Lealui are fascinating ceremonies to watch, but unfortunately the date when they take place is unpredictable. The local curio shop displays Lozi basketwork and carvings.

And the Zambezi plain is itself a fine sight.
Hotel Lyambai,Queen's Drive, Mongu, P.O. Box 193, tel: 271.

NATIONAL PARKS
Kafue National Park
The Kafue National Park through and around which runs the Kafue River, is as large as Wales. Game is plentiful, and includes buffalo, zebra, warthog, hippopotamus, hartebeest, lion and innumerable types of antelope, the rarest of which is the red lechwe which is found in no other part of Africa. Over 400 species of birdlife can be seen and the Kafue Flats is a treasure trove for bird lovers and photographers.

There are seven camps open to the public: Ngoma, Nanzhila, Kalala, Chunga, Lufupa, Moshi and Ntemwa. Ngoma is the largest and has a hotel-type lodge with a restaurant, bar and swimming pool. Accommodation consists of double-roomed chalets. Zambia National Tourist Bureau run a full catering 40 bed Chunga Safari Village in the Kafue National Park. At the camps food and drink must be provided by the visitors but all necessary equipment, bedding and maintenance staff, including a cook, are provided. Cost of accommodation varies according to the camp chosen.

The park is open from June to November and South and Central Kafue National Park are open all year, and all bookings must be made through the Zambia National Tourist Bureau. All weather roads around Ngoma South and Chungi Safari Village, Central, have been constructed for game viewing. Zambia Airways operate flights during the season and the Bureau arranges tours through the park. Entry permits are required.

South Luangwa National Park
Many regard this as one of the finest game parks in Africa. There are six tourist lodges in Luangwa providing com-

fortable accommodation in chalets. The Tourist Bureau offers tours at very reasonable prices to Mfuwe, the largest of the lodges and the only one with catering facilities. Visitors are required to provide their own food and drink at the other lodges, although the necessary cooking equipment, bedding and maintenance staff are provided.

One of the features of the South Luangwa National Park is that visitors can walk about among the animals in company with armed guards—whose instructions must be implicitly obeyed. Children under 12 are not allowed on these walking safaris. At dawn it is possible to see elephants crossing the Luangwa River. Game is prolific and elephant, lion, giraffe, zebra, black rhino, Cape buffalo and the antelopes are all to be found.

All booking must be made through the Tourist Bureau and visitors are not allowed to enter the Park unless they hold an entry permit.

Sumbu National Park

The Park borders the second largest lake in Africa. One can boat and swim and there are luxury launches for picnic cruises. The fishing is excellent, especially from December to March, for Nile perch, tiger fish, *vundu* (a giant catfish), goliath tiger fish, lake salmon and *kupi*.

Accommodation: There are two lodges, Kasaba Bay Lodge, 30 guests, restaurant, bar; and Nkamba Bay Lodge. Sumbu tourist camp.

Zambia Airways flies to Kasaba Bay and Zambia National Tourist Bureau provide transfers and game viewing by Land-Rover and boats.

Lake Kariba

The lake provides good fishing and boating and, at Siavonga, water-skiing.

Accommodation: The Leisure Bay Motel, P.O. Box 15, Siavonga, 20 double rooms. There is also a Rest House at Siavonga, and two camping and caravan sites. At

Sinazongwe there is a rest camp with three chalets.

Lochinvar

This is a National Park devoted to the preservation of the red lechwe, but the visitor will also find many different varieties of birds, and zebra, hippo, baboons, and buffalo. The park also contains an archaeological site.

Accommodation: Game Lodge, 12 guests; bring your own food. Booking is through the Tourist Bureau.

Nyika

Nyika National Park is a small but attractive area adjoining the park of the same name in Malawi. The altitude is over 2,000 m. and the park contains eland, zebra and many kinds of antelope. There is a small non-catering lodge. Details from ZNTB.

Blue Lagoon

Small National Park within convenient reach of Lusaka with plenty of birdlife and the red lechwe. Advance permit required.

HISTORY

Around the 2nd century AD, Zambians began to mine and use iron and to live in villages built on mounds, some of them developing a culture ancestral to the present-day Tonga of Southern Province. The most spectacular archaeological finds come from Ingombe Ilede, a site discovered while digging a bore-hole for the resettlement of the population when Kariba Lake was flooded in 1960-62. Here had been buried several bodies dressed in gold and copper ornaments, near a village which was possibly an outpost of the Rhodesia Zimbabwe empire in the 14th century. These are now in Livingstone Museum.

16th-19th century. From the 16th century small groups of people arrived, some as fugitives, some as conquerors, from the Luba and Lunda empires in Zaire and merged with the earlier population. Most of them set up very small chiefdoms in which the Chief was more a symbolic representative of the people than a figure of authority. However, some large kingdoms did emerge.

Kazembe ruled over the Lunda in Luapula Province, dominating production of the rich copper and salt mines of Katanga, trading with his forebears in Zaire and sporadically with the Portuguese on the East Coast.

Earlier, in Western Province, the Lozi (or Barotse) had organised a highly centralised economic system to exploit the Zambezi food-plain. All the regions sent men to dig canals and build mounds for villages, and all sent their products to the Paramount Chief to be redistributed to other areas.

For some time the Chief refused to sell slaves to traders, partly because he needed people so much in his labour-intensive system.

Zambia suffered greatly during the turbulent 19th century. The Kololo invaded Western Province and the Ngoni Eastern Province. At the same time Portuguese, Arab and Tanzanian slave traders reached Zambia in large numbers bringing guns for sale to those who would help them to collect slaves. So the country was torn by wars and raiding, especially around the fast-growing Bemba kingdom in Northern Province.

The colonial period. In 1890 Cecil Rhodes, who already controlled part of Rodesia had planned to extend British rule from the Cape to Cairo, sent agents to make a treaty with Lewanika, the Lozi Paramount Chief, agreeing to 'protect' him in exchange for the right to mine in much of western Zambia. Gradually, the whole country was incorporated into the Northern Rhodesia protectorate and a railway linked it to South Africa, but in the north the Belgians in Zaire and the Germans in Tanzania foiled Rhodes' grand design.

The copper mines, which had been worked for centuries with simple iron tools, were mechanised in the 1920s and became the basis of Northern Rhodesia's economy, but the profits went largely to shareholders in South Africa and Britain.

Independence. From 1953 to 1963 Zambia was federated with Rhodesia and Malawi, a link which in practice meant economic domination by Rhodesia, and which Africans feared would in future mean political domination by white Rhodesians. African nationalist feeling united in opposition to the Federation until finally Britain allowed the two northern territories to break away and become independent separately.

The independence movement was led by Kenneth Kaunda (Zambia's first President) and the United National Independence Party (UNIP). Independence was formally achieved on 24 October 1964.

A year later, the white ruling group in Rhodesia made their Unilateral Declaration of Independence (UDI). Therefore the early years of Zambia's independence were complicated by the need to disengage the country from the economic stranglehold of past links with Rhodesia.

Zambia remains a member of the Commonwealth but its foreign policy is firmly based on non-alignment, and it is strongly committed to the Organisation of African Unity. It maintains links with its neighbour Tanzania to which it is joined by the Tazara railway line, financed by the Chinese. The Government's commitment to the liberation struggle in southern Africa has brought it into conflict with its white ruled neighbours.

Tension on the Rhodesian border was heightened by the Smith regime's closure of the border in January 1973. When the Rhodesians wished to reopen the border shortly afterwards Zambia refused to allow them to do so.